A PRACTICAL APPROACH TO

COMMERCIAL CONVEYANCING AND PROPERTY

THIRD EDITION

Professor Robert Abbey

Mark Richards

OXFORD

UNIVERSITY PRESS

OXFORD

UNIVERSITY PRESS

Great Clarendon Street, Oxford OX2 6DP

Oxford University Press is a department of the University of Oxford.
It furthers the University's objective of excellence in research, scholarship,
and education by publishing worldwide in

Oxford New York

Auckland Cape Town Dar es Salaam Hong Kong Karachi
Kuala Lumpur Madrid Melbourne Mexico City Nairobi
New Delhi Shanghai Taipei Toronto

With offices in

Argentina Austria Brazil Chile Czech Republic France Greece
Guatemala Hungary Italy Japan South Korea Poland Portugal
Singapore Switzerland Thailand Turkey Ukraine Vietnam

Oxford is a registered trade mark of Oxford University Press
in the UK and in certain other countries

Published in the United States
by Oxford University Press Inc., New York

First published 2006

British Library Cataloguing in Publication Data

Data available

Library of Congress Cataloging in Publication Data

Data available

Typeset by RefineCatch Limited, Bungay, Suffolk
Printed in Great Britain
on acid-free paper by
Ashford Colour Press Ltd, Gosport, Hampshire

ISBN 978–0–19–929150–2

3 5 7 9 10 8 6 4

PREFACE

Why do lawyers practise? Why can't they just work like everyone else? Do plumbers practise? Do truck drivers practise? No, they simply work. But not lawyers. Hell no. They're special, and they practise. With all their damned practising you'd think they'd know what the hell they were doing. You'd think they'd eventually become good at something.

'The Chamber' by
John Grisham

Following the success of *A Practical Approach to Conveyancing* and in response to readers' feedback, we felt a strong need to try something similar in relation to commercial property. It seemed to us that there was no single book on commercial property that was aimed at the busy, cost conscious practitioner seeking a clear reference guide across diverse subject areas. Of course topics in this book are covered elsewhere, but they tend to be found across several disparate and rather expensive practitioner texts. So, spurred on by practitioners, students and others who enjoyed and found *A Practical Approach to Conveyancing* useful, we undertook a project that has proved both academically challenging and hugely enjoyable.

Our aim has been to provide a balanced mix of law and practical guidance, including tips on good drafting, covering a wide area of commercial conveyancing and property. The obvious starting point is the modern commercial lease, as this is the most commonly encountered document in practice. In the lease chapters we consider, amongst other things, rent and rent review, commercial lease covenants, insurance provisions and service charges. We also examine the enforceability of leasehold covenants generally, insolvency, remedies (including forfeiture) and the termination and renewal of business leases under the Landlord and Tenant Act 1954, Pt II. We consider property development including land acquisition, town and country planning, contaminated land issues, construction and finance. We examine the particular concerns when buying and selling tenanted properties, and revenue law generally as it affects commercial property. As with our conveyancing book, we have provided for quick and easy reference, regular key point summaries and practical checklists.

This third edition embraces the latest developments in commercial property including prescribed lease clauses, the 2004 reforms to the Landlord and Tenant Act 1954, Pt II, changes to the Use Classes Order, the impact of the Enterprise Act 2002, stamp duty land tax and the second edition of the Standard Commercial Property Conditions.

Our thanks go to Peter Klim and Ajda Ali at Russell Jones & Walker and commercial property practitioner David Hobbs for his assistance at various stages of the project. We also wish to thank Richard Ross and Lee Portnoi, two of Robert's commercial clients, who contributed substantial amounts of common sense. Finally, thanks as always to the staff at OUP for their continued support and professionalism.

We hope that commercial property practitioners will benefit from having this book on their shelves as well as their support staff, trainee solicitors, licensed conveyancers, legal executives, law students, surveyors, agents and indeed anyone else involved or interested in the subject.

Robert Abbey and Mark Richards
London
January 2006

ACKNOWLEDGEMENTS

The authors wish to acknowledge the kind permission to reproduce copyright material from the following organizations:

- The Standard Commercial Property Conditions (2nd edn), and the standard form business leases are reproduced for educational purposes only by kind permission of the Law Society of England and Wales, and the Solicitors' Law Stationery Society Limited.
- Laserform material is reproduced with the permission of Laserform International Limited.
- The Code of Practice for Commercial Leases in England and Wales is reproduced with the kind permission of the Commercial Leases Working Group and Royal Institute of Chartered Surveyors.
- The Commercial Property Standard Enquiries and Guidance Notes are reproduced with the kind permission of the Practical Law Company Limited.

CONTENTS SUMMARY

CONTENTS

TABLE OF CASES

TABLE OF STATUTES

TABLE OF STATUTORY INSTRUMENTS

THE CLIENT

A   INTRODUCTION

This introductory chapter is intended to provide guidance for the practitioner when advising a client on the grant of a commercial lease, as well as other useful matters including client care and professional conduct issues. It is not intended to be a definitive guide, as each transaction will have its own relevant considerations, but the following sections should alert you to the most important issues that are likely to arise.   **IN.01**

B   MEETING THE CLIENT

IN.02   Quite clearly it is important to establish a good working relationship with the client immediately you receive instructions. The first interview gives you the opportunity to instil confidence in the client in your abilities as a property lawyer. The first interview will of course enable you to gather essential facts, but it should also be used, where necessary, to furnish the client with relevant advice on how to proceed.

IN.03   Always try to see the client in person. Too many firms cut corners by relying solely on the telephone for obtaining instructions but in the long run this can be a false economy, for clients will normally prefer to meet their solicitor at an early stage. It is our view that, ultimately, it is still the high level of service that impresses clients more, not the low level of fees; and a satisfied client is one who will return to you with future instructions. If a personal interview is impossible, at least ensure that the instructions received and advice given over the telephone are clear, and backed up with a letter of confirmation to the client.

C   CHECKLISTS

IN.04   It can be helpful to have a checklist of items that will or may be relevant in the first interview. It is worth obtaining all the information you need from the client at this early stage. This will avoid the need to contact the client for information later on, which is frustrating for you and often annoying to the client. One word of warning on checklists, though; never be a slave to the checklist to the possible exclusion of other relevant matters. Always consider carefully the client's circumstances and ask yourself: 'Is there anything else I need to know from the client? Is there any further advice the client needs from me?'

D   UNDERSTANDING THE LAW OF LANDLORD AND TENANT

IN.05   It should go without saying that when you are involved in the grant of a commercial lease, at the very least you should understand and be able to apply the basic principles of landlord and tenant law. If not, you may find yourself unable to advise your client on its rights and liabilities under the lease in question. It will also assist you when you come to negotiate the terms of the lease.

IN.06   You should appreciate the distinction between a lease and a licence. A lease confers exclusive possession on the tenant, creates an interest in land and entitles the occupying commercial tenant to security of tenure under the Landlord and Tenant Act 1954, Pt II ('the Act'). Be aware of how this twofold security of tenure operates. First, at the end of the contractual term the tenancy will continue until it is terminated by one of the ways prescribed by the Act. Secondly, the tenant may apply to the court for the grant of a new tenancy which the landlord can only oppose on prescribed statutory grounds. Be aware also of the different ways the Act can be avoided, eg, by 'contracting out' of the Act. The detailed provisions of the Act are considered in chapter 7.

You should be knowledgeable about the principles of privity of contract and privity of estate. **IN.07** In particular you should be aware of the substantial changes made to privity of contract by the Landlord and Tenant (Covenants) Act 1995. Remember that for 'new' leases (ie, those created on or after 1 January 1996) an outgoing assignor of a lease is automatically released from future liability under the lease unless it has entered into an authorized guarantee agreement (AGA). AGAs are commonly encountered in practice. This and other matters are considered in detail in chapter 5.

The rules of construction of commercial leases demonstrate the importance of good draft- **IN.08** ing. Generally speaking the court is reluctant to hold a clause void for uncertainty and will find ways to interpret the clause looking at the lease as a whole. But the court usually adopts a literal approach to interpretation unless in the commercial reality of the situation the result would be absurd and one which the parties could not reasonably have intended (see *Broadgate Square plc v Lehman Brothers Ltd* [1995] 01 EG 111). Given the literal approach adopted by the court, this underlines the importance of precise and unambiguous drafting.

E   TAKING INSTRUCTIONS ON THE GRANT OF A COMMERCIAL LEASE

The client, whether landlord or tenant, should normally be in a position to give you full **IN.09** details of the property's location, the parties involved, the initial rent, rent review period and length of the agreed term. However you must ensure that the client considers other key issues as well, such as the precise extent of the premises to be let. This is particularly important when dealing with a letting of part of a building. In this case you should also consider any rights the tenant may require over the landlord's adjoining property and any rights the landlord may require over the demised premises. Consider also what arrangements are to be made for the repair and maintenance of the demised premises and, on a letting of part, the building of which the demised premises form part. The parties will need to agree the permitted use of the premises and be advised on how restrictive the tenant's user covenant should be. As we shall see in chapter 3, a landlord should appreciate that a narrow user clause may not necessarily be in the landlord's best interest when the rent is reviewed. These issues and others are examined in detail in later chapters.

F   DRAFTING, APPROVING, AND NEGOTIATING THE LEASE

If the landlord's reversion is to be sold to an institutional investor, the landlord must have **IN.10** regard to the requirements of such investors who will insist on 'clear' leases. A clear lease places all the costs of repairing and insuring on the tenant so that the landlord receives a clear rental income without the need to 'dip into' the rent to pay for repairs or insurance. Clear leases typically are for fixed terms of 15 years with five yearly upward only rent reviews, although in times of recession they may be shorter. Also, the impact of the Land Registration Act 2002 may give rise to more commercial leases not exceeding seven years in length (see chapter 1).

IN.11 The landlord's solicitor drafts the lease which is usually adapted simply from a commercial lease precedent held by the solicitor's firm. Principles of good drafting dictate that the wording used should be concise but at the same time clear and unambiguous. It is a sad fact that ambiguously worded legal documents are often the cause of much lengthy litigation; and the hallmark of a good non-contentious lawyer is to seek to avoid the client's involvement in future litigation.

IN.12 The landlord's solicitor will send the draft lease in duplicate to the tenant's solicitor ensuring that any copy plans within the lease are correctly coloured. The tenant's solicitor will need to approve the draft lease as quickly as possible ensuring that it adequately reflects the tenant's instructions and, if necessary, is amended to be more favourable to the tenant. Conventionally, tenant's amendments are made in red ink (or red type if the draft is returned electronically). If major points of principle are at stake, eg the frequency of rent review, then to save time these should be put in a letter to the other side at an early stage of the negotiations. When the amended draft lease is returned, the accompanying letter of the tenant's solicitor should explain the reasons for the amendments. The landlord's solicitor can then respond to the amendments either by accepting them or by further amending the draft in green ink (or type) and commenting on these in the covering letter. At this stage the amended draft is known as a 'travelling draft' for the obvious reason that it is travelling between the two firms.

IN.13 Depending upon your relationship with the client you may find it useful to send the client copies of your correspondence with the other side so that the client can see the points at issue. This not only keeps the client informed of progress but also offers the client the opportunity of taking up outstanding matters with the other party direct (or with its agent). Once the travelling draft has gone back and forth a few times it may be advisable to arrange a meeting between solicitors to negotiate any sticking points. Often the meeting takes place with both clients present, so instructions can be taken from them immediately. The meeting will save time, but it also gives the solicitor an opportunity to explain more fully than in correspondence his or her reason for inserting a clause or making an amendment.

IN.14 As with all negotiations, be prepared. Argue your points not on the basis that the amendment is in the best interest of your client but that it is reasonable in all the circumstances. In this way you are more likely to persuade the other side to accept it. Be prepared also for possible counter arguments and be ready to deal with them. As already mentioned, your knowledge of the relevant law is likely to strengthen your position in the negotiations (and impress the client!).

IN.15 Of course your negotiations may be influenced by other factors. The relative bargaining strengths of the parties may be relevant. So a prospective tenant with a good reputation (known as a 'good covenant') is likely to be more appealing to a landlord. The landlord may be keen to get a good covenant signed up and thus be more willing to compromise on the terms of the lease. The state of the letting market in the location of the property can also be a factor in negotiations. How desperate is the landlord to secure a tenant? How desperate is the tenant to move in and start trading? How scarce are available business premises in the area?

IN.16 In the case of a sub-lease the negotiations inevitably will be constrained by the terms of the head lease and the parties have to be realistic about their expectations. This is because the sub-tenant's covenants must be consistent with those in the head lease. In particular the sub-tenant should not be permitted to do anything that the head tenant would be prohibited from doing; otherwise the head tenant may find itself in breach of covenant.

The tenant's solicitor has a duty to explain to the tenant the effect of the terms of the lease **IN.17** and in particular any onerous or unusual clauses (*Sykes v Midland Bank Executor and Trustee Co Ltd* [1970] 2 All ER 471). Without exception, the solicitor should give a full written report to the tenant on the terms of the lease and preferably also go through it in a meeting with the client. A similar duty is imposed on the landlord's solicitor, especially in regard to a business client who may be unfamiliar with commercial leases. In cases where the effect of clauses is not obvious their implications should always be explained to the client.

G CLIENT CARE AND ADVICE ON COSTS

Caring for the client's needs is always of paramount importance to the competent prac- **IN.18** titioner who should naturally be concerned to ensure that the client is happy with the service provided. As part of the continuing drive towards client satisfaction, client care procedures are a formal requirement of the Law Society's Code of Conduct ('the Code') which is expected to be in force in 2006. These are contained in Rule 2 which provides that solicitors shall give their clients information about costs and other matters, and operate a complaints handling procedure in accordance with the Code.

Costs

The Code requires solicitors to give the client the best information possible about the likely **IN.19** overall cost including a breakdown between fees, VAT, and disbursements. At the start of a commercial lease transaction it should be possible to agree an estimate for the whole transaction. You should also advise the client of VAT payable on top of your profit costs together with other expenses such as stamp duty land tax, land registry fees, search fees, and bank transfer fees. If you forget to mention VAT, the client may assume that the quoted figure is inclusive of it (s 89, Value Added Tax Act 1994).

Once you have settled an estimated figure it is sensible to inform the client that you reserve **IN.20** the right to increase your charges should the transaction prove to be unduly complicated or protracted. In this way you are not binding yourself to a fixed, unalterable fee. You may reassure the client, however, by saying that in the vast majority of cases, no increase is usually necessary. You should also discuss how and when the costs are to be met (normally at the conclusion of the transaction). You should confirm the estimate to the client in writing and you must also advise the client immediately in writing if the figure is to be revised. Care is needed here because if you go further than giving an estimate—by committing yourself to a fixed (or 'agreed') fee—then you will not be permitted to charge more even if circumstances arise which make the work unremunerative at that figure.

Complaints handling procedure and client care generally

IN.21 Solicitors are required to operate a complaints handling procedure. It should be in writing and all staff must be made aware of it. You must inform the client of the name and status of the person dealing with the matter, the name of the principal responsible for its overall supervision, and whom the client should contact if there is a problem with the service. You must also ensure that the client is informed about the likely time scale of the transaction.

IN.22 The Code is clear and self-explanatory, and breach of it will raise a question of professional conduct to be investigated by the Law Society or Consumer Complaints Service. However, the Code recognizes that there may be circumstances where it would be inappropriate to provide any or all the information required. For example, when acting for a regular client for whom repetitive work is done the client may already have been provided with the relevant information. It follows that the Code is of particular importance when taking instructions from a new or non-established client.

IN.23 At some stage during the first interview, the practitioner should advise the client of the future action to be taken to progress the matter, the likely time scale of the transaction, and when the practitioner will next contact the client. If the client is unfamiliar with the commercial lease process it is always good practice to offer a brief explanation of the procedures involved. All relevant client care information, including advice on costs, must be confirmed to the client in writing.

H   CLIENT CONFIDENTIALITY AND MONEY LAUNDERING

IN.24 The general rule is that client affairs are confidential and must never be disclosed to a third party without the client's consent, even where the practitioner is no longer acting for the client.

IN.25 One exception to the confidentiality rule which is of importance in the context of commercial conveyancing concerns money laundering. The National Criminal Intelligence Service (NCIS) has highlighted the prevalence of property transactions as a means of laundering criminal funds and the high risk of exposure of professionals offering conveyancing services to the public. The Criminal Justice Act 1993 and the Proceeds of Crime Act 2002 introduced criminal offences for *failing to disclose* to the authorities (ie, the NICS), knowledge or suspicion of others who are involved in laundering the proceeds of a crime, drug trafficking or terrorism. Thus, if you have such knowledge or suspicion, you must report it to your firm's Nominated Officer (see below) as soon as practically possible prior to the transaction taking place. The Law Society has issued a 'blue card warning' to solicitors alerting them to likely circumstances which could amount to assisting in money laundering. These include:

(a) clients who ask you to hold large sums of cash and who then ask for a cheque from your firm,

(b) secretive clients who will not disclose their identity,

(c) unusual instructions, eg, clients instructing you from the other end of the country when they could be using a local firm,

(d) unusual settlement requests, eg, paying for a property with large sums of cash.

Note that it is also an offence to 'tip off' the client that you have made a disclosure to the   **IN.26**
authorities, or that the authorities are investigating a possible laundering offence. This rule
is also contrary to the normal solicitor-client relationship of confidentiality. The duty of
disclosure extends to any party (not just your client) suspected of being involved, so this
covers the other side's client as much as suspicion about your own client.

Solicitors should comply with the Money Laundering Regulations 2003 (SI 2003/3075)   **IN.27**
which came into force on 1 March 2004. In particular:

(a) All staff who handle investment business must be trained to recognize and deal with
     suspicious transactions (eg, a large cash sum received from a client for a deposit on a
     purchase should be treated as suspicious).
(b) Each firm must appoint a reporting officer (known under the 2003 Regulations as a
     Nominated Officer) and establish internal reporting procedures.
(c) There must be procedures for obtaining satisfactory evidence of the client's identity
     where necessary.
(d) A record of each transaction must be maintained for at least five years.
(e) Evidence of clients' identity obtained must be kept for at least five years after the
     relationship with the client has ended.

I   ACTING FOR LANDLORD AND TENANT

Subject to specific exceptions (see below), a solicitor must not act for seller and buyer or   **IN.28**
landlord and tenant in the same arm's length transaction. It is of course a general principle
of professional conduct that a solicitor must not act for two or more clients where there is a
conflict of interest between those clients. It is important to appreciate that the conduct rule
in this area goes much further than the general principle by prohibiting acting for both
parties *even if* there is no actual conflict at the time of acting.

Exceptions

You may act for both buyer and seller (or landlord and tenant) if: **IN.29**

(a) one of the following applies:
     (i)   both parties are established clients, or
     (ii)   the consideration is £10,000 or less and the transaction is not the grant of a lease, or
     (iii) seller and buyer are represented by two separate offices of the same firm in different
            localities
and
(b) the following conditions are satisfied:
     (i)   the written consent of both parties is obtained, and
     (ii)   no conflict of interest exists or arises, and
     (iii) the seller (landlord) is not selling or leasing as a builder or developer, and
     (iv)   when the seller (landlord) and buyer (tenant) are represented by two separate

offices of the same firm in different localities, different individuals who normally work at each office, conduct or supervise the transaction for seller (landlord) and buyer (tenant) and no office of the firm (or an associated firm) referred either client to the office conducting the transactions.

IN.30 If when taking instructions you are in any doubt as to whether a particular situation falls within an exception (including whether a conflict of interest may arise), the best practice is to err on the side of caution and refuse to act for more than one party.

Meaning of 'established client'

IN.31 The most common exception used to justify the inapplicability of the rule against acting for both parties is the established client exception. However, careful consideration should be given to whether the exception properly applies in each case. There needs to be a degree of permanence in the solicitor-client relationship as exemplified by some continuity of instruction over time and the likelihood of future instruction.

Acting for joint landlords or joint tenants

IN.32 This is permitted provided no conflict of interest exists or is likely to arise between them. In most cases, the interests of the joint landlords or tenants are the same, so there is rarely a problem. The practitioner should obtain instructions (or verification of instructions) directly from each client, not simply rely on the word of the other(s).

J USE OF E-MAIL

IN.33 Increasingly clients are keen that their solicitors should communicate by e-mail. However without proper management and guidance the use of e-mail can cause loss for which solicitors may be held liable. There are also professional conduct implications. Solicitors are therefore encouraged to formulate a best practice policy for staff when communicating by e-mail. The following matters should be considered:

- E-mails should include the firm's name and address and a statement about where the names of the partners can be found.
- For ease of use, adopt a standard template for e-mails incorporating the above information (an alternative template should be used for private e-mails, if permitted).
- Because of the risk that an e-mail may be sent to the wrong person, consider an automated confidentiality warning, eg, 'Information in this message is confidential and may be legally privileged. It is intended solely for the person to whom it is addressed. If you are not the intended recipient, please notify the sender, and please delete the message from your system immediately.'
- Incoming e-mails should receive a timely and appropriate response. This may include automated out-of-office responses when staff are away from the office for a day or more.
- A secretary and colleague should have access to an absent person's e-mail to check incoming messages and to deal promptly with urgent enquiries.

- Unless they have no legal significance, e-mails should be printed off and kept on file.
- If a professional undertaking is received by e-mail, check that the context in which it was given provides reasonable assurance of its authenticity. Alternatively, check by telephone/fax that it came from the purported sender.
- Make staff aware that 'deleted' e-mails are capable of being retrieved and can be subject to disclosure in the event of a dispute.
- Make staff aware that the Internet is an insecure medium and vulnerable to hackers and viruses. In particular, staff should be aware that e-mail attachments may contain viruses. Up-to-date virus-scanning software is essential.
- Before downloading a file sent by e-mail, ensure that there will be no breach of copyright.
- The professional conduct principle to 'know your client' applies equally to receiving instructions via e-mail. Make the same checks and enquiries as you would for any other prospective client.
- Do not include confidential information in non-encrypted e-mails without the informed consent of the client who should be advised of the risks. Unless the e-mail is encrypted, ie has a code, there is a risk that it could be accessed by third parties.
- Firms should consider monitoring private e-mails sent between staff in order to maintain professional standards. Because of privacy issues, staff should be asked to give their prior consent to such monitoring.

1

AN INTRODUCTION TO COMMERCIAL CONVEYANCING AND PROPERTY

A   GENERAL INTRODUCTION TO THE SCOPE OF THIS BOOK

1.01   All areas of work conducted by solicitors have, in recent years, become so complex that specialization is the key to the future success of the profession. Conveyancing can no longer be seen as a monolithic area of practice that can be covered by mainstream knowledge of the subject. There has developed over the years a particular area of expertise that services and supports the market in and for commercial property. It is the growth of specific expertise in this area that we examine in this book and call commercial conveyancing.

1.02   Both authors now work as legal academics, but our practice background is in all aspects of conveyancing. We have between us some 50 years' experience of the specialization of commercial conveyancing. Because of this fund of knowledge and experience, we believe we have produced a book that emphasizes a practical approach to the process of commercial conveyancing and, in particular, how to deal with commercial property. However, this is not a book that remains fixed in the past. We both take the view that a successful future for commercial conveyancers must rely upon their thorough appreciation of all aspects of the theory and practice of this speciality, together with the ready embrace of Information Technology (IT) as it applies to this discipline. With these aims in mind, we have produced a book that we believe addresses these objectives as well as offering an understanding to practitioners and law students of the commercial sector as a whole.

1.03   For the sake of clarity, we have adopted the signpost heading method for all the chapters. Consequently, as demonstrated on page 1, you will find at the beginning of each chapter a list of contents. This method has been adopted to help the busy practitioner (or student) find the relevant area of interest as quickly as possible. We appreciate from our own experience of practice that there is nothing worse than spending hours of wasted time, fruitlessly searching through untitled sub-chapter sections trying to locate the desired subject.

1.04   Because this book has been written to assist in a practical understanding and application of commercial conveyancing, we have included in the following chapters appropriate precedent clauses. These lease precedents will be found at the end of each relevant section. The precedent will show a suitable clause from the perspective of the lessor and additions or deletions by way of amendments made to suit the lessee. Deletions will be shown by the original wording being struck through, and additions will be shown as underlined. We will in the main use references to lessors and lessees to try to avoid the gender-specific landlord and tenant descriptions. These are really more suited to short-term residential letting documents. However, we do use both sets of descriptions throughout the book, as happens in practice.

1.05   Within each chapter there are also two further elements designed to assist the busy reader. First, where appropriate, we have included key point summaries highlighting several key elements within a particular topic. These are provided as reminders of matters that should never be overlooked even in the hustle and bustle of the busy modern legal office. Secondly, we have included at the end of each chapter, checklists for the busy practitioner who may be seeking a quick overview of the important elements or the procedures in any particular topic. Two new chapters have been introduced in this edition; the first focusing upon your client; and the second about your practice. Our overall aim is to provide a clear, useful and, in particular, practical approach to commercial conveyancing and property that will help all those who use the book. In this way we hope to assist in the pursuit of an understanding of how commercial conveyancing can be a stimulating and, at times, even exciting legal skill.

B AN OVERVIEW AND AN INTRODUCTION TO COMMERCIAL CONVEYANCING AND PROPERTY

While many areas of commercial conveyancing may resemble similar practices and pro-   **1.06**
cedures utilized in residential conveyancing, the nature of the subject matter has dictated a diversity of approach. We detail below how we have set out to examine and explain that diversity.

A general introduction

We have given this book the title *A Practical Approach to Commercial Conveyancing and*   **1.07**
Property because we consider that commercial conveyancing services and supports the market in and for commercial property. As a result, this book will concentrate on several different topics that all relate to commercial property and which all involve specialist know-ledge of commercial conveyancing. Accordingly, after a general introduction we will offer a detailed examination of the main topic that affects commercial property, namely com-mercial leases. However, before we do, we will in this edition examine how recent statutes have changed and will change commercial conveyancing (see paras 1.18 et seq below). We will also look at possible changes in practice. In the context of commercial leases we will examine complex procedures for the payment and review of rent, as well as the covenants frequently entered into by both lessor and lessee. We will also examine the enforceability of covenants, as well as the remedies available on default. Subsequently we will continue with a comprehensive investigation of the difficult but crucial area relating to the renewal of business leases and the effects of the Landlord and Tenant Act 1954. Thereafter we will move on to consider property development (including land acquisition, planning, construction and finance issues) and the selling and buying of tenanted property with both commercial and residential lessees. In that section we devote some time to the careful examination of the contractual Standard Commercial Property Conditions (SCPCs) and, where relevant, contrast them with the long-established Standard Conditions (SCs) with the intention of seeking to ascertain which set better suits which type of conveyancing transaction. Lastly, we will complete our survey of commercial property by considering some relevant aspects of revenue law in the context of commercial conveyancing. We believe that the subjects we cover should provide a solid foundation to practice in this specialist area.

Commercial conveyancing and property and the Internet

The practice and procedures of commercial conveyancing do not stand still. Technology   **1.08**
affects all aspects of this specialization. Word processors have had a substantial effect on the structure, length and content of commercial leases. But the effects of technology do not stop there. Negotiations are conducted by telephone, e-mail and fax, as well as by

correspondence in the post. Many different types of conveyancing searches can be requested electronically, and now the Internet is exerting its influence over commercial conveyancing and property. The World Wide Web, the most user-friendly and popular section of the Internet, is just as important to commercial conveyancers as it is to their clients. Amongst other things, it is a significant and versatile source of research data that can assist commercial conveyancers in their daily tasks. There are free sites and subscription sites that are of help to commercial conveyancers. To assist, we set out in appendix 1 a list of useful, free access web sites for a commercial conveyancing practitioner. The subscription sites are made available usually by commercial publishing houses that have made their reference works available on the Internet. If you wish to access Internet sites please note, to save time, when using most of the leading web browsers, that you can leave out the prefix 'http://' when inputting one of these site addresses. Web site addresses change frequently. If you have difficulty in locating any of these sites, try searching for them using a web search site such as <www.google.co.uk> and by searching against the main title of the site itself, as listed in appendix 1. This should produce a search result that will take you to the correct location.

C   DEFENSIVE LAWYERING AND THE COMMERCIAL CONVEYANCING PROCESS

1.09   In March 1997, the Managing Director of the Solicitors Indemnity Fund wrote that conveyancing 'accounts for over half of all claims against the fund over all years, by both number and value'. Clearly, this is a reflection both of the pressure on practitioners to expedite transactions at all costs and of inappropriate working practices that provoke negligence claims. It is our view that conveyancers, like the medical professionals, must practise defensively. By this we mean that in our daily conveyancing routine we must build in working practices that protect us from negligence claims as well as looking after the best interests of the client. If doctors can practise in this way, so can conveyancers.

1.10   The worst mistake a practitioner could make would be to fail to spot something fraudulent. The Law Society is as concerned with the incidence of fraud as it affects practitioners as is the Indemnity Fund. You should therefore be fully aware of the pitfalls in practice when fraud occurs. As a form of basic guidance, you should read through the Law Society's 'Green Card' warning on property fraud issued in January 1996 (set out in appendix 5). It makes practical suggestions like 'question unusual instructions' and 'verify signatures', as well as concluding with this warning: 'Any failure to observe these signs and to take the appropriate steps may be used in court as evidence against you if you and your client are prosecuted, or if you are sued for negligence.'

Time limits

1.11   Conveyancing practitioners are constantly up against crucial time limits. The problem is that in a busy modern legal office these can be overlooked all too easily. Your professional negligence insurers will not look kindly upon such simple errors. The use of diaries, either written or electronic, is strongly recommended by us, and we set out below some of the more important time limits to bear in mind. However, in all cases we suggest you use the early warning date system. This puts in your diary a date warning at least a week before the actual deadline. That way, you will have a full, five working days' early warning of the final deadline in which to make sure you take the necessary steps required in any particular transaction. You should always use this system in the following commercial conveyancing cases:

Company mortgage registration period

If you act for a limited company client, any mortgage that it takes out, ie, where the company **1.12** is borrowing the money, *must* be registered at Companies House within 21 days of the completion date (see s 395 of the Companies Act 1985). Remember, the courts almost never extend the time limit. Failure to register within the 21-day period will inevitably mean that you will be held liable in negligence to your client for any loss it may suffer as a consequence of your inaction. Your failure to register will not avoid the debt but the security of the charge is lost (see *Re Molton Finance Limited* [1968] Ch 325, where the court indicated that as a consequence of non-registration there was no right for the lender to retain the borrower's deeds). The lender then becomes a mere unsecured creditor, and it is this loss of status more than anything else that gives rise to claims in negligence against the practitioner at fault. To ensure that the application gets to the appropriate department within Companies House without delay, we recommend that you mark the envelope 'for the Attention of the Mortgage Section' and it should then go straight there. If there are then any queries on the form submitted with the mortgage, you will have sufficient time to deal with the problem so as to allow the actual registration to take place within the 21-day period.

Landlord and Tenant Act 1954 deadlines

Part II of the 1954 Act covers the statutory renewal of commercial or business leases. This is a **1.13** particularly fertile area of negligence claims as the statute is laden with strict time limits: 'The statutory regime is notoriously technical and complex and, consequently, generates much litigation' (see M. Haley, 'The statutory regulation of business tenancies: private property, public interest and political compromise' in (1999) 19(2) LS 227). These lease renewal matters are considered in chapter 7. Some conveyancers will say that this is an area best left to litigators. However, it is also the case that many conveyancers wish to deal with commercial lease renewal cases, which necessitates a secure knowledge of the Act and the time limits concerned. These time limits are not normally capable of extension. You must diarize the date sequence once you have instructions and you know the date the notice was served. These are complicated time constraints, so you must have a proper diary system to protect you from missing a date.

Stamp duty land tax deadlines

After completion of a non-residential purchase where the consideration exceeds (currently) **1.14** £120,000, stamp duty of 1 per cent of the consideration must be paid to the Inland Revenue within 30 days of completion. If the price is more than £250,000, the duty goes up to 3 per cent; and if the price is more than £500,000, the duty increases to 4 per cent of the consideration. New leases attract additional duty calculated on the net present value of the lease. This is in addition to the duty payable on the consideration, ie, the premium. If you fail to pay stamp duty land tax within this period, late payment will be possible only on payment of a penalty fee. On the assumption that you were in funds to pay the duty, there can be no excuse for not paying the duty in time. Moreover, the penalty fee will almost certainly come out of your own funds as the amount will be of such a size that it will not be sufficient to warrant a claim on your indemnity policy. A few of these, and the profit element within your professional charges will soon diminish dramatically. See chapter 10 per more information about stamp duty land tax.

Rent review time limits

1.15   At the core of most (if not all) commercial leases will lie the provisions for the payment and review of rent. These will be looked at in more detail in chapter 2. However, time limits can play an important role in the manner by which rents are periodically reviewed. The procedure for triggering and handling the review is a critical part of the process and another area fraught with timing problems for a commercial conveyancer. Some rent review clauses trigger the process by requiring the lessor to serve a notice upon the lessee calling for a review of the rent at the rent review date. Some trigger notices will be required by the review procedure to state what the lessor requires as a new rent. Others may simply call for the review process to be commenced. If an amount is specified, some lease clauses require the lessee to agree or disagree with the stated amount within a specified period. A trap exists here for the unwary. If time is of the essence for the lessee's response then, should that time limit not be complied with, the rental stated by the lessor, no matter how exaggerated it may be, will prevail as the rent for review. (Exaggeration does not make the notice ineffective, see *Amalgamated Estates Ltd v Joystretch Manufacturing Ltd* (1981) 257 EG 489.)

1.16   Lessors can also be late calling for review by not complying with a time scale stated in the lease rent review provisions. The decision in *United Scientific Holdings Ltd v Burnley BC* [1978] AC 904 held that unless the clause makes it so, time is *not* of the essence for a rent review clause. If the clause makes all of it subject to time being of the essence (or part of the procedure) then the time limits are absolute and incapable of extension. In the absence of express provision, though, delay will not defeat a lessor's claim for a rent review. Nevertheless, time can be of the essence even if the rent review provision does not include that actual wording. If the words of the rent review clause are such that it is possible to show that there was an intention to make time limits absolute then the courts will infer time to be of the essence (see *Henry Smith's Charity Trustees v AWADA Trading & Promotion Services Ltd* [1984] 1 EGLR 116). Time being of the essence can also arise if other wording in the lease supports this possibility. Accordingly, if the lessee can, by notice, terminate the tenancy at the review date, it has been held that this means that time is of the essence for the review (see *Al Saloom v Shirley James Travel Services Ltd* (1981) 42 P & CR 181). The clear moral is that a commercial conveyancer involved in a rent review that contains time limits that are not capable of enlargement, must make clear diary reminders to ensure that vital dates are not overlooked.

Keep a claims record

1.17   Learn from your mistakes. Keep a record of all claims and complaints and see if any pattern is emerging. In this way you can quickly expose any weak links within your firm that require immediate remedial attention. Keep your procedures under constant review and introduce change quickly whenever required. Keep all your staff fully trained and up to date in all aspects of the law, practice and procedure.

D   THE 2002 STATUTES, CODES, AND STANDARDS

For conveyancers and the effect upon conveyancing, the year 2002 may, in due course, **1.18** be seen as a year to rank alongside 1925. First, 2002 saw a major statutory change to the law relating to registered land in the Land Registration Act 2002. Many of the changes impinge upon commercial conveyancing and are outlined below so far as they affect commercial property. The year also saw the passing of the Commonhold and Leasehold Reform Act 2002, which once again may well have a major effect on the theory and practice of commercial conveyancing. The main aspects are set out below. Finally, the year also saw the introduction of a newly revised code of practice for commercial leases and standard enquiries for commercial property. These too are considered below.

The Land Registration Act 2002

The Royal Assent for the Land Registration Act 2002 ('the Act') was given on 26 February **1.19** 2002. The Act came into force on 13 October 2003. The main aspects of the Act that are of major consequence for commercial conveyancers are set out within this section. However, we have also incorporated within other sections of the book reference to the Act where appropriate.

Registration triggers

The intention of the Act is to extend the registration of land to as many legal estates as is **1.20** possible. First, registration matters are covered within Chs 1 and 2 of Pt 2 of the Act. Chapter 1 deals specifically with first registration, covering ss 3 to 14 inclusive. The effect of this is to allow and extend voluntary first registration as well as to extend compulsory first registration triggers to include leases with more than seven years to run. (Indeed the clear intention is to reduce this period down to leases with more than three years to run and the Act contains a power to give effect to this intention.) Section 4 of the Act sets out the triggers for first registration and consolidates the position set out in the Land Registration Act 1997. Section 5 enables the Lord Chancellor to add new compulsory first registration trigger events by way of statutory instruments. Section 6 imposes a requirement upon the estate owner to register within two months of the date of the conveyance or transfer to the new estate owner. Should an estate owner fail to comply with s 6, s 7 provides that a transfer will become void. Should this occur then the transferor would hold the legal estate on a bare trust on behalf of the transferee. If the failure to register arises from the grant of a lease or mortgage they too will be void. They will however, take effect as an agreement to grant the lease or mortgage.

The one major area of concern for practitioners must relate to the reduction in the length of **1.21** leases inducing first registration. This is because, until now, commercial leases in particular have been granted for terms usually between 5 and 21 years but typically 10 to 15 years in length. They have not required registration but have operated as overriding interests. The

Act changes the position by requiring all leases of more than seven years in duration to be subject to compulsory first registration. This could well lead to more commercial leases being granted for terms of not more than seven years in length.

Third party rights; protective entries

1.22 These are notices and restrictions and are dealt with in Pt 4 of the Act covering ss 32 to 47 inclusive. The Act reduces to just two the methods of protecting the interests of third parties over registered land. Cautions and inhibitions are effectively abolished while notices and restrictions are retained. Notices may be used to protect encumbrances affecting land that are intended to bind third parties. A typical example of the kind of encumbrance that could be protected by a notice would be a restrictive covenant. Restrictions regulate the circumstances in which a transaction affecting a registered estate may be the subject of an entry in the register. For example, a restriction might be used where any consents are required to a disposition. The restriction will give notice of the requirement that they be obtained. This will typically arise where a management company is involved and requires a new estate owner to enter into covenants with it before the transfer of the legal estate can be registered, with the prior approval of the company.

1.23 Either form of protective entry can be sought without the consent of the registered proprietor who must be notified and who will be able to apply for cancellation of the notice, or object to an application for a restriction. If a person or company applies for either form of protective entry, they are required by the Act to act reasonably when exercising rights granted by the statute. There is therefore a duty of reasonableness that is owed to any person who suffers damage as a consequence of a breach. No doubt damages will be awarded where an applicant has not acted reasonably.

Charges

1.24 Part 5 of the Act covers the topic of charges and extends from ss 48 to 57 inclusive. The first part covers priority and confirms the established position that priority is the order of registration in the register. Tacking and further advances are covered by s 49 while ss 51 and 52 cover the powers of a chargee. Commercial conveyancing practitioners should remember that by s 25 the Lord Chancellor can prescribe the form and content of any registrable disposition including a registered charge. This could in the future usher in a compulsory standard form of charge in registered land that will cover commercial loans. Presently the Registration Rules merely make provision for a non-compulsory form of registered charge (see para 1.30 below). (Practitioners should remember that mortgages by demise or sub-demise cannot be granted for registered land as s 23 limits the owner's powers by excluding this possibility. All future registered charges over commercial property must be legal charges only.)

Electronic conveyancing

1.25 One of the main purposes of the Act is to usher in electronic conveyancing within the next two to five years. The new legislation aims to create the necessary legal framework that will allow registered land conveyancing to be conducted electronically. It is therefore worth repeating that the fundamental objective of the Act is focused closely upon making e-conveyancing a distinct reality. The Act constructs a framework in which it will be possible to generate and transfer estates and/or interests in registered land by e-conveyancing. The statute does this by authorizing the execution of formal deeds and documents electronically. The Act also contemplates the formation of a secure electronic computer network within which to carry out e-conveyancing. (This is dealt with in Sch 5 to the Act.) It is envisaged that the execution of all such deeds and documents together with their registration will be simultaneous. To do this the process of registration will be initiated by conveyancing practitioners. However, there is state control. The permitting of access to the computer network is to be controlled by the Land Registry, which will also exercise control over the changes that can be made to the land register. The Act also provides for the Lord Chancellor to regulate by rules transactions that can be carried out electronically. Furthermore, the Act gives the Lord Chancellor power to make the use of e-conveyancing compulsory. Compulsory e-conveyancing will only arise after a period of consultation and after a transitional period when conveyancers will move from the existing paper-based system to an electronic system. As such there will necessarily be a period of time while the two systems co-exist.

As a result of para 1 of Sch 5, substantial state control of the conveyancing process and those **1.26** who conduct that process is firmly put in place by this intended model of e-conveyancing. Only those solicitors or licensed conveyancers who have been authorized to do so will be permitted to conduct e-conveyancing. The relationship with the Registry will be contractual, under a 'network access agreement', and the Registry will be obliged to contract with any solicitor or licensed conveyancer who meets specified criteria.

Adverse possession

The stated aim of the Act is to ensure that registration and nothing else should guarantee **1.27** title and ownership as well as all the details of matters affecting the title. The logical extension of this aim is the limitation of title claims by adverse possession. The Act reforms the law of registered land adverse possession. In effect there are two methods by which a party can claim adverse possession. Which method applies to what property depends upon whether or not the property is registered. The old law (the 12-year rule) remains in place for all unregistered titles. For registered land the Act introduces a new scheme for protecting the interests of registered proprietors against the acquisition of title by persons in adverse possession. A person claiming adverse possession of registered land is able to apply to be registered as proprietor after ten years' adverse possession. The registered proprietor must, however, be notified of that application and will, in most cases, be able to object to it. Where the proprietor does object, the application will be rejected unless the 'squatter' can meet one of three limited exceptions. The whole basis of many successful claims for adverse possession previously rested upon the lack of any need to notify the paper title owner of the squatter's occupation. The new law for registered land changes all that and thereby dramatically reduces the number of successful claims.

The proprietor will then have to take steps to evict the squatter, or otherwise regularize the **1.28** position within two years. Should the registered proprietor fail to do so and the squatter remains in adverse possession then after two more years (making 12 in total) the squatter is entitled to be registered as proprietor. It should be noted that the new law places the onus on the squatter to take the initiative. If he or she wants to acquire the land, he or she must apply to be made the registered proprietor of the subject property. This is because the registered proprietor's title will not be barred by mere lapse of time; the ownership must be ousted by an act of registration. Clearly, the purpose of this part of the Act is to make the gaining of title by adverse possession of registered land much harder than is the case for unregistered land. It may well suit owners of commercial property portfolios to seriously consider applying for voluntary registration to bolster their chances of resisting adverse possession claims.

Key points about the Land Registration Act 2002 for the commercial conveyancing practitioner

1.29
- The Act extends compulsory first registration triggers to include leases with more than seven years to run.
- The Act reduces to just two the methods of protecting the interests of third parties over registered land. Cautions and inhibitions are effectively abolished while notices and restrictions are retained.
- Mortgages by demise or sub-demise cannot be granted over registered land as s 23 limits the owner's powers by excluding this possibility. All future registered charges must be legal charges only and may be in a prescribed format.
- The Act constructs a framework in which it will be possible to generate and transfer estates and/or interests in registered land by electronic conveyancing. The statute does this by authorizing the execution of formal deeds and documents electronically.
- The Act also contemplates the formation of a secure electronic computer network within which to carry out e-conveyancing. It is envisaged that the execution of all such deeds and documents together with their registration will be simultaneous.
- A person claiming adverse possession of registered land is able to apply to be registered as proprietor after ten years' adverse possession. The registered proprietor is, however, notified of that application and is able to object to it. Where the proprietor does object, the application is rejected unless the 'squatter' can meet one of three limited exceptions.
- The proprietor will then have to take steps to evict the squatter, or otherwise regularize the position within two years. Should the registered proprietor fail to do so and the squatter remains in adverse possession, then after two more years making 12 in total the squatter will be entitled to be registered as proprietor.

The land registration rules and commercial conveyancing

1.30   The Land Registration Rules 1925 have also been entirely replaced by the rules that were completed in 2003. The Land Registration Rules 2003 are fewer in number than the Rules of 1925. The original draft contained 220 rules, arranged in 16 parts, with 8 schedules. The rules now have a substantial effect upon how registered conveyancing is conducted. For example, the Registry has continued with 'Dematerialization', ie, the process of moving from issuing land or charge certificates to the retention of title details at the Registry. (This was pursuant to s 63 of the Land Registration Act 1925.) The consequence of this is that there are no land or charge certificates and so the rules make no reference to them. A form of paper 'title information document' is issued on first registration or on registration of dispositions involving a change of ownership. However this document will not constitute a guarantee of title. Official copies (the successor to office copies) will have to be used for the purposes of proving title in court.

1.31   Importantly, the rules also contemplate that there will be prescribed standard forms for leases, variations of leases and charges. The rules contemplate that content relevant to the

Land Registry will be brought to the front of these documents. Commercial practitioners need to be aware that where inconsistencies arise, these front elements will override anything in the main body of the lease. It is presently intended by the rules that charge forms will be non-compulsory to enable the use of bespoke forms for commercial or other complex charges. Thus the new rules will introduce new forms that include CH1 (charge), L1 (lease) and VL1 (variation of lease). In January 2003 the Land Registry announced that in the light of responses to the consultation process about the draft rules they had decided to remove their proposals about the mandatory use of forms L1 and VL1. The Registry brought forward revised proposals in the second half of 2003. These were contained in the Land Registration (Amendment) (No 2) Rules 2005 (SI 2005/1982). The compulsory requirements have now been limited to a set number of 'prescribed clauses' with a requirement that these particular clauses must appear at the start of the lease. New Rule 58A states that '. . . . a prescribed clauses lease must begin with the required wording or that wording must appear immediately after any front sheet'. A prescribed clauses lease will cover any lease the term of which triggers compulsory registration and which is granted on or after 19 June 2006. The kind of information that must appear at the lease commencement includes:

- Lessor's title number
- The parties to the lease
- A full description of the property being leased
- Prescribed statements (eg, those required by statute such as those involving a charity or pursuant to the Leasehold Reform and Housing and Urban Development Act 1993)
- The term for which the property is leased
- Any premium
- Prohibitions or restrictions on disposing of the lease
- Rights of acquisition such as a contractual right for the tenant to renew the lease (an option to renew)
- Easements

This information appears straightforward and should not prove to be a major concern to practitioners involved in the drafting of commercial leases. Indeed it would seem sensible to structure all leases, even those that will not be subject to compulsory registration, so as to place this information at the front of them.

The new rules also take account of the competing concerns between freedom of information **1.32** and keeping sensitive commercial information secret. This is because the Freedom of Information Act 2000 provides that government information, including information supplied for land registration purposes, should be released unless there are good reasons not to do so. The good reasons or permissible exceptions are set out in the schedules to the Freedom of Information Act. The main exemption likely to be relevant to the Land Registry is where it is commercially sensitive information. It is likely that commercial conveyancers will need to consider what they include in conveyancing documentation that will go to the Registry, should they wish to keep commercial, sensitive information secret.

The Act therefore allows exemption, ie, for information to be kept out of the public registers, **1.33** to be claimed for commercially sensitive information contained in documents which are otherwise available for inspection under the rules. In this way the new rules seek to strike a balance between the principles of freely available information (under the Freedom of

Information Act 2000) and the right to privacy. The documents that are exempt are naturally called exempt information documents. In relation to these EIDs commercial lessors may be concerned that registered leases will be available to the public as a result of the register being open to review by anyone. The effect of this could be that lessees could find out the lease terms for adjacent or adjoining property and this could be material to lease renewal negotiations in a large estate or could reveal concessions granted to another lessee. However, the Land Registration Rules 2003 allow for applications to remove sensitive material from public view. If the Registry approves an application it will be an EID. An application will be approved if the Registry is satisfied that the document contains 'prejudicial information'. Applications are made on Forms EX1 and EX1A. (As EX1 is a public document, unlike EX1A, do not disclose any sensitive material on this form!) The benefit of an EID is personal to the applicant and cannot be assigned or passed on. On a change of ownership a fresh application will be necessary to 'renew' the EID arrangement.

The Commonhold and Leasehold Reform Act 2002

1.34   The government has introduced another Act which makes substantial changes to leasehold property law and conveyancing. It is called the Commonhold and Leasehold Reform Act 2002. There is another way in which an owner may hold a freehold estate, and it is called commonhold land. The purpose of the new form is to address the current deficiencies in relation to the enforceability of covenants and other lease provisions between lessees. (For the same reason it also addresses the related problems with freehold flats, ie flying freeholds.) Each separate property in a commonhold development will be termed a unit. A unit can be either residential or commercial and the owner will be the unit-holder. Accordingly, commercial conveyancers need to be aware that the Act can apply to a shop or a light industrial unit as well as residential flats.

1.35   There will be a commonhold association that will own and manage the common parts. It will be a company limited by guarantee where all the members will be the unit-holders. Thus unit owners will have duality of ownership. First they will own their unit and secondly they will own a share of the commonhold association and thus indirectly the common parts.

1.36   All commonholds will be registrable at the Land Registry who will require on registration a commonhold community statement (CCS). This statement will contain the rules and regulations for the commonhold. The rules may permit the granting of a business lease out of freehold/commonhold. This would allow shops below flats to be let. It will be possible for owners of existing non-commonhold property to seek to convert their title to a commonhold arrangement but 100 per cent of all owners will have to agree to the conversion. The freeholder must consent to the conversion without which conversion cannot proceed.

1.37   In summary the unit-holders will in effect own, freehold-style, their shop, light industrial unit or flat instead of being a leaseholder. They will share in the running of the commonhold-held common parts and be required to pay a management or service charge. The units will not be wasting assets like leaseholds nor will they be at the whim of a freeholder and/or its management policies.

The Act also makes substantial changes to other aspects of leasehold property law and **1.38** practice that commercial conveyancers may encounter either when dealing with leasehold properties or portfolios of such properties for their commercial clients. The following detail has been prepared from the explanatory notes to the Act prepared by the Lord Chancellor's Department.

A new right to management

The Act introduces a new right for leaseholders of flats to manage their own building. It **1.39** sets out qualifying conditions for exercising the right and provides that eligible leaseholders must set up a company, known as a Right To Manage Company, in order to exercise this new right. The Act decrees the nature and format of the constitution of the company, including its memorandum and articles of association and entitlement to membership. It sets out procedures for exercising the right to manage and for the subsequent management of the building. It includes safeguards to protect the interests of the landlord and any other occupiers of the building such as tenants on short residential leases or commercial tenants.

Changes to the Leasehold Reform Housing and Urban Development Act 1993 ('1993 Act')

The Act seeks to amend the provisions of the Leasehold Reform Housing and Urban **1.40** Development Act 1993 with regard to the right of leaseholders to buy collectively the freehold of their building. The intention is the simplification of the eligibility criteria. It removes the requirements that at least two thirds of the leaseholders in the block must participate and that at least half of the participating group must have lived in their flats for the previous 12 months (or periods totalling three years in the last ten). It removes the low rent test in the limited circumstances where this still applies (leases of less than 35 years). It also increases the proportion of the building that can be occupied for non-residential purposes from 10 per cent to 25 per cent. The purchase of the freehold and subsequent management of the building is to be carried out by a 'Right To Enfranchise Company' of which the participating leaseholders are members. All relevant leaseholders will have the right to participate in the purchase by joining the company.

Finally the Act also seeks to amend the provisions of the 1993 Act covering the right of **1.41** individual leaseholders to buy a new lease. As is the case for leaseholders of houses, the low rent test is removed. The existing requirement that the leaseholder must have lived in the flat for the last three years, or periods totalling three years in the last ten, is replaced by a requirement to have held the lease for at least two years.

Reforms of the Landlord and Tenant Act 1987 ('1987 Act')

The 2002 Act contemplates two changes to this statute. First it extends the right to apply to a **1.42** tribunal for the appointment of a new manager under Pt 2 of the 1987 Act to leaseholders where the lease provides that management is carried out by a third party rather than the landlord. This would cover a company appointed by the lessees and required to manage rather than the lessor. The Act also extends and clarifies the grounds on which application may be made to vary a lease under Pt 4 of the 1987 Act. It also transfers jurisdiction for handling such applications from the county courts to a tribunal.

Other leasehold reforms

1.43 The Commonhold and Leasehold Reform Act introduces a new requirement that ground rent will not be payable unless it has been demanded. The demand is to be made by giving the tenant a prescribed notice. The reforms in the Act prevent the application of any provisions of a lease relating to late or non-payment (for example, additional charges such as interest) if the rent is paid within 30 days of the demand being issued. It also introduces additional restrictions on the commencement of forfeiture proceedings for breaches of covenants or conditions of a lease. It modifies s 81 of the Housing Act 1996 to prohibit the commencement of forfeiture proceedings, including the issue of a notice under s 146 of the Law of Property Act 1925, in respect of non-payment of service charges or administration charges. This is not the case if the charge has been agreed or admitted by the tenant, or a court or Leasehold Valuation Tribunal (LVT) has determined that it is reasonable and due. It also prohibits the commencement of forfeiture proceedings for other breaches unless a court or LVT has determined that a breach has occurred.

Commercial property leases—Code of Practice

1.44 The Department of the Environment as long ago as December 1995 first published a Code of Practice for commercial property leases in England and Wales. April 2002 saw the introduction of a newly revised Code of Practice for Commercial Leases that was issued with the backing of the current Minister for Housing. The code is meant to apply only to new leases and not to existing lettings. The intention of the government-backed Code is to try to ensure that the lease parties deal with each other on an open and honest basis throughout the whole lease term. This means therefore that if the lessee applies for a licence from the lessor, say, for alterations or change of use or assignment then the Code requires the lessor to deal with the application promptly. There are other elements that will be of relevance to both parties, especially where a guarantor is concerned. So if the lessee defaults the lessor will, under the Code, notify any guarantor (who may also be a former lessee) of the default.

1.45 The Code has the support of many elements of the commercial conveyancing market including the British Property Federation, the CBI, the Law Society, the RCIS, the British Retail Consortium and the Small Business Bureau. Consequently, practitioners will no doubt encounter commercial lease provisions as follows:

> The parties hereto confirm that they are aware of the existence of the code of Practice entitled 'Commercial Property Leases in England and Wales—Code of Practice' issued in April 2002 and will use their best endeavours to conform to the terms of it or any subsequent variation or replacement thereof

The Code remains a voluntary arrangement. The government is monitoring the use of the Code and may, in the future, consider that it should be made compulsory should the need arise. Members of the British Property Federation who promote the Code extend to many leading property companies and City solicitors and include British Land Company plc, the Co-operative Insurance Society, Land Securities plc, Linklaters, Lovells, the Prudential Property Investment Managers Ltd, SJ Berwin & Co and Slough Estates plc. Reference is made to 'the Code', meaning the April 2002 revision, where appropriate throughout the text and it is set out in full in appendix 17. Please see <http://www.commercialleasecodeew.co.uk> for more information.

Commercial property—standard enquiries

The London Property Support Lawyers Group has drafted Commercial Property Standard **1.46** Enquiries (CPSEs) with sponsorship coming from the British Property Federation (BPF). They are freely available on the Internet at <http://www.bpf.org.uk> or at <http://www.practical-law.com/0-103-2123>. They may be used on the condition that they are not altered and that the BPF logo remains. Additional enquiries specific to a subject property can be included provided they are clearly identified as such. The CPSEs are based upon a core set of standard general enquiries (CPSE1) which can be used for any transaction, ie, whatever the tenure and possession status of the subject property. Practitioners can then use other supplemental enquiries that are subject-property specific to be selected from the following:

- CPSE2 for tenancies
- CPSE3 for the grant of new leases
- CPSE4 for leasehold assignments

The intention for these forms is that they will be adopted for all commercial transactions and will thereby help to streamline and standardize the process. To assist, detailed and sensible guidance notes accompany the enquiries. However, the enquiries themselves are lengthy and occasionally quite complicated. They may suit the kind of enquiries required for commercial conveyances of a substantial nature but might prove to be too weighty for the more mundane shop or small business unit transfer. The core set of CPSEs are set out in appendix 18 with guidance notes in appendix 19.

Commercial Property—Model Clauses

In February 2003 the British Property Federation and the British Council for Offices published **1.47** a set of model commercial lease clauses. There are nine in total and they are meant to apply to a fifteen year full repairing and insuring office lease of the whole of a building. As a result there are no service charge clauses. The model clauses can be downloaded for use at <http://www.bpf.org.uk/publications>. Using plain English the clauses cover the payment of rent, outgoings, repair and maintenance, alterations and signs, disposals (alienation), insurance costs and definitions. Perhaps their main failing is to ignore service charges and the terms are unlikely to be exported to other kinds of commercial lettings.

E   COMMERCIAL LEASES—AN INTRODUCTION

Commercial property includes shops, offices, and factories, as well as heavy and light **1.48** industrial units. In effect it covers many properties that are not specifically houses or flats used for residential purposes only. All these various types of commercial property can be let on leases. A lease is of course an agreement whereby an estate in land or property is created, but only for a finite term. This seems simple enough, but if there is one area within conveyancing that really demonstrates the client's need for a competent practitioner then this must be it. The reason for this is simply that leasehold commercial conveyancing is so full of pitfalls and problems for the unwary or ill-informed. The explanation for this apparent complexity is contained within the nature and format of the lease document itself. Over time, leases have become longer and longer, with scores of covenants, conditions, provisos and rights being included to try to cover every possible eventuality. Moreover, different types of leases with differing contents are required to deal with different types of property. No one lease is exactly the same as another. It is this uniqueness that demands that, if you act for a lessor or lessee, each lease must be closely scrutinized and amended.

1.49   When a new commercial lease is proposed, the lessor's practitioner will draft a lease and send the draft to the practitioner acting for the lessee, for approval. The draft will then be amended in red on behalf of the lessee, re-amended in green on behalf of the lessor and so on, with the draft lease passing between the two sides. The 'travelling draft' will then pass back and forth between the two until it reaches a form that is agreed between the parties. With the increasing adoption by solicitors of the use of e-mail, sending the draft as an e-mail file attachment can quicken this process. The file is sent as an attached document to the e-mail recipient, and this file will contain coloured amendments in much the same way as is the case for hard copy handwritten amendments. A prudent practitioner will always maintain a file copy of the travelling draft incorporating the several amendments and re-amendments as they appear to ensure that the alterations remain properly recorded. It is also of use to record agreed items just in case the travelling draft is lost between offices. Of course, if matters require expedition then the best method of resolving the lease terms quickly is to arrange a meeting of all the parties around a table.

1.50   Historically many commercial leases were not registered in their own right at the Land Registry because their lease term was not more than 21 years in duration. However, after 13 October 2003 this period is reduced to leases with more than seven years to run by s 4 of the Land Registration Act 2002 (see 1.19 above). As such they exist as overriding interests as a result of the operation of s 29 of the Land Registration Act 2002 and Sch 3 to that Act. They confirm that all leases of registered land not exceeding seven years are overriding interests. If the new lease is not registrable but the superior title is, we would urge practitioners acting for prospective lessees to take advantage of the open registers at the Land Registry and obtain office or official copies of the superior title. This will show covenants imposed on the superior titleholder and which should be reflected in the terms of the proposed lease. It will also highlight any potential conflicts between the covenants in the title and those in the proposed lease. The requirements about deducing title are looked at in more detail at paras 1.92 et seq below. Either way, registered or unregistered, there will exist upon completion a fundamental legal estate with all the usual benefits and burdens attaching to it.

1.51   In the context of commercial property, it is probable that for a majority of cases a property company or an individual will own the freehold or superior title as an investment and will grant a commercial lease to an occupying lessee. The lease terms regulate the basis upon which the lessee will be allowed to occupy the premises for the purposes of carrying on a business. All commercial leases will include covenants given by the parties to the lease, be it the lessor, the lessee, or other parties such as sureties.

1.52   Inevitably this has meant that there is no one common form of commercial or business lease. Practitioners will encounter a multitude of lease formats, none of which is the same. Consequently, when acting for a prospective lessee, the terms must be read carefully to make sure that none of them is of an onerous or unusual nature that might prejudice your client.

When acting for a lessor almost the reverse is true. You will want to be sure that the lease properly restricts the lessee in such a way as to ensure that the property is occupied on the terms dictated by your lessor client. (For example, the rent review clauses can be written by a practitioner for the lessor in such a way as to maximize the rental, while amendments made by a lessee's practitioner will seek to reduce the potential for a rent increase on review. See chapter 2 for further information regarding rent review clauses.) It is this whole area of conflict that requires conveyancing practitioners to consider carefully the detailed contents of commercial leases.

Leases and legal writing

Non-contentious lawyers will almost daily encounter the need successfully to draft a deed or document for their clients. Commercial conveyancers more than most will be involved in legal drafting, especially where leases are concerned. Unfortunately, over the years, leases have become impenetrable in their use of language and lack of punctuation. Like many other examples of orthodox drafting, leases attract heavy criticism for this specific kind of old-fashioned legal writing. Leases are considered wordy, with overlong and complicated sentences full of jargon and arcane language. Indeed, it could be said that a typical lease is founded upon old-fashioned language that is pedantic and pompous. (For example, in *Holicate Ltd v Grandred* [1993] 1 EGLR 135, much judicial time was expended upon the meaning of the word 'said'.)   **1.53**

The obvious remedy is the use of plain English. What is plain English? It is 'The use of plain and straightforward language which conveys its meaning clearly and simply as possible without unnecessary pretension or embellishment' (Richard Wydick, *English for Lawyers* (2nd edn, Durham, NC: Carolina Academic Press, 1985)). Commercial conveyancers, for clear, concise and effective legal writing, should formulate strategies that, wherever appropriate, use short sentences, avoid long paragraphs and, most importantly, avoid legal jargon and/or slang. Remember, when drafting a particular deed or lease, that it will not always be the case that a particular clause will require a long sentence or a long paragraph. The sensible approach is to adopt the use of plain English where it is likely to assist in the easy interpretation of a lease clause.   **1.54**

It is widely understood that the use of correct grammar with some clear punctuation will add to the clarity of the deed. We believe that there can be no uncertainty arising from the sensible use of full stops, colons and semi-colons. It is the injudicious use of commas that can lead to uncertainty. We therefore recommend, for the avoidance of ambiguity, the use of sentences that avoid commas altogether.   **1.55**

Once an appropriate strategy has been formulated for clear, concise and effective legal writing, you will find that by using it you will inevitably adopt correct spelling and punctuation that will lead to the avoidance of ambiguity. However, remember even then to avoid being pompous or verbose. In an effort to adopt this approach, we recommend first that you always strive to take full instructions. Subsequently, reflect carefully upon the proposed purpose of any document such as a lease that may be required to achieve your client's aims. Thereafter, plan the content of the lease to ensure that it is fit for that purpose. If necessary, draft an outline with the intention of creating a deed that has logical sections contained   **1.56** within it. The sensible use of precedents should assist you in this endeavour. However, do not slavishly use precedents without considering whether they suit the intended purpose of the deed. Precedents are there to be adapted. A precedent is only as good as the person drafting it makes it in relation to the needs of the client and the nature of the subject property.

Agreement for lease

1.57   Occasionally it will be necessary for there to be an agreement for lease, and this is issued in draft form along with the form of draft lease. In this situation the two drafts are approved and the agreed form of lease will be attached to the contract on exchange as being the firm basis for the letting forming the main focus of the contract. The agreement will state a date or procedure for completion, at which time the lease will then be granted. Prudent practitioners acting for a lessee should register the agreement as an estate contract (either for registered or unregistered land) while the contract remains uncompleted.

1.58   An agreement for lease may be the preferred method for the grant of a new lease where the parties intend to apply to the court for an order that the letting be exempt from the renewal provisions of the Landlord and Tenant Act 1954 (see para 1.107 below). An agreement for lease will also be the preferred method for the grant of a new lease where the subject property is in the course of construction but the lessor wishes to pre-let the premises so that the lease will be granted on completion of the construction works. In these circumstances there will have to be a provision in the agreement covering a 'certificate of practical completion', ie, when the property is ready for occupation. Such a provision will usually require the certificate to be given by the lessor's architect. It is also possible that in these circumstances the agreement will seek to cover the works to be completed by the lessor. As a result, negotiations may arise whereby the intended lessee will enter into such an agreement only if the lessor completes certain fitting out works to the satisfaction of the proposed lessee and possibly to a fixed time scale. Once again, a conveyancing practitioner will need to ensure that instructions given by the client actually match the provisions in the contract. Reasonableness will have to be incorporated in the agreement when deciding if works have been completed satisfactorily and within time. Lastly, from the perspective of the lessee, it is sensible to ensure that the agreement states that it shall not operate or be deemed to operate as a demise, ie, a lease of the subject property. This precaution is necessary as the courts have held that an agreement for lease can operate as a lease demise. Similarly, it is a wise precaution from the perspective of the lessor that the agreement includes a provision prohibiting the intended lessee from seeking to occupy the subject premises until after completion of the construction works and, indeed, after the lease has actually been completed.

1.59   Lease agreements can be very extensive, and care in their drafting should be exercised at all times to ensure that all the terms are covered properly, including those relating to standard conveyancing considerations such as title, representations, etc.

Principal lease contents

1.60   A business lease should contain specific elements, and these are listed at paras 1.62 to 1.90 below. However, how and where they appear in any one lease will vary greatly. Also remember that registerable leases will all start with prescribed clauses, see para 1.31 for details. Some leases will use schedules, some will not. The retention of precedents for the various constituent parts of a commercial lease on a word processor is made easier by the use of schedules. They can then be incorporated into a lease format for any particular property. In many cases the lease may be referred to as an 'F.R.I.' lease, ie, a full repairing and insuring lease. The phrase has come to signify a lease that makes the tenant wholly responsible for maintaining the structure of the subject property. However, in many cases today the landlord will insure the property but will have the benefit of provisions in the lease that require the tenant to reimburse the landlord fully for the annual premium. The Code's first recommendation for negotiating a business lease states that 'both landlords and tenants should negotiate the terms of a lease openly, constructively and considering each other's views'.

As a consequence of the lack of a standard format for commercial leases, practitioners must **1.61** have in mind a basic list of necessary contents for a commercial lease, as follows.

The heading, date and parties

When reviewing this section, bear in mind that all registrable leases will start with prescribed **1.62** clauses, see para 1.31 above for details. It is a standard convention to start the new deed by calling it a lease, inserting a space for the date and by incorporating all the parties within the heading. Each party will include a description for later use in the deed. Consistency of reference is important, so that 'the lessee' should be called that throughout the deed and not interchangeably with 'the tenant'. Commercial leases will refer to a lessor and lessee, and possibly to a surety or guarantor. These last two are synonymous in that they will both be someone who has given a written undertaking to answer for the payment of a debt or for the performance of an obligation by another party (the lessee) liable in the first instance.

It should be remembered that if the lessee is an individual and that individual dies, the lease **1.63** will devolve upon the personal representatives of the deceased lessee. Indeed, the transmission of title to the executors or administrators will not be a breach of covenant not to assign without the prior consent of the lessor. Such consent is not required in these circumstances. Of course the personal representatives are liable to the lessor under the terms of the lease, possibly to the full extent of the assets held by them in the lessee's estate. Similarly, if the lessee becomes bankrupt the lease vests in the trustee in bankruptcy, and again there is no need to seek the lessor's consent to this devolution of title (see *Re Riggs, ex p Lovell* [1901] 2 KB 16). The trustee in bankruptcy can then either assign with consent or disclaim the lease (see paras 5.63 et seq below). (This position is the same should a lessee company go into liquidation, ie, the lease will pass to the liquidator who can disclaim or assign, if necessary with prior consent from the lessor.) Where there is more than one individual constituting the lessee, such as a business partnership, it is prudent for the lessor to include in the lease a proviso that if the lessee shall be more than one individual (or indeed company) then their liability is both joint and several.

It is also possible, although rare, to see a mortgagee joining in as a party to a lease to give its **1.64** consent to the granting of the leasehold estate out of the mortgaged superior title. (When buying a property subject to a residential lease, other parties to a lease may be encountered, such as a management company.) Some modern lease forms contain a long list of definitions at this point that can include various items such as the parties and the basic lease terms, ie, rent term and review pattern. Other items commonly encountered in such a listing would be rates of interest payable for any penalty provision in the lease (ie, for late payment of rent) and service charge percentages attributable to the lessee.

A clear parcels clause—property description and plan

1.65   This is the term used to describe the section of the lease that is utilized for the setting out of a full description of the property with all attaching rights. Both the property description and the rights attaching can be of fundamental importance when dealing with a commercial letting. For example, if you are granting a new lease of offices within a large block owned by your lessor client, you will need to ensure that the premises' description clearly defines the exact extent of the premises to be let. We recommend the use of scale plans. If the leasehold interest is to be registered, the Land Registry will require a scale plan. If a plan is used and a conflict arises between the plan and the written description of the property, consideration should be given to whether the written description or the plan should prevail over the other. If the written description is to prevail then the plan should be described as being 'for the purposes of identification only'. If the plan is to prevail then the property should be described in the lease as being 'more particularly described [or delineated] on the plan'. In the context of a commercial lease it is generally better for the plan to prevail (provided it is a comprehensive scale plan) as it avoids the need for a detailed and lengthy written description.

1.66   The parcels clause for a letting of the whole premises should not cause any difficulty. The problems arise where there is a letting of part of a larger property. In this situation the lessor's practitioner needs to ensure that the extent of the demise described in the parcels clause clearly links into the repairing liability contemplated by the repairing covenant to appear later in the lease. It may be that the lessor wishes to repair the main structure and to collect a service charge for this work. If this is the case, the parcels clause needs to be drafted to exclude from the demise to the lessee any part of the main structure. Furthermore, where there are several leases in one building there needs to be consistency across the several leases. This will avoid disputes over the location of boundaries and ensure the proper main-tenance of the main structure. Best practice dictates that where the lessor maintains the main structure, the leases to the several lessees demise simply the inner shell of the subject premises covering just the decorated surfaces of the walls together with the floor and ceiling coverings.

1.67   In the same example set out above, rights attaching need to be carefully listed. The offices may be on the fourth floor and so rights of access need to be stated. Additionally, the toilets for the premises may be on another floor. Access to these facilities needs to be referred to in the list of rights. This will also be the case for remote car parking and storage areas. It is therefore best practice to settle with your client a list of rights accruing to the subject prem-ises when taking instructions, including all rights of way inside and outside the building, so that these can be incorporated within the draft lease and included in the parcels clause. Three areas therefore need to be covered. First, rights of way (including the right to use all means of escape in case of fire); secondly, rights for conducting media (such as electricity cables) and connecting to that media; and, thirdly, jointly used structures such as party walls, roofs, sewers, car parking spaces, etc.

The physical layout of the demised premises might necessitate a further important right for **1.68** the lessee, namely to be entitled to enter adjoining land and premises owned by the lessor to carry out repairs or other necessary works to the subject premises. If the demised premises have external walls right on the boundary line then this easement could be very important in ensuring that the lessee complies with its repairing obligations, and indeed all other relevant covenants in the lease.

Lastly, bear in mind that many of the above points will be required on the first page of **1.69** registrable leases, see para 1.31 above.

Exceptions and reservations

These are the converse of the list of rights mentioned in paras 1.65 to 1.68 above, ie, a **1.70** detailed list of all the rights retained by the lessor. These reserved rights are necessary to ensure the continued full enjoyment of the remainder of the property. They will, as mentioned above, cover, first, rights of way, secondly, rights relating to conducting media (gas, water, etc.) and, thirdly, rights for the use of parts of the whole property, eg, shared car parking, toilets, drains, etc. However, these reservations are likely to be extended to include a right of re-entry for the lessor for various purposes. These will include, generally to inspect the premises, to carry out repairs when the lessee is in breach of its repairing covenants and to carry out works for the benefit of adjoining land or premises owned by the lessor. In the same vein there may be the need to include a right for the lessor to connect to media for the benefit of the lessor's adjoining land or premises. Lastly, and to avoid any future dispute with the lessee over the use of the lessor's adjoining land or premises, the lessor should include an absolute right for the lessor to develop that adjoining land or premises.

Start date and lease term

The length of the lease term and the commencement date for that term (not always the **1.71** date of the lease), sometimes known as the *habendum*, will appear at this point in the lease. The most important element here is to ensure certainty by stating a clear, precise and finite term commencing on an appropriate starting date, eg, 15 years from 25 March 2006 (or you can express this fully in words and figures). On renewal the court cannot order a lease for longer than 15 years' duration (see para 7.160 below). Recommendation 4 of the Code states that 'landlords should consider offering tenants a choice of length of term, including break clauses where appropriate and with or without the protection of the Landlord and Tenant Act 1954'.

The date the lease was executed will in many cases be different from the commencement **1.72** date for the term. It is entirely possible for the term commencement date to be either before or after the lease execution date. The only point of concern to note is that if the commencement date is more than 21 years from the date of execution then the lease will be void as a result of s 149(3) of the Law of Property Act 1925. If the commencement date is to be a long period after the execution date then we suggest that instead an agreement for lease is used with the agreed form of lease annexed to it (see paras 1.57 et seq above regarding agreements for leases). A lease term can be continued after the expiry date as a result of the protection given to lessees by Pt II of the Landlord and Tenant Act 1954 (see chapter 7 for details). Section 24 of the Act continues the tenancy on the same terms until the tenancy is terminated under the provisions of the Act. This would be a continuation tenancy continuing on after the expiry date stated in the lease. This could extend the original tenant's liability. However, it was decided in *City of London Corp v Fell* [1994] 1 AC 458 that if the original tenant assigned the lease before the expiry date in the lease then the expiry date is when his or her liability ceases. There is no liability during the continuation tenancy unless the lease expressly defines 'the Term' as including any continuation.

Rent

1.73   The rental details (sometimes known as the *reddendum*) will, where appropriate, include rent review clauses, frequency of payment and payment dates, and whether the rent is paid in arrears or in advance. Modern commercial leases have rent paid quarterly in advance and it will be subject to regular review, usually in an upward direction only. Other rents would be specified at this point, such as service or maintenance charges collected as rent. For details regarding the payment of rent and rent reviews, see chapter 2.

1.74   When taking instructions it is important to ascertain from your lessor client whether or not there is any agreed rental alteration in the way of a rent-free period or some other induce-ment. (A typical inducement is a reverse premium, where the lessor pays a lump sum to induce a lessee to take on a lease.) When the lettings market is weak, lessors will offer these to prospective lessees, and as a consequence of statute it is important to consider whether they should be included in the terms of the lease itself. (This is as a result of s 2 of the Law of Property (Miscellaneous Provisions) Act 1989, where the lease must be signed by both parties and contain all the agreed terms.) Lessors similarly offer such inducements, espe-cially rent-free periods, in exchange for agreements with lessees that they be allowed to complete any fitting out process required at the premises, particularly when the premises are new.

The lessee's covenants

1.75   This is where a long list of obligations with which the lessee must comply is set out. It will usually start with a covenant to pay the rent and will then list other, equally important, obligations such as restrictions upon alienation, changes in use and alterations to the subject property, and repairing obligations that fall to the lessee to perform. If you are acting for a prospective lessee you must, of course, consider carefully the nature and extent of all the lessee's covenants. This is also true if you act for the lessor. You must consider these coven-ants in the light of the intended use of the property and any other salient instructions. However, it is the case that some covenants will be of more consequence to a lessor or lessee than others. For example, will changes of use be allowed? If not, does the lessor appreciate how this could limit the rental income? In relation to the same clause, does the lessee realize that it will not be able to carry on any use in the property other than that stated in the clause (and neither could any assignee)? Can alterations be made at the property; and, if so, on what terms? Will the covenant have any effect upon the rent at review to either the detri-ment or the betterment of a party to the lease? In the following chapters we explore some of the more critical covenants commonly found in commercial leases. The code makes several recommendations covering lessee's covenants. These are also considered in subsequent chapters.

The lessor's covenants

In many commercial leases the list of obligations for the lessor is rather short. In some there **1.76**
will be just two covenants—one for quiet enjoyment, the other regarding insurance. A covenant for quiet enjoyment given by the lessor should be anticipated in virtually all leases.
Indeed, if an express covenant is absent, an implied covenant will apply. A typical express
covenant could read:

> that the lessee paying all the rents reserved by this lease and performing and observing all the
> covenants contained herein shall peaceably hold and enjoy the demised premises without any
> interruption by the lessor or any other company or person rightfully claiming under or in trust
> for the lessor

Where the lessee is a sub-lessee, the clause could be amended to include actions by superior
lessors, thus:

> that the lessee paying all the rents reserved by this lease and performing and observing all the
> covenants contained herein shall peaceably hold and enjoy the demised premises without any
> interruption by the lessor <u>or any superior lessor</u> or any other company or person rightfully
> claiming under or in trust for the lessor <u>or superior lessor</u>

The nature of the covenant is to confirm that the lessee can physically enjoy the complete
benefit of the property without the lessor adversely affecting that enjoyment. It is the extent
of the impact of the covenant that is open to interpretation. In the case of *Owen v Gadd*
[1956] 2 QB 99, where scaffolding was erected by the lessor outside a shop door and window
and consequently affected the lessee's business, it was held that there had been a breach of
covenant by the lessor.

In modern business leases it is common practice for the lessor to insure but for the lessee to **1.77**
covenant to reimburse the lessor for the insurance premium. This is almost always the
arrangement that prevails where there are several commercial lettings within one building.
This is a desirable arrangement as it will be cost-effective to have one policy covering the
whole building and will avoid inconsistencies of insurance cover that might arise if there
were to be a separate policy for each letting. Where the lessee reimburses the lessor, it would
seem that the lessor is under no obligation to consider various insurers to find the cheapest
premium (see *Havenridge Ltd v Boston Dyers Ltd* [1994] 49 EG 111).

The insured risks should be carefully defined and should clearly include damage caused by **1.78**
fire, storm, flooding, subsidence, burst pipes, riot and other usual risks covered by standard
buildings insurance policies. However, practitioners should bear in mind that cover for terrorism needs separate specific cover, and this should be precisely stated in the lease insurance
provisions. (See paras 4.08 et seq generally regarding insurance.)

Quiet enjoyment and insurance covenants are the most commonly encountered lessor's **1.79**
covenants. However, in other circumstances it would be appropriate to insert additional
requirements. For example, if the lessor is responsible for the provision of services then it
should covenant to perform its obligations in that respect. The covenant can be quite simply
a requirement to that effect, ie, to perform its obligations in respect of the provision of such
services. If such a covenant is included in the lease then the lessor will want to make it
conditional upon the lessee paying the service charge and other monies due under the terms

of the lease. It is also fairly common to encounter a covenant by the lessor in a lease of part of a commercial property to decorate the whole block.

1.80   Two further lessor's covenants arise, especially where there are leases that cover retailing. First, if the lease is within a shopping mall or centre, the lessor may agree that all leases granted in that mall or centre should be in a similar format. This would thereby ensure that all lessees were governed by the same covenants regulating service charges, user and other obligations that particularly affect the appearance of the shop premises, eg, not to leave the windows undressed or empty. Secondly, the lessor may agree to include a covenant limiting its right to grant a lease or a licence for an assignment of an existing lease affecting an adjacent property in the mall or centre that is in direct competition with the user allowed in the subject property. This kind of provision could be acceptable to a lessor for the sake of good estate management.

1.81   Lastly, if the lease is actually a sub-lease, the sub-lessee should seek a covenant from the sub-lessor to pay the rent required by the superior lease as well as to comply with the covenants and conditions in that superior lease. Bearing in mind that the sub-lease can be terminated by the forfeiture of the head lease, it is a reasonable precaution to require the sub-lessor to enter into such a covenant. Of course, if the lessor defaults because of a lack of funds or liquidation, there is very little that the sub-lessee can do other than to seek relief from forfeiture from the courts (see para 1.96 below for details).

1.82   The Code covers insurance and repairs and services. Where the landlord is responsible for insurance the policy terms should be competitive and the tenant of an entire building should be given the opportunity of selecting the insurer. Repair costs in service charges should be appropriate to the length of the term and the condition and age of the subject property at the start of the lease.

Any surety covenants

1.83   As has been noted above, commercial leases can refer to a surety or guarantor. These two are synonymous, in that they will both be someone or something that has given a written undertaking to answer for the payment of a debt or for the performance of an obligation by another party (the lessee) liable in the first instance. This section in the lease sets out precisely what is required of a surety, ie, on the default of the tenant is the surety required simply to cover the rent, or, do that and take over the residue of the lease? There can be other requirements for sureties and these should all be clearly set out in this part of the lease. We consider these provisions in chapter 3.

Other provisions

1.84   There will be other important provisions in a commercial lease, including a forfeiture clause (see paras 6.83 et seq below). Other clauses commonly encountered in commercial leases include those regulating the mechanics of the operation of the lease terms, such as a provision for arbitration in case of dispute between the parties or a clause setting out how covenant notices are to be served. Service and/or maintenance charge details could also appear at this point, including accounting details.

1.85   **VAT provisions**   As will be seen in chapter 10, value added tax (VAT) may be payable upon the rent and other sums due under the terms of a commercial lease. If the lessor elects to charge VAT then the lessee must pay it. There should be a covenant included to require payment in addition to the rent. However, there are lessees whose business is concerned only with exempt supplies. If this is so, clearly the lessee will seek a covenant from the lessor not to elect to charge VAT on the rent while that lessee has the benefit of the lease term. The Code recommends that the landlord should disclose the VAT status of the property and the tenant should take advice as to whether any VAT charged on rent is recoverable.

Costs The payment of professional charges can sometimes be the most difficult to resolve   **1.86** when dealing with the approval of a commercial lease. When the market is active and there is a shortage of desirable commercial lettings, lessors will seek to pass on their costs to the lessee. Similarly, when the market is weak and there is an over-supply of commercial property, the lessor will tend to bear its own costs in an effort to secure a lessee. Unless the parties to the lease agree in writing that one party shall be responsible for the other party's costs then each side shall bear its own costs (see s 1, Costs of Leases Act 1958). If the lessee is to pay the lessor's costs, there then needs to be included in the lease a covenant by the lessee to pay these monies. On renewal, there is no discretion for the courts to order a repeat of this covenant by the lessee to pay the lessor's costs notwithstanding the covenant originally included in the lease now being renewed (*Cairnplace v CBL (Property Investments)* [1984] 1 WLR 696, 1 All ER 315).

When the market is strong and as a result favours lessors, they will instruct their solicitors to   **1.87** require an undertaking from the prospective lessee's solicitors to pay their costs whether or not the matter proceeds to completion. This will necessitate two considerations for the lessee to reflect upon. First, whether or not it needs the property so much that it is prepared to risk monies on a potentially abortive transaction. Secondly, if the lessee does wish to proceed on this basis, it will have to put its solicitors in funds for the estimated amount of the potential charges to enable the solicitor to give the undertaking requested. We suggest that if such an undertaking is requested then the lessee's solicitor should first obtain an estimate and advise the client of the level of the potential charges. Also, if an undertaking is to be given it should be subject to a maximum level above which no other monies will be paid. Furthermore, if the undertaking is expressed to be 'whether or not the matter proceeds to completion' then the lessee's solicitor should make it clear that no payment will be required from the lessee if the lessor forces non-completion, ie, the lessor backs out for whatever reason.

The attestation clause

The end of the lease will contain the element demonstrating the proper execution of the   **1.88** lease as a deed. Where the lease includes execution by a company there are alternative methods of sealing. A company is no longer required to have a common seal, and thus a deed can be properly executed by the signature of a director and secretary, or by two of the company's directors (see s 36A of the Companies Act 1985, added by s 130 of the Companies Act 1989 which came into force on 31 July 1990). In this case the attestation clause for execution by the company will read as follows:

> Executed as a deed by A Company Limited acting by
> A Person, Director . . .
> and
> B Person, Secretary . . .

Alternatively, the company's common seal can still be used (and typically is). A more usual form of attestation will read:

> The common seal of A Company Limited was affixed in the presence of:
> [Signature] . . .
> Director of the above named company
> [Signature] . . .
> Secretary of the above named company

As with an individual's attestation, the word 'delivered' is not necessary. The Companies Act 1985, s 36A(5), provides that delivery is presumed at the date of execution unless proved to the contrary. If the deed is to be completed by a foreign company and if that foreign company has a company seal, the execution can be in the format required by the Companies Act and adapted as necessary to take account of any additional requirements. If the foreign company does not have a seal then the following is necessary as the attestation clause:

> Signed as a deed on behalf of (foreign company) a company incorporated in (foreign location) by (full name of signatory) being a person who in accordance with the laws of that territory is acting under the authority of the company.

If either of the above methods of execution is adopted, the buyer from a company incorporated in England and Wales is entitled to assume that proper execution has occurred (Companies Act 1985, s 36A(6)).

1.89 Traditional leases will follow the above format without the use of schedules. As mentioned, the modern practice of compiling leases using word processing and the use of precedents has given rise to the use of schedules to the extent that some leases have all these separate elements within different and discrete schedules. This is to be recommended when compiling documents in this manner in so far as it can assist in the avoidance of confusion in the main body of the lease caused by a lack of structure. This modern usage must grow with the advent of prescribed clauses in registrable leases, see para 1.31 above.

1.90 Many business tenants will benefit from the security of tenure provisions of Pt II of the Landlord and Tenant Act 1954. Full details relating to lease renewals, contracting out and the effect of this statute will be found within chapter 7.

Deducing title—entitlement to inspect the superior or freehold title

1.91 On the grant of a lease, the lessee has no automatic right to investigate the lessor's freehold title unless the lessor agrees otherwise. (Practitioners should be aware that s 44(2) of the Law of Property Act 1925 specifically provides that the intended lessee shall not be entitled to call for the title to the freehold.) If this is the case, the purchase contract should contain a provision requiring the seller to deduce the freehold title. See SC 8.2.4 or SCPC 10.2.4, which require the seller to deduce a title that will enable the buyer to register the lease at HM Land Registry with an absolute title. Of course in these circumstances the freehold title will have to be deduced to ensure the grant of an absolute title. Accordingly, the purchase contract must be checked, first, to ensure that it is drawn up on the basis of the fourth edition of the Standard Conditions and, secondly, to ensure that no attempt has been made in the special conditions of that contract to limit or exclude SC 8.2.4 or SCPC 10.2.4. If the superior title is not investigated, the lessee runs the risk that the lease may not have been validly granted or may not bind a mortgagee of the freehold. For example, the freehold may be in mortgage and the mortgage may specifically preclude the borrower or seller from granting any leases. There is also the risk of being bound by unknown third party interests affecting the freehold, such as overriding interests or minor interests protected by entry on the registers of the freehold title when the lease was granted. These risks are, of course, unacceptable to the lessee.

Deducing title—specific matters when dealing with sub-leases

It is the case that there are special and particular problems in relation to matters of title **1.92** where sub- or under-leases are concerned. These matters are examined in greater detail below.

Rules regarding deduction of title

A sub-lessee can call for the superior lease out of which the sub-lease is to be granted, **1.93** together with all assignments of that lease for the period of the last 15 years. However, s 44(2) of the Law of Property Act 1925 prohibits a call for the superior leasehold and/or freehold title. This is, of course, a problem in unregistered land, but is less so for registered land. This is simply because the registers are now open to public inspection and so the potential lessee can buy official copies of the freehold title (and all superior leasehold titles) direct from the Land Registry. The moral is that if the land is unregistered you should demand a copy of all superior titles before the new sub-lease is granted. Furthermore, the contract SC 8.2.4 (and SCPC 10.2.4) gets around this difficulty by requiring the seller to deduce title to the buyer in such a way so as to enable the buyer to register the sub-lease with title absolute. In other words, the superior titles must be disclosed. This will only apply to leases to be granted for a term exceeding seven years. Shorter leases will fall into the s 44 title trap.

Another real problem arises over the use of the property. The user clause in the sub-lease may **1.94** conflict with the user provisions in an unseen superior title. If this occurs, the practitioner who drew up the sub-lease would be considered to have acted negligently in preparing the lease without regard to the user restrictions in the superior title. Furthermore, the superior title may include a requirement that any sub-lease may only be granted with the superior lessor's consent. Clearly all consents must be obtained before a sub-lease is granted. (Also see SC 8.3 (and SCPC 10.3), which contains provisions that will apply if a consent to sub-let is required from a superior title owner. At worst, if no such consent is forthcoming, rescission is possible.)

Consistency with head lease

It is important to ensure that the covenants and conditions in any sub-lease remain consistent **1.95** with those in any superior lease. It is therefore imperative to see the superior lease to ensure that the terms of the sub-lease do not conflict with the superior lease terms. For example, it would be plainly inconsistent if the head lease required the lessor to repair the subject property while the sub-lease required the sub-lessee to repair the subject property. This is all the more important when you consider that the sub-lessor will almost certainly require an indemnity in the sub-lease, from the sub-lessee, against breaches of the covenants in the superior lease. Consequently, consistency of covenants will make sure that the sub-lessee will be able to ensure compliance with covenants in both leases.

Sub-lessee's right to seek relief from forfeiture

1.96   If a head lease is terminated by forfeiture, all sub-leases will terminate along with the superior lease. To try to prevent this, s 146(4) of the Law of Property Act 1925 allows sub-lessees to apply for relief against forfeiture of the superior lease. This relief is discretionary, and if an order is made it will take effect as a new lease between the lessor and sub-lessee upon the terms deemed appropriate by the court (see para 6.114 below).

Leases and the Landlord and Tenant (Covenants) Act 1995

1.97   This Act is of considerable importance in the context of commercial leases. It applies to all leases granted on or after 1 January 1996. All other leases, ie, those granted before this date, will not normally be affected by the Act (although see para 5.11 below). It reverses the general rule that prevailed before the Act was passed, that a lessee remained liable under the lease covenants throughout the full term of the lease. Unless the lessee has entered into an agreement formulated by the Act as an 'authorized guarantee agreement' (AGA), the lessee will, on assignment, be automatically released from any liability in the future on the lessee's lease covenants. If the lessee has entered into an AGA then the outgoing lessee acts as guarantor for the successor in title, but not beyond the time of ownership of the lease by the incoming lessee. Of course the outgoing lessee cannot escape liability for breaches of covenant that arose during the time prior to the assignment of the legal estate, and the outgoing lessee will remain liable for such breaches after as well as before assignment. Should there be a transfer of the freehold reversion, there is no such automatic release for a lessor under the terms of the statute. However, the reversioner can seek a release by applying for such from the lessee for the time being, either before or within a period of four weeks from the date of the transfer of the reversionary title. If the lessee objects to a release, the lessor can apply to court for a declaration that it is reasonable that it be so released (see s 8 of the 1995 Act). The effect of this Act cannot be excluded or altered by agreement or otherwise.

1.98   What amounts to a new lease can be of material importance, especially where, after 1 January 1996, there is a variation to a lease that was granted before that date. This is because a variation can amount to a surrender and re-grant but without being called a surrender. For example, if the variation concerns either the length of the original term or the extent of the demised property, it will operate as a surrender and re-grant. If this happens then the re-grant will amount to a new lease and will be covered by the terms of the 1995 Act. Practitioners acting for a lessor should always bear this in mind when dealing with variations.

1.99   This important statute will be considered in greater detail in chapter 5 in the context of the enforceability of covenants and remedies generally.

Lease variations

1.100   Where a commercial lease has been granted by deed, practitioners should always bear in mind that an effective variation of the lease must and can only be made by deed. It has been the practice in the past for practitioners to issue 'side letters' to give effect to an agreed variation, such as a rental reduction personal to the lessee in occupation. Frankly, if tested in court, this form of arrangement would be doomed to failure. (Indeed, it should fail as a result of s 2 of the Law of Property (Miscellaneous Provisions) Act 1989, as it is unlikely that such a letter will be signed by both parties or that it will contain all the terms.) Furthermore, if the lease being varied is already registered at the Land Registry, the deed of variation must be submitted to the Registry so that it can note the variation on the title. The deed of variation is ineffective in law until it is properly registered, although it would probably be effective in equity.

Practitioners should remember that where the variation is of a registered lease which affects **1.101** the length of the original term of the lease or the extent of the demised property, the Land Registry considers the deed of variation to be evidence of surrender and re-grant. In effect this means that the 'lease' will be registered and dated from the date of the variation, but will, by implication, refer back to the terms of the original lease. There is therefore a re-grant on the terms as varied by the deed of variation. Furthermore, the new 'lease' will be covered by the terms of the Landlord and Tenant (Covenants) Act 1995 (see para 1.97 above) whereby, without realizing it, a lessor may give a lessee a method of escaping liability under lease covenants that would otherwise not be available. If there is no wish on the part of the lessor to allow such a release to be available to the lessee then a variation should, of course, be avoided.

The Law Society Standard Business Leases

In an effort to standardize leases, the Law Society has made a valiant attempt to produce a **1.102** standard form of lease for commercial lettings. There are two types, one for lettings of whole and the other for lettings of part. Copies are set out in full within appendix 3. They adopt, as far as possible, plain English and are remarkably short in length. (So the parties to the lease are called the landlord and the tenant and the term is called the lease period.) The lease terms are commendably clear and easy to read and understand. This is a fresh and welcome alternative to the labyrinthine sentence construction of many orthodox leases. They also take a balanced view about the sharing of the benefits and burdens arising from the terms of the lease between the landlord and tenant. Sadly, these standard forms are little used in practice, possibly because they are so different in emphasis to the traditional approach where the lessor forces upon the lessee as much as possible in the way of risk and expense.

The Law Society holds the copyright to the leases and will license solicitors to generate **1.103** word-processed versions. Its intention is to underpin the drive towards a standard format. To that end it requires users to follow as far as possible the pre-printed format and to leave unaltered various core elements of the lease. These core elements include all the tenant's obligations, rent review provisions and the landlord's obligation and forfeiture rights.

The form starts with a page of definitions setting out the date, the parties, the property **1.104** description, the lease period, the use by the tenant allowed by the landlord and the amount of the rent, the payment dates and the review pattern. (In the lease of part, the first page also includes a definition of the building of which the subject premises form part.) The first page concludes with the simple statement that 'This lease is granted on the terms printed on pages 2 to 5, as added to or varied by any terms appearing on . . . any attached continuation page.' Pages 2 to 4 contain the rest of the lease provisions and start with the tenant's obligations.

1.105   One of the more controversial elements of the lease covers the section called 'Condition and Work' and which is the equivalent to a repairing covenant in a traditional lease. A commercial lease of whole will usually place an obligation upon the lessee to keep the subject property in a good and substantial condition, which may be interpreted as an obligation virtually to replace the whole property should this prove necessary. The Law Society takes a far more even-handed approach. Its provision simply requires the tenant 'to maintain the state and condition of the inside of the property but the Tenant need not alter or improve it except if required in clause 6.10'. Furthermore, the tenant need only paint the inside and out every five years and in the last three months of the lease period. Many orthodox leases will require a lessee to paint the exterior every three years and in the last three months of the term. Clearly the standard lease is much softer on the lessee, and it may well be that this has led practitioners to spurn its use. (Although they may also find it difficult to maintain fee levels when producing a light, four or five page deed!)

1.106   Provided your client is aware of your intentions, you could adopt the pre-printed format where it is cost-efficient to do so. For example, if the rent is very low or the lease term very short, issuing a 'standard' 60 page commercial lease would really be a case of 'using a sledge hammer to crack a nut'. This being so, a short form of lease following the Law Society format could well suit the client and allow you to issue a draft that will be approved quickly. You will then be able to charge fees commensurate with the limited nature of the letting and thus maintain good relations with your client. Otherwise we would not recommend the wholesale adoption of the Law Society Standard Business Leases as they really would not suit larger-scale lettings, or indeed long-term commercial leases, ie, over ten years or more.

Landlord and Tenant Act 1954—security of tenure

1.107   Part II of the 1954 Act covers the statutory renewal of business leases and affords a powerful element of security of tenure for many commercial lettings. At the end of a commercial letting, be it by lease or by a mere periodic tenancy, the effect of the Act is to extend by statute the lease term until the lessor serves upon the lessee at least a six-month notice to quit in the form prescribed by the Act. Until that notice expires the lessee is entitled to remain in the subject premises on the same terms and conditions as prevailed at the end of the original letting (see s 24). It is important for lessors to appreciate that this includes the rent, so that no increase in the rent can be made until appropriate steps are taken in accordance with the terms of the statute. Thereafter the lessee has the right to apply to court for an order that the lease is renewed, and the lessor can oppose that application only on several statutory grounds defined in the Act. It is possible to contract out of the effects of this statute. This important Act is considered in detail in chapter 7.

1.108   The 1954 Act does not apply to mere licences of commercial premises. This has led to attempts to avoid the effects of the Act by calling lettings 'licences'. This is doomed to failure as a result of the decision in the important case of *Street v Mountford* [1985] AC 809. The court decided that whatever the relevant document might call itself, if the arrangement it regulated allowed a party exclusive possession of premises for a certain term and at a rent, the result was a tenancy. The court considered that there were two elements that were paramount in a test for a tenancy—exclusive possession and a certain term. If these are present then the court will set aside any attempt to avoid the 1954 Act by calling the arrangement a licence. Although the case was about a residential letting, it is clear that the decision applies to all types of tenancies, including commercial lettings. Consequently the courts will consider bogus any attempt by a lessor to avoid the Act by misdescribing a lease as a licence. The moral is not to attempt this avoidance procedure, as it is fraught with danger and is likely to fail.

Break clauses

A break clause is normally understood to mean a clause in the lease allowing either or both **1.109** parties to the lease to break and end the lease term prematurely, ie, prior to the determination of the lease term by effluxion of time. From the lessor's perspective a break clause is especially useful if it intends to redevelop the site. It enables the lessor to receive a rental right up to the time when redevelopment of the site is physically possible and after all planning and other matters have been resolved. From the lessee's perspective it is particularly useful in avoiding excessive increases in rent at times of review. It will also free a lessee from a lease of premises that have grown either too small or too costly.

Break clauses are usually drafted so as to operate in two different ways. First, the entitlement **1.110** to serve a break clause may be triggered by simply reaching a specific date or dates. The clause will therefore indicate that the break clause will be triggered upon a giving of notice at specific dates, such as the end of the fifth and tenth years of the lease term. Secondly, the break clause entitlement may possibly come into operation upon the happening of a specified event, such as the lessor receiving a planning consent from the local planning authority.

If the lessee has the right to break the lease, the lessor should ensure that any existing rights **1.111** that the lessor may have against the lessee are not lost with the exercise of the break option. The clause should therefore be drafted so as to stipulate that the lease break will not affect any rights subsisting and accruing to the lessor such as may arise from rent arrears or subsisting breaches of covenant. The clause may therefore be drafted to stipulate that the lessee can break the lease only if all the lease covenants have been complied with. If it does, the lessee must ensure that if it intends to exercise a break option no breaches are subsisting (see *Trane (UK) Limited v Provident Mutual Life Association* [1995] 3 EG 122).

The timing of the notice is critical, as the courts have taken the view that time will be of the **1.112** essence unless the break clause provides otherwise (see *Chiltern Court (Baker Street) Residents Limited v Wallabrook Property Co Limited* [1989] 43 EG 173). (However, minor errors in the timing of the operation of the break clause that could not mislead the recipient of a notice will be overlooked by the courts—see *Mannai Investment Co Limited v Eagle Star Life Assurance Co Limited* [1997] 24 EG 122.) To that end a lessor may therefore require a strict timetable while the lessee will try to avoid such formulations. Accordingly, the break clause should require the notice to break to be made in writing and to state that it must be served upon the lessor/lessee and/or the lessor's/lessee's solicitor.

If the lessor has the right to break the lease, the most efficient way of breaking it, without **1.113** falling into problems with the operation of Pt II of the Landlord and Tenant Act 1954 (see para 1.107 above), is simply to provide in the break clause that the mechanism for the exercise of it, is to be the same as that for the 1954 statute. If this formulation is adopted, the form of notice and period of notice will coincide for both elements and make the necessity for two notices superfluous. The one notice made by the lessor will thereby comply with the requirements of statute as well as the terms of the lease break clause. The point to bear in mind is that it could be possible for the break clause to be given by the lessor without regard for the provisions of this statute. This could lead to the dilemma of having complied with the terms of the break clause but not with the statute. The dilemma is avoided if the notice serves both purposes.

1.114   One case highlights the need for practitioners to check all the lease terms when exercising a break clause. In *Secretary of State v Unicorn* [2001] EG 27 January 138 when exercising a break clause some extra rent became payable. Although the break clause notice was valid the extra rent was not paid. It was held that consequently the break clause was ineffective. This case highlights the need to look through all the lease to check for any action required when exercising a break clause.

Options to renew

1.115   If the lessor wishes to give an intended lessee some additional assurances about the period of time that the lessee may remain in the subject premises, it can include in the original lease an option for the lessee to renew the tenancy at the expiry of the term. If that option is in the deed then the lessor will be obliged to honour the term and renew the lease. However, the option may be conditional, ie, it may arise only if the lessee has complied with various preconditions such as fulfilling all the covenants and conditions in the original lease. There will also be a prerequisite mechanism to comply with, ie, the lessee must exercise the option by notice in writing to the lessor at a fixed point in the lease term and probably before a fixed date.

1.116   If the precondition is full compliance with all lease covenants then the courts will construe this strictly (see *West Country Cleaners (Falmouth) Limited v Saly* [1966] 1 WLR 1485, CA— cyclical repainting must be up to date if the option is to be exercised and binding upon the lessor). Breaches that occurred during the term of the original tenancy but which were remedied will not, however, preclude the lessee from succeeding with an option to renew (see *Bass Holdings Limited v Morton Music Limited* [1987] 2 All ER 1001, CA).

1.117   If the renewal is to proceed, it will usually be on the same terms and conditions as were contained in the previous lease. However, it is vital that the option is worded to ensure that two sections in the original lease are not repeated in the renewed lease. First, the rent will, of course, be at the market level at the time of renewal. Indeed, it is imperative that there is a clearly stated and precise mechanism for ascertaining the rent to be paid at the time of renewal. Without this complete mechanism the courts will consider an option void for uncertainty (see *King's Motors (Oxford) Ltd v Lax* [1970] 1 WLR 426). We suggest that the incorporation of the operation of the old lease rent review mechanism could be a way of achieving this. Alternatively, there should be a repeat of such a review mechanism within the option clause itself but with any alterations to take account of the circumstances surrounding the option to renew. Secondly, the option to renew clause must itself be excluded, failing which there would be a perpetually renewable lease (made into a lease for 2,000 years by reason of s 145 of the Law of Property Act 1922).

Lastly, practitioners for a lessee should remember to register the option by a notice or **1.118** restriction on the lessor's registered title, or as a Class C(iv) land charge if the title is unregistered. If the option is not protected in this way, the lessee could have difficulty in exercising the option against a purchaser of the reversionary interest.

KEY POINTS SUMMARY: LEASE CONTENTS

- If there is a conditional aspect to the start of the lease, eg, the subject property is still to be **1.119** built, consider carefully the likely terms in any agreement for lease to ensure that it complies with your client's instructions.
- In the light of the type of lease to be given or taken by your client, are the terms contained within it suitable to a lease of that kind? Try to step back and take an overview to ensure that the contents are suitable.
- Commercial conveyancers, for clear, concise and effective legal writing, when drafting leases, should, ideally and where appropriate, formulate strategies that use short sentences, avoid long paragraphs and (most importantly) avoid legal jargon and/or slang.
- Work out with the lessor how the lease will cover, first, rights (and exceptions) of way, secondly, rights (and exceptions) relating to conducting media (gas, water, etc.) and, thirdly, rights (and exceptions) for the use of parts of the whole property, eg, shared car parking, toilets, drains, etc.
- Deal with all the obligations/covenants required by your client from the proposed lessee and consider the nature and effect of the covenants to be given by the lessor, if any other than to allow quiet enjoyment and to insure.
- Does either party require the lease to include either or both options to break or to renew? If so, what are the terms upon which they may operate? If either involve notices, consider the timing of them and the service arrangements necessary to complete the arrangements contemplated.
- Include the correct attestation clause for your client company, be it one created in England and Wales or outside the home territory. Remember, in England and Wales a company may execute/seal a deed without actually using a company seal.
- Is the commercial letting sufficiently simple, or are the rents passing so low or is the term so short that you might be able to use the standard form of lease issued by the Law Society?
- Consider the recommendations in the April 2002 Code of Practice for Commercial Leases in England and Wales ('the Code').
- If the lease is registrable, have you placed the prescribed clauses at the front of the deed?

PRACTICAL CHECKLIST: LEASE CONTENTS

When dealing with the drafting or the basic contents of a new commercial lease, have **1.120** particular regard to the draft terms and the contents of the following provisions to make sure that the details accord with your clients' needs and instructions:

- The exact parties, length of the lease term and the start date.
- Is the extent of the subject property clearly defined and is a scale plan appropriate?
- How will the lease cover, first, rights (and exceptions) of way, secondly, rights (and exceptions) relating to conducting media (gas, water, etc.) and, thirdly, rights (and exceptions) for the use of parts of the whole property, eg, shared car parking, toilets, drains, etc?
- The rental level and payment days, as well as the necessity to pay other rents, eg, for insurance and/or service charges.
- The rent review provisions, frequency and mechanics. Avoid items that make time of the essence.
- Who is to insure? If it is the lessor, whether the lease terms are sufficient to ensure that the property is fully insured and that the lessee must fully reimburse the lessor for all premiums.
- Alienation provisions. Will the lease allow dealings with part of the property? What conditions will be expressly imposed if permission is forthcoming?
- Will changes of use be allowed? If not, does the lessor appreciate how this could limit the rental income?
- Can alterations be made at the property; and, if so, on what terms? Will the covenant have any effect upon the rent at review?
- What are the surety provisions, if any?
- Is the lessee to pay for your costs? If so, have you included an appropriate covenant on the lessee's part to make such a payment upon completion of the lease; and have you obtained an undertaking from the lessee's solicitor to pay those costs whether or not the matter proceeds to completion?
- Are the other terms appropriate to a commercial letting of the nature contemplated by your client as well as the subject property itself?
- If the lease contains a break clause, the clause should be drafted so as to stipulate that the lease break will not affect any rights subsisting and accruing to the lessor such as may arise from rent arrears or subsisting breaches of covenant.
- If the lease contains an option to renew, make sure that it has within it a rent review mechanism set out to operate at the time of renewal and that the renewal provision itself is excluded at the time of renewal to avoid any possibility of a perpetually renewable lease.
- Consider the recommendations in the April 2002 Code of Practice for Commercial Leases.
- If the lease term exceeds seven years, submit the lease to the Land Registry upon completion for first registration of the new leasehold title.
- Will the lease include reference to the Code of Practice for Commercial Leases?
- If the lease is registrable, have you placed the prescribed clauses at the start of it?

KEY DOCUMENTS

1.121
- Land Registration Act 2002
- Commonhold and Leasehold Reform Act 2002
- Landlord and Tenant (Covenants) Act 1995
- Landlord and Tenant Act 1954

- Code of Practice for Commercial Leases in England and Wales (2nd edn)
- Commercial Property Standard Enquiries
- Standard Commercial Property Conditions (2nd edn)
- Standard Property Conditions (4th edn)

Printed copies of legislation can be ordered from The Stationery Office (<http://www.tsoshop.co.uk>). Legislation from 1988 onwards can be downloaded free of charge from <http://www.opsi.gov.uk/acts.htm>.

The Code of Practice for Commercial Leases in England and Wales is set out in appendix 17.

The Commercial Property Standard Enquiries are set out in appendix 18 with guidance notes on the Enquiries set out in appendix 19.

The Standard Commercial Property Conditions are set out in appendix 4.

2

RENT AND RENT REVIEW

A RENT

Definition

Rent is commonly defined as a contractual sum designed to compensate the landlord for the **2.01**
tenant's right to possess the land during the term (see *CH Bailey Ltd v Memorial Enterprises Ltd*
[1974] 1 All ER 1003). Capital payments made at the beginning of the term (eg, on the grant

of a long lease of a flat) do not constitute rent; these are known as 'premiums'. Similarly, other tenant's payments under the lease, such as insurance premiums, service charges and VAT on rent, are at common law not classified as rent. However, the parties may agree expressly to define these other payments as 'rent', and this is often a requirement of the landlord before agreeing to grant the lease. There are two reasons why this benefits the landlord. First, the procedure for forfeiting a lease for 'non-payment of rent' is easier than it is for breaches of other covenants, in that there is no requirement to serve on the tenant a notice under s 146 of the Law of Property Act 1925. Secondly, the landlord's ancient remedy of distress is available to recover 'arrears of rent' only (s 146 notices and distress are considered in detail in chapter 6).

2.02   The landlord should also seek to include within the definition of rent any 'interim rent' payable under s 24A of the Landlord and Tenant Act 1954 (see para 7.101 below). Otherwise the tenant may be liable only for the contractual rent during any holding over period (see *Herbert Duncan Ltd v Cluttons* [1993] 04 EG 115).

Rent not essential in a lease

2.03   Payment of rent under a lease is quite usual but it is not an essential characteristic of a lease. Lord Templeman's judgment in *Street v Mountford* [1985] AC 809 is sometimes mis-interpreted as imposing a requirement for rent, but the Court of Appeal in *Ashburn Anstalt v Arnold* [1989] 1 Ch 1 said that the remarks in *Street v Mountford* should not be treated as introducing such a requirement. Moreover, the Law of Property Act 1925, s 205(1)(xxvii), defines a term of years absolute as 'a term of years ... (whether or not at a rent)', and other provisions in the Law of Property Act 1925 imply that a valid lease can exist without payment of rent (see s 149(3) and (6)). The principle that a lease can exist without payment of rent was reaffirmed in *Skipton Building Society v Clayton* (1993) 66 P & CR 223.

2.04   In the absence of an express covenant to pay rent, it should be noted that the common law will generally imply such a covenant if, as is usually the case, it is shown to be the parties' intention (see *Youngmin v Heath* [1974] 1 All ER 461).

2.05   The landlord may allow the tenant a rent-free period at the beginning of the term to enable the tenant to fit out the premises, or perhaps as an inducement for the tenant to take the lease if the landlord is having difficulty finding a tenant. This may have VAT implications (see para 2.13 below).

Rent must be certain

2.06   Rent need not necessarily be a money payment; it can take the form of payment in kind or the performance of services. However, the rent must be certain or capable of being calculated with certainty at the date when payment becomes due. Thus in *King's Motors (Oxford) Ltd v Lax* [1970] 1 WLR 426, an option to renew a lease was insufficiently certain when it stated that the new tenancy should be 'at such a rental as may be agreed upon between the parties'. The option should have gone on to outline a formula by which the rent could be calculated (eg, by reference to the market value of the premises). Alternatively it could have provided for the rent to be fixed by a third party, eg, the President of the Royal

Institution of Chartered Surveyors (see *Lloyds Bank Ltd v Marcan* [1973] 3 All ER 754). The detailed provisions for the review of rent during the lease term are considered below at paras 2.24 et seq.

Time and manner of payment

A well-drafted lease on behalf of a landlord will provide for payment of rent in advance on **2.07** specified dates (eg, '. . . by equal monthly payments made in advance on the first day of each month'). It is usual to state that the first payment of rent (or an apportioned amount) shall be made on the date the lease is granted. If the lease does not expressly provide for rent to be paid in advance then the common law implies payment in arrears, ie, it falls due at the end of each period by reference to which the rent has been calculated. Thus for a term of years the rent becomes due at the end of each year; for a monthly (or weekly) periodic tenancy, it becomes due at the end of each month (or week). Business leases normally provide for rent to be paid in advance on the traditional quarter days—25 March, 24 June, 29 September and 25 December—or the modern quarter days—1 January, 1 April, 1 July and 1 October. Rent unpaid by midnight on the appropriate day is deemed to be in arrears (*Dibble v Bowater* (1853) 2 E & B 564).

The landlord will want to prevent the tenant from exercising any right of set-off or making **2.08** any deductions from the rent. Set-off occurs where the tenant is sued by the landlord for non-payment of rent and the tenant cross-claims for breach of covenant by the landlord. The draft lease should require the tenant to pay rent 'without any set-off or deduction whatsoever'. For landlords, the risk of delay in payment of rent can be reduced by requiring the tenant to pay rent by standing order or direct debit.

Interest on rent

At common law the landlord cannot charge interest on late payment of rent until judgment **2.09** is obtained. Accordingly, the landlord should expressly provide for the tenant to pay interest on any late payment of rent both before and after any judgment up until the date cleared funds are received. The rate of interest should be sufficiently harsh as an incentive to pay on time, and the usual rate is 4 per cent above the base rate of one of the clearing banks. A landlord who is concerned that banks may in future abolish base rates should consider adding the words, 'or such other equivalent rate as the landlord shall reasonably specify'.

VAT on rent

The issues concerning VAT on commercial property are considered in chapter 10. The land- **2.10** lord may wish to add VAT to the rent and other payments due from the tenant. The landlord's solicitor should include a provision in the draft lease that the rent and other sums payable by the tenant are exclusive of VAT and that the tenant covenants to pay any VAT in addition to any other sums payable under the lease. If such a provision is not included and the landlord before the grant of the lease elects to charge VAT (ie, 'waive the exemption from VAT') then the landlord will have to account to HM Customs and Excise for the VAT out of the net rent received. If the landlord makes the VAT election after the grant of the lease, it can rely on s 89 of the Value Added Tax Act 1994 which effects a change from exempt to standard rated supply (ie, from 0 per cent to 17.5 per cent). However, best practice is to insist on the tenant's express covenant.

2.11 Conversely, the tenant may wish to limit its liability to pay VAT, especially where the tenant is an exempt supplier and cannot reclaim VAT. A tenant which is an exempt supplier would have to absorb any VAT as an increased overhead of its business. An express clause in the lease forbidding the landlord from adding VAT to the rent will effectively protect the tenant from paying VAT (s 42, Value Added Tax Act 1983). An example of such a clause would be:

> No VAT shall be added to the rent reserved by this lease notwithstanding that the landlord has elected to waive any exemption from VAT in relation to the demised premises or the building of which it forms part

Alternatively the tenant could seek to prevent the landlord (and its successors) from making the election for VAT in the first place:

> The landlord covenants not to elect to waive any exemption from VAT in relation to the demised premises or the building of which it forms part and on any assignment of the reversion the landlord will procure that the assignee gives a covenant in the terms of this clause

Stamp duty land tax on rent

2.12 Stamp duty land tax is assessed on the rental element of leases. Duty is payable at a flat rate of 1 per cent on the 'net present value' (NPV) of the total rent payable over the lease term. The NPV is calculated by discounting rent payable in future years by 3.5 per cent per annum. Where the NPV of the total rent does not exceed £150,000, no duty is payable. Duty will not be chargeable on the VAT element of the rent provided the landlord has not opted to charge VAT by the time the lease is granted. There is further consideration of stamp duty land tax at paras 10.24 et seq below.

VAT and rent-free periods

2.13 The landlord may allow the tenant a rent-free period at the beginning of the term to enable the tenant to fit out the premises, or perhaps as an inducement for the tenant to take the lease if the landlord is having difficulty finding a tenant. There are no VAT implications if the purpose of the rent-free period is genuinely to permit the tenant to fit out in readiness for trading or to arrange a sub-letting; in this case the tenant is giving the landlord nothing in return for the rent-free period.

2.14 However, the position is different either if the tenant is obliged by the landlord to do the fitting-out works (ie, they are for the landlord's benefit), or if the rent-free period is an inducement for the tenant to take the lease. In these situations HM Customs and Excise will treat the tenant as making a supply to the landlord of an amount equivalent to the rent foregone; thus the tenant must pay VAT on the rent not paid during the rent-free period! (See *Ridgeons Bulk v Commissioners of Customs and Excise* [1992] 37 EG 97.)

Rent abatement and insurance

At common law the tenant will continue to pay rent even if the premises are damaged or **2.15** destroyed and cannot be used (*Matthey v Curling* [1922] 2 AC 180). Tenants may try to plead frustration of the contract, but frustration will rarely apply to leases unless the circumstances are exceptional (see *National Carriers Ltd v Panalpina (Northern) Ltd* [1981] AC 675, where the House of Lords suggested that a property affected by coastal erosion might invoke the doctrine). Accordingly, the tenant should insist on an appropriate rent abatement clause in the lease so that the payment of rent is suspended until the premises are restored, fit for use. If the tenant pays a service charge, suspension of this would also be advisable. To protect against rent abatement, landlords should insure against loss of rent and provide for the premium to be recoverable from the tenant. Rent abatement and insurance against loss of rent are considered further at paras 4.20 et seq below.

Rent deposits

The parties will sometimes agree a rent deposit. This is a means of conferring on the landlord **2.16** additional security in the event of the tenant's non-payment of rent or other monies due under the lease. The tenant deposits a sum of money in an interest-bearing account, which the landlord is able to call upon if the tenant defaults. The actual sum deposited is of course a matter for negotiation, but it can be rent for a quarter, six months or even a year. The parties will normally enter into a rent deposit deed to record the terms upon which the deposit is held and the situations in which the landlord can withdraw from it. The Code of Practice for Commercial Leases in England and Wales recommends that the terms on which any cash, ie rent deposit, is to be held should be agreed and documented.

A distinction must be drawn between rent deposits for leases granted before 1 January 1996 **2.17** ('old leases') and those granted on or after this date ('new leases'). The changes brought about by the Landlord and Tenant (Covenants) Act 1995 as they affect rent deposits may be summarized as follows.

Old leases

For old leases the obligations in the rent deposit deed do not bind successors in title because **2.18** they do not touch and concern the land, ie, they are merely personal obligations between the original landlord and tenant. Thus a buyer of the reversion cannot be compelled to repay the deposit at the end of the term (*Hua Chiao Commercial Bank Ltd v Chiaphua Industries Ltd* [1987] 1 AC 99). Accordingly, the tenant should insist on a clause in the rent deposit deed in which the landlord, if it sells the reversion, agrees to procure from the buyer a deed in the tenant's favour in which the buyer takes over the obligations of the landlord in the rent deposit deed. A prudent tenant will also require the deposit to be repaid to it when it lawfully assigns the lease, leaving the landlord to take a new deposit from the assignee if it deems it necessary.

New leases

The 'touch and concern' test no longer applies to new leases so that the benefit and burden **2.19** of all obligations will pass to successors unless they are expressed to be personal. Thus a buyer of the reversion generally can be compelled to repay the deposit at the end of the term and an assignee of the lease is entitled to be repaid it. Accordingly, on an assignment of a new lease, the assignor should insist that the assignee pays to the assignor on completion a sum equivalent to the deposit at the time of the assignment. Alternatively, the tenant can require the deposit to be repaid to it when it lawfully assigns the lease, leaving the landlord to take a new deposit from the assignee.

2.20 A seller of the reversion of a new lease, before passing the rent deposit to the buyer, should secure from the tenant a release under the Landlord and Tenant (Covenants) Act 1995 of the covenant to repay the deposit. If the tenant will not release the covenant the landlord can apply to the court for a release. A less cumbersome means of protection would be simply to retain the deposit as the buyer's attorney, allowing the buyer to access it if the tenant defaults. However, this may not be such an attractive option for the buyer who may prefer to have closer control of the deposit.

2.21 The position as it was with old leases can still be achieved if the rent deposit obligations are expressed in the deed to be personal. In this way the benefit and burden of the obligations will not pass to successors.

Drafting the rent deposit deed

2.22 The following factors should be considered when drafting the rent deposit deed:

(a) In what situations should the landlord be entitled to withdraw from the account? Essentially, the landlord will want to call upon the deposit if (i) the tenant defaults in paying the rent or other monies, (ii) if the tenant becomes insolvent or makes arrangements with its creditors, or (iii) if the lease is forfeited or disclaimed. So far as (i) is concerned, the tenant should ensure that the landlord can take only so much of the deposit as is needed to cover the unpaid amount so that, eg, one missed rental payment would not trigger forfeiture of the whole deposit.

(b) The monies are normally held in a separate account in the landlord's name but the tenant retains beneficial ownership of them. This protects the tenant in the event of the landlord's insolvency, ie, the landlord's liquidator could not claim the monies as they do not belong to the landlord. The tenant will then normally charge the deposit to the landlord so that the landlord has first claim on the monies in the event of the tenant's insolvency. If the tenant is a company, remember that any charge must be registered at the Companies Registry under s 395 of the Companies Act 1985.

(c) When is the deposit to be returned to the tenant? Again this is a matter for negotiation. The landlord may want to keep the deposit for the whole of the lease term. The tenant, on the other hand, may suggest that it gets it back after a fixed period (say two years) once it has demonstrated that it is a good tenant which pays its rent on time. Another possibility for the tenant is to allow for the deposit to be returned to it once accounts can be produced showing a net annual profit exceeding, say, three times the annual rent. Lastly, the tenant should consider a provision for the repayment of the deposit if it assigns the lease, leaving the landlord to negotiate a new deposit, if necessary, from the assignee.

(d) If the landlord withdraws monies from the account, it will want the tenant to 'top up' the account so that the original agreed sum is maintained.

(e) Some landlords will seek an increased deposit if the rent is raised at review. Tenants should resist this unless it was specifically agreed at the negotiation stage.

(f) Who is entitled to receive interest on the deposit? If the parties cannot agree, the fairest solution may be simply to credit interest to the account. Then, if the tenant does not default, ultimately the tenant will get the interest when the deposit is repaid.

KEY POINTS SUMMARY: RENT

- Rent is not essential for a lease, but where it exists it must be certain.   **2.23**
- The landlord should define other payments under the lease as 'rent' to make it easier to forfeit the lease and use the distress remedy; also, include as 'rent' any interim rent payable under s 24A of the Landlord and Tenant Act 1954.
- The landlord should require rent to be paid in advance by standing order or direct debit and without set-off or deduction.
- The landlord should require the tenant to pay interest on late payment of rent (the rate should be sufficiently penal, eg, 4 per cent above base rate).
- The landlord should require the tenant to pay any VAT on top of the rent. The tenant should resist this if an exempt supplier.
- If the tenant is granted a rent-free period as an inducement to enter into the lease, it must pay VAT on the rent foregone.
- The tenant requires a rent abatement clause to cover a situation where the premises become incapable of use due to fire, etc.
- The landlord should insure against loss of rent, with the premium being recoverable from the tenant.
- The obligations in a rent deposit deed for leases granted before 1996 do not bind successors as they do not touch and concern the land. Conversely, for leases granted on or after 1 January 1996, the obligations in a rent deposit deed are binding on successors unless they are expressed to be personal.
- There are important considerations when drafting a rent deposit deed, in particular: In what circumstances can the landlord withdraw monies? When will the tenant get the deposit back? Should the deposit be held in a separate account? Who gets the interest?

B   RENT REVIEW

Introduction

For the landlord, the rent review clause is arguably the most important provision in the   **2.24** whole lease. The landlord is an investor, and as such will wish to maximize its investment. A fixed rent throughout a lease will in times of inflation obviously result in losses to the landlord. Accordingly, in leases granted for more than just a few years the landlord will want to ensure that the rent is increased periodically throughout the term.

In this important section of the book we shall examine the different methods of rent review   **2.25** with particular emphasis on the most popular current method, the open market revaluation. We shall also consider drafting matters and interpretation together with the mechanics of the review itself.

Upward and downward review

2.26   Traditionally, rent review clauses were drafted on the basis of upward review only so that they benefited landlords alone. However, since the recession of the early 1990s, tenants have appreciated that rent review can naturally assist them if the lease allows for review downwards. While now sympathetic to the notion that rents can fall as well as rise, landlords are still reluctant to countenance any downward shift at review. This has more to it than simple greed; it is because the perceived requirement of the institutional investor is for 'upward only reviews' so that a lease that does not conform to this stereotype is by definition a poor investment. Much will depend on the bargaining strengths of the parties, but as a general rule tenants should insist that the review clause allows for downward as well as upward review.

Penultimate day rent review

2.27   Some landlords will provide in the draft lease for a rent review to occur on the penultimate day of the contractual term, ie, the last day but one. This is to enable the rent to be raised to the current market level during any renewal procedure initiated by the tenant. The landlord can of course apply to the court for an interim rent to be fixed (see paras 7.99 et seq below), but this is likely to be 10–15 per cent below the market rent. It follows that tenants should resist attempts by landlords to insert penultimate day reviews.

Different methods of review

2.28   The principal methods of review are now examined. These are index-linked rents, turnover rents, sub-lease rents, premium rents, fixed increases and, most importantly, revaluation to open market rent. This last method is by far the most popular method of review in occupational business leases and is considered fully at paras 2.35 et seq below.

Index-linked rents

2.29   This is a review of rent linked to the rise or fall of an index (eg, retail prices index) where the rent is normally increased annually. Although common on mainland Europe, it is not a popular method of rent review in England and Wales. The main reason for this is that an index can move in ways that are unrelated to property rental values. The rate of general inflation shown by the index may have no bearing on the state of the property market in a particular area; and this may lead to rent reviews that are unrealistic. There is also the problem of which index to use in the first place, and the fact that the index may in future cease to exist or possibly be re-evaluated in times of high inflation. For a case concerning an index-linked review clause, see *Blumenthal v Gallery Five Ltd* (1971) 220 EG 33 (where problems occurred due to a change in the composition of the index).

Turnover rents

2.30   This is where the rent is linked to the turnover of the tenant's business—the higher the turnover, the higher the rent. For the tenant, the difficulty with this concept is that high turnover does not necessarily mean high profit. One solution is to couple the rent review to profit instead of turnover, but landlords are usually reluctant to see rental levels fluctuate according to the relative business efficiency of the tenant.

Turnover rents are sometimes used in conjunction with ordinary rents where the parties **2.31** agree a basic rent of, say, 75 per cent of the market annual rent, and then a turnover rent on top. This arrangement was quite popular in the 1980s in lettings of units in shopping centres, hotels and restaurants.

Sub-lease rents

Sub-lease rents operate in a similar way to turnover rents in that the rent is linked to the level **2.32** of rental income generated by sub-letting the premises. The higher the rental income received by the tenant from its sub-tenants, the higher the rent the tenant pays under the head lease. As with turnover rents, a hybrid form is sometimes used in which a sub-lease rent is paid on top of the base rent.

Premium rents

A premium rent arises where the parties agree an initially higher rent, in return for which the **2.33** landlord concedes to a longer period than normal between review (eg, the tenant pays 20 per cent more than market rent in return for reviews every ten years instead of every five). If the commencing rent is high enough the landlord may agree to no reviews at all. Both parties are saved the trouble and expense (eg, professionals' fees) of conducting a review, but there is the risk that the total rent payable during the term may, in the event, be higher or lower than that which would have been payable in normal circumstances. Consequently, premium rents are very rare.

Fixed increases

These are simply fixed increases of rent at specified intervals during the term, eg, £20,000 **2.34** for the first five years, £30,000 for the next five years, etc. As with premium rents, the parties are saved the trouble and expense of going through the review process. Fixed increases are widespread in assessing low ground rents in long leases of residential property, but they are unpopular in commercial leases at market rents because of the difficulty in predicting realistic increases.

Revaluation to open market rent

This is the most common method of rent review found in commercial leases. Accordingly, **2.35** the drafting and implementation of this type of clause will now be considered at length. A precedent for a valuation formula (with suggested tenant's amendments) is set out at para 2.103 below.

Introduction

The aim of the revaluation clause is to establish the market rent for the leasehold interest in **2.36** the premises at the agreed review dates during the term. One should appreciate that it is the leasehold *interest* in the premises that is being valued, not the premises themselves. In assessing the market rent for a leasehold interest the clause will make certain assumptions regarding a hypothetical letting of the premises (eg, duration, term and other conditions) and will disregard certain matters that may actually exist. These 'assumptions' and 'disregards' are an important feature of the rent review clause and are examined in detail at paras 2.44 to 2.80 below. Thus it is a *hypothetical* interest in the premises that is valued, not the actual tenant's interest itself. As explained more fully below, the reason for this is to avoid potential problems and injustices to both sides.

2.37   At each rent review the landlord and tenant will seek to negotiate a new rental figure based on the terms of the hypothetical letting and the assumptions and disregards contained in the review clause. It is, of course, the terms of the review clause itself that will determine the outcome and this is why the precise wording of the clause is so important.

Take specialist advice

2.38   Each side would normally instruct a chartered surveyor who specializes in rent review to advise them during their negotiations. This specialist advice is crucial throughout the drafting and negotiating process because solicitors, however experienced, cannot always identify all the valuation difficulties that may arise. This is particularly so for unusual premises where a departure from the standard office precedent may be essential. One interesting example of this is where the tenant gains access to the subject premises through adjoining premises, which the tenant also occupies. In this case, to protect the landlord, the review clause should assume an alternative access to the subject premises to counter the tenant's potential argument that the premises cannot be let to anyone else and should therefore attract a reduced rent (see *Jefferies v O'Neill* (1983) 269 EG 131).

2.39   In some leases (usually older ones) the review clause may require the parties to begin negotiations by serving notices and counter-notices. Ultimately, if the parties fail to agree a revised rent, the review clause will usually refer the matter to an independent third party to determine the outcome, eg, an expert surveyor or arbitrator (the differences are outlined at para 2.96 below). Even then, the expert or arbitrator will accord the terms of the review clause firm respect.

2.40   It can be seen, therefore, that the drafting and negotiation of the review clause by solicitors at the initial stage when the lease is actually granted is crucial to the outcome of future rent reviews. We shall now consider closely the key elements of this type of rent review clause and the matters of importance for solicitors negotiating the terms.

Defining the rent

2.41   The most commonly used formula for defining the rent is as follows:

> the rent at which the demised premises might reasonably be expected to be let in the open market on the review date by a willing landlord to a willing tenant

The express reference to willing landlord and willing tenant is useful for the landlord. It rebuffs any contention by the tenant that the property would not be let at the time of the review, eg, because the market is dead (see *Evans (FR) (Leeds) Ltd v English Electric Co Ltd* (1978) 36 P & CR 185). However, even if the words are omitted the courts have held that a willing tenant can be assumed (*Dennis & Robinson Ltd v Kiossos Establishment* [1987] 1 EGLR 133).

2.42   Certain other phrases should be avoided as they can create injustice and uncertainty. The words 'a reasonable rent for the demised premises' could result in the tenant's improvements being taken into account when assessing the rent. This is unfair as the tenant would be paying for the improvements twice over—once when they were carried out and again in the consequential rental uplift (see *Ponsford v HMS Aerosols Ltd* [1979] AC 63). Tenants' voluntary improvements are normally expressly disregarded (see paras 2.74 et seq below).

A clause that directs the surveyor to assess the rent 'having regard to rental values' current at **2.43** the review date should also be avoided. This injects a subjective element into the assessment calculation and causes uncertainty. It also begs the question, 'What if there are no comparable rental values for that property?' (see generally *English Exporters (London) Ltd v Eldonwall Ltd* [1973] 1 All ER 726). In particular, tenants should resist the phrase 'best rent'. This allows a valuer to take into account a 'special purchaser's bid' that may be well in excess of the market rent, eg, from someone trading next door who is keen to acquire and expand into the subject premises (see *First Leisure Trading v Dorita Properties* [1991] 1 EGLR 133).

Assumptions

Rent and rent review   The rent review clause should provide for the terms of the hypo- **2.44** thetical letting to be the same as the actual lease, save obviously for the amount of rent (as this is to be reviewed). Unscrupulous landlords may also try to exclude the rent review clause itself from the hypothetical letting. Tenants must be on their guard against this, as it will normally have a dramatically uplifting effect on the rent at review. The reason for the uplift is that a hypothetical tenant would be willing to bid a higher rent to secure a lease with a fixed rent throughout the term (ie, with no rent reviews). See *National Westminster Bank plc v Arthur Young McClelland Moores & Co* [1985] 1 WLR 1123. (Tenants must also be on their guard against user assumptions, see paras 2.67 et seq below.)

If there is no mention of the rent review clause in the hypothetical letting, the courts should **2.45** give effect to the underlying purpose of the clause and assume rent review to be included on the same terms as the actual lease (see *British Gas Corp v Universities Superannuation Scheme* [1986] 1 WLR 398 and *Arnold v National Westminster Bank plc* [1991] 2 WLR 1177). However, tenants must beware of express wording that excludes the rent review clause as a court would be bound to follow it. Examples of wording to be avoided are 'on the terms of this lease save for this proviso' and 'disregarding the provisions of this clause'.

We suggest that the following wording should make it clear that rent review will be a feature **2.46** of the hypothetical letting (and should be acceptable to both parties):

> upon the terms of this lease other than the amount of rent but including provisions as to rent review

Some landlords' solicitors will seek to include an assumption to ignore the effect of any statute, order, instrument, regulation or direction then in force which has the effect of regulating or restricting the amount of rent which might be payable in respect of the demised premises. This is to protect landlords against any future statutory control of rents that may come into force (as occurred between 1972 and 1975 as a part of government anti-inflation measures). The courts upheld such a clause in *Langham House Developments Ltd v Brompton Securities Ltd* (1980) 256 EG 719. In negotiations the tenant should argue against agreeing to this assumption on the basis that if a statutory law is in force it should be complied with.

Vacant possession   Most rent review clauses will make an assumption in the hypothetical **2.47** letting that the property is to be let with vacant possession, ie, that the tenant has moved out. This reflects the reality of the situation immediately before the start of a lease if the tenant is to occupy the whole of the building. However, if the property is or will be sub-let, an assumption of vacant possession will distort reality because it will ignore any sub-lettings in existence at the date of the review. Depending on the circumstances, this could benefit the landlord or the tenant. For example, if the sub-letting is lucrative with profitable sub-rents (eg, a high-class shop) this should increase the rental value of the head leasehold interest. In this situation the landlord would want the sub-letting taken into account. Conversely, if the sub-rent is low (eg, a residential letting) the landlord would prefer it to be ignored. We suggest that the fairest approach where there are sub-lettings would be to accord with reality. In other words, the review clause should assume vacant possession relating to those parts occupied by the tenant on the review date, but any existing sub-tenancies at that time should be taken into account.

2.48   Although vacant possession is normally assumed, the landlord will resist the corollary that the tenant has removed its fixtures. Moreover, the landlord will seek an assumption that the premises are fully fitted out. The reasons for this are now considered.

2.49   **Premises fit for use**   It is usual to include an assumption that the premises are fit for immediate occupation and use for the purposes permitted by the lease. 'Fit for immediate occupation' means only that the premises are fit to be occupied for fitting-out purposes (*Pontsarn Investments Ltd v Kansallis-Osake-Pankki* [1992] 22 EG 103). The landlord's solicitor must go further and include an assumption that the premises are 'fully fitted out'. This is to counter a tenant's argument that an incoming hypothetical tenant would ask for a rent-free period for notional fitting-out works (in a hypothetical vacant possession letting, removal of tenant's fittings would otherwise be assumed: see *Young v Dalgety plc* [1987] 1 EGLR 116, CA). A notional rent-free period would effectively reduce the overall rent payable during the period until the next review. For example:

- No rent-free period: £50,000 per annum for five years = £50,000 per annum
- Initial three-month rent-free period: £50,000 × 4.75 ÷ 5 = £47,500 per annum

If the premises are assumed to be 'fully fitted out', the clause should go on to say at whose expense it was done. If, as usual, the actual tenant paid for it, the hypothetical tenant's expense should be taken into account. But if the actual landlord contributed, the hypothetical landlord's contribution should be taken into account, ie, by rentalizing the cost (*Pontsarn Investments Ltd v Kansallis-Osake-Pankki* [1992] 22 EG 103).

2.50   **Length of hypothetical term**   The preferred length of term of the hypothetical letting will vary depending on market conditions. If a longer term is attractive to tenants then a hypothetical tenant would bid a higher rent to secure it. If so, the landlord would wish to specify a long hypothetical term (eg, in a 25-year lease, 'a term equal to the original term of this lease'). Conversely, in times of recession a tenant may prefer a shorter term and would bid a higher rent for a short lease (in which case the landlord would want 'a term equal to the unexpired residue of this lease').

2.51   The parties should take specialist advice from surveyors as to the preferred length of term for the subject premises at any given time. Much will depend on the nature of the premises and their location. As a compromise it is a generally held view that a formula based on the unexpired residue, possibly with a minimum period (eg, 10 or 15 years) is the best option.

Even so, solicitors should still take expert advice from local surveyors familiar with similar commercial lettings in the area.

The valuer is allowed to take into account any likelihood that the lease will be renewed **2.52** under the Landlord and Tenant Act 1954 (*Secretary of State for Employment v Pivot Properties Ltd* (1980) 256 EG 1176). If renewal is a strong possibility, the rent will obviously be higher as the lease is more attractive to tenants.

If the rent review clause is silent as to the hypothetical term, a letting for the residue of the **2.53** term will be presumed (*Norwich Union Life Assurance Society v Trustee Savings Bank Central Board* [1986] 1 EGLR 136).

The rent review clause should also state the commencement date of the hypothetical term, **2.54** otherwise the position may be unclear. In *Lynnthorpe Enterprises Ltd v Sydney Smith (Chelsea) Ltd* [1990] 2 EGLR 131, the court held that the commencement date was assumed to be the same day as the actual lease. However in *Canary Wharf Investments (Three) v Telegraph Group Ltd* [2003] 46 EG 132, the commencement date of the hypothetical lease was assumed to be the review date itself.

Consideration and rent-free periods   The rent review clause will normally assume that no **2.55** premium (ie, capital sum) is paid on the grant of the hypothetical lease, either by the tenant or by the landlord (ie, reverse premium). This is because payment of a premium could distort the amount of rent payable. For example, the landlord might offer the tenant a reverse premium as an inducement to enter into the lease at the market rent. Without such induce- ment the tenant might only be willing to take the lease at a lower rent. Similarly, if the tenant pays a premium to the landlord, the tenant might argue for a reduction in rent as compensation.

The same issue arises over a rent-free period given to a tenant at the start of the lease as it **2.56** could distort the market rent if taken into account on review. If the rent-free period is an inducement to the tenant to take the lease, the hypothetical tenant could argue that without such inducement he would insist on a lower rent. Consequently, for the landlord's benefit, the rent review clause will normally assume that no rent-free period is included in the hypothetical lease (or, alternatively, that any rent-free period has expired). The impact of a rent-free period on rent review calculations can also be illustrated as follows:

- Assume headline rent £10,000 per annum for five years with first year rent-free: total rent over five years = £40,000
- Landlord's preferred option: disregard rent-free period (first year): market rent is £40,000 divided by four years = £10,000 per annum
- Tenant's preferred option: take rent-free period into account: market rent is £40,000 divided by five years = £8,000 per annum

If the rent review clause is silent as to how rent-free periods are to be treated, the courts will **2.57** consider the purpose of the rent-free period. Was it given as an inducement for the tenant to take the lease, or was it genuinely to allow the tenant to fit-out the premises before trading? If it was an inducement it will be taken into account on rent review and the tenant's argument should succeed, ie, a lower rent will result. However, if it was given to allow genuine fitting-out, it will be disregarded and the rent should be higher as a result (see *Broadgate Square plc v Lehman Brothers Ltd* [1995] 01 EG 111, CA). Remember that this is the case only where the lease is silent on the point. If the wording of the rent review clause is clear and unambiguous the courts are bound to follow it.

2.58   **Break clause**   If the actual lease contains a break clause, the parties must decide whether a break clause should feature in the hypothetical letting. A tenant's break option would generally make the lease more attractive and increase the market rent. Conversely, a landlord's break option could disrupt the tenant's business, thus reducing the market rent. A common arrangement is to include a break clause in the hypothetical lease but only in respect of rent reviews that occur before the date the actual break can be exercised. Another method is to include the clause in all the rent reviews but have an assumption as to the date on which it is exercisable, eg, five years after the grant of the hypothetical lease. A mutual break date at least five years away is generally treated as a neutral position for valuation purposes.

2.59   **Compliance with covenants**   Most rent review clauses will assume that the tenant has complied with its covenants. If this were not the case the tenant could simply allow the premises to fall into disrepair before a review date (ie, in breach of its repairing covenant) and claim a lower rent for premises in poor condition. If the review clause were silent on this point, a court would imply the assumption anyway on the general principle that a person should not profit from his own wrongdoing. A landlord should obviously resist any suggestion from the tenant that the tenant's compliance with its covenants should not be assumed!

2.60   Tenants should resist any assumption that the landlord's covenants have been performed. This would permit a landlord who has failed in its repairing obligations to claim a higher rent on the assumption that the premises are in perfect condition—a situation patently unfair to the tenant. Landlords will argue that tenants have their remedies for breach of covenant and should use them. They will also argue that the landlord should not be penalized for the whole review period simply for a temporary breach just before review. Both arguments should be firmly resisted by the tenant's solicitor. After all, a landlord which performs its covenants will have no cause for complaint.

2.61   **Premises restored**   Landlords often require an assumption that, if the premises have been destroyed or damaged at the review date, they have been fully restored. Landlords will argue that this assumption will not adversely affect the tenant if the lease allows for suspension of rent. However, suspension of rent is normally limited in time and operates only if the premises are damaged by an insured risk so as to make them unfit for occupation and use. The damage may also have occurred as a result of the landlord's breach of covenant. There is a compromise solution, which should be acceptable to both parties. This is to allow the assumption that the premises are restored, but only in relation to damage or destruction that the tenant is under an obligation to repair or caused by an insured risk.

2.62   **Recovery of VAT**   The hypothetical market for the letting of the premises might consist of organizations that make VAT exempt supplies (eg, banks and insurance companies in city centre locations). These organizations cannot reclaim the VAT they pay and have to absorb it as an increased overhead of their businesses. As a result, such a hypothetical tenant would bid a lower rent. To overcome this situation a landlord will include an assumption that the hypothetical tenant can recover any VAT payable under the lease. Alternatively, the landlord may try to introduce an assumption that the hypothetical letting includes a covenant by the landlord not to waive the exemption for VAT (ie, not to 'opt to tax'). Tenants should resist such assumptions by arguing that the premises should be valued as they really are.

Assumptions concerning other terms of the hypothetical lease: alienation and user In **2.63** the absence of any direction to the contrary, the valuer on review will take into account all the other terms of the actual lease. This is known as the presumption in favour of reality and has been favoured by the courts in many cases. See, in particular, *Basingstoke and Deane BC v Host Group Ltd* [1988] 1 All ER 824, *Lynnthorpe Enterprises v Sidney Smith (Chelsea)* [1990] 2 EGLR 131 and *St Martins Property Ltd v (1) CIB Properties Ltd (2) Citibank International Plc* [1998] EGCS 161. Note that the presumption in favour of reality will include any variations to the lease that the parties may have agreed.

It follows that when negotiating the rent review clause, if either party feels that a term in the **2.64** lease will have an adverse effect on the rental value then they should try to exclude it from the hypothetical letting, by use of an appropriate assumption or disregard. The valuer will have particular regard to the terms of the tenant's alienation and user covenants, which are now considered.

(a) Alienation covenant The more restrictive the alienation covenant, the less attractive **2.65** the lease will be on the open market (ie, to the hypothetical tenant). It follows that if the lease is unattractive to tenants, the market rent will be depressed, ie, lowered. Landlords should therefore be wary of making the alienation covenant in the actual lease more restrictive than is necessary to protect the interest of the landlord. For example, in a lease of a large building, an absolute prohibition against sub-letting would confine the market to those tenants capable of occupying the whole. This is likely to depress the rent. A balancing act is thus needed for the landlord as to the degree of severity of the covenant. The landlord will obviously want control over the tenant's ability to dispose of the premises, but not at the expense of depressing the rent.

Any attempt by the landlord to introduce into the hypothetical lease assumptions regarding **2.66** alienation that do not exist in reality should be firmly resisted by the tenant. For instance, an assumption that the lease permits sub-letting of whole or part when the lease actually prohibits it. This assumption would be patently unfair on the tenant, as it would make the hypothetical lease more attractive to tenants and, as a result, increase the rent (see paras 3.54 et seq generally regarding the alienation covenant).

(b) User covenant The same considerations apply to the tenant's user covenant. If the **2.67** permitted use is unduly restrictive, the lease will be less attractive to tenants on the open market and will thus depress the rent on review. Again, a balancing act will be needed for the landlord—the restrictions on the tenant's use should do no more than is necessary to protect the interest of the landlord (see paras 3.85 et seq regarding the user covenant).

Some landlords' solicitors when drafting the rent review clause try to circumvent this **2.68** dilemma by including an assumption that the hypothetical lease has no restriction on use at all. This is patently unfair on the tenant because it does not reflect the reality of the tenant's position. Why should the tenant be paying for something it does not in fact have? The tenant's solicitor should always resist such a provision (indeed, the tenant's solicitor would be negligent in advising his or her client to accept it). The trouble in a very long clause is that the words 'with any use' can be easily overlooked.

2.69   A clever landlord might try to argue that the rent should be higher because the landlord *would have* allowed a wider use than that permitted by the lease. This argument will not succeed. The courts have said they will ignore any possibility that the landlord might allow a wider use of the premises than the covenant actually permits, ie, effectively waive a breach of covenant or unilaterally vary it. This principle was confirmed in *Plinth Property Investments Ltd v Mott, Hay & Anderson* [1979] 1 EGLR 17, and applies to other tenant's covenants as well, where a landlord's consent to change is required (see also *C&A Pensions Trustees Ltd v British Vita Investments Ltd* (1984) 272 EG 63).

Disregards

2.70   In the interests of fairness it is appropriate that certain matters are disregarded when assessing the rent to be paid under the hypothetical lease. These are matters that arise either from the presence of the tenant, or as a result of the tenant's labour. The three main 'disregards' discussed below are based on the statutory disregards contained in s 34 of the Landlord and Tenant Act 1954, Pt II (see para 7.165 below). It is better not to incorporate these by reference because they are too restrictive; the disregards (in expanded form) should be expressly stated in the rent review clause itself and are as follows.

2.71   **Occupation**   The tenant's occupation of the premises should be disregarded. This is to counter any suggestion by the landlord that the tenant would bid a higher than market rent to avoid the expense of moving to other premises.

2.72   The tenant's solicitor should also seek to disregard the occupation of any sub-tenants, predecessors in title or other lawful occupiers of the whole or any part of the demised premises. Moreover, if the tenant occupies adjoining premises in addition to the subject property, the tenant's occupation of those adjoining premises should also be disregarded. The inference is that a tenant in this situation would bid a higher rent to secure premises into which it could expand ('marriage value': see *First Leisure Trading v Dorita Properties* [1991] 1 EGLR 133).

2.73   **Goodwill**   If the tenant has generated goodwill of its business (eg, a good name and reputation) then it is fair that this should be disregarded on rent review; otherwise the tenant would be penalized for its business expertise. The tenant's solicitor should also seek to disregard the goodwill of any predecessors in title (including those in business before the grant of the lease), sub-tenants, or other lawful occupiers of the whole or any part of the demised premises. If the lease disregards the tenant's occupation but omits to disregard goodwill, the courts will normally imply the latter as being a product of occupation (*Prudential Assurance Co v Grand Metropolitan Estates* [1993] EGCS 58).

2.74   **Improvements**   If the tenant pays for improvements to the premises then it would generally be unfair for the tenant to pay a higher rent because of it. This is because the tenant would effectively be paying for the improvements twice over—once when carrying them out and again as a result of paying the higher rent (see *Ponsford v HMS Aerosols Ltd* [1979] AC 63). Not all alterations will constitute improvements; the alterations must go beyond repair and be seen as improvements from the tenant's point of view (*Post Office v Aquarius Properties Ltd* [1987] 1 All ER 1055, CA). (For a further discussion of alterations that constitute improvements, please refer to the discussion of the tenant's alterations covenant at paras 3.36 et seq below)

Accordingly, the rent review clause will generally provide for tenant's improvements to be **2.75** disregarded on review unless they were made pursuant to an obligation to the landlord, or at the landlord's expense. Landlords may also wish to limit the disregard to tenant's improvements made only with the consent of the landlord. This acts as an incentive for the tenant to comply with the usual lease covenant that landlord's consent is required for alterations. It also avoids arguments over what improvements have actually been made. If the landlord's solicitor proposes this limitation, the tenant's solicitor should amend the clause to say that improvements can still be disregarded if consent was not required under the lease, or, if required, was unreasonably withheld.

Examples of situations where it *would* be appropriate to take improvements into account are **2.76** as follows:

(a) where the improvements are part of the tenant's consideration for the grant of the lease;
(b) where the tenant is obliged to carry out improvements under an agreement for lease or other document;
(c) where the improvements are carried out at the landlord's expense;
(d) where the tenant is required by statute to carry out improvements (eg, fire escapes, fire doors, etc.). (Note—if the tenant feels it should not be penalized on review for statutory obligations, insert after 'otherwise than pursuant to an obligation to the landlord', 'except obligations requiring compliance with statutes or directions of local authorities or other bodies exercising powers under statute or Royal Charter'.)

As with the occupation and goodwill disregards, the tenant's solicitor should ensure that **2.77** improvements made by sub-tenants, predecessors in title and other lawful occupiers are also disregarded. This must include any improvements made under an earlier lease or during any pre-letting period of occupation for fitting-out purposes (although the latter may be implied anyway, see *Hambros Bank Executor & Trustee Co Ltd v Superdrug Stores Ltd* [1985] 1 EGLR 99).

As mentioned, tenant's improvements made pursuant to an obligation to the landlord are **2.78** not normally disregarded on review. The question arises whether a landlord's licence to make alterations could be construed as an obligation for this purpose, especially if the tenant covenants to do works in the licence. In *Godbold v Martin the Newsagents Ltd* (1938) 268 EG 1202, the court confirmed that such an obligation may be contained in a contractual document other than the lease. Accordingly, a tenant's solicitor when negotiating the terms of a licence for alterations must ensure that the licence is expressed to be permissive in nature rather than obligatory. In other words, the licence should *allow* the tenant to do the works without a covenant on the tenant's part to do so. This should ensure that the alterations allowed under the licence are not rentalized on review (see also *Historic Houses Hotels Ltd v Cadogan Estates* [1993] 30 EG 94).

For further reading on the disregard of improvements and the courts' interpretation, see the **2.79** judgments of Forbes J in *GREA Real Property Investments Ltd v Williams* (1979) 250 EG 651 and *Estates Projects Ltd v Greenwich LBC* (1979) 251 EG 851. On a more general note, tenants' advisers should also be aware of hidden obligations to carry out improvements in the lease. For example, a covenant to comply with Acts of Parliament may impose an obligation to carry out statutory improvements, eg, installing fire doors. Obligations to improve may also be concealed in the repairing clause. For further commentary on this, see paras 3.07 et seq below.

2.80   The tenant should firmly resist attempts by the landlord to disregard other matters that would have a depressing effect on the rent (eg, restrictive user and alienation clauses). Interestingly, there is a view that too many assumptions and disregards in the landlord's favour could ultimately backfire on the landlord. The astute tenant could argue that, as the terms of the hypothetical letting are more onerous than the norm, the rent should be discounted.

Defining review dates

2.81   By the time solicitors are instructed, the parties will usually have agreed how frequently the review is to take place. Tenants' solicitors must be careful, however, when considering the definition of review dates in the lease. It is better not to specify the actual dates but to define them instead by reference to the anniversaries of the commencement of the lease. An example of this preferred definition would be:

> The Rent Review Dates shall be every fifth anniversary of the Term Commencement Date during the Term

2.82   The dangers to the tenant of specifying the actual dates can be seen in the following scenario:

(a)   The hypothetical lease is for 25 years from the relevant rent review date but otherwise on the terms of the actual lease.

(b)   The review dates are specified as 25 March 2011, 25 March 2016, 25 March 2021 and 25 March 2026.

(c)   At each review the hypothetical lease is for 25 years, but with no rent reviews after 2026 (because that is specified as the last one).

(d)   Thus at each review the hypothetical tenant will bid a higher and higher rent to secure a hypothetical lease where no review (ie increase) occurs after 2026. (At the 2026 review he gets a hypothetical 25-year term with no review at all!)

(e)   This will have an increasingly uplifting effect on the rent at each review.

Rent review procedure

Introduction

2.83   This section considers the means by which the parties will conduct the review process. The rent review clause should specify the procedure to be adopted in agreeing the new rent and, if the parties cannot agree, allow the matter to be referred to an independent third party for adjudication.

2.84   These days, modern leases generally adopt an informal approach to negotiations. They simply provide for the matter to be referred to a third party if the parties have not agreed the new rent by the review date (or a period before the review date, eg, three months). Tenants' solicitors should ensure that the tenant as well as the landlord has the option of referral. This protects a tenant who might want a speedy settlement of the new rent to enable him to sell on more easily.

In older leases a more traditional approach is often employed. This is to impose a requirement **2.85** for the service of formal notices between the parties (known as 'trigger notices'). The lease might impose notice provisions similar to those for ending a lease under the Landlord and Tenant Act 1954. Typically, a landlord's trigger notice suggesting a new rent would need to be served on the tenant between 6 and 12 months before the relevant review date. The tenant would then have, say, two months to serve a counter-notice indicating the tenant's preferred new rental figure. The parties would then have, say, three months to reach agreement, failing which the matter could be referred to a third party. If the trigger notice method is adopted, tenants' solicitors should ensure that the tenant, as well as the landlord, is given the option to initiate the review, ie, by serving the first notice.

Because of the inherent risks in the 'trigger notice' method, when drafting and negotiating a **2.86** new rent review clause we recommend that the parties adopt the modern, informal method of initiating the review. A precedent for rent review procedure is set out at para 2.104 below.

Is time to be of the essence?

Whichever approach is used, it will be necessary to establish whether time is of the essence **2.87** of the time limits. This is important, because where time is of the essence and there is delay, however slight, the party who breaks the time limit will lose its rights. So a landlord could forfeit its right to review the rent until the next review date. Or a tenant could forget to respond in time to a landlord's trigger notice suggesting an excessively high increase (and be stuck with it; see *Amalgamated Estates Ltd v Joystretch Manufacturing Ltd* (1980) 257 EG 489).

The leading authority on this question is the House of Lords' decision in *United Scientific* **2.88** *Holdings Ltd v Burnley BC* [1978] AC 904. Their Lordships held that time will not be of the essence unless there are express words or contraindications in the rent review clause itself, or the interrelation of the rent review clause with other clauses in the lease dictates otherwise (see also *McDonald's Property Co Ltd v HSBC Bank plc* [2001] 36 EG 181 and *Lancecrest Ltd v Asiwaju* [2005] 16 EG 146).

Express wording or contraindications in the review clause   The situation will be clear if **2.89** unambiguous wording is used, eg, 'time is of the essence of this clause'. Even if these words are not used, the courts may construe other words to mean the same thing (eg, 'within three months after the review date but not otherwise' was held to make time of the essence in *Drebbond Ltd v Horsham DC* (1978) 246 EG 1013; similarly, '12 months before the relevant review date but not at any other time' was held to make time of the essence in *First Property Growth Partnership v Royal and Sun Alliance Services Ltd* [2003] 1 All ER 533). Other cases indicate that the courts will not easily rebut the presumption that time is not of the essence (see *Phipps-Faire Ltd v Malbern Construction Ltd* [1987] 1 EGLR 129 and *North Hertfordshire DC v Hitchin Industrial Estate Ltd* [1992] 2 EGLR 121). Ultimately each case will turn on the interpretation of the particular words used in the clause, and the parties' solicitors should endeavour to make the drafting clear.

Some leases allow landlords to serve a notice for proposing a new rent, and if the tenant does **2.90** not serve a counter-notice within a given period (eg one month), then the landlord's proposed rent is deemed to be the new rent. This is known as a 'deeming provision'. The Court of Appeal in *Starmark v CPL* [2002] Ch 306 held that, in these circumstances, time is of the essence because the deeming provision is a 'contraindication' in the rent review clause. As a result of this important case, tenants should, on rent reviews, check carefully to establish whether any deeming provisions are included in their leases. If they are, and they fail to respond to the landlord's notice in time, they will be stuck with the landlord's proposed figure (which could be a high opening bid). Tenants are advised to strike out any deeming provisions in new leases being negotiated.

2.91   It is usually the case that the parties agree that time shall not be of the essence. In this way the landlord averts the risk of forfeiting the review and the tenant at least gets the certainty of knowing what the new rent will be. Accordingly, and to remove doubt, the best practice is to state the position expressly, eg, '. . . and time shall not be of the essence of this clause'. In this case it follows that the parties should avoid stipulating timetables for action because, without sanction, any breach becomes meaningless. See also the precedent at para 2.105 below.

2.92   **Interrelation of the review clause with other clauses in the lease**   The most common example of how another clause can make time of the essence of rent review is where a break option is linked to rent review. For example, the parties may have agreed that if the tenant is unhappy with the rental increase he can end the lease. Time is of the essence of a break clause unless the lease states otherwise (see paras 1.109 et seq on break clauses). Thus the interrelation to rent review will make time of the essence of the latter as well. This applies even if the break option is mutual or linked to only one of many rent reviews (see *Central Estates Ltd v Secretary of State for the Environment* [1977] 1 EGLR 239).

2.93   To avoid a break clause impacting on rent review in this way, the parties simply need to provide clearly in the rent review clause that time is not to be of the essence of that clause. However, in this case, tenants should bear in mind that the exercise of their break option (where the time limit is strict) may have to be given without knowing what the new rent will be (where time limits are not strict).

Third party adjudicator

2.94   If the parties fail to reach agreement on the new rent by the review date (or, say, three months before the relevant review date), the review clause should allow for either party (not just the landlord) to refer the matter to an independent third party adjudicator. If the tenant is intending to dispose of the lease it will want to finalize the review as soon as possible and must be given the option of activating the referral. Accordingly, the tenant's solicitor must ensure that the rent review clause allows the tenant to refer as well. If the lease is silent on the point, either party may refer (*United Scientific Holdings Ltd v Burnley BC* [1978] AC 904, 960).

2.95   The clause will normally allow for the parties to agree who shall determine the new rent (normally a surveyor). But if the parties cannot reach agreement, the clause should permit either party to apply to the President (or his nominee) of the Royal Institution of Chartered Surveyors (RICS) to appoint an adjudicator. The RICS will then appoint a surveyor with experience and knowledge of similar leases in the area.

2.96   The surveyor appointed to determine the revised rent may act either as an expert or as an arbitrator, and the lease will normally make it clear which of these is to apply. Alternatively, the lease may allow the party who refers the matter to choose whether to appoint an expert or an arbitrator. The essential differences between expert and arbitrator are as follows:

- An expert exercises his or her own skill and judgement and sorts out the relevant facts for himself or herself. He or she is not bound by the procedure under the Arbitration Act 1996.
- An arbitrator performs a quasi-judicial function by hearing evidence and submissions from the parties, and deciding the outcome from the evidence presented to him or her (ie, like a court). The arbitrator is bound by the procedure under the Arbitration Act 1996, allowing him or her to order attendance of witnesses and discovery of documents.
- Determination by an expert is normally cheaper and quicker than determination by an arbitrator, as arbitration will incur all the costs associated with a full-blown hearing.
- An expert can be sued in negligence; an arbitrator cannot be sued in negligence.
- An expert's decision is final and binding unless it can be shown that he or she failed to perform the assigned task (*Jones v Sherwood Computer Services Plc* [1992] 2 All ER 170). To this end the parties should insist that the expert gives a written report of the reasons for his or her decision (a 'reasoned award').
- Against an arbitrator's award there is a limited right of appeal to the High Court on a point of law.

It can be seen that cost is an important factor. Arbitration is generally more suitable where the stakes are high and the costs of a fully-argued arbitration can be justified. Arbitration may also be preferred where points of law are involved, or where the property is unconventional in character and perhaps difficult to value.

For ordinary properties at moderate rents, where comparable properties are numerous, for both parties the appointment of an expert will generally be more appropriate. The parties should be entitled to submit to the expert in writing their own valuation and representations, and to comment on or reply to the valuation and/or representations of the other party. **2.97**

Additional rent review provisions

As is often the case, the revised rent may not be agreed or determined until after the relevant review date. In this case the parties will normally agree (ie, the lease will provide) that the old rent is paid on account of the new rent until the latter is known. Once the new rent is fixed, the shortfall between the old and new rent becomes due together with interest if agreed. A fair rate of interest would be the current base rate or possibly 1 or 2 per cent above the base rate (not the harsh rate of 4 per cent above base rate, applicable to late payment of rent arising from tenant default). If, unusually, the rent is revised downwards, the lease should oblige the landlord to refund the difference to the tenant, with interest if agreed. If the lease is silent on this point, it may be implied (see *Royal Bank of Scotland v Jennings* [1997] 19 EG 152). **2.98**

Additionally, from the tenant's perspective, the lease should make it clear that the date of valuation is the review date itself. The date of valuation should not be a date fixed by a landlord's notice, or the date the parties reach agreement on the rent or the date that a third party determines the rent. Such provisions would allow a unscrupulous landlord in a rising market to delay negotiations to achieve a later valuation date and higher rent. **2.99**

2.100 Lastly, the rent review clause should provide that after the revised rent has been agreed or determined, a memorandum should be drafted in duplicate recording the new rental figure. The landlord and tenant then sign the memoranda and one copy is affixed to the original lease and the other to the counterpart lease. In this way, those reading the documents, eg, prospective assignees of the lease or reversion, will see how the rent has been reviewed.

The Code of Practice for Commercial Leases and Rent Review

2.101 Recommendations 6 and 13 of the Code relate to rent review. Recommendation 6 states that 'The basis of rent review should generally be to open market rent. Wherever possible, landlords should offer alternatives which are priced on a risk-adjusted basis, including alternatives to upwards only rent reviews; these might include up/down reviews to open market rent with a minimum of the initial rent, or another basis such as annual indexation.' Of course financiers of property often require landlords to ensure that rental income will not fall below a particular level. Such a constraint would be likely to restrict a landlord's ability to agree an upward or downward review. However the Code's recommendation goes on to state that 'Those funding property should make every effort to avoid imposing restrictions on the type of rent review that landlords, developers and/or investors may offer'. Recommendation 13 of the Code is concerned with rent review and the conduct of the parties during the lease. It states that 'Landlords and tenants should ensure that they understand the basis upon which rent may be reviewed and the procedure to be followed, including the existence of any strict time limits which could create pitfalls'. It further recommends that parties should take professional advice well before the review date and also immediately upon receiving (and before responding to) any notices or correspondence.

Precedents for rent review clause for occupational lease

2.102 *(Note: suggested tenant's amendments and additions are shown struck through and underlined.)*

Valuation formula

2.103 1. The revised rent shall be the amount agreed between the Lessor and the Lessee as being the ~~best~~ <u>market</u> rent for the time being taking into account the following assumptions:

(a) that the Premises are available to be let by a willing landlord to a willing tenant on a letting of whole;

(b) that the letting is for a term of years equivalent to the residue of the term of this lease or ~~fifteen~~ <u>ten</u> years (whichever is the longer) on the open market commencing from the date of review;

(c) that the Premises are let with vacant possession (<u>but taking into account any sub-tenancies existing at the date of review</u>);

(d) that there is no payment of any premium or fine;

(e) ~~that there is no restriction as to the purpose for which the Premises may be used;~~

(f) that the Premises are ~~fitted out~~ ready for use and occupation by a lessee;

(g) ~~that all rent-free or reduced rent periods or allowances which might be made to a lessee have expired or been otherwise allowed (and there shall be ignored for the purposes of~~

~~determining the said market rent all such periods and allowances and also any depreciatory effect on rent of this provision~~);

(h) that ~~the Lessor and~~ the Lessee ~~have~~ has complied with all ~~their~~ its obligations as to repair and decoration and for compliance with statutory requirements imposed on the Lessee (but without prejudice to any rights or remedies of the Lessor);

(i) that the letting is otherwise upon terms (other than the amount of the rent hereby reserved) and subject to covenants conditions and provisions (~~excluding~~ including provisions as to rent review) similar to those contained in this lease

2. In assessing the revised rent there shall be disregarded any effect on rent of:

(a) the fact that the Lessee its sub-lessees their respective predecessors in title or other lawful occupiers may have ~~has~~ been in occupation of the Premises or any part thereof

(b) any goodwill attached to the Premises as a result of any trade or business carried on in the Premises by the Lessee its sub-lessees their respective predecessors in title or other lawful occupiers

(c) any improvements to the Premises or any part of the Premises (to which the Lessor shall have given written consent or to which the Lessor could not unreasonably have withheld consent) carried out by the Lessee its sub-lessees their respective predecessors in title or other lawful occupiers at ~~his~~ their own expense ~~during the currency of this lease~~ whether before or after the date of this lease and otherwise than as a result of an obligation to the Lessor except obligations requiring compliance with statutes or directions of local authorities or other bodies exercising powers under statute or Royal Charter

(d) the fact that the Premises ~~or any means of access thereto~~ have been destroyed or damaged either by an insured risk or for which the Lessee is under an obligation to repair and in such a case for the purposes of establishing the market rent the Premises ~~and any means of access thereto~~ shall be deemed to have been fully reinstated and rendered fit for occupation and use immediately prior to the date of review

(e) ~~The charging of Value Added Tax or such other similar tax~~

(f) ~~any statute order instrument regulation or direction then in force which regulates or restricts the amount of rent which may be payable~~

Rent review procedure

(a) If the market rent shall not have been agreed three months before the relevant review date then the question may be referred by either the Lessor or the Lessee to the decision of a surveyor ('the Surveyor') to be mutually agreed by the Lessor and the Lessee or in default of agreement to be nominated by the President for the time being of The Royal Institution of Chartered Surveyors or his or her nominee **2.104**

(b) The Surveyor whether agreed or nominated shall be a Chartered Surveyor having knowledge of rental values in the area in which the Premises are situated and the Surveyor shall act either as an expert or at the option of the Lessor or the Lessee as an arbitrator under a reference which shall be deemed to be a submission to arbitration within the meaning of the Arbitration Act 1996 or any statutory modification or re-enactment for the time being in force

(c) If the Surveyor acts as expert each party shall be entitled to submit to him in writing within four weeks after his appointment a valuation and representations and within a further two weeks written comments on or replies to the valuation and/or representations of the other party and the Surveyor shall not be limited or fettered by any submission by either party and shall determine the market rent in accordance with his own judgement and his decision shall be binding on both the Lessor and the Lessee

(d) ~~at the expense of the Lessee~~ a memorandum recording the agreement or determination of the market rent shall be signed by the Lessor and the Lessee in duplicate immediately after the same has been agreed or determined and annexed to this lease and the counterpart

(e) In the event of the market rent not having been agreed or determined prior to the relevant review date then in respect of the period of time (hereinafter called 'the said interval') beginning with the relevant review date and ending on the quarter day immediately following the date on which such agreement or determination shall have been made the Lessee shall pay to the Lessor the previous rent at the yearly rate payable immediately before the relevant review date

(f) At the expiration of the interval there shall be due as a debt payable by the Lessee to the Lessor on demand a sum of money equal to the amount whereby the yearly rent agreed or determined as aforesaid shall exceed the previous rent at the yearly rate aforesaid but duly apportioned on a daily basis in respect of the said interval together with interest on such sum of money at ~~four per cent (4%) above~~ the base lending rate of Barclays Bank Plc from time to time from the date of the commencement of the said interval until the date of actual payment

Statement that time shall not be of the essence

2.105   For the purposes of the rent review time shall not be of the essence and the Lessor shall not be prevented from requiring a rent review in respect of any period of this Lease by reason of any delay on its part (whether before during or after the period in question) and any such delay shall not in any circumstances amount to an abandonment of the right to review the rent

---

PRACTICAL CHECKLISTS: RENT AND RENT REVIEW

Acting for the tenant—negotiating the draft rent review clause

2.106
- Allow for the rent to be reviewed downwards as well as upwards, ie, resist 'upwards only'. The Code recommends that landlords should offer alternatives to upwards only reviews.
- Define the rent as 'the rent at which the Premises might reasonably be expected to be let in the open market on the review date by a willing landlord to a willing tenant'. Avoid the phrase 'best rent'.
- Take a valuer's advice on the preferred length of the hypothetical term. A formula based on the unexpired residue of the term, possibly with a minimum period (eg, 10 or 15 years) is normally the best option for the tenant.
- Generally, the terms of the hypothetical lease should reflect reality.
- Do not accept assumptions that do not exist, eg, unrestricted alienation or user covenants. Why should the tenant be paying for something it does not in fact have?
- Ensure that the rent review clause is not excluded from the hypothetical lease.

- Resist attempts by the landlord to disregard any future statutory control of rents (on the basis that the parties should abide by the law).
- Resist an assumption of vacant possession if the premises will be sub-let at review.
- Resist an assumption of the premises being 'fully fitted out' as the hypothetical tenant may ask for a rent-free period for notional fitting-out works.
- If a rent-free period is given as an inducement at the start of the lease then it should be taken into account on review.
- Any landlord's break option should be taken into account on review.
- Resist any assumption that the landlord's covenants have been performed.
- Resist an assumption that the hypothetical tenant can recover VAT as this may not be the case in reality.
- Always include the 'statutory' disregards of occupation, goodwill and improvements. Extend these to cover sub-tenants, predecessors in title and other lawful occupiers.
- Disregard tenant's occupation of adjoining premises if this is the case.
- Define the review dates by reference to the anniversaries of the commencement date, not by specifying the dates themselves.
- Take specialist advice generally from a valuer or surveyor on the terms of the clause.

Rent review procedure—checklist of sensible provisions for both parties

- Preferably adopt the informal method of implementing the review rather than the 'trigger   **2.107** notice' method.
- State expressly that time shall *not* be of the essence of any time limits in the review clause.
- In the absence of agreement on the new rent, either party to be allowed to refer to a third party adjudicator.
- For orthodox properties with modest rents, appoint an expert.
- For unorthodox properties or properties with high rents, appoint an arbitrator.
- Until the new rent is fixed, the old rent to be paid on account and the difference forwarded (plus interest at base rate) once the new rent is known.
- The date of the rent review valuation should be the review date itself.
- Provide for rent review memoranda to be affixed to the lease and counterpart lease.

KEY DOCUMENTS

- Landlord and Tenant (Covenants) Act 1995   **2.108**
- Value Added Tax Act 1983
- Landlord and Tenant Act 1954
- Code of Practice for Commercial Leases in England and Wales (2nd edn)

Printed copies of legislation can be ordered from The Stationery Office (<http://www.tsoshop.co.uk>). Legislation from 1988 onwards can be downloaded free of charge from <http://www.opsi.gov.uk/acts.htm>.

The Code of Practice for Commercial Leases in England and Wales is set out in appendix 17.

3

COMMERCIAL LEASE COVENANTS I

A   GENERAL INTRODUCTION

A covenant, being an obligation within a contract drawn up under a seal, eg, a lease, is the   **3.01**
fundamental basis for all the regulatory elements of the lessor–lessee relationship. In modern leases the need, on the part of lessors' practitioners, to cover all eventualities has led to
the appearance of excessively long lists of covenants all for the lessee to perform. (The
number of covenants for the lessor is, unsurprisingly, considerably limited, and is dealt with
in chapter 1 at paras 1.76 et seq and in full in chapter 4. In the main, the lessor's covenants
are usually concerned only with quiet enjoyment, insurance matters and sometimes with
the provision of various services.)

In this chapter, we have concentrated upon those lessee covenants that will, in one form or   **3.02**
another, appear in most if not all modern commercial leases. They will usually regulate
who is responsible for repairing the subject property, obligations limiting or permitting

alterations, who can occupy the subject premises as a result of the terms of the lease, and details of what the subject property can be used for.

B   COVENANTS BY THE LESSEE

3.03   The covenants by the lessee will often comprise a long list of obligations for the lessee to adhere to. It will usually start with a covenant to pay the rents due under the lease terms and will then list other important obligations, such as restrictions upon alienation, changes in use and alterations to the subject property, as well as repairing obligations that fall to the lessee to perform. If you are acting for a prospective lessee you must of course consider carefully the nature and extent of all the lessee's covenants. You must do so in the light of the client's intended use of the property and any other salient instructions. However, it is the case that some covenants will be of more consequence to a lessee than others. We set out below details of some of the more important covenants commonly found in commercial leases, all of which must be considered carefully by a practitioner acting for either lessor or lessee.The Code of Practice for Commercial Leases in England and Wales (April 2002 edition) ('the Code') covers many of these important topics. It does so from two perspectives. First, when negotiating for a business lease and, secondly, it considers the conduct of the parties to a lease during the lease term. The Code will be considered in each section below where relevant and will cover both recommendations of good practice along with appropriate explanations.

Payment covenants

3.04   All commercial leases should start their list of lessee's covenants with one for the payment of rent. The covenant should also make clear whether the rent is to be paid in arrears or in advance and upon what days, eg, most leases still mention the usual (ie traditional) quarter days (25 March, 24 June, 29 September and 25 December in each year). The modern alternative will refer to 1 January, 1 April, 1 July and 1 October. Other payment dates are of course possible, such as monthly payments on a particular date, eg, the first day of each month. The amount to be paid will, of course, be covered earlier in the lease, as will any revision of the rent pursuant to rent review obligations. The rental covenant should also cover the payment of additional rent required on review as well as other rents required by the lease, such as service charge payments to be treated as rent as a consequence of the lease terms. Accordingly, insurance payments can be dealt with as rent as can interest on rent arising as a result of late payment. Some lessors will require the rent to be paid in a particular way, such as by banker's standing order or possibly even direct debit. If your lessor client requires payment in a particular format, it is best to include a reference to this specific payment method within this first covenant.

3.05   If a lease does not include a covenant by the lessee to pay interest upon rent paid after the due date then there is a discretionary power for the courts to award interest to a lessor claimant. However, certainty for the lessor dictates the need for such a distinct covenant, which will also enable the lessor to stipulate the level of interest payable (usually expressed to be a percentage above a bank base rate, eg, 4 per cent above Barclays Bank plc base rate).

Excessively high interest rates are subject to scrutiny by the courts to ascertain whether they might, as a result of the high level, constitute an unfair penalty rather than a measure of damages for loss caused by the lessee's breach. Consequently, a reasonable interest rate in the lease, such as that shown in the example above, will not be open to attack. The Late Payment of Commercial Debts (Interest) Act 1998 does not cover commercial leases.

The lease should also contain a covenant by the lessee to pay all taxes, rates, assessments and **3.06** outgoings in respect of the demised premises. This will include in particular all business rates and water rates. A prudent tenant, when approving such a covenant, should include a proviso that the covenant does not extend to any taxes properly payable by the lessor arising from the receipt of rent or as a result of any dealing by the lessor with the reversion.

Repairing obligations

This is a common area of dispute between the parties to a commercial letting. It is therefore **3.07** critical that the lease repairs clauses are as clear as they can be in defining which of the parties to the lease is responsible for repairing the subject property and to what standard. As a result, this is an area of great difficulty in two principal ways. First, deciding what part of the subject property must be repaired by the lessee does rather depend on the extent of the definition of the lessee's property in the lease. Secondly, when the extent of the property is known the measure of the burden of the repairing liability must then be clearly defined— from simple repairs necessary to deal with ordinary wear and tear, right up to the lessee being under a strict obligation virtually to replace the whole property.

Conventional commercial leases usually tackle repairs in a tripartite fashion. First, the lessee **3.08** is required to keep the subject premises in repair throughout the lease term; secondly, the lessee must yield up the premises in repair; and thirdly the lessee must redecorate either inside or out (or both) at fixed times throughout the lease term and at its end. There will usually be an enforcing fourth provision requiring the lessee to repair within a period on notice served upon the lessee after inspecting the premises, ie, the lessee will be required to comply with a schedule of dilapidations setting out the required repairs.

Some repairing covenants will not just require the lessee to keep the subject property in **3.09** repair but will actually require the lessee to put the premises in repair. While keeping in repair does include putting in repair (and indeed yielding up in repair), the courts have decided that the obligation to put in repair is of no greater consequence to a lessee at the commencement of the lease term. If the premises are not in repair at the time the lease commences then the obligation to keep the premises in repair will require the lessee actually to put them in repair at the start of the term (see *Proudfoot v Hart* (1890) 25 QBD 42, at para 3.15 below). The additional wording adds little, as is the case for inserting 'good' or 'sufficient' or 'tenantable' within the repairing covenant (see *Anstruther-Gough-Calthorpe v McOscar* [1924] 1 KB 716).

It used to be the case that lessees could argue that they were not responsible for repairs **3.10** arising from inherent defects in the subject property, ie, for repairs arising from any defects in the design and/or construction of the particular premises. The modern view is that this 'defence' is no longer viable and that a lessee may be required to make such repairs where the repairing covenant requires it notwithstanding that the repairs may arise from such a defect.

The case that made this liability plain is *Ravenseft Properties Limited v Davstone (Holdings) Limited* [1980] QB 12. As was observed in the case, 'It is always a question of degree' whether the tenant is required merely to repair the property as opposed to completing such extensive works that the lessee will eventually give back to the lessor 'a wholly different thing from that which he demised'. It is therefore of consequence to ascertain how substantial the works may be. For example, in *Post Office v Aquarius Properties Ltd* [1987] 1 All ER 1055, the works were concerned with a porous area of concrete in a basement that allowed the immediate vicinity to be flooded, but it did no actual harm and thus did not give rise to any disrepair. The lessee was therefore not required to repair the defect. Clearly, the simple method of avoiding any doubt is to draft the repairing clause so as to make it quite clear that the lessee will be obliged to repair any such design or construction defects.

3.11 A typical repairing covenant is set out below (as is the case throughout this book, tenant's amendments and additions are struck through and underlined). This example is appropriate for a lease that gives to the lessee the whole of the subject property and thus the whole repairing responsibility for the property. The deletions made by the lessee are to reduce wherever possible liability for works, and the additions are made with the same purpose in mind. The precedent is in a somewhat anodyne format, in that it has not been tailored for a particular type of property. Practitioners should remember to adjust these clauses to cover any specific requirements that may arise because of the nature of the subject premises. For example, if the lease was for a shop and upper part, the first clause should be extended to include reference to the shop front and fascia to make sure that this is kept in repair by the lessee. Furthermore, a proposed lessee of an older or dilapidated property would want to limit liability by reference to a schedule of condition. See para 3.17 below for details of such schedules.

3.12 At all times during the term <u>fair wear and tear excepted</u>:

1. to well and substantially cleanse repair ~~renew~~ and renovate ~~and when necessary replace and rebuild~~ to the satisfaction of the lessor~~'s surveyor~~
    1.1 all present and future structures or buildings forming all or any part of the demised premises and
    1.2 all fixtures additions and improvements which may at any time be attached placed or made upon the demised premises and
    1.3 to clean and repair the external stone and brickwork ~~replacing such stone and brickwork as required~~
2. to repair and ~~to put and~~ keep:
    2.1 the exterior and interior of the demised premises and all additions thereto including any machinery and fixtures boundary walls and fences drains soil and other pipes and sanitary water gas electrical central heating telephony and computer apparatus within the demised premises
    2.2 doors and windows floors ceilings walls stairways landings lifts roofs guttering and foundations
    in good and substantial repair ~~including any arising from inherent defects~~ throughout the term.

Repairs—who does what?

As to which party will be required by the lease to be responsible for repairs, this is likely to be **3.13**
dictated by the nature of the premises. Where there is a property in multiple occupation—
say an office block containing several office suites, all let to different lessees—the usual
repairing arrangement is for the lessee to be required to keep in good repair only the
inner skin of its property. This would therefore require the lessee to keep properly maintained the plaster, the ceiling and flooring materials, but not much else. All structural elements of the property, including the floor and ceiling joists, the load-bearing or main bearing
walls, the roof and foundations, should all be repairable by the lessor. This would then mean
that all the lessees would have to covenant to pay a service charge to reimburse the lessor for
the expense of repairing these main structures. (Consequently, the further need for clear and
appropriate service charge covenants arises from this form of repairing arrangement, see
paras 4.45 et seq below.) The rationale for this procedure is that there is a need for a single,
consistent approach to the whole subject of structural repairs and maintenance. On the
other hand, if the lease is of all the building—such as a lease of a shop and upper part, or
indeed one office building let to one lessee—then it is common for the sole lessee to be
responsible for all the repairs to the building, both inside and out.

Whether the lessee is required to repair the whole of the demised premises or just the inner **3.14**
shell, it is clear that the repairing covenant must be drafted in terms that are unequivocal
and where there is no possibility of doubt about the extent of the liability. This being so,
elements of this rigorous obligation will now be analysed.

What is the standard of repair?

The precise standard of repair required was set out in the case of *Proudfoot v Hart* (1890) **3.15**
25 QBD 42. Here it was held that the standard of repair is to be determined according to
several factors, including the subject property's age and character and the environment in
which the property is located. In effect this has meant that there is a clear difference in the
expected standard of repair for a Victorian property and that for one that was built in the late
1990s. As to the meaning of 'repair', the courts have made it clear that this includes elements
of renewal (see *Lurcott v Wakeley & Wheeler* [1911] 1 KB 905). However, the courts have also
considered where repair ends and renewal begins. Clearly this is likely to be an indistinct
boundary, but the case of *McDougall v Easington DC* (1989) 58 P & CR 201, CA, contains a
three-part test for the distinction between repairs and renewals. The test had:

> to be approached in the light of the nature and age of the premises, their condition when the
> tenant went into occupation, and the other express terms of the tenancy:
>
> (i)   whether the alterations went to the whole or substantially the whole of the structure or to
>   only a subsidiary part;
> (ii) whether the effect of the alterations was to produce a building of a wholly different
>   character from that which had been let;
> (iii) what was the cost of the works in relation to the previous value of the building, and what
>   was their effect on the value and lifespan of the building?

It should also be remembered that a covenant requiring the lessee 'to put and keep the **3.16**
property in good and substantial repair' is a covenant that can be construed in the courts as
being particularly substantial in its effect. This is because the obligation amounts to a burden

that could be considered to be above mere repair. As a consequence, it is likely that the courts will interpret full repairing covenants as requiring the lessee to carry out all repairs and renewals, substantial or not, right from the start of the lease (see *Elite Investments Limited v TI Bainbridge Silencers Limited* [1986] 2 EGLR 43). It should be noted that where the covenant contains the obligation 'to keep' the premises in repair then the courts have decided that this means that the premises must be kept in repair at all times throughout the term of the lease. If a defect arises then there is an immediate breach of covenant (see *British Telecommunications plc v Sun Life Assurance Society plc* [1995] 3 WLR 622).

3.17   As a result, each lease repairing covenant, seen in the light of the subject property, will dictate the nature and extent of the repairs required. However, this will not mean that a lessee of an old property can argue that as a result of the age of the subject property the lessee need not honour a full repairing covenant (see *Lurcott v Wakeley & Wheeler* [1911] 1 KB 905). If a lessee is faced with an old property and a full repairing covenant then it would be well advised to try to define the repairing liability as being no greater than the condition of the property at the start of the lease. This can be achieved by preparing a schedule of condition setting out the state the property is in at the time the lease is granted. The schedule can then be referred to in the repairing covenant so that the document is incorporated into the deed. The lessee is then stated in the covenant not to be liable for repairs over and above those set out in the schedule. To assist, the inclusion of a set of photographs will help to fix exactly the condition of the property at the lease commencement date.

3.18   In summary, 'repair is restoration by renewal or replacement of subsidiary parts of a whole. Renewal, as distinguished from repair is reconstruction of the entirety, meaning by the entirety not necessarily the whole but substantially the whole' (*Lurcott v Wakeley & Wheeler*, above). The standard is 'such repair as having regard to the age, character and locality would make it reasonably fit for the occupation of a reasonably minded tenant of the class likely to take it (*Proudfoot v Hart* (1890) 25 QBD 42). But that does not mean that an old property limits liability. A tenant 'can never say "The house was so old that it relieved me from my covenant to keep it in good condition" '. (*Lurcott v Wakeley & Wheeler*, above).

3.19   It is quite possible for the wording of a repairing covenant to require the lessee to do more than merely repair, by the inclusion of words such as 'reconstruct', 'replace', 'rebuild' or 'restructure' within the body of the repairing covenant. Quite how far this takes the responsibility beyond keeping in repair depends upon the circumstances, and indeed upon the actual wording of the covenant. For example, in the case of *Norwich Union Life Assurance Society v British Railways Board* [1987] 2 EGLR 137, it was held that a repairing obligation expressed to be 'where necessary to rebuild reconstruct or replace' dictated a liability to rebuild the entirety of the subject premises. Similarly, in *Welsh v Greenwich LBC* (2001) 33 HLR 40, where the premises had to be in 'good condition', it was held in the Court of Appeal that this was sufficient to extend the repairing obligation to defects that were not structural.

3.20   A practitioner acting for a lessee may seek to limit liability by including in the lease covenant additional wording stating that repairs are 'fair wear and tear excepted'. This was defined in *Haskell v Marlow* [1928] 2 KB 45, where it was stated that a lessee was not responsible for repairs arising from what is due to reasonable wear and tear: 'Reasonable wear and tear means the reasonable use of the house by the tenant and the ordinary operation of natural forces.' It is up to the lessee to demonstrate that any want of repair arises from reasonable wear and tear.

Where insurance monies are potentially available to fund repairs or to rebuild the subject **3.21** premises, it is clearly fair to limit the lessee's liability under the repairing covenants to take account of this possibility. Accordingly, it is common to encounter in repairing covenants an exemption in the lessee's favour in respect of damage and consequent repairs caused by an insured risk. It is also the case that such exemptions will have a precondition that the exemption will apply only so long as the insurance cover has not been negatived by reason of the lessee's act or default. There is then a further concern, and that is if there is a shortfall on the insurance payment. In these circumstances a prudent lessor will seek to make the lessee responsible for this shortfall; while the lessee might argue that it is for the lessor to cover, bearing in mind that the lessor insures. Plainly this is a topic that will be open to negotiation between the parties at the time the draft lease is settled. For more on insurance, see paras 4.08 et seq below.

Cyclical decorations

Most commercial leases will also include clauses calling upon the lessee to decorate intern- **3.22** ally (and externally if the lessee has the total repairing liability of the demised premises) at regular intervals during the term of the lease. Common repainting and redecorating intervals are every five years internally and every three years externally. The sequence can be larger or smaller. Many such covenants call upon the lessee to decorate and repaint in the final year of the term, whether or not this coincides with the fixed intervals.

Some clauses of this kind go on to stipulate the kind of resources the lessee should use when **3.23** repainting or redecorating. This can lead to inappropriate items being referred to that are either out of date, or unsuited to the subject premises. For example, some old-fashioned leases will refer to the use of good quality lead-based paints, something health and safety concerns would now disallow. We suggest that generic terms be used, such as 'good quality paint' or 'good quality materials'. This clause can also give an additional element of control to the lessor by enabling it to first approve the materials used with the commencing phrase, 'In colours and materials first approved by the lessor . . .'.

Overall, the purpose of clauses such as these is to define clearly the nature and extent of **3.24** the lessee's cyclical decorating liability, so as to ensure the proper upkeep of the subject property. A typical clause of this kind will read:

> To decorate all of the outside of the demised premises every third year of the term and to decorate the inside of the demised premises every fifth year and in both cases in the last year of the term using good quality paint and materials in colours first approved by the lessor's surveyor (such approval not to be unreasonably withheld) but the lessee will not be required to redecorate in the last year of the term if the lessee has redecorated within the previous twelve months

The amendment by the lessee at the end requires the decision about colours to be reasonable **3.25** and to be made by the lessor's surveyor, who may take a more professional view than a business lessor. The final addition covers the situation where, because of the length of the lease term, there may be a duplication of effort. For example, if the lease was for ten years, the lessee would be required to carry out cyclical redecoration in the ninth year and then again soon after in the tenth and last year. Plainly, this would be unacceptable to the lessee.

Repairs enforcement provisions

3.26   To ensure compliance with repairing obligations, modern leases will always include a covenant allowing the lessor to enter the demised premises, on prior written notice, to view the state of repair. If the lessee is in breach of the repairing covenant, the lessor will then be able to serve a notice on the lessee calling for repair to be carried out. Moreover, the lessor, in the case of default by the lessee, will have the benefit of a further provision enabling the lessor to enter the subject property to carry out the necessary repairs and to charge the lessee for the cost of the work required. If the costs incurred by the lessor are described as a simple debt, due from the lessee, this can be to the advantage of the lessor. This is because if the cost of repair is described as a simple debt, it is not caught by statutory limitations upon the recovery of damages. For the rationale for this approach, see below regarding the limitations imposed by the Landlord and Tenant Act 1927 and the Leasehold Property (Repairs) Act 1938 in relation to damages. Nevertheless, practitioners need to advise lessors in these circumstances that if they do effect entry to make repairs, they will potentially become liable for claims arising under the terms of the Defective Premises Act 1972 since lessors will be under a duty to make sure that the premises are in a condition that ensures the safety of persons within them.

3.27   The lessor can also serve a notice pursuant to the terms of s 146 of the Law of Property Act 1925, calling for the lessee to comply with the lease repairing covenants. The notice will give the lessee a fixed amount of time to comply with those covenants, failing which the lessor can seek to forfeit the lease for breach of covenant. Practitioners should remember that the lessor's rights in this regard are limited by the effect of the Leasehold Property (Repairs) Act 1938. If the original term of the lease was for seven years or more and there are at least three years left unexpired of the term, the s 146 notice must refer to the 1938 Act and inform the lessee of his right to serve a counter-notice claiming the benefit of the Act. This counter-notice must be served upon the lessor within 28 days of the service of the s 146 notice. If the lessee obtains the benefit of the Act by serving a counter-notice within the time limit, the lessor cannot forfeit the lease without leave of the court. In effect, it means that the lessor can neither sue for damages nor forfeit the lease without a court order allowing the lessor so to do. When making an order the court has a complete discretion to impose such conditions in the order as it deems appropriate to the particular circumstances of the case. Precedents for s 146 notices are set out in appendix 12.

3.28   Practitioners should bear in mind, however, the effect of the decision in *SEDAC Investments Ltd v Tanner* [1982] 1 WLR 1342. In this case the lessor carried out works of repair on an emergency basis without giving the lessee an opportunity of carrying out the required works. As a result the lessor could not serve a s146 notice as the works were complete and the breach remedied. Because of these circumstances no notice could be served under the 1938 Act, and therefore the court was unable to grant the lessor leave to commence proceedings for an action in damages against the lessee arising from the breach of covenant. Furthermore, s 18 of the Landlord and Tenant Act 1927 makes it clear that no damages can be awarded if it is apparent that the premises are to be demolished at the end of the lease or shortly thereafter, or there are alterations intended that would make the repairs pointless.

3.29   As well as forfeiture, a lessor can also seek damages for a breach of the repairing covenants. (Normally specific performance will not be an available remedy except in exceptional circumstances, as to allow it could lead to the statutory provisions set out above being circumvented.) During the lease term the measure of damages is the diminution in the value of the reversion caused by the breach. At the end of the lease the measure of damages is the amount that is required to put the premises into the condition in which the lessee would have had to leave them, had it left the premises with no subsisting breach of covenant (see *James v Hutton* [1950] KB 9 and *Joyner v Weeks* [1891] 2 QB 31).

Yielding up in repair

Most commercial leases will include a covenant by the lessee to yield up the subject property **3.30** in repair at the end of the lease term. The clause can be brief and to the point:

> At the expiration of the lease term howsoever determined and at the cost of the lessee to yield up the demised premises in good repair and in accordance with all the covenants terms and conditions of this lease.

Of course the lessor need not stop there. The obligation to yield up to a requisite standard or **3.31** condition can be extended to other matters. So, when yielding up at the end of the term the lessee may also be required to replace any of the lessor's fixtures and fittings, or to compensate the lessor for their loss or damage. Similarly, the lessee may be required to remove from the demised premises any sign or writing that was an advert for the name or business conducted by the lessee within the subject premises. The lessee can also be required to remove all the lessee's fixtures and fittings and on yielding up to make good all damage caused by their removal.

It is also a common problem with lessees at the end of the term that they abandon unwanted **3.32** furniture and other effects in or about the demised premises. To try to avoid this the lessor could include within the yielding up provisions a requirement for the lessee to remove all such items on the determination of the lease term. Should the lessee fail to comply within a fixed period, say seven days, then the clause should state that the lessor will be entitled to sell these items and to account to the lessee for the net proceeds less all reasonable costs of storage and sale. Should there be a loss then that loss should be repayable by the former lessee.

Lastly, the clause should state that should the lessee fail to comply with it then the lessor can **3.33** carry out the works required in default and then charge the lessee for the cost of the works.

From the lessee's perspective it really is the case with these provisions that the less said the **3.34** better. Accordingly, when approving the draft the best practical tactic would be to try to delete as many of these additional elements leaving no more than the main clause as indicated above.

The Code and repairs

Recommendation 7 of the Code relates to repairs and services. It states that 'the tenant's **3.35** repairing obligations, and any repair costs included in service charges, should be appropriate to the length of the term and the condition and age of the property at the start of the lease. Where appropriate the landlord should consider appropriately priced alternatives to full repairing terms.' Recommendation 18 states that 'tenants should take the advice of a property professional about their repairing obligations near the end of the term of the lease and also immediately upon receiving a notice to repair or a schedule of dilapidations'. The explanatory notes make it clear that disagreement about the scope and content of such schedules 'are not uncommon and the law on repairing obligations is complex'. This would seem to be borne out by the details of paras 3.07 to 3.35 generally.

Alteration provisions

3.36 It is common for lessees to want to alter the subject premises either at the commencement, or during the term of the lease. If they do want to change the structure physically in some way they will need to consider, as a result of the lease covenants, if that alteration requires the prior consent of the lessor. Modern leases will almost always include a covenant limiting what the lessee may do to the demised premises. Lessors will require the lease to contain such a provision to make sure that at the end of the lease they get back premises that are in the same style and format as existed at the start of the lease. It is also possible that some alterations could in theory depress the rental value of the premises, and no business lessor would therefore want to permit such alterations in these circumstances.

3.37 However, while the above is true in principle, in practice the nature of the alterations clause is very much dictated by the length of the lease term. If the lease term is short then the lessor will want to and will be able to limit the possible alterations. Once the lease term is for 21 years or more then the position starts to reverse itself. Such long-term lessees will want to have more control over the possible alterations they can make at the premises, especially when the lease term is substantial. Indeed, prospective lessees for long-term leases could be put off from taking the lease should the alterations clause be too restrictive.

3.38 Modern leases will seek to stop the lessee from carrying out any permanent alterations, especially where they alter the structure (or sometimes the appearance) of the subject premises. Such leases will go on, though, to allow the lessee to carry out alterations of a non-structural nature, including the erection of demountable partitions. A typical clause reads as follows:

>   1.   Not to alter cut harm or remove any of the principal or load bearing walls floors or other structures of or enclosing the demised premises nor to make any other alterations improvements or additions of a structural nature
>   2.   Not to make any alterations or additions of a non-structural nature to the demised premises <u>without having first obtained the prior written consent of the lessor such consent not to be unreasonably withheld</u> except that the lessee may install alter and remove demountable partitioning
>   3.   ~~The lessor may as a condition of giving consent require the lessee to enter into any covenants as the lessor shall require regarding the implementation of any such works and the reinstatement of the demised premises at the end or sooner determination of the term of this lease~~

3.39 The alterations to the covenant by the lessee are made to try to loosen the restrictions and are based upon a twofold approach. First, the limited consent is made subject to the test of reasonableness and therefore statute may intervene: see para 3.43 below. Secondly, the lessee will want to try to delete all of clause 3 as this gives an extremely wide discretion to the lessor to impose virtually any condition it chooses on the giving of permission for alterations.

Alteration covenants can be drafted to exclude absolutely any alterations, or may permit **3.40** alterations but only with the prior approval of the lessor. We consider each in further detail below:

Absolute covenants

A covenant dealing with alterations can include an absolute bar, such as: **3.41**

> . . . not to make or allow to be made any alterations additions or improvements to the demised premises.

If this is the lease alterations covenant, the lessee cannot carry out any such works whatsoever. This could be seen to be unfair to a long leaseholder, and consequently such clauses are sometimes qualified to allow the lessee to carry out non-structural alterations within the demised premises. An absolute bar on alterations or additions must therefore be considered unacceptable in a long lease, ie, a lease term of 21 years or more. If one appears in a draft, the lease should be amended to allow alterations with the lessor's written consent, and preferably with the consent subject to a test of reasonableness (see para 3.43 below).

If the lease does contain an absolute covenant, alterations or improvements may still be **3.42** possible. First, the lessee can seek to obtain the lessor's consent notwithstanding the absolute covenant, and the lessor can give consent subject to whatever conditions it seeks to impose. The lessor has a complete and virtually unfettered discretion when working with an absolute covenant. Secondly, statute may intervene and require works to be carried out notwithstanding the lease terms, ie, alterations required for means of escape in case of fire pursuant to the provisions of the Fire Precautions Act 1971. Thirdly, in relation to improvements one specific statute may apply. Section 3 of the Landlord and Tenant Act 1927 allows a lessee to apply to court for an order that the lessee may be permitted to carry out improvements even though the alteration covenant contains an absolute bar. As to what amounts to an improvement, this was considered in *Lambert v FW Woolworth & Co Ltd* [1938] 2 All ER 664. In this case it was decided that an improvement will be considered as such from the lessee's viewpoint and if it makes the subject premises more useful or more valuable to the lessee.

Qualified covenants

A covenant dealing with alterations can include a qualified approach, such as: **3.43**

> . . . not to make or allow to be made any alterations additions or improvements to the demised premises without the prior written approval of the lessor.

If this is the lease covenant, the lessee can carry out any work only with the prior written consent of the lessor. The lease therefore allows alterations to the property with the lessor's written consent. To the extent that proposed alterations amount to improvements, s 19(2) of the Landlord and Tenant Act 1927 will then apply so that consent cannot be unreasonably withheld. As to what amounts to an improvement, see para 3.42 above. The court will require the lessee to supply to the lessor, in support of the lessee's application for a licence for alterations, all appropriate information required to enable the lessor to make an informed decision (*Kalford Ltd v Peterborough City Council* [2001] EGCS 42).

The lessor cannot demand any payment beyond reasonable legal and other expenses **3.44** incurred in the granting of consent for the relevant works. It should be noted that the 1927 Act does not stop the lessor from seeking a reasonable sum should the proposed amendments diminish the value of the premises, or indeed any adjacent premises in the ownership of the same lessor. Similarly, if the alteration or addition does not add to the letting value of the premises, the Act does not prevent the lessor from obtaining from the lessee a covenant to reinstate the premises to their former condition at the end (or sooner determination) of the lease.

3.45 Where the lessor is prepared to grant its consent to the lessee's application to carry out alterations, the lessor may wish to impose conditions upon the lessee as part of that consent. The most commonly encountered conditions are that plans must be approved by the lessor, together with the specification for the proposed building works. Clearly the lessee will have to comply with the approved plans and complete the works in accordance with the approved specification. The lessor may require the lessee to obtain all other necessary consents and approvals and to produce them to the lessor prior to the commencement of the works. If the lease is silent on this point, the licence for alterations should include a provision requiring the lessee to reinstate the premises at the end of the lease if the lessor wants them back in their former condition. Such a clause requiring reinstatement is not implied, it must be express (see *Never-Stop Railway (Wembley) Limited v British Empire Exhibition Incorporated* [1926] 1 Ch 877).

3.46 Lastly, and in relation to improvements, there is a concern for the lessee in relation to the payment and recovery of VAT. Under the terms of the Landlord and Tenant Act 1927, the lessee can apply to the lessor to carry out improvements. In response the lessor can opt to carry out the proposed works of improvement itself and rentalize the expense of those works (see s 27). In effect the lessor takes over the works constituting the improvements desired by the lessee. It will pay for them and then include the cost as part of the rent paid by the lessee. If this occurs, the lessee will not be in a position to recover any element of the VAT on the cost of the improvements made by and paid for by the lessor.

Related covenants

3.47 Leases may also contain clauses that prohibit what items the lessee may erect upon or affix to the subject premises. The lessor can seek to stop the erection of aerials and masts as well as any alterations to the electrical wiring on the premises. These restrictions are all meant to ensure that the premises and anyone occupying them are kept safe. For example, defective electrical wiring could lead to substantial problems within the demised premises, so that by this kind of provision the lessor seeks to stop the lessee from making alterations that could overload the system.

3.48 The alterations made to the covenant below, written in by the lessee, are another attempt to impose the test of reasonableness on decisions made by the lessor. A typical clause reads:

> 1. Not to erect upon or affix to the demised premises any machinery or scientific apparatus save as reasonably required by the use of the demised premises; and
> 2. Not <u>without the previous consent in writing of the lessor such consent not to be unreasonably withheld</u> to affix any wireless television or other aerial to the exterior of the demised premise; and

3.   Not <u>without the written consent of the lessor such consent not to be unreasonably with-held</u> to alter or add to any electric wiring or system in the demised premises

Although not strictly speaking an alteration, most lessees will want to erect a sign advertising   **3.49**
their occupation of the subject property. Many commercial leases place restrictions on
this by requiring the lessee to submit plans for the sign for prior approval by the lessor.
Alternatively, some commercial leases include a provision requiring signs to be placed in one
particular location and to a specific format. This is usually used where there is, say, a signboard
within an entrance hall on which all the businesses are listed for that building.

Lastly, and linked to the whole topic of alterations, the lessor may seek to control whether or   **3.50**
not a lessee can apply for planning consents. This covenant should be linked to the alterations covenant and be similarly absolute or qualified. Thus, if the alterations clause is
absolute then the planning covenant should be similarly drafted. Notwithstanding the absolute provisions, it is always open to a lessor to grant consent with a condition that the lessee
obtains all consents (see para 3.45 above).

Compensation for improvements

Part I of the Landlord and Tenant Act 1927, as amended by the Landlord and Tenant Act   **3.51**
1954, gives a lessee the right to claim at the end of the lease compensation for improvements
made by the lessee. It will only apply to authorized improvements, and the improvements
must have added to the letting value of the subject property. To be authorized, the lessee
must comply with the terms of the Act and serve upon the lessor a notice indicating that the
lessee intends to carry out works of improvement. The lessor has three months to object,
failing which the lessee can assume that the works are approved. If the lessor objects, the
lessee can apply to court for approval.

The amount to be paid will be the sum deemed to be the additional value to the subject   **3.52**
property occasioned by the improvements. Alternatively, the compensation can be the reasonable cost of carrying out the improvement. Of course, if the lessor wishes to avoid this
problem it should simply ensure that the lease includes a requirement for reinstatement at
the end of the lease so that no compensation need be paid. Should the lessor fail to pay and
the lessor has served a s 25 notice under the terms of the Landlord and Tenant Act 1954, the
lessee must apply to court for compensation within three months of the receipt of that
notice. This whole procedure is rarely used and the Law Commission has recommended that
the 1927 Act in this respect be abolished (see *Compensation for Tenant's Improvements* (Law
Com No 187, 1989)).

The Code and alterations

Recommendation 10 of the Code states that the 'landlord's control over alterations . . .   **3.53**
should not be more restrictive than is necessary to protect the value of the premises and
any adjoining or neighbouring premises of the landlord. At the end of the lease the
tenant should not be required to remove and make good permitted alterations unless this
is reasonably required.' The explanatory notes make the point that if the provisions of
the lease are very restrictive this can hinder the assignment of the lease to a different
business.

Alienation restrictions

3.54 Alienation restrictions cover covenants against assignments, underlettings, mortgages, and other material dealings with the leasehold estate. Here we consider the enforcement of alienation covenants in relation both to leases granted before the start of 1996 and leases created after the end of 1995. We also consider absolute and qualified alienation covenants so far as they affect the parties to a lease. Of course, if the lease is silent about alienation, ie, there is no covenant covering the topic, then the lessee is free to assign or otherwise deal with the lease without reference to the lessor (see *Leith Properties Ltd v Byrne* [1983] QB 433).

Introduction

3.55 This area involves covenants that are of great concern for business leases from the perspective of both the lessee and the lessor. The reason for this is that a business lessor will want to know who is in occupation of the property, and in particular that the person or company in occupation has the financial strength such that the rents required by the lease will be paid. Similarly, the lessee will want to be sure that, should circumstances require it, the lessee can readily dispose of the premises either completely by way of an assignment, or by way of a sub-letting. A covenant covering alienation will encompass dealings with the whole of the title as well as part, and will include assignments, underlettings, parting with possession or sharing possession, as well as mortgages and possibly declaring a trust of the leasehold premises.

Covenants on assignment

3.56 As a consequence of the concerns mentioned above, the lessor will seek to validate intending lessees to try to be sure that they will be able to pay the rents and comply with all the lease covenants. It will do so by asking for references from the applicant's bankers, solicitors, accountants and, if appropriate, a trade referee. It is also common and sensible to ask for the last three years' audited accounts for the proposed assignee to try to measure the financial worth of the applicant. A former landlord's reference may also be required.

3.57 Once the lessor has approved the status of the incoming lessee, the lessor will normally require the proposed assignee to enter into a deed of licence. This will incorporate direct covenants between the lessor and assignee requiring the assignee to comply with the lease terms while the assignee is the lessee. This provision is now subject to the terms of the Landlord and Tenant (Covenants) Act 1995; as to the enforceability of covenants, see paras 3.58 et seq below. However, it should be noted that the 1995 Act contains valuable anti-avoidance provisions that favour the lessee. In particular, the assignee effectively cannot covenant with the lessor for the whole of the residue of the lease term. The Act limits the covenant to the period of time during which it is the lessee.

Enforceability of covenants

3.58 Until recently, the original lessor and original lessee were liable to each other under the covenants in their lease for the full term granted by the first lessor to the first lessee. As a consequence of the effects of privity of contract, this liability remained enforceable in the courts, even if the lessee had subsequently assigned the residue of the term of the lease. The practical effect of this used to be that a lessee could be sued for arrears of rent even though that lessee had not been the lessee in occupation for many years. (Indeed, the liability could be extended even after assignment. In *Selous Street Properties Ltd v Oronel Fabrics Ltd* [1984] 1 EGLR 50, it was held that where a later lessee carried out improvements that increased the rental value, the original lessee had to pay rent at that higher level, even though the works were carried out after the original lessee ceased to be involved as a result of having assigned the residue of the term of the lease.) Clearly this ancient element of landlord and tenant law led to some very unfair situations where an original lessee was called upon to pay rent many years after assigning its legal estate in the subject property. However, this is still the law for all leases granted before the end of 1995.

The provisions of the Landlord and Tenant (Covenants) Act 1995 introduced a measure of **3.59** reform, and the details of the changes are set out below (as well as at paras 5.02 et seq). Practitioners should be aware that these provisions generally apply only to new leases created on or after 1 January 1996. The Act does not apply to leases created on or after this date if they were made pursuant to an agreement made before 1 January 1996. In essence, a lessee who assigns such a lease automatically enjoys a release through statute for any continuing liability under the lease covenants. However, a lessor can require the outgoing lessee to enter into a form of guarantee designated by the statute as an 'authorized guarantee agreement' (AGA). Further details are given below. The 1995 Act has made a major change to the law. It means that the benefit and burden of lease covenants now pass on assignment automatically without any question of whether or not they touch and concern the land. The successor in title, the assignee, will take the benefit and burden of the lease covenants by reason of statute and the assignor, the original lessee, will be released from liability.

Unless the lessee has entered into an agreement formulated by the Landlord and Tenant **3.60** (Covenants) Act 1995 as an AGA, the lessee will, on assignment, be automatically released from any liability in the future on the lessee's lease covenants. If the lessee has entered into an AGA then the outgoing lessee acts as guarantor for the successor in title, but not beyond the time of ownership of the lease by the incoming lessee. Of course the outgoing lessee cannot escape liability for breaches of covenant that arose during the time prior to the assignment of the legal estate, and will remain liable for such breaches after as well as before assignment.

Should there be a transfer of the freehold reversion, there is no such automatic release for an **3.61** outgoing lessor under the terms of the statute. However, the reversioner can seek a release by applying for such from the lessee, either before or within a period of four weeks from the date of the transfer of the reversionary title. It would seem that the logic behind this arrangement is that, because the lessee has no control over a new lessor, no release should be automatically given. However, because the lessor can control who becomes lessee, there should as a result of that control be an automatic release. The lessor can apply to court for a release should this not be forthcoming from the lessee. The effect of the 1995 Act cannot be excluded or altered by agreement or otherwise.

What constitutes a new lease can be of material importance, especially where there is a **3.62** variation to a lease that was granted before 1 January 1996. This is because a variation can amount to a surrender and re-grant of a new term, but without being called a surrender. For example, if the variation concerns either the length of the original term or the extent of the leased property, it will operate as a surrender and re-grant. If this happens then the re-grant will amount to a new lease and will be covered by the terms of the 1995 Act. Practitioners acting for a lessor should always bear this in mind when dealing with variations, especially where the rent or the extent of the demised property is involved.

Absolute covenants

3.63 An absolute covenant will have the effect of giving the lessor a predominant position over the lessee, leaving the lessee powerless so far as requests for alienation are concerned. It may give the lessor absolute control, but it might also adversely affect the rental value on review precisely because of the highly restrictive nature of the covenant.

3.64 An absolute covenant against alienation might read:

> Not to assign transfer charge sub-let dispose or share or part with possession of all or any part of the demised premises.

It is therefore an unequivocal attempt by the lessor to restrict the occupation of the demised premises to the lessee named in the lease or tenancy agreement. As a consequence, should the lessee actually assign or sub-let, etc., it will immediately be in breach of this restrictive covenant. The lessor has a complete discretion whether or not to consider waiving the prohibition, but can arbitrarily refuse and does not need to give reasons for refusal. There are statutory limitations in that the lessor must not breach the provisions of the Disability Discrimination Act 1995, the Race Relations Act 1976 or the Sex Discrimination Act 1975, but otherwise it may refuse to waive its rights come what may. These statutes will come into play if it can be shown that the lessor refused consent based upon an applicant's disability, race or sex.

3.65 If the lease states that the lessor's consent is required but does not refer to reasonableness then statute adds this qualification (see s 19(1)(a) of the Landlord and Tenant Act 1927). This kind of clause is a qualified covenant and might read:

> Not without the lessor's prior written consent to assign transfer charge sub-let dispose or share or part with possession of all or any part of the demised premises.

This statutory addition is covered in more detail in paras 3.68 to 3.74 below. The parties to a lease cannot exclude this statutory provision.

3.66 The lessor is entitled, should it decide to grant a licence for the desired form of alienation proposed by the lessee, to charge reasonable legal fees and surveyors' charges in connection with the application. Other relevant reasonable expenses incurred by the lessor will also be chargeable and payable by the lessee as a condition of granting the consent. However, s 144 of the Law of Property Act 1925 makes it quite clear that no fine or sum of money in the nature of a fine shall be payable for the granting of the lessor's consent. A fine is now understood to be a sum of money exacted as a penalty. Thus the reasonable fees mentioned above would not amount to a fine but a demand for extra rent would (see *Jenkins v Price* [1907] 2 Ch 229). Lessors sometimes require a lessee to provide a security deposit, particularly if their covenant is weak. The deposit is taken by the lessor to ensure that the lessee complies with all the lease covenants, and in particular that the covenant to pay rent is honoured in full. Failure to comply would enable the lessor to have recourse to the deposit. This security deposit condition has been held not to be by way of a fine (see *Re Cosh's Contract* [1897] 1 Ch 9). The subject of rent deposits is covered in detail in paras 2.16 et seq above.

Many modern business leases will include an absolute covenant against dealing with part of **3.67** the subject premises. There are two good reasons for including such a provision. First, good estate management practice dictates that the fewer the number of lessees there are in a block the easier it is to manage the building as a whole. However, the second reason is far more compelling. Under the Landlord and Tenant Act 1954, business lessees in occupation at the end of a business lease are entitled by statute to renew their lease. If there have been sub-lettings of part the lessor may be required by statute to issue new leases to all the sub-lessees in occupation and not to the original lessee who became the sub-lessor but did not remain in occupation. In this way the superior lessor could end up accidentally with several lessees where originally there was only one.

Qualified covenants

There is no restriction against alienation unless there is express provision to that effect **3.68** within the lease (see *Keeves v Dean; Nunn v Pellegrini* [1924] 1 KB 685 and *Leith Properties Ltd v Byrne* [1983] QB 433). Many commercial leases include a covenant whereby the lessee cannot assign the lease without the prior written consent of the lessor, such consent not to be unreasonably withheld. This is known as a fully qualified covenant. Some leases extend this provision to include sub-lettings as well as assignments. If the lease states that the lessor's consent is required but does not refer to reasonableness, statute adds this qualification (see s 19(1)(a) of the Landlord and Tenant Act 1927). The effect of this statutory intervention is that the lessor cannot unreasonably withhold consent if the lease requires the lessor to grant such consent. (The Court of Appeal issued guidelines as to what amounts to reasonableness in the context of s 19 in *International Drilling Fluids Ltd v Louisville Investments (Uxbridge) Ltd* [1986] 1 All ER 321, and see paras 3.71 et seq below.) However, if the lease includes an absolute prohibition then the lessee simply cannot assign the lease and must remain in the premises for the residue of the term.

Section 19(1A) of the Landlord and Tenant Act 1927 (introduced by s 22 of the Landlord and **3.69** Tenant (Covenants) Act 1995) allows the parties to a lease to agree conditions or circumstances which must be satisfied before the lessor will give consent (see paras 3.71 et seq below). Section 19(1A) relates to qualified covenants against assigning only, ie not sub-letting or charging. If the lease requires the lessee to offer a surrender of the lease back to the lessor prior to seeking an assignment, that provision may be unenforceable (see *Allnatt London Properties Ltd v Newton* [1984] 1 All ER 423).

Practitioners acting for the lessee should remember that even though a lessor may not **3.70** unreasonably withhold licence, that does not mean that the lessee can progress an act of alienation prior to seeking consent. If the lessee fails to seek licence and progresses the matter regardless, it will be in breach of covenant and liable to a claim for possession by the lessor (see *Wilson v Fynn* [1948] 2 All ER 40).

Section 19(1), Landlord and Tenant Act 1927

If the lease states that the lessor's consent is required for an act of alienation but does not **3.71** refer to reasonableness, s 19(1)(a) of the 1927 Act adds this qualification. The effect of this statutory intervention is that the lessor cannot unreasonably withhold consent if the lease requires the lessor to grant such consent. There is a further provision to this section. Section 19(1)(b) provides that if there is a lease for more than 40 years that is made in consideration of the erection or substantial improvement or alterations to a building, and there is a qualified covenant, then no consent or licence is required. This is sometimes called a building lease. There is one condition, and that is that notice in writing must be given to the lessor of the particular act of alienation within six months of completion. The act of alienation must take place more than seven years before the end of the building lease. (It would seem that for building leases granted on or after 1 January 1996, this section will not apply where s 19(1A) applies; see below.)

3.72 In deciding what is reasonable refusal the courts have taken the view that each case must be considered individually, bearing in mind the circumstances that existed at the time the lessor decided to refuse. The Court of Appeal issued guidelines as to what amounts to reasonableness in the context of s 19 in *International Drilling Fluids Ltd v Louisville Investments (Uxbridge) Ltd* [1986] 1 All ER 321. The Court set out six guidelines:

(a) that the covenant exists to protect the lessor from an undesirable use or lessee (the House of Lords in *Ashworth Frazer Ltd v Gloucester City Council* [2001] 1 WLR 2180 considered the effect of a proposed use in relation to a licence to assign and decided that the case of *Killick v Second Covent Garden Property Co Ltd* [1973] 1 WLR 658, CA had been wrongly decided. The court held that it could not be said that a refusal of consent was necessarily unreasonable where it was founded on the landlord's belief, reasonable or otherwise, that the proposed assignee intended to use the demised premises for a purpose that would give rise to a breach of a user covenant. The courts should consider what the reasonable landlord would do when asked to consent in the particular circumstances. Therefore it may not be unreasonable to refuse consent if the landlord considers the intended use to be prohibited under the lease covenants.);

(b) therefore a lessor cannot refuse consent because of an unconnected ground giving the lessor an advantage not contemplated by the lease covenants (see *Bromley Park Gardens Estates Limited v Moss* [1982] 2 All ER 890);

(c) the lessor must show that the reasons for refusal would be those that a reasonable man would make;

(d) refusal may be reasonable on the basis of the intended use even though the use is within the lease user covenant (see *Bates v Donaldson* [1896] 2 QB 241);

(e) it may be unreasonable for the lessor to withhold consent if it is likely to lead to disproportionate harm to the lessee (see *International Drilling Fluids Ltd v Louisville Investments (Uxbridge) Ltd* [1986] 1 All ER 321);

(f) subject to the above, it is a question of fact as to reasonableness based upon all the circumstances of the case.

3.73 Section 19(1A) of the Landlord and Tenant Act 1927 (introduced by s 22 of the Landlord and Tenant (Covenants) Act 1995) allows the parties to a lease to agree conditions or circumstances which must be satisfied before the lessor will give consent. Section 19(1A) relates to qualified covenants against assigning only, ie, not sub-letting or charging. It also applies only to leases granted on or after 1 January 1996. The effect of this provision is that if those circumstances do not exist or the conditions have not been fulfilled at the time of the application for licence to assign, the lessor may refuse licence and such refusal will not be deemed unreasonable. If the reasons for denying consent are outside the stated conditions or circumstances then the ordinary provisions of s 19(1)(a) will apply, ie, the reasonableness test. Section 19(1C) contemplates that the conditions or circumstances will be objectively verifiable, or they may be such that the lessor has discretion. If objectively verifiable, the best example is the requirement that the proposed assignee be able to show pre-tax profits that exceed three times the current rental payable for the subject premises. Where discretionary, the lessor must agree to act reasonably or there must be a right to refer matters to an independent third party. Here an example would be the lessor's right to refuse an assignment where the assignee's intended use would conflict with another in adjoining premises owned and let by the lessor. However, such refusal must be based on reasonableness, ie, in the reasonable opinion of the lessor there would be a conflicting user. Should the lessee disagree with a decision of the lessor then a suitable independent third party could include an arbitrator, expert or local surveyor not acting for the lessor.

A common precondition to a consent, particularly where a limited company is the intended **3.74** assignee, is the requirement for sureties to guarantee the performance of the proposed assignee. This can also be a requirement where the lessor may doubt the financial viability of the lessee. This is examined further at para 3.107 below, together with a precedent covenant.

The licence process

The Landlord and Tenant Act 1988, s 1(3), requires the lessor to deal with applications for **3.75** consent to an assignment within a reasonable time of the making of the application. Should the lessor fail to do so, the lessee can, if the lessee has suffered loss as a consequence, sue the lessor for damages.

The lessor can attach conditions to any consent, but those conditions themselves must be **3.76** reasonable (see s 1(4)). As to reasonableness, the courts have held that a serious outstanding breach of a repairing covenant will be sufficient cause to allow a lessor to refuse to grant licence to assign (see *Goldstein v Sanders* [1915] 1 Ch 549). On the other hand, an example of a case in which refusal to grant licence was held to be unreasonable was *Re Smith's lease, Smith v Richards* [1951] 1 All ER 346, where the lessor required possession of the subject premises for his own use. This was not sufficient to allow the lessor to withhold consent. Mere delay in dealing with the application for consent can amount to unreasonableness (see *Lewis and Allenby (1909) Ltd v Pegge* [1914] 1 Ch 782). The burden of proof is upon the lessee to show that the lessor has acted unreasonably. The lessee must make a court application seeking a declaration to that effect. If successful, the lessee can seek an award for costs and the lessor may also be liable for damages where the claimant has suffered loss (s 4, Landlord and Tenant Act 1988).

Most commercial leases will include a requirement for the lessee to give notice of a permitted **3.77** act of alienation to the lessor's solicitor. There will also usually be a requirement to pay a registration fee. This enables the lessor to know when a permitted act of alienation has actually been completed, eg, when the assignment permitted by the lessor has taken place. Where assignments are concerned, this will then enable the lessor to issue all future rent demands in the name of the appropriate person or company. The notice requirement can simply call for written notice, or go on to call for a copy of the actual form of disposition, such as a copy of the deed of assignment.

Some commercial leases allow lessees to share occupation of the demised premises with **3.78** other companies within the same group. This will usually mean any company within a group that comes within the definition of a group of associated companies that is set out in s 42(1) of the Landlord and Tenant Act 1954. Some lessees, particularly of larger shop premises, will seek permission to 'franchise' out parts of the sales area to other parties. Such parties will be granted licences that do not give them exclusive possession but merely the right to use a sales counter. This is clearly an attempt by the lessees to share occupation and to avoid granting a formal or 'informal' lease. Whether or not this is so depends upon the facts and the view of the courts (see *Street v Mountford* [1985] AC 809). They are, however, sharing occupation, and for this reason lessees contemplating this arrangement should always seek prior approval from the lessor.

3.79   The Court of Appeal in *Allied Dunbar Assurance plc v Homebase Ltd* [2002] 27 EG 144 held that side letters, even those personal to the parties, cannot normally be used to get around onerous underletting restrictions in leases. In this case, although a proposed form of underlease conformed to the lease requirements, a side letter tried to circumvent such requirements. The court said that allowed the landlord to refuse licence to sublet.

An alienation example precedent

3.80   The following covenant contemplates allowing the lessee to assign or underlet the whole of the demised premises, but not any other form of alienation including dispositions of part and mortgages. It also refers to authorized guarantee agreements and reasons why a licence can be refused, ie, a list of circumstances in which the parties agree that the lessor cannot be accused of unreasonableness. To aid understanding of the construction of the clause and to assist its readability, paragraph headings have been used. This is an increasingly common feature of better-drafted commercial leases and is to be recommended. Tenant's amendments and additions are shown struck through and underlined.

No alienation without express consent

1.   Unless expressly permitted by a component of this covenant not to part with possession assign transfer charge mortgage underlet or hold upon trust for another or share the occupation of the whole or any part of the demised premises

Consents for dealings with the whole premises

2.   Not to assign or underlet the whole of the demised premises except by an assignment or underlease of the whole of the demised premises in accordance with the following stipulations

Consent for assignment and guarantee agreement

3.   Not without first receiving the written consent of the lessor such consent not to be unreasonably withheld or delayed to assign or transfer the whole of the demised premises. When giving consent the lessor requires:

    3.1   That the proposed assignee completes a deed of licence to be prepared by the lessor's solicitors in such form as they shall reasonably require containing a covenant by the proposed assignee with the lessors to observe and perform all the lessee lease covenants and

    3.2   That the out-going lessee enters into an agreement pursuant to section 16 of the Landlord and Tenant (Covenants) Act 1995 in such form as the lessor shall <u>reasonably</u> require whereby the lessee will:

        3.2.1   guarantee the performance of the proposed assignee of the covenants on the part of the lessee contained in the Lease; and

        3.2.2   be liable to the lessor as principal debtor and is not released from that liability even if the lessor gives the proposed assignee extra time to comply with any covenant; and

3.2.3 agree that in the event that the Lease is disclaimed the out-going lessee will take the grant of a fresh lease of the demised premises on the same terms and covenants for the residue of the term at the time of disclaimer; and

3.3 That the outgoing lessee pays the costs and expenses <u>reasonably</u> incurred by the lessor in connection with the application for licence including all <u>reasonable</u> solicitor's costs and surveyor's fees.

Consent for underletting of the whole premises

4. Not without first receiving the written consent of the lessor such consent not to be unreasonably withheld or delayed to underlet the whole of the demised premises. When giving consent the lessor requires:

4.1 that any underlease shall be in a form first reasonably approved in writing by the lessor <u>and such approval is not to be unreasonably withheld</u> AND that the lessee and proposed underlessee complete a deed of licence to be prepared by the lessor's solicitors in such form as they shall <u>reasonably</u> require

4.2 that any underlease shall contain covenants by the underlessee and rent review provisions identical in all material respects as those on the part of the lessee contained in this Lease

4.3 that any underlessee shall covenant with the lessor to observe and perform the covenants and conditions contained in this Lease (<u>excluding the covenant to pay the rent</u>)

4.4 any underlease shall
   (a) be at a rent which is the ~~greater of either the~~ current rent payable by the lessee ~~and the current market rent that would be payable had there been a rent review at the time of the underletting;~~ and
   (b) any underlease shall provide that reviews of rent shall be upwards only on the basis and on the dates for review of the rent specified in this Lease; and
   (c) the lessee shall not agree the yearly rent payable by any underlessee whether initially or upon any rent review or renewal without first obtaining the prior written consent of the lessor <u>such consent not to be unreasonably witheld</u>; and shall
   (d) contain a covenant not to assign or transfer the demised premises without the prior consent in writing of the lessor <u>such consent not to be unreasonably withheld or delayed;</u> and
   (e) contain an absolute covenant not to assign part with possession or share the occupation of any part of the demised premises; and
   (f) contain an absolute covenant by the underlessee not to further underlet or part with possession of the demised premises

4.5 The lessee covenants to pay the costs and expenses <u>reasonably</u> incurred by the lessor in connection with the application for licence to underlet including all <u>reasonable</u> solicitor's costs and surveyor's fees.

Guarantees

5. The lessor may reasonably require persons or corporate bodies to act as guarantors for the proposed assignee and may require them prior to the assignment to enter into joint and several covenants in favour of the lessor in such form as the lessor may <u>reasonably</u> require

Reasons for not giving consent

6. It is agreed between the parties that the lessor shall be entitled to withhold consent to an

assignment or transfer of the whole of the demised premises in one or more of the following situations where:

6.1   there are arrears of any of the rents payable under the terms of the Lease

6.2   the lessee is in breach of one or more covenants conditions or terms of the Lease

6.3   where the proposed assignee cannot show that it had net profits before tax (calculated in accordance with recognized accounting procedures) for each of the three completed financial years of the proposed assignee immediately before the date of the application for licence

6.4   where the proposed assignee cannot show the net profits indicated in 6.3 and is not willing to deposit with the lessor an amount representing one quarter of the annual rent payable by the lessee at the time of the application for licence

6.5   ~~where the lessor reasonably believes that if the licence were to be granted it would adversely affect the lessor's reversionary interest~~

6.6   ~~where the lessor reasonably believes that if the licence were to be granted it would adversely affect any current or imminent rent review~~

6.7   ~~where the lessor reasonably believes that the proposed assignee offers a weaker covenant than that of the lessee as a consequence of the proposed assignee's weaker financial status~~

3.81   It is our view that it would be prudent for the lessor to add an additional clause 4.4(g) above in the following format

(g)   be contracted out of the security of tenure provisions of the Landlord and Tenant Act 1954, Part II

The reason for this recommendation is that it ensures that the lessor will always be able to control who is in occupation of the subject property at the end of the lease, even if there is an approved sub-lessee in occupation. Without the additional provision, the position at the end of the lease will be that the sub-lessee in occupation will be entitled to the security provisions of Pt II of the Landlord and Tenant Act 1954. If this occurs then the lessor will be saddled with the sub-lessee as its direct lessee.

3.82   Lastly, it should be noted that this particular precedent does not include an actual form for an authorized guarantee agreement. It is becoming the case that commercial leases actually include a form of guarantee, possibly within a schedule to the lease. You will find an example of a simple form of guarantee agreement authorized as a consequence of s 16 of the Landlord and Tenant (Covenants) Act 1995 set out in appendix 2.

The Code and alienation restrictions

3.83   Recommendation 9 of the Code covers the assigning and subletting of commercial property. It states that 'unless the particular circumstances of the letting justify greater control, the only restriction on assignment of the whole premises should be obtaining the landlord's consent which is not to be unreasonably withheld. Landlords are urged to consider requiring Authorised Guarantee Agreements only where the assignee is of lower financial standing than the assignor at the date of the assignment.' Recommendation 12 covers requests for consents such as applications for a licence to assign. It states that 'when seeking a consent from the landlord, the tenant should supply full information about his/her proposal. The landlord should respond without undue delay and should where practicable give the tenant an estimate of the costs that the tenant will have to pay. The landlord should ensure that the request is passed promptly to any superior landlord or mortgagee whose agreement is needed and should give details to the tenant so that any problems can be speedily resolved.' These recommendations are then clarified in subsequent notes.

The explanatory notes go on to explain that there are two ways in which the tenant may pass   **3.84**
on the lease obligations to a third party. The first is by assignment (selling, giving away or paying someone to take over, the lease), and the second is by subletting. Leases generally control assignment and subletting. Most require the tenant to obtain the landlord's consent (which cannot be unreasonably withheld) but some leases completely prohibit certain acts such as sub-letting part of the premises. The notes continue with a consideration of the position for post-1995 new leases. It states that 'A new lease, and an existing lease granted since 1995, may expand the landlord's right to control assignments by imposing credit ratings or other financial criteria for assignees. It may also require the assigning tenant to stand as guarantor for any assignee by giving the landlord an "Authorised Guarantee Agreement"; alternatives include giving this guarantee only if it is reasonably required by the landlord, such as where the assignee is of lower financial standing than the assigning tenant.'

User

A lessee may find that its use of the subject premises will be limited in several different ways,   **3.85**
including by statute, planning control, covenants on the lessor's title or any superior title and by the terms of the lease itself. A lessor may wish to control the use of the premises for several different reasons. These might include the need to maintain the value of the premises for rental purposes, to avoid competing trades in a parade or estate owned by the lessor, and to ensure that nothing is done in the property of an illegal or immoral nature. The problem for the lessor is that the more control it exerts over the use of the premises, the greater likelihood there is that this may have a depressing effect on the rental it can recover. See below at para 3.88 for further details in this regard.

A user clause can be either negative or positive. If the covenant is positive there is a benefit   **3.86**
for the lessor. Should the lessee cease to trade or occupy the premises, there is a breach of the positive covenant. If the lessor suffers loss as a result, the lessee may be liable in damages as a consequence of its failure to use the premises as the positive covenant requires. (This whole topic was considered in *Transworld Land Co Limited v J Sainsbury plc* [1990] 2 EGLR 255.) The problem can also be addressed, especially in relation to shops, by including another covenant requiring the lessee to keep the premises open during normal business hours. The lessor may also require the lessee not to allow the premises to remain vacant (see *Co-operative Insurance Society Limited v Argyll Stores (Holdings) Limited* [1997] 2 WLR 898, HL). This case reaffirmed the orthodox approach that the courts will not grant specific performance to lessors to force their lessees to keep premises open except in wholly exceptional cases.

Absolute covenants

It is possible for the lease to include a covenant imposing an absolute restriction on the   **3.87**
lessee changing the use from any stated user precisely defined by the lease. Because the covenant is absolute, the lessor cannot be compelled to allow a change of use. If a change is agreed in subsequent negotiations, it can be effected by a deed of variation to the terms of the original lease. Of course in some circumstances an absolute covenant will be acceptable if

it is widely drawn, eg: 'Not to use the demised premises other than as offices'. If that clause is then extended to say what business is to be carried on in those offices, the absolute restriction will bite, eg, '. . . for the business of solicitors'. In this example the offices can only be used by solicitors and can only be assigned to an in-coming lessee that will adopt this very restricted office use.

Qualified covenants

3.88   The lease user covenant can be qualified by including a precondition requiring the lessor's consent before the use can be changed. This type of qualification is more commonly seen in commercial leases. In these leases the inclusion of an absolute user covenant will mean that the rental on review could be subject to a reduction in valuation. This is because a restriction on the user makes the lease less attractive to tenants and it will therefore command less as a rental. However, a fully qualified covenant will avoid this limitation on the rental income, ie, by including wording such as '. . . such consent not to be unreasonably withheld'. Note that in user covenants there is no statutory provision that implies that the lessor's consent cannot be unreasonably withheld, as is the case with alienation covenants (see paras 3.54 et seq above). The downside to this wording is, of course, that the lessor will lose absolute control of the user within the demised premises. It is therefore a decision for the lessor to make between maximizing the rent or having control over what happens in the subject premises.

3.89   A covenant that is partly qualified, ie, that says changes of user can be made with the lessor's prior written consent but does not go on to apply reasonableness as mentioned above, does not really assist the lessee any more than an absolute covenant. This is again because there is no statutory intervention importing reasonableness and, consequently, the lessor may decline to approve a change of user quite arbitrarily. However, there is a small statutory measure of comfort for the lessee. Section 19(3) of the Landlord and Tenant Act 1927 provides that if a consent for a change of use is required, the lessor is not in any circumstances allowed to demand a premium or extra rent for the giving of that consent. The lessor can require costs to be paid by the applicant, including all legal fees. A premium or extra rent can be demanded if alterations to the structure of the property are also proposed. Accordingly, the use by the lessee of the subject premises can be greatly limited by the covenants required by the lessor over and above the limitations that may be imposed by the actual user clause.

Other related covenants

3.90   In addition to the stated user clause, the modern business lease will include other clauses concerned with the use of the property. For example, there will be a covenant requiring the lessee to comply with the Planning Acts, including changes of use, so that there is no breach of planning as a result of the lessee's use of the property. The provision can in the alternative prohibit the lessee from making any application for planning consent, so that there can be no change to the stated use if that change of use requires planning permission. Business leases will also require the lessee to covenant not to reside at the property or to sleep overnight, as to do so could be a breach of planning law. Most, if not all, commercial leases will include a lessee's covenant not to use the property for an illegal or immoral purpose and to do nothing within the subject premises that is a nuisance or annoyance to other neighbouring lessees. Certain business leases may prohibit a user that might in some way adversely affect the lessor's insurance, eg, by stopping the lessee from bringing on to the demised premises materials required by the lessee but which are dangerous because they are inflammable or some other form of dangerous material. If the premises are to be used for light (or even heavy) industrial purposes, the lessor may require the lessee not to use the demised premises in such a way as to overload the floors of the premises by the installation of very heavy machinery.

Covenants naming a use class or the lessee

Some commercial leases will define the permitted use at the subject premises either by reference to the lessee by name, or by reference to a planning law use class. **3.91**

Generic use descriptors are contained within the Town and Country Planning (Use Classes) Order 1987, SI 1987/764. Thus, should the proposed user covenant simply need to be linked to a user such as 'shop for the retail sale of goods' or 'warehouse for storage or distribution' then the Order will enable exact descriptors to be adopted. There can be traps for the unwary, though, in the adoption of use classes. First, the Order may be subject to amendment by the legislators. To address this, the covenant can be expressed to be construed with reference to the 1987 Order and not any subsequent amendments to it. Indeed, to emphasize this concern, from 21 April 2005 there are changes to the use classes that were created by the 1987 Order. That order has been amended by the Town and Country Planning (Use Classes) (Amendment) (England) Order 2005 which substitutes for the former A3 (food and drink) three new use classes, (i) restaurants and cafes—A3, (ii) drinking establishments (pubs and bars)—A4, and (iii) hot food takeaways—A5. So had a lease user covenant simply referred to a user by reference to A3, this could by reason of a change to use classes cause confusion about whether or not a use is lawful; old A3 or new A3, old food and drink or new restaurants and cafes? The moral here is to define the user by exact descriptors rather than by reference to a mere use class title. Secondly, if the user simply refers to the code within the Order, eg, A1 retail, care should be taken to ensure that this does not widen the use beyond that originally contemplated by the parties. The codes cover extensive lists; for example, A1 includes a post office, funeral directors and premises for the washing and cleaning of clothes or fabrics on the property. Accordingly, care needs to be taken if referring only to a use code. For more on the Use Classes Order, see paras 8.68 et seq below. **3.92**

Sometimes commercial leases contain a user covenant that actually names the lessee, usually to try to avoid identifying the nature of the lessee's business. However, this too can lead to problems of interpretation and may have particularly adverse effects on the rental value at review. First, if the lessee is named in the user clause it effectively means that the lease cannot be assigned to anyone else. This extreme restriction will depress the rental value (see *Law Land Co Limited v Consumers Association Limited* (1980) 255 EG 617). This problem can be resolved by the lessor inserting in the rent review clauses a condition that the rent for the 'hypothetical lease' should be reviewed on the basis of any use on an open market basis, notwithstanding that the actual use is highly restrictive. (This whole area of difficulty was further considered in *Post Office Counters Limited v Harlow DC* [1991] 36 EG 151, as well as in *Sterling Land Office Developments Limited v Lloyds Bank plc* (1984) 271 EG 894.) Secondly, problems can also be encountered should the lease refer to the 'business of the lessee' as being the permitted user. The problem is the interpretation of this phrase; does it mean the original or the existing lessee, or the original user or the use **3.93** made by an assignee after assignment? This is a phrase best avoided to ensure certainty of purpose.

Precedent use clauses

3.94 User clauses can be straightforward and need not be lengthy. A typical clause is set out below which allows changes of use with consent and includes a qualification that will maximize the rental income. It adds another element outlawing one particular kind of use:

> Not without the lessor's prior written consent such consent not to be unreasonably withheld or delayed
> (1) to use the demised premises other than as offices for the business of solicitors and
> (2) not to use the demised premises for the sale of alcohol or other intoxicating liquors

3.95 Another user clause referring to the Use Classes Order 1987 might read as follows:

> Not to use the demised premises or any part thereof for any purpose other than for the manufacture and ancillary storage of electrical equipment or (subject to the lessor's consent not to be unreasonably withheld) for any other light industrial use within class B1 of the Town and Country (Use Classes) Order 1987

Note in the precedent above how the items to be manufactured are specified and then followed by a fully qualified prohibition against change of use within the relevant use class. This should have a neutral effect for rental valuation purposes.

The Code and user covenants

3.96 Recommendation 10 of the Code covers changes of use. It states that the 'landlord's control over alterations and changes of use should not be more restrictive than is necessary to protect the value of the premises and any adjoining or neighbouring premises of the landlord'.

3.97 The explanatory notes go on to explain that 'the permitted use of the premises may be very narrowly defined or there may be a wide class of use. Consent for changes of use can be at the landlord's discretion or, alternatively, the lease may provide that consent is not to be unreasonably withheld. If the provisions of the lease are very restrictive this can hinder the assignment of the lease or the subletting of the property to a different business.'

C   SURETY COVENANTS

3.98 Lessors will always be concerned about the 'strength of the lessee's covenant', ie, whether the lessee will be able to afford the lease rental. A lease and/or a deed of licence may therefore include covenants affecting parties called sureties or guarantors. The following paragraphs explore their use and impact.

At the time the lease was granted

3.99 Commercial leases will invariably refer to a lessor and a lessee, and possibly to a surety or guarantor. These last two parties are synonymous in that they will both be someone or something that has given a written undertaking to answer for the payment of a debt or for the performance of an obligation by another party (ie, the lessee) who is liable in the first instance. Accordingly, if the lessor is unsure about the financial viability of the lessee, it can require a surety or guarantor to guarantee the lessee's liability arising from the lease terms. The lessor will usually also require a third party of this kind when letting to a private limited company, and may ask for two directors of the company to act as sureties. The advantage to the lessor is, of course, to ensure that liability for the performance of the lease covenants may extend on default by the company to the directors on a personal basis.

If the original lessee remains the lessee throughout the lease term, the liability for a surety **3.100** should normally cease at the end of that lease term (see *Junction Estates Limited v Cope* (1974) 27 P & CR 482). This case confirmed that the liability for a guarantor would not continue during a statutory extension arising from the operation of Pt II of the Landlord and Tenant Act 1954. Of course a lessor can continue the liability by defining the term in the lease as including any statutory extension. If there is coupled with this a requirement for the guarantee to continue throughout the defined term, the guarantor will then also be liable throughout any extension period.

The termination of liability in other circumstances is now examined. **3.101**

Leases granted before 1 January 1996

An original guarantor will remain liable under the original lessee's liability throughout the **3.102** full term of the lease. Accordingly, the lessor can sue and recover unpaid rent from the surety of the original lessee even though the original lessee is no longer the lessee in occupation (see *Selous Street Properties Ltd v Oronel Fabrics Ltd* (1984) 270 EG 643). (However the surety can sue the surety of the defaulting successor in title of the original lessee. The surety can, of course, also seek to recover losses from the lessee whose performance it was guaranteeing.)

Leases granted after 31 December 1995

Section 24(2) of the Landlord and Tenant (Covenants) Act 1995 affords some protection for **3.103** guarantors. It does so by providing that if a lessee is released from liability then the guarantor is similarly released. There is one limitation. It would seem to be the case that a guarantor may be asked to guarantee the performance of an outgoing lessee in regard to its obligations under an authorized guarantee agreement formulated within the terms of this statute. Clearly, it would be appropriate for practitioners acting for a surety to try to resist liability for their client under any authorized guarantee agreement. An example of a typical authorized guarantee agreement is set out in appendix 2.

Other forms of release

There are circumstances in which the actions or conduct of the lessor will be interpreted by **3.104** the courts as a release. If the lessor agrees to vary the terms of the lease without reference to the guarantor, this will operate as a release. The usual example for this is the case of *Holme v Brunskill* (1878) 3 QBD 495, CA where it was held that a guarantor could be released as a consequence of the part of the demised premises being surrendered. (By the same token, a complete surrender would also provide a release for the guarantor from the surrender date.) Accordingly, a lease variation that is not merely of a minor nature and effect will act as a release for the guarantor.

3.105 If a lessor 'gives time' to a lessee, ie, in a binding format allows the lessee to have more time to pay rents, this too can act as a release for the guarantor (see *Swire v Redman* (1876) 1 QBD 536).

3.106 Practitioners acting for a lessor should therefore ensure that any authorized guarantee agreement includes conditions that seek to negative the effects of these other forms of release. See the example of a typical authorized guarantee agreement set out in appendix 2.

At the time of an assignment

3.107 Similarly, the lessor may insert into the lease a precondition to a proposed assignment that the proposed assignee must put forward guarantors to support the application for licence to assign. Thus a clause within the alienation covenant could appear as follows:

> If an intended assignee shall be a company limited by shares ('the company') then:
> (a) if the lessor so <u>reasonably</u> requires ~~at least~~ two of the directors of the company shall be parties to the licence to assign as sureties for the company
> (b) the sureties shall in the licence jointly and severally covenant with the lessor <u>only so long as the company shall be the lessee</u>:
> (i) that the company will observe and perform all the lease covenants and
> (ii) that if the company shall be in breach of any of the lease covenants or any other terms of the lease then they will indemnify the lessor against all losses damages demands costs claims and expenses arising from the breach.

3.108 The lessee alterations are all made to try to limit the impact of the covenant should the lessor ever activate it because of any lessee default. The practitioner acting for the surety could also contemplate one further addition to the clause. If the covenant is activated through default, the surety should be able to call for an assignment of the residue of the term of the lease. In doing so the surety will be seeking to reduce losses and to control, as far as possible in these limiting circumstances, the ultimate disposal of the lease to another party.

Professional conduct issues and guarantors

3.109 There is a concern for a practitioner acting for a lessee and (coincidentally) sureties in that a conflict of interest will arise between acting for the company and then for sureties being the directors of that company. Because there is a conflict of interest, sureties or guarantors should always be advised to take separate and independent legal advice with regard to their lease and/or licence obligations and liabilities.

The Code and surety covenants

3.110 Recommendation 15 of the Code covers varying the lease—the effect on guarantors, and states that 'landlords and tenants should seek the agreement of any guarantors to proposed material changes to the terms of the lease, or even minor changes which could increase the guarantor's liability'. The explanatory notes go on to explain that a 'guarantor may not be liable if the terms of the lease are changed without the guarantor's consent. In some cases the variation may release a guarantor from all liability.'

Recommendation 16 covers holding former tenants and their guarantors liable. It states that **3.111** 'when previous tenants or their guarantors are liable to a landlord for defaults by the current tenant, landlords should notify them before the current tenant accumulates excessive liabilities. All defaults should be handled with speed and landlords should seek to assist the tenant and guarantor in minimizing losses. An assignor who wishes to remain informed of the outcome of rent reviews should keep in touch with the landlord and the landlord should provide the information. Assignors should take professional advice on what methods are open to them to minimize their losses caused by defaults by the current occupier.' The explanatory notes go on to explain that a 'tenant who assigns a lease may remain liable for a period for any subsequent breach of the lease terms including failure to pay rent. This liability may also apply to a guarantor for the former tenant. Where payment is made to the landlord under this liability, the former tenant may be entitled to take an overriding lease of the property in order to have some control over the current tenants; legal advice can be obtained about these matters. In certain circumstances, insurance against losses following an assignment may be possible. Landlords must notify previous tenants about arrears of rent and service charges within six months of the amount becoming due, in order to make them liable.'

KEY POINTS SUMMARY: LEASE COVENANTS

- Commercial leases usually handle repairs in a tripartite fashion. The lessee covenants (i) to **3.112** keep the subject premises in repair, (ii) to yield up the premises in repair, and (iii) to redecorate at fixed times throughout the lease term and at its end.
- If the premises are not in repair at the start of the lease then the obligation to keep the premises in repair will require the lessee actually to put them in repair at the beginning of the term.
- Repair is restoration by renewal or replacement of subsidiary parts of a whole. Renewal, as distinguished from repair, is reconstruction of the entirety, meaning not necessarily the whole but substantially the whole.
- The standard for repair is 'such repair as having regard to the age, character and locality would make it reasonably fit for the occupation of a reasonably minded tenant of the class likely to take it'.
- Modern leases will stop the lessee from carrying out any permanent alterations, especially where they alter the structure or the appearance of the subject premises. They will go on to allow the lessee to carry out alterations of a non-structural nature, including demountable partitioning.
- To the extent that proposed alterations amount to improvements, s 19(2) of the Landlord and Tenant Act 1927 will then apply so that consent cannot be unreasonably withheld.
- A lessee who assigns a lease created on or after 1 January 1996 automatically enjoys a release through the Landlord and Tenant (Covenants) Act 1995 for any continuing liability under the lease covenants. However, a lessor usually requires the outgoing lessee to enter into a form of guarantee designated by the statute as an 'authorized guarantee agreement'.
- If a lease states that the lessor's consent is required for an act of alienation but does not

refer to reasonableness, statute adds this qualification (s 19(1)(a) of the Landlord and Tenant Act 1927). The effect of this is that the lessor cannot unreasonably withhold consent.

- The Landlord and Tenant Act 1988, s 1(3), requires the lessor to deal with applications for consent to an assignment within a reasonable time of the making of the application. Should the lessor fail to do so, the lessee can, if it has suffered loss as a consequence of the lessor's delay, sue the lessor for damages.
- In business leases an absolute user covenant will mean that the rental on review may be subject to a reduction in valuation. This is because a restriction on the user makes the lease less attractive to tenants and it will therefore command less as a rental.
- Lessors will always be concerned about the 'strength of the lessee's covenant', ie, whether it will be able to afford the lease rental. A lease and/or a deed of licence may therefore include covenants affecting parties called sureties or guarantors.
- The practitioner acting for a surety should ensure that if the surety covenant is activated through default, the surety should be able to call for an assignment of the residue of the term of the lease. In doing so the surety will be seeking to reduce losses and to control the ultimate disposal of the lease to another party.
- If sureties are required, bear in mind they will need to be separately represented to avoid a conflict of interest.
- Does the client/lessor want you to include reference in the new lease to the Code?

PRACTICAL CHECKLIST: LEASE COVENANTS

3.113 The following list sets out the principal practical points from this important chapter as a quick summary for practitioners to use as an *aide-mémoire* when drafting or approving a business lease:

- Regarding repairing obligations, it is critical that the lease repairs clauses are as clear as they can be in defining which of the parties to the lease is responsible for repairing the subject property and to what standard.
- Lessors must consider drafting the repairing clause so as to make it quite clear that the lessee will be obliged to repair any design or construction defects (inherent defects).
- If a lessee is faced with an old property and a full repairing covenant then, if acting for the lessee, prepare a schedule of condition setting out the state the property was in at the time the lease is granted, to be included in the lease.
- A practitioner acting for a lessee may seek to limit the repairing liabilities by including in the lease covenant additional wording stating that repairs are 'fair wear and tear excepted'.
- The lessee can, under the Landlord and Tenant Act 1927, apply to the lessor to carry out improvements. The lessor, in reply, can opt to carry out the proposed works of improvement and rentalize the cost of those works. The lessee will not be in a position to recover any element of the VAT on the cost of such improvements.
- If the lessor wishes to avoid paying compensation for improvements pursuant to Pt I of the Landlord and Tenant Act 1927, it should ensure that the lease includes a requirement for reinstatement at the lease end and no compensation need then be paid.

- Through the Landlord and Tenant (Covenants) Act 1995, a lessor can and should always require an outgoing lessee to enter into a form of guarantee designated by the statute as an 'authorized guarantee agreement' guaranteeing the performance of the new lessee.
- Should there be a transfer of the freehold reversion, there is no automatic release for an outgoing lessor under the terms of the 1995 Act. However, the reversioner can and should seek a release by applying for such from the lessee, either before or within a period of four weeks from the date of the transfer of the reversionary title.
- A user clause can be either negative or positive. If the covenant is positive there is a benefit for the lessor. Should the lessee cease to occupy or trade from the premises, there is a breach of the positive covenant. If the lessor suffers loss as a result, the lessee may be liable in damages as a consequence of its failure to use the premises as the positive covenant requires.
- Generic use descriptors are contained in the Use Classes Order 1987. There can be traps for the unwary in the adoption of use classes. The Order may be subject to amendment, but the covenant can be drafted with reference to the 1987 Order and not any subsequent amendments to it. Also, if the user refers to the code within the Order, eg, A1 retail, care should be taken to ensure that this does not widen the use too far.
- There is a concern for a practitioner acting for a lessee and (coincidentally) sureties in that a conflict of interest will arise between acting for the company and then for sureties being the directors of that company. Because there is a conflict, sureties or guarantors should always be advised to take separate, independent legal advice.
- If the Code applies, do the covenants comply with it?

KEY DOCUMENTS

- Land Registration Act 2002   **3.114**
- Landlord and Tenant (Covenants) Act 1995
- Landlord and Tenant Act 1927
- Law of Property Act 1925
- Code of Practice for Commercial Leases in England and Wales (2nd edn)

Printed copies of legislation can be ordered from The Stationary Office (<http://www.tsoshop.co.uk>). Legislation from 1988 onwards can be downloaded free of charge from <http://www.opsi.gov.uk/acts.htm>.

The Code of Practice for Commercial Leases in England and Wales is set out in appendix 17.

4

COMMERCIAL LEASE COVENANTS II

A LESSOR'S COVENANTS

It has been noted that for many commercial leases the list of covenants given by the lessor **4.01**
will be considerably shorter than those given by the lessee. We set out below details of some
of the more important lessor covenants.

Quiet enjoyment

The purpose of the covenant for quiet enjoyment is to confirm that the lessee can physically **4.02**
enjoy the complete benefit of the property without the lessor adversely affecting that
enjoyment. A covenant for quiet enjoyment given by the lessor should be anticipated in

virtually all leases. Indeed, if an express covenant is absent, an implied covenant will apply. See paras 1.76 et seq above for further detail concerning this covenant and an example of it. The case of *Southwark LBC v Mills; Baxter v Camden LBC* [1999] 3 WLR 939, HL makes it clear that quiet enjoyment covers direct interference (*Owen v Gadd* [1956] 2 QB 99) as well as noise, ie, loud noises from neighbouring property.

Lessor's repairing covenants

4.03 Where the lessor enters into a covenant to keep the subject premises in repair then the rules that apply to tenant's covenants apply equally to the lessor. Thus, the lessor cannot be liable for breaches under the terms of the repairing covenant unless it has been served with a notice of disrepair (see *O'Brien v Robinson* [1973] AC 912). However a notice of repair is not required if the lessor is responsible for repairs beyond merely the subject property. If the lessor is obliged to repair the building of which the subject property forms part, there is an immediate liability without notice (see *British Telecommunications plc v Sun Life Assurance Society plc* [1995] 3 WLR 622). In these circumstances, lessors would be well advised to include in a lease that makes them responsible for repairs of the whole building containing several commercial lettings, a condition that it will be liable for repairs only once a formal notice of repair is served by the lessee.

4.04 Where the lessor is under an obligation to keep a building of which the subject property forms part in good repair, the cost of those repairs will usually be recoverable from the lessee. That cost, along with other expenses incurred by the lessor in providing the services (eg, lighting and heating of common parts) on behalf of all lessees, will form a service charge. If it is described as a rent in the lease then that enables the lessor to distrain for arrears of a service charge rental. Normally there will be a service charge payable as a rent, with payments on account made quarterly at a level to be decided by the lessor's surveyor (whose decision shall be final, save for manifest error). These payments will usually be at the start of each year, but having regard to the expenditure during the previous year. At the end of the year accounts are prepared to reconcile the figures as to payments made and received. Any balance due will be demanded, but if there is an excess there should be a provision allowing the lessor to retain the excess monies against liabilities arising in the following year. Service charges are examined in more detail at paras 4.45 et seq below.

4.05 In a commercial lease of part of a building the lessor should be obliged by a covenant to carry out clearly defined obligations listed in a schedule to the lease. These will include repairs and renovations to the main structure and common parts, as well as lighting and heating the common parts and external decoration. These obligations are usually made conditional upon the lessee paying the service charge.

4.06 A lessor's repairing covenant is subject to the same rules of construction as a tenant's covenant. Accordingly, the lessor is not obliged to carry out works that would provide the lessee with something wholly different from that originally demised. Although there is an implied right for the lessor to enter the demised premises to carry out the repairs, this right of entry should always be expressly set out in the lease. Lessees would be wise to qualify the lessor's right of entry so that it is only exercisable at reasonable times upon prior written notice (except in the case of emergencies).

The effect of the Defective Premises Act 1972 on the lessor's repairing obligations should also **4.07** be mentioned here. Under the Act, a lessor who is under an express or implied obligation to repair the demised premises owes a duty to all persons who might reasonably be expected to be affected by defects in the state of the premises to take such care as is reasonable in all the circumstances to see that they are reasonably safe from personal injury or damage to their property. This duty arises immediately the lessor knows or ought to have known of the defect (*Sykes v Harry* [2001] 3 WLR 62).

Insurance

It is always imperative in a lessor/lessee relationship to ensure that there is recorded who will **4.08** insure the subject premises to make certain that one or the other actually arranges cover. In modern business leases, it is common practice for the lessor to insure but for the lessee to covenant to reimburse the lessor for the insurance premium. However, this is by no means a complete standard, as the following paragraphs will confirm.

Introduction

At the drafting and negotiating stage of a new commercial lease, both landlord and tenant **4.09** will need to address their minds to the question of insurance. It is important to appreciate that at common law there is no implied obligation on either party to insure the demised premises. Accordingly, express provision should always be made in the lease. This section considers the recommended terms of the insurance provisions, including who should insure, the risks to be covered and the amount of cover. It also looks at the consequences of destruction or damage and how the insurance monies should be applied.

Whose obligation to insure?

Occasionally you will find a tenant insuring where the demised premises are the whole of a **4.10** building and are self-contained. This has the advantage of tying in with a tenant's full repairing covenant. However, generally speaking, in a commercial lease the landlord will assume responsibility for insurance. There are a number of possible reasons for this:

(a) The landlord may be under a pre-existing duty to insure. For example, if the landlord has a mortgage, it may be a condition of the mortgage that the landlord must insure the property. Similarly, if the landlord is granting a sub-lease, it may be under an obligation in its own lease to insure.

(b) The landlord may prefer to insure in order to retain control; it would rather claim against its own insurance policy, which it knows is adequate, than risk suing a penniless tenant who has underinsured.

(c) Importantly, the nature of the premises may dictate that the landlord insures. On a letting of part of a building the landlord should always insure the whole building, including common parts, forecourts, car parking areas, etc. In this way, one policy will cover the whole building, eliminating the risk that part of it (eg, common parts or unlet units) might remain uninsured.

(d) Lastly, the landlord may realize that the party which insures could be entitled to receive commission!

The name of the insured

4.11 Although under the terms of the lease the responsibility to insure normally rests with the landlord, the tenant will prefer the policy to be in the joint names of the landlord and tenant. The reasons for this are as follows:

(a) it ensures that both parties will be notified by the insurance company before the policy is allowed to lapse;

(b) any insurance proceeds paid out will go jointly to the landlord and tenant, thus giving the tenant a measure of control over how the proceeds are spent. This is also beneficial to the tenant should the landlord go into liquidation as it prevents all the proceeds passing into the hands of the landlord's liquidator;

(c) subrogation against the tenant is avoided. Subrogation is the right of an insurance company, which has paid out on a claim, to step into the shoes of the insured and pursue any claims that the insured has against third parties. Thus, in a situation where the policy is in the landlord's sole name and the premises are destroyed by an act or omission of the tenant entitling the landlord to sue the tenant, the insurance company can claim against the tenant.

An insurance company cannot subrogate against the insured, so it follows that if the tenant is one of the insured it is impossible to subrogate against the tenant. For decisions involving subrogation against a tenant, see *Mark Rowlands Ltd v Berni Inns Ltd* [1986] QB 211 and *Lambert v Keymood Ltd* [1997] 43 EG 131. In the *Mark Rowlands* case, the insurance was in the landlord's name and some doubt was cast on the principle of subrogation against a tenant. This was on the basis that the insurance was for the parties' mutual benefit and the tenant had reimbursed the insurance premiums to the landlord. A foolproof approach for the tenant would be to insist that the insurance policy includes a waiver of subrogation rights against the tenant (or at least the insurer writes confirming that it will not subrogate).

4.12 Of course, it may not be practicable for insurance to be in joint names, eg, where the demised premises are part of a larger building, such as a unit in a shopping centre. In this case, or if the landlord cannot be persuaded to agree to joint insurance, the tenant should insist that the tenant's interest is at least noted on the landlord's policy. Although this does not give the tenant any right to claim under the policy, it should ensure that the insurance company notifies the tenant if the policy is about to lapse.

Conversely, if (unusually) the tenant has the obligation to insure, the roles will be reversed. Now it is the landlord who wants the policy in joint names (or to have its interest noted).

Sum insured

4.13 It is a fundamental principle of insurance law that the insurance contract is one of indemnity for loss suffered but no more than that (*Castellain v Preston* (1883) 11 QBD 380, CA). In the context of real property, indemnity is usually based on the market value of the building rather than the higher cost of reinstating it. Accordingly, the parties should expressly provide in the lease for insurance to be on a full reinstatement basis to include site-clearance and demolition costs, professionals' fees, planning application fees and any VAT payable. The reinstatement cost should be calculated as the cost that might properly be expected to be incurred at the time reinstatement takes place, not at the date when the annual insurance premium is paid (*Gleniffer Finance Corp Ltd v Bamar Wood and Products Ltd* [1978] 2 Lloyd's Rep 49).

The parties will need to take expert advice from a reputable insurance broker as to the **4.14** appropriate level of cover in each case. As well as assessing a figure for full reinstatement value, an allowance will also need to be made for inflation in respect of building costs. Assessing the appropriate level of cover may be relatively easy for a modern building, but problems can occur with an older building where it may be impossible to replace with anything similar, eg, an old building converted for use as offices. The moral is clear—take expert advice.

Risks insured

It is generally in both parties' interests to have a clear and comprehensive range of insured **4.15** risks against which the premises must be insured. Ambiguous statements such as 'fire and other normal risks', 'insurable risks' or 'comprehensive risks' should be avoided. A typical list of risks would include fire, lightning, explosion, impact, storm, tempest, flood, bursting and overflowing of water tanks or pipes, riot and civil commotion. For flexibility, the landlord should include a sweeping-up provision at the end as follows: '. . . and such other risks as the landlord may from time to time reasonably consider necessary'. Note the word 'reasonably' to protect the tenant. The landlord should also insure against loss of rent (see para 4.22 below).

There are two principal reasons why the tenant in particular should insist on a full range **4.16** of insured risks:

(a) The tenant's repairing covenant will normally contain a proviso that the tenant will not be required to repair damage caused by an insured risk (see para 3.21 above). Naturally, this is because the insurance monies will pay for it. However, unless the range of insured risks is comprehensive, the tenant may find itself having to repair damage caused by a risk against which the landlord has not insured, eg, if the premises suffer flood damage but flooding is not listed as an insured risk. If the risk is at least mentioned in the landlord's insurance covenant, the tenant will be protected because even if the landlord failed *actually* to insure against flooding, the tenant still has a claim against the landlord for breach of covenant to insure.

(b) The prudent tenant will insist on a rent abatement clause in the lease so that if the premises are damaged and become unfit for use the rent will be suspended (see para 4.20 below). The landlord will insist on qualifying this provision so that the rent is suspended only if the damage is caused by an insured risk (ie, the damage is outside the tenant's repairing liability; see (a) above). Accordingly, unless the range of insured risks is fully comprehensive, there is a danger that the rent suspension may not come into operation and the tenant is left paying rent for a building it cannot use.

The landlord should seek to qualify its obligation to insure in two situations: **4.17**

(a) Landlords should exclude any risk against which insurance may not from time to time be reasonably available, eg, acts of terrorism (this has serious repercussions for the tenant; see below). It may also be difficult to obtain cover for subsidence (and the tenant may need to consider its own separate cover for this). The fact that insurance is not available for a particular risk is no defence to a claim by the tenant for breach of covenant (*Enlayde Ltd v Roberts* [1917] 1 Ch 109).

(b) The covenant to insure should be subject to any exclusions, limitations and excesses imposed by the landlord's insurer.

4.18 If acts of terrorism are excluded from the list of insured risks, this is potentially very serious for the tenant. As we have seen, insured risks will normally be excluded from the tenant's repairing liability. However, if damage is caused by an uninsured risk (eg, acts of terrorism) the tenant must repair the damage. Similarly, rent abatement will operate only where damage is caused by an insured risk. The net effect is the tenant must repair the damage and continue to pay rent for premises it may be unable to use.

4.19 It is still possible to obtain insurance against acts of terrorism. Although since 1 January 1993 insurers have limited cover for such acts to £100,000, further cover can be acquired through the Pool Reinsurance Company (known as Pool Re). The balance above £100,000 up to the sum insured is paid by Pool Re. If Pool Re's funds become exhausted, the insurers who are members of Pool Re pay 10 per cent of the total premiums paid, with the Government agreeing to meet the balance (see Reinsurance (Acts of Terrorism) Act 1993). Further guidance is given at <http://www.hm-treasury.gov.uk>.

Rent abatement and insurance against loss of rent

4.20 At common law the tenant is obliged to continue paying rent even if the premises are rendered unfit for use. Notwithstanding that the tenant may be paying for the loss of rent insurance cover (see below), rent suspension will not be implied (*Cleveland Shoe Co Ltd v Murray's Book Sales (Kings Cross) Ltd* (1973) 229 EG 1465). Furthermore, the doctrine of frustration generally has no part to play in leases (*National Carriers Ltd v Panalpina (Northern) Ltd* [1981] AC 675). Accordingly, the tenant must always ensure that a suitable rent abatement clause is included in the lease allowing for the suspension of rent if the premises become unfit for use, or access to them is denied, as a result of damage through an insured risk.

4.21 In a lease of part of a building the tenant will want any service charges to be suspended too, because if it is not occupying the premises it cannot receive the benefit of the services. However, a landlord is unlikely to agree to this on the grounds that damage to the tenant's premises alone is unlikely to reduce the level of services provided to the rest of the building (a weak argument, in our view). Understandably, the landlord will want a proviso that rent abatement does not occur if an act or omission of the tenant vitiates or invalidates the insurance policy (see para 4.30 below). Rent abatement is considered further at para 2.15 above and there is a precedent below at para 4.44.

4.22 As the lease will normally include a rent abatement clause in the event of damage by an insured risk, the landlord should insure against loss of rent during the rent suspension period. The premium for loss of rent insurance will normally be borne by the tenant. The landlord will need to calculate how long it would take to demolish, obtain consents and rebuild the premises. As the tenant will no doubt be reimbursing the landlord's premium for the loss of rent cover, the tenant should ensure that the period is no longer than reasonably necessary (two years is usually sufficient for most commercial properties).

Lease provisions regarding insurance

The following insurance provisions are typically found in a business lease. **4.23**

Landlord's covenant to insure   As previously mentioned, the landlord will normally cov- **4.24**
enant to insure the demised premises. If they comprise part of a larger building the landlord
should obviously covenant to insure the whole building, recovering a proportion of the
premium from each tenant. On the question of which insurer to use, the landlord may prefer
to have no limitations so as to give flexibility when the policy comes up for renewal. However, the tenant should always insist on an express proviso that the insurance is with a
'reputable' insurance company.

The landlord should not agree to 'shop around' for competitive quotes. This is because it has **4.25**
no obligation to do so at common law (see *Tredegar v Harwood* [1929] AC 72 and *Havenridge
Ltd v Boston Dyers Ltd* [1994] EGCS 53). In spite of that, the *Havenridge* case confirmed the
general principle that a landlord's power to insure must be exercised in a bona fide manner.
Thus, a premium which is deemed excessive may fall foul of this principle.

Landlord to produce insurance policy and premium receipt   If the landlord insures, the **4.26**
tenant will want to know that the policy is in force and for what amount. The lease should
therefore require the landlord, if requested, to produce the insurance policy and the last
receipt for any insurance premium, and to notify the tenant of any changes. These provisions will normally be built into the landlord's covenant to insure. If the insurance policy
covers other buildings as well (eg, under the landlord's block policy), the landlord may be
reluctant to produce the insurance policy on the grounds of confidentiality. In this case the
tenant should at least require sight of the schedule to the policy detailing the relevant
insurance cover for the demised premises. Alternatively, the landlord could authorize the
tenant to correspond directly with the insurers for this information.

Tenant's covenant to reimburse insurance premium   Where the landlord covenants to **4.27**
insure the premises, the tenant will covenant to reimburse the landlord for the insurance
premium and any taxes or charges levied on the premium. This reciprocal obligation is dealt
with either through the service charge provisions, or, if there is no service charge, by a simple
reimbursement covenant. The tenant will agree to repay the premium itself, but should
resist any attempt by the landlord to recover fees or expenses incurred in determining the
reinstatement cost, or effecting or maintaining the insurance or claims under it.

In a lease of part of a building where the landlord insures the whole, the tenant's reimburse- **4.28**
ment should of course be limited to a proportion of the premium attributable to the demised
premises. The tenant's share of the premium is usually calculated as the same percentage as
the tenant's floor area bears to the whole building. In each case, however, the tenant's
solicitor must consider carefully whether this is reasonable. There may be cases where it is
unreasonable, eg, where other businesses in the building have a higher fire risk. A fairer
approach in this situation might be to provide for 'a reasonable proportion to be determined
by the landlord's surveyor acting as expert'.

As with all tenant obligations to pay money, a prudent landlord will ensure that the tenant's **4.29**
covenant to reimburse the insurance premium is reserved as rent. This allows distress to be
levied and makes it easier to forfeit the lease for non-payment, ie, without serving a notice
under s 146 of the Law of Property Act 1925.

4.30 **Tenant not to vitiate or invalidate insurance** It is usual to include a covenant on the tenant's part not to do (or omit to do) anything which would cause the landlord's policy to be avoided or vitiated, or to render irrecoverable any of the insurance monies (eg by bringing in inflammable goods). If the tenant vitiates the policy, it is likely that neither the rent suspension clause nor the proviso to the tenant's repairing covenant (ie, no obligation to repair for damage caused by insured risks) will operate. This is potentially disastrous for the tenant, and it is even more reason why the tenant will want to know exactly what the policy says and insist that the landlord produces it on request.

4.31 **Landlord's covenant to reinstate premises** In the event of damage or destruction there is no general obligation on the landlord who insures to use the insurance monies to reinstate the demised premises (although see *Mumford Hotels Ltd v Wheeler* [1963] 3 All ER 250, a case which turned on its own facts). Accordingly, where the landlord insures the property, the tenant should insist on an express covenant by the landlord to apply the proceeds of the policy in reinstating the demised premises. The landlord should also covenant, in the event of a shortfall, to make up any deficiency out of its own funds (this acts as an incentive to the landlord to insure to the full reinstatement cost!). If the landlord is obliged to reinstate, it must do so within a reasonable time (*Farimani v Gates* (1984) 271 EG 887).

4.32 As we have seen, the landlord will want to qualify its reinstatement covenant so that it is not liable to reinstate if an act or omission of the tenant vitiates the insurance. The tenant usually accepts this as reasonable. However, the landlord may also wish to exclude or suspend its liability to reinstate where it is prevented from doing so by circumstances beyond its control (eg, strikes, lockouts, or shortage of materials). The tenant should resist this on the basis that unless the tenant is at fault, reinstatement must be assured.

4.33 If the lease omits to include an express provision to reinstate, the Fires (Prevention) Metropolis Act 1774 may be of some assistance. Section 83 of that Act entitles the occupier or owner of a building damaged by fire to require the insurers to apply the proceeds of a fire policy towards the building's repair or replacement instead of paying them to the insured. It should be noted that the Act applies only to damage by fire and that the application to the insurer must be made *before* the insurance monies are laid out.

4.34 For a precedent for a landlord's insurance and reinstatement covenant, see para 4.44 below.

4.35 **Option to terminate lease if no reinstatement** A tenant should consider including an option to terminate the lease if reinstatement has not taken place within a reasonable specified time (say, two or three years). A tenant may even consider a provision allowing it to terminate the lease as soon as the premises become unfit for use or occupation, thus allowing it to relocate permanently. This would seem particularly appropriate in a short lease. Similarly, an option to terminate the lease may prove attractive to a landlord who would prefer to redevelop (perhaps with adjoining land) rather than seek to reconstitute premises which are destroyed.

4.36 In any event, the parties should make appropriate provision in the lease to allow either of them to terminate it if reimbursement proves impossible, eg, as a result of planning consent being refused. The lease should provide for either party to serve notice of termination on the other. If the lease is protected under the Landlord and Tenant Act 1954, Pt II, termination must occur in accordance with the Act's provisions (see chapter 7 generally regarding these procedures). The parties should also consider a termination provision in the event that neither party desires reinstatement.

The worst-case scenario for a tenant would be to enter a lease with no provision for rent **4.37** abatement and no provision for termination if the premises cannot be reinstated. In the event of the premises being destroyed the tenant would have no premises to occupy, no prospect of reinstatement but still be required to pay rent!

If reinstatement does not take place, what happens to the insurance monies? The position at **4.38** common law is unclear, as the court must establish the intentions of the parties by looking at the lease as a whole. In *Beacon Carpets Ltd v Kirby* [1984] 2 All ER 726, the landlord insured and the court divided the proceeds between the parties in shares proportionate to their respective interests in the premises. However, in *King, Robinson, Re v Gray* [1963] 1 All ER 781, the tenant insured and the court held that as the purpose of the insurance was to secure performance of the tenant's obligations, the insurance monies should belong to the tenant alone.

Due to this uncertainty, the lease should expressly provide for ownership of the insurance **4.39** monies in the event of reinstatement proving impossible or mutually undesirable. Opinions vary as to how the monies should fairly be apportioned. In the usual situation, where the landlord insures, the tenant would argue that the proceeds should be split according to the value of the parties' respective interests (see *Beacon Carpets*, above). Conversely, a landlord who has paid good money for the reversion would argue that the proceeds should rightfully belong to it. It would point out that any loss suffered to the tenant's business will be covered by the tenant's own insurance. Ultimately, it is a matter of negotiation and the bargaining strengths of the parties, but one avenue to consider is to provide, in the absence of agreement, for the matter to be referred to an arbitrator. For a precedent, see below at para 4.44.

Tenant's covenant to insure premises   As we have seen, it is rarely the case that the tenant **4.40** will covenant to insure the premises. However, if (unusually) this is the case, the landlord will have concerns corresponding to those of the tenant mentioned above. In particular, the following points should be borne in mind when acting for the landlord:

(a)   the tenant should always covenant to reinstate the premises;

(b)   the landlord would prefer the insurance to be in joint names for the reasons stated at para 4.11 above;

(c)   the landlord would wish to oversee and approve the terms of the insurance policy, including the sum insured and the risks covered.

Additional provisions

The following additional tenant's covenants relevant to insurance will often be included in a **4.41** commercial lease:

(a)   not to bring dangerous, inflammable or explosive items on to the premises;

(b)   not to do or permit anything that would cause the insurance premiums to be increased;

(c)   to pay any additional premiums that may become due as a result of the tenant's activities on the premises;

(d)   to comply with the recommendations and requirements of the landlord's insurer and the fire authority. If the tenant's use contravenes the insurer's recommendations and results in an increased premium being payable, the landlord may consider seeking an injunction restraining the use (*Chapman v Mason* (1910) 103 LT 390);

(e)   to pay any excess liability under the landlord's insurance policy (tenant to resist this if possible);

(f)   to pay the cost of the landlord's annual valuation fees for insurance purposes (tenant to resist this if possible);

(g)   to insure any plate glass at the premises, eg, a glass-fronted shop. It is normally more convenient for insurance of plate glass to be dealt with under a policy separate from the buildings insurance.

Lastly, when acting for a tenant, it is worth remembering that in running a business the tenant will no doubt be required to maintain employer's liability and public liability insurance policies. You should remind the tenant to notify these insurers of any acquisition of new premises as this is normally a condition of these policies.

The Code of Practice for Commercial Leases and Insurance

4.42   Recommendations 8 and 14 of the Code relate to insurance. Recommendation 8 states that 'where the landlord is responsible for insuring the property, the policy terms should be competitive. The tenant of an entire building should, in appropriate cases, be given the opportunity to influence the choice of insurer. If the premises are so damaged by an uninsured risk as to prevent occupation, the tenant should be allowed to terminate the lease unless the landlord agrees to rebuild at his own cost.' The explanatory notes go on to say that such uninsured risks might include terrorist damage and that, unless suitable provisions are included in the lease, the tenant might have to meet the cost of rebuilding in that situation. Recommendation 14 is concerned with insurance during the currency of the lease. It states 'where the landlord has arranged insurance, the terms should be made known to the tenant and any interest of the tenant covered by the policy. Any material change in the insurance should be notified to the tenant. Tenants should consider taking out their own insurance against loss or damage to contents and their business (loss of profits etc.) and any other risks not covered by the landlord's policy.' Both landlord and tenant are encouraged to take professional advice as soon as any damage occurs.

KEY POINTS SUMMARY: INSURANCE PROVISIONS

4.43   • Always make sure that there is express provision in the lease for insurance.

• The landlord normally insures, and should always do so in a lease of part of a building (where the landlord must insure the whole building, not just the demised premises).

• The tenant will reimburse the landlord's insurance premium (or a proportion attributable to the demised premises) reserved as rent, but should not repay other associated costs, eg, valuation fees.

• The tenant will prefer the policy to be in the joint names of landlord and tenant, or at least have its interest noted on the policy.

• The sum insured should be for the full reinstatement cost, including site clearance, demolition costs and all fees; take expert advice.

• Include in the insurance covenant a comprehensive list of insured risks, plus a sweeping-up provision at the end.

- The tenant must insist on a rent abatement clause if the premises become unfit for use as a result of damage by an insured risk; as a result, the landlord should insure, at the tenant's expense, for loss of rent.
- The tenant should require the landlord to produce on request a copy of the policy and receipt for the last premium paid.
- The tenant will covenant not to vitiate the insurance.
- The landlord will covenant to use the insurance proceeds to reinstate the premises, and the tenant will require the landlord to make up any deficiency out of its own monies.
- The parties should provide for termination of the lease if reinstatement proves impossible, or if neither party wants it.
- If reinstatement does not occur, the parties should make express provision for ownership of the insurance monies.
- The tenant should notify its employer's liability and public liability insurers of any acquisition of new premises.

Precedents: lessor's covenants

(Note: tenant's amendments and additions are struck through and underlined.) **4.44**

Landlord's covenant to insure and reinstate (lease of part of building)

(1) To keep the Building insured with an insurance company of repute against loss or damage by fire and such other risks as the Landlord thinks fit lightning explosion impact by vehicle aircraft (or other aerial device) or articles falling from them civil commotion riot malicious persons acts of terrorism earthquake landslide subsidence storm flood tempest overflowing and bursting of water pipes tanks and other apparatus and such other risks as the landlord may from time to time reasonably consider necessary ('the Insured Risks') for an amount equal to the full reinstatement cost of the Building (including debris removal demolition site clearance and all professional fees and VAT) and two years' loss of rent

(2) The obligation to insure is subject to any exclusions limitations and excesses imposed by the insurers and to any risk being ordinarily available from a reputable insurer for the Building

(3) To produce to the Tenant on demand a copy of the insurance policy (or an extract of the terms) maintained by the Landlord and the receipt for the last premium payable and to procure that the interest of the Tenant is noted or endorsed on the policy

(4) If the Building is destroyed or damaged by any of the Insured Risks and the policy of insurance has not been vitiated by some act or omission of the Tenant to apply the insurance monies in reinstating the Building or such part of it as may have been destroyed or damaged as soon as possible and to make up any deficiency out of its own monies

(5) If it is impossible or impracticable to reinstate in accordance with the preceding clause any monies received under the insurance policy shall belong to the Landlord absolutely (except payments for loss of rent which shall belong to the Landlord) shall be divided between the Landlord and the Tenant according to the value of their respective interests in the demised premises as at the date of the damage or destruction (to be determined in default of agreement by an arbitrator appointed by the President of the Royal Institution of Chartered Surveyors)

Termination clause

(1) If the demised premises is so damaged or destroyed by any of the Insured Risks as to become unfit for occupation or use and it remains so unfit two years after the damage or destruction (the 'Two Year Period') then either party may end this Lease by serving on the

other not less than three months' written notice given at any time after the Two Year period

(2) Termination under the preceding clause shall not affect the rights that either party may have against the other and any monies received under the insurance policy ~~shall belong to the Landlord absolutely~~ (except payments for loss of rent which shall belong to the Landlord) shall be divided between the Landlord and the Tenant according to the value of their respective interests in the demised premises as at the date of the damage or destruction (to be determined in default of agreement by an arbitrator appointed by the President of the Royal Institution of Chartered Surveyors)

Rent abatement clause

(1) If the demised premises or the main access thereto is so damaged or destroyed by an Insured Risk in whole or in part as to become unfit for occupation or use and the sum insured is not irrecoverable as a result of any act or omission by the Tenant then the rent or a fair proportion of it according to the nature and extent of the damage shall be suspended until the demised premises are again fit for occupation and use or until two years after the damage or destruction whichever is the shorter

(2) Any dispute as to a fair proportion of the rent to be suspended shall be determined by an arbitrator appointed by the President of the Royal Institution of Chartered Surveyors

---

B   SERVICE CHARGES IN A COMMERCIAL LEASE

4.45 It may be that the landlord wishes to repair the main structure and to collect a service charge for this work. If this is the case, where there are several leases in one building there needs to be consistency across them. This will ensure the proper maintenance of the main structure. The issue of service charges is now considered in detail.

Introduction

4.46 A service charge is appropriate in a lease of part, where the landlord covenants to repair, maintain and insure the whole building and to provide other services to the occupying tenants. The landlord has the primary responsibility for payment of these items but recovers a proportion of the recurring annual cost (ie, the service charge) from each tenant. In this way, the landlord will not have to 'dip into' the rent to recover its expenses; it keeps a 'clear' rent in a 'clear' lease. Importantly, as far as the value of the landlord's reversionary interest is concerned, this type of lease (ie, a lease of part subject to service charge) is the form generally acceptable to an institutional investor. It is seen in leases within office blocks, industrial estates and shopping centres.

4.47 The service charge provisions must be drafted and negotiated with care. For the tenant's part, onerous provisions may result in the tenant paying a higher service charge than it ought to. Equally, for the landlord, unduly harsh provisions on the tenant could possibly reduce the rental value on review. Unlike the rent, the service charge is likely to vary each year according to the landlord's actual annual expenditure. In some leases service charge funds are set aside in separate sinking or reserve funds to pay for future items of expenditure that do not occur every year, eg, decorating the outside of the building (see para 4.68 below).

On a lease of the whole of a building the tenant normally assumes direct responsibility for **4.48** maintenance and repair under its repairing covenant. In this case a service charge is not appropriate, as the landlord is not actively involved in the management of the building. Similarly, if the tenant is granted the right to share a private road or sewer where no regular maintenance is required, a standard service charge is not appropriate. In this case the landlord simply includes a covenant by the tenant to reimburse a fair proportion of the landlord's cost as and when maintenance works are required. This is really a service charge payable on demand rather than one paid regularly in advance.

Services provided and expenditure recoverable

The landlord's solicitor's objective in drafting the service charge provisions is to ensure that **4.49** all the landlord's expenditure on the building is recoverable from the occupying tenants. If there is no obligation in the lease for the tenant to pay for a particular service then the law will not imply one (*Rapid Results College Ltd v Angell* [1986] 1 EGLR 53). Accordingly, the landlord must list all the services it will provide and include a sweeping-up clause to cover unforeseen items of expenditure. The tenant's solicitor, in considering these provisions, will appreciate that the landlord is effectively spending the tenant's money. The solicitor will therefore try to limit the tenant's liability to pay only the reasonable cost of those services that are reasonably necessary. The tenant's cause is aided by *Finchbourne v Rodrigues* [1976] 3 All ER 581, which held that the amount charged to the tenant must be fair and reasonable, and also by s 15 of the Supply of Goods and Services Act 1982 which implies such a term. Nevertheless, instead of relying on case law and statute, it is better for the tenant to have express provisos as to reasonableness.

Typical services

The following are fairly typical of the services provided by a landlord in a commercial lease **4.50** (although not exclusively so).

Maintenance and repair of the building

This can be a contentious area. The landlord will obviously want to recover all its expenditure **4.51** on the property. This will include maintaining and repairing the structure, roof, foundations and plant, as well as the repair and decoration of the outside of the building, common parts and conducting media. However, the tenant must ensure that the landlord's simple covenant to 'repair' does not extend to allowing the landlord, at the tenant's expense, to improve, alter, rebuild or renew the premises. The tenant's solicitor must strike out such wording as a court will interpret the clause strictly (*Mullany v Maybourne Grange (Croydon) Management Co Ltd* [1986] 1 EGLR 70). Moreover, the tenant will not wish to pay for remedying inherent or latent defects in the property, eg, a design defect in a new building. The landlord must carry out such repairs at its own expense, not as part of the services it provides to the tenant (for an appropriate precedent, see para 4.75 below). The cost of the building insurance is also often included in the service charge (for insurance generally, see paras 4.08 et seq).

In *Fluor Daniel v Shortlands* [2001] 2 EGLR 103 the court reduced a proposed refurbishment **4.52** bill of £2.1 million to £300,000, declaring that landlords should look at such proposals from the perspective of a reasonably minded tenant. The court held that the standard of works should be such as the tenants, given the length of their leases, could be fairly expected to pay. In this case the majority of leases ended within just a few years and the court considered this to be significant. Landlords could not overlook the limited interest of tenants who were having to pay by carrying out works which were calculated to serve an interest extending beyond that of the tenants. Subject always to the terms of the individual leases, landlords should bear such additional costs themselves. This important decision clearly assists tenants faced with landlords wishing to unfairly dictate works, for which tenants will see no benefit in the lifetime of their lease.

Staff costs and managing agents

4.53 These are the landlord's costs of employing its staff, ie, caretakers, receptionists, porters, security personnel and others involved in the management and security of the building. The costs will include salary, National Insurance contributions, any pension contributions and any staff accommodation costs. Staff employed by the landlord's managing agents for the building should also be included. The tenant should not agree to pay the full-time salary of staff unless they are wholly engaged in providing the services in the lease. Accordingly, the tenant should consider the following qualification in the drafting: '. . . to the extent that the staff are performing the services referred to in this lease . . .'. The professional fees of the managing agents should also be included, or else the landlord will be unable to recover them (*Embassy Court Residents Association v Lipman* (1984) 271 EG 545). The tenant should only agree to pay managing agents' fees that are reasonably and properly incurred.

Other services such as heating, lighting of common parts, water, etc.

4.54 Landlords will usually provide tenants with hot and cold water and, in some premises, air conditioning. The cost of lighting and heating the building will also be included in the service charge, but heating may only be for specified periods, eg, 1 October to 1 May. Landlords may be reluctant to switch on the heating outside the specified periods if they cannot recover the cost (which explains why some premises feel cold in late September or early May!). In some leases these services may be confined only to the common parts of the building. Other items of expenditure may include refuse disposal, fire-fighting equipment, window cleaning, landscaping, and maintaining lifts, boilers and other plant and machinery. A tenant of ground-floor premises who clearly does not use the lift should try to exclude any liability for lift maintenance (or replacement) costs.

Sweeping up

4.55 The sweeping-up clause will permit the landlord to recover the cost of other services not specifically mentioned, and also take account of any new services that the landlord may want to provide later. The tenant should resist a sweeping-up clause that is too widely drawn. Additional costs should be recoverable only if they plainly benefit the tenant. A tenant should seek notification in advance of any proposed new services, or even possibly a right of prior consultation. (For an interesting case on sweeping-up clauses, see *Sun Alliance & London Assurance Co Ltd v British Railways Board* [1989] 2 EGLR 237.) If the landlord agrees a consultation provision in the lease, it cannot recover the cost of the relevant works unless consultation actually takes place. This principle applies generally to services that are at the landlord's discretion and is not confined to the sweeping-up clause (see *Northways Flats Management Co (Camden) Ltd v Wimpey Pension Trustees Ltd* [1992] 2 EGLR 42).

Landlord's covenant to provide services

The landlord's services are normally categorized into those services that are obligatory **4.56** (ie, essential services such as repairing, maintaining the structure, lighting and heating) and those services that are discretionary (eg, security, promotional items, installing plants, flowers, etc.). The tenant must obviously ensure that the list of essential services is fully comprehensive. As far as discretionary items are concerned, the tenant should introduce a qualification that the landlord's discretion is exercised reasonably.

At common law, the fact that the tenant pays a service charge does not mean that the **4.57** landlord is obliged to provide the services (*Russell v Laimond Properties* (1984) 269 EG 947). The tenant should therefore ensure that the landlord covenants unconditionally to provide all essential services 'in an efficient and economical manner, to a reasonable standard and in accordance with the principles of good estate management'. The tenant should not accept merely a standard that the landlord considers reasonable or adequate. Neither should the tenant accept a conditional covenant in which the landlord is obliged to provide the services only if the tenant pays the service charge; these are independent obligations in the lease and should remain so. In the absence of clear wording to the contrary, a court generally would not allow a landlord to withhold services just because the tenant is in arrears with its payments (*Yorkbrook Investments Ltd v Batten* [1985] 2 EGLR 100). In any event, the landlord in practice would be unable to withdraw services to the whole building unless all the tenants were in arrears.

Another way for landlords to dilute their obligation to provide services is to say that they will **4.58** use their 'best' or 'reasonable' endeavours to provide them. A joint committee of the RICS and Law Society has recommended using the words 'to use all reasonable efforts' (see [1986] LS Gaz 1057), but in spite of this a tenant in a strong bargaining position would still hold out for an absolute covenant simply 'to provide' the services.

If the landlord agrees an absolute covenant, it should qualify it by excusing itself from **4.59** liability for interruptions to the services caused by factors beyond its control (eg, strikes and lockouts). Of course a tenant may object to this, but there will be few landlords who are willing to give a cast iron assurance of an unqualified absolute covenant. As a compromise we recommend that the parties agree the following:

(a) absolute covenant by landlord to provide services; but
(b) no liability for failure or interruptions caused by factors beyond its control; unless
(c) such failure or interruptions could reasonably have been prevented or shortened by the landlord; and
(d) landlord must use best endeavours to restore services as soon as possible.

Landlord excluding liability for employees' negligence

Some landlords seek to exclude their liability for any act, omission or negligence of their **4.60** employees in performing the services. They say that the tenant will have its own insurance against such accidents and it would be a waste of money for the landlord to insure for this as well (at the tenant's expense). Tenants should resist such a clause on the basis that it would contravene the Unfair Contract Terms Act 1977. This Act prevents a party from:

(a) excluding liability for death or personal injury due to negligence; and

(b) excluding liability for any other loss due to negligence if it is unreasonable.

(Although the 1977 Act does not apply to contracts relating to land, it is generally accepted that a contract to provide services is not a land contract; see *Regis Property Co Ltd v Redman* [1956] 2 QB 612.) If the landlord insists on the exclusion for employees' negligence, to avoid doubt the tenant should include the proviso, 'the Unfair Contract Terms Act 1977 shall apply to this clause'.

Calculating the tenant's share of service charge

4.61   The service charge clause will set out how the landlord's expenditure is to be apportioned between the different tenants in the building. One important preliminary point is that tenants should insist the landlord pays the service charge for any units in the building that are not let, ie, 'voids'. The risk of voids should properly fall on the landlord, not on the occupying tenants.

4.62   Various methods can be used to calculate the tenant's share. The most common of these are:

(a) By reference to rateable values, ie, the higher the rateable value of the tenant's premises, the higher the service charge. This method lacks flexibility and rateable values can fluctuate for reasons unconnected with the level of services provided to the unit (see *Moorcroft Estates Ltd v Doxford* (1979) 254 EG 871).

(b) By reference to floor areas, ie, the bigger the tenant's floor area, the higher the service charge. This method is very popular, especially in shopping centres. To avoid dispute, the means of measuring floor areas should be agreed in advance, eg, by reference to the current edition of the *Code of Measuring Practice* produced jointly by the Royal Institution of Chartered Surveyors (RICS) and the Incorporated Society of Valuers and Auctioneers (ISVA).

(c) Based on the tenants' anticipated use of the services, ie, the tenant who uses more services pays a higher service charge (eg, a restaurant will use more hot water than a shop). However, this method is widely seen as impracticable and difficult to assess accurately.

(d) Fixed percentages (usually based on rateable value or floor area). This has the merit of certainty and avoids dispute, but also lacks flexibility. To make it more flexible the parties can provide for the fixed share to be reassessed if necessary, eg, on a change from shop to restaurant where hot water use is increased, or where the landlord extends the building and introduces additional tenants. The tenant should insist on a condition that the aggregate of the proportions payable by all tenants should not exceed 100 per cent, thus preventing the landlord from unfairly making a profit.

(e) A 'fair proportion'. This is the most flexible method allowing all relevant circumstances to be taken into account. However, one disadvantage for the landlord is that it gives the tenant scope for disputing the figure. What is fair? A landlord will usually provide for the fair proportion to be assessed by its own surveyor whose decision shall be final and conclusive (see *Morgan Sindall v Sawston Farms (Cambs) Ltd* [1999] 1 EGLR 90). A tenant should at the very least add the words, 'save for manifest error'.

Payment of the service charge

The landlord will want the service charge to be paid by the tenant in advance of the expend- **4.63** iture to be incurred for any given year. This obviously saves the landlord from paying for the services out of its own funds. The payment dates on account are usually the same as the rental payment dates, ie, the usual quarter days. There are two main ways of calculating the payments. They are based either on the previous year's actual expenditure, or on an estimate of the anticipated expenditure for the current year. Acting for the landlord, the lease should provide expressly for the estimate to be given by the landlord's surveyor in his or her capacity as expert (otherwise the law implies that the expert must be independent; *Finch-bourne v Rodrigues* [1976] 3 All ER 581). An expert must act impartially and cannot be the landlord or the landlord's managing agent (see *Concorde Graphics Ltd v Andromeda Investments SA* (1982) 265 EG 386).

The landlord will usually provide for the expert's certificate to be final and conclusive, but **4.64** the tenant should add the words 'save for manifest error' and ensure that the expert acts reasonably. The tenant should also consider including a provision referring any dispute over the service charge to an independent expert or arbitrator. The landlord is likely to resist this, but the tenant must have regard to the decisions in *Morgan Sindall v Sawston Farms (Cambs) Ltd* [1999] 1 EGLR 90 and *National Grid Co Plc v M25 Group Ltd* [1999] 08 EG 169, which held that where the parties intend to exclude the jurisdiction of the courts an expert's determin-ation on questions of law is likely to be binding even if it is wrong. Lastly, the tenant should not have to pay the service charge until it receives the estimate.

The landlord should prepare annual service charge accounts showing the actual expenditure **4.65** for the year. These should be properly certified by the landlord's accountant. Once again the landlord will want the accountant's certificate to be final and conclusive, but the tenant will have the same concerns as mentioned above. After the actual expenditure for any given year is established, adjustments can be made to correct any overpayment or underpayment. The lease will, of course, provide for the tenant to make up any shortfall within a specified time. Unfortunately for the tenant, any overpayments are not normally returned. They are simply credited to the service charge account and held on account for the following year. The tenant should try to ensure that advance payments for service charges are held in an interest-bearing account which is separate from the landlord's own money. In this way the funds will be protected if the landlord becomes insolvent.

Service charge reserved as rent

As with all tenants' covenants to pay money under a lease, the service charge should be **4.66** reserved as rent. This benefits the landlord in two ways:

(a) the procedure for forfeiting a lease for 'non-payment of rent' is easier than it is for breaches of other covenants, in that there is no requirement to serve on the tenant a notice under s 146 of the Law of Property Act 1925; and

(b) the landlord's ancient remedy of distress is only available to recover 'arrears of rent'.

Service charge abatement

4.67 As we have seen, the tenant will insist on a rent suspension clause in the event of damage to the premises by an insured risk (rent abatement is considered at paras 4.20 et seq above). Similarly, a well-advised tenant would ask for service charge abatement as well—after all, why should a tenant pay for services it cannot use? Landlords should resist service charge abatement on the basis that if the whole building or development is totally destroyed there will be no services to provide. However, if part of the building or development is still open the landlord will be providing services for which it wants reimbursement. Perhaps a fair compromise would be to provide for no abatement except to the extent that services are not provided to the tenant.

Reserve and sinking funds

4.68 These are separate sums of money set aside to cover the cost of services that are not carried out every year. A reserve fund will meet the cost of major items of expenditure that may occur perhaps only every four or five years, eg, decorating the outside of an office block. To save the tenants having to pay an extra large service charge for the year in which the decoration is carried out, a part of the anticipated cost is set aside annually and paid into the reserve fund. Thus the cost is effectively spread over the four- or five-year period.

4.69 A sinking fund is slightly different in that it covers the cost of replacing major items of plant or other equipment in a building, eg, a lift or boiler. Again, the idea is to spread the cost over several years.

4.70 The tenant should insist that the reserve or sinking fund is held in a separate trust account. This ensures that if the landlord becomes insolvent, the landlord's liquidator or trustee in bankruptcy cannot claim the fund as part of the landlord's assets. The tenant should also ensure that the lease clearly sets out the purpose of the fund and the occasions on which it can be accessed. This will prevent any sharp practice from a landlord who is considering using the fund for his own purposes, eg, rebuilding the property at the end of the lease term.

4.71 On an assignment of the lease the assignor may seek to recover its unused contributions to the fund(s) from the assignee. The assignor will argue that it is the assignee who will benefit when the fund is utilized in the future and so the assignee should effectively pay for it. The assignee will argue that the cost of major expenditure should be spread across the whole term so that every tenant contributes, not just the occupying tenant in the year the work is done.

Taxation difficulties of reserve or sinking funds

4.72 There can be complex taxation difficulties for both parties in connection with these funds, the details of which are beyond the scope of this book. However, very broadly, the potential difficulties are as follows. For the lessor, if the fund is payable to the lessor 'as rent' (ie, not into a trust), the lessor will be liable to income tax under Schedule A of the Income and Corporation Taxes Act 1988. The lessor can of course offset its annual expenditure against income, but in the case of these funds it probably cannot do so until the year in which the expenditure is actually incurred. Likewise for a lessee, service charge payments are normally deductible for income tax purposes. However, if the monies are paid into a trust, it is likely that they will not be deductible from income until the year in which the trust actually lays out the monies (see generally, ss 25–31 of the 1988 Act). There may also be inheritance tax implications for the lessee, as the trust could amount to a settlement for inheritance tax purposes. The parties should each take specialist tax advice before setting up and agreeing the terms of any sinking or reserve fund.

The Guide to Good Practice on Service Charges

Recommendation 20 of the Code of Practice for Commercial Leases states that 'landlords should observe the Guide to Good Practice on Service Charges in Commercial Properties. Tenants should familiarize themselves with that Guide and should take professional advice if they think they are being asked to pay excessive service charges.' The Guide to Good Practice on Service Charges has been fully endorsed by several leading property industry and professional bodies including the British Property Federation, the Royal Institution of Chartered Surveyors, the Property Managers Association and the British Council for Offices. These organizations encourage all practitioners within the property industry to use the Guide. The Guide sets out principles for good practice designed to cover all types of commercial properties. The principles are laid down in the overall context of managing property but apply particularly to the delivery of common services and their costs on multi-let properties. The Guide encourages good working relationships through consultation and communication about what services are required, their quality and cost. Although the Guide cannot override the provisions of existing leases it is recommended that parties in negotiations should seek, where possible, to interpret and apply the lease in accordance with the principles of the Guide. The full text of the Guide (now in its second edition) can be downloaded from <http://www.bpf.org.uk>. **4.73**

KEY POINTS SUMMARY: SERVICE CHARGES

- Service charges are appropriate in a lease of part of a building where the landlord requires a clear rent. **4.74**
- The landlord should list all services for which it requires reimbursement and include a sweeping-up provision.
- Typical services include: repair, maintenance and insurance of the building; staffing costs; managing agent's fees; heating and lighting; and the provision of other services to common parts.
- For staffing costs, the tenant should not agree to pay the full-time salary of staff unless they are wholly engaged in providing the services in the lease.
- The tenant must ensure that it does not pay indirectly by way of service charge for the renewal or improvement of the building, or for remedying inherent defects.
- The tenant must ensure that any additional services are allowable only if they plainly benefit the tenant.
- Any discretionary services should be exercised by the landlord reasonably.
- The landlord should covenant unconditionally to provide all essential services 'in an efficient and economical manner, to a reasonable standard and in accordance with the principles of good estate management'.
- The tenant should resist a 'best or reasonable endeavours' covenant by the landlord to

provide services. It is better to agree an absolute covenant with the concession that the landlord has no liability for failure or interruptions caused by factors beyond its control, unless such failure or interruptions could reasonably have been prevented or shortened by the landlord. Also, the landlord must use its best endeavours to restore services as soon as possible.

- The landlord should not exclude liability for employees' negligence.
- The landlord should pay any service charge for unlet units.
- Various methods can be used to calculate tenants' shares, eg, by reference to rateable values, floor areas, tenants' anticipated use of services, fixed percentage or 'fair proportion'.
- If the fair proportion approach is employed, the landlord will want it assessed by its own surveyor whose decision is final.
- Service charges are usually paid in advance on the rent payment dates and reserved as rent.
- The amount is usually based either on previous years' expenditure, or on an estimate of anticipated expenditure for the current year.
- The landlord requires any estimate to be given by its own surveyor acting as an expert whose decision is final.
- The tenant will want to refer any dispute to an independent expert or arbitrator.
- The landlord should be required to prepare properly audited annual accounts.
- Advance payments for service charges should be held in an interest-bearing account separate from the landlord's own money.
- Include provision for adjustment of figures when the final accounts are known.
- The tenant should seek service charge abatement in the event of damage by insured risks.
- Consider whether a reserve or sinking fund is appropriate; there are potential taxation difficulties and expert advice should be obtained.
- Landlords and tenants should observe the Guide to Good Practice for Service Charges (see para 4.73 above).

Precedents: service charges

4.75   *(Note: tenant's amendments and additions are struck through and underlined)*

Landlord's covenant to provide services

~~Subject to the Tenant paying the Service Charge~~ the Landlord shall ~~use its reasonable endeavours to~~ provide the following services <u>in an efficient and economical manner to a reasonable standard and in accordance with the principles of good estate management</u>: [add full list of services]

Sweeping-up clause

Any further costs and expenses which the Landlord may incur in providing such other services as the Landlord may in its ~~absolute~~ <u>reasonable</u> discretion deem necessary or desirable for the benefit of the Building or any part of it or for enhancing or securing any amenity of the Building or in the interest of good estate management <u>provided always that the Landlord shall consult with and have regard to the wishes of the Tenant before providing any such other services</u>

Sinking fund

Such annual provision as the Landlord may, in its ~~absolute~~ <u>reasonable</u> discretion, decide as being proper <u>and reasonable</u> and in the interest of good estate management for the establishment and maintenance of a sinking fund for the replacement of any plant boilers machinery apparatus and equipment in the Building provided that the Tenant shall not be required to contribute towards expenditure by the Landlord that will be incurred after the expiry of this lease

Tenant's exclusions from service charge (relevant to new buildings except (d) below, which is relevant to all buildings)
The Tenant shall not be required to pay as part of the Service Charge:
(a)   The initial capital cost of the construction of the Building, or
(b)   The initial capital cost of the fixtures equipment plant and machinery within the Building, or
(c)   The initial capital cost of providing the services to the Building including the heating and air conditioning, or
(d)   The cost of remedying any damage caused by an Insured Risk, or
(e)   The cost of remedying any damage caused by an Inherent Defect in the Building
['Inherent Defect' means any defect in the Building attributable to defective design, supervision, construction, workmanship or materials]

Empty units
The Service Charge payable by the Tenant shall not be increased owing to any part of the Building being unlet at any time

---

KEY DOCUMENTS

- Income and Corporation Taxes Act 1988   **4.76**
- Unfair Contract Terms Act 1977
- Defective Premises Act 1972
- Law of Property Act 1925
- Fires (Prevention) Metropolis Act 1774
- Code of Practice for Commercial Leases in England and Wales (2nd edn)
- Guide to Good Practice on Service Charges

Printed copies of all legislation can be ordered from The Stationery Office (<http://www.tsoshop.co.uk>. Legislation from 1988 onwards can be downloaded free of charge from <http://www.opsi.gov.uk/acts.htm>.

The Code of Practice for Commercial Leases in England and Wales is set out in appendix 17.

5

MISCELLANEOUS LEASE CONCERNS: ENFORCEABILITY OF LEASE COVENANTS, INSOLVENCY AND DISCLAIMER, SURRENDER AND MERGER

5.01 In this chapter we focus on other various lease concerns, including the important and complex area of enforceability of covenants. We explain the widespread reforms brought about in this field by the Landlord and Tenant (Covenants) Act 1995 and reflect on the impact on commercial leases of the Contracts (Rights of Third Parties) Act 1999. In the sphere of insolvency we consider the consequences of a tenant's bankruptcy or liquidation and the effect of a subsequent disclaimer of the lease. We analyse briefly receivership and administration orders. To conclude, we consider the termination of commercial leases by surrender and merger.

A   ENFORCEABILITY OF LEASE COVENANTS

Introduction

5.02 A lease naturally creates a contractual relationship between the parties to it. Accordingly, under the principle of privity of contract, the original landlord and tenant, provided they stay the same throughout the term, remain liable under their respective covenants (*Thursby v Plant* (1690) 1 Saund 230). This is the easy part. More complex issues are involved if the identities of the parties change during the lifetime of the lease, eg, if the tenant assigns the lease or the landlord assigns the reversion, or the tenant sub-lets. In this context it is necessary to consider the impact of the Landlord and Tenant (Covenants) Act 1995 ('the 1995 Act'), which created a new set of rules for leases created on or after 1 January 1996. Thus, with some exceptions, we have one set of rules for leases granted before 1 January 1996 ('old tenancies') and another for leases created on or after that date ('new tenancies'). It follows that practitioners faced with an enforceability scenario, where either the current landlord or the tenant is not the original, should first ask the question: What is the date of the lease? This will determine the correct set of rules you should use. Note that parts of the 1995 Act apply to old tenancies as well (these are ss 17–20, considered in paras 5.09 to 5.12 below). Further, the 1995 Act does not apply to tenancies granted after 1 January 1996 made pursuant to an agreement or court order made before that date. 'Agreement' in this context includes an option or right of pre-emption (eg, an option to renew contained in an old tenancy).

Enforceability of lease covenants following an assignment of lease and/or reversion

We shall first consider the liability of the original landlord and tenant where a lease and/or **5.03** reversion has been assigned, and then go on to discuss the liability of the assignees of the lease and reversion. We shall examine the rules for both old and new tenancies. Although the 1995 Act applies principally to new tenancies, you should bear in mind that ss 17–20 of the Act, discussed below, apply to both old and new tenancies.

Liability of original landlord and tenant—rules for old tenancies

Under an old tenancy, the original parties remain liable throughout the lifetime of the **5.04** tenancy, even after they have disposed of their interests. This is based on the contractual principle of privity of contract. So, for example, if a tenant has contracted to pay rent or repair the premises under, say, a 25-year term then the landlord can enforce those obligations against the original tenant at any time during the term even after the tenant has sold the lease to someone else (see *Estates Gazette v Benjamin Restaurants* (1994) 26 EG 140, CA, and *Thames Manufacturing Co Ltd v Perrotts (Nichol & Peyton) Ltd* (1984) EG 284). Sometimes this obligation is set out expressly in the lease. If not, under s 79 of the Law of Property Act 1925, it is implied that the original tenant will be responsible for the acts and omissions of the tenant's successors in title (ie, assignees) and persons deriving title under the tenant (ie, sub-tenants). It is possible that the parties may have excluded this rule by providing in the lease that the tenant's liability will cease after it assigns. Although this would be very unusual, practitioners should still check the precise wording of the lease.

Likewise, under s 79 of the 1925 Act it is implied that the original landlord will be respon- **5.05** sible for the acts and omissions of the landlord's successors in title. Thus the original landlord's liability survives the assignment of the reversion (*Stuart v Joy* [1904] 1 KB 362). Of course the parties may have excluded this common law rule by providing in the lease that the landlord's liability will cease when he assigns the reversion (*Bath v Bowles* (1905) 93 LT 801). Again, although this would be very unusual, the wording of the lease should still be checked.

The original tenant will not be liable for any additional obligations agreed by the landlord **5.06** and assignee that were not contemplated in the original contract (eg, as in a deed of variation of the lease) (*Friends' Provident Life Office v British Railways Board* [1996] 1 All ER 336). However, this does not apply to rent reviews contemplated by the original lease. Thus the original tenant will still be liable for the reviewed rent, even though it was not a party to the review negotiations (see *Selous Street Properties Ltd v Oronel Fabrics Ltd* (1984) 270 EG 643 and *Friends' Provident Life Office v British Railways Board*, above). This common law position is now affirmed by statute (s 18 of the 1995 Act, which applies to both old and new tenancies).

In most cases the landlord will seek to enforce covenants against the current tenant rather **5.07** than against the original tenant (as we shall see, the burden of most lease covenants will pass on the assignment of the lease or reversion). This is simply because the current tenant's whereabouts will be known, whereas the original tenant may have disappeared. However, if the current tenant is 'a man of straw', eg, bankrupt, then the landlord will want to pursue the original tenant if it can. This happened frequently during the recession of the early 1990s and helped precipitate the reforms brought in by the 1995 Act. These reforms helped to protect former tenants caught out in this way by changing the privity of contract rule. Nevertheless, as we shall see, the 1995 Act did not apply retrospectively and so old tenancies remain largely unaffected by the reforms. (Of course, if the original tenant is a well-known strong covenant, eg, Tesco, then this may make it an automatic first choice.)

5.08 For old tenancies, if the landlord decides to pursue the original tenant, the latter is entitled to be indemnified by its immediate assignee (Law of Property Act 1925, s 77 for unregistered land; Land Registration Act 1925, s 24(1) for registered land). However, this is small comfort to the original tenant if the assignee is insolvent. In addition, the common law rule in *Moule v Garrett* (1872) LR 7 Ex 101 may assist the original tenant. This provides that 'where one person is compelled to pay damages by the legal default of another, he is entitled to recover from [that person] the sum so paid'. This would enable the original tenant to claim an indemnity from the current tenant at fault even if the current tenant were not the original tenant's immediate assignee. But once again, the assignee is probably a man of straw, otherwise the landlord would have recovered from it in the first place!

5.09 Section 17 of the 1995 Act is a valuable aid for former tenants and is one of the few provisions of the 1995 Act that applies retrospectively, ie, to old as well as new tenancies (the other sections applying to all tenancies are ss 18–20). Under s 17, where a landlord wishes to recover a fixed charge (which includes rent or service charge) from a former tenant, the landlord must serve notice on the tenant within six months of the charge becoming due. After that period the landlord's right to recover the money is lost. The procedure is that the landlord must serve a notice on the former tenant informing it that the money is due and stating that the landlord intends to recover such amount as is specified in the notice (s 17(2)). The relevant notice under s 17 is set out in appendix 6. One effect of this rule is to prevent landlords allowing arrears to accumulate over a period of time without the former tenant being aware of the breach by the current tenant.

5.10 Under s 19 of the 1995 Act, an original tenant who has made such a payment under s 17 may require the landlord to grant it an 'overriding lease'. This is a concurrent lease in which the original tenant becomes the immediate landlord of the defaulting current tenant. The term of the overriding lease is equal to the remainder of the term of the relevant tenancy plus three days (s 19(2)). Thus, if there are further breaches, the original tenant can take action to remedy them, eg, by forfeiting the overriding lease and regaining possession of the premises. If the original tenant requires an overriding lease it must demand it in writing, either at the time of making the payment under s 17 or within 12 months of that payment being made (s 19(5)). A precedent request for an overriding lease is set out in appendix 10 and a precedent for the overriding lease itself is set out in appendix 11.

5.11 The landlord must grant the overriding lease within a reasonable time, and the tenant must pay the landlord's reasonable costs (including surveyor's fees) in granting the lease (s 19(6)). If the landlord fails to provide the overriding lease within a reasonable time then the tenant may have an action for damages (s 20(3)). The lease will be a 'new tenancy' only if the relevant tenancy was a new tenancy (s 20(1)); otherwise it will be an old tenancy and subject to the old rules (even though it was granted after 1 January 1996). The lease must state that it is a lease under s 19 and whether it is a lease to which the new or old rules apply (s 20(2)). Covenants in the original lease which are expressed to be personal or which have been spent should not be included in the overriding lease (s 19(3) and s 19(4)(b)). The overriding lease will automatically bind a mortgagee of the landlord's interest without the need for the mortgagee's consent. However, if the mortgagee holds the landlord's title deeds the landlord must send the counterpart overriding lease to the mortgagee within one month from the date of the lease (s 20(4)). Importantly, practitioners should note that the demand for an overriding lease creates an estate contract which should be protected by a notice for registered land, or a Class C(iv) land charge for unregistered land (s 20(6)).

Lastly, it should be noted that ss 17–20 of the 1995 Act, which protect former tenants of both old and new tenancies, apply also to guarantors or sureties of the former tenant. **5.12**

KEY POINTS SUMMARY: LIABILITY OF ORIGINAL LANDLORD AND TENANT—RULES FOR OLD TENANCIES

- If the original parties remain the same then they stay liable to each other throughout the term. **5.13**
- Moreover, the original parties remain liable throughout the lifetime of the tenancy, even after they have disposed of their interests (privity of contract).
- Unusually, the parties may expressly limit this liability so that it ceases on disposal of their interest; check the terms of the lease to be sure.
- Generally, the original tenant is not liable for any additional obligations agreed by the landlord and assignee that were not contemplated in the original lease; check for any deeds of variation.
- If, following an assignment, the original tenant is sued, it can seek an indemnity from the assignee (implied by s 77 of the Law of Property Act 1925 or s 24(1) of the Land Registration Act 1925 and also the rule in *Moule v Garrett*) but this may be worthless.
- If a landlord wishes to recover a fixed charge (which includes rent or service charge) from a former tenant, the landlord must serve notice on the former tenant within six months of the charge becoming due (s 17 of the 1995 Act).
- Under s 19 of the 1995 Act, an original tenant who has made a payment under s 17 can require the landlord to grant it an overriding lease.
- The advantage of an overriding lease is that if there is further default the original tenant can take action to remedy it, eg, by forfeiting the overriding lease.
- A demand for an overriding lease should be protected by a notice registered against the landlord's title (or by a Class C(iv) land charge if the landlord's title is unregistered).

Liability of original landlord and tenant—rules for new tenancies

Here we consider the release of the outgoing tenant under s 5 of the 1995 Act, excluded assignments, assignments of part, authorized guarantee agreements and the release of the outgoing landlord under ss 6–8 of the 1995 Act. **5.14**

Release of tenant under s 5 of the Landlord and Tenant (Covenants) Act 1995 Original tenants have long objected to the unfairness of being sued many years after they have disposed of their interest, when they know nothing of the current tenant and have no control over it. The major change introduced by the 1995 Act affecting new tenancies is the release of the tenant on the assignment of the lease. This constitutes a fundamental reform of the privity of contract rule as it affects leasehold covenants. Section 5 provides that on an assignment of the whole of the leasehold premises, the tenant is automatically released from **5.15**

the tenant covenants in the lease. A 'tenant covenant' is defined simply as a covenant falling to be complied with by the tenant of the premises demised by the tenancy (s 28(1)), ie, there is no 'touch and concern' test restricting the covenant to one that affects the parties in their capacities as landlord and tenant (*Spencer's Case* (1583) 5 Co Rep 16a).

5.16 The release under s 5 applies to all assigning tenants, not just the original tenant, so that each time the lease is assigned the relevant assignor is released (provided it is not an 'excluded assignment', see para 5.19 below). However, any liability of the tenant that arose from a breach of covenant occurring before the assignment will continue (s 24(1)). A perhaps inadvertent result of this provision (applying to new tenancies only) is to change the rule that a landlord who assigns its reversion loses the right to sue for a previous breach of the tenant's covenant.

5.17 The release also applies to any other person, eg, a guarantor, who is bound by the covenants in the tenancy, to the same extent that the tenant is released (s 24(2)). Correspondingly, the tenant ceases to be entitled to the benefit of the landlord covenants in the lease as from the date of the assignment (s 5(2)). A 'landlord covenant' is defined as a covenant falling to be complied with by the landlord of the premises demised by the tenancy (s 28(1)).

5.18 Sections 77 and 79 of the Law of Property Act 1925 and s 24(1) of the Land Registration Act 1925 (discussed at 5.04 et seq above) do not apply to new tenancies. The reason for this is quite simple. As a result of the statutory release, the tenant no longer impliedly covenants on behalf of its successors and thus no longer requires an indemnity from its assignee (s 30).

5.19 **Excluded assignments**   The 1995 Act provides that the tenant shall not be released from its covenants if the assignment is classified as 'excluded'. Excluded assignments are either assignments in breach of a covenant in the tenancy (eg, a covenant not to assign), or assignments by operation of law (eg, on death or bankruptcy) (s 11(1)). If a subsequent assignment occurs that is not an excluded assignment then the tenant will be released at that time (s 11(2)(b)), unless it is required to give an authorized guarantee agreement (see para 5.21 below). The concept of excluded assignments also applies to assignments of the reversion (see para 5.30 below).

5.20 **Assignments of part**   If, unusually, the tenant assigns part only of the premises then the release will apply to the extent that the relevant covenants can be attributed to the part assigned (s 5(3)). So, for example, in a lease of an office and flat above, where the office is sold but the flat retained, the tenant would be released from the user covenant relating to the office but not that for the flat. If the position is less clear (eg, a general covenant to repair the whole building), the assignor and assignee may agree to apportion liability between them (s 9) and decide that the agreed apportionment should be binding on the landlord (s 10 and s 27). The relevant notice for service on the landlord is set out in appendix 9. If agreement cannot be reached, s 13 of the 1995 Act provides for joint and several liability on the assignor and assignee.

5.21 **Authorized guarantee agreements**   As a concession to landlords who have lost their privity of contract rights under new tenancies, the 1995 Act allows landlords to require tenants assigning their leases to enter into an authorized guarantee agreement (AGA). This is an agreement between the landlord and tenant in which the tenant who is released under s 5 guarantees the liability of its immediate successor, ie, the incoming assignee. Note that the guarantee cannot extend to any further assignees after that; or, for that matter, to the liabilities of any other person except the immediate assignee (s 16(4)).

Under s 16 of the 1995 Act, an AGA can be imposed only if the following conditions are met: **5.22**

(a)   there is an absolute or qualified covenant against assignment in the tenancy;

(b)   any landlord's consent thereby required is given subject to a condition (lawfully imposed) that requires the tenant to enter into an agreement guaranteeing the performance of the relevant covenant(s) by the assignee;

(c)   the agreement is entered into by the tenant pursuant to that condition.

Prudent landlords will want to include a provision in the lease requiring the tenant to enter **5.23** into an AGA on assignment. Indeed, this is now a standard requirement in most commercial leases and is usually imposed as a precondition to consent to assignment pursuant to s 19(1A) of the Landlord and Tenant Act 1927 (see para 3.71 above). If the former tenant under an AGA is forced to pay damages in respect of the assignee's breach of covenant or the assignee's unpaid rent, it should be remembered that it can request an overriding lease under s 19 (see para 5.10 above). In this way the former tenant will become the defaulting assignee's landlord and can take appropriate action if necessary (eg, forfeiture of the overriding lease).

The AGA may also require that if, following the assignee's insolvency, the trustee in bank- **5.24** ruptcy or liquidator disclaims the lease, the landlord can require the guarantor under the AGA to take a new tenancy expiring no later and on no more onerous terms than the assigned tenancy (s 16(5), and see the AGA precedent in appendix 2). Lastly, on a second assignment after an excluded assignment, the landlord may require the original assignor to give an AGA as well as the second assignor (s 16(6)).

Release of landlord under ss 6 to 8 of the Landlord and Tenant (Covenants) Act **5.25** **1995**   The release provisions for landlords are slightly different from those for tenants. Under s 6 of the 1995 Act, when a landlord assigns the reversion in the whole of the premises of a new tenancy, it is not, as is the case with tenants, automatically released from its obligations under the lease. Instead the landlord must apply to the tenant to be released. The reason for this is that whereas the landlord will usually have some measure of control over who comes in as tenant (through the alienation provisions), the tenant will have no corres- ponding control in respect of the assignee of the reversion. The landlord can basically sell to whomever it wants. Thus the requirement that the landlord applies for release goes some way to redress this balance.

If the landlord assigns the reversion in part only of the premises then it can apply to be **5.26** released to the extent that the relevant covenants fall to be complied with in relation to that part of those premises (s 6(3)(a)). The relevant notice for this is set out in appendix 7.

The procedure for the landlord's release is set out in s 8. It requires the landlord to serve **5.27** notice on the tenant either before or within four weeks beginning with the date of the assignment. The notice must be in a prescribed form (s 27(1)) (see appendix 7). It must inform the tenant of the assignment that has taken place (or the proposed assignment) and request that the covenant be released.

If the tenant makes no objection to the application, the covenant is released to the **5.28** extent mentioned in the notice (s 8(2)(a)). If the tenant wishes to object it must serve a counter-notice within four weeks (see precedent for this in appendix 8). The prudent tenant may decide to object if it has doubts over the creditworthiness of the proposed new landlord. This is particularly relevant where the landlord has repairing obligations under the lease. If the tenant chooses to object, the landlord may apply to the county court for a declaration that it is reasonable for the landlord to be released (s 8(2)(b)).

5.29   In similar vein to the tenant's release provisions, when the landlord is released from the covenants it ceases to be entitled to the benefit of the tenant covenants of the tenancy from the date of the assignment of the reversion (s 6(2)(b)). On a release of part, the landlord will cease to be entitled to the benefit of the tenant covenants to the extent that they fall to be complied with in relation to that part of those premises (s 6(3)(b)). However, any liability that arose from a breach of covenant occurring before the assignment will continue (s 24(1)).

5.30   As with the tenant's release provisions, the 1995 Act does not allow the landlord to be released from its covenants if the assignment of the reversion is classified as 'excluded' (for the definition of excluded assignments, see para 5.19 above). Thus an assignment of the reversion by operation of law, eg, on death or bankruptcy, would not end the continuing liability of the original landlord (s 11(1)). However, if a subsequent assignment occurs that is not excluded, the landlord can apply to be released at that time (s 11(3)(b)).

5.31   Lastly, a former landlord who on an earlier assignment of the reversion has previously applied for a release and failed (or simply failed to apply earlier), can apply for release if the present landlord makes a further assignment of the reversion (s 7). When selling a reversion prudent sellers will insist on a special condition in the contract requiring the buyer to inform them of any future sale so that they can apply for release if necessary (see generally chapter 9).

KEY POINTS SUMMARY: LIABILITY OF ORIGINAL LANDLORD AND TENANT—RULES FOR NEW TENANCIES

5.32   • If the original parties remain the same then they stay liable to each other throughout the term.
     • On an assignment of the whole of the leasehold premises the tenant is automatically released from the tenant covenants in the lease unless it has entered into an AGA.
     • Any liability that arose from a breach of covenant occurring before the assignment will continue.
     • The tenant's release does not apply to excluded assignments, ie, those in breach of covenant or following death or bankruptcy.
     • If the tenant assigns part only of the premises then the release will apply to the extent that the relevant covenants can be attributed to the part assigned.
     • The tenant ceases to be entitled to the benefit of the landlord covenants in the lease as from the date of the assignment.
     • If the tenant enters into an AGA, it guarantees the liabilities of its immediate successor/assignee.
     • Landlords should include a provision in the lease requiring the tenant to enter into an AGA on assignment.
     • When the landlord assigns its reversion it is not automatically released from its covenants; it must apply to the tenant for release.

- The landlord must serve a prescribed form of notice on the tenant either before or within four weeks from the date of the assignment.
- If the tenant wishes to object it must serve a counter-notice within four weeks.
- If the tenant objects, the landlord may apply to the county court for a declaration that it is reasonable for the landlord to be released.
- The landlord ceases to be entitled to the benefit of the tenant covenants in the lease as from the date of the assignment of the reversion.
- The landlord cannot be released if the assignment of the reversion is 'excluded', ie, in breach of covenant or following death or bankruptcy.
- A former landlord who on an earlier assignment of the reversion has previously applied for a release and failed (or simply failed to apply earlier), can apply for release if the present landlord makes a further assignment of the reversion.

Liability of assignees from original landlord and tenant

We shall now consider the liability of the assignees of the lease and reversion (ie, A or L2 in **5.33** Figure 5.1 below). Can A be sued by L or L2? Can L2 be sued by T or A? The rules that follow apply equally to subsequent assignees from L2 and A.

Figure 5.1 Assignees from original landlord and tenant

$$L \rightarrow L2$$
$$\downarrow$$
$$T \rightarrow A$$

As we have seen, with the advent of the 1995 Act there are now different rules for leases **5.34** created before 1 January 1996 ('old tenancies') and those created on or after that date ('new tenancies'). We shall discuss the effect of these rules both on an assignment of the lease and on an assignment of the reversion, in each case considering the rules for old and new tenancies respectively.

Where the lease has been assigned—rules for old tenancies Consider Figure 5.2 below **5.35** where L is the current landlord, A is the current tenant and the lease is an *old* tenancy. L and A are in a relationship of landlord and tenant and there is said to be privity of estate between them. As long as privity of estate exists, L and A will be able to sue each other for breach of covenant (ie, the benefit and burden of the covenants will run) provided the relevant covenants 'touch and concern' the demised premises (*Spencer's Case* (1583) 5 Co Rep 16a). A covenant will probably satisfy the touch and concern test if it affects the parties in their capacities as landlord and tenant (*Breams Property Investment Co Ltd v Stoulger* [1948] 2 KB 1). Thus typical covenants found in a commercial lease will

Figure 5.2 Assignment of an old tenancy

$$L$$
$$\downarrow$$
$$T \rightarrow A$$

undoubtedly 'touch and concern', eg, repair, rent, user, alienation, etc. However, a covenant giving the tenant an option to buy the reversion will not touch and concern the land because it affects the parties as seller and buyer, not as landlord and tenant (*Woodall v Clifton* [1905] 2 Ch 257). Other covenants that have been held *not* to touch and concern the demised premises are:

(a) a tenant covenant to repair property other than the demised premises (*Dewar v Goodman* [1909] AC 72);

(b) a tenant covenant to pay rates on property other than the demised premises (*Gower v Postmaster General* (1887) 57 LT 527); and

(c) a covenant allowing a tenant to erect advertising on land other than the demised premises (*Re No 1 Albermarle Street, Re* [1959] Ch 531).

5.36 An assignee of the tenant's interest (A) under an old tenancy can sue the original landlord (L) for breach of a landlord's covenant which occurs while the assignee holds the tenancy. Note that an assignee cannot sue for a breach which occurred before that time unless that right is expressly assigned to it by the assignor who had the right to sue in respect of the breach. Without such express assignment, the right to sue for a pre-assignment breach remains with the assignor (T).

5.37 **Where the lease has been assigned—rules for new tenancies** Again consider the same scenario as in Figure 5.2, but this time for a *new* tenancy.

5.38 The important point for new tenancies is that the 'touch and concern' test disappears. The 1995 Act provides that the benefit and burden of all landlord and tenant covenants will pass whether or not they have reference to the subject matter of the tenancy (s 2(1)(a)). Section 3 provides:

> (1) The benefit and burden of all landlord and tenant covenants of a tenancy
>   (a) shall be annexed and incident to the whole, and to each and every part, of the premises demised by the tenancy and of the reversion in them, and
>   (b) shall in accordance with this section pass on assignment of the whole or any part of those premises or the reversion in them.

5.39 Section 3(2) provides that the assignee of the tenancy (A) is bound by the tenant's covenants in the lease and is entitled to the benefit of the landlord's covenants. Thus L and A will usually be able to sue each other. However, there are exceptions:

(a) If the covenants did not bind the assignor (T) immediately before the assignment (s 3(2)(a)(i)), eg, where the landlord has released the tenant (T) from its covenant or has waived the right to enforce it.

(b) If the covenants relate to other premises not comprised in the assignment (s 3(2)(a)(ii)). This is to cover the situation where part of the premises is assigned.

(c) Another important exception, sometimes overlooked, is that covenants that are 'expressed to be personal' will not pass (s 3(6)(a)). It follows that if either party does not wish a covenant to bind successors, they should ensure that the lease describes it as a personal covenant.

5.40 **Where the reversion has been assigned—rules for old tenancies** Consider Figure 5.3 below, where L2 is the current landlord, T is the current tenant and the lease is an *old*

Figure 5.3 Assignment of reversion under an old tenancy

$$L \rightarrow L2$$
$$\downarrow$$
$$T$$

tenancy. Again there is privity of estate between L2 and T. The question now is whether L2 has acquired the benefit of the tenant's covenants (ie, can L2 sue T?) and whether the burden of L's covenants has passed to L2 (ie, can T sue L2?).

Section 141 of the Law of Property Act 1925 provides that the benefit of all the covenants in a lease 'which refer to the subject-matter of the lease' will run to benefit the assignee of the reversion. Likewise, s 142 of the 1925 Act provides that the burden of a covenant in a lease will run to bind an assignee of the reversion provided also that it 'has reference to the subject-matter of the lease'. This is similar to the common law 'touch and concern' test referred to above (para 5.35) and the same criteria will apply (*Hua Chiao Commercial Bank Ltd v Chiaphua Industries Ltd* [1987] AC 99, PC). However, unlike the common law test, the statutory rules do not require there to be privity of estate between the parties (*Arlesford Trading Co Ltd v Servansingh* [1971] 1 WLR 1080). Moreover, under s 141(2), L2 can sue T for breach of covenant (including arrears of rent) that occurred even before the assignment of the reversion took place. As we have seen (para 5.35 above), this is not the case where the assignee of the lease (A) sues L. In this case A cannot sue L for a breach which occurred before the assignment of the lease unless that right is expressly assigned to it by the assignor (T) who had the right to sue in respect of the breach. **5.41**

Where the reversion has been assigned—rules for new tenancies Again consider the same scenario as in Figure 5.3 above, but this time for a *new* tenancy. **5.42**

Sections 141 and 142 of the Law of Property Act 1925 do not apply to new tenancies (s 30(4)(b) of the 1995 Act). They are, of course, governed by the 1995 Act. The provisions are similar to those applicable to the assignment of a tenancy. Section 3(3) provides that the assignee of the reversion (L2) is bound by the landlord's covenants in the lease and is entitled to the benefit of the tenant's covenants. This is unless the covenants did not bind the assignor (L) immediately before the assignment (s 3(3)(a)(i)) or relate to other premises not comprised in the assignment (s 3(3)(a)(ii)). Similarly, covenants expressed to be personal will not pass (s 3(6)(a)). Section 4 provides that the benefit of the landlord's right of re-entry will pass on assignment of the reversion. This right of re-entry may be used by L2 in respect of any breach of covenant, even one occurring before the reversion was assigned (s 23(3)). **5.43**

KEY POINTS SUMMARY: LIABILITY OF ASSIGNEES OF LEASE AND REVERSION

- There are different rules for old tenancies (created before 1 January 1996) and new tenancies (created on or after that date). **5.44**
- On an assignment of an *old* tenancy, the benefit and burden of leasehold covenants will pass to the assignee of the lease provided the covenants touch and concern the demised premises (the usual lease covenants will do this); the relevant parties can then sue provided there is privity of estate.

- On an assignment of an *old* tenancy, the assignee (A) cannot sue L for a breach which occurred before the assignment of the lease unless that right was expressly assigned to it by the assignor (T) who had the right to sue in respect of the breach.
- On an assignment of a *new* tenancy, under the 1995 Act the benefit and burden of all leasehold covenants will generally pass to the new tenant unless they are expressed to be personal. There is no need to consider whether they 'touch and concern' the demised premises.
- On an assignment of the reversion of an *old* tenancy, the benefit and burden of the leasehold covenants will pass to the assignee of the reversion provided the covenants have reference to the subject matter of the lease (ss 141 and 142 of the Law of Property Act 1925); privity of estate is not essential.
- On an assignment of the reversion of an *old* tenancy, L2 can sue T for breach of covenant (including arrears of rent) that occurred even before the assignment of the reversion took place (s 141(2) of the 1925 Act).
- On an assignment of the reversion of a *new* tenancy, under the 1995 Act the benefit and burden of all leasehold covenants will generally pass to the new landlord unless they are expressed to be personal. There is no need to consider whether they have reference to the subject matter of the lease.

Enforceability of lease covenants following a sub-letting

Introduction

5.45 Here we are concerned with the enforceability of covenants between L and S, as shown in Figure 5.4 below.

Figure 5.4 Creation of a sub-lease

L
↓ Head lease
T
↓ Sub-lease
S

5.46 Although there is privity of contract and privity of estate between L and T and T and S respectively, there is neither of these between L and S. This is because L and S do not have a contract and do not enjoy a relationship with each other of landlord and tenant. Thus the general rule (subject to exceptions considered below) is that a head landlord cannot sue a sub-tenant (and vice versa). L can enforce against T but not S, and S can enforce against T but not L. Remember that T is responsible for the actions of persons deriving title under it (s 79 of the Law of Property Act 1925 for old tenancies: see para 5.04 above). Of course if L forfeits the head lease for breach of covenant then the sub-lease will become forfeited too (subject to S's right to apply for relief from forfeiture, see paras 6.114 et seq below). This would be an indirect way of L taking enforcement action against S. In addition, where rent under the head lease is in arrears, L can serve notice on S directing S to pay its rent direct to L until the arrears are discharged (Law of Distress Amendment Act 1908, s 6; see para 6.78 below).

There is an exception to the general rule that a head landlord cannot sue a sub-tenant direct. **5.47** L can enforce *restrictive* covenants against S provided the rules deriving from *Tulk v Moxhay* (1848) 2 Ph 774 are satisfied, ie, essentially if they are protected by registration (notice/ caution in registered land or a Class D(ii) land charge in unregistered land). An example of this occurred in *Hemingway Securities Ltd v Dunraven Ltd* [1995] 1 EGLR 51, where a covenant not to assign or sub-let without the landlord's consent was enforceable directly against the sub-tenant. In addition, where the head leasehold title is registered, the sub-tenant will be bound by any covenants registered against that title.

As far as new tenancies are concerned (ie, those granted on or after 1 January 1996), coven- **5.48** ants restrictive of the user of the land are enforceable against sub-tenants. Section 3(5) of the Landlord and Tenant (Covenants) Act 1995 provides that:

> Any landlord or tenant covenant of a tenancy which is restrictive of the user of the land shall, as well as being capable of enforcement against an assignee, be capable of being enforced against any other person who is the owner or occupier of any demised premises to which the covenant relates, even though there is no express provision in the tenancy to that effect.

The same principles apply even if the current head landlord and sub-tenant are not the original parties to their respective leases, ie, if L has assigned its reversion or S has assigned its sub-lease. Provided the above rules are satisfied, the current head landlord will be able to sue the current sub-tenant, and vice versa.

Our discussion so far has centred on whether L can enforce covenants in the head lease **5.49** against S. We must also consider whether L can enforce the covenants in the sub-lease (to which it was not a party) against S. It seems that this may be possible under s 56 of the Law of Property Act 1925, which provides that:

> a person may take . . . the benefit of any . . . covenant . . . respecting land, although he may not be named as a party to the conveyance [in which the covenant is made].

In *Amsprop Trading Ltd v Harris Distribution Ltd* [1997] 1 WLR 1025, the sub-tenant cov- **5.50** enanted with its immediate landlord that if it did not carry out repairs then it would allow the head landlord to do them at the sub-tenant's expense. The head landlord tried to enforce the covenant against the sub-tenant, relying on s 56 of the 1925 Act. The court rejected the argument because the covenant was not actually made with the head landlord. However, it seems that the claim would have succeeded if this had been the case. Moreover, with the Contracts (Rights of Third Parties) Act 1999 now in force, a clause in the sub-lease conferring a right on the head landlord would be enforceable by the latter notwithstanding that it was not a party to the covenant (see paras 5.53 et seq below for more on this Act).

A sub-tenant seeking to enforce a covenant against the head landlord could possibly use the **5.51** argument accepted in *Smith and Snipes Hall Farm Ltd v River Douglas Catchment Board* [1949] 2 KB 500. In this case it was held that s 78 of the Law of Property Act 1925 had the effect of extending the right to enforce a covenant to a tenant who derived title under a freeholder. However, this would not help a tenant under a new tenancy, as s 78 of the 1925 Act does not apply to new tenancies (s 30(4) of the 1995 Act).

In practice the head landlord and sub-tenant will usually create their own privity of contract. **5.52** This is because the alienation provisions of most commercial leases require the landlord's written consent before the tenant can sub-let. This consent is normally given in the form of a licence to sub-let. The head landlord will generally insist that the sub-tenant is a party to the licence and covenants directly with the head landlord to observe and perform the tenant's covenants (other than payment of rent) in the head lease so far as they relate to the sub-let premises. This is something all landlords of commercial premises should require as a matter of good practice.

Contracts (Rights of Third Parties) Act 1999—effect on sub-lettings

5.53   The head landlord and sub-tenant are both assisted by the Contracts (Rights of Third Parties) Act 1999. Section 1 of the Act provides that a person not a party to a contract will be able to enforce a term of the contract if:

(a)   the contract expressly provides that the third party should have the right to do so; or

(b)   the term of the contract purports to confer a benefit on the third party unless, on a proper construction of the contract, it appears that the parties did not intend the contract to be enforceable by the third party.

5.54   Thus a covenant by the head landlord in the head lease to insure the premises or provide services will clearly benefit a sub-tenant. Under the 1999 Act the sub-tenant will be able to enforce the covenants against the head landlord even though there is no privity of estate. Similarly, if the terms of s 1 are satisfied, the head landlord can enforce a breach of covenant by the sub-tenant in the sub-lease. Unlike s 56 of the Law of Property Act 1925, the identity or even existence of the third party taking the benefit need not be ascertained at the time the contract is entered into (s 1(3)). Moreover, the third party can be named merely as a class of persons whom the obligation is intended to benefit (eg, 'occupiers of the premises'), rather than as a specific individual.

5.55   The provisions of the 1999 Act can be excluded. Section 1(2) provides: '[unless] on a proper construction of the contract, it appears that the parties did not intend the term to be enforceable by the third party'. This is something that practitioners will need to consider at the drafting stage of the lease. If your client does not wish third parties to take the benefit of the lease covenants then, as a safety valve, the lease should expressly exclude third parties from taking the benefit. A suitable clause will read:

> The parties hereto agree and declare that the Contracts (Rights of Third Parties) Act 1999 shall not apply to this lease

5.56   Whether the third party can take the benefit of the particular covenant will depend on whether the original lease expressly provides for this or purports to confer such a benefit. The wording, 'purports to confer' (s 1(1)(b)) is important, as it will be sufficient for enforcement by identifiable third parties that the parties to the contract have not indicated otherwise. One option to overcome such a wide application would be to include a contractual term excluding s 1(1)(b) so that only third parties expressly given rights under the lease would benefit.

KEY POINTS SUMMARY: ENFORCEABILITY OF LEASE COVENANTS FOLLOWING A SUB-LETTING

5.57   • The general rule is that the head landlord and sub-tenant cannot sue each other because there is no privity of contract or privity of estate.

- A licence to sub-let will be in place for most sub-lettings, in which the sub-tenant covenants directly with the head landlord, thereby creating privity of contract.

Otherwise: **5.58**

- A head landlord can enforce *restrictive* covenants against a sub-tenant provided the rules deriving from *Tulk v Moxhay* are satisfied.
- Where the head leasehold title is registered the sub-tenant will be bound by any covenants registered against the head leasehold title.
- For new tenancies, any landlord or tenant covenant which is restrictive of the user of the land can be enforced against any other person who is the owner or occupier of the demised premises, eg, a sub-tenant (s 3(5) of the 1995 Act).
- The head landlord may be able to enforce covenants in a sub-lease against a sub-tenant by virtue of s 56 or s 78 of the Law of Property Act 1925.
- The Contracts (Rights of Third Parties) Act 1999 makes the enforcement of covenants between head landlord and sub-tenant much easier.

Contracts (Rights of Third Parties) Act 1999—enforcement of lease covenants by other tenants in a building or development

The Contracts (Rights of Third Parties) Act 1999 may also assist other tenants or occupiers in **5.59** a building or development that has a common landlord. Before the Act came into force, such tenants generally could not enforce covenants against each other. This was because they did not have privity of contract (or estate). They had to insist on a covenant by the landlord in their lease to insert similar covenants in the other leases and enforce them against the other tenants if requested (on reimbursement of costs). Clearly there will be many tenant covenants that confer benefit on other tenants in a building or development, eg, a covenant not to cause nuisance, or a covenant to use shop premises for a specified retail use. As a consequence of the 1999 Act, breach of these covenants, prima facie, will be enforceable by the other tenants directly, without recourse to the landlord.

Equitable leases

It is necessary to consider briefly the enforceability of covenants in equitable leases. An **5.60** equitable lease will arise where the formalities for a legal lease have not been observed (the lease being construed as an agreement for a lease), or where an agreement for a lease has simply never been completed. Remember the general rule that for a lease to be legal it must be by deed (s 52(1), Law of Property Act 1925) unless it is for a period not exceeding three years, in which case it can be created in writing or orally.

As against each other, the original parties will be bound in much the same way as for legal **5.61** leases (*Walsh v Lonsdale* (1882) 21 Ch D 9). For 'new tenancies', liability following an assignment of an equitable tenancy is the same as for legal tenancies (see s 28(1) of the 1995 Act, which defines a tenancy as including an 'agreement for a tenancy'). Thus the benefit and burden of all covenants will pass unless expressed to be personal. As far as an assignment of an equitable 'old tenancy' is concerned, again the position appears to be broadly equivalent to legal tenancies. Essentially, the rule in *Spencer's Case* (1583) 5 Co Rep 16a is likely to apply in the same way, so it is a matter of whether the covenants 'touch and concern' the land (*Boyer v Warbey* [1953] 1 QB 234). Assignments of the reversion to equitable 'old tenan-cies' will also be governed by ss 141 and 142 of the Law of Property Act 1925 (s 154 of the 1925 Act defines a 'lease' as including 'an under lease or other tenancy'). Thus, as with legal leases, the question is whether the covenants have reference to the subject matter of the lease.

The Code of Practice for Commercial Leases

5.62 Recommendation 16 of the Code relates to the liability of former tenants and their guaran-tors. It states, 'when previous tenants or their guarantors are liable to a landlord for defaults by the current tenant, landlords should notify them before the current tenant accumulates excessive liabilities. All defaults should be handled with speed and landlords should seek to assist the tenant and guarantor in minimising losses.' Recommendation 17 goes on to encourage landlords who sell their reversionary interest to take legal advice about ending their ongoing liability under the lease. As previously mentioned in this chapter, landlords can seek agreement from the tenant to end their liability or apply to the court for a release (see paras 5.25 et seq above).

B   INSOLVENCY AND DISCLAIMER

5.63 A commercial lease will usually allow the landlord to forfeit the lease upon the first stage of a tenant's insolvency, eg, the presentation of a petition for bankruptcy or an administration order. Thus the landlord may already have recovered the premises before any insolvency proceedings have become fully operational. The following is intended only as a brief sum-mary of the important aspects of insolvency as it affects landlords, tenants and other con-nected persons (eg, guarantors). For a more detailed analysis of this area of law, you are recommended to consult a specialized insolvency text. This applies particularly to the com-plex problems that can arise when a tenant is seeking to enforce covenants against an insolvent landlord.

Background

5.64 Insolvency (ie, bankruptcy) proceedings are normally begun by a creditor presenting a peti-tion in bankruptcy against a debtor (although it is possible to petition for one's own bank-ruptcy). If it is shown that the potential bankrupt is unable to pay his debts as they become due, the court will make a bankruptcy order. The control of the bankrupt's assets passes initially to the Official Receiver. A trustee in bankruptcy is then appointed and the bank-rupt's assets vest automatically in the trustee by virtue of the Insolvency Act 1986, s 306. Where the bankrupt is a company the insolvency proceedings are known as liquidation and the equivalent of the trustee in bankruptcy is called a liquidator.

5.65 A petition in bankruptcy or liquidation is registered by the bankruptcy court against the name of the potential bankrupt in the register of pending actions at the central Land Charges Department in Plymouth. This will be revealed by any land charges search against the potential bankrupt's name. If in addition the potential bankrupt owns registered land, the court will register a creditor's notice in the proprietorship register of the registered title. The effect of this is that any subsequent disposition of the registered title will be subject to the claims of the creditors (unless the subsequent disposition has been afforded priority protection by an official search).

Tenant's bankruptcy

When a tenant becomes bankrupt the lease will vest in the trustee in bankruptcy who takes **5.66** over the obligation to pay rent and observe and perform the other tenant's covenants in the lease. This is classed as an involuntary assignment and will not breach the tenant's alien- ation covenant in the lease. The trustee may seek to raise money by selling the lease, but, in most cases, a commercial lease at a rack rent has little or no capital value. The trustee therefore usually views the lease as an onerous liability, which he or she will wish to disclaim as soon as possible. The trustee may disclaim onerous property under s 315 of the Insolvency Act 1986. Notice of disclaimer of a lease must be given to the landlord on a prescribed form. A landlord who is anxious to know whether the trustee will disclaim can serve a request on the trustee under s 316. The trustee then has 28 days to disclaim, after which the right to disclaim is lost. The effect of disclaimer is considered below (para 5.69).

Once a petition in bankruptcy has been presented, the court is able to order a stay on any **5.67** action, execution or other legal process against the property of the debtor (Insolvency Act 1986, s 285(1)). Moreover, once a bankruptcy order is made, leave of the court is required before creditors can seek a remedy against the bankrupt's property in respect of a provable debt in the bankruptcy (s 285(3)). This may obviously affect a landlord, although it seems that the remedy of forfeiture remains unaffected by this provision (see *Razzaq v Pala* [1997] 38 EG 157).

Tenant's liquidation

Unlike bankruptcy, when a company tenant goes into liquidation the lease does not pass **5.68** to the liquidator but remains vested in the tenant which retains the obligations to pay rent, etc. The disclaimer provisions are very similar to those of the trustee in bankruptcy (see ss 178–181, Insolvency Act 1986). Although it would be quite usual to see a disclaimer of a lease in a creditor's voluntary liquidation or a compulsory liquidation, it is unlikely to occur in a member's voluntary liquidation. In the latter case, the landlord can make an unliquidated claim for any loss arising from the disclaimer. In a compulsory liquidation, once a winding- up order has been made, no proceedings against the company can be continued or initiated without leave of the court (this includes forfeiture proceedings but not peaceable re-entry). In a voluntary liquidation, the court may stay proceedings upon application by the liquid- ator. A stay in proceedings might adversely affect a landlord seeking to enforce a tenant's covenants. However, it would not prevent a landlord from serving notice on a sub-tenant under s 6 of the Law of Distress Amendment Act 1908 (ie, requiring the sub-tenant to pay its rent direct to the head landlord; see para 6.78 below).

The consequences of disclaimer

If the trustee in bankruptcy or liquidator disclaims the lease, the effect will be to terminate **5.69** all rights, liabilities and interests of the bankrupt in the lease. It will also discharge the trustee from personal liability in respect of the property. If the landlord wishes to claim unpaid rent or damages for breach of covenant then it must do so by proving in the bank-ruptcy as an unsecured creditor. If the bankrupt was the original tenant (with no guarantor or sub-leases in place) then the lease will end and the landlord can recover possession. However, where there are guarantors or sub-tenants, or the bankrupt tenant is an assignee, the position is more complex. These issues are now considered.

Guarantors, sub-tenants and assignees

5.70   In most cases the liability of any guarantor of the bankrupt tenant under its guarantee will not cease on a disclaimer of the lease by the trustee or liquidator. This will include the liability of any guarantor under an authorized guarantee agreement (AGA) (see paras 5.21 et seq above). The reason for this is that carefully drafted guarantees (ie, those contained in the lease or AGA) ought to require the guarantor to take a new lease from the landlord if disclaimer occurs. The new lease will usually be for a term commencing on the date of disclaimer and ending on the expiry date of the disclaimed lease, at the rent payable at the time of disclaimer and upon the same terms and conditions of the disclaimed lease (see AGA precedent in appendix 2).

5.71   Section 315(3) of the Insolvency Act 1986 provides that the disclaimer 'does not . . . affect the rights or liabilities of any other person'. Accordingly, although the lease will have ended, the landlord may be able to pursue other persons who have covenanted directly with it, eg, the original tenant (if the bankrupt was an assignee), intermediate assignees and their guarantors, a former tenant under an AGA, or a sub-tenant. Effectively, the tenancy is deemed to continue for the purpose of preserving the liability of these persons (see the important House of Lords' decision in *Hindcastle Ltd v Barbara Attenborough Associates Ltd* [1996] 15 EG 103). Under s 320 of the Insolvency Act 1986 such persons have the option to apply to the court for an order for the lease to be vested in them. In this way the guarantor, former tenant or sub-tenant can assume greater control by taking possession of the property. More commonly, however, they will try to divest themselves of continuing liability by assigning the lease to a tenant more acceptable to the landlord. If a vesting order is made in favour of a sub-tenant, the effect is to make the sub-tenant the immediate tenant of the landlord.

Tenant in receivership

5.72   A tenant is in receivership when a chargee or mortgagee of the tenant under the provisions of its charge appoints a receiver. A receiver under the Law of Property Act 1925 can be appointed under a fixed charge of land, but this would be rare in the context of a commercial lease. As we have seen, this is due to the fact that commercial leases at rack rents have little or no capital value and are thus usually worthless in their own right as security. An administra-tive receiver may be appointed under a floating charge secured on the whole undertaking and assets of the company, provided the floating charge is dated before 15 September 2003. Indeed, if a company is in financial difficulty a mortgagee will normally wish to appoint an administrative receiver under its floating charge before an administrator can be appointed by the court (see para 5.75 below). In this way the chargee will retain control over the conduct and timing of the sale of the company's assets.

The receiver's job essentially is to seize and dispose of the charged assets in order to repay **5.73** the outstanding indebtedness to the chargee. This may involve assigning the lease with the landlord's consent, but the landlord will probably insist that all arrears of rent and other losses are discharged before giving its consent. The receiver is instructed by the chargee but acts as agent for the borrower, and thus incurs no personal liability under the covenants in any lease. If the lease is onerous the receiver cannot disclaim it. Instead, the chargee will either release the property from the charge, or instruct the receiver to seek a surrender of the lease to the landlord. The fact that the tenant is in receivership will not adversely affect the landlord's ability to forfeit the lease.

On 15 September 2003 the corporate insolvency provisions of the Enterprise Act 2002 came **5.74** into force, and for most floating charges created on or after this date it is no longer possible to appoint an administrative receiver (there are very limited exceptions). The charge holder can now appoint an administrator under a new fast-track procedure by completing a set of forms which are then filed at court. However the administrator as an officer of the court owes allegiance to all creditors, not just the charge holder. Administration is now considered.

Administration

On 15 September 2003 the Enterprise Act 2002 introduced a new fast-track procedure to **5.75** enable floating charge holders (as well as the company, its directors and the court) to appoint an administrator. Administration is a process designed to assist companies in financial difficulty. The administrator is an officer of the court and must do all that is necessary for the management of the affairs, business and property of the company with a view to rescuing it. This management will include handling the company's obligations under a commercial lease and possibly the disposal of any premises that are surplus to requirements. The administrator is an agent of the company and thus incurs no personal liability under the lease. Unlike a liquidator or trustee in bankruptcy, the administrator cannot disclaim the lease.

While a company is in administration any new or existing proceedings cannot be brought or **5.76** continued against the company without leave of the court or the administrator. This includes forfeiture by way of peaceable re-entry. Leave for forfeiture will normally be granted unless it would seriously hinder the administration or impose loss on others greater than the landlord's loss. For further consideration of the grounds when a court will grant leave, see *Re Atlantic Computer Systems Plc* [1992] 1 All ER 476. Note that generally leave will not be given while the purpose of the administration is still attainable.

KEY POINTS SUMMARY: INSOLVENCY AND DISCLAIMER

- A landlord of a commercial lease will usually want to be able to forfeit the lease upon the **5.77** tenant's insolvency; check to see whether it has been built into the forfeiture clause.
- On a bankruptcy (ie, non-corporate tenant) the lease will vest in the trustee in bankruptcy who takes over the obligations to pay rent and observe and perform the other tenant's covenants in the lease.
- The trustee in bankruptcy of a commercial tenant will normally wish to disclaim a rack rented business lease because it has little or no capital value, ie, it is onerous.

- The effect of disclaimer is to terminate all rights, liabilities and interests of the bankrupt in the lease. It will also discharge the trustee from personal liability in respect of the property.
- Notice of disclaimer must be given to the landlord in a prescribed form.
- Insolvency proceedings will result in a stay in proceedings against the bankrupt's property, although a landlord's right to forfeiture is normally unaffected.
- On a liquidation (ie, corporate tenant) the lease does not pass to the liquidator but remains vested in the tenant who retains the obligations to pay rent, etc.
- Following a disclaimer, depending on the terms of the guarantee, a guarantor (including one under an AGA) may be required to take a new lease of the property; check the guarantee.
- Notwithstanding disclaimer, the tenancy is deemed to continue for the purpose of preserving the liability of other persons, eg, intermediate, directly covenanting assignees, their guarantors and directly covenanting sub-tenants.
- Such persons have the option to apply to the court for an order for the lease to be vested in them.
- A charge holder can no longer appoint an administrative receiver under a floating charge if the charge is dated on or after 15 September 2003.
- A new fast-track procedure is available to appoint an administrator, but an administrator is an officer of the court and owes allegiance to all creditors of the company, not just the charge holder.
- The administrator's aim is to rescue the ailing company by managing the company's business, including handling the company's obligations under a commercial lease and possibly disposing of the lease.
- While a company is in administration, any new or existing proceedings cannot be brought or continued against the company without leave of the court or the administrator.

C SURRENDER

5.78 A lease is surrendered when the tenant, with the landlord's consent, gives back the remainder of the tenant's interest to the landlord. On surrender the lease is simply extinguished by being absorbed back into the reversion. The lease is said, therefore, to 'merge' in the reversion (the concept of merger is considered further at paras 5.91 to 5.92 below). So if, for example, the landlord is the freeholder, the lease would merge in the freehold and disappear, and we would be back to one estate instead of two. Note that the landlord must agree to the surrender (which can be implied); the tenant cannot surrender unilaterally.

5.79 Following surrender, the landlord and tenant can still sue each other for pre-surrender breaches of covenant (*Dalton v Pickard* [1926] 2 KB 545; *Brown v Blake* (1912) 47 LJ 495). This is unless they agree to release their liability in respect of past breaches as well (*Deanplan v Mahmoud* (1992) 64 P & CR 409). When advising a tenant you should always seek a full release of all breaches by the tenant. If there is more than one tenant, the surrender will be ineffective unless all tenants join in the surrender (*Greenwich LBC v McGrady* (1982) 81 LGR 288).

Surrender may occur expressly or impliedly by operation of law. For the sake of certainty, **5.80** practitioners should endeavour to document all surrenders expressly by deed, rather than rely on operation of law. Moreover, it is no longer possible to avoid stamp duty by taking the operation of law route (see para 5.86 below).

Express surrender

An express surrender must be made by deed since it is a dealing with a legal estate in land **5.81** (s 52, Law of Property Act 1925). The exemption for short leases, ie, less than three years (s 54(2), 1925 Act), applies to their grant but not to their surrender. Even if the formalities for surrender are not observed, the surrender may be implied from the circumstances (an implied surrender does not require a deed (s 52(2)(c), Law of Property Act 1925)). More-over, if the deed is defective in some way (eg, unwitnessed), the surrender may take effect in equity as a contract to surrender, provided it complies with s 2 of the Law of Property (Miscellaneous Provisions) Act 1989. If the consideration exceeds the stamp duty threshold then the transaction will, prima facie, be subject to stamp duty land tax.

Agreements to surrender

A landlord and tenant must take care when agreeing to surrender in the future a business **5.82** lease protected by Pt II of the Landlord and Tenant Act 1954. Under the 1954 Act, as amended by the 2004 reforms, parties wishing to make this sort of agreement have to follow similar arrangements as for contracting out of the 1954 Act (see para 7.11 below). The landlord must give the tenant a warning notice explaining the implications of agreeing to surrender the tenancy, ie, that the tenant's renewal rights will be lost. The landlord must send the notice at least 14 days before the agreement to surrender (not the surrender itself) comes into effect. The tenant must sign a simple declaration that he or she has read and understood the notice and accepted its consequences. Alternatively, if the parties cannot wait for 14 days, or do not wish to, the tenant must sign a statutory declaration before a solicitor confirming that he or she has read and understood the notice and accepted its consequences. The lease must then include wording or be endorsed to say that the landlord has served the notice and that the parties have followed the correct procedure.

Rarely, you will find a business lease requiring the tenant to offer to surrender the lease **5.83** before seeking the landlord's consent to assign (known as a 'surrender-back' clause). In this case, any resulting agreement to surrender will be void and unenforceable. This is because the agreement to surrender effectively precludes the tenant from applying at the end of the term for a new tenancy under the 1954 Act (see *Allnatt London Properties Ltd v Newton* [1984] 1 All ER 423).

Implied surrender

An implied surrender occurs by operation of law where the parties' conduct unequivocally **5.84** amounts to an acceptance that the tenancy has ended. As Peter Gibson J stated in *Tarjomani v Panther Securities Ltd* (1982) 46 P & CR 32, at 41: 'There must either be relinquishment of possession and its acceptance by the landlord, or other conduct consistent only with the cesser of the tenancy, and the circumstances must be such as to render it inequitable for the tenant to dispute that the tenancy has ceased.' From this it can be seen that the principle of implied surrender is very much based on the doctrine of estoppel. Mere inaction on the landlord's part will generally not amount to an acceptance of a surrender (*Belcourt Estates Ltd v Adesina* [2005] All ER (D) 293).

5.85 There have been several cases that shed light on the type of conduct that is sufficient to amount to an implied surrender. If the landlord grants a new tenancy to the tenant while the old tenancy is still subsisting then, irrespective of the parties' intentions, the old tenancy will be surrendered by operation of law (*Jenkin R Lewis & Son Ltd v Kerman* [1970] 3 All ER 414). The tenant who gives back possession to the landlord is another obvious example. However, in *Hoggett v Hoggett and Wallis* (1979) 39 P & CR 121, it was held that the fact that the tenant's wife was still living in the premises prevented a valid surrender. In *Preston BC v Fairclough* (1982) 8 HLR 70 it was held that if the tenant abandoned the premises it would not constitute a surrender if the landlord took no action to indicate that it thought the tenancy was at an end. Handing back keys is often considered good enough, but the act of giving back a key to a landlord will constitute surrender only if the landlord's intention is sufficient and the act is unequivocal. Thus in *Proudreed Ltd v Microgen Holdings Plc* [1996] 1 EGLR 89, CA, although the landlord accepted the keys he did not intend to accept the offer of surrender until the property was successfully re-let to another tenant. Further, in *Boynton-Wood v Trueman* (1961) 177 EG 191, there was no surrender as the key was handed back to enable the landlord to carry out repairs; the act was thus not unequivocal. In *Arundel Corp v The Financial Training Co Ltd* [2000] 3 All ER 456 the tenant left the key with the landlord who accepted it as surrender by re-letting the premises. If the tenant agrees to remain in the property as a rent-free licensee instead of a tenant then an implied surrender of the tenancy will occur (*Foster v Robinson* [1951] 1 KB 149, CA).

5.86 Practitioners should be aware that a surrender by deed or by operation of law is a land transaction for the purposes of stamp duty land tax. Accordingly, when applying to close a registered leasehold title, the Land Registry will require not only evidence of the acts which gave rise to the surrender, but also a Land Transaction Return Certificate or self certificate. For a surrender by operation of law a statutory declaration will be needed giving evidence of the facts of the implied surrender. The statutory declaration should:

(a)   contain detailed information about the acts that amount to the surrender;

(b)   confirm that no instrument of surrender was entered into; and

(c)   recite any consideration paid for the surrender.

Surrender and re-grant

5.87 As we have seen, if the landlord grants a new tenancy to the tenant while the old tenancy is still subsisting then, irrespective of the parties' intentions, the old tenancy will be surrendered by operation of law. Additionally, in certain circumstances a variation of a lease can amount to a surrender and re-grant of the lease. This will be so where the variation has the effect of increasing either the extent of the let premises or the length of term (*Friends' Provident Life Office v British Railways Board* [1996] 1 All ER 336). Otherwise, whether a particular variation is sufficient to constitute a surrender and re-grant will be a question of degree in all the circumstances.

A surrender and re-grant can have serious repercussions where the original lease was granted **5.88** before 1 January 1996. Under the original lease, the original tenant is of course liable for the entire duration of the term. However, as the re-granted lease will be governed by the Landlord and Tenant (Covenants) Act 1995, the landlord will lose its privity of contract. Practitioners should therefore take great care when agreeing variations to leases to ensure that they do not inadvertently effect a surrender and re-grant. (See also how variations can operate to discharge a guarantor's liability, at paras 3.104 to 3.105 above.)

Effect of surrender on sub-leases

Any sub-lease in existence remains unaffected by the surrender of the head lease. The sub- **5.89** tenant becomes the immediate tenant of the head landlord under the terms of the sub-lease (s 139 of the Law of Property Act 1925). This is so even if the sub-lease was created in breach of covenant. On a surrender and re-grant of a head lease, any sub-lease remains unaffected; the sub-tenant continues to hold as sub-tenant just as if the head lease had never been surrendered (s 150, Law of Property Act 1925).

KEY POINTS SUMMARY: SURRENDER

- On surrender the lease is extinguished and absorbed back into the reversion. **5.90**
- Both sides must agree for the surrender to be effective.
- Acting for a tenant, try to agree that *all* breaches of covenant will be released; otherwise pre-surrender breaches will still be actionable.
- Ideally all surrenders should be made expressly and, if so, they must be by deed (s 52, Law of Property Act 1925).
- An implied surrender will occur by operation of law where the parties act in a way which is inconsistent with the continuation of the lease, eg, vacating the property, handing back keys, landlord re-letting, same parties completing a new lease before the old one ends.
- A surrender by deed or operation of law is a land transaction for the purposes of stamp duty land tax.
- An agreement to surrender a business lease will be void unless prescribed procedures are followed.
- Beware that certain variations of leases may operate as a surrender and re-grant, eg, increasing the extent of the let premises or the length of the term.
- Any sub-lease remains unaffected by the surrender of a head lease; the sub-tenant becomes the immediate tenant of the head landlord under the terms of the sub-lease.

D MERGER

Merger occurs where the tenant acquires the immediate reversion to its lease, or a third party **5.91** acquires both the lease and the immediate reversion. It is not possible for the same person to own both freehold and leasehold estates in the same property and so the lease disappears, ie, it merges into the reversion. In addition, as we have seen, a surrender of a lease also effects a merger; this is where the landlord acquires the tenant's interest. As with surrender, the covenants in the tenancy are extinguished (*Webb v Russell* (1789) 3 Term Rep 393) and any sub-lease remains unaffected by the merger of the head lease (s 139, Law of Property Act 1925). In *Golden Lion Hotel (Hunstanton) v Carter* [1965] 3 All ER 506, a landlord entered into a covenant restricting his right to build on an adjoining plot. The freehold and leasehold estates became merged and the covenant was held to be unenforceable against a subsequent buyer.

5.92 No merger will be implied if there would have been no merger in equity (s 185 Law of Property Act 1925). In equity, the two separate estates were retained if it was in a party's interest to keep them apart, or if it was a party's duty to ensure that they should not be merged. This might occur where one person owned the estates in different capacities eg, one estate as tenant for life under a trust and the other beneficially.

PRACTICAL CHECKLISTS: MISCELLANEOUS LEASE CONCERNS

Enforcing lease covenants

5.93 • If you act for an original landlord or tenant seeking to enforce lease covenants against an original landlord or tenant then both parties are mutually liable under their respective covenants (privity of contract and estate).
• If there has been an assignment of the lease or reversion, you must first ask: Was the lease granted before or after 1 January 1996, ie, is it an old tenancy or a new tenancy? This will determine which set of rules applies.
• Check the lease wording to see whether liability ceases when the party's interest is assigned (this would be unusual).
• Has there been a subsequent deed of variation of the lease? This could have the effect of releasing the original parties from their obligations.
• For *old* tenancies, the landlord will usually seek to enforce against the current tenant. However, if the current tenant is not worth suing, the landlord can pursue the original tenant or any intermediate assignees who have given direct covenants in the licence to assign; check the terms of the licences.
• Former tenants of old tenancies sued in this way are entitled to be indemnified by their immediate assignee or under the rule in *Moule v Garrett*.
• For *all* tenancies, if the landlord is seeking to recover a fixed charge from a former tenant, remember to serve notice on the former tenant within six months of the charge becoming due (s 17 of the 1995 Act)—see appendix 6.
• If you act for a former tenant who is served with a s 17 notice, consider whether the tenant should apply for an overriding lease under s 19 of the 1995 Act—see appendix 10 for a precedent.
• If you demand an overriding lease, remember that the demand creates an estate contract and must be protected by notice or a Class C(iv) land charge.
• For *new* tenancies, a tenant which assigns the lease will be released from liability unless it has entered into an AGA; when considering whom to sue, check whether an AGA is in place.
• Did the former tenant's breach occur before it assigned the lease? If so, any liability will continue in any event.

- Check that the assignment of the new tenancy was not 'excluded', ie, in breach of covenant or following death or bankruptcy. In this case the tenant will not be released from its obligations.
- If, as landlord of a new tenancy, you assign your reversion, you must apply to the tenant to be released from your obligations in the lease (see appendix 7 for a precedent)—this will not happen automatically.
- A landlord of a new tenancy can also apply for release upon the occasion of a later assignment of the reversion by its successors in title.
- To determine the liability of an assignee of the lease or reversion, refer to para 5.33 above and the key points summary that follows.
- To determine the liability of a sub-tenant and head landlord, refer to para 5.45 above and the key points summary that follows.

Insolvency and disclaimer

- The landlord may be able to forfeit the lease following the tenant's insolvency; check the **5.94** terms of the forfeiture clause in the lease.
- The trustee in bankruptcy or liquidator will normally wish to disclaim a commercial lease. This will terminate all rights, liabilities and interests of the bankrupt.
- Remember that notice of disclaimer must be served on the landlord in a prescribed form.
- Is there an AGA or other guarantee? Following a disclaimer, the guarantor may be required to take a new lease of the property; check the terms of the AGA/guarantee.
- Following a disclaimer, the landlord may still be able to sue other persons, eg, intermediate, directly covenanting assignees or sub-tenants, or their guarantors.
- Even after the appointment of an administrative receiver or administrator, the landlord may still take forfeiture proceedings (with the leave of the court or the administrator if the company is in administration).

Surrender and merger

- If the parties agree to surrender the lease, remember to document it expressly in a deed. **5.95**
- Tenants should aim to obtain a release from all liabilities, including any breaches that may have occurred pre-surrender.
- Before entering into an agreement to surrender a business lease protected by the 1954 Act, remember to follow the correct procedures; otherwise the agreement will be void.
- Be careful when agreeing a variation of a lease—it may be construed as a surrender and re-grant and turn an old tenancy into a new tenancy governed by the 1995 Act.
- On surrender of a head lease, any sub-tenant will become the immediate tenant of the head landlord under the terms of the sub-lease.
- Merger occurs where the tenant acquires the immediate reversion to its lease, or a third party acquires both the lease and the immediate reversion. A surrender of a lease will also effect a merger.

KEY DOCUMENTS

5.96 • Enterprise Act 2002
• Contracts (Rights of Third Parties) Act 1999
• Landlord and Tenant (Covenants) Act 1995
• Insolvency Act 1986
• Landlord and Tenant Act 1927
• Law of Property Act 1925
• Code of Practice for Commercial Leases in England and Wales (2nd edn)

Printed copies of legislation can be ordered from The Stationery Office (<http://www.tsoshop.co.uk>). Legislation from 1988 onwards can be downloaded free of charge from <http://www.opsi.gov.uk/acts.htm>.

The Code of Practice for Commercial Leases in England and Wales is set out in appendix 17.

6

REMEDIES

6.01   This chapter concentrates upon what can be done if a contractual party delays or defaults and if a party to a lease is in breach of a lease obligation. The first part concentrates upon contractual delays and remedies, and at the same time will highlight any differences in how these two elements are treated in the Standard Conditions of Sale (4th edn) and the Standard Commercial Property Conditions (2nd edn). The second part highlights in particular what the lessor can do if the lessee is in breach of a lease obligation, especially if there are rent arrears.

CONTRACTUAL DELAYS AND REMEDIES

A   DELAYS

6.02   In most commercial transactions, where there is to be a written agreement, practitioners will draft a form of contract to regulate all the terms of the transaction. In the rare event of an open contract where there is no agreed completion date, completion must take place within a 'reasonable time' (see *Johnson v Humphrey* [1946] 1 All ER 460). In the more likely event of a contract regulated by either the Standard Conditions (SCs) or the Standard Commercial Property Conditions (SCPCs), the completion date will be specified either on the front page of the agreement within the particulars, or (more rarely) by SC 6.1/SCPC 8.1, 20 working days after the date of the contract.

6.03   This arrangement for completion is straightforward, but what is the position if completion is delayed? This is a potential difficulty for a seller of a commercial property or lease in that buyers may exchange at an early stage when they think they have an attractive deal and will worry about the funding of the transaction after exchange of contracts. In these circumstances the seller may be kept waiting while the buyer completes the financial arrangements required to fund the purchase. The seller therefore needs to know what can be done to speed up the buyer to force completion, and thereby to compel the buyer to comply with the terms of the contract. Of course, there are circumstances where a buyer may be entitled to refuse to complete a transaction, eg, where there has been an act of fraudulent misrepresentation (see *Derry v Peek* (1889) 14 App Cas 337, HL). Alternatively, if the contract is for a sale with vacant possession then if there is an occupant in the subject premises at the time for completion, the buyer will be entitled to refuse to complete because of this extremely serious breach of the terms of the agreement. This would also apply if the seller failed to show good title. These aspects are considered later in this chapter (see paras 6.29 et seq below).

Late completion

A major problem for commercial property practitioners is what can be done if one of the **6.04**
parties delays completion. As with all conveyancing contracts, the agreement will state a
date for completion. If completion does not take place on the date stipulated in the contract,
completion will be delayed, probably as a result of the conduct of one of the parties to the
agreement. It is plain that such a delay will be a breach of contract, and it was so held in the
House of Lords in *Raineri v Miles* [1981] AC 1050—that failure to complete was a breach
entitling the innocent party to a claim for damages arising from the delay.

Can an injured party, immediately upon the happening of the breach, terminate the con- **6.05**
tract? It would seem not, because this remedy is available to the innocent party only if time
is of the essence for the completion date. When time is of the essence, there is no leeway for
delay; completion must be on the date specified, failing which all remedies will be available
to the aggrieved party. Section 41 of the Law of Property Act 1925 tried to regulate time
clauses in property contracts but only achieved further confusion (see *Stickney v Keeble* [1915]
AC 386 albeit on the similar predecessor clause to s 41, and *United Scientific Holdings Ltd v
Burnley BC* [1978] AC 604 for an idea of how differently the courts have interpreted this
statutory provision).

The position now seems to be that if a contract states a completion date without qualifica- **6.06**
tion, that date is not a strict and binding date such that it would entitle the innocent party to
withdraw from the contract as a result of the breach. On the other hand, if the completion
date is expressed to be 'time of the essence' then a strict interpretation arises. If there is a
failure to complete on the stipulated date, there will be a breach of contract of such
magnitude that the innocent party will be free to pursue all remedies, which can include
immediate termination or rescission of the contract.

Essentially, therefore, time will be of the essence for a conveyancing contract if: **6.07**

(a) the parties agree to it being written into the contract; or
(b) a notice to complete has been correctly served; or
(c) time is of the essence by necessary implication from the surrounding circumstances of
     the case.

In a contract regulated by either of the Standard Conditions, SC 6.1/SCPC 8.1 specifically **6.08**
states that time is not of the essence unless a notice to complete is served. (See para 6.19
below.) The parties to the contract can vary this term to make time of the essence, but of
course this cannot be achieved unilaterally. To make time of the essence, both of the forms
of Standard Conditions should be varied to delete the word 'not' from SC 6.1/SCPC 8.1, and
the words 'unless a notice to complete has been served' should be replaced with 'without the
necessity for the service of a notice to complete'. In addition, the words 'time shall be of the
essence of the contract' should be inserted next to the stated completion date. Although this
second element is not essential, it nevertheless will remind all parties of this critical element
of the agreement.

In the absence of a provision in the form of SC 6.1/SCPC 8.1, 'time of the essence' can also **6.09**
arise where there is no express provision referring to time being of the essence but where
the time of completion is clearly expressed to be an essential, almost paramount term.

(Examples are *Harold Wood Brick v Ferris* [1935] 1 KB 168, where completion was required 'not later than . . .', and *Barclay v Messenger* (1874) 43 LJ Ch 446, where if the purchase monies were not paid by a certain date the contract would be null and void.) Time being of the essence will also arise on the giving of a notice to complete (see para 6.19 below).

6.10 Lastly, time being of the essence will also arise by necessary implication (see *Parkin v Thorold* (1852) 16 Beav 56), and in particular from the surrounding circumstances of the transaction. For example, time being of the essence will be implied in a contract concerned with the sale of a business as a going concern where delay would have a material (and probably adverse) effect (see *Smith v Hamilton* [1951] Ch 174, regarding the sale of a shop as a going concern). The same would be true for a sale of a wasting asset such as a short leasehold interest (see *Pips (Leisure Productions) Ltd v Walton* (1980) 43 P & CR 414, which was concerned with the sale of a 21-year lease with 15 years unexpired). However, in all these cases, if the express contract terms are to the contrary, ie, they include a provision such as SC 6.1/SCPC 8.1, then the express term in the agreement will override any implication of time being of the essence. (See *Ellis v Lawrence* (1969) 210 EG 215, where the contract included express terms for the service of a notice to complete. Even though the sale was of a business as a going concern, the express terms negated any implication of time being of the essence.)

6.11 What, then, are the implications where time is not of the essence and yet one party has delayed completion? One element of this predicament is clear—the injured party cannot refuse to complete the contract. If the injured party wishes to seek to establish grounds for terminating the agreement then the appropriate course of action is to make time of the essence, and a notice to complete should be served upon the delaying party without delay. (See paras 6.19 et seq below.)

Consequences of delay: compensation

6.12 Both sets of Standard Conditions stipulate a time for completion, ie, 2 pm, after which the receipt of the completion monies is to be treated as taking place on the next working day. This will affect apportionments as well as interest payments. Thus, where there is delay in completing a transaction, that delay, however short, will amount to a breach of contract. If there is delay, even of a matter of hours (or even minutes), the innocent party is entitled to seek damages for any loss occasioned as a result of the delay. Of course in the circumstances of a brief delay of a few hours, any loss sustained is unlikely to be such as to justify taking action in the courts for breach of contract. As a result it has become the norm to include compensation provisions within the express contract terms. These compensatory terms do not preclude an action in the courts, but where such steps are taken any compensation paid under the contractual terms must be taken into account when computing damages. (Both sets of Standard Conditions include a condition (SC 7.3/SCPC 9.3) that clearly states that any loss claimed for late completion must be reduced by any contractual compensation paid by the defaulting party.)

6.13 The common law has made provision for compensation, but if certainty is required compensation terms should always be included in a commercial conveyancing contract. The common law position is that where completion is delayed in an open contract, the buyer will be entitled to any income from the property but must bear all outgoings. Furthermore, if the seller remains in the subject property, it will be required to pay a fee for occupation unless the delay has arisen as a consequence of any default by the buyer.

The seller will be entitled to interest on the unpaid purchase monies. The level of interest is   **6.14** likely to be the variable rate allowed on the court short-term investment account under the Administration of Justice Act 1965 (see *Bartlett v Barclays Bank Trust Co Ltd* [1980] Ch 515). If the seller causes the delay then he or she must pay the outgoings. Accordingly, the position at common law seems to be that the intention is to deal with the parties as if completion had actually taken place even though in reality no such step has been taken. Notwithstanding that the innocent party will be entitled to seek damages, it is clear that to allow open contract provisions to prevail in these circumstances would be unwise.

Conditions 7 and 9 in the forms of Standard Conditions cover explicit remedies where there   **6.15** is default. Little of this particular condition is changed from the SC to the SCPC, although there is one alteration of consequence for buyers. It should be noted that SCPC 9.3.1 provides that liability for interest arises only on the default of the buyer. If the seller defaults and delays completion, in the absence of a special condition all that a buyer can do is sue the defaulting seller for damages. Moreover, SCPC 9.3.4 states that if completion is delayed, the seller may give notice to the buyer that it will take the net income from the subject property until completion takes place as well as any interest due pursuant to SCPC 9.3.1. Accordingly, both sets of Conditions contain clear and precise provisions for compensation for a breach of contract that arises from delayed completion, but the SCPC clearly favour the seller. Practitioners acting for a buyer should amend this condition to make it applicable to both parties to the contract.

In contrast, SC 7.3 states that if a party to the contract defaults and delays completion, the   **6.16** defaulting party must pay compensation to the innocent party. Both parties can be liable to pay compensation, and compensation is quantified as being interest at the rate specified in the agreement as the 'contract rate' (see below) to the intent that the interest is on the unpaid purchase price. If a deposit has been paid and the buyer is in default, interest is calculated on the unpaid balance of the purchase price, or the total purchase price if the seller is in default. Interest is payable for each day that there is delay. SC 9.3.4 states that if the subject property is tenanted then the seller can elect to take the rent rather than interest. Accordingly, if the rent is likely to exceed the value of the interest, notice should be served upon the defaulting buyer to confirm that the rent is to be taken by the seller rather than interest. Of course this Standard Condition can be varied in the special conditions to allow the seller to take the interest and the rent should the buyer default and delay completion. SC 7.3 also contemplates the possibility of both parties being in default. In these circumstances, the party at greater fault must pay compensation. SCPC 9.3 simply covers compensation for default by the buyer. However, it does say in SCPC 9.3.2 that if the seller is in default, interest will not accrue if the buyer is also in default, ie, the buyer will only have to pay compensatory interest once the seller is no longer in default.

The interest rate defined by the two sets of Standard Conditions as being the 'contract rate' is   **6.17** 'The Law Society's interest rate from time to time in force'. This is declared each week in the *Law Society's Gazette*. Of course there is a gap on the front of the contract for an alternative rate to be declared, and this could be, eg, 4 per cent above the base rate of Lloyds TSB Bank Plc or such other lending rate as the Bank shall declare in place thereof'.

6.18   As mentioned above, where compensatory interest is sanctioned by the contract it will be payable on completion being delayed, even if this is only by a matter of minutes. Both sets of Standard Conditions stipulate a time and day for completion (see SC 6.1.2 and 6.1.3 and SCPC 8.1.1 and 8.1.2). It should be noted that there is no equivalent condition in the SCPCs because SC 8.1.3 stipulates that the 2 pm deadline does not apply where the seller is selling with vacant possession and has not vacated by the 2 pm limit. The omission arises from the assumption that the seller will not be in occupation of commercial premises as they will be sold subject to the occupation of the seller's commercial tenant. If the time limit is breached but completion takes place on the contractual date, completion is deemed to take place on the next working day and interest will arise. The worst time for this to occur is on a Friday, when three days' interest will arise for the period over the weekend to the next working day, being the following Monday. All this will be allowed by the contract even though completion actually took place late on the previous Friday. If the SCPCs are used this penalty is even greater, because SCPC 9.3.4 allows the seller to claim interest for the three days and rent for the same period.

Notices to complete

6.19   As we have seen, in any conveyancing contract, time is not of the essence if regulated by either of the Standard Conditions unless the special conditions provide otherwise. As a result, an innocent party suffering from a delayed completion cannot consider the agreement as repudiated as a result of the defaulting party's delay. This is an unsatisfactory position, because the defaulting party may have no intention whatsoever of completing and yet the contract would in theory subsist. To bring the matter to a head and to terminate the agreement the innocent party must take steps to precipitate a change, and this will be by way of a notice to complete. The notice will in all cases give a final date for completion, failing which there will be no further time for the defaulting party. Time is now of the essence of the contract. The notice can inform the defaulting party that unless completion takes place by the date stated in the notice, the party serving the notice will be entitled to all remedies, including a repudiation of the agreement.

6.20   Because notices to complete deal with timing, practitioners need to reflect upon two elements: first, when can the notice be served; and, secondly, how long must the notice period be before it expires?

When can a notice to complete be served?

6.21   Where there is an open contract this is open to doubt. The reason for this is that a notice to complete can be served only if sufficient time has elapsed so as to mean that any further delay would be unreasonable and unfair so far as the innocent party is concerned. The party serving the notice must be ready willing and able to complete, failing which the notice will be invalid.

6.22   Where either of the Standard Conditions apply the position is perfectly clear. SC 6.8/SCPC 8.8 states that at any time on or after the date fixed for completion, either party who is ready, able and willing to complete may give the other a notice to complete. SC 6.8/SCPC 1.1.3 goes on to define when a party is ready, able and willing, ie, it would have been in a position and ready to complete but for the default of the other party.

How long should the notice to complete period be?

In an open contract the period for completion should be what would be reasonable to allow **6.23** completion to be effected when all the outstanding steps are taken into consideration. Again this is open to doubt, and so where either of the Standard Conditions are being used, SC 6.8.3/SCPC 8.8.3 states that the parties are to complete the agreement within ten working days of the giving of the notice to complete. However, practitioners should note that the ten-day period *excludes* the day on which the notice is given. The condition goes on to state the essential wording, namely 'for this purpose, time is of the essence of the contract'. Lastly, and for what it is worth, SC 6.8.3 does say that a buyer who delays completion and has paid less than a 10 per cent deposit at exchange must pay the remaining monies required to make up a full 10 per cent deposit and must pay these monies immediately on receipt of the notice. In practice this is unlikely to happen if the reason for not completing is a lack of finance! However, under either set of Standard Conditions the seller has the authority of a written condition to claim a part of or the full 10 per cent deposit.

If there is still no completion even after the service and expiry of a notice to complete, the **6.24** Standard Conditions set out what is to be done. SC 7.5/SCPC 9.5 applies where the buyer is in default and SC 7.6/SCPC 9.6 applies where the seller defaults. There is no difference here between the two sets of conditions. If SC 7.5/SCPC 9.5 comes into operation the seller may rescind; and if there is rescission the seller may forfeit the deposit, resell the property and claim damages. These provisions are not exclusive, and the seller therefore retains all other rights and remedies that may also be available. If SC 7.6/SCPC 9.6 are operative the buyer may rescind; and if there is rescission the buyer can demand repayment of the deposit with any interest thereon. Again, these provisions are not exclusive and the buyer therefore retains all other rights and remedies that may otherwise be available. (Also see s 46 of the Law of Property Act 1925, as discussed at para 6.33 below.) In both cases the conveyancing papers must be returned and any protective registrations cancelled. Practitioners should note that the notice is binding upon *both* parties and not just the party that was originally in default (see *Quadrangle Development and Construction Co Ltd v Jenner* [1974] 1 All ER 726, CA). Thus time is of the essence for both the seller and the buyer (see *Oakdown Ltd v Bernstein & Co* (1984) 49 P & CR 282).

If you need to serve a notice to complete in connection with a contract incorporating either **6.25** of the Standard Conditions, the following is a suitable precedent. It will be addressed to the defaulting party:

> On behalf of the [insert your client seller/buyer and address] we hereby give you NOTICE that with reference to the contract dated [insert the date of the agreement] and made between [insert the seller's full names and the buyer's full names] whereby you contracted to buy [insert the property address or description in the contract] we place on record the fact that the sale/ purchase of the property has not been completed on the date fixed in the contract for completion. We further give you NOTICE that the seller/buyer [delete the party not ready] is ready able and willing to complete. We therefore give you NOTICE pursuant to condition 6.8 of the Standard Conditions of Sale (4th edition)/Standard Commercial Property Conditions (2nd edition) and require you to complete the contract in compliance with that condition.

This can be given by letter or a separate form, but whichever means is used, it should be sent **6.26** to the defaulting party in such a way that you will be able to prove delivery, ie, service of the notice. (We suggest at the very least the Special Delivery service through the Royal Mail.) If you send a letter you can also draw the recipient's attention to the period of notice (ten working days excluding the day of service) and to what the contract provides in SC 7.5/SCPC 9.5 (buyer's failure) or 7.6/9.6 (seller's failure) should completion not take place within the time limit set by the notice.

B   REMEDIES

6.27   In the large majority of conveyancing transactions, completion occurs without difficulty and the title passes unhindered from seller to buyer. However, there will always be cases where completion does not occur, or if it does occur a dispute over the subject property will arise after completion. The following paragraphs cover, first, what remedies are available if completion has not taken place, and, secondly, what remedies are available if a dispute and potential consequential claim arise after completion. In all cases where a claim is necessary, specialist litigation assistance should be suggested to the client as the best way of advancing a claim.

6.28   Of course it is always open to a party to a conveyancing contract to try to limit any liability by an exclusion clause excluding liability for a breach of contract. To be valid the exclusion clause must be contained within the written agreement and must deal with the kind of breach that has arisen (see *Curtis v Chemical Cleaning Co* [1951] 1 KB 805). Exclusion clauses must be very carefully worded, as the courts will construe any ambiguity within the clause against the party seeking to rely upon it. Practitioners should remember that conveyancing contracts do not fall within the ambit of the Unfair Contract Terms Act 1977, save for claims arising out of misrepresentation, and as such there is no test of reasonableness that can apply to an exclusion clause in a conveyancing contract (other than for misrepresentation). (See, however, the Unfair Terms in Consumer Contracts Regulations 1999 (SI 1999/2083), which came into effect from 1 October 1999 which may cover a 'non-commercial' party to the contract.)

Where the contract has not been completed

6.29   In the circumstances where a contract has not been completed, and where a cause of action has arisen, an innocent party to that contract can consider four available and different remedies. These remedies are:

(a)   specific performance;

(b)   a claim for compensation by way of damages;

(c)   rescission; and

(d)   a vendor and purchaser summons.

Specific performance

6.30   Specific performance is an equitable remedy by way of a discretionary order of the court that is intended to compel the defaulting party to perform and complete the contract for the sale and purchase of land. The remedy is available to both buyer and seller where the other party has committed a breach of contract and where an award of damages would be insufficient compensation for the party suffering loss. (This would be the case in most conveyancing matters, bearing in mind the unique nature of the subject matter of most conveyancing contracts.) The remedy can be sought along with a claim for damages or rescission, or indeed on its own, depending on the nature of the contractual dispute and the claims arising therefrom. However, in due course, and certainly by the time of the hearing, the claimant must elect to select one remedy. If a judgment for that one remedy is granted, it will thereby preclude recourse to the other remedies. Both SC 7.5 and 7.6/SCPC 9.5 and 9.6 make it clear that an innocent party's right to apply for an order for specific performance is not precluded by the fact that a notice to complete has been served and not complied with.

Completion need not have passed by before commencing an action for specific perform- **6.31** ance. In *Hasham v Zenab* [1960] AC 316, the seller, after signing the contract, then tore it up, plainly with the intention of trying to avoid the contractual liability. Immediately after, and before completion, the buyer applied for specific performance. The position of delay must also be considered in this context. In the case of *Lazard Bros & Co v Fairfield Properties* [1977] 121 SJ 793, the court held that simple delay without possession of the property is not in itself a bar to the remedy of specific performance. In this case a delay of two years was held not to be a bar because the defendant had not been prejudiced by the delay. It is therefore apparent that delay ('laches') will not necessarily defeat a claim for specific performance unless the defendant is going to be prejudiced as a consequence. Indeed, if the buyer actually takes occupation, it can rely upon its, his, or her equitable title and not take action for specific performance for as long as ten years without losing the right to the award (see *Williams v Greatrex* [1956] 3 All ER 705, CA).

Practitioners should bear in mind that this is an equitable remedy, and as such the principles **6.32** of equity will prohibit an award for specific performance where it would breach equitable principles. So, for example, where there is an element of fraud or illegality, or the award would cause one party exceptional hardship, the court will refrain from granting an order for specific performance. Furthermore, it should always be remembered that if damages would properly compensate the innocent party for the loss sustained then the court will order damages and not specific performance. Indeed, even where an order for specific performance is obtained, damages can still subsequently be ordered if the innocent party cannot enforce the order (see *Johnson v Agnew* [1980] AC 367). An award for damages can be made pursuant to s 50 of the Supreme Court Act 1981. On the other hand, it should be remembered that specific performance can be awarded before the completion of the transaction, ie, where a serious breach is likely to occur steps can be taken to seek an order for specific performance even though a breach of contract has yet to arise. (See *Manchester Diocesan Council for Education v Commercial and General Investments Ltd* [1966] 3 All ER 1563 and *Oakacre Ltd v Clare Cleaners (Holdings) Ltd* [1982] 3 All ER 667, for examples of how the courts will make such decisions.)

Damages, including forfeiting or returning the deposit

A general consideration of damages is more fully set out below at paras 6.61 et seq. However, **6.33** it is appropriate to consider at this point the question of damages and the forfeiting of any deposit. In essence, where a claim for damages is to be advanced, credit must be given for any deposit forfeited by the seller. (Indeed, this is also true for any compensation payments made pursuant to either set of Standard Conditions: SC 7.3.1/SCPC 9.3.1.) It should be borne in mind that s 46(2) of the Law of Property Act 1925 empowers the court, if it thinks it appropriate, to order the repayment of any deposit and where the court has refused to make an order for specific performance. Indeed, it has been held that the court has an unfettered discretion to order the return of the deposit if this is the fairest way of dealing with the dispute (see *Universal Corp v Five Ways Properties Ltd* [1979] 1 All ER 522, CA). This particular provision does not seem to allow a partial return of the deposit.

Rescission

6.34 Rescission has over time gathered two meanings. First, it can mean an order of the court under which the parties are put back into such a state as would have prevailed had the contract never existed. In effect the court will order the 'undoing' of the conveyancing contract. This occurs where there has been a claim arising out of some vitiating factor such as fraud, mistake or misrepresentation. This form of rescission is dealt with at paras 6.52 et seq below. Secondly, rescission can mean the result of the innocent party accepting the repudiation of the agreement as a consequence of the defaulting party's breach of a major term in the agreement. Rescission can arise in the following ways:

(a)   by a term in the conveyancing contract; or

(b)   by agreement; or

(c)   by an order of the court.

6.35 The Standard Conditions refer to rescission in three different circumstances, as discussed below.

6.36 **Condition 5.1**   This is the SC insurance clause where the risk on the property remains with the seller and, as a consequence of some catastrophic event (eg, fire), the subject property is unusable for its purpose (eg, as a residential property) and this event has taken place after exchange but before completion. The same condition in the SCPC reverses the position so that the seller is under no obligation to the buyer to insure. There is therefore no reference to rescission. SCPC 7 covers the position if the property is subject to a lease.

6.37 **Condition 7.1**   This condition (in the SCPC it is 9.1 and is the same) allows rescission for misrepresentation. Condition 7 permits rescission where any statement or plan in the contract or the negotiations leading to it is or was misleading or inaccurate as a consequence of an error or omission. However, SC 7.1.3/SCPC 9.1.3 limits this provision by allowing rescission only where there is an element of fraud or recklessness, or if, where the innocent party took the property, it would prejudicially be substantially different from that which the innocent party expected as a result of the error or omission. You should note that this is the one area of conveyancing contracts where an exclusion clause is subject to the reasonableness test within s 11 of the Unfair Contract Terms Act 1977.

6.38 **Condition 8.3**   Where the subject property is leasehold, and where the lease terms require the landlord's consent or licence to a change of tenant, under SC 8.3, if that licence to assign is not forthcoming either party can seek rescission. The SCPCs are different—SCPC 10.3.6 states that at any time after four months from the original completion date either party may rescind if the lessor's licence to assign has not been given and there is no court declaration of unreasonableness on the part of the lessor. The purpose of this provision is to take into account the fact that when licences to assign are sought in commercial transactions, lessors can be slow in giving consent.

It is always open to the parties to a contract mutually to agree to rescind the contract. This is **6.39** rescission by agreement, ie, the parties mutually agree to put aside the agreement and to undo its effect.

In the past the courts have been reluctant to allow a claimant to seek rescission and, in the **6.40** alternative, damages. However, it would seem that the modern position is to allow this alternative claim (see *Johnson v Agnew* [1976] 1 All ER 883). It seems that where the contract is rescinded as a result of the other side's breach, rescission and damages will be allowed. If rescission is sought as a consequence of a vitiating element then there can be no claim for damages. (This is not the case for misrepresentation, where s 2(1) of the Misrepresentation Act 1967 permits the innocent party to claim damages and rescission.)

To summarize, if there is misrepresentation or mistake, rescission can arise on the funda- **6.41** mental basis of the undoing of the contract. If there is a defective title, failure to complete or misdescription, rescission can arise for the breach of contract. Lastly, rescission can of course also arise under the terms of the contract. If this is the case then, when it is exercisable, the ramifications are also governed by the contract terms.

Vendor and purchaser summons

Section 49(1) of the Law of Property Act 1925 provides that 'a vendor or purchaser of any **6.42** interest in land may apply in a summary way to the court in respect of any requisitions or objections, or any claim for compensation or any other question arising out of or connected with the contract', and if such an application is made the court can 'make such order upon the application as to the court may appear just'.

This procedure allows either party to a conveyancing contract to apply to court for its delib- **6.43** eration on a point of dispute without having to apply for specific performance. An example of what could give rise to a summons of this kind is a reference to the court to ascertain if the seller has shown good title and thus complied with the terms in the contract to that effect. If the court did decide that good title had not been shown, the court could order the return of the deposit with interest and costs. Other examples of the kind of dispute that can be referred to the court are whether or not a requisition is valid and whether or not there has been a valid notice to complete. However, the procedure cannot be used to test the validity, or indeed existence, of a contract.

Post-completion

Completion of a conveyancing contract narrows down the available remedies. In the main it **6.44** is the buyer who will commence proceedings as the seller will have the sale proceeds. If, unusually, the doctrine of merger effectively puts paid to the terms of the contract (see paras 6.45 et seq below), the aggrieved buyer can only sue for damages on the covenants for title through title guarantee, implied in the purchase deed. Other post-completion remedies are considered at paras 6.52 et seq below.

Covenants for title and title guarantee—the new regime

6.45 The doctrine of merger stipulates that, subject to any contractual terms to the contrary, on completion the contract terms merge with the purchase deed and are thereby extinguished. (However, see SC 7.4/SCPC 9.4, which states that completion does not cancel liability to perform any outstanding obligation under the contract.) As a consequence, after completion the primary remedy is an action for breach of title guarantee where completion was effected after 1 July 1995, and an action for breach of implied covenants for title for cases completed before that date. The new regime of title guarantee is governed by the Law of Property (Miscellaneous Provisions) Act 1994, while the old regime was regulated by s 76 of the Law of Property Act 1925. It is probable that most practitioners will not encounter a dispute centred upon the old regime and so we shall concentrate upon the new scheme.

6.46 The new title guarantee regime contemplates just three alternatives: full title guarantee, limited title guarantee, or no guarantee at all. In the last situation the contract will offer no form of guarantee whatsoever, to the intent that there will be no post-completion remedy arising out of the guarantee available to an innocent party in the event of a dispute occurring after completion. The remaining two possibilities are full and limited guarantees, which are in effect statutory guarantees that will be implied in a purchase deed by the use of brief phrases declared by the 1994 Act to be 'with full guarantee' or 'with limited guarantee'. In both sets of Standard Conditions, condition 4.5.2 stipulates that where the contract is silent as to title guarantee, the seller is to transfer with full title guarantee.

6.47 The concept of title guarantee is a new approach that is a distinct change from the old regime where the capacity of the seller implied differing covenants for title. For example, in the old regime more detailed covenants were implied by 'beneficial owners' than by 'trustees'. This is not the case in the new regime, where the contract need not refer to the capacity of the seller and need only refer to the level of guarantee on offer. Indeed, there is nothing in the 1994 Act that prohibits the extent or the level of guarantee being modified further by the terms of the contract.

6.48 If the seller sells with full title guarantee, the seller covenants:

- (a) that the seller has the right to sell the property;
- (b) that the seller will at the seller's cost do all things that can be reasonably done to give to the buyer the title the seller purports to give;
- (c) if the nature of the title to the subject property is not clear, that it is therefore freehold;
- (d) if the property is registered, that the buyer will receive at least the class of title that prevailed before the transfer;
- (e) that the seller will provide reasonable assistance to enable the recipient to be registered as proprietor of the registered land;
- (f) if the interest is registered, that it must be presumed that the disposition is of the whole interest;
- (g) where the interest passing is leasehold, that the disposition is of the whole of the unexpired portion of the term of years created by the lease, that the lease still subsists and that there is no subsisting breach that could give rise to forfeiture;
- (h) that the person making the disposition disposes of it free from all charges and encumbrances and from all other rights exercisable by third parties other than those

that the person does not and could not reasonably be expected to know about. (Remember that the contract will include specific reference to encumbrances expressly subject to which the property will be sold.)

If the seller sells with limited title guarantee, the seller covenants that all the covenants set **6.49** out above will be complied with, save in relation to the last covenant which is replaced by a covenant that the person making the disposition has not since the last disposition for value charged or encumbered the property which still exists, or granted third party rights which still exist.

Title guarantees are covenants that run with the land and can therefore be enforced by **6.50** successors in title. A breach of these implied covenants gives rise to a remedy equivalent to an action for a breach of contract, with all the attaching rights and claims. Because completion has taken place it is probable that the only likely result would be for an order for damages.

A practitioner will normally advise the client to offer a full title guarantee. However, a **6.51** limited title should be suggested for a sale by a personal representative or trustee. No doubt sellers of commercial property will seek to sell with limited title guarantee, but there is really no reason why the buyer should accept this, on the assumption that there is no difficulty with the subject title.

Other post-completion remedies

These remedies cover, inter alia, fraud, innocent misrepresentation and mistake, as well as **6.52** rectification. They in effect exist to cover situations where one or more of these factors apply and the transaction could as a consequence be set aside. (This has become known as rescission, in respect of which there will be a complete undoing of the conveyancing agreement, provided of course that there is an entitlement to rescind.)

A misrepresentation is an untrue factual statement made by one party and relied upon by **6.53** the other, and which induces the other party to enter into the contract who as a consequence suffers loss. A misrepresentation can be deliberately dishonest and is then termed a fraudulent misrepresentation. To a lesser degree, the misrepresentation can be simply careless, when it is termed a negligent misrepresentation. Alternatively, and to a lesser degree again, the misrepresentation may be made innocently and be a genuine mistake, when it will be termed an innocent misrepresentation.

If there is a suggested fraud (see *Derry v Peek* (1880) 14 App Cas 337 for a test of what will **6.54** amount to fraud), the aggrieved party may sue for damages (by way of the tort of deceit) and rescind the contract. The problem here is that the party alleging fraud must prove it. This is likely to be difficult and costly. Consequently, actions are more usual at the lower level of negligent misrepresentation. Where this is so, the innocent party may take action pursuant to s 2 of the Misrepresentation Act 1967 for either damages or rescission of the contract. If the misrepresentation was innocent, the only remedy available is rescission.

A misdescription is an error in the property particulars of the contract. A patent example **6.55** would be to state incorrectly the tenure as freehold when it is in fact leasehold, or vice versa. If the misdescription is sufficiently significant it will entitle the innocent party to seek rescission and damages. A significant misdescription is one that would lead to the innocent party being deprived of what it thought it was going to receive under the terms of the contract (see *Watson v Burton* [1956] 3 All ER 626). Since the enactment of the Misrepresentation Act 1967, most such cases will fall within a claim for misrepresentation.

6.56 Non-disclosure can arise where the seller has not complied with its obligation to disclose matters in the contract or within documents referred to in the contract. Again, if the non-disclosure is sufficiently significant, so as to lead to the innocent party being deprived of what it thought it was going to receive under the terms of the contract, that party may seek to rescind the contract.

6.57 Rectification can arise in different ways. Both the contract and purchase deed can be the subject of rectification. If the contract is involved then an application to the court can be made. If rectification is ordered to correct either an omission or an incorrectly recorded contract term, the court has the discretion to set the date upon which the contract is effective. If the purchase deed is involved, again an application to the court can be made to ensure that all the terms in the contract (and which should be in the purchase deed) are indeed incorporated within it.

6.58 Whereas the Land Registration Act 1925 talked about 'rectification' of the register, the Land Registration Act 2002 ('the Act') provides for 'alteration' of the register of title (s 65, Sch 4) (ss 20–21). Under the Act, rectification is just one kind of alteration and is defined as one which involves the correction of a mistake *and* which prejudicially affects the title of a registered proprietor (Sch 4, para 1). As a result of the latter, a right to indemnity will naturally flow from rectification. The court and the registrar are both given powers under the Act to alter the register (Sch 4, paras 2–7).

6.59 The Act contains a specific rule-making power to enable the registrar to correct a mistake in an application or accompanying document. In the circumstances prescribed in such rules, the correction will have the same effect as if made by the applicant or interested parties (Sch 10, para 6(e)). This effectively replicates r 13 of the Land Registration Rules 1925, which presently allows the registrar to correct clerical errors.

6.60 The Act sets out the circumstances in which a person who suffers loss is entitled to be indemnified (Sch 8, para 1(1)). Importantly, the substance of the indemnity provisions in the Act does not differ in any significant way from the existing indemnity provisions in the 1925 Act (as amended by s 2 of the Land Registration Act 1997).

Damages

6.61 A claimant involved in a claim arising from an uncompleted or completed conveyancing contract may be entitled to damages. A successful commercial conveyancing contract claim will give rise to damages in just the same way as for all other contracts (see *Hadley v Baxendale* (1854) 6 Exch 341 for remoteness of damages), in that the general common law rules will apply. Consequently, the party entitled to claim will be able to seek to recover losses arising naturally from the breach, or losses that can reasonably be supposed to have been contemplated by both parties to the agreement as the probable result of the breach of contract.

6.62 Substantial damages can be claimed, especially where the contract has not been completed.

In *Beard v Porter* [1948] 1 KB 321, the transaction was not completed because the seller could not comply with the contract and give vacant possession to the buyer. As a consequence, substantial damages were awarded to the purchaser, based upon the difference between the purchase price and the value of the property still subject to the tenancy, as well as other consequential costs. Similarly, in *Cottrill v Steyning and Littlehampton Building Society* [1966] 2 All ER 265, a seller knew that the buyer was intending to develop the subject property. The seller failed to complete. The substantial damages awarded were based upon the potential profit the buyer would have made had the transaction been completed properly. Wasted expenses can also be claimed, including wasted legal fees and proper surveying fees. Other expenses claims are likely to fail, eg, the cost of carpets and curtains purchased before the property purchase has actually taken place. The courts take the view that these are expenses a prudent buyer should not incur until completion has taken place.

Both sets of Standard Conditions limit any potential claim for damages in cases of misrepresentation. SC 7.1.2/SCPC 9.1.2 state that when there is a material difference between the description or value of the subject property as represented and as it is, the injured party is entitled to damages. This effectively limits any claim for damages for misrepresentation to just this difference. **6.63**

Damages will be assessed as at the date of the breach (see *Johnson v Agnew* [1980] AC 367), but if that principle is likely to cause injustice the court will assess damages at another date (see *Forster v Silvermere Golf and Equestrian Centre Ltd* (1981) 42 P & CR 255). However, damages are not a mechanism by which the claimant can be put into a better position than that which would have prevailed had the transaction been completed. In all cases there is a duty to mitigate the loss, ie, the claimant must take all reasonable steps to reduce (or even avoid) the loss (*Raineri v Miles* [1976] 3 All ER 763, at 774). This duty applies to either a buyer or a seller seeking damages. For example, if a buyer is forced to store furniture as a result of a breach of contract by the seller, the storage charges should be at a reasonable level, ie, not the most expensive, as the buyer will be under a duty to keep these costs down. **6.64**

Liens

A seller will be entitled to claim a lien (ie, a right to retain possession of another's property pending discharge of a debt) over the subject property in relation to any unpaid element of the purchase price. The lien is in effect an equitable charge enforceable by the court by way of an order for the sale of the property or for the setting aside of the contract. The lien should always be protected by a caution or notice on the title for registered land and as a class C(iii) registration for unregistered land. **6.65**

A complication relating to the existence of a lien arises when the contractual parties agree to leave monies unpaid at completion. As a matter of course, conveyancing practitioners routinely include in a purchase deed a receipt clause. For unregistered land, s 68 of the Law of Property Act 1925 states that the inclusion of such a receipt clause is good evidence of the discharge of the seller's lien because it confirms full payment. For registered land, in the absence of a protective entry on the register a subsequent buyer will take free of a lien. **6.66**

Accordingly, if the seller agrees to allow a part of the purchase monies to be unpaid on completion, the purchase deed should exclude the routine receipt clause. If this approach is adopted the Land Registry will assume that there is a vendor's lien and will make an entry on the register to record it. A mortgage given by the buyer to the seller to protect the unpaid portion of the purchase price will override any lien.

6.67 A buyer is entitled to claim a lien if the deposit is returnable and was paid over originally to the seller's practitioner as agent for the seller. The lien claimed will be in respect of the deposit monies. The lien should also be protected by registration. Practitioners must remember that SC 6.5.1 prohibits any entitlement on the seller's part to a lien over the title deeds after completion and after the buyer has tendered all the money due to be paid over at completion. SCPC 8.5.1 is different, in that it says that the seller must part with the documents of title as soon as the buyer has complied with all its obligations. This is in contrast to SC 8.5.1, where it says that the deeds must be given over once the completion monies are tendered. It would therefore appear that there is more scope to claim a lien if you use the SCPCs. If the seller wants this entitlement to be available, the contract terms must be varied to that effect to enable enforcement of other payments or the performance of other contractual obligations.

6.68 Lastly, practitioners may care to note that the common law allows a solicitor a lien over a client's deeds until outstanding costs are paid in full. However, the Law Society is entitled to order a solicitor to release deeds, and the lien will not apply to deeds that the solicitor may be holding for the mortgagee of a client.

KEY POINTS SUMMARY: DELAYS AND REMEDIES

6.69
- If the other party is late for completion, remember under the SCs either party is entitled to claim compensation for delay at the contract rate of interest on a daily basis until completion takes place, but under the SCPCs only the seller is so entitled.
- If you decide to serve a notice to complete, always do so in such a way that enables you to prove service (personal delivery, recorded or special delivery, etc.), and remember the period of notice *excludes* the day on which the notice is given.
- Remember that, once issued, a notice to complete cannot be withdrawn, although the time period set out in the notice can, by mutual agreement, be extended provided both parties acknowledge that time remains of the essence.
- Specific performance can be claimed along with damages and rescission, but the claimant must at the eventual hearing select one remedy in respect of which judgment is to be sought.
- Does the contract include any form of exclusion clause that might limit liability? If it does, is it in any way ambiguous? If it is, remember that ambiguity is construed against the person seeking to rely upon the exclusion clause.

PRACTICAL CHECKLIST: DELAYS AND REMEDIES

- Has the time for completion set out in the contract elapsed?   **6.70**
- If it has, does the client want you to serve a notice to complete, ie, have you taken instructions for approval for this step?
- If you have instructions, have you served a notice using the appropriate wording and in such a way as to enable you to prove service of the notice?
- Has the period set out in the notice expired and, if so, does the client want to rescind the agreement, sell the property elsewhere and sue for damages?
- Is there some other form of breach of contract? If so, have you obtained a full history of the conveyancing transaction with all supporting papers; and what remedy does the innocent party want?
- Are you able to quantify the client's loss arising from the breach? If so, how much is that loss?
- In the light of the above, does it make economic sense to commence proceedings bearing in mind the costs that will be incurred?
- Apart from the other party to the contract, might there be a claim elsewhere, eg, against a conveyancing practitioner or surveyor, in negligence?

COMMERCIAL LEASE REMEDIES

A lessor will want to select a remedy to deal with two common acts of default by a lessee: **6.71**

(a) where there are rent arrears; and/or
(b) where there is a breach or breaches of the other lease covenants beyond the obligation to pay rent.

However, the major need for a lessor's remedy arises most commonly from rent arrears. Figure 6.1 below sets out the main remedies available to a lessor in these circumstances.

The choice of remedy depends upon each particular situation where rent arrears occur.   **6.72** However, it is our experience that in commercial property transactions the lessor will have a good idea of the financial strength of its tenant. Depending upon this information, the lessor will be able to select the best remedy in any particular set of circumstances that surround the rent arrears. For example, the lessee may not want to disturb the lessee's ability to carry on in business. This being so, the lessor may simply select a court action. Alternatively, the lessor may consider that the lessee is just being idle and that 'a shock to the system' is in order. Here the remedy of distress is a good selection, or possibly a statutory notice.

In the special circumstances where a lessee has sub-let and nevertheless allowed rent arrears   **6.73** to accrue, the head lessor is able to serve notice on the sub-lessee to collect rent direct to pay off the arrears. This is covered at para 6.78 below. Court action is straightforward; it requires the commencement of proceedings in either the county court or the High Court (further details are set out at paras 6.127 et seq). This is also the case for the use of statutory demands,

Figure 6.1 Remedies available where lessee defaults on payment of rent

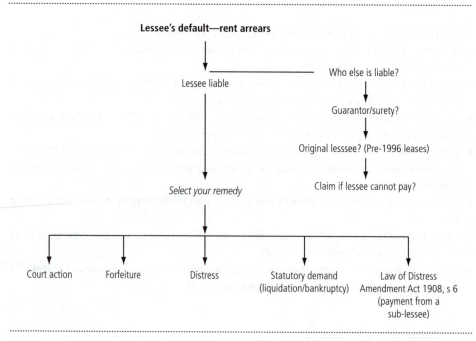

and these are also discussed at paras 6.127 et seq below. However, if this last remedy is selected the lessor should bear in mind that the amount to be recovered this way may well be diluted by other monies due to other creditors.

C   DISTRESS FOR RENT

6.74 Distress is the taking of personal property belonging to another to force that person to perform an obligation, such as a lease covenant, or to obtain satisfaction for a debt. To distrain is to take goods or chattels by way of distress. Distress is a very ancient remedy stretching back to the time of Magna Carta and feudal law. Perhaps because of the great age and nature of the remedy, it has in recent years been described as having fallen into disuse (see *Abingdon Rural DC v O'Gorman* [1968] 2 QB 811). However, both writers of this book have encountered this swift and challenging remedy in the context of commercial conveyancing and property. That experience has been from both sides of a lease, and it is therefore clear that this is a far from archaic or redundant remedy. Indeed, used in the right way, for the lessor, it can be both effective and rapid in recovering outstanding rent. Practitioners must remember that this remedy is available only where there is a landlord and tenant relationship and there are outstanding rent arrears.

6.75 Section 5 of the Limitation Act 1980 sets a time limit for distress, ie, the expiration of six years from the date on which the cause of action accrued—here, the formation of the rent arrears. (The time limit also applies to court claims.) Accordingly, where there are rent arrears the lessor may either by itself or through a certificated bailiff seize goods owned by the lessee.

The goods seized must be proportionate to the size of the rent arrears (The Statute of Marlborough 1267 requires distress to be reasonable.) The lessor may then hold onto those goods pending one of two resolutions to this 'self-help' remedy—either the lessee will pay to have the goods released, or the lessor will sell them to pay off the rent arrears. For a person to act as a certificated bailiff, he or she must first be so certified through the county court. (The actions of such a certificated bailiff are regulated by the Distress for Rent Rules 1988, SI 1988/ 2050, and a certificate to act as a bailiff is granted under s 7 of the Law of Distress Amendment Act 1888, as amended by the Law of Distress Amendment Act 1895.) The right to sell stems from statute (see the Distress for Rent Act 1689).

Somewhat archaic rules restrict the goods that can be affected by distress. For example, s 4 of the Law of Distress Amendment Act 1888 states that trade tools to a stated value (£150) are exempt, as are clothes and bedding. There are also rules about how distress can be implemented. No force can be used to effect entry to the subject premises; accordingly, the lessor must re-enter peaceably (see *Crabtree v Robinson* (1885) 12 QBD 312). Lessors should be aware of s 6 of the Criminal Law Act 1977, which makes it a criminal offence to use or to threaten violence so as to secure entry into the subject premises and where there is someone present who is opposed to that re-entry. Peaceable re-entry cannot take place on a Sunday or during the hours of darkness. **6.76**

Section 10 of the Distress for Rent Act 1737 allows goods to be impounded within the subject premises without their prior removal. The lessor is said to go into 'walking possession' of the impounded goods while they are in the demised premises. If a third party is unaware of the existence of a walking possession arrangement then that third party is at liberty to remove its goods (see *Abingdon Rural DC v O'Gorman* [1968] 2 QB 811). If a third party is aware of the distress, it must serve a written declaration upon the lessor to enable its goods to be exempted. If the lessor proceeds notwithstanding the service of the declaration, the third party can apply to a magistrate for an order for restoration of the goods belonging to the third party. **6.77**

Distress and sub-lessees

Section 6 of the Law of Distress Amendment Act 1908 covers the situation where a lessee has sub-let and nevertheless allows rent arrears to accrue. In this situation the head lessor is able to serve notice on the sub-lessee to collect rent direct to pay off the arrears. While the arrears subsist the sub-lessee is required to pay rent direct to the head lessor. Accordingly, where there are rent arrears, and there are sub-lessees, the superior lessor can serve upon any sub-lessee a notice by registered post and addressed to the sub-lessee at the subject premises. The notice should state the amount of the arrears and require all future rental payments payable by the named sub-lessee to be made direct to the superior lessor who gave the notice. The payments are to be made until the arrears have been paid in full. The notice operates so as to transfer to the superior lessor the right to recover, receive and give a discharge for such rent. Practitioners should therefore note that this is a process by which distress is actually avoided and replaced by the process contemplated in the notice. It is therefore of consequence to a superior lessor to know just who is in occupation of the property by way of sub-lessees. This is another reason why the lease's covenants for the lessee to perform should include a covenant requiring the lessee to give notice to the lessor of the creation of all sub-leases. **6.78**

Distress and the Human Rights Act 1998

6.79   The Human Rights Act 1998 came into force on 2 October 2000 and incorporates into English law the Articles contained in the European Convention on Human Rights ('the ECHR'). The effect of this is that the provisions of the ECHR will be applicable to all aspects of English law, and property law is no exception. Article 8 ECHR covers the right to respect for private and family life. The purpose of the Article is to ensure that all citizens have a right to respect for their private family life and home, ie, the Act will apply to property. Furthermore, the European Court of Human Rights has held that Article 8 will apply to commercial premises when they are occupied by an individual for the purposes of that citizen's business. Additionally, Article 6 ECHR gives all citizens the right to a fair trial, and in particular a right to have recourse to the courts.

6.80   The scope of the 1998 Act is not as obvious as it might be, in that judicial interpretation is likely to set it as the cases proceed. In particular, there is no precise guidance as to whether the Act applies to citizens seeking to enforce rights against other citizens or non-governmental bodies within the confines of private litigation. A narrow interpretation of the law would disallow such an application, limiting the effect of the 1998 Act to cases involving claims by individuals against governmental bodies (and their ilk) and not other individuals. However, a wider interpretation is possible applying s 7(1), so that the Act would apply to 'any legal proceedings'. If this view is taken then it would seem possible that the 1998 Act will be interpreted as applying to claims between citizens as to their human rights.

6.81   It is our view that it may prove difficult for a litigant to show that distress is a breach of human rights, for two important reasons. First, the lessee is not prohibited from making applications to the court to ameliorate the effects of the lessor's action. Indeed, there are specific third party protections set out in statute that would underpin this view. (If a third party is aware of the distress, it must serve a written declaration upon the lessor to enable its goods to be exempted (see s 1 of the Law of Distress Amendment Act 1908).) If the lessor proceeds notwithstanding the service of the declaration, the third party can apply to a magistrate for an order for restoration of its goods (see s 2 of the Law of Distress Amendment Act 1908). Secondly, and perhaps more importantly, there are cases that have come before the European Court in Strasbourg that show a clear trend which indicates a reluctance on the Court's part to get involved in reviewing the effects of civil litigation between citizens in the context of the 1998 Act. Only with the passage of time and the outcome of cases under the Act as they apply to distress will the position become clearer. In the meantime, currently, there is nothing to stop a commercial lessor from using the quick and inexpensive 'self-help' remedy of distress (see *Fuller v Happy Shopper Markets Limited* [2001] 1 WLR 1681).

6.82   The Law Commission has recommended abolition of the right to distress (see *Distress for Rent* (Law Com No 194, 1991).

D   FORFEITURE

6.83   The remedy of forfeiture (or right of entry) is available only to a landlord. It is the process whereby, following a tenant's breach of covenant or condition, a landlord is able to end the lease prematurely and recover possession of the property. A right of entry included in a lease confers on the landlord a legal interest in land (Law of Property Act 1925, s 1(2)(e)). This ultimate sanction is clearly a powerful weapon, but, as we shall see, the law, in order to protect the tenant, limits the landlord's right to forfeit in several ways. This includes the tenant's ability to apply to the court for relief against forfeiture (see paras 6.110 et seq below).

The first point to be made concerning forfeiture is that there is no implied right to forfeit for **6.84** breach of covenant. In other words, for a landlord to exercise the remedy there must be express provision in the lease. This is commonly found in all leases, and failure to include a forfeiture clause in a lease will constitute negligence on the part of the landlord's solicitor (unless, unusually, the client agrees otherwise). For an example of a forfeiture clause (or 'right of re-entry') in a commercial lease, see appendix 3, clause 14. Note that the clause permits the landlord to forfeit for non-payment of rent, breach of covenant and upon the tenant's bankruptcy. Although these are typical forfeiting events in a commercial lease, practitioners should appreciate that a clause allowing forfeiture on a tenant's bankruptcy would make a lease unmortgageable. However, this is really only a problem for residential long leases, as business leases are rarely offered as security due to their minimal capital value.

One minor point, not always appreciated by practitioners, is that where there has been a **6.85** breach of *condition* in a lease (as opposed to a breach of covenant), forfeiture is an automatic right (ie, there is no need for an express forfeiture clause). A 'condition' arises where the continuation of the term is clearly expressed to be conditional upon the observance of the tenant's obligations (*Doe d Henniker v Watt* (1828) 8 B & C 308). A condition is rarely seen in modern commercial leases, and in any event the courts will generally lean towards interpreting lease obligations as covenants. The point is thus primarily of academic interest only and the moral for lessors' practitioners is clear—always include a forfeiture clause in your lease!

Another crucial point in the understanding of how forfeiture works is that a breach of **6.86** covenant does not in itself effect forfeiture. A breach only *entitles* the landlord to forfeit the lease. Thus, in order to forfeit, the landlord must exercise that right by performing some unequivocal act, demonstrating that it considers the relationship of landlord and tenant to be at an end. This can be done either by issuing proceedings for recovery of possession, or by taking peaceable re-entry (see paras 6.107 to 6.109). As we shall see, if the landlord does nothing and treats the lease as continuing, it may waive (ie, lose) its right to forfeit. The landlord should also consider whether forfeiting the lease is a sensible remedy in the circumstances. Can the premises be easily re-let? Depending on the state of the market, the landlord could be left without a tenant for some time which would make forfeiture counter-productive.

Waiver

Nature of waiver

Waiver occurs where, despite an event giving rise to the right to forfeit, the landlord does **6.87** some act, perhaps unwittingly, resulting in it giving up that right. Before issuing proceedings to forfeit, you should always consider whether waiver has occurred. If it has, your client will lose its action and probably be forced to pay the tenant's costs. Waiver is based upon the principle of law that a person should not benefit from two remedies where those remedies are inconsistent with each other—the individual must elect for one or the other. In the case of forfeiture, the landlord must elect whether to exercise the right to forfeit, or to continue to enjoy its rights under the lease by affirming the lease.

6.88 Waiver can be express, but more commonly it is effected by an unknowing act of the landlord. It is unnecessary to have an intention to waive and the understanding or belief of the tenant is irrelevant (see *Central Estates (Belgravia) v Woolgar (No 2)* [1972] 1 WLR 1048). Non-express waiver arises where the landlord first knows that a breach has occurred and then acts in such a way that it treats the lease as still continuing and communicates this to the tenant. Knowledge of the breach may be imputed where the landlord's employee or agent is aware of the facts, provided the employee had a reasonable time to inform the landlord of the breach (see *Blackstone (David) v Burnetts (West End)* [1973] 1 WLR 1487 and *Metropolitan Properties v Cordery* (1979) 39 P & CR 10).

6.89 The classic case of non-express waiver is where the landlord, knowing of the breach, claims or accepts rent from the tenant (see *Segal Securities Ltd v Thoseby* [1963] 1 QB 887). Accordingly, if you, as the landlord's solicitor, become aware of the tenant's breach and your client is contemplating forfeiture, you should immediately advise your client to stop demanding or accepting rent. This may involve cancelling standing orders and contacting the landlord's agent who issues the demands. Even accepting rent by mistake or 'without prejudice' will still constitute waiver (see *Segal Securities Ltd v Thoseby*, above). The idea of refusing rent may seem anathema to the landlord, but it is essential to preserve the landlord's position. Note, however, that there is no waiver if a rent demand is issued but never received by the tenant (see *Trustees of Henry Smith's Charity v Wilson* [1983] QB 316). This is because waiver must be communicated to the tenant.

6.90 Accepting rent is a straightforward act of waiver. As far as other acts of non-express waiver are concerned, the courts will 'look at all the circumstances of the case to consider whether the act . . . relied on [as constituting waiver] is so unequivocal that, when considered objectively, it could only be regarded as having been done consistently with the continued operation of a tenancy' (*per* Slade LJ in *Expert Clothing Service & Sales Ltd v Hillgate House Ltd* [1986] 1 Ch 340, at 360). Some examples of acts which have been held to affirm the existence of a tenancy, and thus constitute waiver, are:

(a) serving notice under a repairing covenant (*Doe d Rutzen v Lewis* (1836) 5 A & E 227);
(b) levying distress for rent (*Ward v Day* (1863–64) 4 B & S 337);
(c) serving notice to quit requiring the tenant to give up possession (*Marche v Christodoulakis* (1948) 64 TLR 466).

6.91 The effect of waiver will vary according to whether the breach of covenant is a once and for all breach or a continuing breach. If the breach is once and for all, eg, breach of a covenant against assignment, then once the landlord has waived the breach it will lose any right to forfeit for that particular breach in the future. Conversely, if the breach is continuing in nature, eg, failure to repair or an unauthorized change of use, the right to forfeit will arise again the next day. Thus for continuing breaches the adverse effect of waiver on the landlord's position is likely to be minimal.

Reform of the law relating to waiver: Termination of Tenancies Bill

Under this draft Bill, the landlord may seek a 'termination order' for the lease by relying on a **6.92** 'termination order event' (ie, a breach of covenant). Clause 11 provides that the landlord will only waive its right to rely on a termination order event if:

(a) its conduct, after the event came to its knowledge, would have led a reasonable tenant to believe, and in fact led the tenant to believe, that the landlord would not seek to rely on it; or

(b) its conduct, after the event came to its knowledge, would have led a reasonable tenant to believe, and in fact led the tenant to believe, that the landlord would not seek to rely on it if a particular condition were fulfilled, and the condition was fulfilled.

Essentially this new style waiver is based upon estoppel and concentrates on what is believed by the reasonable tenant. Whether it will achieve the desired certainty and simplicity remains to be seen.

A question was recently asked in the Commons about these potential changes to the law in **6.93** this area. A Commons Written Answer was given on 11 March 2002 to the effect that the scope of the current work being carried out by the Law Commission is that 'an examination be made of the law relating to the termination of tenancies, to facilitate the implementation of the report previously published [*Landlord and Tenant Law, Termination of Tenancies Bill* (Law Com No 221, 1994)], with a view to modernising and simplification of the law in this area'. The Law Commission has reconsidered the draft Bill (attached to the 1994 report) in order that it might be brought into line with changes in civil court procedure, the enactment of the Human Rights Act 1998 and changes in case law. The Law Commission published a further consultation paper with revised proposals. The consultation period ended in 2004. The Law Commission expects to issue a revised draft bill in early 2006.

KEY POINTS SUMMARY: WAIVER OF THE RIGHT TO FORFEIT

- Waiver occurs where: **6.94**
    (a) there has (have) been breach(es) of covenant entitling the landlord to forfeit the lease; and
    (b) the landlord has knowledge of the breach(es) (real or imputed); and
    (c) the landlord has orally or by its conduct acknowledged the continued existence of the lease; and
    (d) the landlord has communicated that acknowledgement to the tenant.
- Demanding or accepting rent following a breach will be a clear non-express waiver; this will be so even if the landlord accepts the rent 'without prejudice'.
- If the breach is once and for all, waiver will result in the right to forfeit being lost for good.
- If the breach is continuing then, despite waiver, the right to forfeit should arise again the next day.

Forfeiture procedure

The procedure for forfeiting a lease varies according to whether the breach of covenant **6.95** involves non-payment of rent or not. The Law Commission has recommended that this distinction be abolished and that one system is adopted for all breaches (see *Forfeiture of Tenancies* (Law Com No 142, 1985)).

Forfeiture for non-payment of rent

6.96 The forfeiture procedure for non-payment of rent is far easier than for breach of other covenants. This is because the landlord has no need to serve a notice under s 146 of the Law of Property Act 1925 (s 146(11)). Accordingly, at the drafting stage of the lease, a prudent landlord will ensure that the payments of service charges, insurance payments and other payments under the lease are 'reserved as rent'.

6.97 At common law, before the landlord can proceed to forfeit for non-payment of rent it must first make a formal demand for the rent. In practice this is usually unnecessary, as a well-drafted forfeiture clause will contain the words, 'whether formally demanded or not'. In addition, under s 210 of the Common Law Procedure Act 1852 (High Court proceedings) and s 139(1) of the County Courts Act 1984 (county court proceedings), a formal demand is unnecessary where the rent is at least half a year in arrears and there are insufficient goods on the premises to satisfy the debt.

6.98 The tenant may apply to the court for relief from forfeiture (see paras 6.110 et seq below). This will usually be granted in respect of non-payment of rent, provided the tenant discharges the arrears together with the landlord's costs (often done 'at the door of the court').

Forfeiture for breach of covenants other than non-payment of rent

6.99 Before the landlord can forfeit for other breaches, it must serve on the tenant notice under s 146 of the Law of Property Act 1925 (although there are exceptions, see para 6.103 below). The policy behind service of the s 146 notice is to give the tenant warning of the breach and allow it the opportunity to remedy the breach if possible. For breach of a covenant against assignment, the s 146 notice must be served on the assignee. Specimen s 146 notices are contained in appendix 12.

6.100 To be valid, s 146(1) prescribes that the s 146 notice must:

(a) specify the breach; and
(b) require the breach to be remedied within a reasonable time, if it is capable of being remedied; and
(c) require the tenant to pay compensation for the breach, if the landlord so requires.

6.101 Concerning (b) above, there has been much judicial argument and academic debate over whether certain covenants are capable of remedy or not. Generally, breach of a positive covenant (eg, a covenant to repair) is remediable, but breach of a negative covenant may be either remediable or irremediable depending on the facts. Essentially the test is whether it is possible for the tenant to remedy the harm that has been caused to the landlord, ie, whether the mischief can be removed. The modern judicial view, following the Court of Appeal decisions in *Expert Clothing Service & Sales Ltd v Hillgate House Ltd* [1986] 1 Ch 340 and *Savva v Hussein* (1997) 73 P & CR 150, is that most breaches, positive or negative, will prima facie be capable of remedy. You should be aware, however, that breach of a covenant against assigning or sub-letting (ie, alienation) is classified as a once and for all breach and cannot be remedied (see *Scala House & District Property Co Ltd v Forbes* [1974] QB 575 approved in *Expert Clothing* and *Savva v Hussain*, above).

If you are unsure whether the breach is capable of remedy, the practical solution when **6.102** drafting the s 146 notice is simply to require the tenant to remedy the breach 'if it is capable of remedy'. This will prevent an invalidation of the s 146 notice on this point. If a s 146 notice requiring remedy has been served, the landlord must allow the tenant a reasonable time to remedy the breach (s 146(1)). If no remedy has occurred within a reasonable time then the landlord can proceed to forfeit the lease. Of course, if you are certain that the breach cannot be remedied then the landlord can forfeit straight away. All it need do is specify the breach in the s 146 notice and then proceed to forfeit without waiting for the tenant to do anything.

Situations where s 146 notice not required   A s 146 notice is not required in the situations **6.103** described in s 146(9) and (10) of the Law of Property Act 1925. These are:

(a) where more than one year has elapsed since the bankruptcy of the tenant (which also loses its right to relief from forfeiture). However, if the tenant's interest is sold during that year, the assignee retains the protection of s 146 indefinitely (see *Pearson v Gee and Braceborough Spa Ltd* [1934] AC 272);

(b) leases of agricultural or pastoral land;

(c) leases of mines or minerals;

(d) leases of a public house or beershop;

(e) leases of furnished dwelling houses;

(f) leases of property where the personal qualifications of the tenant are important to the landlord or any person holding under it, for the preservation of its value or character, or because of the neighbourhood (see generally *Earl Bathurst v Fine* [1974] 1 WLR 905 and *Hockley Engineering Co Ltd v V & P Midlands Ltd* [1993] 1 EGLR 76).

Leasehold Property (Repairs) Act 1938   There are additional rules if the breach is of a **6.104** repairing covenant and the lease was granted for seven years or more and still has three or more years left to run. In this case the s 146 notice must contain a statement of the tenant's right to serve a counter-notice within 28 days, claiming the benefit of the Leasehold Property (Repairs) Act 1938. If the tenant serves the counter-notice, the landlord must seek leave of the court before forfeiting the lease (see paras 6.117 et seq below).

Recent reforms and long leases   In relation to long leases (over 21 years) the law relating **6.105** to forfeiture has been reformed by recent legislation. The Commonhold and Leasehold Reform Act 2002 provides that a long leaseholder will only be liable for any ground rent payable under a lease where the tenant has received a written notice from the landlord in a prescribed form. The notice must specify the amount due, the date by which payment is to be made and (if different) the date on which the amount would have been payable under the terms of the lease. The date payment is to be made must be at least 30 days and not more than 60 days after the day the notice is given, and must not be before the date it would normally be payable under the terms of the lease. The landlord will also be prevented from starting forfeiture action unless it has issued a written notice, and the ground rent is still unpaid after the due date. These provisions came into force on 28 February 2005.

6.106   The 2002 Act also introduced new restrictions on the commencement of forfeiture proceedings, including the service of notices under s 146 of the Law of Property Act 1925. Landlords will only be able to take action when a court or Leasehold Valuation Tribunal has determined that a breach of a covenant or condition of a lease has occurred. The Act also prevents the use of forfeiture for outstanding debts that are less than a prescribed amount, unless the amount or any part of it has been outstanding for more than a prescribed period. The prescribed amount cannot exceed £500. This will apply to outstanding debts of rent, service charges and administration charges. These provisions came into force on 28 February 2005.

Effecting forfeiture

6.107   Once the above procedures have been complied with, the landlord can effect forfeiture either by peaceable re-entry or through court proceedings. Forfeiture through peaceable re-entry is generally quicker and cheaper than court proceedings, but it is recommended only where business premises are left unoccupied. This is because s 6(1) of the Criminal Law Act 1977 provides that:

> ...any person who, without lawful authority, uses or threatens violence for the purpose of securing entry into any premises for himself or for any other person is guilty of an offence, provided that—
>
> (a)   there is someone present on those premises at the time who is opposed to the entry; and
>
> (b)   the person using or threatening the violence knows this.

6.108   The fact that the landlord effecting re-entry has an interest in or right to possession does not constitute lawful authority for the purpose of seeking possession (s 6(2)). (Note: for residential premises, peaceable re-entry should never be used unless the premises have been abandoned. Section 2 of the Protection from Eviction Act 1977 provides that only proceedings through the courts are permitted while any person is in lawful residence.)

6.109   The most practical way of effecting re-entry of business premises is to turn up after business hours or early in the morning, check that no one is occupying the premises and simply change the locks. However, you should remember that if the breach of covenant is other than non-payment of rent, you must still serve a s 146 notice on the tenant *before* you effect peaceable re-entry (see para 6.99 above). In most cases forfeiture will be effected through court proceedings under the Civil Procedure Rules 1998 which came into force on 26 April 1999. The detail of these procedures is beyond the scope of this book and practitioners are advised to consult a specialist litigation text. One further obstacle that can prevent the landlord from forfeiting the lease is the tenant's right to apply to the court for relief from forfeiture. This is now considered.

Tenant's right to relief from forfeiture

6.110   Section 146(2) of the Law of Property Act 1925 is the relevant statutory provision dealing with the tenant's right to relief from forfeiture and is worth quoting in full:

> (2) Where a lessor is proceeding, by action or otherwise, to enforce such a right of re-entry or forfeiture, the lessee may, in the lessor's action, if any, or in any action brought by himself, apply to the court for relief; and the court may grant or refuse relief, as the court, having regard

to the proceedings and conduct of the parties under the foregoing provisions of this section, and to all the other circumstances, thinks fit; and in case of relief may grant it on such terms, if any, as to costs, expenses, damages, compensation, penalty, or otherwise, including the granting of an injunction to restrain any like breach in the future, as the court, in the circumstances of each case, thinks fit.

As we have seen, if the landlord is seeking forfeiture for non-payment of rent the tenant is **6.111** likely to obtain relief from forfeiture provided it discharges the arrears of rent and the landlord's costs. As far as breach of other covenants is concerned, generally the tenant can apply to the court for relief at any time up until the landlord has actually re-entered the premises (see *Rogers v Rice* [1892] 2 Ch 170). However, if the landlord has peaceably re-entered (as opposed to issuing proceedings), the court may still grant relief even after the landlord has re-entered (see the important House of Lords' decision in *Billson v Residential Apartments Ltd* [1992] 1 AC 494). Nevertheless, the tenant should act quickly as any delay in making the application may prejudice the tenant's case.

In deciding whether to grant relief the court has a very wide discretion. It will often try to **6.112** weigh up the harm that the breach causes to the landlord against the advantage the landlord will gain in forfeiting the lease. Thus, in *Van Haarlem v Kasner* (1992) 64 P & CR 214, the court considered that forfeiture would be too Draconian a remedy for a lease that still had 80 years left to run. The court will also examine whether the breach is capable of remedy. If it is, and the tenant is willing and able to remedy it within a reasonable time, relief will probably be granted, provided the breach is unlikely to re-occur. However, it does not follow that relief will be refused simply because the breach is irremediable. As we saw in *Scala House & District Property Co Ltd v Forbes* at para 6.101 above, the breach of covenant against sub-letting was classified as irremediable. Nevertheless, the court held that the unlawful sub-letting was one to which the landlord would not have been able reasonably to withhold consent had the tenant asked for it; and accordingly relief was available.

Other factors that the courts will consider before deciding whether to grant relief are: **6.113**

(a) the conduct of the parties (see *Segal Securities v Thoseby* [1963] 1 All ER 500);
(b) the nature and seriousness of the breach;
(c) the value of the property (see *Ropemaker v Noonhaven* [1989] 2 EGLR 50); and
(d) the extent of any damage caused by the breach.

Before granting relief, the court may of course impose such terms as it thinks fit (see generally *Duke of Westminster v Swinton* [1948] 1 KB 524).

Effect of forfeiture on sub-tenants and mortgagees

At common law, forfeiture of a head lease will automatically forfeit a sub-lease (*Moore* **6.114** *Properties (Ilford) Ltd v McKeon* [1977] 1 All ER 262). However, under the Law of Property Act 1925, s 146(4), a sub-tenant can apply to the court for relief against forfeiture of the head lease even where the tenant itself has no right to relief. If the court grants relief, a vesting order will be made. This creates a new leasehold estate in which the sub-tenant becomes the immediate tenant of the head landlord and the intermediate tenant disappears. The court can impose such conditions as it thinks fit, including a requirement that the sub-tenant complies with the terms of the head lease and pays a higher rent than under the sub-lease

(*Ewart v Fryer* [1901] 1 Ch 499). The aim is to put the landlord back into the same position as it was before the forfeiture took place. Accordingly, the court will normally require the sub-tenant to pay off all rent arrears and costs and remedy any outstanding breaches of covenant (see *Belgravia Insurance Co Ltd v Meah* [1964] 1 QB 436, CA).

6.115   The new term is normally for the duration of the sub-lease, although it cannot be longer and may finish sooner (see *Hammersmith and Fulham LBC v Top Shop Centres* [1990] Ch 237). A business sub-tenant protected by the Landlord and Tenant Act 1954 will be entitled not only to the residue of its contractual term, but also to a continuation of it under the 1954 Act (*Cadogan v Dimovic* [1984] 2 All ER 168). Unlike for tenants, the relief order for sub-tenants cannot be made retrospectively. This means that between the time when the head lease is forfeited and relief is granted to the sub-tenant, the sub-tenant is a trespasser and can be required to pay mesne profits to the landlord. Mesne profits are those profits lost to the owner of land as a result of it being wrongfully dispossessed. This amount could conceivably be more than the sub-tenant was paying in rent (eg, if it was a long lease).

6.116   A mortgagee of the leasehold interest is also treated as a sub-tenant for the purposes of s 146(4) of the Law of Property Act 1925, and is thus able to apply for relief from forfeiture. This is an important protection for lenders who would otherwise lose their security. However, this is more appropriate for residential long leases, as lenders would not normally consider a commercial lease as security due to its minimal capital value.

E   REMEDIES FOR BREACH OF LESSEE REPAIRING COVENANTS

6.117   To ensure compliance with repairing obligations, modern leases will always include a covenant allowing the lessor to enter the demised premises, on prior written notice, to view the state of repair. If the lessee is in breach of the repairing covenant, the lessor will then be able to serve a notice on the lessee calling for repair to be carried out. Moreover, the lessor, in the case of default by the lessee, will have the benefit of a further provision enabling the lessor to enter the subject property to carry out the necessary repairs and to charge the lessee for the cost of the work required. If the costs incurred by the lessor are described as a simple debt due from the lessee, this can be to the advantage of the lessor. This is because if the cost of repair is described as a simple debt it is not caught by statutory limitations upon the recovery of damages. For the rationale for this approach, see below regarding the limitations imposed by the Landlord and Tenant Act 1927 and the Leasehold Property Repairs Act 1938 in relation to damages. Practitioners need to advise lessors in these circumstances that if they do effect entry to make repairs, they will potentially become liable for claims arising under the terms of the Defective Premises Act 1972. This is because the lessor will be under a duty to make sure that the premises are in a condition that ensures the safety of persons within them.

6.118   The lessor can also serve a notice pursuant to the terms of s 146 of the Law of Property Act 1925, calling for the lessee to comply with the lease repairing covenants (see appendix 12). The notice will give the lessee a fixed period of time to comply with those covenants, failing which the lessor can seek to forfeit the lease for breach of covenant. Practitioners should remember that the lessor's rights in this regard are limited by the effect of the Leasehold Property (Repairs) Act 1938. If the original term of the lease was for seven years or more and there are at least three years left unexpired of the term, the s 146 notice must refer to the 1938 Act and inform the lessee of its right to serve a counter-notice claiming the benefit of the Act. This counter-notice must be served upon the lessor within 28 days of the service of the s 146 notice. If the lessee obtains the benefit of the Act by serving a counter-notice within the time limit, the lessor cannot forfeit the lease without leave of the court. In effect it means that the lessor can neither sue for damages nor forfeit the lease without a court order allowing it so to do. When making an order the court has a complete discretion to impose such conditions as it deems appropriate in the particular circumstances of the case.

Practitioners should bear in mind, however, the effect of the decision in *SEDAC Investments*   **6.119**
Ltd v Tanner [1982] 1 WLR 1342. In this case the lessor carried out works of repair on an emergency basis without giving the lessee the opportunity of carrying out the required works. As a result the lessor could not serve a s 146 notice as the works were complete and the breach remedied. Because of these circumstances, no notice could be served under the 1938 Act and therefore the court was unable to grant the lessor leave to commence proceedings for an action in damages against the lessee arising from the breach of covenant. Further-more, s 18 of the Landlord and Tenant Act 1927 makes it clear that no damages can be awarded if it is apparent that the premises are to be demolished at the end of the lease or shortly thereafter, or there are alterations intended that would make the repairs pointless.

As well as forfeiture, a lessor can seek damages for a breach of the repairing covenants.   **6.120**
(Normally, specific performance will not be an available remedy except in exceptional cir-cumstances, as to allow it could lead to the statutory provisions set out above being circum-vented.) During the lease term the measure of damages is the diminution to the value of the reversion caused by the breach. At the end of the lease, the measure of damages is the amount that is required to put the premises into the condition in which the lessee would have had to leave them had it left them with no subsisting breach of covenant (see *James v Hutton* [1950] KB 9 and *Joyner v Weeks* [1891] 2 QB 31).

F   REMEDIES AVAILABLE TO THE LESSEE

If a commercial lease contains covenants for the lessor to perform then the lessee is entitled   **6.121**
to bring an action for damages where the lessor is in breach and the lessee has suffered loss. In just the same way as there are other remedies available to the lessor, so the lessee could also claim further redress by way of injunctive relief or specific performance. If the lessee is in a part of a property that is subject to multiple lettings then, if the lessee has commenced proceedings for breach of covenant, the lessee can also apply for a receiver to be appointed pursuant to s 37 of the Supreme Court Act 1981. The receiver should be appointed to manage the several properties involved and to collect the rents from the lessees. This appointment is appropriate where the lessor is in breach of a repairing covenant, or indeed a covenant to provide services.

6.122   Most commercial leases contain a covenant given by the lessor to allow the lessee quiet enjoyment of the subject premises (see paras 1.76 and 4.02 above). The existence of such a covenant allows the lessee to seek an appropriate remedy for unlawful eviction, ie, the unlawful repossession of the subject property by the lessor when there was no entitlement to do so. Accordingly, the lessee can claim damages (possibly exemplary where the lessor's actions justify such a punitive award) to compensate the lessee for loss occasioned by the lessor's unlawful act. As well as damages the court may grant an injunction against the defaulting lessor should it deem it appropriate to do so.

Breach of the lessor's covenant to repair

6.123   Where the lessor enters into a covenant to keep the subject premises in repair then the rules that apply to tenants' covenants apply equally to the lessor. Thus, the lessor cannot be liable for breaches under the terms of the repairing covenant unless it has been served with a notice of repair (see *O'Brien v Robinson* [1973] AC 912). A notice of repair is not required, however, if the lessor is responsible for repairs beyond merely the subject property. If the lessor is obliged to repair the building of which the subject property forms part, there is an immediate liability without notice (see *British Telecommunications plc v Sun Life Assurance Society plc* [1995] 3 WLR 622).

6.124   If the lessor is in breach of a covenant to repair then the lessee can commence proceedings for damages, seek the appointment of a receiver, consider specific performance or possibly carry out the work itself. Each of these remedies is considered further below.

6.125   Proceedings for damages will be the usual course of action. The measure of the lessee's damages should be the difference between the value of the premises to the lessee had the covenant been complied with and the value at the time of the damages assessment, ie, when there was a breach of the covenant. A receiver could also be appointed pursuant to s 37 of the Supreme Court Act 1981. The receiver will manage the property in conformity with the lessor's lease covenants (and collect the rents) and will be nominated by the lessee to be a person qualified to carry out this duty. Specific performance is available to a lessee, but is a discretionary order that may not be granted should the court decide that damages are a sufficient remedy. Lastly, the lessee could carry out the repairs itself. If it does, the lessee can deduct the cost (at a reasonable level) from future rents (see *Lee-Parker v Izzet* [1971] 1 WLR 1688).

Derogation from grant

6.126   The courts will imply a covenant on the part of the lessor not to derogate (not to deviate in standard or quality) from its grant, ie, the making of the commercial lease itself. This provision supports the covenant for quiet enjoyment in that the lessor cannot do or allow something that adversely affects the lessee's enjoyment of its premises. In effect this means that 'a grantor having given a thing with one hand is not to take away the means of enjoying it with the other' (see *Birmingham Dudley and District Banking Co v Ross* (1888) 38 Ch 295). This can apply to rights granted in a lease. Accordingly, if a right of way is granted and the lessor blocks that right of way, it will amount to a derogation from grant. This can extend to adjoining lessees. In *Chartered Trading Plc v Davies* [1997] 49 EG 135, the court held that there would be a derogation from grant where a lessor fails to stop an adjoining lessee who commits acts of nuisance that adversely affect the claiming lessee. The logical extension of this decision is that where a lessor lets a development to several lessees it must enforce breaches against all, failing which a lessee that suffers loss through another defaulting lessee can claim a remedy through derogation of grant.

G   LITIGATION AND OTHER COMMERCIAL LEASE REMEDIES

Should the lessee fail to pay, the lessor has recourse to the courts or to the provisions of the   **6.127** Companies Acts for further remedies. The lessor can advance a claim through the courts to seek an order for payment of the debt (and/or for forfeiture; see 6.83 et seq above). Once there is a court order in place, enforcement proceedings are available, such as the use of court bailiffs or insolvency remedies. There is also the possibility of using a statutory demand under the terms of the Companies Acts. These alternative routes are now examined.

Court action

Section 5 of the Limitation Act 1980 sets a time limit for court actions founded on contracts   **6.128** (including leases and/or tenancy agreements). The Act sets that limit at the expiration of six years from the date on which the cause of action accrued, ie, at the time of the formation of the rent arrears. (The time limit also applies to the remedy of distress.) The choice of where to commence proceedings is usually dictated by the size of the debt. Larger debts will normally be dealt with in the High Court, but most will be the subject of proceedings in the county court.

Statutory demands

Provided the debt is in excess of £750, the lessor can opt to serve a statutory demand upon   **6.129** the lessee with a view to pursuing an insolvency remedy. If the lessee is a company, winding-up proceedings will be threatened; if an individual, bankruptcy proceedings will be appropriate. Should the lessee fail to comply with the terms of the demand then, under the Insolvency Act 1986, action can be taken for redress through these remedies.

There is one word of caution necessary when dealing with a remedy reliant upon insolvency   **6.130** action—should the proceedings reach the bitter end of a bankruptcy or winding-up order, the claimant will rank as a mere ordinary, unsecured creditor. This will mean that there is a distinct possibility that the claim may get diluted by all the other, similar debts. As a result, the possibility of being paid in full will be adversely affected. Where there are creditors ranking in priority (usually secured creditors such as the lessee's bankers), receiving a payment less than the full claim is a very real possibility.

Who else might be liable?

Practitioners should remember that if the lease was granted prior to 1 January 1996, the   **6.131** original lessee might be liable in privity of contract for breaches by the current lessee. Leases granted after this date will be treated in a different manner. The Landlord and Tenant (Covenants) Act 1995 is of considerable importance in the context of commercial leases. It applies to all leases granted on or after 1 January 1996. All other leases, ie, granted before this date, will not normally be affected by the Act. It reverses the previous general rule that a lessee remained liable under the lease covenants throughout the full term of the lease. Unless the lessee has entered into an agreement formulated by the Act as an 'authorized guarantee agreement' (AGA), the lessee will, on assignment, be automatically released from any liability in the future on the lessee's lease covenants. Thus a lessor dealing with a breach arising from a lease granted before the Act will also be able to take action against an original lessee. If the lease is a post-Act lease then, if there is an AGA in place, the previous lessee may also be liable.

6.132   The lessor may also be entitled to pursue a surety or guarantor under the terms of the subject lease. Commercial leases can refer to a surety or guarantor. These two terms are synonymous in that they both refer to someone or something that has given a written undertaking to answer for the payment of a debt or for the performance of an obligation by another party (the lessee) liable in the first instance. On the default of the lessee, the surety or guarantor will be required to cover the rent and/or take over the residue of the lease.

6.133   Lastly, there is also a possibility that a previous lessee entered into direct covenants with the lessor (in the licence to assign) where the obligation remains in place notwithstanding that that lessee has since assigned and is no longer the lessee in occupation. In this situation the lessor could also consider seeking redress against that former lessee.

Pursuing 'fixed charges'

6.134   A 'fixed charge' will be the rent, service charge or other pre-determined amount due under the terms of the lease, including any interest on these amounts. The Landlord and Tenant (Covenants) Act 1995 makes reference to this group of payments in s 17, and imposes an obligation upon the lessor to serve a written notice of the intended claim upon a guarantor or former lessee within six months of the existing lessee's default. The importance of this provision is that, should the lessor fail to serve such a notice, the lessor will be barred by the effect of this statute from recovering its loss from the guarantor or former lessee. If a former lessee does receive a valid notice then it may call for the lessor to grant to it an overriding lease of the subject premises. A precedent for this kind of lease can be found in appendix 11. The former lessee can, by reason of the benefit of the overriding lease, thereby acquire an interest that will enable it to arrange for an assignment, possibly for value, rather than just be liable to pay rent for a property where it does not hold the legal estate. The lessor can also benefit in that it can take action to remedy any further breaches, eg, by forfeiting the overriding lease and taking possession. Accordingly, an overriding lease can provide benefits to both parties and should not necessarily be considered as an unnecessary complication by lessors required to grant one.

KEY POINTS SUMMARY: COMMERCIAL LEASE REMEDIES

- If the other party is late for completion, remember that under the SCs either party is **6.135** entitled to claim compensation for delay at the contract rate of interest on a daily basis, until completion takes place.
- It should be noted that SCPC 9.3.1 provides that liability for interest arises only on the default of the buyer. If the seller defaults and delays completion, in the absence of a special condition all that a buyer can do is sue the defaulting seller for damages.
- If you decide to serve a notice to complete, always do so in such a way that enables you to prove service (personal delivery, recorded or special delivery, etc.), and remember that the period of notice excludes the day on which the notice is given.
- Remember, once issued, a notice to complete cannot be withdrawn, although the time period set out in the notice can, by mutual agreement, be extended provided both parties acknowledge that time remains of the essence.
- Specific performance can be claimed along with damages and rescission, but the claimant must at the eventual hearing select one remedy in respect of which judgment is to be sought.
- Does the contract include any form of exclusion clause that might limit liability? If it does, is it in any way ambiguous? If it is, remember that ambiguity is construed against the person seeking to rely upon the exclusion clause.

PRACTICAL CHECKLISTS: COMMERCIAL LEASE REMEDIES

Delays and remedies

- Has the time for completion set out in the contract elapsed?   **6.136**
- If it has, does the client want you to serve a notice to complete, ie, have you taken instructions for approval for this step?
- If you have instructions, have you served a notice using the appropriate wording and in such a way as to enable you to prove service of the notice?
- Has the period set out in the notice expired; and, if so, does the client want to rescind the agreement, sell the property elsewhere and sue for damages?
- Is there some other form of breach of contract? If so, have you obtained a full history of the transaction with all supporting papers, and what remedy does the innocent party want?
- Are you able to quantify the client's loss arising from the breach? If so, how much is that loss?
- In the light of the above, does it make economic sense to commence proceedings bearing in mind the costs that will be incurred?
- Apart from the other party to the contract, might there be a claim elsewhere, eg, against a conveyancing practitioner or surveyor in negligence?

Forfeiture

6.137 • There is no implied right to forfeit for breach of covenant. Acting for a landlord and
         drafting a lease, always ensure that the lease gives the landlord an express right to forfeit.

       • Ensure that the events giving rise to forfeiture are comprehensive. For a commercial lease,
         include forfeiture on the tenant's bankruptcy.

       • Consider whether forfeiture is a sensible remedy in the circumstances; can the landlord
         easily re-let the premises?

       • The landlord must avoid waiving the right to forfeit; consider whether the breach is once
         and for all (eg, alienation) or continuing (eg, repairs). If necessary, do not demand or
         accept rent and instruct the landlord's agents accordingly.

       • To exercise forfeiture the landlord must perform some unequivocal act, demonstrating
         that it considers the relationship of landlord and tenant to be at an end—either issue
         proceedings or effect peaceable re-entry.

       • Before forfeiting for breach of covenant other than non-payment of rent, the landlord
         must serve a s 146 notice on the tenant.

       • If unsure whether the breach is capable of remedy, include in the s 146 notice the words 'if
         it is capable of remedy'.

       • If the breach is of a repairing covenant and the lease was granted for seven years or more
         and still has three or more years left to run, the s 146 notice must contain a statement of
         the tenant's right to serve a counter-notice within 28 days, claiming the benefit of the
         Leasehold Property (Repairs) Act 1938.

       • Effect peaceable re-entry only where the business premises are left unoccupied and after
         the expiry of any notice under the s 146 notice.

       • Consider effecting peaceable re-entry after business hours or early in the morning by
         changing the locks; however, always check that no one is occupying the premises.

       • Alternatively, issue court proceedings.

       • The tenant can apply for relief from forfeiture at the court's discretion; this can be done
         even after peaceable re-entry has taken place (*Billson v Residential Apartments Ltd* [1992]
         1 AC 494).

       • If the tenant is willing and able to remedy the breach within a reasonable time, relief will
         probably be granted provided the breach is unlikely to re-occur.

       • Forfeiture of a head lease automatically ends a sub-lease, but the sub-tenant (and any
         mortgagee) can apply to the court for relief under s 146(4) of the Law of Property Act 1925.

       • Before granting relief the court will normally require the sub-tenant to pay off all rent
         arrears and costs and remedy any outstanding breaches of covenant.

KEY DOCUMENTS

6.138 • Land Registration Act 2002
       • Landlord and Tenant Act 1954
       • Law of Property Act 1925
       • Code of Practice for Commercial Leases in England and Wales (2nd edn)
       • Commercial Property Standard Enquiries

- Standard Commercial Property Conditions (2nd edn)
- Standard Property Conditions (4th edn)

Printed copies of legislation can be ordered from The Stationery Office (<http://www.tsoshop.co.uk>). Legislation from 1988 onwards can be downloaded free of charge from <http://www.opsi.gov.uk/acts.htm>.

The Code of Practice for Commercial Leases in England and Wales is set out in appendix 17.

The Commercial Property Standard Enquiries are set out in appendix 18 with guidance notes on the Enquiries set out in appendix 19.

The Standard Commercial Property Conditions are set out in appendix 4.

7

THE LANDLORD AND TENANT ACT 1954, PT II: SECURITY OF TENURE FOR BUSINESS TENANTS AND THE TERMINATION AND RENEWAL OF BUSINESS TENANCIES

A INTRODUCTION

It is probably true to say that the Landlord and Tenant Act 1954, Pt II ('the Act') has been one **7.01**
of the most successful property statutes in the last 60 years. This is due in large part to the fair
balance that it appears to strike between achieving a reasonable degree of security for business tenants while at the same time avoiding unnecessary harshness to landlords. As we shall
see, the complex provisions of the Act regulate the ways in which business tenancies can be
terminated and provide business tenants with much needed security of tenure.

Security of tenure for a business tenant under the Act is twofold: **7.02**

(a) The right for the tenancy to continue automatically at the end of the contractual term.
     Accordingly a fixed term lease does not end on the expiry date and a periodic tenancy is
     not terminated by the landlord's usual notice to quit. Section 24 of the Act continues
     the tenancy on the same terms (except for termination provisions) and at the same rent
     until it is terminated in one of the ways prescribed by the Act.
(b) The right for the tenant to apply to the court for a statutory renewal of the tenancy
     which can only be opposed by the landlord on grounds specified in the Act. In addition,
     the tenant has a right to compensation for disturbance if the application for renewal of
     the lease is unsuccessful.

Strict time limits are enforced for service of the various notices under the Act and for the **7.03**
tenant's application to the court for a new tenancy. Failure to adhere to these time limits
represents one of the most common examples of solicitors' negligence. Consequently attention to detail and a fail-safe diary or computer entry system are essential when dealing with
business tenancy renewals.

Although the Act has been very successful, it was reformed by the Regulatory Reform (Business **7.04**
Tenancies) (England and Wales) Order 2003, SI 2003/3096, which came into force on 1 June
2004. The reforms do not alter the substance of the Act and are largely procedural in nature.
They are incorporated into the text but a summary of them can be found at para 7.190 below.

B QUALIFYING AGREEMENTS

The Act applies to 'any tenancy where the property comprised in the tenancy is or includes **7.05**
premises which are occupied by the tenant and are so occupied for the purposes of a business
carried on by him or for those and other purposes' (s 23(1)). Thus to qualify for protection
under the Act *a tenant must be occupying premises for the purposes of a business*. The wording of
s 23(1) as interpreted by the courts is now considered.

C NEED FOR 'TENANCY'

Section 23(1) uses the word 'tenancy', which is defined in s 69(1) of the 1954 Act as **7.06**
being a:

> . . . tenancy created either immediately or derivatively out of the freehold, whether by a lease or

underlease, by an agreement for a lease or underlease or by a tenancy agreement or in pursuance of any enactment (including this Act), but does not include a mortgage term or any interest arising in favour of a mortgagor by his attorning tenant to his mortgagee . . .

It follows that a licence cannot be protected by the Act because it is not a tenancy. However, there are dangers for landlords who seek to avoid the Act by purporting to grant a licence to occupiers of their premises. The courts have construed many so-called licences to be mere fabrications, and have held them instead to be tenancies. If the agreement has the hallmarks of a tenancy (exclusive possession, for a term, and at a rent) then the courts will generally construe it as such, notwithstanding that the parties may call it a licence (see *Bruton v London & Quadrant Housing Trust Ltd* [1999] 3 WLR 150, HL). A tenancy includes an equitable interest under an agreement for a lease as well as a sub-lease, even if the sub-lease has not been authorized by the superior landlord (see *D'Silva v Lister House Developments Ltd* [1971] Ch 17).

7.07   It is well known that the key factor in determining whether an arrangement is a tenancy or licence is whether the occupier has been granted exclusive possession of the property (*Street v Mountford* [1985] 2 All ER 289, HL). Exclusive possession by the occupier will connote a tenancy, and this has been confirmed in several cases involving commercial property. In *Esso Petroleum Ltd v Fumegrange Ltd* [1994] 2 EGLR 90, the Court of Appeal held that exclusive possession of a petrol station had not been granted because the licensor had reserved extensive rights over the property. These included control over the way in which the occupier's business was to be operated as well as the physical layout of the site. It should be noted that a reservation of a simple right of entry or access onto the occupier's premises will be insufficient to negate exclusive possession (see *Addiscombe Garden Estates Ltd v Crabbe* [1957] 3 All ER 563, CA). In *National Car Parks Ltd v Trinity Development Company (Banbury) Ltd* [2000] EGCS 128, the court held that an agreement to occupy premises as a car park did not constitute a tenancy and was a mere licence. Here the fact that the agreement allowed the licensor potentially to use the premises itself to park cars, and also laid down regulations as to the conduct of the licensee's business, was sufficient to deny exclusive possession.

D   TENANCIES WHERE STATUTORY PROTECTION IS EXCLUDED

7.08   Certain tenancies are excluded from the protection of the Act. The principal exclusions relevant to conveyancing practice are discussed in paras 7.09 to 7.22 below.

Fixed term tenancies not exceeding six months (s 43(3))

7.09   Although generally excluded, it should be noted that these short fixed term tenancies will be protected under the Act in two situations:

(a) if they contain provisions for renewing the term or extending it beyond six months (s 43(3)(a)), or

(b) if the tenant (including any predecessor in the same business) has already been in occupation for a period exceeding 12 months (s 43(3)(b)). For the tenant to have protection, such occupation must be under either a fixed term or a periodic tenancy, ie, not as licensee, tenant at will, or trespasser. Note that any predecessor in the tenant's business need not necessarily have been a tenant and may have been occupying as a mere licensee, or even as freeholder (see *Cricket Ltd v Shaftesbury plc* [1999] 3 All ER 283).

The exception under s 43(3)(b) allows a tenant starting up in business to be granted up to **7.10** three successive tenancies of less than six months each. This is because by the time the third tenancy is granted, the tenant will not have been in occupation for 12 months.

Contracted out tenancies

Under s 38A of the Act, the prospective landlord and tenant may agree to exclude from the **7.11** lease the security of tenure provisions of the Act (ss 24–28). Importantly, the agreement must satisfy three statutory requirements, failing which the agreement will be void with the consequence that the tenancy will be protected under the Act. For landlords, it is therefore vital that these requirements are observed. They are:

Landlord's health warning

Before the tenant enters into the tenancy (or, if earlier, before the tenant is contractually **7.12** bound to do so) the landlord must serve on the tenant a 'health warning' notice in the form, or substantially the form, set out below. The notice should be served 14 days before the tenant commits itself to the lease.

IMPORTANT NOTICE

You are being offered a lease without security of tenure. Do not commit yourself to the lease unless you have read this message carefully and have discussed it with a professional adviser.

Business tenants normally have security of tenure—the right to stay in their business premises when the lease ends.

If you commit yourself to the lease you will be giving up these important legal rights.

- You will have no right to stay in the premises when the lease ends.
- Unless the landlord chooses to offer you another lease, you will need to leave the premises.
- You will be unable to claim compensation for the loss of your business premises unless the lease specifically gives you this right.
- If the landlord offers you another lease, you will have no right to ask the court to fix the rent.

It is, therefore, important to get professional advice—from a qualified surveyor, lawyer, or accountant—before agreeing to give up these rights.

If you receive this notice at least 14 days before committing yourself to the lease, you will need to sign a simple declaration that you have received this notice and have accepted its consequences, before signing the lease.

But if you do not receive at least 14 days notice, you will need to sign a 'statutory' declaration. To do so, you will need to visit an independent solicitor (or someone else empowered to administer oaths).

Unless there is a special reason for committing yourself to the lease sooner, you may want to ask the landlord to let you have at least 14 days to consider whether you wish to give up your statutory rights. If you then decided to go ahead with the agreement to exclude the protection of the Landlord and Tenant Act 1954, you would only need to make a simple declaration, and so you would not need to make a separate visit to an independent solicitor.

Tenant's declaration

7.13   After receiving the health warning notice the tenant (or someone authorized by the tenant, eg, his solicitor) must take the following action before entering into the tenancy (or, if earlier, becoming contractually bound to do so). The tenant (or authorized person) must sign a declaration that the tenant has received the health warning and accepts the consequences of contracting out of the Act. Provided the tenant receives the health warning at least 14 days before committing himself to the lease, the tenant (or authorized person) merely signs a simple declaration (not requiring a witness), stating that the tenant has received the notice and accepts the consequences of contracting out of the Act.

7.14   However, the landlord is permitted to serve the health warning notice less than 14 days before the tenant enters into the tenancy (or, if earlier, becomes contractually bound to do so). In this case, the tenant must sign a more formal statutory declaration in front of an independent solicitor (or someone else empowered to administer oaths). Thus the parties can effectively waive the 14-day period. Notwithstanding this, it is important to appreciate that however late the health warning is served, it must always be served *before* the tenant actually enters into the tenancy (or becomes contractually bound to do so). Failure to do so will make the agreement to contract out of the Act void.

Reference in the lease

7.15   The third requirement is that the lease must contain reference to (a) the health warning, (b) the tenant's declaration or statutory declaration, and (c) the agreement to contract out. Typically this will all be contained in a separate clause in the lease. Alternatively, a separate endorsement to this effect can be attached to the lease.

Tenancies at will

7.16   Tenancies at will may occur where a person occupies property with the permission of the owner but does not pay rent (see *Wheeler v Mercer* [1957] AC 416). The owner/landlord can withdraw permission to occupy at any time ('at will'), but the tenant must also have the right to terminate the tenancy at any time. Tenancies at will cannot be granted for a fixed term. They can be made expressly but often arise by implication. Examples of implied tenancies at will include where the tenant takes possession before the lease is formally granted (see *Javad v Aqil* [1991] 1 WLR 1007, CA), or where the tenant holds over at the end of a fixed-term tenancy (see *Cardiothoracic Institute v Shrewdcrest Ltd* [1986] 1 WLR 368). In *Hagee (London) Ltd v AB Erikson and Larson* [1975] 3 All ER 234, the Court of Appeal confirmed that an express tenancy at will did not fall within the Act. A tenancy at will is not a legal estate, as it does not fall within the definition of a term of years absolute in the Law of Property Act 1925. Landlords should beware that if they accept rent a tenancy at will may be converted into an implied tenancy, which would prima facie confer statutory protection on the tenant.

Service tenancies

7.17   These are tenancies granted to persons in connection with their office or employment (eg, school caretaker) and end when the office or employment is terminated. A service tenancy granted after 1 October 1954 (the commencement date of the Act) must be in writing and express the purpose for which it was granted. Provided this occurs, a service tenancy is not protected under the Act (s 43(2)).

Agricultural holdings

Agricultural holdings are not protected by the Act (s 43(1)(a)). They are protected under a **7.18** different statute, the Agricultural Holdings Act 1986. For the purposes of the 1954 Act 'agricultural holding' has the same meaning as in s 1(1) of the 1986 Act. If the tenancy appears to qualify as both an agricultural holding and a business tenancy, it will be protected as an agricultural holding only, not as a business tenancy under the 1954 Act (*Short v Greeves* [1988] 1 EGLR 1, CA). Neither the 1954 Act nor the 1986 Act applies to new lettings to new tenants since 1 September 1995. These are known as 'farm business tenancies' and are governed by the Agricultural Tenancies Act 1995.

Mining leases

Section 43(1)(b) provides that the Act does not apply where land is let under a mining lease. **7.19** Under s 46, 'mining lease' has the same meaning as in the Landlord and Tenant Act 1927, s 25(1), which provides:

> The expression 'mining lease' means a lease for any mining purpose or purposes connected therewith, and 'mining purposes' include the sinking and searching for, winning, working, getting, making merchantable, smelting or otherwise converting or working for the purposes of any manufacture, carrying away, and disposing of mines and minerals, in or under land, and the erection of buildings, and the execution of engineering and other works suitable for those purposes . . .

The Court of Appeal in *O'Callaghan v Elliott* [1965] 3 All ER 111 held that the Act did not **7.20** apply to a lease granted for the extraction of sand and gravel.

Tenancies of premises licensed to sell alcohol, not including hotels etc

The protection of the 1954 Act does not extend to tenancies of premises licensed to sell **7.21** alcohol, not including hotels, restaurants and other premises where the sale of alcohol is not the main use of the premises, which were granted before 11 July 1989. Tenancies of premises licensed to sell alcohol granted on or after 11 July 1989 are protected by the 1954 Act (Landlord and Tenant (Licensed Premises) Act 1990, s 1(1)). Off licences have consistently enjoyed full statutory protection.

Other exclusions

The Act will also not apply in the following situations: **7.22**

(a) *National security and public interest.* Sections 57 and 58 of the Act permit the determination of business tenancies on the grounds of national security and public interest. A public interest certificate may be issued where the premises are required for the purposes of a government body such as a local authority, or development corporation, or even the National Trust (see *R v Secretary of State for the Environment, ex p Powis* [1981]

1 All ER 788). A tenant who is precluded from obtaining a new tenancy will in certain circumstances be entitled to compensation (s 59). Sections 60, 60A and 60B contain similar provisions applying to premises where the landlord is the Minister of Technology, the Urban Regeneration Agency, the Welsh Development Agency, or the Development Board for Rural Wales.

(b) *Where the parties to a lease agree that the tenant will be granted a new tenancy in the future (s 28).* The agreement must specify the date of the future tenancy, and the current tenancy will end on that date. It is for the period between the date of the agreement and the date of the new tenancy that the tenant will not be protected by the Act. The agreement must comply with s 2 of the Law of Property (Miscellaneous Provisions) Act 1989 and be binding and enforceable between the parties (*RJ Stratton Ltd v Wallis Tomlin & Co Ltd* [1986] 1 EGLR 104, CA). To protect the agreement against any potential assignee of the reversion the tenant should register it as an estate contract. This will be a class C(iv) land charge in unregistered land, or a notice in registered land.

(c) *Where the court revokes an order for a new tenancy following an application by the tenant under s 36(2) of the Act* (see para 7.180 below). This section allows the tenant to apply for a revocation within 14 days of the order for a new lease. It will be used by a tenant who is not satisfied with the new terms granted by the court. Following the revocation, the Act will not apply to the current tenancy, which will continue under s 36(2) for such period as the court may specify.

E   NEED FOR 'OCCUPATION'

7.23 In most cases it will be fairly clear whether the tenant is in occupation of the premises. The courts have held that the important factors to be taken into account are the tenant's physical occupation or presence, and the measure of control the tenant exercises over those who use the premises (see *Wandsworth LBC v Singh* (1991) 62 P & CR 219, CA, in particular the judgment of Ralph Gibson LJ at 227–230). In *Hancock and Willis v GMS Syndicate Ltd* [1983] 1 EGLR 70, CA, Eveleigh LJ said (at 72):

> The words with which we are concerned import, in my judgment, an element of control and use and they involve the notion of physical occupation. That does not mean physical occupation every minute of the day provided the right to occupy continues. But it is necessary for the judge trying the case to assess the whole situation where the element of control and use may exist in variable degrees. At the end of the day it is a question of fact for the tribunal to decide, treating the words as ordinary words in the way in which I have referred to them.

7.24 If the tenant is forced to leave the premises because of something over which it has no control, eg, fire damage or to allow lessor's repairs, the tenant remains in occupation for the purposes of the Act (*Morrison Holdings Ltd v Manders Property (Wolverhampton) Ltd* [1976] 2 All ER 205). However, the tenant must continue to exert and claim a right to occupy the premises (see *Demetriou v Poolaction* [1991] 1 EGLR 100, CA and *Fairline Properties Ltd v Hassan* [1998] EGCS 169). If the tenant leaves the premises voluntarily it will be a question of fact as to whether the 'thread of business continuity' has been broken. If the thread is broken the tenant will have ceased to occupy for the purposes of the Act (see *Aspinall Finance Ltd v Viscount Chelsea* [1989] 1 EGLR 103). The longer the period of absence, the more likely it is that the thread will have been broken. For shorter periods, Simon Brown LJ in *Bacchiocchi v Academic Agency Ltd* [1998] 2 All ER 241 said (at 249):

> . . . whenever business premises are empty for only a short period, whether mid-term or before or after trading at either end of the lease, I would be disinclined to find that the business occupancy has ceased (or not started) for that period provided always that during it there exists no rival for the role of business occupant and that the premises are not being used for some other, non-business purposes. That to my mind is how Part II of the 1954 Act should operate in logic and in justice.

If the tenant is a seasonal occupier, eg, it is a summer holiday business where the tenant is absent during the winter months, the tenant normally will be regarded as in occupation for the whole year (*Artemiou v Procopiou* [1965] 3 All ER 539, CA).   **7.25**

Occupation by a manager or agent of the tenant may be sufficient to constitute occupation by the tenant, provided the management or agency arrangement is genuine (see *Pegler v Craven* [1952] 1 All ER 685 and *Cafeteria (Keighley) Ltd v Harrison* (1956) 168 EG 668, CA). A limited company's business that is managed by another company may also be in occupation (*Ross Auto Wash Ltd v Herbert* (1978) 250 EG 971); and where another company within the same group occupies the premises, the occupation is treated as occupation by the tenant (s 42). Under the 2004 reforms the protection of the Act is extended to tenancies where the tenant and the business are not the same, as long as one controls the other. For example a company which is in occupation and is controlled by the tenant will be protected by the Act (s 23(1A)).   **7.26**

Generally, if the tenant sub-lets or parts with possession of the premises it can no longer be said to be in occupation of the part (or whole) that has been sub-let. It would therefore not qualify for statutory protection in respect of the part (or whole) of the premises occupied by the sub-tenant. In *Graysim Holdings Ltd v P&O Property Holdings Ltd* [1995] 3 WLR 854, the tenant of a market hall managed it by sub-letting to stallholders who had exclusive possession of their stalls. Unusually, the Court of Appeal held that both the tenant and sub-tenant could be 'in occupation' for the purposes of the Act. However, the House of Lords held that there could be no dual occupation and reversed the decision. Importantly, their Lordships left open the possibility that the tenant may, exceptionally, reserve sufficient rights over the sub-let part to enable it to remain the 'occupier' at law. The Court of Appeal has subsequently applied the reasoning in *Graysim* (see *Bassari Ltd v Camden LBC* [1998] EGCS 27, CA).   **7.27**

F   NEED FOR 'THE PURPOSES OF A BUSINESS'

To qualify for protection under the Act, the tenant is required to occupy the premises for the purposes of a business. The fact that they are occupied for business purposes does not necessarily mean that the tenant must carry on the business there. What is important is that the premises must be occupied for that purpose (see *Bracey v Read* [1962] 3 All ER 472 and *Methodist Secondary Schools Trust Deed Trustees v O'Leary* [1993] 1 EGLR 105, CA). A business carried on by one member of a group of companies of which the tenant company is a member is treated as a business of the tenant (s 42(2)(a)). Similarly, where a tenancy is held   **7.28** on trust, the carrying on of a business by the beneficiaries under the trust is treated as being the business of the tenant (s 41(1)).

7.29 The definition of 'business' in s 23(2) includes a 'trade, profession or employment and includes any activity carried on by a body of persons, whether corporate or unincorporate'. It can be seen that the definition is narrower for an individual ('trade, profession or employment') than it is for a body of persons ('any activity'). Thus a body of persons running a tennis club was held to be a business (*Addiscombe Garden Estates v Crabbe* [1958] 1 QB 513, CA), as was the administration of a hospital by a board of governors (*Hills (Patents) Ltd v University College Hospital Board of Governors* [1956] 1 QB 90, CA). Similarly, a local authority's maintenance of a park was classified as a business activity under the Act (*Wandsworth LBC v Singh* (1991) 62 P & CR 219, CA). However, an individual running a Sunday school has been held not to be within the definition of 'trade, profession or employment'. The provision of residential accommodation by way of a business venture has been classified as a business activity (*Lee-Verhulst (Investments) Ltd v Harwood Trust* [1973] QB 204).

7.30 If the premises are used partly for business and partly for residential purposes (eg, a flat above a shop), the test is whether the business activity is a significant purpose of the occupation, or whether it is merely incidental to the occupation as a residence. It is a question of degree in each case. For example, an office block might have sleeping accommodation for staff on the top floor. Although residential in nature, the sleeping accommodation would only be incidental to the building's principal use as business premises. Conversely, one room in a dwellinghouse set aside exclusively for business purposes (eg, a doctor's private consultation room at home) would not alter the fact that the significant purpose of the occupation of the property was residential. This occurred in *Royal Life Savings Society v Page* [1978] 1 WLR 1329. In *Gurton v Parrot* [1991] 1 EGLR 98, a residential tenant's conversion of outbuildings into dog kennels was held to be merely incidental to the property's use as a dwellinghouse. Similarly in *Wright v Mortimer* (1996) 28 HLR 719, CA, an art historian's use of his flat for writing was held to be merely incidental to his residential use. On the other hand, a seafood importer who received business visitors and kept files, a telephone and typewriter in his flat, and had no other business premises, was held to occupy the flat for business purposes (*Cheryl Investments Ltd v Saldanha* [1979] 1 All ER 5, CA).

7.31 If the lease prohibits business use generally (eg, 'not to use the premises for business purposes'), the tenant cannot obtain protection from the Act simply by carrying on a business in breach of the covenant (s 23(4)). However, the Act may apply if the landlord consented to or acquiesced in the breach (see *Bell v Alfred Franks and Bartlett Co Ltd* [1980] 1 All ER 356 and *Methodist Secondary Schools Trust Deed Trustees v O'Leary* [1993] 1 EGLR 105, CA). The tenancy will still come within the Act if the tenant's user is merely in breach of a covenant in the lease. For example, a covenant:

(a) prohibiting use for a specified business (eg, 'not to use as a modelling agency'—if in breach of covenant the premises are used as a modelling agency, the Act would still apply), or

(b) prohibiting use for any business except a specified business (eg, 'not to use except as a modelling agency'—if in breach of covenant the premises are used for a business other than a modelling agency, again the Act would still apply).

G WAYS OF TERMINATING TENANCIES UNDER THE ACT

A business tenancy protected by the Act can be terminated only in one of the ways **7.32** prescribed by the Act. Until that occurs the tenancy simply continues on the same terms as the original tenancy (except for the termination provisions). The landlord or the tenant can seek an increased rent by applying to the court for an interim rent under s 24A of the Act (see para 7.99 below).

The most widely used methods of termination are the landlord's s 25 notice and the tenant's **7.33** s 26 request. These are considered below at paras 7.43 and 7.64 respectively. The other methods of termination are:

(a) a tenant's notice under s 27(1) or s 27(2) of the Act where the tenancy is for a fixed term (these notices are used where the tenant does not wish the lease to continue or be renewed: see para 7.34 below),

(b) a tenant's notice to quit in a periodic tenancy (provided the tenant has been in occupation for at least one month),

(c) surrender,

(d) forfeiture,

(e) forfeiture of a superior lease,

(f) notice to quit served by a mesne landlord on the superior landlord, and

(g) an agreement between the parties for a future tenancy under s 28 of the Act (see para 7.22 above).

Tenant's notice under s 27

If the tenant has a fixed term tenancy and does not wish it to continue, the tenant can **7.34** terminate the lease by serving on the immediate landlord a statutory notice under s 27 of the 1954 Act. There are two types of notice. A notice under s 27(1) is served before the end of the contractual term; whereas a notice under s 27(2) is served after the end of the contractual term where the tenant is holding over.

Before the end of the contractual term—tenant's notice under s 27(1)

A tenant who has been in occupation under a business tenancy for at least one month and **7.35** who does not wish to renew its fixed term tenancy can serve a notice in writing on its immediate landlord under s 27(1). This notice must be served not later than three months before the end of the fixed term. The tenancy will then come to an end on the expiry of the contractual term. Section 27(1) applies only to 'a term of years certain', ie, a fixed term. This would exclude periodic tenancies, but would include a fixed term of less than one year (see *Re Land and Premises at Liss, Hants* [1971] 3 All ER 380). It has been held that 'a term of years certain' would not include a term of 12 months and thereafter from year to year determinable on the landlord giving 12 months' notice (*Nicholls v Kinsey* [1994] 2 WLR 622, CA).

There is no prescribed form, but a typical notice might read as follows: **7.36**

To [name of landlord]
of [address of landlord]

From [name of tenant]
of [address of tenant]

1.   I am the tenant of [address of property] under a lease dated [date of lease] ('the Lease') made between [original parties to lease].
2.   The Lease expires on [contractual expiry date].
3.   I hereby give you notice under s 27(1) of the Landlord and Tenant Act 1954 ('the Act') that I do not wish my tenancy to be continued under the provisions of Part II of the Act.

Dated:
Signed:
[signature of tenant, or on behalf of tenant]

A tenant who has served a s 27(1) notice is not permitted to serve a s 26 request (s 26(4)). A s 27(1) notice will not affect any sub-tenancy protected by the Act.

7.37   What is the position if the tenant vacates the premises before the contractual expiry date? Is a s 27(1) notice needed? In *Esselte AB v Pearl Assurance plc* [1997] 02 EG 124, it was held that a s 27(1) notice is strictly not necessary if the tenant has ceased to occupy the premises for business purposes on or before the contractual expiry date. This is because the tenancy is no longer one to which the 1954 Act applies (ie, not in occupation for the purposes of a business) and so cannot be continued under s 24.

7.38   The 2004 reforms amend the Act to reflect the decision in *Esselte AB v Pearl Assurance plc* [1997] 02 EG 124. Section 27(1A) provides, in effect, that a fixed term tenancy will not continue under the Act if the tenant was not in occupation at the contractual expiry date. However, in cases of doubt as to whether the tenant has fully quit the premises, it is still best practice for the tenant to serve a s 27(1) notice.

After the end of the contractual term—tenant's notice under s 27(2)

7.39   A notice under s 27(2) differs slightly from a s 27(1) notice. It is served by a tenant who is holding over after the contractual expiry date has passed and who does not wish to renew the tenancy. As with a s 27(1) notice, the tenant must have been in occupation for at least one month. It is served on the immediate landlord, who must be given at least three months' notice expiring on any day. This is a change from the position before 1 June 2004 where the three months' notice had to expire on a quarter day.

7.40   There is no prescribed form, but a typical notice might read as follows:

To [name of landlord]
of [address of landlord]
From [name of tenant]
of [address of tenant]

1.   I am the tenant of [address of property] under a lease dated [date of lease] ('the Lease') made between [original parties to lease].
2.   The Lease expired on [contractual expiry date] and my tenancy continues under s 24 of the Landlord and Tenant Act 1954 ('the Act').
3.   I hereby give you notice under s 27(2) of the Act that my tenancy will come to an end on [date tenancy to end] by virtue of this notice.

Dated:
Signed:
[signature of tenant, or on behalf of tenant]

A tenant who has served a s 27(2) notice is not permitted to serve a s 26 request (s 26(4)). A **7.41**
s 27(2) notice will not affect any sub-tenancy protected by the Act. If the tenant vacates the
premises after the end of the contractual term, it cannot rely on the effect of *Esselte AB v Pearl
Assurance plc* [1997] 02 EG 124 and the new s 27(1A) (see para 7.38 above). This is because
s 27(2) provides that where a fixed term continues under s 24 the tenancy will not end
merely because the tenant ceases to occupy the premises. The tenant must therefore serve a
s 27(2) notice to bring the tenancy to an end.

Under a new s 27(3), provision is made for the appropriate apportionment of rent to be made **7.42**
in the tenant's favour as at the expiry of a s 27(2) notice. The tenant may therefore recover
any overpayment of rent.

Landlord's notice under s 25

If the tenant is protected under the Act and the landlord requires the premises back at the **7.43**
end of the lease, the landlord must serve a s 25 notice on the tenant specifying the grounds
on which the landlord is claiming possession. This is known as a 'hostile notice'. The specified grounds for possession are contained in s 30(1) of the Act and are considered at paras
7.110 et seq below. Even if the landlord is content for the tenant to remain in possession
under a negotiated new lease, the landlord must still serve a s 25 notice to end the existing
lease. This is known as a 'non-hostile notice'. The landlord cannot serve a s 25 notice if the
tenant has already served a s 26 request or a s 27 notice.

The s 25 notice is effective only if it is in a prescribed form. Moreover, there are strict **7.44**
time limits for service in that the notice must be given not less than six months, or more
than 12 months, before the *termination date specified in the notice*. As will be seen, the termination date cannot be earlier than the contractual expiry date, and may well be later. If the
time limits are not observed the notice will be invalid and of no effect. If the landlord client
suffers loss as a result of an invalid notice, a negligence claim against the solicitors is likely to
ensue.

Prescribed form and content of s 25 notice

The current prescribed form for a s 25 notice is set out in appendix 14. A form 'substantially **7.45**
to the like effect' can be used, but this is not to be recommended. To ensure that the most
current form is used, the safest practice is to use a printed form from law stationers or a
computer software form. If firms use their own word-processed forms there is always a danger that errors or omissions could occur, leading to possible negligence claims. Do not use
forms in use before 1 June 2004.

The s 25 notice must: **7.46**

(a) specify the date at which the tenancy is to end (s 25(1)). This termination date must not
be earlier than the date on which the tenancy could have been terminated at common
law. Thus for a normal fixed term without a break clause, the specified termination date
cannot be earlier than the last day of the contractual term. And for a fixed term lease
with a break clause (as well as a periodic tenancy), the specified termination date cannot
be earlier than the date upon which the landlord could have ended the tenancy by
common law notice;

(b)   state whether the landlord would oppose the tenant's application to the court for a new tenancy, and if so on which statutory grounds (s 25(6) and (7)). Thus the landlord must decide whether the notice is 'hostile' or 'non-hostile'. The statutory grounds of opposition are considered at paras 7.110 et seq below. The notice cannot be amended once it has been served, so the landlord should specify all the grounds on which it wishes to rely (*Hutchinson v Lambeth* [1984] 1 EGLR 75, CA);

(c)   if the s 25 notice states that the landlord would not oppose the tenant's application for a new tenancy, it must set out the landlord's proposals as to (i) the property to be comprised in the new tenancy (either the whole or part of the property comprised in the current tenancy); (ii) the new rent; and (iii) the other terms of the new tenancy (s 25(8)). This is a new provision introduced by the 2004 reforms;

(d)   be given and signed by, or on behalf of, the landlord. If there is more than one landlord, all their names must be given (*Pearson v Alyo* [1990] 1 EGLR 114). If there are joint tenants, the notice must be served on all of them unless the joint tenancy is held by a partnership. In this case, s 41A of the Act permits the landlord to serve only those tenants who are partners involved in running the business;

(e)   relate to the whole of the demised premises not part only (*Southport Old Links Ltd v Naylor* [1985] 1 EGLR 129). This applies even where the tenant has sub-let part of the premises. Where, after the grant of the tenancy, the reversion becomes vested in different landlords, the landlords should either serve a notice jointly, or serve separate notices which can be read together (see *M & P Enterprises (London) Ltd v Norfolk Square Hotels Ltd* [1994] 1 EGLR 129);

(f)   be served on any sub-tenant where the tenant has sub-let the *whole* of the premises. This is provided the sub-tenancy satisfies s 23 (see also paras 7.87 et seq regarding s 40).

7.47   If the prescribed information is omitted from the s 25 notice, is it still valid? The test, as laid down by Barry J in *Barclays Bank Ltd v Ascott* [1961] 1 WLR 717, is whether the notice gives 'the proper information to the tenant which will enable the tenant to deal in a proper way with the situation, whatever it may be, referred to in the statement of the notice'. The Court of Appeal approved this test in the later cases of *Tegerdine v Brooks* (1977) 36 P & CR 261, *Morrow v Nadim* [1986] 1 WLR 1381 and *Bridgers v Stanford* [1991] 2 EGLR 265. Ultimately it will be a question of whether a reasonable recipient would have been misled by the notice (see *Sabella Ltd v Montgomery* [1998] 1 EGLR65, CA, where a notice omitting the 'Act Quick' warning and other notes was held to be invalid). Accordingly, if the form is not materially different from the prescribed form then it will generally be considered valid (*Sun Alliance and London Assurance Co Ltd v Hayman* [1975] 1 WLR 177).

7.48   If the notice contains an error or is incorrectly completed, is it still valid? The test was laid down by the House of Lords in *Mannai Investment Co Ltd v Eagle Star Life Assurance Ltd* [1997] 3 All ER 352. Essentially, the court has to decide, first, whether the error in the notice is obvious or evident and, secondly, whether, despite the error, the notice read in its context is sufficiently clear to leave a reasonable recipient in no reasonable doubt as to the terms of the notice. Although the notice in this case was a contractual one, the Court of Appeal in *Garston v Scottish Widows' Fund and Life Assurance Society* [1998] 3 All ER 596 approved the *Mannai* test in the context of a statutory notice under the 1954 Act. The test before *Mannai* was very similar, namely, whether '. . . the notice is quite clear to a reasonable tenant receiving it . . . Is it plain enough that he cannot be misled by it?' (*per* Goulding J in *Carradine Properties Ltd v*

Aslam [1976] 1 WLR 442). (The pre-*Mannai* test was subsequently approved by the Court of Appeal in *Germax Securities Ltd v Spiegal* (1978) 37 P & CR 204 and *Bridgers v Stanford* [1991] 2 EGLR 265.) Although each case will turn on its own facts, it may be useful to consider examples of where defects have and have not invalidated a notice.

Examples of defects which have invalidated a s 25 notice: **7.49**

- failure to name all joint landlords in the notice (*Smith v Draper* [1990] 2 EGLR 69, CA; *Pearson v Alyo* [1990] 1 EGLR 261);
- naming the wrong person as landlord (*Morrow v Nadeem* [1986] 1 WLR 1381, CA);
- an assignor serving a notice after the reversion had been assigned (*Yamaha-Kemble Music (UK) Ltd v ARC Properties* [1990] 1 EGLR 261).

Examples of defects which have *not* invalidated a s 25 notice: **7.50**

- the notice was not signed but the covering letter made it apparent that the notice was served on behalf of the landlord (*Stidolph v American School in London Educational Trust* (1969) 20 P & CR 802, CA);
- the notice stated the wrong termination date but the covering letter made it apparent what date was intended (*Germax Securities Ltd v Spiegal* (1978) 37 P & CR 204);
- failure to date the notice (*Falcon Pipes Ltd v Stanhope Gate Property Co Ltd* (1967) 204 EG 1243);
- failure to refer to a tiny part of the premises (*Safeway Food Stores Ltd v Morris* [1980] 1 EGLR 59).

If the landlord discovers that a s 25 notice it has served is defective in some way (eg, it   **7.51** contains an error or has been incorrectly served), best practice is to serve a fresh notice without prejudice to the validity of the original notice. Then if the original notice is subsequently held to be invalid, the second notice will become effective (*Smith v Draper* [1990] 2 EGLR 69, CA; see also *Barclays Bank v Bee* [2001] EWCA Civ 1126, concerning a third notice held to be valid)).

Time limits for service of s 25 notice

The notice must be given not more than 12 months or less than six months, before the date   **7.52** of termination specified in the notice (s 25(2)). Moreover, this date of termination cannot be earlier than the date upon which the tenancy can be terminated at common law. There are thus different considerations for a normal fixed term, a fixed term with a break clause, and a periodic tenancy. These are considered below. In computing time limits under the Act the corresponding date rule is used, and 'month' means calendar month (ss 5 and 22(1) and Sch 2, para 4(1), Interpretation Act 1975). This means that the relevant period will end on the corresponding date in the appropriate subsequent month. So, for example, two months starting on 2 May will end on 2 July; but two months starting on 31 July will end on 30 September, and two months starting on 31 December will end on 28 (or 29) February. (See Lord Diplock's judgment in *Dodds v Walker* [1981] 1 WLR 1027, HL, at 1029.) These time limits are strictly enforced by the courts and it is therefore vitally important for practitioners to abide by them.

Normal fixed term tenancies without a break clause   In the usual case of a fixed term   **7.53** lease, the earliest time a landlord can serve the notice is one year before the end of the contractual term. For example, if the lease is due to end on 30 September 2005, the landlord cannot serve the notice earlier than 30 September 2004 (and for the avoidance of doubt it is probably safer to wait until the next day, 1 October 2004).

7.54 If the landlord delays serving notice until less than six months remain of the fixed term, it must still give the tenant at least six months' notice. In this situation the landlord would have to specify a termination date in the notice later than the contractual expiry date. In the example above, the lease is due to expire on 30 September 2005. If the landlord delays giving notice until after 30 March 2005, the termination date he specifies in the notice will inevitably need to be later than the contractual expiry date (30 September 2005). Even if the landlord delays serving notice until after the contractual expiry date has passed (ie, when the lease is continuing under s 24), the tenant must still be given a minimum of six months' notice.

7.55 **Fixed term tenancies with a break clause** Landlords' advisers must take great care when exercising a break option to end a lease before the contractual expiry date. How many notices must be served? One under the contract and one under the Act, or just one covering both contract and Act? The answer is that a single notice will suffice provided it fulfils both the statutory requirements and the requirements of the break clause (*Scholl Manufacturing Co Ltd v Clifton (Slim-Line) Ltd* [1967] Ch 41). If the notice fails to fulfil the requirements of s 25, the tenancy will not end but will continue under s 24. If the notice fails to fulfil the requirements of the contractual break clause, the lease will not 'break' and the opportunity for the landlord to break at this stage will have been lost. To be sure, it is recommended that landlords should serve both notices.

7.56 **Periodic tenancies** The notice required to end a periodic tenancy at common law is at least one full period of the lease expiring on the last day of a completed period of the tenancy (ie, on a rent day). The landlord serving a s 25 notice must ensure that the date of termination specified in the notice is not earlier than the date at which the tenancy could have been terminated by notice to quit (*Commercial Properties Ltd v Wood* [1968] 1 QB 15, CA). However, the s 25 notice must be given not more than 12 months, or less than six months, before the date of termination specified in the notice (s 25(2)). The following examples show how this works with both a monthly and a yearly tenancy:

- *Monthly tenancy*: assume that a tenant has a monthly periodic tenancy running from the 20th of each month. To end the tenancy at common law the landlord would need to serve notice to quit, on say, 19 April to expire on 20 May. But to comply with the requirements of the Act the landlord would need to give at least six months' notice. The notice served on 19 April could not therefore specify a termination date earlier than 20 October.
- *Yearly tenancy*: if the periodic tenancy were yearly from, say, 20 May, the minimum notice period at common law would be at least *six* months ending on the last day of a completed period, ie, 19 May. Thus if the landlord were to serve notice, say, on 10 August, he would have to specify a termination date between 19 May and 10 August of the following year.

7.57 If the periodic tenancy requires more than six months' notice (eg, contractually), s 25(3)(b) of the Act provides that the maximum period in the s 25 notice shall be six months longer than the length of notice required under the tenancy agreement. This circumvents the difficulty of a contractual notice period of more than 12 months. Without the assistance of s 25(3)(b) a landlord could never comply with the general statutory rule that notice must be given not more than 12 months before the termination date specified in the notice.

The tenant's counter-notice

The requirement for the tenant to serve a counter-notice is abolished in relation to s 25 notices given on or after 1 June 2004. **7.58**

Tenant's and landlord's applications to the court for a new tenancy

Before 1 June 2004 only the tenant could apply to the court for an order for the grant of a new tenancy. As from 1 June 2004 three important statutory changes have been made. First, both the tenant and the landlord can now apply to the court for a new tenancy, secondly, the time limit for making the court application is extended and, thirdly, the landlord and tenant may agree to extend that time limit. These procedures are now considered. **7.59**

Section 24(1) of the Act, as amended, enables either the tenant or the landlord to apply to the court for an order for the grant of a new tenancy. The application can be made only after the service of a landlord's s 25 notice or a tenant's s 26 request (the latter is considered at paras 7.64 et seq below) and must be made within the time limits referred to below. Neither party may make an application if the other has already made an application under s 24(1) and the application has been served. Nor can either party make a s 24(1) application if the landlord has already made an application under the new s 29(2) for an order for the termination of the current tenancy and the application has been served (see paras 7.72 et seq regarding such applications). **7.60**

Time limits Section 29A provides that an application to the court by either party under s 24(1) must be made on or before the date specified in the landlord's s 25 notice or immediately before the date specified in the tenant's s 26 request. These are the latest dates by which the application can be made (unless there is an agreement to extend, see below). The deadline is strictly enforced and so, for example, if the tenant fails to apply within the required time the tenancy will come to an end on the date specified in the s 25 notice or immediately before the date specified in the s 26 request, as the case may be. As such the tenant's right to apply for a new tenancy will be lost and the tenant's solicitor is likely to be sued in negligence. A fail safe diary system is therefore essential. Even if the landlord has indicated that he is willing to grant a new tenancy and terms are nearly agreed, the tenant must still apply to the court as a 'fallback'. Without the back-up of the court application, the landlord could simply change his mind and there would be nothing the tenant could do about it (save possibly a claim in estoppel (see *Bristol Cars Ltd v RKH Hotels Ltd* (1979) 38 P & CR 411) or that the landlord has waived its rights (see *Kammins Ballrooms Co Ltd v Zenith Investments (Torquay) Ltd* [1971] AC 850)). **7.61**

Where the tenant has made a s 26 request, the landlord or the tenant may not apply to the court until the landlord has served the required counter-notice, or the two-month period for service of the counter-notice has expired, whichever occurs first (s 29A(3)). Without this provision, a court application might be made at a time when it was not known whether the landlord opposed renewal and, if so, on what grounds. Once the landlord's counter-notice has been served, either party may apply to the court without waiting for the two months to elapse. The position in respect of a s 25 notice is much simpler. If the landlord has served a **7.62** s 25 notice, there is no two-month waiting period and either party may apply to the court immediately.

7.63 Section 29B allows the parties to agree to extend the latest time for applying to the court, provided they do so before the current time limit expires. The agreement must be made in writing. The parties may agree further postponements from time to time provided the agreement is made before the end of the period of postponement specified in the current agreement (s 29B(2)). The effect of such an agreement is that the s 25 notice or s 26 request is treated as terminating the tenancy at the end of the period specified in the agreement (s 29B(4)). It is hoped that this new provision, introduced in the 2004 reforms, will assist in reducing the number of court applications.

Tenant's request under s 26

7.64 This method of termination is not available to periodic tenants and those with fixed terms of one year or less. However, such tenants still have security of tenure and can apply for a new tenancy if the landlord has served them with a s 25 notice. Accordingly, to be able to serve a s 26 request the tenant must have been granted a term of years certain exceeding one year (whether or not continued by s 24), or a term of years certain and thereafter from year to year (s 26(1)).

7.65 A s 26 request must be served on the tenant's 'competent' landlord, or its agent, otherwise it will be invalid (*Railtrack plc v Gojra* [1998] 1 EGLR 63, CA). The tenant's competent landlord may not necessarily be the same as the tenant's immediate landlord (see paras 7.79 et seq for a discussion of competent landlord). A s 26 request cannot be served if the landlord has already served a s 25 notice, or the tenant has already served a s 27 notice (see paras 7.34 et seq above). Once the tenant has served a valid s 26 request it cannot later withdraw it and serve another amended one (*Polyviou v Seeley* [1980] 1 WLR 55).

Situations in which a tenant would be advised to serve a s 26 request

7.66 If a tenant has security of tenure then the tenancy will continue under s 24 until it is terminated by one of the ways under the Act. This gives rise to the question, why, if the tenant can continue in occupation under s 24, paying the existing rent, should it want to end the lease by serving a s 26 request? Why not wait until the landlord serves a s 25 notice and in the meantime carry on paying rent that is probably less than the market rent under any new lease? The following are situations in which a tenant would be advised to serve a s 26 request:

(a) *Tenant's tactical pre-emptive strike*. In a normal rising market, the tenant will wish to pay the current rent as long as possible because it will be lower than the market rent. In these circumstances, a prudent landlord would end the lease as early as possible by serving a s 25 notice one year before the expiry date (the termination date in the notice would be the expiry date of the contractual term, ie, 12 months hence). However, if the landlord is dilatory and forgets to serve a s 25 notice, the tenant could serve a s 26 request, say, six months before the expiry date, in which the tenant specifies a date 12 months ahead as the termination date. In this way the tenant would get six months longer paying the old rent. As an example, assume a lease has a contractual expiry date of 31 December. If by the middle of the previous June the landlord has not served a s 25 notice, the tenant could serve a s 26 request specifying a termination date 12 months ahead, ie, in June of the following year. That would be six months after the earliest date the landlord could have ended the lease.

(b) *Proposed improvements*. If the tenant intends to spend money improving the premises, it may prefer the certainty of a new fixed term lease before doing so.

(c) *Proposed sale*. If the tenant intends to assign the lease, a prospective buyer will probably want the certainty of a new fixed term lease being in place.

(d) *Fall in market rent*. If the market rent has fallen (eg, during a recession) and is less than the existing rent under the lease, the tenant will want a new lease with a lower market rent in place as soon as possible. The landlord, of course, will be happy for the old (higher) rent to continue.

Prescribed form and content of s 26 request

The current prescribed form for a s 26 request is set out in appendix 15. A form 'substantially to **7.67** the like effect' can be used, but this is not to be recommended. For cases on defects in notices and whether they invalidate them, see paras 7.48 et seq above, in particular *Mannai Investment Co Ltd v Eagle Star Life Assurance Ltd* [1997] 3 All ER 352. To ensure that the most current form is used, the safest practice is to use a printed form from law stationers or a computer software form. If firms use their own word-processed forms there is always a danger that errors could occur, leading to possible negligence claims. Do not use forms in use before 1 June 2004.

The s 26 request must: **7.68**

(a) specify a date for the commencement of the new tenancy (the existing tenancy will end immediately before this date). This commencement date must not be more than 12 months or less than six months after the making of the request. Nor must it be earlier than the date on which the tenancy could have been terminated at common law. Thus for a normal fixed term without a break clause, the specified termination date cannot be earlier than the last day of the contractual term. And for a fixed term lease with a break clause, the specified termination date cannot be earlier than the date upon which the tenant could have ended the tenancy by common law notice. In *Garston v Scottish Widows Fund and Life Assurance Society* [1998] 3 All ER 596, CA, the tenant effectively tried to engineer a downwards rent review by serving a break notice as permitted by the lease, and at the same time serving a s 26 request. The court disallowed this practice as being contrary to the spirit and purpose of the Act;

(b) set out the tenant's proposals for the new lease, namely—

   (i) the property to be comprised in the new tenancy. This can be either the whole or part of the property in the current tenancy (compare this with a s 25 notice in which the whole of the property must be specified),

   (ii) the new rent (valuation advice should be taken before doing so),

   (iii) the other terms of the new tenancy.

These proposals must be genuine and the tenant must have a real intention of taking up the new tenancy. Thus a request served merely as a precautionary measure will be invalid (*Sun Life Assurance plc v Racal Tracs Ltd* [2000] 1 EGLR 138);

(c) be given and signed by, or on behalf of, the tenant. If there is more than one tenant, all their names must be given (*Jacobs v Chaudhuri* [1968] 1 QB 470, CA) unless the joint tenancy is held by a partnership. In this case, s 41A of the Act allows only those tenants who are partners carrying on the business to be named in the request. If there are joint landlords the notice must be served on all of them.

Time limits for service of s 26 request

7.69 As mentioned above, the date specified in the s 26 request as the date for the commencement of the new tenancy must not be more than 12 months or less than six months after the request is served on the landlord. Accordingly, the earliest time a tenant can serve a request is one year before the contractual expiry date. In the case of a 'tenant's pre-emptive strike' (see para 7.66 above) the tenant will often specify a commencement date 12 months ahead, having given the request between 12 and six months before the contractual expiry date.

The landlord's counter-notice

7.70 Upon receiving a tenant's s 26 request the landlord has two months in which to notify the tenant if he intends to oppose the tenant's application to the court for a new tenancy (s 26(6)). There is no prescribed form of 'counter-notice' so a clear letter will suffice, but the landlord must state on which grounds in s 30 of the Act the landlord opposes the application (see paras 7.110 et seq below).

7.71 The landlord should be certain of his grounds because they cannot be amended later. If the landlord fails to serve a counter-notice within the two months he will lose his right to oppose the new tenancy. If the reversion is assigned after the counter-notice has been given, the incoming landlord steps into the shoes of the outgoing landlord and can rely on the grounds specified in the counter-notice (*Morris Marks v British Waterways Board* [1963] 1 WLR 1008). Needless to say, there have been many cases of negligence against landlords' solicitors who have overlooked this two-month deadline. A typical form of counter-notice might read as follows:

> To [name of tenant]
> of [address of tenant]
>
> I [name of landlord] of [address of landlord] received on [date of receipt] your request under s 26 of the Landlord and Tenant Act 1954 Part II ('the Act') for a new tenancy of [description of property] ('the Property').
> I hereby give you notice that I will oppose your application to the court for a new tenancy of the Property on the following ground(s) contained in s 30(1) of the Act, namely paragraph(s) [insert paragraph letter(s)].
>
> Dated:
> Signed:
> [signature of landlord, or on behalf of landlord]

Landlord's application to the court for an order for the termination of the current tenancy without the grant of a new tenancy

7.72 A new provision, introduced on 1 June 2004, enables the landlord to apply to the court for an order for the termination of the current tenancy without the grant of a new tenancy (s 29(2)). This is permitted either:

(a) where the landlord has given notice under s 25 that he is opposed to the grant of a new tenancy, or

(b) where the tenant has made a s 26 request and the landlord indicated in his counter-notice that he will oppose an application for a new tenancy, stating the ground(s) on which he will do so.

The landlord is not permitted to make an application for termination of the current tenancy if the tenant or the landlord has already made an application (albeit not served) for the grant of a new tenancy under s 24(1). **7.73**

Accordingly, if the landlord opposes the grant of a new tenancy on one or more of the grounds in s 30(1), the landlord has two options. He can either make his own application for termination of the current tenancy without the grant of a new tenancy under s 29(2) or he can defend the tenant's application under s 24(1) for the grant of a new tenancy. **7.74**

Where the landlord has made and served his application for an order for the termination of the tenancy, the tenant is not permitted to make an application for an order for a new tenancy (s 24(2B)). But if the landlord fails to establish any of the s 30(1) grounds of opposition, how does the tenant get his new tenancy? The answer lies in the new s 29(4)(b), which provides that the court 'shall make an order for the grant of a new tenancy and accordingly for the termination of the current tenancy immediately before the commencement of the new tenancy'. The clever landlord might try to defeat such an order by withdrawing his application. However, s 29(6) prevents this by providing that the landlord may not withdraw his application for an order for termination unless the tenant consents. Of course, if the tenant wants a new tenancy he should not simply consent to the withdrawal of the landlord's application. In doing so, he would lose his right to an order for a new tenancy! **7.75**

H   DEFINITION OF 'THE HOLDING'

On an application for a renewal of the lease the tenant will only be entitled to a renewal of 'the holding' as defined by the Act in s 23(3). The holding is defined as: **7.76**

> ... the property comprised in the tenancy, there being excluded any part thereof which is occupied neither by the tenant nor by a person employed by the tenant and so employed for the purposes of a business by reason of which the tenancy is one to which this Part of this Act applies.

It follows that the holding will not include the following, in respect of which the tenant cannot claim a new lease: **7.77**

(a) any part of the premises presently sub-let by the tenant will generally not form part of the holding unless the tenant can show that it remains in occupation of that part for business purposes (see paras 7.23 et seq above and *Graysim Holdings Ltd v P&O Property Holdings Ltd* [1995] 3 WLR 854);

(b) any part of the premises occupied by a third party;

(c) any part of the premises that is unoccupied;

(d) any part of the premises occupied by the tenant's employees in connection with another of the tenant's businesses.

It should be noted, however, that as long as the tenant occupies part of the premises for **7.78** business purposes the holding will include other parts of the premises that the tenant occupies for other purposes, eg, residential use. The extent of the holding is determined on the date on which the order for the grant of the new tenancy is made (s 32(1)). Some of the landlord's statutory grounds of opposition also refer to 'the holding'.

I DEFINITION OF 'COMPETENT LANDLORD'

7.79 A tenant's request for a new tenancy under s 26 must be served on the 'competent landlord' as defined by s 44(1) of the Act. Similarly, the 'competent landlord' must serve a landlord's s 25 notice. There can only be one competent landlord at any given time, and his or her identity may change during the course of the renewal procedure. If this occurs, the new competent landlord must be a made a party to any proceedings under the Act (*Piper v Muggleton* [1956] 2 All ER 875, CA). The time for determining the competent landlord is the date of service of the s 25 notice or s 26 request.

7.80 Where the tenant's immediate landlord is the freeholder, establishing the identity of the competent landlord will be easy (as it will obviously be the freeholder). However, in the case of sub-leases it is necessary to consider s 44(1) of the Act. This provides that where a landlord is a tenant himself, he will be the competent landlord to his immediate tenant only if his own tenancy will *not* come to an end within 14 months. If it will end within 14 months, the competent landlord will be the next landlord up the chain of tenancies whose tenancy satisfies this criterion (or the freeholder if you reach the top). This may be illustrated by Examples 1 and 2 involving a sub-lease. In each case, consider who is the sub-tenant's competent landlord.

EXAMPLE 1	EXAMPLE 2
L	L
↓ Fixed-term headlease	↓ Fixed-term headlease
T	T
↓ Sub-lease of whole	↓ Sub-lease of part
ST	ST
Example 1: L (freeholder) lets premises to T on fixed-term; T sub-lets *whole* of premises to ST.	Example 2: L (freeholder) lets premises to T on fixed term; T sub-lets *part* of premises to ST.

7.81 In example 1, because T has sub-let the whole, T is not 'in occupation', will not have the protection of the Act, and T's lease will not continue under s 24 (ie, it ends on the contractual expiry date). Thus, once T's lease (L–T) has less than 14 months to run, it will certainly come to an end within 14 months. ST's competent landlord will be L (freeholder) in any event.

7.82 In example 2, T occupies that part of the premises he has not sub-let to ST. Accordingly, T is protected by the Act ('in occupation') and T's lease (L–T) will continue under the Act (s 24). Thus, even during the last 14 months of T's lease, it will *not* come to an end within 14 months because it continues under the Act (see *Bowes-Lyon v Green* [1963] AC 420). ST's competent landlord will be T.

7.83 Importantly, however, the situation in Example 2 is reversed if L serves T with a s 25 notice, or T serves L with a s 26 request or s 27 notice. In this case T's lease *will* come to an end within 14 months because it is being terminated by one of the ways prescribed by the Act. In this case, ST's competent landlord will be L (freeholder).

In Example 2, for ST of part where T remains in occupation of the remainder, it is crucial for **7.84** ST to know, in respect of T's lease (L–T), whether T has been served with a s 25 notice (by L), or whether T has himself served a s 27 notice or s 26 request (on L). To establish the position, ST can serve a notice on T under s 40 of the Act. Section 40 notices are considered below (paras 7.87 et seq).

The following should also be considered where there is a sub-lease or sub-leases. If the **7.85** immediate landlord is the competent landlord and the immediate landlord's own lease has less than 16 months to run from the date of service or receipt, he is obliged to send a copy of the s 25 notice or s 26 request to his own landlord (1954 Act, Sch 6, para 7). The superior landlord, if he becomes the competent landlord within two months of service of the s 25 notice, may serve notice withdrawing the s 25 notice (1954 Act, Sch 6, para 6). The superior landlord may then choose whether to serve his own s 25 notice on the sub-tenant.

Similarly, where the superior landlord is not himself the freeholder, he must send a copy to **7.86** his landlord who has the same rights as described above. The superior/competent landlord will bind the intermediate landlord(s) in relation to s 25 notices that he gives to the sub-tenant. Moreover, the terms of any new tenancy that the superior/competent landlord agrees with the sub-tenant are binding on the intermediate landlord(s). However, the latter must give its/their consent (such consent not to be unreasonably withheld), failing which the superior/competent landlord will be liable to pay compensation for any loss arising from the making of the agreement (1954 Act, Sch 6, para 4).

J   SECTION 40 NOTICES

The identity of the competent landlord can change more than once during the course of the **7.87** litigation and renewal procedure. In Example 2 in para 7.80 above, the identity of the competent landlord will depend on whether notices or requests have been given to terminate T's lease (L–T) under the Act. To request information about superior leases and sub-leases, and whether notices or requests have been given, landlords and tenants can serve on each other a notice under s 40 of the Act. The 2004 reforms have increased the amount of information required to be given. Ideally, the s 40 notice should be served before or simultaneously with the notices or requests under ss 25, 26, and 27. For the consequences of a tenant serving the wrong person, see *Re 55 and 57 Holmes Road, Kentish Town, Beardmore Motors Ltd v Birch Bros (Properties) Ltd* [1959] Ch 298. A tenant can also serve a s 40 notice on any person being a mortgagee in possession. A s 40 notice may not be served earlier than two years before the date on which, apart from the Act, the tenancy would end by effluxion of time, or could be brought to an end by notice to quit given by the landlord (s 40(6)).

As a matter of good practice, the only time one can safely dispense with a s 40 notice is where **7.88** one is certain that the landlord is the freeholder and the tenant occupies the whole of the premises. (Perhaps a tenant should also resist serving a s 40 notice where he intends to serve a s 26 request and does not wish to prompt his landlord into serving a s 25 notice!) Only a tenant who is entitled to serve a s 26 request may serve a s 40 notice; thus a periodic tenant cannot serve one.

7.89   A tenant who receives a s 40 notice must indicate within one month whether he occupies the premises or any part of them wholly or partly for business purposes. The tenant must also indicate whether he has sub-let; and if so, must provide information about the sub-letting, including whether there has been a contracting-out and whether a s 25 notice has been served or a s 26 request made. The tenant must state the identity of any known reversioner. Conversely, a landlord who receives a s 40 notice must indicate within one month whether he owns the freehold; and if not, must give the identity of his immediate landlord and when his own tenancy will expire. A landlord must also state whether there is a mortgagee in possession and, if so, its name and address. Where there is a superior lease the landlord must state whether a s 25 notice has been served or a s 26 request has been made. The landlord must also state the identity of any known reversioner. There is a statutory duty on both landlord and tenant to update the information given for a period of six months from the date of service of the s 40 notice, where it ceases to be correct (s 40(5)).

7.90   A landlord may learn from a tenant in response to a s 40 notice that the premises have been sub-let. If the landlord has served a s 25 notice on the tenant, the landlord will now be the competent landlord of the sub-tenant. In these circumstances, generally it will be good practice for the landlord to serve a s 25 notice on the sub-tenant to prevent the sub-tenant making a s 26 request.

7.91   Section 40A, introduced on 1 June 2004, deals with cases concerning the transfer of an interest following the service of a s 40 notice. Section 40A(1) deals with the case of a recipient of a s 40 notice (either landlord or tenant) who subsequently transfers his interest in the property. Provided notice in writing of the transfer and of the name and address of the transferee is given to the server of the s 40 notice, the recipient of the s 40 notice ceases to be under a duty to comply with the original s 40 notice. This includes the duty to update any information already given. It follows that the server of the s 40 notice must serve a fresh s 40 notice on the transferee of the interest if they wish to receive up-to-date information.

7.92   Likewise, a new s 40A(2) deals with the case of the server of a s 40 notice who subsequently transfers his interest in the property. Here, the server (or his transferee) must give the recipient of the s 40 notice a notice in writing of the transfer and the name and address of the transferee. Once this is done, the duty to provide information becomes owed to the transferee of the interest. Where there has been no notice given of the transfer of an interest by the server of the s 40 notice, the recipient of the s 40 notice can perform his duty by providing the information either to the server of the s 40 notice or to the transferee of the interest (s 40A(3)).

7.93   Failure to comply with any of the s 40 requirements may result in civil proceedings in tort for breach of statutory duty. This is expressly laid down in s 40B. The court may make an order requiring compliance and make an award of damages. This new provision, introduced by the 2004 reforms, will mean that many landlords and tenants will need to take a far more serious attitude to their responses to s 40 notices than they have done in the past.

K   RULES FOR SERVICE OF NOTICES

Section 66(4) of the 1954 Act provides that the service of notices under the Act is governed **7.94** by s 23 of the Landlord and Tenant Act 1927. The prescribed methods of service are:

(a) personal service;
(b) leaving at the last known place of abode in England and Wales (or place of business: *Price v West London Investment Building Society* [1964] 2 All ER 318);
(c) sending by registered post or recorded delivery to the last known place of abode in England and Wales (or business). The benefit of using registered post or recorded delivery is that, even if the notice is not received, service is presumed (although it can be rebutted; see *Lex Service plc v Johns* [1990] 1 EGLR 92, CA, and *Italica Holdings SA v Bayadea* [1985] 1 EGLR 70). Another benefit is that the notice or request is deemed to have been served on the day it was posted (*Railtrack plc v Gojra* [1998] 08 EG 158). This makes calculating dates easier, eg, the termination date in a s 25 notice. If the notice is sent by recorded delivery but there is no one in the recipient's office when the post office attempts delivery, delivery is still deemed to have taken place (see *WX Investments v Begg* [2002] EWHC 925 (Ch)).

Service by ordinary post is also effective, provided the sender can prove that the posted item **7.95** was received. This allows the obvious risk that the notice could get lost in the post (see *Chiswell v Griffon Land and Estates Ltd* [1975] 2 All ER 665). Unlike registered post or recorded delivery, when service is effected by ordinary post the date of service is deemed to be the date of actual receipt. For companies, service can be effected at their registered offices (s 725, Companies Act 1985; see *National Westminster Bank v Betchworth Investments* [1975] 1 EGLR 57, CA). Service by fax is permitted provided the facsimile copy received is in a complete and legible state (*Hastie & Jenkerson v McMahon* [1990] RVR 172, CA). Service by fax is not recommended, because the recipient's fax machine may not be operating correctly or it may be using poor quality paper.

What if the person carrying on the business is resident abroad? In this case, if the property **7.96** contained in the tenancy is the only territorial link that person has in England and Wales then the tenanted property may be used as the place of abode (*Italica Holdings SA v Bayadea* [1985] 1 EGLR 70). Notice may be served on the landlord's agent where the agent has been duly authorized to receive notice (s 23(1) of the 1927 Act).

KEY POINTS SUMMARY: S 25 NOTICES AND S 26 REQUESTS

Landlord

- If you want the tenant to leave at the end of the lease, serve a hostile s 25 notice and be **7.97** sure of your statutory grounds for opposing a new lease.
- Be sure you are the 'competent' landlord for the tenant in question (see paras 7.79 et seq above). It may be necessary to serve a notice under s 40 to be sure (see paras 7.87 et seq above).
- The s 25 notice must be given not more than 12 months or less than six months before the date of termination specified in the notice; this termination date must not be earlier than

the date on which the tenancy could have been terminated at common law (eg, the contractual expiry date of a fixed term).

- If you are happy for the tenant to continue in occupation under a new lease and wish the new lease to be in place as soon as possible, serve a non-hostile s 25 notice one year before the contractual expiry date specifying the contractual expiry date as the termination date in the notice.
- Ensure that any s 25 notice is in the prescribed form and contains the prescribed content.
- If you receive a tenant's s 26 request and you want the tenant to leave, you must serve a counter-notice within two months specifying your statutory grounds for opposing a new lease.
- Serve by registered post or recorded delivery (in which case service is deemed to be the date of postage).

Tenant

7.98
- If you receive a landlord's s 25 notice and you want to renew your lease, ensure that you apply to the court for a new lease on or before the date specified in the s 25 notice.
- If you have not received a s 25 notice by the time there is less than 12 months to go on the lease, consider a 'pre-emptive strike' by serving a s 26 request and specifying a commencement date for the new lease 12 months hence.
- Serve the s 26 notice on your 'competent' landlord (see paras 7.79 et seq above). It may be necessary to serve a notice under s 40 to be sure (see paras 7.87 et seq above).
- Ensure that your s 26 request is in the prescribed form and contains the prescribed content.
- If you serve a s 26 request, be sure to apply to the court for a new lease before the date specified in the s 26 request.
- Serve by registered post or recorded delivery (in which case service is deemed to be the date of postage).

L   LANDLORD'S APPLICATION FOR INTERIM RENT

7.99   After an application to the court for a new lease, the current tenancy continues at the old contractual rent until three months after the conclusion of the proceedings (by virtue of s 64). This is clearly disadvantageous to a landlord seeking a higher market rent under the new lease, and it is also an incentive for the tenant to extend the proceedings for as long as possible. To remedy this unreasonable state of affairs the Law of Property Act 1969 inserted a new s 24A into the Act to allow the competent landlord to apply to the court for an interim rent to be fixed until the current tenancy comes to an end. In the case of a sub-tenancy where the head tenancy is also being continued under s 24, the competent landlord will be the head landlord. Thus, rather curiously, the head landlord will be applying for an interim rent which is payable to the intermediate landlord.

7.100   Under the 2004 reforms both landlords and tenants now have the right to make applications for interim rent. The reason for allowing the tenant to apply as well is because there may be market conditions under which rents are falling, and in this situation it is only fair to allow tenants to benefit from such market conditions.

A new s 24A was introduced on 1 June 2004. It states that provided either a s 25 notice has **7.101** been served or a s 26 request has been made, both landlords and tenants may apply for an interim rent while the tenancy is continuing under s 24. However no application may be made later than six months after the termination of the contractual tenancy. To avoid duplication of proceedings, neither party may apply if the other party has already done so, unless that application has been withdrawn.

Under s 24B the interim rent is payable from: **7.102**

(a) the earliest date that could have been specified for termination of the tenancy, where a s 25 notice has been served (s 24B(2)), or
(b) the earliest date that could have been specified for commencement of the new tenancy, where a s 26 request has been made (s 24B(3)).

This is intended to rule out the tactical use of s 25 notices and s 26 requests.

The basis for valuation of interim rent

The court is given a discretion to determine an interim rent which the tenant is to pay **7.103** while the current tenancy continues under s 24. There are two different methods for determining the amount of the interim rent. These are contained in s 24C and s 24D respectively and are now considered.

Section 24C valuation

The method of valuation contained in s 24C applies where the landlord grants a new ten- **7.104** ancy of the whole of the property previously let to the tenant, whether pursuant to a court order or otherwise, and three conditions are met. They are:

(a) that the landlord's s 25 notice or the tenant's s 26 request applies to the whole of the property let; and
(b) that the tenant is in business occupation of the whole of that property; and
(c) that the landlord does not oppose the grant of a new tenancy.

Subject to the two exceptions referred to below, under s 24C the market rent payable at the **7.105** commencement of the new tenancy shall also be the interim rent. Significantly therefore, unlike the position before 1 June 2004, the landlord should receive the full market rent as interim rent and, as such, the interim rent will have no 'cushioning effect' on the tenant (explained at para 7.107 below).

The two exceptions to this basis of valuation are as follows: **7.106**

(a) A substantial change in the market rent since the date when the interim rent became payable. Where either party is able to establish that the rent for the new tenancy differs substantially from the rent (determined on the same basis) that the court would have ordered had it been fixed to run from the date at which interim rent became payable, the latter becomes the interim rent.
(b) A substantial change in rent caused by a change in terms of the new tenancy. Where either party is able to establish that the occupational terms of the new tenancy are so different from those of the old one that they would affect the rent for the new tenancy,

had it been granted on the same occupational terms as the old one, the interim rent becomes the rent it would be reasonable for the tenant to pay.

Where both these exceptions apply, the court can use its discretion to fix a rent that it would be reasonable for the tenant to pay.

Section 24D valuation

7.107 The second method of valuation is contained in s 24D and applies in every other case, eg, where the landlord opposes the renewal. Essentially this is the same as the method used before 1 June 2004. The interim rent is 'the rent which is reasonable for the tenant to pay while the relevant tenancy continues by virtue of s 24' (s 24D(1)). It is assessed on the basis of a yearly tenancy and will generally be 10–15 per cent lower than the market rent for a fixed term lease (see *Janes (Gowns) Ltd v Harlow Development Corpn* (1979) 253 EG 799). The interim rent thus acts as a 'cushion' protecting the tenant from the blow of moving to a much higher market rent (see generally *English Exporters (London) Ltd v Eldonwall Ltd* [1973] Ch 415 and *Baptist v Masters of the Bench and Trustees of the Honourable Society of Gray's Inn* [1993] 2 EGLR 159). However, the level of interim rent is entirely at the court's discretion. In *Department of the Environment v Allied Freehold Property Trust Ltd* [1992] 45 EG 156 the court fixed a full market rent because the tenant had been paying a low contractual rent for a long period. In *Fawkes v Viscount Chelsea* [1980] QB 441 the court ordered a much lower rent until the landlord remedied breach of his repairing obligations. Additionally, and introduced by the 2004 reforms, the court must also have regard to the rent payable under any sub-tenancy of part of the property.

7.108 In a normal rising market the landlord will generally apply for an interim rent as early as possible, namely as soon as the s 25 notice or s 26 request has been given or received. Conversely, in a falling market the landlord will have no need for an interim rent if the contractual rent is higher than the prevailing market rent. Here, it is the tenant who would be advised to apply for an interim rent. Another instance when it should be unnecessary for a landlord to apply for an interim rent will be where the rent was reviewed immediately before the contractual expiry date (a 'penultimate day rent review'); in this case the tenant should already be paying the market rent.

7.109 The tenant will be required to start paying interim rent as soon as the court determines it. Interest will also be payable from this date, unless the lease provides that interest will be payable from a period after the rent becomes due, eg, 14 days. Interim rent continues to be payable until the date on which the current tenancy comes to an end.

M   LANDLORD'S STATUTORY GROUNDS OF OPPOSITION

7.110 There are seven statutory grounds in s 30(1) of the 1954 Act which entitle a landlord to resist a tenant's application for a new lease. If the landlord is successful in proving one or more of those grounds then the tenant's application should fail. It should be noted that some grounds are subject to the court's discretion. The landlord must state the relevant ground(s) in its s 25 notice or counter-notice to the tenant's s 26 request. No later amendments or additions to the grounds are allowed, so it is important that the landlord specifies the correct grounds at this early stage. However, the landlord's stated grounds must be genuine; if the grounds are false and made fraudulently, the notice may be rendered invalid and unenforceable (see *Rous v Mitchell* [1991] 1 All ER 676, CA). A subsequent purchaser of the landlord's interest will also be bound by the original landlord's choice of ground(s) (*Morris Marks v British Waterways Board* [1963] 3 All ER 28, CA).

In summary, the grounds of opposition are: **7.111**

(a) tenant's failure to carry out repairing obligations,
(b) tenant's persistent delay in paying rent,
(c) tenant's substantial breaches of other obligations,
(d) suitable alternative accommodation is available for the tenant,
(e) on sub-letting of part, the landlord requires the whole property for subsequent letting,
(f) the landlord intends to demolish or reconstruct the premises,
(g) the landlord intends to occupy the holding.

Grounds (a), (b), (c), and (e) are discretionary. Thus even if the landlord establishes the **7.112** ground, the court may decide to order a new tenancy in any event, eg, because of the tenant's good conduct. Examples of situations where the court may decide to use its discretion are considered below under the individual grounds. The remaining grounds—(d), (f), and (g)—are mandatory, so that if the landlord establishes the ground the court must refuse to order a new tenancy.

The specific grounds are now considered; and to assist in interpretation, the precise wording **7.113** of the grounds is set out followed by commentary and reference to cases.

Ground (a): tenant's failure to carry out repairing obligations

(a) where under the current tenancy the tenant has any obligations as respects the repair and maintenance of the holding, that the tenant ought not to be granted a new tenancy in view of the state of repair of the holding, being a state resulting from the tenant's failure to comply with the said obligations . . .

Ground (a) only applies to failure to repair the tenant's 'holding' as defined by the Act (see **7.114** paras 7.76 et seq above). Thus it would not apply to a part of the demised premises in disrepair which is occupied by a sub-tenant. Moreover, a substantial breach of covenant on the tenant's part may on its own be insufficient to establish the ground. The landlord must go further and show that the breach is serious enough that the 'tenant ought not to be granted a new tenancy'. Because of the ground's discretionary nature, the court may grant a new tenancy despite the breach (see *Nihad v Chain* (1956) 167 EG 139). The grant could be on the basis of an undertaking by the tenant to remedy the breach (see *Lyons v Central Commercial Properties Ltd* [1958] 2 All ER 767, CA, at 775; although a grant was actually refused in this case). In exercising its discretion the court will consider whether a new tenancy would be unfair to the landlord, having regard to the tenant's past performances and conduct. It will also consider the reasons for the tenant's breach of covenant to repair (see generally *Lyons v Central Commercial Properties Ltd*, above, applied subsequently in *Eichner v Midland Bank Executor & Trustee Co Ltd* [1970] 2 All ER 597, CA).

If the landlord intends to rely on this ground, it (or its surveyor) should first serve on the **7.115** tenant a schedule of dilapidations with a request that the repairs be carried out (on the assumption that there is a lease repairing covenant). The landlord may also consider forfeit-ure of the lease as an alternative to ground (a). A tenant faced with opposition under ground (a) should consider giving the landlord an undertaking to carry out the repairs within a set time. A court may take such an undertaking into account when exercising its discretion, but may also seek evidence that the tenant has sufficient funds to carry out the works. If the tenant is refused a new lease under ground (a), the tenant is not entitled to compensation.

Ground (b): tenant's persistent delay in paying rent

> (b)   that the tenant ought not to be granted a new tenancy in view of his persistent delay in paying rent which has become due . . .

7.116   The word 'persistent' is significant as it clearly means more than one incident of delay. The court will consider the frequency and extent of the delays (*Hopcutt v Carver* (1969) 209 EG 1069, CA), the steps the landlord had to take to secure payment, and how the landlord may be protected against delay in any future tenancy (*Rawashdeh v Lane* [1988] 2 EGLR 109, CA). In *Hazel v Akhtar* [2001] EWCA Civ 1883, the Court of Appeal held, interestingly, that the longer the practice of late payment continued, the easier it was for the tenant to argue that the landlord had accepted the tenant's conduct and was estopped from using ground (b). The ground is discretionary, so that even if persistent delay is proven the court may decide to order a new tenancy if the tenant can offer a satisfactory explanation for the delay. This occurred in *Hurstfell Ltd v Leicester Square Property Co Ltd* [1988] 2 EGLR 105, where the Court of Appeal declined to interfere with a decision of the county court judge who accepted the tenant's reasons for persistent delays over a period of more than two and a half years.

7.117   The word 'rent' may include other payments due under the lease if these are reserved as rent, eg, service charges. The landlord should prepare a full schedule of arrears which, if possible, should be agreed with the tenant. In the absence of agreement, the landlord should serve it on the tenant with a 'Notice to Admit Facts' under CPR, r 32.18. The tenant seeking to resist an opposition under ground (b) should ensure that no further arrears accrue and, if appropriate, suggest means of guaranteeing future payments (eg, a rent deposit or guaran-tor). If the tenant is refused a new lease under ground (b), the tenant is not entitled to compensation.

Ground (c): tenant's substantial breaches of other obligations

> (c)   that the tenant ought not to be granted a new tenancy in view of other substantial breaches by him of his obligations under the current tenancy, or for any other reason connected with the tenant's use or management of the holding . . .

7.118   This is another discretionary ground. It concerns the tenant's substantial breaches (note the use of the word 'substantial') of *other* obligations in the lease (ie, other than repair or rent), and it also extends to reasons linked generally with the tenant's use or management of the holding. Thus a court can refuse to grant a new lease if the tenant is at fault in some way even though the tenant has performed all his obligations under the lease. This occurred in *Turner & Bell v Searles (Stanford-le-Hope) Ltd* (1977) 33 P & CR 208, where the Court of Appeal allowed the landlord to succeed on this ground because the tenant's use of the premises contravened a planning enforcement notice. The court must have regard to all relevant circumstances, including whether the landlord's interest has been prejudiced, the general conduct of the tenant, and any proposals for remedying the breach (see *Eichner v Midland Bank Executor and Trustee Co Ltd* [1970] 2 All ER 597 and *Beard v Williams* [1986] 1 EGLR 148).

Whether a breach is 'substantial' is a question of fact in each case. In addition, the reference **7.119** to 'breaches' would not preclude a single substantial breach. This is because in an Act of Parliament, unless a contrary intention appears, words in the singular include the plural and vice versa (s 6, Interpretation Act 1978). It is not necessary for the breaches to relate to 'the holding' and so substantial breaches relating to any sub-let part of the premises may be included. If the tenant is refused a new lease under ground (c), the tenant is not entitled to compensation.

Ground (d): suitable alternative accommodation is available for tenant

(d)   that the landlord has offered and is willing to provide or secure the provision of alternative accommodation for the tenant, that the terms on which the alternative accommodation is available are reasonable having regard to the terms of the current tenancy and to all other relevant circumstances, and that the accommodation and the time at which it will be available are suitable for the tenant's requirements (including the requirement to preserve goodwill) having regard to the nature and class of his business and to the situation and extent of, and facilities afforded by, the holding . . .

This ground is not discretionary, so if the landlord can provide suitable alternative accom- **7.120** modation based on the above criteria the court must dismiss the tenant's application for a new tenancy (*Betty's Cafes Ltd v Phillips Furnishing Stores Ltd* [1957] Ch 67, at 84). The relevant date to assess the reasonableness of the terms and the suitability of the alternative accommodation is the date of the hearing. Interestingly, the landlord may offer part of the tenant's existing premises as alternative accommodation (as is the case under the Rent Act 1977). The landlord must show, however, that the part in question is sufficient for the tenant's business purposes as at the date of the hearing (see *Mykolyshyn v Noah* [1971] 1 All ER 48).

Alternative accommodation in the future may also be sufficient for the landlord. If he **7.121** can establish that it will be available at a later date (ie, even after the termination date in the s 25 notice or s 26 request), he may still be able to succeed on ground (d) (see s 31(2) of the Act; see also 'near miss' cases at para 7.144 below). If the tenant is refused a new lease under ground (d), the tenant is not entitled to compensation.

Ground (e): on sub-letting of part, landlord requires the whole property for subsequent letting

(e)   where the current tenancy was created by the sub-letting of part only of the property comprised in a superior tenancy and the landlord is the owner of an interest in reversion expectant on the termination of that superior tenancy, that the aggregate of the rents reasonably obtainable on separate lettings of the holding and the remainder of that property would be substantially less than the rent reasonably obtainable on a letting of that property as a whole, that on the termination of the current tenancy the landlord requires possession of the holding for the purpose of letting or otherwise disposing of the said property as a whole, and that in view there of the tenant ought not to be granted a new tenancy . . .

7.122 Ground (e) is another discretionary ground and is the least used of all the grounds (indeed, there are no reported cases on how the discretion is to be exercised). It applies only where there is a sub-letting of part and the 'competent' landlord of the sub-tenant is the superior landlord, ie, not the sub-tenant's immediate landlord. As previously explained at para 7.80 above, the intermediate lease will in these circumstances have less than 14 months to run.

7.123 The landlord must show two things:

(a) the rent obtainable on separate lettings of the whole building would be substantially less than the rent obtainable on a letting of the whole. It should be noted that the rent has to be substantially less, not merely less (see *Greaves Organisation Ltd v Stanhope Gate Property Co Ltd* (1973) 228 EG 725); and

(b) on the termination of the sub-tenancy the landlord requires possession of the sub-let part to let or otherwise dispose of the property as a whole. The landlord may have difficulty in establishing this unless the intermediate lease is due to end before the sub-tenancy is terminated (on the basis that he cannot re-let the whole if the intermediate tenant is still in occupation).

7.124 In exercising its discretion a court would have regard to whether the landlord originally consented to the sub-letting. Section 31(2) of the Act also applies to ground (e), ie, if the landlord can establish the ground at a later date (see 'near miss' cases at para 7.144 below). If the tenant is refused a new lease under ground (e), the tenant is entitled to compensation (see paras 7.147 et seq below).

Ground (f): landlord intends to demolish or reconstruct premises

(f) that on the termination of the current tenancy the landlord intends to demolish or reconstruct the premises comprised in the holding or a substantial part of those premises or to carry out substantial work of construction on the holding or part thereof and that he could not reasonably do so without obtaining possession of the holding . . .

7.125 This is the most frequently used ground. To rely on it the landlord must show on the termination of the tenancy the following three elements:

(a) the landlord's intention;

(b) to demolish or reconstruct the premises in the holding (or a substantial part thereof), or to carry out substantial work of construction on the holding (or part thereof); and

(c) that he could not reasonably do so without obtaining possession of the holding.

Each of these three elements is now considered.

Landlord's intention

7.126 The landlord's intention to carry out the work must be more than a simple desire to bring it about. The intention must be firm and settled. It must have 'moved out of the zone of contemplation—out of the sphere of the tentative, the provisional and the exploratory—into the valley of decision' (*per* Asquith LJ in *Cunliffe v Goodman* [1950] 2 KB 237, and subsequently approved by Viscount Simonds in *Betty's Cafes Ltd v Phillips Furnishing Stores*

Ltd [1959] AC 20, HL). Further, as a question of fact, there must be a reasonable prospect that the landlord's plan will succeed, although he does not need to prove that it will be a commercial success (*Dolgellau Golf Club v Hett* [1998] 2 EGLR 75, CA).

The time when the landlord's intention must be established is the date of the court hearing **7.127** (*Betty's Cafes Ltd v Phillips Furnishing Stores Ltd*, above). The fact that the landlord (or his predecessor) had no such intention at the time of serving the s 25 notice (or counter-notice to s 26 request) is irrelevant (see *Marks v British Waterways Board* [1963] 3 All ER 28). Provided the landlord can prove the ground as a matter of fact, the court will not examine the landlord's motives for using the ground. Thus in *Fisher v Taylors Furnishing Stores Ltd* [1956] 2 QB 78, it did not matter that the landlord's primary object was to occupy the reconstructed premises himself.

The necessary intention is a question of fact in each case, but the landlord's position will be **7.128** strengthened if, by the time of the hearing, he has taken appropriate steps. These would include: instructing professionals, obtaining quotations, preparing plans and drawings, securing any necessary planning permissions, arranging finance, and, for a company landlord, passing a board resolution. The less the landlord has to do by the time he gets to court, the better (see *Gregson v Cyril Lord* [1962] 3 All ER 907). Where planning permission has been applied for but not obtained by the date of the hearing, the test the court will use is whether there is a reasonable prospect that permission will be granted (*Westminster City Council v British Waterways Board* [1984] 3 WLR 1047, HL). This 'reasonable prospect' test was applied in *Aberdeen Steak Houses Group Ltd v Crown Estates Commissioners* [1997] 31 EG 101, *Coppin v Bruce-Smith* [1998] EGCS 55, CA, and *Gatwick Parking Service Ltd v Sargent* [2000] 25 EG 141, CA.

The works must be carried out 'on the termination of the current tenancy'. The Court of **7.129** Appeal has held this to include within a reasonable time from the date of the termination of the tenancy (*London Hilton Jewellers Ltd v Hilton International Hotels Ltd* [1990] 1 EGLR 112). For practical purposes, 'termination of the current tenancy' would include any continuation tenancy under s 64 of the Act, as the landlord would clearly be entitled to possession before the works were carried out. A reasonable time will, of course, be a question of fact in each case.

Demolish, reconstruct or carry out substantial work of construction

In addition to establishing an intention, the landlord must also show that the proposed **7.130** works fall within the express wording of ground (f). This will depend upon the nature and extent of the works and is a question of fact in each case. The key words used are 'demolish', 'reconstruct', and 'substantial work of construction'. 'Demolish' is easily understood and there must be some property on the holding which is capable of being demolished, eg, a building or wall (see *Housleys Ltd v Bloomer-Holt Ltd* [1966] 2 All ER 966, CA, involving a wall and garage). If part of the premises are to be demolished then they must be 'substantial', which is a question of fact (see *Atkinson v Bettison* [1953] 3 All ER 340, CA). 'Reconstruct' has been held to involve rebuilding and a substantial interference with the structure of the building. The work need not be confined necessarily to the outside of the premises or to load-bearing walls (see *Percy E Cadle & Co Ltd v Jacmarch Properties Ltd* [1957] 1 QB 323, CA, and *Romulus Trading Co Ltd v Henry Smith's Charity Trustees* [1990] 2 EGLR 75, CA).

7.131 'Substantial work of construction' implies a new building or adding to what was already there (see *per* Ormerod LJ in *Cook v Mott* (1961) 178 EG 637). It connotes more than mere refurbishment or improvement. In *Barth v Pritchard* [1990] 1 EGLR 109, CA, an intention to re-wire, re-roof, redecorate, install central heating and reposition a staircase was held to be insufficient. Yet in *Joel v Swaddle* [1957] 1WLR 1094, a proposal to convert a shop with two storage rooms into part of a large amusement arcade came within the ground. Other successful works of 'construction' have been the laying of pipes, wires, cables and drains, and the laying of a road (see *Housleys v Bloomer-Holt Ltd*, above).

7.132 On the question of what amounts to a reconstruction of a substantial part of the holding, the court in *Joel v Swaddle* (above) said the proper approach was to look at the position as a whole. One should compare the result after carrying out the proposed work with the condition and state of the premises before the work was begun.

Landlord could not reasonably carry out the work without obtaining possession of the holding

7.133 The landlord must show that he needs legal possession of the holding, not merely physical possession. In other words, he must show that he needs to terminate the tenancy in order to carry out the work. If the landlord can do the work simply by exercising his right of entry under the terms of the lease, ground (f) will not be established (this right is often reserved by landlords to enable them to execute improvements and alterations; see *Heath v Drown* [1973] AC 496, HL).

Tenant's defences under s 31A

7.134 Even if the landlord can show that he requires possession to carry out work, the tenant may be assisted by s 31A of the Act (inserted by s 7(1) of the Law of Property Act 1969). This effectively prevents the landlord from using ground (f) in circumstances where the proposed work would be over quickly, or where the work will affect only part of the premises. Section 31A provides that a court cannot hold that the landlord could not reasonably carry out the demolition or other work without obtaining possession if either of the following occurs:

(a) The tenant agrees to the inclusion in the terms of the new tenancy of terms giving the landlord access and other facilities for carrying out the work intended and, given that access and those facilities, the landlord could reasonably carry out the work without obtaining possession of the holding and without interfering to a substantial extent or for a substantial time with the use of the holding for the purposes of the business carried on by the tenant.

   The tenant may decide to rely on this defence where the landlord has failed to reserve adequate rights in the lease to allow him to carry out the work (*Heath v Drown* [1973] AC 496, HL). 'The work' means the landlord's intended works and the court has no power to consider whether the landlord should be carrying out different works (*The Decca Navigator Co Ltd v Greater London Council* [1974] 1 All ER 1178). The word 'interfering' refers to interference with the tenant's use of the holding for its business purposes, not the business itself or the goodwill. Thus a tenant intending to leave while the works are being carried out and then return with its goodwill unaffected cannot use s 31A (*Redfern v Reeves* [1978] 2 EGLR 52, CA).

(b) If the tenant is willing to accept a tenancy of an economically separable part of the holding and either paragraph (a) above is satisfied with respect to that part, or possession of the remainder of the holding would be reasonably sufficient to enable the landlord to carry out the intended work.

Here, a part of the holding will be an economically separable part if, and only if, the aggregate of the rents which, after completion of the intended work, would be reasonably obtainable on separate lettings of that part and the remainder of the premises affected by or resulting from the work would not be substantially less than the rent which would then be reasonably obtainable on a letting of those premises as a whole (s 31A(2)). If the tenant establishes defence (b), the order for the new tenancy will be only of the economically separable part (s 32(1A)).

Section 31(2) of the Act applies to ground (f), ie, the landlord has a second chance if he can **7.135** establish the ground at a later date (see 'near miss' cases at para 7.144 below). However, ground (f) must be established within one year of the termination date specified in the s 25 notice or s 26 request. If the tenant is refused a new lease under ground (f), the tenant is entitled to compensation (see paras 7.147 et seq below).

Ground (g): landlord intends to occupy the holding

(g)   ... that on the termination of the current tenancy the landlord intends to occupy the holding for the purposes, or partly for the purposes, of a business to be carried on by him therein, or as his residence.

This is another frequently used ground which has three important elements: the five-year **7.136** rule; the landlord's intention; and the occupation of the holding. These are now considered.

The five-year rule

The five-year rule is an integral part of ground (g) and is set out in s 30(2) of the Act. It **7.137** provides that the landlord cannot rely on ground (g) if the landlord's interest 'was purchased or created after the beginning of the period of five years which ends with the termination of the current tenancy'. So to rely on ground (g) the landlord effectively must have owned the reversion for at least five years before the termination date specified in the s 25 notice or s 26 request. The word 'purchased' means 'bought for money', and the time at which the purchase occurs is the date of exchange of contracts (*HL Bolton (Engineering) Co Ltd v TJ Graham & Sons Ltd* [1957] 1 QB 159, CA). Where the landlord has a leasehold interest, it is 'created' when the lease is executed, not when the term begins or the lease is registered (*Northcote Laundry Ltd v Frederick Donnelly Ltd* [1968] 1 WLR 562, CA).

The purpose of this rule is to prevent persons from buying the landlord's interest towards the **7.138** end of the tenancy simply in order to gain possession for themselves. The rule applies only where the premises have been let on a tenancy or series of tenancies within the Act's protection throughout the five-year period. So for example, if three years before the end of a tenancy a purchaser buys the reversion (subject to the tenancy), the five-year restriction would prevent him from using ground (g). However, if the same purchaser bought the freehold with vacant possession and then subsequently granted a lease, the five-year restriction would not apply.

7.139 A landlord requiring possession can circumvent the five-year rule if he can prove ground (f) instead, ie, an intention to demolish or reconstruct the premises (see para 7.125 above). The court will not examine the landlord's motives for using ground (f), so he could lawfully move in after the construction works have been completed. In addition, the future application of the five-year rule can be avoided if the current landlord is a company. Here, if the purchaser acquires the company by share acquisition it will not be purchasing the 'landlord's interest' (see *Wates Estate Agency Services Ltd v Bartleys Ltd* [1989] 2 EGLR 87).

Landlord's intention

7.140 The landlord must intend to occupy the premises either for business purposes, or as his residence. As with ground (f), the landlord must be able to show by the date of the hearing a firm and settled intention. The matters considered at paras 7.126 et seq above are therefore equally applicable here. One relevant factor will be the likely prospect of the landlord succeeding in his plans to occupy. For example, if planning permission were to be refused for the landlord's intended business use, this could make the necessary intention harder to establish (see *Westminster City Council v Bristol Waterways Board* [1985] AC 676, HL, and *Gatwick Parking Service Ltd v Sargent* [2000] 25 EG 141, CA). However, the likely failure of the landlord's proposed business is not a relevant consideration (see *Cox v Binfield* [1989] 1 EGLR 97, CA).

The occupation of the holding

7.141 The landlord must intend to occupy the holding for the purposes, or partly for the purposes, of a business to be carried on by him in the premises, or as his residence. The words 'carried on by him' enable occupation through the landlord's manager (see *Skeet v Powell-Sheddon* [1988] 2 EGLR 112) or agent (see *Parkes v Westminster Roman Catholic Diocese Trustee* (1978) 36 P & CR 22 where trustees occupied through the agency of a parish priest). The landlord may also occupy in partnership with others (see *Re Crowhurst Park, Sims-Hilditch v Simmons* [1974] 1 All ER 991).

7.142 Section 42(3) enables a landlord which is a company in a group of companies to rely on ground (g) where another member of the group is to occupy the premises. Section 41(2) enables a landlord who is a trustee to rely on ground (g) where there is an intention to occupy by a beneficiary under the trust. Under the 2004 reforms, ground (g) is extended to a wider category of landlords. Section 30(1A) provides that where a landlord has a controlling interest in a company, then a reference in ground (g) to the landlord is a reference either to the landlord or to the company. Similarly s 30(1B) provides that where the landlord is a company, and a person has a controlling interest in that company, then a reference in ground (g) to the landlord is a reference either to the landlord or that person.

7.143 If the tenant is refused a new lease under ground (g), the tenant is entitled to compensation (see paras 7.147 et seq below).

'Near miss' cases

7.144 If the landlord fails to establish grounds (d), (e), or (f) (alternative accommodation, uneconomic sub-lease, or intention to demolish or reconstruct) at the date of the hearing, he may still be saved by s 31(2) of the Act. If the landlord can show that he would have been able to establish one of these grounds had the termination date in the s 25 notice or s 26 request been up to 12 months later, the court must refuse the tenant's application for a new tenancy. In this case the tenant can ask the court to substitute that later date for the original termination date in the s 25 notice or s 26 request and the tenancy will continue until the later date. For a case involving the application of s 31(2), see *Accountancy Personnel Ltd v Worshipful Company of Salters* (1972) 222 EG 1589, CA.

Compensation for misrepresentation

Where a misrepresentation has been made to the court or there has been concealment of **7.145** material facts, the court may order compensation to be paid by the landlord to the tenant or vice versa. The tenant can claim compensation if he is induced not to apply to court, or to withdraw an application for renewal, because of a misrepresentation. The detailed provisions are contained in s 37A, which was introduced in the 2004 reforms.

KEY POINTS SUMMARY: STATUTORY GROUNDS UNDER S 30(1)

- Four of the seven grounds are discretionary. They are the tenant's 'fault' grounds—(a) **7.146** tenant's failure to repair; (b) tenant's delay in paying rent; and (c) tenant's breaches of other obligations—and ground (e) on sub-letting of part, where the superior landlord requires the whole property for subsequent letting.
- You cannot amend your grounds at a later date, so be sure of them when the notices are served.
- Grounds (f) (demolish/reconstruct) and (g) (landlord's occupation) are the most frequently used grounds. They require a firm and settled intention on the landlord's part, to be established at the date of the hearing.
- Ground (f) (demolish/reconstruct) will not be established if the tenant is willing to accept a new tenancy of part of the holding, or under the new lease the landlord is allowed access to carry out the works.
- Ground (g) (landlord's occupation) will not be established if the landlord acquired the reversion less than five years before the end of the current tenancy.
- Grounds (d), (e), or (f) may be proven under the 'near miss' rule if the landlord can show he could have established them within 12 months.

N TENANT'S RIGHT TO COMPENSATION FOR FAILURE TO OBTAIN A NEW TENANCY

The tenant can claim financial compensation from the landlord if the landlord succeeds in **7.147** establishing one or more of the 'non-fault' grounds (e), (f), or (g). This is often referred to as 'compensation for disturbance'. The tenant's right to compensation on quitting the premises is contained in s 37(1) of the Act. The basis for compensation is that the tenant is being denied a new tenancy through no fault of its own. Conversely, if one of the 'fault' grounds (a), (b), or (c) is established then the tenant properly will have no right to compensation. Similarly, there will be no right to compensation if the landlord can provide suitable alternative accommodation under ground (d) (on the basis that the tenant has suffered no loss).

7.148 It should be noted that s 37(1) allows the tenant compensation on quitting the holding where the landlord in his s 25 notice (or counter-notice to a s 26 request) has specified grounds (e), (f), or (g) in the notice and the tenant has either:

(a) not applied to the court for a new tenancy (see *Re 14 Grafton Street London W1, De Havilland (Antiques) Ltd v Centrovincial Estates (Mayfair) Ltd* [1971] 2 All ER 1); or

(b) made and then withdrawn an application for a new tenancy; or

(c) applied to the court for a new tenancy but has been defeated on one or more of grounds (e), (f), or (g).

7.149 Where the landlord has opposed on both fault and non-fault grounds and has been successful, the tenant must, in order to claim compensation, apply to the court for a certificate confirming that the landlord was successful only on grounds (e), (f), or (g) and on no other ground (s 37(4)). This is normally done at the hearing of the application for the new lease and the certificate is then incorporated into the court order. The landlord's stated grounds must be genuine; if the grounds are false and made fraudulently, eg, by stating a fault ground in an attempt to avoid paying compensation, the notice may be rendered invalid and unenforceable (see *Rous v Mitchell* [1991] 1 All ER 676, CA).

Amount of compensation

7.150 The amount of compensation is calculated by multiplying the rateable value of the holding (as at the date of service of the s 25 notice or s 26 request) by the 'appropriate multiplier' set from time to time by the Secretary of State. The current multiplier at the time of writing is 1, as prescribed by the Landlord and Tenant Act 1954 (Appropriate Multiplier) Order 1990, SI 1990/363, which came into force on 1 April 1990 (before that date the multiplier was 3). The rateable value to be used is taken from the valuation list in force at the date of service of the landlord's s 25 notice or s 26(6) counter-notice (s 37(5)(a); *Plessey & Co. Ltd v Eagle Pension Funds Ltd* [1989] EGCS 149). Any disputes over rateable value are determined by a valuation officer appointed by the Commissioners of the Inland Revenue under the Landlord and Tenant (Determination of Rateable Value Procedure) Rules 1954, SI 1954/1255. A right of appeal against the decision of the valuation officer lies to the Lands Tribunal.

7.151 Double compensation is payable where the tenant or his predecessors in the same business have been in occupation for at least 14 years prior to the termination of the current tenancy (s 37(3)). The date of termination is either the date of termination specified in the s 25 notice, or the date specified in the s 26 request as being the date from which the new tenancy is to start (s 37(7)). In these circumstances, double compensation is calculated by multiplying twice the rateable value by the appropriate multiplier (presently 1). If the tenant vacates for a short period (eg, before the end of the tenancy) it should not lose its right to double compensation, provided, during the vacation period, the premises were not being used by another business or for non-business purposes (see *Bacchiochi v Academic Agency Ltd* [1998] 2 All ER 241, CA, where the tenant closed down 12 days early). Notwithstanding the decision in *Bacchiochi*, best practice for tenants wishing to secure double compensation is not to vacate until the date specified in the s 25 notice or s 26 request has passed.

Importantly, double compensation can still be claimed even if only part of the holding has **7.152**
been occupied for 14 years for the purposes of the business (*Edicron Ltd v William Whiteley
Ltd* [1984] 1 All ER 219, CA). An example of this might occur where the tenant surrenders its
lease and takes a new lease of the same premises together with other premises in the same
building. Here the tenant will be entitled to double compensation in respect of the entire
holding even though it has not been in occupation of all of it for 14 years. The tenant may
wish to consider moving back into part of the premises it has vacated in order to secure
increased compensation. Moreover, where the tenant has occupied for nearly 14 years, the
timing of a s 26 request or s 25 notice may be crucial in determining whether double
compensation is payable.

Excluding compensation by agreement

The landlord and tenant may agree (eg, in the lease) to exclude or modify the tenant's right **7.153**
to compensation for failure to obtain a new tenancy (s 38(3)). However, s 38(2) provides that
such agreement will be void where the tenant or his predecessors in the same business have
been in occupation for five years or more prior to the date the tenant quits the premises. A
prospective tenant would be wise to resist attempts by the landlord to 'contract out' of
compensation, as such a provision may adversely affect the marketability of the lease during
the last five years of the term.

Compensation is also available in special circumstances, eg, a failure to be granted a new **7.154**
tenancy on the grounds of public interest or national security (see ss 57–60 of the Act).

O   THE TERMS OF THE NEW TENANCY

If the tenant properly applies to the court after following all the correct procedures, the court **7.155**
will order a new lease where, (i) the landlord fails to establish an opposition ground under
s 30, or (ii) the landlord has not opposed the tenant's application. In (ii), it is rare for the
matter to get to court, as the parties' solicitors, after a period of negotiation, will normally be
able to agree on the terms of the new lease. The tenant's application in this situation is simply
a back-up in case the negotiations break down, and if the parties reach agreement on the
terms of the new lease the tenant can simply instruct the court to close its file on the matter.

When conducting negotiations it is important to know the powers of the court, and in **7.156**
particular the lease terms that the court would be likely to impose. Practitioners are clearly in
a far stronger position if they can argue for the inclusion of a particular clause on the basis
that the court would agree with them. Accordingly, this section will concentrate on the terms
a court would be likely to impose in a renewed tenancy. If the parties agree some terms but
not others, the court will rule on the unresolved matters, leaving the agreed terms to stand.

The premises

Generally the new lease will be of 'the holding' (s 32), which is all the property comprised **7.157**
in the existing tenancy, excluding any part not occupied by the tenant (eg, a sub-let part).

The parties may of course agree as to the extent of the premises to be comprised in the new lease.

7.158   In the following situations the premises in the new lease may be more or less than 'the holding':

(a)   *More than the holding.* Under s 32(2), the landlord (but not the tenant) can require the new tenancy to be of the whole of the premises in the current tenancy. A landlord may wish to do this where the tenant has sub-let part of the premises but the landlord has no interest in recovering possession of the sub-let part (eg, a flat over an office). The landlord would prefer instead to grant a new tenancy of the whole.

(b)   *Less than the holding.* Where the landlord has succeeded under ground (f) (demolition or reconstruction; see para 7.125 above) and the tenant has agreed to accept a tenancy of an 'economically separable part' of the holding (see s 31A).

7.159   If the current lease includes rights enjoyed by the tenant in connection with the holding, those rights will be included in the new lease unless the parties agree to the contrary (s 32(3)). If the parties fail to agree, the court will decide which rights should be included. In *Re No 1 Albermarle Street W1* [1959] Ch 531, the court included in the new tenancy the tenant's existing 'right' to display advertising signs on the outside of the property. However, this was not by virtue of s 32(3) as it was merely personal in nature. Instead the court allowed the right to be included as one of the 'other terms' by virtue of s 35 (see paras 7.170 et seq below). Only existing legal rights will be permitted under s 32(3), not equitable rights. In *G Orlik (Meat Products) Ltd v Hastings and Thanet Building Society* [1974] 29 P & CR 126, an informal right to park delivery vans on adjoining land was not granted in the new lease.

Duration

7.160   The parties are free to agree whatever length of term they like, but in default of agreement, the maximum fixed term that the court can order is 15 years (s 33). The court has a wide discretion and may order such term as it considers reasonable in all the circumstances (subject to the 15-year maximum). The court also has the power to order a periodic tenancy (although this is rare). In the absence of agreement between the parties the new tenancy will commence when the current tenancy ends under s 64, ie, three months after the application finally has been disposed of. The court should also specify an end date for the new tenancy.

7.161   The court will consider such matters as:

•   duration of current tenancy (see *Betty's Cafes Ltd v Phillips Furnishing Stores Ltd* [1959] AC 20);

•   length of time tenant has held over under the current tenancy (see *London and Provincial Millinery Stores Ltd v Barclays Bank Ltd* [1962] 2 All ER 163);

•   comparative hardship caused to either party (see *Amika Motors Ltd v Colebrook Holdings Ltd* (1981) 259 EG 243);

•   landlord's future plans for the property. The court may decide to order a short term where although the landlord at the date of the hearing is unable to show sufficient intention under ground (f) (demolition/reconstruction), the court is satisfied that he will do so in the near future (see *Roehorn v Barry Corporation* [1956] 2 All ER 742, CA). Similarly, the court may order a short term if the landlord narrowly missed being able to rely on ground (g) (own occupation; see para 7.136 above) because of the five-year rule in s 30(2) (see *Upsons Ltd v E. Robins Ltd* [1956] 1 QB 131). The court may include a break clause in the lease, which would allow the landlord to end the lease early to carry out future development plans (see *National Car Parks Ltd v Paternoster Consortium Ltd* [1990] 2 EGLR 99);

- any other factors relevant to the particular case (see *Becker v Hill Street Properties Ltd* [1990] 2 EGLR 78).

Rent

Rent is usually the most contentious matter between the parties. Section 34(1) provides that **7.162** the rent shall be that at which '. . . having regard to the terms of the tenancy (other than those relating to rent), the holding might reasonably be expected to be let in the open market by a willing lessor'. In assessing the rent, the court will usually hear evidence from surveyors or valuers and consider comparable rents in the area ('comparables'). If relevant comparables are not available, the court will consider generally any increases of rent in the locality (*National Car Parks Ltd v Colebrook Estates Ltd* [1983] 1 EGLR 78).

As the other terms of the tenancy will have a bearing on the rent, such other terms are **7.163** normally agreed before the rent. The courts have approved this as being the most sensible approach (see *Cardshops Ltd v Davies* [1971] 2 All ER 721, CA). The tenant's user covenant in the new lease will be especially relevant when determining the new rent. Landlords often seek a wider use clause so as to command a higher rent (on the basis that a wider use is more attractive to a tenant, thus increasing the rent a tenant in the open market would be willing to pay). In general the courts have been reluctant to permit a relaxation of the user covenant for this purpose (see *Gorleston Golf Club Ltd v Links Estates (Gorleston) Ltd* [1959] CLY 1830 and *Charles Clements (London) Ltd v Rank City Wall Ltd* [1978] 1 EGLR 47).

Disregards when assessing rent

Under s 34(1), the court when assessing the rent must disregard certain factors which would **7.164** otherwise work against the tenant. These 'disregards' are similar to those found in a typical rent review clause in a business lease. For further reference on rent review and cases interpreting these disregards, see chapter 2.

The 'disregards' in s 34(1) are: **7.165**

(a) Occupation: '. . . *any effect on rent of the fact that the tenant has or his predecessors in title have been in occupation of the holding*'. Thus the landlord cannot argue for a higher rent on the basis that a tenant in occupation would pay more rent to avoid the expense of moving elsewhere.

(b) Goodwill: '. . . *any goodwill attached to the holding by reason of the carrying on thereat of the business of the tenant (whether by him or by a predecessor of his in that business)*'. If the tenant has through his own efforts generated goodwill in his business then he should not be penalized for it by having to pay a higher rent.

(c) Improvements: '. . . *any effect on rent of an improvement . . . carried out by a person who at the time it was carried out was the tenant . . . otherwise than in pursuance of an obligation to his immediate landlord*'. This effectively avoids the tenant paying for the improvements twice over; once when the tenant carries them out and again through a consequential uplift in the rent. The words 'otherwise than in pursuance of an obligation to his immediate landlord' (s 34(2)), mean that improvements to the premises that the tenant was obliged to carry out (eg, under the terms of the lease) will not be disregarded. In other words, such obligatory improvements will be taken into account when assessing the rent.

In addition under s 34(2), a voluntary improvement will be disregarded only if it has been carried out during the current tenancy, or:

(i)   it was completed not more than 21 years before the application for the new tenancy was made; and

(ii) the holding or any part of it affected by the improvement has at all times since been comprised in tenancies to which the Act applies; and

(iii) at the termination of each of those tenancies the tenant did not quit the premises.

(d) For licensed premises only, eg, a public house, any addition to the value of the premises attributable to the tenant's licence is disregarded (s 34(1)(d)). This includes betting shops licensed under the Betting Gaming and Lotteries Act 1963 (*Ganton House Investments v Crossman Investments* [1995] 1 EGLR 239).

Effect on rent of premises in disrepair

7.166   If the premises are in disrepair due to the tenant's breach of repairing covenant, should the court disregard the disrepair in assessing the new rent? The courts have supported conflicting approaches to the problem.

7.167   The tenant would argue that the disrepair should be taken into account to reflect the actual condition of the premises (thus resulting in a lower rent). The tenant would say that the landlord could always sue him for breach and in that way recover any diminution in the value of the reversion. The tenant would further argue that there is nothing in s 34 directing the court to assume that the premises are in good repair. The tenant's approach was supported by the Court of Appeal in *Fawke v Viscount Chelsea* [1980] QB 441, where the Court accepted that the rent should be assessed having regard to the actual state of repair of the property. (This case actually concerned a landlord's failure to repair.)

7.168   Conversely, the landlord would argue that the disrepair should be disregarded so as to prevent the tenant from prospering from his own wrongdoing. In other words, there should be an assumption that the tenant has performed his repairing obligations. Such an approach was supported by the Court of Appeal in *Family Management v Gray* (1979) 253 EG 369 and later in *Crown Estate Commissioners v Town Investments Ltd* [1992] 1 EGLR 61.

Rent review in new tenancy

7.169   The court is permitted, if it thinks fit, to include a provision in the new lease for varying the rent, ie, a rent review clause (s 34(3)). This applies irrespective of whether a rent review clause was included in the current lease. However, a court will normally include a review clause if one is present in the current lease. The scope and frequency of the rent review is entirely at the court's discretion. Upward only reviews are common, but tenants have successfully argued for the inclusion of downward reviews if market rents have fallen (see *Forbouys plc v Newport BC* [1994] 1 EGLR 138).

Other terms of the new tenancy

In default of agreement the other terms of the lease 'may be determined by the court; and in   **7.170** determining those terms the court shall have regard to the terms of the current tenancy and to all relevant circumstances' (s 35(1)). This includes the operation of the provisions of the Landlord and Tenant (Covenants) Act 1995 (see paras 7.175 et seq below). Accordingly, if either party wishes to introduce terms that were not included in the current lease, they must justify this by showing that it is fair and reasonable in all the circumstances.

It is usually the landlord who seeks to introduce new terms under the guise of 'modernizing'   **7.171** the lease. Predictably, these new terms are usually more onerous on the tenant. Such modernization provisions should of course be resisted by the tenant, who is assisted by the House of Lords decision in *O'May v City of London Real Property Co Ltd* [1983] 2 AC 726. In *O'May* Lord Hailsham gave the following guidance:

> . . . the court must begin by considering the terms of the current tenancy, that the burden of persuading the court to impose a change in those terms against the will of either party must rest on the party proposing the change and the change proposed must in the circumstances of the case be fair and reasonable and should take into account, amongst other things, the compara- tively weak negotiating position of a sitting tenant requiring renewal, particularly in conditions of scarcity, and the general purpose of the Act which is to protect the business interests of the tenant so far as they are affected by the approaching termination of the current lease, in particular as regards his security of tenure.

The landlord in *O'May* failed to show that a proposed new term requiring the tenant to pay a   **7.172** service charge was reasonable, even though the tenant was offered a reduction in rent. The court could see that the landlord's true intention was to shift the burden of maintenance and repair of the building onto the tenant, and this was unjustified.

Landlords have understandably been critical of *O'May* and maintain that the courts should   **7.173** not shield tenants from commercial reality. They argue that if tenants were taking alterna- tive premises in the area, they would probably have to accept modern provisions in a *new* lease, so why should they not do so in a renewed lease? The landlord is naturally concerned to maintain the value of his reversion, and the acceptability of lease terms to institutional investors is a crucial factor in this. Yet the tenant must not be unfairly disadvantaged in carrying on his business; this is a general purpose of the Act (see the judgment of Denning LJ in *Gold v Brighton Corporation* [1956] 3 All ER 442). Ultimately it is a question of general policy towards commercial property and balancing the respective interests of the landlord and tenant.

The court is able to require the tenant to provide guarantors for the new tenancy (see *Cairn-*   **7.174** *place Ltd v CBL (Property Investment) Co Ltd* [1984] 1 All ER 315). This is likely to occur where the tenant has a poor record of paying rent or performing other covenants, or where the tenant is a recent assignee or newly formed company.

Effect of the Landlord and Tenant (Covenants) Act 1995

One area in which the courts may be sympathetic to a landlord seeking to introduce new   **7.175** terms is with regard to the tenant's alienation covenant. If the current lease was granted before 1 January 1996, the old privity of contract rules meant that the original tenant was bound for the entire duration of the lease even after he or she had assigned it. The change to the privity of contract rule introduced by the Landlord and Tenant (Covenants) Act 1995 ('the 1995 Act') benefited tenants, in that for leases granted on or after 1 January 1996 the tenant was released from liability after assignment. A renewed lease today is therefore a 'new lease' under the 1995 Act and the landlord's position will be worse than it was under the current lease (assuming the current lease was granted before 1 January 1996).

7.176 To reflect the changes introduced by the 1995 Act, new leases generally contain more restrictive alienation obligations on the tenant, eg, pre-conditions to be satisfied before assignment and the use of authorized guarantee agreements (AGAs). Accordingly, to counteract the landlord's loss of privity, the courts will generally permit a modernization of the alienation covenant in the renewed lease to reflect current practice on the grant of new leases. This is reinforced by Sch 1, para 4 to the 1995 Act, which amends s 35 of the 1954 Act to provide that the reference to 'all relevant circumstances' includes the operation of the provisions of the 1995 Act (s 35(2)). In *Wallis Fashion Group Ltd v CGU Life Assurance Ltd* [2000] 27 EG 145, the landlord argued that the renewal lease should entitle the landlord to an automatic AGA from the assigning tenant. However, Neuberger J held that although there could be an AGA condition, it should be qualified by the words 'where reasonable'. This decision is important for tenants, who can now properly resist any claim by the landlord for an automatic AGA. An AGA is appropriate only if it is reasonable in all the circumstances.

7.177 Alternatively, the landlord's loss of privity under the 1995 Act may be counter-balanced by changes to other terms in the lease, including the level of rent. To underline the point, the 1995 Act amends s 34 of the 1954 Act by inserting a new s 34(4) as follows:

> It is hereby declared that the matters which are to be taken into account by the court in determining the rent include any effect on rent of the operation of the provisions of the Landlord and Tenant (Covenants) Act 1995.

Costs of the new tenancy

7.178 The question of whether the tenant agrees to pay the landlord's costs in connection with the new lease will, of course, depend upon the parties' relative bargaining strengths. However, the tenant should endeavour to resist this as it is highly unlikely that the tenant will be forced to do so by the court (see *Cairnplace Ltd v CBL (Property Investment) Co Ltd* [1984] 1 All ER 315). The Costs of Leases Act 1958, s 1, provides that, unless the parties otherwise agree in writing, each party should be responsible for its own costs.

KEY POINTS SUMMARY: TERMS OF THE NEW LEASE

7.179 • The parties' advisers should appreciate the terms a court is likely to order in the lease. This puts them in a stronger negotiating position. In particular:
   • The court will order a new lease of 'the holding' which generally excludes sub-let parts.
   • The maximum fixed term the court can order is 15 years. The duration of the current tenancy will be an important consideration, but there are other factors (see paras 7.160 to 7.161 above).
   • In assessing the rent the court will consider comparable rents in the area and disregard the matters in s 34 of the 1954 Act.

- The court will take into account the effect of the Landlord and Tenant (Covenants) Act 1995 (ie, landlord's loss of privity) when fixing the rent and other terms (eg, alienation provisions).
- Tenants are within their rights to resist a landlord's demand for an automatic AGA; accept an AGA only 'where reasonable'.

P COURT ORDER FOR NEW TENANCY

If the court orders a new tenancy it will not commence until three months after the **7.180** proceedings are 'finally disposed of' (s 64). The landlord and tenant should execute a lease and counterpart lease respectively (s 36(1)). The parties may agree not to act upon the order if they so wish, but such an agreement should be in writing (s 69(2)) and comply with the ordinary principles of contract law.

If the tenant is not satisfied with the terms of the new lease as ordered by the court, it has a **7.181** last chance to apply to the court within 14 days for the order to be revoked (s 36(2)). In this case the current tenancy will continue for such period as the parties agree, or the court determines, to enable the landlord to re-let or otherwise dispose of the property (s 36(2)). A tenancy which continues under s 36(2) will not be a tenancy to which the 1954 Act applies. Where an order for a new tenancy is revoked, the court may also vary, revoke, or award an order for costs (s 36(3)).

PRACTICAL CHECKLISTS

Summary of the 1954 Act

- The Act affords statutory protection to 'a tenant who occupies premises for the purposes **7.182** of a business'.
- The tenant's statutory protection is twofold: the tenancy automatically continues at the end of the contractual tenancy; and the tenant can apply to the court for a statutory renewal of the tenancy.
- Certain tenancies are excluded from statutory protection, eg, fixed-term tenancies not exceeding six months and contracted out tenancies.
- For an agreement to contract out of the security of tenure provisions to be valid, the landlord must first serve a 'health warning' on the tenant who, in turn, must sign a declaration that he has received it.
- Tenancies protected by the Act can be terminated only by one of the methods prescribed by the Act.
- The most common methods of termination are by landlord's s 25 notice or tenant's s 26 request.
- The landlord can oppose the tenant's application for a new lease by relying on one or more of the statutory grounds for opposition in s 30. Some of these grounds are at the discretion of the court.
- Section 25 notices and s 26 requests must be in prescribed form and contain prescribed

information. There are strict deadlines for service (see key point summaries earlier in the chapter).

- The s 25 notice/s 26 request must be served by/upon the 'competent landlord'. Consider serving a s 40 notice to establish the identity of the competent landlord.
- The competent landlord should consider applying to the court for an interim rent to be assessed. If market rents have fallen, the tenant should consider doing so.
- If the landlord successfully opposes a new tenancy under grounds (e), (f), or (g), the landlord will have to pay the tenant compensation for disturbance.
- In default of agreement the court will determine the terms of the new lease.
- In assessing the new rent the court will disregard certain matters such as tenant's occupation, goodwill, and voluntary improvements (s 34).
- If the landlord wishes to impose new terms in the renewed tenancy, the landlord will have to show that it is fair and reasonable in all the circumstances (*O'May v City of London Real Property Co. Ltd* [1983] 2 AC 726).

Acting for landlord

Serving a s 25 notice

7.183
- If you want the tenant to leave at the end of the lease, serve a hostile s 25 notice and be sure of your statutory grounds for opposing a new lease.
- Be sure you are the 'competent' landlord for the tenant in question (see paras 7.79 et seq above). It may be necessary to serve a notice under s 40 to be sure.
- The s 25 notice must be given not more than 12 months or less than six months before the date of termination specified in the notice; this termination date must not be earlier than the date on which the tenancy could have been terminated at common law (eg, the contractual expiry date of a fixed term).
- If you are happy for the tenant to continue in occupation under a new lease and wish the new lease to be in place as soon as possible, serve a non-hostile s 25 notice one year before the contractual expiry date specifying the contractual expiry date as the termination date in the notice.
- Ensure that the s 25 notice is in the prescribed form and contains the prescribed content.
- If you receive a tenant's s 26 request and you want the tenant to leave, you must serve a counter-notice within two months specifying your statutory grounds for opposing a new lease.
- Serve by registered post or recorded delivery (in which case service is deemed to be the date of postage).

Landlord's statutory grounds under s 30(1)

7.184
- Four of the seven grounds are discretionary. They are the tenant's 'fault' grounds—(a) tenant's failure to repair; (b) tenant's delay in paying rent; and (c) tenant's breaches of other obligations—and ground (e) on sub-letting of part where the superior landlord requires the whole property for subsequent letting.
- You cannot amend your grounds at a later date, so be sure of them when the notices are served.
- Grounds (f) (demolish/reconstruct) and (g) (landlord's occupation) are the most frequently

used grounds. They require a firm and settled intention on the landlord's part, to be established at the date of the hearing.

- Ground (f) (demolish/reconstruct) will not be established if the tenant is willing to accept a new tenancy of part of the holding, or under the new lease the landlord is allowed access to do the works.
- Ground (g) (landlord's occupation) will not be established if the landlord acquired the reversion less than five years before the end of the current tenancy.
- Grounds (d), (e), or (f) may be proven under the 'near miss' rule if the landlord can show he could have established them within 12 months.

Landlord's obligation to pay compensation

- The landlord must pay the tenant compensation for disturbance if he establishes one or more of the 'non fault' grounds (e, f, or g). **7.185**
- The amount of compensation is the rateable value of the holding x 1. However, the landlord must pay double compensation if the tenant or predecessors in the same business have occupied for at least 14 years.
- The parties may exclude compensation by agreement, unless the tenant or predecessor in the same business has been in occupation for five years or more.

Acting for tenant

Responding to a s 25 notice

- If you receive a landlord's s 25 notice and you want to renew your lease, ensure that you apply to the court for a new lease on or before the date specified in the s 25 notice. **7.186**
- If you have not received a s 25 notice by the time there is less than 12 months to go on the lease, consider a 'pre-emptive strike' by serving a s 26 request and specifying a commencement date for the new lease 12 months hence.

Serving a s 26 request

- Serve the s 26 request on your 'competent' landlord (see paras 7.79 et seq above). It may be necessary to serve a notice under s 40 to be sure. **7.187**
- Ensure that your s 26 request is in the prescribed form and contains the prescribed content.
- If you serve a s 26 request, be sure to apply to the court for a new lease before the date specified in the s 26 request.
- Serve by registered post or recorded delivery (in which case service is deemed to be the date of postage).

Tenant's right to compensation for failure to secure new lease

- The landlord must pay the tenant compensation for disturbance if he establishes one or more of the 'non-fault' grounds (e, f, or g). **7.188**
- The current amount of compensation is the rateable value of the holding x 1. However, the landlord must pay double compensation if the tenant or predecessors in the same business have occupied for at least 14 years.
- The parties may exclude compensation by agreement, unless the tenant or predecessor in the same business has been in occupation for five years or more.

Negotiating the terms of the renewed lease

7.189 Appreciate what terms a court would be likely to order in the lease. This puts you in a stronger negotiating position. In particular:

- The court will order a new lease of 'the holding' which generally excludes sub-let parts.
- The maximum fixed term the court can order is 15 years. The duration of the current tenancy will be an important consideration, but there are other factors too.
- In assessing the rent the court will consider comparable rents in the area and disregard the matters in s 34 of the 1954 Act.
- The court will take into account the effect of the Landlord and Tenant (Covenants) Act 1995 (ie, landlord's loss of privity) when fixing the rent and other terms (eg, alienation provisions).
- Consider the case of *O'May v City of London Real Property Co Ltd* [1983] 2 AC 726. Any variations from the current lease must be fair and reasonable in all the circumstances. This will prevent the landlord from 'modernizing' the lease unfairly.

Key reforms introduced on 1 June 2004

7.190 - *Contracting out.* It is no longer necessary to apply to the court for an order approving an agreement to contract out of the security of tenure provisions of the Act. The landlord must serve a prior 'health warning' notice on the tenant. The tenant must sign a declaration that he has received and accepted the consequences of the notice.
- The prescribed form of s 25 notice and s 26 request has changed. Use the up-to-date forms.
- The requirement for the tenant to serve a counter-notice to a landlord's s 25 notice is abolished.
- When serving a 'non-hostile' s 25 notice, the landlord must include in the notice the key terms of the proposed new tenancy.
- Following service of a s 40 notice, the recipient has a duty to revise the information supplied if circumstances change.
- Both landlords and tenants are now permitted to apply to the court for the terms of a new tenancy to be settled.
- There are new time limits for applications to the court to renew tenancies and the parties can agree to extend these.
- Landlords are permitted to apply for an order that the tenancy be terminated without renewal if they can make out one of the statutory grounds for opposition.
- Ownership and control of businesses. The circumstances in which landlords and tenants can operate the procedures under the Act are widened. In particular, an individual and any company he controls should be treated as one and the same and companies controlled by one individual should be treated as members of a group of companies.
- *Interim rent.* Tenants as well as landlords can apply to the court for an interim rent. The date from which interim rent is payable becomes the earliest date for renewal of the tenancy which could have been specified in the s 25 notice or s 26 request. Where the landlord does not oppose the renewal, the interim rent is likely to be set at the same level as the rent for the new tenancy, ie, the market rent.

KEY DOCUMENTS

- Landlord and Tenant Act 1954, Pt 2   **7.191**
- Landlord and Tenant Act 1927
- Landlord and Tenant Act 1954, Part 2 (Notices) Regulations 2004 SI 2004/1005
- Regulatory Reform (Business Tenancies) (England and Wales) Order SI 2003/3096
- Landlord and Tenant Act 1954 (Appropriate Multiplier) Order SI 1990/363

Printed copies of legislation can be ordered from The Stationery Office (<http://www.tsoshop.co.uk>). Legislation from 1988 onwards can be downloaded free of charge from <http://www.opsi.gov.uk/acts.htm>. Statutory instruments are available from <http://www.opsi.gov.uk/stat.htm>.

8

PROPERTY DEVELOPMENT: LAND ACQUISITION, PLANNING, CONSTRUCTION AND FINANCE

A INTRODUCTION

8.01 In this chapter we consider the key issues that may arise when acting for a prospective developer of land. We shall be dealing with the core elements relating to the acquisition of land as they affect the commercial conveyancer, including investigation of title, drafting the contract (including conditional contracts and option agreements), relevant searches and enquiries, and the problems associated with contaminated land. We shall then go on to consider important planning matters such as the initial requirement for planning consent for development purposes, the operation of the General Permitted Development Order and the Use Classes Order, the procedure when applying for express permission, planning obligations (including agreements under s 106 of the Town and Country Planning Act 1990), appeals and enforcement. We then examine the construction project itself, including the liabilities of the design and construction team and the methods employed to protect third parties interested in the project (eg, collateral warranties). Lastly, we introduce the specialized field of development finance and explain the issues that will concern a practitioner acting for a secured lender of a development site.

B ACQUIRING LAND FOR DEVELOPMENT

The title

8.02 The solicitor acting for the purchaser/developer of land must ensure that the title is good and marketable and free from encumbrances that may adversely affect the developer's proposals. The most obvious examples would be an adverse restriction on use (eg, agricultural use only), or a restrictive covenant against building on the land. In addition, there may be easements that burden the land, such as a right of way in favour of a third party. If such covenants or easements exist, your client will need to consider various possibilities to resolve the problem. You could negotiate through the draft contract for the seller to remedy the problem prior to completion, but to protect your client care will be needed over the precise wording used. Indemnity insurance is another possibility, if cover is available for the problem area. Another option is for you or the seller to seek a release or modification of the easement or covenant from the person with whom the benefit lies. Lastly, perhaps as a last resort, your client or the seller could consider applying to the Lands Tribunal for the covenant to be removed from the title. These alternatives are considered below. As far as indemnity insurance is concerned, it should be noted that a common requirement of insurance companies is that no one (eg, the covenantee) should have been contacted in connection with the breach. Accordingly, it may be prudent to try the indemnity route first before approaching the person with the benefit of the covenant or right.

Indemnity insurance

This involves arranging an indemnity insurance policy with a reputable insurance company, **8.03** in which the buyer, successors in title and any mortgagee are insured against loss which may arise as a result of the breach. The insurer will normally require a copy of the conveyance or Land Registry entry imposing the restriction, a statutory declaration from the owner of the property confirming that no enforcement action has been taken, and counsel's opinion (if taken). It should be noted that insurance is unlikely to be offered if the covenant was created recently (ie, within the last 10–15 years). This is because of the increased risk of enforcement. Of course this does not preclude problems with older covenants that can still be enforceable.

Practitioners should be aware that since January 2005 carrying on insurance mediation **8.04** activities for remuneration by way of business requires authorization from the Financial Services Authority. This would include arranging restrictive covenant indemnity insurance where remuneration is received, such as commission payments or perhaps where there is some other economic benefit to the firm, eg, receiving discounts on one's own insurance premiums in return for introducing clients.

Consent or release by covenantee

You may consider contacting the person who has the benefit of the covenant to obtain his **8.05** or her retrospective consent to the breach. Alternatively, you may be seeking his or her agreement to a release or variation of the covenant(s). Such person may require payment for the release or variation.

The Land Registry's approach is also worth noting here; restrictive covenants will be **8.06** removed from the register only provided clear evidence is produced showing that the benefitor who is purporting to release the covenant has the right to do so. The Registry will thus need to inspect the title to the benefiting land to establish who currently has the benefit of the covenant. Obviously, this may not be easy in respect of covenants created many years ago. Indeed it is often the case that the evidence produced as to ownership is insufficient. If so, the Registry will actually add an entry to the register indicating that a deed is only 'expressed' to release the land from the covenant(s). Naturally, such an entry is not conclusive and should be approached with caution by intending developers.

Application to Lands Tribunal

An application can be made to the Lands Tribunal for an order that a covenant be removed **8.07** from the title (Law of Property Act 1925, s 84). This is unlikely to be successful unless the covenant is old and redundant. It is seen rather as an act of last resort, and can be expensive, but it may be a price worth paying if the size of the proposed development is substantial.

8.08 If a breach of covenant or easement burden problem cannot be resolved, the buyer (and any lender) should be advised very carefully about the various options available to remedy the situation and, if a proper solution cannot be found, to withdraw from the transaction.

8.09 Establishing the benefit of easements is also important, as it will be necessary to ascertain if the subject property has all necessary rights. This is particularly important in the context of acquiring land for development. Easements for development land will include rights of access and the right to run and connect into existing services (eg, foul and surface water drainage for the proposed development). All these matters must be addressed before contracts are exchanged, and a full title investigation is essential. If the land is a greenfield site, it may well be that title is unregistered, in which case the investigation is likely to be more complicated than for registered land. For a full consideration of the issues that may arise in the investigation of unregistered title, refer to Abbey, R. and Richards, M., *A Practical Approach to Conveyancing* (7th edn, OUP, 2005) ch 5.

8.10 As far as registered titles are concerned, you will need to check carefully the official copies and other documents referred to on the register and compare them against the information given in the draft contract. Remember that the official copies should be as up-to-date as possible. You should in particular consider the following:

(a) confirm whether the estate is freehold or leasehold. Is the title number correct?

(b) Consider the class of title; is it absolute, possessory, good leasehold or qualified? (Anything less than absolute title will generally be considered as adverse.)

(c) Does the land being acquired correspond with the title description? (Consider the title plan—does it indicate that land has been removed from the title?)

(d) Is the seller in the contract the same as the registered proprietor?

(e) Are there any encumbrances in the charges register, and how will these affect the developer's proposals?

The contract

Standard unconditional contract

8.11 The parties may be quite willing to proceed on the basis of a standard unconditional contract. Naturally, in this case neither party would be able to withdraw without incurring liability for breach. An unconditional contract would be appropriate where the buyer is satisfied with the title investigation and the results of all searches and enquiries, and has secured relevant planning permission for the proposed development. Of course a seller would always prefer an unconditional contract because it does not allow the buyer to pull out unless the seller is in default. For a full consideration of the issues that may arise in the drafting and negotiation of unconditional contracts, see Abbey and Richards, op cit at para 8.09 above, ch 3. In addition, the following special conditions should be considered in a contract for the sale of land for commercial development:

(a) The seller may be selling the land with the benefit of pre-existing planning permission for development. If so, the buyer will probably want to develop the site in accordance with the plans and specifications used in the application. As the copyright will no doubt remain vested in the architect who drew up the plans, it will be necessary for the seller to procure the assignment of the benefit of those plans from the architect to the buyer, or at least a licence to use them. The buyer's solicitor should ensure that a special condition is inserted to this effect. A typical clause protecting the buyer might read:

> The Seller shall procure that [name and address of seller's architect] ('the Architect') employed by the Seller in connection with the Seller's planning application dated [insert date] for the Property shall without charge to the Buyer grant to the Buyer a licence in respect of all copyright material produced by the Architect entitling the Buyer to use all such copyright material as the Buyer thinks fit.

(b) A condition dealing with value added tax (VAT). The buyer will want to know whether VAT will be payable on top of the purchase price. Both the Standard Conditions of Sale (SC 1.4) and the Standard Commercial Property Conditions of Sale (SCPC 1.4) provide for all sums payable under the contract to be exclusive of VAT, ie, any VAT is *added* to the purchase price. If the buyer wishes to avoid paying VAT, it will require a special condition to this effect. The condition will say either that the purchase price is to be inclusive of any VAT, or that the seller warrants that it has not elected to waive any exemption to VAT and will not do so on or before completion. This is especially important for buyers who make exempt supplies in the course of their businesses, eg, banks, building societies and insurance companies, because they are unable to recover their VAT payments. See paras 10.02 et seq below for a full consideration of VAT. Typical clauses protecting the buyer might read:

> All sums payable under this agreement are inclusive of VAT

or

> The Seller warrants that it has not prior to the date of this agreement and will not before completion elect to waive any exemption for VAT in respect of the Property.

(c) A condition preventing any sub-sale. The seller wants the best price for the property and would not be pleased to learn following exchange that the buyer has 'turned' the property by way of a sub-sale. This means that the buyer between exchange and completion exchanges contracts with a third party at a higher price than that agreed with the seller. The buyer then directs the seller in the purchase deed to transfer the property to the third party. The buyer naturally pockets the difference between the original price and the price paid by the third party without ever actually owning the land. To avoid this scenario, the seller will normally want a special condition stipulating that the seller is only required to transfer the property to the buyer and not to any other person. Although this condition will prevent a sub-sale, it will not of course prevent the buyer from executing its own transfer to a third party. However, the disadvantage of having two transfers instead of one is that there will be two charges to stamp duty land tax (assuming the price exceeds the initial stamp duty land tax threshold). It can therefore act as a disincentive to the prospective entrepreneurial buyer. The special condition may also go on to prevent the buyer from assigning the benefit of the contract to a third party. A typical clause protecting the seller might read:

> This agreement is personal to the Buyer and the Seller shall not be required to transfer

the Property other than by a single transfer to the Buyer and the Buyer shall not assign or otherwise dispose of this agreement without the consent of the Seller.

(d) If the seller is retaining land for possible future development, careful consideration should be given to the reservation of easements and the imposition of covenants, including the negation of any implied easements in favour of the buyer. This is an important aspect of any sale of part contract and is covered in more detail in Abbey and Richards, op cit at para 8.09 above, ch 3.

(e) Lastly, the seller may consider a special condition allowing it to rescind the contract if the buyer becomes subject to bankruptcy, liquidation or other insolvency proceedings before completion. This will avoid the delay of waiting for completion and then having to serve notice to complete before the seller can rescind and sell to another buyer.

Other types of contract

8.12 An unconditional contract may not be satisfactory for a buyer if the land is being acquired for development. In this situation there may be certain matters that are outstanding when the parties are otherwise ready to enter into a binding commitment. Typically, the grant of planning permission for the proposed development is one. In this case, the parties may consider a different contractual arrangement, eg, a conditional contract or an option agreement. These types of contract (considered below) protect the buyer essentially by preventing the seller from selling the land to another party during the subsistence of the contract.

Conditional contracts

8.13 A conditional contract may be proposed where the parties are ready to exchange but perhaps one important matter is still outstanding, eg, where the buyer is waiting for a satisfactory local search, offer of funding or planning permission. If the contract is created conditional upon, say, satisfactory planning permission, this is a condition precedent to the performance of the contract. It means that there can be no enforceable contract unless and until the condition is satisfied. A seller would normally be advised to resist such a condition for the obvious reason that it would allow the buyer to walk away from the contract if the condition remained unfulfilled. However, it may be the only way in which the buyer is willing to proceed.

8.14 One danger with conditional contracts is that the law in this area is complex, and unless great care is taken in drafting the condition(s) a court may declare the condition void for uncertainty. In *Lee Parker v Izzett (No 2)* [1972] 2 All ER 800, a contract expressed to be 'subject to the purchaser obtaining a satisfactory mortgage' was held to be void for uncertainty because the condition was too imprecise. However, in *Janmohamed v Hassam* (1976) 241 EG 609, a condition referring to 'a mortgage offer satisfactory to the buyer' was held to be valid on the basis that the buyer ought to act reasonably in coming to a decision.

8.15 Conditional contracts are generally less flexible for buyers/developers than option agreements (see paras 8.20 et seq below). Conditional contracts should never be used where either party has a related unconditional sale or purchase. However, this is unlikely to be the case in the sale of land for development where there are normally only two parties involved and no 'chain' either side.

8.16 In general terms, the following principles of good practice should be noted when drafting conditional contracts:

(a) Define the condition precisely:
   (i) If it relates to the buyer obtaining satisfactory planning permission, specify the exact nature of the permission required and what conditions annexed to the consent would entitle the buyer to withdraw.
   (ii) If the condition relates to the buyer's mortgage offer, specify the amount required, details of the proposed lender and acceptable interest rates.
   (iii) If the condition relates to the buyer's local search, specify those adverse replies which would entitle the buyer to withdraw.
   (iv) If the condition relates to the buyer's survey, specify the type of survey, the name of the surveyor and those defects revealed by the survey which would entitle the buyer to withdraw.
(b) Set time limits for fulfilment of the condition. For example, by what date must the mortgage offer, local search or planning consent be received? It is important to get this right, because time for the performance of the condition is of the essence and cannot be extended (see *Aberfoyle Plantations Ltd v Cheng* [1960] AC 115).
(c) Rather than make up the condition yourself, find a precedent (eg, from the *Encyclopedia of Forms and Precedents* (Butterworths)) and adapt it carefully to suit your client's needs.
(d) Note the following specific drafting points concerning contracts conditional on planning permission, buyer's finance and local search respectively:

Conditional on planning permission (see paras 8.63 et seq generally regarding planning)

- Define the buyer's proposed development.   **8.17**
- Define the relevant planning permission as the planning permission for the buyer's proposed development, and state whether the planning permission should be outline or detailed.
- Oblige the buyer to submit an application to the planning authority within a prescribed time and pay all necessary fees.
- Oblige the buyer to take all necessary steps to procure the grant of the permission as soon as possible, including possibly submitting an amended application or appealing against a refusal.
- Oblige the buyer to keep the seller informed as to the progress of the planning application.
- Stipulate that completion of the sale shall take place a given number of days after the grant of planning permission (eg, 14 days).
- The buyer will not want to complete if planning permission is granted subject to any 'unreasonable conditions'.
- Define 'unreasonable conditions', eg, one that materially affects the cost of construction or the marketability of the development.
- If the parties cannot agree whether a condition is unreasonable, refer the matter to an independent surveyor for determination.
- If the relevant planning permission is not granted by a pre-determined long-stop date then either party may rescind the contract and the deposit is returned to the buyer.

Conditional on buyer's finance

- Buyer to take all necessary steps to procure a relevant offer of finance, including completing all documents required by the mortgagee.   **8.18**

- Define a relevant offer of finance as being for not less than a stipulated sum and which is not subject to any 'unusually onerous conditions'.
- Define 'unusually onerous conditions', eg, an interest rate above a certain percentage or an excessive arrangement fee.
- Alternatively, the buyer may wish to retain control by deciding for itself whether any offer of finance is satisfactory.
- Purchase to be subject to the buyer receiving by the contractual completion date (set realistic date) the relevant offer of finance, failing which the contract ends and the deposit is returned to the buyer.

Conditional on buyer's local search

8.19   - Buyer not obliged to complete contract unless satisfactory local search received by the contractual completion date (set realistic date).
- Define 'satisfactory local search', eg, one that does not reveal entries which materially and adversely affect the market value of the property or the buyer's proposed use/development.
- Alternatively, the buyer may wish to retain control by deciding for itself whether the result of any local search is satisfactory (unlikely that the seller will agree to this).
- Consider a clause whereby, if the parties cannot agree whether a local search is satisfactory, the matter is referred to an independent surveyor for determination.
- Seller to impose long-stop date for fulfilment of the condition (time being of the essence), after which the seller can withdraw from the contract and repay the deposit.

Option agreements

8.20   In simple terms, a typical option agreement is a contract in which the grantee of the option (the buyer) is able, within a fixed period, to serve notice on the owner requiring the latter to transfer the land to the buyer. The option is a particularly useful tool for developers wishing to acquire several pieces of land from different owners in order to develop a larger site. Once the developer has secured options over all the pieces of land, it has effectively gained control of the development site and can safely apply for planning permission. Then, once planning permission is obtained, the developer can exercise all the options to ensure that it owns every part of the proposed development site. Note that the grant of an option to purchase a new freehold commercial building which is less than three years old is standard rated for VAT purposes.

8.21   When the option is exercised, a binding contract for the sale and purchase of the land comes into existence at that point. The exercise of the option does not have to satisfy s 2 of the Law of Property (Miscellaneous Provisions) Act 1989, and thus only requires the signature of the grantee of the option (*Spiro v Glencrown Properties Ltd* [1991] Ch 537). However, the original option agreement itself is a land contract and must satisfy that provision. In other words, the option agreement must be in writing, incorporate all the agreed terms and be signed by both parties.

8.22   The courts will construe time limits in option agreements strictly, ie, time is of the essence (*Hare v Nicoll* [1966] 2 QB 130). The option must be exercised within the maximum permitted period of 21 years so as not to infringe the rule against perpetuities (Perpetuities and Accumulations Act 1964). Most option periods are for much shorter periods than this (eg, one to five years).

In return for the grant of the option the grantee will normally pay the owner an option fee as **8.23** consideration. The fee may be nominal, but is more likely to be substantial if the owner recognizes the development potential of his land. The option fee is sometimes deducted from the purchase price if and when the option is exercised and the land transferred. The method of calculating the purchase price for the land will normally be agreed at the time the option is granted. It will either be a fixed price, or the market value at the time the option is exercised or the development value to be determined by a valuation formula in the option agreement. The option agreement is liable to stamp duty land tax and so a certificate of value should be incorporated if necessary.

The grantee of the option will normally be expected to investigate title before entering **8.24** into the option. The option agreement will record this by stating that, title having been deduced, the grantee shall not raise any requisition or objection to it. The agreement should provide for a completion date for the purchase, eg, ten working days after service of the buyer's notice exercising the option. The method of service of the notice should also be made clear, eg, 'notice in writing served on the grantor on or before. . .'. As with ordinary contracts, the agreement should also provide for the incorporation of general conditions of sale, eg, the latest Standard Commercial Property Conditions. This avoids an 'open' contract and the consequent complexities of consulting common law and statute if there is a dispute. The grantee may require a warranty from the owner that it will not encumber the land without the grantee's consent.

Owners who grant options must of course appreciate that the land will be tied up for the **8.25** length of the option period and that any sale of the land by the owner will be subject to the rights under the option (provided the option is registered). An option is an estate contract, and as such the grantee must protect it by registration. This is done either by lodging a notice or a caution for registered land, or, for unregistered land, by registering a class C(iv) land charge. Only registration of the option will make it binding on any subsequent purchaser of the land; actual notice of the option by a subsequent purchaser will be irrelevant (*Midland Bank Trust Co Ltd v Green* [1981] AC 513).

The classic form of option described above is known as a 'call option'. There is, however, **8.26** another, rarer form of option, which is the reverse of the above, known as a 'put option'. This is where the grantor is the prospective buyer and the grantee the prospective seller. In a put option it is the seller who is able to require the buyer to purchase the land. This may occur, for example, where the seller wants the buyer to be locked into a fixed price in a potentially falling market. The remaining terms of the put option will be substantially the same as those of a call option, eg, establishing price, setting completion date, prior deduction of title, etc.

Rights of pre-emption

An owner may grant a prospective buyer a right of pre-emption over land. A right of pre- **8.27** emption is slightly different from an option in that the grantee cannot force the grantor to sell the property to the grantee. It merely gives the grantee a right of first refusal so that if, and only if, the owner decides to sell during the currency of the pre-emption agreement, the owner must offer the land to the grantee first. Clearly this is less restrictive on the owner because it may decide not to sell at all. The grantee meanwhile has no control over the acquisition, which is entirely dependent on the will of the owner. Of course if the owner offers the land to the grantee, the grantee is under no duty to accept (compare this with a 'put option' described at para 8.26 above). A right of pre-emption is an estate contract and, similar to an option, should be protected by registration in the usual way (ie, by notice or caution, or as a class C(iv) land charge).

Comparing option agreements, conditional contracts and rights of pre-emption

8.28   A typical option agreement will generally give the buyer more flexibility than a conditional contract. In a conditional contract, the buyer will be forced to complete the contract once the condition has been fulfilled. However, with an option agreement the buyer can choose at a later stage whether to exercise the option or not, as the case may be. Thus if, say, market conditions have changed since the option was granted and the buyer no longer requires the land, it can simply allow the option to lapse. Buyers will normally be advised to steer clear of pre-emption agreements because of the uncertainty of whether the seller will proceed.

KEY POINTS SUMMARY: THE CONTRACT

8.29   • A scale plan is normally essential when describing the property.
   • Consider whether a conditional contract or option agreement may be more suitable to the needs of your developer client.
   • For conditional contracts, typical conditions might be: subject to planning consent, subject to satisfactory finance for the buyer, or possibly subject to satisfactory local searches.
   • Any terms making the contract conditional must be drafted with care and defined precisely; uncertainty will make the condition invalid.
   • Option agreements generally give greater flexibility to the buyer/developer and are appropriate when the buyer is seeking to acquire and later develop several pieces of land from different sellers.
   • Remember to protect an option or right of pre-emption by registering it.
   • In a development scenario, always consider what special conditions should be included.
   • Examples of special conditions:
      — grant and reservation of new easements
      — negation of any implied grant of easement
      — imposition of new covenants
      — whether VAT is payable in addition to the purchase price
      — where there are pre-existing plans for development, procuring the assignment to the buyer of the benefit of the copyright in them (or licence to use plans)
      — prevention of any sub-sale by the buyer or assignment of the benefit of the contract to a third party
      — seller able to rescind contract if buyer becomes insolvent.

Pre-contract searches and enquiries

8.30   Here we discuss the additional matters regarding pre-contract searches and enquiries, which will be relevant when buying land for development purposes. For more comprehensive information regarding pre-contract searches and enquiries generally, see Abbey and Richards, op cit at para 8.09 above, ch 4.

Commons registration search

When purchasing a greenfield site, ie, land that has not previously been built upon, a **8.31** commons registration search is essential. The search may also be necessary if the land has been previously been built upon. For instance, the land may adjoin existing common land such as a village cricket pitch. If in doubt, you should always conduct the search, because failure to carry out a commons search where one is appropriate will be negligent (*G & K Ladenbau (UK) Ltd v Crawley and de Reya* [1978] 1 WLR 266). The search is made in the register maintained under the Commons Registration Act 1965 and it will disclose whether the land in question is common land. If it is subject to rights of common then clearly it cannot be developed.

Local authority search

A local authority search will always be made in the case of every purchase of land. This will **8.32** reveal any local land charges pertaining to the subject property, eg, tree preservation orders that could jeopardize the proposed development. In residential conveyancing, solicitors typically ask only the compulsory enquiries in Part 1 of the search form. These are of course relevant for development land as well. For example, details of the planning history will be revealed. This will show whether any previous planning applications have been made and, importantly, whether any have been refused. The answers to the highways questions will give details of any access from adopted highways and whether any new highways are proposed. A separate water search of the local sewerage company will be required on form CON29DW. This will give details of how any foul and surface water drains away from the property to the public sewers, and indeed the location of the nearest public sewer. These answers will help the developer to assess how many new drains will be needed to service the development.

In addition to the above, you must consider which of the optional Part 2 enquiries are **8.33** appropriate. These must be specifically selected on the form and an additional nominal fee paid. The question relating to public paths or byways is particularly relevant when buying a greenfield site. This is because if a public footpath or bridleway crosses the land, the developer will need to apply to the local authority for it to be diverted. Further, the additional enquiry concerning gas pipelines is pertinent. This will disclose whether a gas pipeline has been laid pursuant to the Pipelines Act 1962 or the Gas Act 1986 through, or within 100 feet of, the subject property. If it has, this could of course affect the development of the land. There is no provision for registration of the existence of a pipeline or works, but a map showing the route is deposited with local authorities and is open to inspection. In relation to potentially contaminated land and the effects of pollution, one question asks for information about environmental and pollution notices. Another question asks for details of all entries in the council's register pursuant to s 28 of the Planning (Hazardous Substances) Act 1990. It is the presence of hazardous substances on land that requires consent.

In relation to environmental matters that could affect the property a standard question asks **8.34** if the property is in an area where precautions against radon gas are required in new buildings. Buyers in parts of Devon, Cornwall, Derbyshire, Northamptonshire and Somerset in particular are advised to ask this question, as these are all areas that could be affected by natural radon gas emissions. Radon gas might cause lung damage, and possibly lung cancer.

This question is therefore an important one in these particular areas. A guide containing further information about *Radon Affected Areas* is available free from DEFRA, Warehouse Publications, Admail 6000, London SWIA 2XX (tel 08459 556000; fax 020 8957 5012), or from DEFRA, Radioactive Substances Division, Zone 4/E7, Ashdown House, 123 Victoria Street, London SW1E. Further information can be obtained from the National Radiological Protection Board at Chilton, Didcot, Oxfordshire OX11 0RG (tel 01235 822622). Lastly, the enquiries now include questions to ascertain whether the local authority has served or resolved to serve any notices relating to contaminated land (see paras 8.51 et seq below regarding contaminated land generally).

8.35 Some practitioners and commentators recommend raising all Part 2 enquiries whenever acquiring commercial property. We believe this to be poor conveyancing practice (as well as a waste of time and money). Is it really necessary to ask if the greenfield site is part of an inner urban improvement area? We recommend that you simply raise the Part 2 enquiries that are relevant, and possibly add extra ones of your own, eg, whether the council is aware of any possible contamination of the site.

8.36 It should be noted that some local authorities will answer these enquiries for personal applicants, but they will not guarantee the accuracy of their replies. Perhaps of greater importance is that in many personal search applications the council will not answer all the questions in Part 1. As such, a personal search is really of very limited use and should be used only as a last resort with the client being made fully aware of its limitations. Remember that if an answer in a personal search is wrong, it is your word against the word of the local authority. It is unlikely that any commercial lender would accept a personal search result in any event.

8.37 Lastly, on a local search of a development site, always attach a plan to the search form. This is necessary because the subject property is unlikely to be readily identifiable from its description (even if it is, some local authorities still insist on a plan).

Inspection and survey

8.38 Your developer client will no doubt have made a thorough physical inspection of the land before instructing you, but an early inspection by the solicitor will also be useful. Remember that the seller has no duty to disclose patent defects, ie, those apparent on inspection. When visiting the site, ask yourself the following:

- Are any public footpaths, bridleways or other rights of way apparent? Look for signs, styles, used pathways, gates etc.
- Is there evidence of farming or other occupation on the land (eg, sheep grazing)? The client will want vacant possession, but this may be difficult if the land, or part of it, is let to a farmer who has security of tenure.
- Are there any electricity power lines overhead? If so, will they impede the proposed development? Ask the seller for copies of any wayleaves or consents granted to the electricity company.
- Is there any indication as to who is responsible for the boundaries? Take a look at any fences, hedges and walls. Does the location of the boundaries on the ground accord with the boundaries shown on the title plan(s)?
- Consider the neighbouring land. Could the proposed development possibly interfere with

any neighbours' rights to light or air? It may be necessary to investigate whether adjoining owners have such rights.

- Investigate how the site is to be accessed and serviced. Where is the nearest public highway? Will it be necessary to have new easements over neighbouring land for access, drainage and other services?

In addition to a physical inspection a formal site survey is essential. The client should **8.39** instruct the surveyor formally to assess the site's drainage and access requirements and to report generally on the suitability of the site for development. One area of special concern is the matter of contaminated land. It may be necessary to commission an environmental survey to rule out the possibility of contamination (see paras 8.51 et seq below).

Other searches

The following additional searches should also be conducted if appropriate. For a full discus- **8.40** sion of these, see Abbey and Richards, op cit at para 8.09 above, ch 4.

Mining searches   You should consider whether the land is in a mining area. For coal min- **8.41** ing, consult the Law Society's *Coal Mining Directory* to see if the property is located within a coal mining area. The Law Society's *Guidance Notes* of 1994 contain a list of towns and parishes that may be affected by mining, either in the past, or at present or in the future. However, in this regard the guiding principle should be, if in doubt, always make a search. Consider also whether searches are necessary for limestone mining, clay mining, tin mining or brine extraction. This will depend again on the particular location of the subject property. (See Abbey and Richards, op cit at para 8.09 above, for details of these searches.)

Index map search   An index map search should be carried out at the Land Registry when- **8.42** ever the subject land has an unregistered title. The search will disclose any cautions against first registration and confirm that the land is definitely unregistered. If the title has been previously registered, the title number will be disclosed.

Land charges search   Again, this is necessary where the subject land is unregistered. It will **8.43** reveal any land charges registered against the seller and former estate owners, as well bank-ruptcy entries and pending actions.

Company search   This is always necessary where the seller is a company. The search will **8.44** confirm whether the selling company has the power to sell property under the constitution of the company and indicate if the company is being wound up. On-line searches are avail-able from the Companies House website at <http://www.companies-house.gov.uk>.

Rivers   The National Rivers Authority maintains details of all rivers, streams and brooks. If **8.45** the subject property is next to a watercourse then a search will be necessary. It will provide details of liability for repairs and maintenance of riverbanks as well as for floods from the river, etc.

Canals   The British Waterways Board maintains details of all canals in the country. If the **8.46** subject property is next to a canal then (for the same reasons as for rivers) a search should be sent to the Board. The search can also enquire as to rights of way, etc. affecting the towpath.

Railways   If the subject property is alongside a railway or over a railway tunnel then a **8.47** search can be made of Railtrack, who should be able to provide information about any matters affecting the property. Items of concern could be tunnel routes, boundary maintenance and entrance for the purpose of carrying out repairs.

8.48   **Verderers of the New Forest**   This is relevant if the property is situated in parts of Hampshire or Dorset in or near to the New Forest. The Forest has its own common land registration system, which is not governed by the Commons Registration Act 1965.

8.49   **Agricultural credits search**   Where agricultural land is being purchased, an agricultural credits search should be made where a working farmer occupies farm buildings either as an owner or as a tenant farmer. The Agricultural Credits Act 1928 allows farmers to arrange bank floating charges. If there is a registration by the bank at the Land Charges Registry, a buyer will take subject to it; hence the need for this search.

Enquiries of the seller's solicitor

8.50   The buyer's solicitor will of course raise the standard enquiries that are used in any conveyancing transaction, but there will be additional matters to think about where the client is acquiring land for development. In particular, you should ask:

- whether the land has ever been subject to flooding
- if the seller has details of the planning history of the land, including previous applications, refusals, etc.
- whether the land has ever been contaminated
- whether the seller is aware of any changes in the boundaries from those indicated on the title plans
- whether the seller has elected to waive any exemption for VAT and, if not, confirmation that the seller will not do so before completion (see paras 10.02 et seq below for a full consideration of VAT issues)
- for confirmation of the use of any adjacent property that could possibly conflict with your client's proposed development
- whether the seller has information concerning any previous uses to which the subject property has been put and copies of relevant planning consents
- general environmental enquiries of the seller (for examples of these, see appendix 16).

Contaminated land

8.51   One area of special concern for a buyer of intended development land is the possibility that the site may be contaminated. Contamination in itself may have practical implications, in that the site may not sensibly be used for development, but there are also legal and financial implications that flow from contamination. The most important of these is the potential liability for remediation (or 'clean-up') costs of the contamination. Practitioners should be aware that clean-up costs can run as high as £1 million per hectare.

Liability under the Environment Act 1995

8.52   It is necessary to consider whether the subject property falls within the definition of 'contaminated land' in the Environment Act 1995. The Act defines contaminated land as land which appears to the local authority to be in such a condition that:

(a)   significant harm is being caused; or

(b) there is a significant possibility of such harm being caused; or

(c) water pollution is being or is likely to be caused.

It is estimated that some 100,000 sites are contaminated in the UK, with up to 300,000 hectares affected in some way.

A statutory regime for the identification and remediation of contaminated land was intro- **8.53** duced on 1 April 2000. In essence, local authorities are able to serve remediation notices on 'appropriate persons' requiring them to clean up contaminated land. To identify contaminated land each authority must inspect its area and produce a written strategy setting out its approach.

Under the terms of the statutory guidance the local authority is directed to consider the **8.54** following:

(a) Whether a 'pollutant linkage' is established. This means all of the following:
    (i) a *source* of contamination, ie, a contaminant on the land that has potential to cause harm or water pollution;
    (ii) a *receptor or target*, ie, something which may be harmed by the contaminant, such as humans, living organisms, ecological systems, buildings, livestock or crops;
    (iii) a *pathway*, ie, a route through which the receptor could be exposed to the contaminant.
(b) If a pollutant linkage is established, the question of significant harm or water pollution is considered. Significant harm for humans includes harm which would result in death, disease, serious injury, genetic mutation, birth defects or the impairment of reproductive functions. Significant harm for buildings includes structural failure, substantial damage or substantial interference with any associated property rights. Significant harm for livestock and crops includes death, disease or other physical damage causing a loss in value or loss of yield of 20 per cent or more.
(c) Whether remediation of the contamination is required so that the land is suitable for current use, including any likely informal recreational use, eg, children playing on the land. The guidelines direct the local authority to assess whether remediation is reasonable, having regard to the cost of the remediation and the seriousness of the harm or pollution involved. Remediation will not be reasonable if the costs to be incurred outweigh the benefits to be achieved.
(d) If the local authority decides that remediation is required, unless remediation is being carried out voluntarily, it will serve a remediation notice on the 'appropriate person', as defined by s 78F of the Environmental Protection Act 1990. In the first instance this is the original polluter who 'caused or knowingly permitted' the land to be contaminated (Class A person). Importantly, a purchaser who buys with knowledge of contamination, and who has had a reasonable opportunity to act, may be classified as a knowing permitter. Moreover, if the buyer is a 'large commercial organization or public body' and the seller permitted the buyer to carry out investigations as to the condition of the land, this will indicate that the buyer had sufficient knowledge of the contamination.
(e) If a Class A person cannot be found, the 'appropriate person' is the current owner or occupier of the land (Class B person).
(f) All remediation notices will be kept on a public register. Even after successful

remediation, there is no provision for sites to be removed from the register. This may blight the land making it difficult to sell or mortgage.

(g) The local authority has power to carry out the remediation works itself at the expense of the 'appropriate person'.

8.55 Information and guidance on the detailed provisions of the regulations can be viewed at <http://www.environment.detr.gov.uk//contaminated/land/index.htm>. The relevant statutory provisions are ss 78A–78YC of the Environmental Protection Act 1990 (inserted by the Environment Act 1995). They came into force on 1 April 2000 and require local authorities to identify contaminated sites within their area.

Other liability

8.56 In addition to the potential statutory liability for clean-up costs, an owner of contaminated land may have other legal risks associated with 'migrating pollution', ie, where waste escapes from the land causing pollution damage. These risks include criminal liability under s 34 of the Environmental Protection Act 1990 and potential civil liability in nuisance. An example of a case involving the latter is *Cambridge Water Co v Eastern Counties Leather Ltd* [1994] 2 WLR 53. Here, although the actual defendant escaped liability, it was held that it would be possible to establish civil liability without proof of fault or negligence. The House of Lords held that an owner who brought a noxious substance on to its land, and who should have reasonably foreseen the consequences of its escape, prima facie would be strictly liable.

Environmental searches (including flooding)

8.57 A practitioner acting for a buyer is required to make all prudent searches and enquiries, and this should certainly include an environmental search. Furthermore, practitioners should not merely rely upon any contaminated land information obtained from the local authority in their replies to enquiries in the local authority search. This is because the detail supplied is likely to be insufficient, being limited to land identified by the local authority as contaminated or potentially affected by nearby contaminated land. It is possible to make a search with the Environment Agency but the results can take time to be issued and the information likely to be available may not be widespread enough to be of real benefit.

8.58 However, environmental searches can be obtained from the Landmark Information Group (<http://www.landmark-information.co.uk>) and they can assist with both commercial and residential properties (telephone 020 7593 2370 or 020 7958 4949). The result should cover historical land use, current contaminating and polluting processes, coal mining areas, radon affected areas as well as risk of subsidence and flooding.

8.59 At a more basic level environmental risk can be checked without cost on the internet at another site—<http://www.homecheck.co.uk>. Furthermore the Environment Agency has put details by way of maps on the internet that show areas potentially liable to flooding. This is a free service and can be accessed using a property post-code at <www.environment-agency.gov.uk>. The maps however do not indicate the level of risk. An additional pre-contract enquiry of the seller asking whether the subject property had ever been affected by flooding would also seem prudent.

8.60 There may be an alternative approach. Enquiries should be made of commercial insurers to see if an indemnity insurance policy might offer an insurance solution. Such an insurance policy should offer cover against the potential liability for remediation costs of any contaminants found on their land. Either way conveyancing practitioners need to effect either a search or, if possible, insurance to cover this potential area of concern.

KEY POINTS SUMMARY: CHECKING FOR CONTAMINATION

The prudent buyer's solicitor is able to take a number of steps to establish whether the **8.61** subject property might be contaminated and, if so, the extent of any contamination:

* One obvious step (often overlooked) is to read the title deeds carefully to try to ascertain earlier uses of the land. If the land has a registered title it will be necessary to consider the pre-registration deeds, if these are available, including plans. Evidence of a previous industrial use, eg, gas works, will obviously raise concerns.
* In addition to title plans, the ordnance survey map of the area can be a useful aid. The map may indicate that the land is near a potential source of contamination, eg, a landfill site, or an old quarry or mine.
* Enquiry can be made of the Environment Agency to see if any incidents of pollution have been reported on or near the site.
* Specific enquiry of the seller or other occupier of the site can be made to establish whether they are aware of any possible contamination (see environmental enquiries in appendix 16).
* An additional enquiry on your local search can be raised asking whether the council is aware of any possible contamination. At the same time a full planning history of the site can be requested, as previous planning consents may show an earlier industrial use.
* A personal site inspection is advisable is all cases, but particularly if you suspect the land may be contaminated.
* Homesight (<http://www.homesight.co.uk>) will provide a postcode-specific report on contaminated land for a fixed fee. Note that this report can be used only if the property has a postcode and is therefore of little use for a greenfield site.
* Environmental survey. If you or your client establish that the site is at high risk of contamination, you must advise the client to institute an environmental site survey and/or soil test to be carried out by a specialist surveyor or engineer.
* If the buyer is worried about potential liability for clean-up costs it can:
  — renegotiate the price of the land, or
  — expressly agree in the contract that responsibility for remediation costs remains with the seller, or
  — take an indemnity from the seller against future remediation costs. Before an indemnity is taken, the buyer should check the seller's financial position and consider whether a guarantor or environmental insurance is appropriate.

Reporting to the client

Once the buyer's practitioner has carried out all necessary searches and enquiries, approved **8.62** the form of contract and investigated title, it will be necessary to prepare a comprehensive written report to the client dealing with all aspects of the proposed acquisition. It is especially important to *highlight any adverse matters* to the client, eg, possible land contamination, restrictive covenants on the title, planning difficulties (see paras 8.63 et seq below) or an adverse search result. The report will of course assist the client in deciding whether to commit itself to a binding contract, but it will also serve to protect the solicitor if there is any future dispute with the client as to the advice given at the time of purchase. Naturally the solicitor will keep a complete copy of the report on file.

C TOWN AND COUNTRY PLANNING

Development

8.63 The current extensive town planning legislation seeks to control the development of land and buildings (Town and Country Planning Act 1990 ('the Act'), s 57(1)). In particular, s 57 stipulates that 'planning permission is required for the carrying out of any development of land'. Development is defined by s 55 of the Act as consisting of:

(a) 'the carrying out of building, engineering, mining or other operations in on over or under land'; and

(b) 'the making of any material change in the use of any buildings or other land'.

8.64 By this definition legislation has been put in place to control almost all aspects of the use, enjoyment and redevelopment of land throughout the country. As a consequence, it is important that practitioners know the basics of planning law in sufficient detail to enable them to advise their clients about any effect the legislation might have on the subject property. For a detailed appraisal of planning law and procedure, we recommend Victor Moore, *A Practical Approach to Planning Law* (9th edn, OUP, 2005).

Town and Country Planning (General Permitted Development) Order 1995

8.65 If a client intends to carry out development in the manner defined by the 1990 Act then planning permission will be required. This can be obtained in one of two ways:

(a) by permission deemed to have been given as a consequence of the effects of the Town and Country Planning (General Permitted Development) Order (GPDO) 1995, SI 1995/418; or

(b) by a formal express application for planning permission submitted to the local planning authority.

8.66 The GPDO 1995 grants blanket permission for certain kinds of specific development. For example, the erection of fences is a development (subject to particular height restrictions) that will not require express planning consent. Similarly, the exterior painting of a property is covered by the Order, subject to the painting not amounting to advertising. Perhaps the most important blanket approval is that for small extensions to an existing dwelling house. These small extensions (such as a rear kitchen extension) are subject to restrictions on size and position, but otherwise can be made without the necessity for express planning permission. If the GPDO 1995 does not apply (eg, as in the case of full-scale property development on a greenfield site) then an express application for planning permission will be needed.

8.67 Planning authorities can exclude the effect of all or part of the GPDO 1995 if they deem it expedient to do so. This provision is termed an 'Article 4 Direction', Article 4 of the Order providing authority for such exclusions. The purpose of this restrictive provision is to allow a planning authority to control all aspects of development in great detail. It allows the authority to control even minor development activities, such as the installation of double glazing or a plastic front door, where it is appropriate to do so, say, in a conservation area.

Town and Country Planning (Use Classes) Order 1987

Types of use are defined within the Town and Country Planning (Use Classes) Order 1987, SI 1987/764, which lists 16 separate use classes. Practitioners should appreciate that a change of use *within* a use class does not require planning consent (ie, it is not 'development'), whereas a change of use from one use class to another will generally require planning consent if it amounts to a material change of use (see *Rann v Secretary of State for the Environment* [1980] JPL 109). Note, however, that the GPDO 1995 provides that certain changes made between different use classes are permitted development without express permission (see below). **8.68**

The following use classes are of greatest importance to a commercial conveyancing practitioner: **8.69**

(a) *Class A1: shops.* This class includes a post office, travel agency, sandwich bar, hairdressers, dry cleaning agency and the retail sale of goods other than hot food. Thus a greengrocery can change to a travel agent, and because it is in the same class no planning consent is required. This class will also include a retail warehouse used as a point of sale of goods to the public, even though the size is such that it is not exactly a shop. This will still be the case even if a part of the building is used for storage. (If however, the main element is storage then Class A1 cannot apply and the relevant class will be Class B8 covering storage and distribution centres.)

(b) *Class A2: financial and professional services.* This allows property to be used for the provision of financial services or professional services (not being health or medical services), or any other service appropriate to a shopping area where such services are intended for visiting members of the public. This class has been declared in an effort to support the growing advice and financial services industry. Accordingly, insurance brokers, solicitors, accountants, surveyors, architects and mortgage brokers will all be covered by the one class. Furthermore, the class will also include betting shops and law centres, as well as banks and building societies. However, the critical element is the availability of the service to visiting members of the public.

(c) *Class A3: food and drink.* This class was amended on 21 April 2005 and is now restricted to restaurants and cafes. The class will therefore not cover pubs, takeaways and bars (see para 8.70 below).

(d) *Class B1: business.* This class covers offices other than those covered by Class A2, for research and development of products or processes, or for any other industrial process. At first sight this would seem a very wide class. However, there is a restrictive condition, in that the use is permitted only if it can be carried out when in a residential area without detriment to the amenity of the area. This detriment could be by way of noise, vibration, smell, fumes, smoke, soot, ash, dust, or grit. Accordingly, this form of business use is clearly going to be a problem if it is intended for an area that is primarily residential and the use could be noisy, etc.

(e) *Class B2: general industrial.* This is the class that permits any use for the carrying on of an industrial process not covered by Class B1 or by other provisions in the Order covering special industrial processes (eg, alkaline works and other types of heavy industry that tend to emit noxious fumes or effluent).

(f) *Class C1: hotels and hostels.* This class clearly covers the use of buildings as hotels or hostels and will include boarding houses as well as guest houses. However, none of these will fall within this class if the use includes a serious element of care for persons in residence. In these circumstances, class C2 below will apply. If the nature of the 'care' is in doubt, it should be noted that there is a definition of 'care' within Article 2 of the 1987 Order.

(g) *Class C2: residential institutions.* This class covers buildings used for the provision of personal care or treatment, as well as residential educational facilities.

(h) *Class C3: dwelling houses.* This class will allow the use of property for the accommodation of a family, as well as the coming together of up to six individuals as a single household. This would therefore allow the accommodation of five persons suffering from a disability with a warden or other person caring for them. The limit is fixed at six and the property must be used as a single household. This ensures that other forms of multiple occupation cannot fall within this class. The use of a single dwelling house as two or more separate dwelling houses (ie, the conversion of a house into several flats) is stated by the Act to be a material change of use for which planning consent will be required (s 55(3)(a), Town and Country Planning Act 1990).

Changes to the 1987 Use Classes Order

8.70 From 21 April 2005 there are changes to the use classes that were created by the 1987 Order. That order has been amended by the Town and Country Planning (Use Classes) (Amendment) (England) Order 2005 which substitutes for the former A3 (food and drink) three new use classes:

(a) Restaurants and cafes (A3),

(b) Drinking establishments (Pubs and bars) (A4), and

(c) Hot food takeaways (A5).

Accordingly A3 is restricted to just restaurants and cafes and excludes pubs, bars and takeaways. Pubs and bars have their own use class, A4, and takeaways are given a new Use Class, A5. (Planning consent will not be needed for a change of use from A4 or A5 to A3 but any other change of use will require planning permission.)

8.71 Internet cafes are now within Use Class A1 (shops) and motorcar showrooms are excluded from A1, meaning that planning permission will be needed for such a change of use.

8.72 The GPDO 1995 allows as permitted development specific changes between different use classes (unless an Article 4 direction (see para 8.67 above) is in force). The following permissions should be noted as being particularly relevant:

From	*To*
A2, financial and professional services	A1 shop
(In this case the subject premises must have a display window at street or ground floor level.)	

A3, restaurants and cafes	A1 shop, or A2 financial and professional services
A4, drinking establishments (pubs and bars)	A1 shop, or A2 financial and professional services
A5, hot food takeaways	A1 shop, or A2 financial and professional services
B2 (general industrial)	B1 (business)
B2 (general industrial), but limited to changes of use of not more than 235 square metres of floorspace	B8 (storage and distribution)
B8 (storage and distribution), but limited to changes of use of not more than 235 square metres of floorspace	B1 (business)

Applying for express planning permission

This will be done by a formal application submitted to the local planning authority. The **8.73** client's architect will normally prepare and submit the application. An applicant has the choice of making an application either for outline planning permission, or for full planning permission. An outline application will elicit a response from the planning authority without the expense of having to prepare a full and comprehensive application involving full plans. The planning authority can impose conditions attaching to the outline consent. If an outline consent is granted, it can be expressed to be subject to 'reserved matters', thereafter being resolved to the satisfaction of the planning authority. Reserved matters will relate to the detail of the application, such as the external appearance of the property, means of access to it and landscaping. If there are reserved matters, it will mean that a full application will be necessary to obtain approval for the applicant's proposals in relation to the reserved matters. This must be made within three years of the outline consent. The work itself must start within five years of the outline consent, or two years from approval of the reserved matters, whichever is the later (see ss 91–93 of the Act). The planning authority may prescribe alternative time limits if it deems it appropriate on planning grounds.

The alternative to an application for outline approval is, of course, a full planning applica- **8.74** tion. The planning authority can impose conditions attaching to the full planning consent. Moreover, as for outline consents, the work itself must start within five years from the date of the full planning consent (unless an alternative period is substituted). Practitioners should advise applicants who envisage any delay that the planning authority has further powers under s 94 of the 1990 Act. These are that if the work has started but not progressed very far, and/or if the authority is of the view that the development will not be completed within a reasonable period, the authority can serve a completion notice upon the owner or developer. This notice stipulates that the planning permission will cease to have effect after the expiry of a stated period, which must not be less than 12 months later. If work is carried out after the end of the notice period, it will in effect be unlawful as the consent will no longer be valid.

The decision of the planning authority is registered in the planning register, and the appli- **8.75** cant must be given written notification of the decision with reasons for any refusal or conditions attached to a permission. Practitioners should appreciate that the grant of planning permission is entirely independent of building regulation consent and listed building consent (for which separate applications will be necessary). In addition, it may be obvious (but worth saying) that planning permission does not give any right to breach an enforceable covenant affecting land. Covenants are, of course, contractual matters between private individuals and must be considered separately (see paras 8.02 et seq regarding title investigation).

8.76 Planning permission enures for the benefit of the land and all persons interested in the land (s 75(1) of the Act). Its permissive nature means that the owner of the land, provided work has not already started, cannot be compelled by the planning authority to commence the permitted development.

8.77 Any conditions attached to the permission are subject to the constraints imposed by a landmark decision of the House of Lords in 1981. The conditions must be for a planning purpose and not for any ulterior purpose; they must fairly and reasonably relate to the permitted development; and they must not be so unreasonable that no reasonable planning authority could have imposed them (see *Newbury DC v Secretary of State for the Environment* [1981] AC 578, HL, *per* Viscount Dilhorne at 599). (See also the Annex to DoE Circular 11/95, which gives detailed guidance to planning authorities on the subject of planning conditions.) Notwithstanding the above, there is a way in which the planning authority can counter these restraints on conditions. That is to utilize 'planning obligations' under an agreement pursuant to s 106 of the 1990 Act or a unilateral undertaking given by the developer. These are considered in paras 8.78 et seq below.

Planning obligations, s 106 agreements and unilateral undertakings

Planning obligations and s 106 agreements

8.78 Planning obligations agreed between a developer and the local planning authority pursuant to an agreement under s 106 of the 1990 Act are not subject to the constraints mentioned at para 8.77 above. Given the flexibility of the s 106 agreement, it has become a popular method of achieving, through negotiation, what the parties require from the proposed development, independently of the limitations of the planning permission itself. The s 106 agreement is registrable by the local planning authority as a local land charge and so will be revealed by a local search of the subject property.

8.79 Various formalities have to be followed. The agreement must be by deed and state that it is a planning obligation for the purposes of s 106 of the Act. It must identify the land and the parties concerned, including the interest of the developer. Any person 'interested in land' in the area of the local planning authority may, 'by agreement or otherwise', enter into a planning obligation. Importantly, a person 'interested in land' means someone with a legal estate or interest in the land and so would not include, for instance, a developer with an equitable interest under an option to purchase. The reference to 'agreement or otherwise' means that a planning obligation can also be created by a unilateral undertaking given by the developer (see para 8.84 below).

8.80 The planning obligation may, pursuant to s 106(1):

(a) restrict the development or use of the land in any specified way; or

(b) require specified operations or activities to be carried out in, on, under or over the land; or

(c) require the land to be used in any specified way; or

(d) require a sum or sums to be paid to the authority on a specified date, or dates or periodically.

The obligations may be imposed indefinitely or for specified periods (s 106(2)). They may **8.81** also be conditional. The obligations are enforceable by the planning authority not only against the person entering into them, but also against any person deriving title from that person (s 106(3)). One interesting feature of this is that both negative and positive obligations are capable of binding successors in title (eg, the payment of money or building works). Compare this to land law principles relating to freehold covenants, where the burden of positive covenants generally will not bind successors. Note, however, that liability is limited to the time during which a person has an interest in the land (s 106(4)).

There are policy and common law restraints on what may be included in a s 106 agreement. **8.82** These deterrents are necessary to prevent unfair obligations being imposed, which would be contrary to the public interest. These are known as 'planning gain'. Examples of such abuse would be for parties to agree 'bribes' or other improper inducements given by developers to planning authorities to secure planning permission. A detailed statement of policy in this regard is contained in Circular 1/97 issued by the Secretary of State for the Environment. Planning obligations will be allowable only if they are:

(a) necessary to make a proposal acceptable in land use terms;
(b) relevant to planning;
(c) directly related to the proposed development;
(d) fairly and reasonably related in scale and kind to the proposed development;
(e) reasonable in all other respects.

There is relevant case law in this area, and interested practitioners should consult *Tesco Stores* **8.83** *Ltd v Secretary of State for the Environment* [1995] JPL 581, HL; *Good v Epping Forest DC* [1994] JPL 372, CA; and *R v Plymouth City Council, ex p Plymouth & South Devon Co-operative Society Ltd* [1993] 36 EG 135, CA. These cases concern the reasonableness of benefits in planning obligations and the importance that should be given to them in determining whether planning permission should be granted.

Unilateral undertakings

As an alternative to s 106 agreements, the developer may give a unilateral undertaking **8.84** (binding on it and its successors in title) to carry out certain works. The advantage of an undertaking is that, unlike a s 106 agreement, the planning authority does not need to agree the terms of the undertaking. Thus it avoids the problem of the 'difficult' planning authority which plays for time or holds out for excessive gain.

In considering a related planning application (or appeal), the planning authority (or **8.85** Secretary of State) can take into account the terms of any undertaking that the developer is willing to give. The developer can also offer further undertakings during the course of appeal proceedings.

Modification and discharge of planning obligations

Any person against whom a planning obligation is enforceable may apply to the local plan- **8.86** ning authority for the obligation to be modified or discharged (s 106A of the 1990 Act). The application can be made at any time after the expiry of five years from the date of the planning obligation, or such other period as the Secretary of State may prescribe.

Planning appeals

8.87   The applicant for planning permission may appeal against the refusal of planning permission, the conditions imposed in a permission, the refusal of reserved matters or the failure to notify a decision within the prescribed time (usually eight weeks). The appeal must be made to the Secretary of State for the Environment within six months of the notice of the decision or failure to determine the case, as the case may be. There are three distinct forms of appeal procedure, which we examine below: written representations, public inquiries, and informal hearings. In each case the grounds for appeal must be set out in the appeal form.

Written representations

8.88   The written representation method accounts for the vast majority of appeals, as it is much quicker and cheaper than inquiries or hearings. The detailed procedure is contained in the Town and Country Planning (Appeals) (Written Representations Procedure) (England) Regulations 2000, SI 2000/1028. Strict time limits are imposed for the submission of representations and any further comments on representations. Time runs from the 'starting date' notified by the Secretary of State, which is usually the date he receives all relevant documents necessary to consider the appeal. The planning authority can veto an appeal by written representation and opt for a public inquiry instead, eg, if it wishes to test the other side's evidence by cross-examination. However, planning authorities rarely exercise this power and are usually content to proceed with a written representation appeal if requested by the appellant.

Public inquiries

8.89   Public inquiries are normally appropriate for large-scale developments where complex issues are involved, or where there is significant local or public interest in the proposed development. If the Secretary of State decides to determine the appeal himself, the Town and Country Planning (Inquiries Procedure) (England) Rules 2000, SI 2000/1624 will govern the procedure. Alternatively, the Secretary of State may simply transfer the decision for determination by an inspector. In this case the procedure is governed by the Town and Country Planning (Determination by Inspectors) (Inquiries Procedure) (England) Rules 2000, SI 2000/1625). The detailed procedure leading to and at the inquiry is beyond the scope of this book; for further reading in this area we recommend Moore, op cit at para 8.64 above.

Hearings

8.90   As an alternative to a formal inquiry, the Secretary of State can invite the parties to agree to the appeal being dealt with by an informal hearing before a planning inspector. A hearing is recommended in the following circumstances:

(a)   for small-scale developments where there is little or no third party interest;

(b)   where complex or technical issues are unlikely to arise;

(c)   where there is no likelihood that formal cross-examination will be needed to test the evidence.

Naturally, the danger to the parties of an informal hearing is that the more relaxed **8.91** atmosphere may lead to a less thorough examination of the issues (see *Dyason v Secretary of State for the Environment and Chiltern DC* [1998] JPL 778, where the Court of Appeal levelled criticism at the hearing procedure).

The Town and Country Planning (Hearings Procedure) (England) Rules 2000 govern the **8.92** procedure for informal hearings (replacing a previous Code of Practice). Essentially the procedure consists of inspector-led discussions between the parties. As with the written representations procedure, the hearing procedure is geared to a strict timetable that runs from the 'starting date' notified by the Secretary of State. Local authorities are obliged to notify certain interested parties of the appeal within two weeks of the starting date.

Further appeals

The appeal decision may be further challenged by an appeal to the High Court (s 288 of the **8.93** 1990 Act), but only if the procedural requirements have not been met or if the decision was not within the powers of the Act. An application for judicial review is another possibility.

Enforcement

If the local authority becomes aware of a breach of planning control, it has the power to issue **8.94** and serve an enforcement notice (s 172(1) of the 1990 Act). Failure to comply with an enforcement notice can amount to a criminal offence for which magistrates can impose a fine of up to £20,000. Accordingly, where development has been carried out without permission or a condition has not been complied with, the authority can serve such a notice upon the owner or occupier or anyone else interested in the subject property. A breach of condition notice may also be served, requiring compliance with a condition attached to a planning permission.

The time limits for enforcement action are contained in s 171B of the Act. Enforcement **8.95** action must be taken within four years of any operational development, such as a new building. The four-year period runs from the date when the operations were substantially completed. Similarly, a four-year period for enforcement operates for changes of use of any building to use as a single dwelling house, running from when the fresh use commenced. In the case of any other breach of planning law the enforcement action period is ten years from the date of any breach. Any other breach will be all breaches including changes of use other than operational development or a change of use to a single dwelling house. The four-year rule also applies to building works such as a flat conversion. Failure by the planning authority to take enforcement action within the relevant time limit will render any breach lawful. If a notice is validly served then the recipient can appeal to the Secretary of State on one or more of the grounds for appeal set out in s 174 of the Act. These grounds include indicating that planning permission ought to be granted and that the proposals, if they occur, do not constitute a breach of planning control.

While an enforcement notice is under appeal it has no effect. The consequence of this is that **8.96** the alleged improper use can continue. If the authority wishes to terminate the use immediately upon service of an enforcement notice then it must also issue and serve a stop notice. The planning authority can rely upon s 183 of the Act, which empowers it to issue stop notices which effectively prohibit any use or activity contained or mentioned in the allied enforcement notice. A stop notice will not prohibit the use of any building as a dwelling house (s 183(4) of the Act). Accordingly, a stop notice will arise only in the context of an enforcement notice and not otherwise.

8.97 Before deciding whether to issue an enforcement notice, the planning authority can enter land on 24 hours' notice to ascertain whether there has been breach of planning control. If it identifies a breach it may serve a planning contravention notice under ss 171C–171D of the 1990 Act. The notice will require the person on whom it is served to give detailed information regarding any operations, use or activities on the land. The person served will commit an offence unless he or she replies to the notice within 21 days (barring a reasonable excuse).

8.98 If the local planning authority wishes to secure compliance with conditions or limitations attaching to an existing planning consent, it may serve a breach of condition notice under s 187A of the Act. The notice is served on any person who is carrying out or has carried out the development, or on any person having control of the land. The notice must state a compliance period of not less than 28 days.

8.99 The local planning authority may also apply to the court for an injunction to restrain any existing or potential breach of planning control. An injunction is, of course, an equitable remedy at the discretion of the court. For examples of its use in a planning context (see *Wealden DC v Nelson James Krushandal* [1999] JPL 174, CA, and *Croydon LBC v Gladden* [1994] JPL 723 (a case involving the removal of a replica Spitfire from a garden!).

Building regulation approval

8.100 Regulations about the standards for building works were issued in 1991 (the Building Regulations 1991, SI 1991/2768) and came into force on 1 June 1992. Building works must comply with these Regulations. Practitioners should advise their clients of the need to obtain building regulation approval as an entirely separate requirement from planning. It is in effect an additional requirement. Before the works start, the developer should advise the local authority and deposit with it plans of the proposed works. Once the works have been completed, the developer should seek from the local authority a final certificate. This is a certificate of compliance confirming that the works have been carried out to the satisfaction of the local authority and in accordance with the Regulations.

8.101 If the local authority intends to take action as a consequence of any suspected breach of the Regulations, it must do so within 12 months of the alleged breach (s 36(1), Building Act 1984 and s 65, Public Health Act 1936). As a result, many buyers' practitioners take the view that sight of a building regulation consent is necessary only if the works have been carried out within the last 12 months. However, the effect of a recent Chancery Division case, *Cottingham v Attey Bower & Jones* [2000] EGCS 48 has been that practitioners, to avoid negligence, must now always insist on seeing a copy of the consent. In this case, the buyer's solicitor sent standard enquiries asking for copies of building regulation consents. The seller's solicitors replied that the seller did not have any, and that works had been carried out seven years previously. The buyer's solicitor did not pursue the matter because of the length of time since the completion of the works. Nevertheless, the judge held that while there could be no prosecution later than 12 months after the works, the local authority could still obtain an injunction in respect of the unauthorized works under s 36(6) of the Buildings Act 1984. The buyer's solicitor was therefore negligent in not taking further steps to establish whether consent had been given. The moral is now very clear—if you know that works have been carried out at any time, ensure that you obtain a copy of the relevant building regulation approval (or arrange indemnity insurance cover).

KEY POINTS SUMMARY: TOWN AND COUNTRY PLANNING

- Planning permission is needed for 'development', ie, the carrying out of building, engin- eering, mining or other operations in, on, over, or under land (operational development), or the making of any material change in the use of any buildings or other land (change of use). **8.102**
- The GPDO 1995 may grant permission for certain types of development (subject to size and volume limits) but will not cover full-scale property development, eg, of a greenfield site, where an express application will be necessary.
- Changes of use within the same use class of the Town and Country Planning (Use Classes) Order 1987 are not 'development' and are thus permitted.
- Changes of use between different use classes are 'development' and will require express permission if they amount to material changes of use. However, certain changes between use classes are permitted by the GPDO 1995 (provided an Article 4 direction does not restrict them).
- An express application may be for outline or full consent. Outline consent will normally require approval of reserved matters, ie, detailed plans, within three years.
- Work must normally start within five years of the planning consent, otherwise the permission will lapse.
- Any condition attached to the planning consent must fairly and reasonably relate to the permitted development and must not be so unreasonable that no reasonable planning authority could have imposed it (*Newbury DC v Secretary of State for the Environment* [1981] AC 578).
- To counter these constraints, the developer can enter into separate planning obligations with the planning authority either through a s 106 agreement, or by offering a unilateral undertaking.
- Certain planning obligations will not be allowed if they constitute 'planning gain', eg, improper inducements to secure planning permission.
- Appeals against refusal of planning consent or objectionable conditions attached to a consent may be made to the Secretary of State within six months, by written representa- tions, public inquiry or an informal hearing.
- Enforcement action is normally taken by service of an enforcement notice; the enforce- ment period for a new building is four years.
- The local authority may also serve a planning contravention notice or breach of condition notice, and may seek an injunction at the discretion of the court.
- Building regulation approval is an additional requirement and is separate from planning; buyers should obtain copies of all relevant consents even if the works were carried out more than 12 months previously.

D   DESIGN AND CONSTRUCTION

Introduction

8.103   The property developer, having acquired the site, must now embark on the design and construction of the development. For this purpose it will need to employ a team of professionals to assist in the development project (assuming it is not itself such a professional). Typically the team will comprise a building contractor and architect and, for larger projects, quantity surveyors and consulting engineers, all of whom will be employed by the developer. The building contractor may decide to employ subcontractors to carry out different parts of the development. The terms of the traditional building contract will normally require the main contractor to complete the building works in accordance with the plans and specifications drawn up by the developer's architect. Alternatively, the developer and building contractor may enter into a 'design-and-build' contract in which the contractor assumes responsibility for both design (through its own architect) and construction.

8.104   On completion of the development the developer may wish to sell the whole site to a third party purchaser, or grant leases of the units within the development to commercial tenants. If the development is residential, the developer will wish to sell individual freeholds or grant long leases of the dwellings to individual purchasers.

Liability of the design and construction team

Contract

8.105   The developer who employs professionals will have contracts with them. If the completed building is defective either because of its design, or because of the type of materials used or the way it was constructed, the developer will of course have a claim against the professional(s) at fault for breach of contract. Although the developer has no privity of contract with any subcontractors, the building contractor may also be liable for the acts of its subcontractors, depending on the terms of the main contract. Contractual damages are assessed under the normal *Hadley v Baxendale* (1854) 9 Exch 341 principles. Thus the innocent party can recover losses arising naturally from the breach, or losses that can reasonably be supposed to have been contemplated by both parties to the agreement as the probable result of the breach of contract.

Tort

8.106   Establishing liability in tort for a defective building is far more difficult. The rulings of the House of Lords in *D & F Estates Ltd v Church Commissioners for England* [1989] AC 177 and *Murphy v Brentwood DC* [1990] 2 All ER 908 have established that liability in tort for pure economic loss is not recoverable (unless it arises as a result of negligent misstatement or advice under the principle in *Hedley Byrne & Co Ltd v Heller & Partners Ltd* [1964] AC 465). Pure economic loss in this sense means loss not connected to physical injury. Thus, for example, loss of earnings as a result of personal injury is recoverable ('economic loss'), but the cost of repairing a defective building which is not connected to physical injury ('pure economic loss') is irrecoverable.

Protecting third parties

As there is no redress in tort, it follows that a person suffering loss as a result of a defective **8.107** new building must try to establish some other liability. Of course the developer has a contract with each member of the design and construction team and can, if necessary, sue for breach of contract. But there remains the problem of others who may suffer loss, eg, a subsequent purchaser of the site, the developer's financier/mortgagee, or the individual tenants or purchasers of the units or plots. In the absence of any collateral warranty (see paras 8.109 et seq below) none of these people can ordinarily sue for breach of contract (although see the effect of the new Contracts (Rights of Third Parties) Act 1999 at paras 8.114 et seq below).

Various methods have been employed to protect third parties. One method is latent defects **8.108** insurance, and this has worked quite successfully for new residential buildings, eg, the National House Building Council (NHBC) ten-year insurance cover plan. Similar schemes are available for commercial properties, but have been less popular due to hefty premiums and excesses (eg, the first £50,000 of a claim is often not covered). Of course lessees of commercial leases can protect themselves from liability for repairing inherent defects by negotiating an appropriate form of wording in the lease to ensure that the lessor, not the lessee, is responsible. Lessees should also be careful that they do not become indirectly responsible for the cost of remedying inherent defects through the service charge. Other methods of protection have been used, such as the developer agreeing to assign any contractual rights against the professionals, or declaring that it holds such rights upon trust for the benefit of itself and specified third parties. However, by far the most common method of protection is the collateral warranty considered at paras 8.109 et seq below.

Collateral warranties

A collateral warranty is a binding promise given by one or more members of the design and **8.109** construction team in favour of a third party who would not otherwise have a contractual relationship with them. For example, a warranty may be given by the developer's architect to the developer's mortgagee, or by the developer's building contractor to a tenant of one of the new units.

The essential elements of the collateral warranty are normally as follows: **8.110**

(a) that reasonable skill and care has been and will continue to be exercised in the performance of their duties under the contract with the developer;
(b) that deleterious materials will not be used in the construction of the development, eg, high alumina cement, wood wool slabs in permanent formwork to concrete, calcium chloride in admixtures for reinforced concrete, asbestos products and naturally occurring aggregates in reinforced concrete that do not comply with British standards;
(c) that any mortgagee/financier shall be given a licence to copy and use the plans, drawings and specifications of the development in case it has to call in the loan and finish off the construction;
(d) that professional indemnity insurance will be maintained by the design and construction team up to an agreed amount.

There is a standard form of warranty published by the British Property Federation **8.111** and approved by the Association of Consulting Engineers, the Royal Institute of British Architects and the Royal Institution of Chartered Surveyors, which is widely used. It can be seen that in the absence of recovering pure economic loss in tort, the collateral warranty has the benefit of creating a contractual duty of care enabling the third party, if necessary, to sue in contract to recover pure economic loss. It would simply be necessary to show that the loss suffered could reasonably be said to have been in the contemplation of the parties when the warranty was given.

8.112   As well as benefiting third parties, the developer may itself also require a collateral warranty from any subcontractor with whom it would not otherwise have a contractual relationship. (Note that it may be possible to establish an implied collateral contract between developer and subcontractor; see *Shanklin Pier Co Ltd v Detel Products* [1951] 2 KB 854.)

8.113   The limitation period for a collateral warranty under hand is six years; for one given by deed the period is 12 years. It follows that the person receiving the benefit of the warranty should insist on a warranty given by deed. The Latent Damage Act 1986, which can extend the limitation period for civil actions, does not apply to breach of contract claims.

Effect of Contracts (Rights of Third Parties) Act 1999

8.114   Third parties who do not have a contractual relationship with the design and construction team may also be helped by the Contracts (Rights of Third Parties) Act 1999. Section 1 of the Act provides that a person not a party to a contract will be able to enforce a term of the contract if:

(a)   the contract expressly provides that the third party should have the right to do so; or
(b)   the term of the contract purports to confer a benefit on the third party unless, on a proper construction of the contract, it appears that the parties did not intend the contract to be enforceable by the third party.

8.115   Thus an architect and a landlord/developer could agree under the architect's contract of engagement that a future tenant of the building could take the benefit of rights under the contract. This would confer on the tenant direct rights of action against the architect.

8.116   The identity, or even the existence, of the third party taking the benefit need not be ascertained at the time the contract is entered into (s 1(3)). Moreover, the third party can be named merely as a class of persons whom the obligation is intended to benefit (eg, 'occupiers of the premises'), rather than a specific individual. Whether the third party can take the benefit of the particular contract will depend on whether the original contract expressly provides for this or purports to confer such a benefit (see *Nisshin Shipping Co Ltd v Gleaves & Co Ltd* [2003] EWHC 2602 (Comm)). The wording, 'purports to confer' (s 1(1)(b)) is important, as it will be sufficient for enforcement by identifiable third parties that the parties to the contract have not indicated otherwise. One option to overcome such a wide application of the Act would be to include a contractual term excluding s 1(1)(b), so that only third parties who are expressly given rights under the contract would benefit. Practitioners for third parties will still need to inspect the contracts carefully to establish whether their clients can benefit and perhaps negotiate additional provisions on their behalf. Ultimately a 'belt and braces' approach may be preferable for third parties, by insisting on a separate collateral contract anyway.

As mentioned above, the provisions of the Act can be excluded. Section 1(2) provides, **8.117** '[unless] on a proper construction of the contract, it appears that the parties did not intend the term to be enforceable by the third party'. This is something that practitioners will need to consider at the drafting stage of the particular contract. If, for example, the architect or building constructor does not wish third parties (eg, tenant end-users) to take the benefit of the contract of engagement then, as a safety valve, the contract should expressly exclude third parties from taking any benefit.

One last point should be noted regarding the 1999 Act. Where a third party has an enforce- **8.118** able right under a contract and has already relied on that right, the parties to the contract can vary that right only with the third party's consent (s 2). This right can be expressly excluded by the contractual parties or waived by the court (s 2(4)), eg, if the whereabouts of the third party is unknown.

KEY POINTS SUMMARY: PROTECTING OTHER PARTIES INTERESTED IN A NEW DEVELOPMENT

- Typically, the developer employs a design and construction team in the construction of **8.119** the development, eg, architects, building contractors and quantity surveyors. Their terms of engagement create a contractual relationship with the developer.
- The design and construction team cannot be sued in tort for pure economic loss (*D & F Estates Ltd v Church Commissioners for England* [1989] AC 177).
- Other parties interested in the development, eg, tenant end-users, mortgagees and subsequent purchasers, prima facie have no contractual relationship with the design and construction team.
- To protect these parties it is advisable to create a contractual relationship by taking collateral warranties from members of the design and construction team. They can then be sued in contract for pure economic loss.
- The developer should also consider taking a collateral warranty from any subcontractor with whom it would not otherwise have a contract.
- The limitation period for a collateral warranty given by deed is 12 years (six years under hand).
- Other methods of protecting third parties are available, eg, latent defects insurance, but are not widely used.
- The financier/mortgagee may wish to take an assignment of the benefit of the copyright in the plans, drawings and specifications (or a licence to copy and use the same) in case it has to call in the loan and finish off the development (usually by appointing a receiver).
- Other parties interested in the development, eg, tenant end-users, mortgagees and subsequent purchasers may be able to enforce obligations in contracts to which they are not parties by utilizing the Contracts (Rights of Third Parties) Act 1999.
- Under the 1999 Act, a person not a party to a contract will be able to enforce a term of the contract if the contract expressly provides that the third party should have the right to do so, or the term of the contract purports to confer a benefit on the third party unless, on a proper construction of the contract, it appears that the parties did not intend the contract to be enforceable by the third party.

E DEVELOPMENT FINANCE AND SECURED LENDING

Introduction

8.120 Here we introduce some different methods of financing a property development and the key issues to be considered when acting for a lender. Practitioners should appreciate, however, that development finance can be a highly specialized area of practice involving diverse and complex issues of corporate law and accountancy, including taxation. A detailed consideration of development funding and corporate finance is therefore beyond the scope of this book and practitioners may wish to refer to specialist works in the field. We shall concentrate primarily on the developer who is seeking funding from a financial institution in order to purchase and develop a greenfield site.

8.121 Unless the property developer is cash-rich or is itself a financial institution, it will require a source of funding to finance the proposed development. The developer will usually be looking to finance the purchase price of the land (assuming it does not already own it), together with its professionals' fees and the subsequent costs of construction. The funding source may be a clearing, secondary or merchant bank, or possibly a building society or insurance company. In each case the funder will normally instruct its own solicitors (as opposed to those of the developer) to act on the funding arrangements, including the completion and perfection of the security to be given by the developer. The lender's solicitor will liaise with the developer's solicitor in setting out the detailed requirements to be satisfied before the loan monies can be drawn down (see paras 8.134 et seq below). This type of arrangement is called 'secured lending'.

Secured lending

8.122 Property development projects are normally funded by loans from commercial lending institutions. Typically, the lender will require as primary security for the loan a first legal charge on the development site. In addition, it may require a fixed and floating charge over the undertaking and assets of the development company itself. If this is the case, the overall strength and profitability of the company will obviously be an important factor for the lender.

8.123 One advantage of having a floating charge used to be the lender's ability to appoint an administrative receiver under its charge. This had the effect of pre-empting any appointment of an administrator by the court and meant that the lender retained control, through the administrative receiver, of the timing and conduct of any subsequent disposal of the development site. Whereas administrative receivers owed allegiance to the charge holder who appointed them, importantly administrators owe allegiance to all the creditors of the company.

8.124 On 15 September 2003 the corporate insolvency provisions of the Enterprise Act 2002 came into force and for most floating charges created on or after this date it is no longer possible to appoint an administrative receiver (there are very limited exceptions). The reason for this change was the government's perception that rescues of businesses were being frustrated by the appointment of administrative receivers.

8.125 The charge holder can now appoint an administrator under a new fast-track procedure by completing a set of forms which are then filed at court. However the administrator as an officer of the court still owes allegiance to all creditors, not just the charge holder. It should be noted that it is still possible to appoint an administrative receiver under a charge created before 15 September 2003.

As collateral security, funding institutions may insist on personal guarantees from directors **8.126** of the development company, and possibly a guarantee from any parent company as well. Another important element of the lender's security requirements is that collateral warranties from the design and construction team must be in place. These ensure that the lender can bring an action in contract against the professionals should it suffer loss arising from defect-ive design, materials, or workmanship. Remember that pure economic loss is generally irrecoverable in tort (see para 8.111 above). In addition, the prudent lender will ask for an assignment from the professionals of the copyright in the plans, drawings, and specifica-tions of the development. If the professionals will not agree to this then, at the very least, the lender must insist on a letter from the person(s) in whom the copyright is vested authorizing the lender to use and take copies of any plans, drawings or specifications relating to the proposed development. This is important in case the lender has to call in the loan and finish off the development itself (usually by appointing a receiver).

In some cases the lender may also ask for life policies on the directors' lives to be assigned to **8.127** the lender so that it has the benefit of the proceeds in the event of the directors' premature deaths. In addition, if the loan exceeds a certain percentage of the lender's valuation of the development project (normally between 70 and 80 per cent, depending on the lender), the lender may require additional security. This is to cover a situation in which the borrower defaults and the lender is subsequently forced to sell the property at a loss (ie, for less than the outstanding debt). The additional security takes the form of a separate indemnity guar-antee policy protecting the lender against this risk. The insurance company offering the guarantee charges a single premium (normally several hundred pounds) which the lender will pay initially and then either deduct from the mortgage advance, or add to the loan account. Either way, the borrower ends up paying the premium.

An extended 'belt and braces' approach is for the lender to require second charges on the **8.128** directors' private houses. If these houses are jointly owned, eg, with a spouse, the lender must be satisfied that the spouse is independently advised. In *Royal Bank of Scotland v Etridge (No 2)* [2001] 4 All ER 449 the House of Lords laid down guidelines for solicitors advising a spouse being asked to agree a husband's (or wife's) business debts being secured on the matrimonial home. These guidelines also apply to cases where anyone in a non-commercial relationship has offered to guarantee the debts of another, eg, a parent and child. Before the case came to the Lords, the Court of Appeal had imposed on solicitors the onerous task of ensuring that the transaction was one into which the wife 'could sensibly be advised to enter'. This seemed to presuppose expertise in accountancy and marriage guidance as well as law! The House of Lords has reversed the Court of Appeal's decision, adopting a more com-mercially realistic approach. Although a solicitor should exercise his own skill and judgment in advising on the merits of each transaction, the 'core minimum' guidelines when advising a spouse are as follows:

- Be satisfied that you can properly act for the wife as well as the husband, ie, that there is no conflict of interest.

- Meet the wife face to face in the absence of the husband (telephone calls and letters are not sufficient).
- Confirm what is the wife's understanding of the transaction and correct any misapprehension she may have.
- Explain in non-technical language the nature of the documents and their practical consequences, eg, if the husband's business fails the risk of losing her home and being made bankrupt.
- Emphasize the seriousness of the risks involved.
- Explain the length of time the security will last.
- Explain that the wife has a choice and that the decision to proceed is hers and hers alone.
- If the wife wishes to proceed there should be clear confirmation from her that this is the case and she should authorize you to provide written confirmation of this to the lender.

8.129   You should also consider the following matters of good professional practice:

- Before agreeing to act, consider whether you have the time and expertise to advise fully on interpreting what may be very detailed financial information.
- Who will pay your fee for advising the wife? If the wife decides not to guarantee the proposed loan will your fees get paid at all?
- Open a separate file and send the wife a retainer letter which clearly defines your relationship with her.
- Keep a clear record of your advice, especially if the transaction appears to be to the wife's disadvantage. Consider asking the wife to counter-sign a copy of that advice.
- The wife's authority for you to provide a 'certificate' to the lender should be given in writing.

8.130   Some lenders require a transfer of the development site to the funding institution once the development has been completed and units let to occupational tenants. In this case the funder, in return for becoming the reversioner of the development, will pay a capital sum to the developer. The sum it pays will represent the capital value of the site less the sums owed to the lender by the developer under the terms of the funding agreement.

8.131   Before the lending institution will be willing to make an offer of funding in principle, it will require sight of a comprehensive feasibility study of the intended development. This will normally include an appraisal of the estimated costs of the development, the likely timescale to completion, the quality and reputation of the design and construction team and the overall viability of the project. Once the lender approves the funding in principle, it will issue a facility letter (or funding agreement) detailing the terms of the offer and setting out its required security. The letter will also set out the developer's side of the bargain, namely to acquire the land and develop it within an agreed timescale and in accordance with agreed plans and specifications. If the development is to be let to occupational tenants (eg, in a new shopping centre) the lender will normally stipulate the nature of the lettings. Typically, a lender requires 'clear' institutional-type leases at specified commencing rentals with upward-only rent reviews.

8.132   Typically the loan will not be drawn down all at once. If the developer is in the course of purchasing the site, an initial 'tranche' will be offered for the site acquisition cost (and associated fees) and then further tranches will be advanced to cover construction costs and professional fees as they arise. If the developer approves the funding agreement, it will sign by way of acceptance and return the facility letter to the lender. It is normally at this stage that the lender will formally instruct solicitors and send them a copy of the facility letter setting out the agreed terms.

KEY POINTS SUMMARY: SECURED LENDING FOR DEVELOPMENT—SECURITY OPTIONS

- First legal charge on development site.   **8.133**
- Fixed and floating charge on undertaking and assets of development company.
- Personal guarantees from directors of development company.
- Assignment of life policies on the directors' lives.
- Second charges on directors' private houses (any spouses must be separately advised).
- Guarantee from any parent company.
- Collateral warranties from the professionals, ie, design and construction team.
- Facility letter or funding agreement duly signed for and on behalf of the developer.
- Assignment of copyright in the plans, drawings and specifications of the development (or licence to use them).
- Mortgage indemnity guarantee policy.
- If the development is to be let, institutional-type commercial leases with upward-only rent reviews.

Practical considerations when acting for the lender

As solicitor for the lender you will write to the borrower/developer's solicitors setting out   **8.134**
your requirements to be satisfied before you can report to the lender recommending the
matter to proceed.

Costs

The lender will expect the borrower to be responsible for its costs and so you must at the   **8.135**
outset ask the solicitors for an undertaking to be responsible for them, whether or not the
matter proceeds to completion. The undertaking should extend to responsibility for all
costs, including disbursements, stamp duty, land registry fees and VAT. You can explain that
in the normal course of events the total costs incurred on behalf of the lender will be
deducted from the advance monies on completion, and before completion a full statement
of the net advance will be given. However, to enable matters to proceed without delay you
will need to protect your client against costs should the matter become abortive. Accordingly, you should ask at this stage for an undertaking limited to, say, £500 plus disbursements and VAT. The borrower's solicitor should give such an undertaking only with the
borrower's express authority. The borrower's solicitor should always consider the merit of
obtaining monies in advance from the client before giving such an undertaking.

Title, searches and enquiries

Your other requirements will be concerned mainly with ensuring that the title to the subject   **8.136**
property is good and marketable and constitutes acceptable security for the lender. You will
ask for up-to-date official copies of the registered title, or, if the land is unregistered, a full
abstract or epitome of title. You will ask to see local searches and enquiries with replies no

more than two months old (including replies to all relevant Part 2 enquiries). Assuming the loan facility is for development purposes, you will want to see evidence that the proposed use is authorized. You will therefore want a copy of the planning application and subsequent planning permission authorizing the proposed development, together with all other necessary consents (eg, by-law consents). It is worth checking that all conditions imposed by the planning consents can be fully satisfied within the curtilage of the property without access to other land.

8.137 In a development there should be an approved drainage layout for the site showing the run of foul and surface water sewers and their connection to the mains. You can ask the developer's solicitors to indicate on this plan the location of the existing adopted sewers. If the sewers do not immediately connect up to the boundary of the subject property, or are not within the boundary, you must ensure that appropriate easements are in place for connection of the new services. Moreover, you will check that all services in relation to water, gas, electricity, telephone, etc. are readily available to the site to serve the whole development without the need for the borrower to secure consents other than from the statutory authorities. Check also that excessive connection charges will not be incurred.

8.138 For a greenfield site you will ask to see a commons registration search and mining search (or a certificate from the developer's solicitors that the land is not in a mining area). A public index map search will be necessary if the land is unregistered. If the land is not already owned by the developer, you will want to see the contract for purchase, requisitions on title with replies, the results of pre-completion searches (if already carried out) and the approved draft purchase deed. Bankruptcy searches will be needed against any personal guarantors and an up-to-date company search would be necessary against a corporate borrower.

8.139 You will also want to consider the replies to pre-contract enquiries given by the current owner/seller. One area you will want to check is whether there are any adverse claims by neighbouring owners or occupiers. If the subject property is occupied, full details must be supplied of the occupiers and any interest they may have. The lender will not wish to be bound by any pre-existing third party interest, eg, an overriding interest. If the property is let, replies to standard tenancy enquiries will also be needed. As can be seen, the lender's solicitor is essentially double-checking the work of the borrower/developer's solicitor. Inevitably this results in duplication of work, but this is unavoidable unless the lender is willing to accept a certificate of title from the borrower's solicitor.

Corporate borrowers

8.140 For corporate borrowers (and corporate guarantors), you will ask for a certified copy of the company's memorandum and articles of association. In considering these you will check that the company can properly acquire the land and that it is acting within its powers to enter into the proposed loan facility (or guarantee). You will ask for clarification that no alteration will be made to the memorandum and articles of association before or during the currency of the proposed advance other than at the request or with the consent of the lender. You will also ask to see a certified copy of the company's board minutes authorizing acceptance of the loan facility and resolving to execute the legal charge and other security documentation.

Insurance

If the property is capable of insurance, ie, there are completed buildings on it, you should **8.141** request a copy of the insurance policy and confirmation that the last premium has been paid. Procure a letter from the insurer confirming that the lender's interest will be noted on the policy on completion of the charge. It is also worth asking the insurer to confirm that the policy will not be allowed to lapse without prior reference to the lender. The legal charge should contain a provision whereby any insurance proceeds are either charged, or held on trust for the mortgagee. Some lenders will insist on insurance in the joint names of borrower and lender so that the lender can influence the basis of cover and be involved in negotiations consequent upon loss or damage. In this case the lender will want to retain the original policy. On a development site, where property is in the course of construction, the building contract will deal with insurance, with the building contractor normally assuming responsibility for cover.

Some lenders require life policies on the directors' lives to be assigned to the lender. If this **8.142** is the case, you will require full details of the policy(ies), including the amount of cover, life company, policy number and confirmation that the policy is on risk, ie, in force. The original policies must be handed over on completion and the life companies notified of the assignment.

Security documentation

If the lender's solicitor has any queries on the information provided, these should be raised **8.143** with the borrower's solicitor as formal requisitions. If the land is being acquired by the developer, the developer's solicitor will probably raise these in turn with the seller's solicitor. Once the lender's solicitor is satisfied that all requisitions have been properly dealt with, he or she will prepare the security documentation for execution by the borrower and any guarantors or directors. This will comprise the legal charge and other relevant collateral security such as any floating charge, guarantees of directors and/or parent company and any deed of assignment of life policy(ies). The legal charge should be an 'all monies' charge so that any default by the borrower would entitle the lender to call in any other loans made to the borrower. If the borrower later defaults and the lender decides to call in the loan and complete the development (or collect rents), it may wish to appoint a receiver under the Law of Property Act 1925 (an 'LPA receiver'). Accordingly, in addition to conferring on the lender fully comprehensive powers of enforcement, the charge should extend the powers given to an LPA receiver by the Law of Property Act 1925. Such additional powers would include the ability to go on to the land, complete the development and grant leases.

Completion and post-completion

Although the lender's solicitor will attend to the post-completion work, the borrower's **8.144** solicitor will normally be expected to supply a completed Land Registry application cover and a Land Transaction Return Certificate (for stamp duty land tax purposes). Unless completion occurs at a meeting attended by the lender's solicitor, the latter will normally appoint the borrower's solicitor to act as its agent on completion. This is on the basis that the borrower's solicitor undertakes to hold the mortgage advance to order pending completion and undertakes to supply immediately thereafter the following items:

- all relevant documents of title, ie, land/charge certificate (where they still exist) or documents of title as abstracted, with all copies marked as examined as appropriate
- executed purchase deed
- form DS1 (ie, Land Registry form of discharge of registered charge) or seller's vacated charge (or acceptable form of undertaking)
- all appropriate security documentation duly executed (list them)
- originals of all relevant planning permissions
- original life policies
- completed and signed Land Registry application cover
- Land Transaction Return Certificate
- Company Form(s) 395
- certified copy board minutes of the corporate borrower's resolution to accept the offer and execute the security documentation
- certificate signed by a director of the corporate borrower confirming that no alteration will be made to the company's memorandum and articles of association except with the lender's consent
- buildings insurance policy (if relevant) with lender's interest noted.

8.145 Assuming the transaction proceeds to completion, the lender's practitioner's costs and other payments, such as stamp duty land tax and Land Registry fees, will be deducted from the mortgage advance. The lender's solicitor is thus paid directly by the client, but not at the client's expense! Your fee note will be a third party bill addressed to your client lender but expressed in parenthesis to be payable by the borrower.

8.146 Following completion the developer's solicitor will forward all relevant documentation to the lender's solicitor in compliance with the undertaking given shortly before completion. The lender's solicitor will check carefully that all the documentation has been correctly executed and received. If the borrower is a company, the lender's solicitor must register the newly created charge(s) at the Companies Registry within 21 days of completion (accompanied by Companies Form(s) 395). If appropriate, notice of assignment of life policies must be given. The lender's solicitor will then attend to payment of stamp duty land tax and registration at the Land Registry. After completion of the registration at the Land Registry, the solicitor will check the Title Information Document and deal with the deeds and documents of title and security documentation in accordance with the lender's instructions. Usually the lender requires all documentation to be forwarded to it for retention for the duration of the loan facility.

KEY POINTS SUMMARY: PRACTICAL CONSIDERATIONS WHEN ACTING FOR A COMMERCIAL LENDER

8.147
- Consider carefully your instructions and the terms of the facility letter.
- Set out all your requirements in your initial letter to the developer's solicitor.
- First obtain an undertaking for costs whether or not the matter proceeds.
- See and approve the following items before reporting to your client lender:
  — title, ie, official copies or abstract/epitome
  — all relevant searches, including up-to-date local search (and replies to all relevant Part 2 enquiries), commons search and possibly mining search

— public index map search if property is unregistered
— copies of all relevant planning permissions
— replies to pre-contract enquiries, including details of any occupiers of the land
— contract, replies to requisitions and approved purchase deed
— results of all pre-completion searches, including bankruptcy searches against any personal guarantors
— memorandum and articles of any corporate borrower, plus board minutes
— company search against corporate borrower
— buildings insurance details (if appropriate)
— life policy details if to be assigned to lender
— buildings insurance details (if relevant).

- Prepare the security documentation in accordance with your client's instructions.
- Instruct borrower's solicitor to act as your agents on completion on the understanding that he or she will undertake to send you all relevant documentation (list them) immediately following completion.
- Receive payment of your costs and any stamp duty land tax direct from the lender.
- Following completion, register the charge(s) at Companies Registry, pay any stamp duty land tax and attend to registration at the Land Registry.
- Give notice of assignment of life policies (if relevant).
- Forward all documentation to the lender, if instructed to do so; otherwise retain in the firm's strongroom.

Equity finance and joint ventures

Practitioners should be aware that another method of development finance occurs where **8.148** the funder takes an equity stake in the development itself. The effect of this is that the funder takes a 'share of the cake', ie, it participates in the profits (or losses) of the development project or development company. This is sometimes known as 'equity finance'. In putting up the development finance and sharing in the expected profits the funder is effectively entering into a joint venture with the developer or developers. The parties to the joint venture will typically form a joint venture limited company to acquire the site and undertake the development. The principal funder in the joint venture will ideally wish to take preference shares in the company to enable it to make a priority return on its investment, ie, through a fixed dividend.

Joint venture partnerships are also possible. One disadvantage of these, though, as opposed **8.149** to corporate joint ventures, is of course unlimited liability. However, there are benefits to a non-corporate joint venture. These include avoiding the need to file annual returns and keeping partnership accounts private, thus assuring anonymity. There are also taxation considerations when choosing the appropriate joint venture vehicle, which are beyond the scope of this book.

It is possible to mix a secured loan with a joint venture. The way it works is that a loan is **8.150** made up to a certain percentage of the development costs (eg, 70 per cent) secured in the normal way by a first legal charge, etc. The funder is then prepared to inject additional capital in return for a share in the profits of the development. This is sometimes called 'mezzanine finance'.

8.151   Those seeking advice from practitioners regarding joint ventures should be warned that if the development fails, those participating in it would stand to lose everything they have invested. You should advise the intending investors that in a liquidation they would rank in priority behind secured lenders, preferential creditors and unsecured creditors.

Sale and leaseback

8.152   Lastly, it should be noted that the lender and developer may, if they wish, agree a sale and leaseback arrangement. Figure 8.1 below shows how a sale and leaseback usually operates.

Figure 8.1 Sale and leaseback arrangement

1. L → LOAN → D
2. D → TRANSFERS FREEHOLD → L
3. L → GRANTS LONG LEASE → D
4. D
   ↓ SUB-LETS UNITS
   ST

1. The lender (L) makes a capital loan to the developer (D), in return for which
2. D transfers the freehold of the development site to L
3. L grants a long lease to D (eg, 99 or 125 years) which is the 'leaseback'. The annual rent that D pays L under the lease represents the annual payments of the loan
4. D then sub-lets the completed units to occupational tenants under institutional-type leases in the normal way. L may want to take a share in the sub-lease rents as well.

Key: L = LENDER   D = DEVELOPER   ST = SUB-TENANTS

PRACTICAL CHECKLISTS: PROPERTY DEVELOPMENT

Land acquisition

8.153   • Check that the title is good and marketable and free from encumbrances that may adversely affect the developer's proposals.
   • When drafting and negotiating the contract, describe the land accurately (usually by reference to a plan) and consider carefully the terms of the special conditions, eg, VAT, easements and covenants.
   • Consider whether a conditional contract or option agreement may be more suitable.
   • Carry out all relevant pre-contract searches and enquiries, especially in relation to contaminated land, and inspect the site.
   • Ensure that the land is not contaminated, otherwise substantial clean-up costs may be incurred; carry out an environmental survey if necessary.

- Always give the purchaser client a full written report before a binding contract is entered into, highlighting any adverse matters.

Planning

- Planning permission is required for 'development', ie, the carrying out of building, engin-   **8.154** eering, mining or other operations in, on, over, or under land (operational development), or the making of any material change in the use of any buildings or other land (change of use).
- The GPDO 1995 may grant permission for certain types of development (subject to size and volume limits), but will not cover full-scale property development, eg, of a greenfield site, where an express application will be necessary.
- Changes of use within the same use class of the Town and Country Planning (Use Classes) Order 1987 are not 'development' and are thus permitted.
- Changes of use between different use classes are development and will require express permission if they amount to material changes of use. However, certain changes between use classes are permitted (provided an Article 4 direction does not restrict them).
- An express application may be for outline or full consent. Outline consent will normally require approval of reserved matters, ie, detailed plans, within three years.
- Work must normally start within five years of the planning consent, otherwise the permission will lapse.
- Any condition attached to the planning consent must fairly and reasonably relate to the permitted development and must not be so unreasonable that no reasonable planning authority could have imposed it (*Newbury DC v Secretary of State for the Environment* [1981] AC 578).
- To counter these constraints, the developer can enter into separate planning obligations with the planning authority either through a s 106 agreement, or by offering a unilateral undertaking.
- Certain planning obligations will not be allowed if they constitute 'planning gain', eg, improper inducements to secure planning permission.
- Appeals against refusal of planning consent or objectionable conditions attached to a consent may be made to the Secretary of State within six months, by written representations, public inquiry or an informal hearing.
- Enforcement action is normally taken by service of an enforcement notice; the enforcement period for a new building is four years.
- The local authority may also serve a planning contravention notice or breach of condition notice, and may seek an injunction at the discretion of the court.
- Building regulation approval is an additional requirement and is separate from planning; buyers should obtain copies of all relevant consents, even if the works were carried out more than 12 months previously.

Design and construction

- The professionals working on the development project will typically comprise a building   **8.155** contractor, architect, quantity surveyor, and consulting engineer, employed by the developer. The building contractor may employ subcontractors.

- The terms of the traditional building contract normally require the main contractor to complete the building works in accordance with the plans and specifications drawn up by the developer's architect.
- Alternatively, the developer and building contractor may enter into a 'design-and-build' contract in which the contractor assumes responsibility for both design (through its own architect) and construction.
- As there is generally no liability in tort for pure economic loss, the professionals will be asked to give contractual warranties to third parties who may be adversely affected by design defects, eg, lenders, tenants.
- Other methods of protecting third parties are available, eg, latent defects insurance, but are not widely used.
- Other parties interested in the development, eg, tenant end-users, mortgagees and subsequent purchasers, may be able to enforce obligations in contracts to which they are not parties by utilizing the Contracts (Rights of Third Parties) Act 1999.

Finance

8.156
- The most likely funding source for a development will be a clearing, secondary or merchant bank, or possibly a building society or insurance company.
- Before making an offer the lender will require from the developer a comprehensive feasibility study of the development project.
- The lender's security will typically comprise a first charge on the development site together with a floating charge from a corporate borrower and possibly personal guarantees from directors; additional security may be required—see Key Points Summary at para 8.133 above.
- The lender will also require collateral warranties from the professional team and a licence to use the plans and drawings in the event of it having to finish off the development.
- The loan will be drawn down in several stages to cover acquisition costs, professional fees and construction costs.
- There are important practical considerations when acting for a lender—see Key Points Summary at para 8.147 above.
- Equity finance is another method of funding a development. This is where the financier directly participates in the profits of the development ('a share of the cake'); it is usually achieved through a joint venture limited company.
- Sale and leaseback is another funding possibility.

KEY DOCUMENTS

8.157
- Enterprise Act 2002
- Contracts (Rights of Third Parties) Act 1999
- Environment Act 1995
- Environmental Protection Act 1990
- Town and Country Planning Act 1990
- Commons Registration Act 1965

- Law of Property Act 1925
- Town and Country Planning (Use Classes) (Amendment) (England) Order 2005, SI 2005/84
- Town and Country Planning (General Permitted Development) Order 1995, SI 1995/418
- Building Regulations 1991, SI 1991/2768
- Town and Country Planning (Use Classes) Order 1987, SI 1987/764

Printed copies of legislation can be ordered from The Stationery Office (<http://www.tsoshop.co.uk>). Legislation from 1988 onwards can be downloaded free of charge from <http://www.opsi.gov.uk/acts.htm>. Statutory instruments are available from <http://www.opsi.gov.uk/stat.htm>.

9

SELLING AND BUYING TENANTED PROPERTIES

A GENERAL INTRODUCTION

9.01 There is a considerable commercial market in the sale and purchase of properties that are subject to the occupation of lessees with statutory security of tenure. This is particularly so in relation to property occupied by business tenants. However, many of the special factors required in transactions involving commercial property will also apply to properties sold with residential tenants. In this chapter we consider special factors, first from the seller's perspective and then from the buyer's. We also consider completion matters and, in the context of selling and buying tenanted properties, company acquisitions. When considering contractual matters for the seller, we compare and contrast two sets of standard contractual conditions to analyse where each should be used, and we look at selecting appropriate preliminary enquiries for a buyer. At the core of all these activities, the precise nature and extent of the terms of the letting will be of material importance to both seller and buyer. This will therefore be the case in relation to the title, contract enquiries and requisitions. All these elements are examined below.

B TENANTED PROPERTIES: THE SELLER'S PERSPECTIVE; CONTRACTUAL MATTERS

An introduction

9.02 In the case of simple residential transactions, the pre-printed Standard Conditions of Sale (4th edn) form of contract is almost universally used by conveyancing practitioners (see paras 9.34 et seq below). But is this a satisfactory form of agreement for the sale of a reversion subject to tenancies? When preparing the contract the seller's practitioner will want to be sure that there are specific items in the agreement covering all the relevant features of the sale, and in particular to take account of the nature of the letting or lettings. If the tenant in occupation is a mere residential tenant, the basic terms of the Standard Conditions could suffice. If the commercial element in the proposed agreement is more complicated, and in particular if the lessee in occupation is a commercial tenant, the Standard Commercial Property Conditions are likely to be more appropriate. A more detailed consideration of the two competing sets of Conditions within standard forms of contract is set out at para 9.43 below. However, we will begin with a detailed look at the Standard Commercial Property Conditions.

The Standard Commercial Property Conditions

9.03 The Standard Commercial Property Conditions (SCPCs) were issued on 17 May 1999 for use in commercial transactions. A second edition of the SCPC was issued on 1 June 2004. The second edition takes into account the changes in the law and practice arising from the Land Registration Act 2002 as well as the Commonhold and Leasehold Reform Act 2002. It also builds upon the fourth edition of the Standard Conditions (SCs) that were issued in October 2003. For ease of reference the SCPCs are reproduced in full in appendix 4.

The SCPCs are now divided into two distinct parts. Part 1 contains general conditions build- **9.04** ing upon those in the first edition, while Part 2 contains new clauses and in particular detailed provisions covering VAT, capital allowances and reversionary interests in flats. As such the emphasis is clearly upon more complex commercial transactions. In general Part 1 applies unless expressly excluded while Part 2 will only apply if expressly incorporated. Completing tick boxes on the back page of the agreement effects express incorporation, see SCPC 1.1.4 (a) and (b).

Both sets of conditions have a front page that allows practitioners to insert basic yet vital **9.05** details for the agreement such as details of the seller, buyer, the property, title information and specified incumbrances. (By SCPC 3.1.2(a) the seller sells subject to incumbrances speci- fied in the contract, ie, on the front page). The front page on the second edition of the SCPC now allows for the sale of chattels to be included in the purchase price. On the back page a special condition will provide for vacant possession or for a sale subject to listed tenancies. Another special condition provides for chattels to be included in the sale or to be sold separately. Finally there is a special condition on the back page that has tick boxes enabling the specific incorporation of Part 2 conditions, eg, conditions covering VAT, capital allowances and reversionary interests in flats.

Part 1 Conditions

Part 1 contains general conditions building upon those in the first edition. It is of interest **9.06** that there is no mention on the front page of the SCPC within the general details of the contract of title guarantee. There is such a provision within the SCPC at 6.6.2. However, this is subject to any incumbrances affecting the subject property and covered by SCPC 3.1.2. The following section is an examination of some of the more important features of the SCPC.

Condition 1 General   In this section there is a definition for 'direct credit'. The effect of **9.07** this is that payments at exchange and completion cannot be by bankers draft and can only be by bank telegraphic CHAPS payment transfers. The purpose of this inclusion is to take account of the general commercial practice of requiring completely cleared funds at exchange or completion. SCPC 1.1.3 defines when a party is ready able and willing to com- plete, ie, when they might be able to serve upon the other party who is not so ready a notice to complete. (Such a notice is also defined as a notice requiring completion of the contract in accordance with SCPC 8.)

SCPC 1.5.1 prohibits the transfer of the benefit of the contract. Practitioners should also be **9.08** aware that SCPC 1.5.2 is a total prohibition against sub-sales in whole or in part. The buyer must be named as the transferee in the purchase deed and no other party can be mentioned unless they are a named party in the agreement. This section is therefore close to the terms of the SCs and is there to ensure that the named buyer and only the named buyer completes with the seller.

SCPC 1.3 recognizes the use of e-mail to deliver and serve a notice (as well as by fax). If the **9.09** recipient's e-mail is stated in the contract (on the back page within the section for details of the seller's and buyer's conveyancers), then adding the e-mail address authorizes service by e-mail, see SCPC 1.3.3(b). An e-mail is treated as being received before 4 pm on the first working day after despatch, see SCPC 1.3.7(e).

9.10   **Condition 2 Formation**   As to the date of the formation of the agreement, the terms cover the moment of exchange, ie, it will be at the time of posting or at the time of deposit in the DX or by some other procedure agreed between the parties. SCPC 2.2 regarding the deposit states that the deposit (at 10 per cent) except by auction sale must be paid by direct credit, (see para 9.07 above). In contrast to domestic conveyances, most transactions where the parties are selling and/or buying tenanted properties are unlikely to be part of a chain of transactions. Consequently the deposit is paid to the seller's solicitor as stakeholder and is to be released to the seller on completion with accrued interest. However, where there is an auction sale the deposit is to be held by the auctioneer as agent for the seller thus enabling the seller to get hold of the deposit prior to completion. Furthermore, if there is a deposit paid at an auction sale by cheque and all or any part of the payment is dishonoured on first presentation then the seller has an option to terminate on dishonour. The seller does not need to re-present the cheque as the provision talks of first presentation and can simply give notice to the buyer that the contract has been discharged by the buyer's breach.

9.11   **Condition 3 Matters affecting the property, Condition 4 Occupational leases**   SCPC 3.1.2 (d) has been written to put the burden upon the buyer to carry out all searches and enquiries that a prudent buyer would make before entering into a contract of this type. In essence the property is sold subject to all matters that would be disclosed in, say, a local authority search save for monetary charges. SCPC now also states that the incumbrances affecting the subject property are either specified in the contract, discoverable upon inspection or disclosable in searches or enquiries. SCPC also states that a leasehold property is sold subject to any subsisting breach of covenant regarding the condition of the property.

9.12   Otherwise the major changes within this section of the SCPC between the first and second editions are located in Condition 4 concerned with leases affecting the subject property. Condition 4 covers leases and applies if any part of the property is sold subject to a lease (and a lease is defined as including a sub-lease tenancy and agreement for a lease or sub-lease). SCPC 4.1.3 states that the seller is not to serve a notice to end the lease or accept surrender and is to inform the buyer without delay if the lease ends. These elements are included in the SCPC to prevent the seller from taking unilateral action that might adversely affect the value of the premises by ensuring that the seller cannot after exchange and before completion force the tenant out of the subject property or take steps towards ejecting the tenant. SCPC 4.2 is a major innovation by seeking to cover property management for the period between exchange and completion. It sets out extensive provisions for the conduct of litigation proceedings affecting leasehold premises in court or by arbitration. (However, you should note that this does not cover rent review matters that are covered by condition 5, see para 9.13 below.) Furthermore, the seller is not to grant or formally withhold any licence consent or approval required by the terms of the occupational lease. In effect this means that once contracts are exchanged the seller must always seek the buyer's permission in relation to any matters that arise from the lease terms and that need the consent or involvement of the lessor. However SCPC 4.2.7 provides that the buyer is not to withhold consent so as to place the seller in breach of a statutory duty or of an obligation to the lessee. So if the circumstances are such that the lessor should grant a licence to assign and by refusing would be in breach of a statutory duty, the buyer cannot dictate that the sellers adopt this stance. SCPC 4.2.9 requires the seller to manage the property in accordance with the principles of good estate management until completion. Quite whether parties to a contract in dispute can agree as to what might amount to good estate management is open to debate.

Condition 5 Rent reviews   This is a wholly new condition included in the second edition **9.13** that covers some of the details in the first edition with expanded and new items. The purpose of the condition is explicitly to cover rent review matters that will arise between exchange and completion. SCPC 5.4 imposes upon both the seller and the buyer an obligation to co-operate promptly and effectively regarding the process of the rent review and the documentation required to facilitate the review process. Most importantly, neither can approve a rent without the written approval of the other, SCPC 5.5. The condition also covers how the cost of the rent review should be paid as between the seller and the buyer. For example SCPC 5.6 states that the seller and the buyer are to bear their own costs of the rent review process. More detailed time related provisions follow relating to the payment of costs, see SCPC 5.7 and 5.8.

Condition 6 Title and Transfer   Conditions 6.1 through to 6.4 are the same in both sets of **9.14** conditions. In effect, without cost to the buyer the seller is to provide proof of the title to the subject property as well as the seller's entitlement to transfer it. (Requirements for both registered and unregistered titles are set out in 6.1.2 and 3.) However 6.6.4 has been drafted so that where the seller will, after completion, be bound by an obligation affecting the property, then provided the obligation is disclosed to the buyer before exchange the seller is entitled to an indemnity from the buyer. There must be disclosure failing which there is no binding obligation to afford any such indemnity. Accordingly, if the contract makes no provision as to title guarantee, then by SCPC 6.6.2 and subject to SCPC 6.6.3 the seller is to transfer the property with full title guarantee. (Condition 6.6.3 states that the transfer will operate on the basis that it is expressly made subject to all matters to which the subject property is sold under the terms of the agreement.)

If the property is registered there may be exempt information documents (EIDs) such that **9.15** they may not be disclosed on or with the official copies of the registers. Accordingly, where there are any such EIDs, the buyer should make sure that the seller is obliged by a contractual term to provide the buyer with full copies. As a precautionary measure, it may be appropriate to include this in all contracts. (EIDs are discussed in detail at para 1.33 above). In the first edition of SCPC old condition 5 allowed for circumstances in which the buyer might be permitted to go into occupation prior to completion. The second edition no longer permits this and the condition has been removed.

Condition 7 Insurance   This new clause brings together detailed arrangements for the **9.16** insurance of the subject property many of which were contained in condition 5 of the first edition. SCPC 7.1.4 states that the seller is under no obligation to insure unless 7.1.2 applies. This provision applies where the contract terms require the seller to continue with its insurance between exchange and completion. SCPC 7.1.3 will apply if the subject property is let on terms where the seller is obliged to insure (either as lessor or lessee). Accordingly the clause, inter alia, requires the seller to do everything required to maintain the policy, including paying promptly any premium which falls due. The buyer is to pay to the seller a proportionate part of the insurance premium from the date when the contract is made to the date of actual completion. If after exchange and before completion the property is damaged by an insured risk, the seller is obliged to pay to the buyer on completion the amount of the policy monies received by the seller. If no final insurance payment has been made then the seller is to assign to the buyer all rights to monies under the insurance policy and to hold any monies received in trust for the buyer.

9.17 Accordingly, if condition 7.1.4 applies, the buyer must assume the risk from exchange and if necessary arrange insurance from that time. This replicates the position that prevailed with the National Conditions, before they were subsumed into the SCs, first and subsequent editions. Furthermore if there is double insurance, ie, the seller and the buyer have the property insured, and the subject property is damaged by an insured risk, then the contract consideration is to be abated by any reduction in the payment made by the buyer's insurance as a result of the seller's cover.

9.18 **Condition 8 Completion**   In this section, being the condition regulating all matters at completion, the buyer instead of the seller is assumed to own the property from the start of the completion date. The completion date will be the actual date of completion where the whole property is sold with vacant possession, otherwise it is the date specified in the agreement. This clearly affects apportionments (see SCPC 8.3.3). These are further regulated at SCPC 8.3.4 where the detailed arrangements required for completion date apportionments are set out. Sums are to be treated as accruing from day to day throughout the period for which payment is or has to be made and at the rate applicable for that period. The SCPC also covers unquantified sums such as final year-end service charges, see SCPC 8.3.5. These are to be payable with interest on late payment, but because of the larger amounts involved in commercial property we suggest that it would be safer to set up an agreed retention with the buyer's solicitor, by way of the special conditions. Alternatively, the seller's solicitor could retain the monies in a designated client deposit account pending settlement with the interest accruing to the seller in any event. This provision should also be covered by way of a special condition in the agreement.

9.19 SCPC 8.3.6 applies where a lease affects the property being sold and where there is a service charge. On completion the buyer is to pay to the seller any element of the service charge incurred by the seller but not yet due from the tenant. In the light of this provision it is vital that practitioners acting for a buyer in these circumstances raise detailed enquiries about any such expenditure. It is therefore important that proof of payment be produced along with proof that it was necessarily incurred and repayable under the terms and conditions of the lease. This is of course required to avoid subsequent problems with the lessee in obtaining reimbursement and is covered by SCPC 8.3.6 (a).

9.20 SCPC 8.3.7 and 8 both seek to cover the position where there are arrears. The terms of these clauses are complicated and should be considered in detail for each subject property and amended as necessary. SCPC 8.3.7 states that SCPC 8.3.8 applies if there are arrears, there is no contractual assignment to the seller of the right to collect those arrears, and the seller is not entitled to recover any arrears from the tenant. In these circumstances SCPC 8.3.8 requires the buyer to seek to collect all the arrears in the ordinary course of management but is not obliged to commence court proceedings for their recovery. Any monies received are to be apportioned between the parties in the ratio of the sums owed to each. New leases granted post-1995 are covered by s 3 and s 23 of the Landlord and Tenant (Covenants) Act 1995 to the extent that unless specifically assigned to the buyer, the right to collect arrears remains with the seller. This is relevant in the context of these SCPCs and the conditions required to bring SCPC 8.3.8 into operation. It also means that pre-1996 leases are such that the seller will not be able to recover arrears by commencing proceedings or instructing bailiffs after completion, (see s 141, Law of Property Act 1925).

Finally in this section SCPC 8.5 says that as soon as the buyer has performed all its obliga- **9.21** tions on completion the seller must part with the title documents. SCPC 8.7 requires payment to be by direct credit, (see para 9.07 above for the meaning of direct credit). SCPC 8.8 states that at any time on or after the completion date a party who is ready able and willing to complete may give to the other a notice to complete. Ten working days is the notice period excluding the day on which the notice is given. For this purpose time is of the essence, see SCPC 8.8.2.

Condition 9 Remedies Little of this particular condition is changed from the SC to the **9.22** SCPC although there is one alteration of consequence for buyers. It should be noted that SCPC 9.3.1 provides that liability for interest arises only on the default of the buyer. If the seller defaults and delays completion in the absence of a special condition, all that a buyer can do is sue the defaulting seller for damages. Moreover, SCPC 9.3.4 states that if completion is delayed the seller may give notice to the buyer that it will take the net income from the subject property until completion takes place as well as any interest due pursuant to SCPC 9.3.1.

Otherwise either party may, if so entitled, by SCPC 9.2 rescind the contract. SCPCs 9.5 and **9.23** 9.6 set out the position should either the buyer or the seller fail to comply with a notice to complete.

Condition 10 Leasehold property As one might anticipate for a set of conditions **9.24** designed to cover commercial transactions and especially those dealing with the selling and buying of tenanted properties, this section contains substantial provisions. There are of course detailed alterations from the terms of the SCs where leases are concerned and in particular in relation to the normal requirement to obtain the consent of the lessor in a commercial lease assignment or transfer.

Dealing firstly with new leases, (ie, a contract for the grant of a new lease), SCPC 10.2 **9.25** reiterates the provisions of the SCs as to definitions and under the SCPC the lease is to be in the form of a draft attached to the agreement itself. Accordingly it is contemplated that new leases will be part of the actual agreement by attachment. If the lease term exceeds seven years the seller is to deduce title to enable the buyer to register with absolute title. This means that a lessor will have to show the lessee their superior title. To avoid this disclosure, lessors should only grant seven year leases or less.

SCPC 10.3 deals with the landlord's consent and has been substantially reworked. For **9.26** example, SCPC 10.3.3(b) states that the seller is to enter into an authorized guarantee agreement if so required. Similarly the buyer is to use reasonable endeavours to provide guarantees of the performance and observance of the tenant's covenants and the conditions in the seller's lease. (SCPC 10.3.1(b) defines consent as 'consent in a form which satisfies the requirement to obtain it'—see *Aubergine Enterprises Ltd v Lakewood International Ltd* [2002] 1 WLR 2149.) Completion can now be postponed for up to four months if there is a delay in obtaining the consent of the lessor (SCPC 10.3.4 and 10.3.5). The commercial conditions also require both parties to perform obligations in support of the application for the lessor's consent, and while those contractual obligations remain incomplete the party in breach cannot rescind the contract (SCPC 10.3.8).

9.27   Condition 11 Commonhold   This condition contains new requirements for commonhold transactions. It first makes it clear that the buyer having received from the seller the memorandum and articles of the commonhold association and the Commonhold Community Statement is treated as having accepted all their terms. If the transaction affects part of a commonhold the seller is to apply for consent to the sale of part and if the consent is not forthcoming there are provisions allowing either party, on giving of notice, to rescind the agreement, see SCPC 11.4.

9.28   Condition 12 Chattels   The only change to this condition is within SCPC 12.3 where it now provides that ownership of any chattels covered by the agreement passes to the buyer at completion, but that the chattels are at the buyer's risk from exchange. This in effect reflects the provision in the SCPC relating to the insurance risk for the subject property, where the risk also passes at the contract date. The reverse is the case for both the subject property and the chattels in the SCs. (SC 9.3 states that ownership of the chattels passes to the buyer on actual completion.)

Part 2 conditions

9.29   Part 2 of the SCPCs contains new clauses and in particular detailed provisions covering VAT, capital allowances and reversionary interests in flats. They are completely new and there is nothing in the SCs that matches them. The main details of these three new provisions are as follows.

9.30   VAT   The standard position in Part 1 is that the seller warrants that the sale of the property does not constitute a supply that is taxable for VAT purposes. Part 2 changes this in two possible ways. First, A1 states that the sale does constitute a supply that is taxable for VAT purposes. A1.3 requires the buyer to pay VAT on top of the purchase price in exchange for a proper VAT invoice. Secondly, Condition A2 covers a transfer of a going concern. In this case the seller warrants that it is using the property for the business of letting to produce a rental income. VAT at the standard rate or VAT for a transfer as a going concern can be selected by tick boxes set out within the Special Conditions on the back page of the contract.

9.31   Capital allowances   Condition B supports a buyer in any claims it may make pursuant to the terms of the Capital Allowances Act 2001. In doing so it requires the seller to provide copies of relevant information as well as co-operation and assistance as the buyer may reasonably require. In the special conditions there is a specific clause for the purposes of the Capital Allowances Act 2001 stating the amount of the purchase price apportioned to plant and machinery at the subject property.

9.32   Reversionary interests in flats   C1 covers the provisions of the Landlord and Tenant Act 1987 and the tenants' rights of pre-emption on a sale. The condition requires the seller to warrant that on the facts the tenants do not have any rights arising from this statute, ie, the relevant notice has been served but no response was forthcoming. Condition C2 covers the position where the tenants are entitled to a right of first refusal. Again tick boxes on the back page of the contract within the Special Conditions will allow practitioners to select either position with regard to the tenant's rights of first refusal.

Conclusion

The SCPCs have been expanded and greatly improved by the additional provisions included **9.33** in the second edition. They are now likely to be adopted for all appropriate sales of commercial property especially where there is a tenant in occupation or where there are VAT considerations and/or capital allowances to be taken into consideration. While it is true that much of the SCPCs replicate the terms of the SCs, this can only be of benefit to practitioners by ensuring that most will be acquainted with the contract details and will therefore be prepared to use these new commercial conditions.

The Standard Conditions of Sale

The Standard Conditions of Sale (SCs) are best suited to, and were really drafted for, **9.34** residential transactions, but may be used for selling and buying tenanted properties if the agreement terms are suitably amended. For example, where the subject property is sold subject to a residential letting, clause 5 of the special conditions should be amended so as to delete the first alternative, leaving the contract term thus: 'The property is sold subject to the following leases or tenancies:'. Thereafter the simple details of the residential lettings should be inserted. These details should refer to the lessee by name, to the type of tenancy, ie, weekly, monthly, quarterly, etc., and to the amount of the rent, together with the part of the property occupied if the tenancy is not of the whole of the subject property.

The following SCs are of material importance. SC 3.3 covers leases affecting the property. **9.35** (A lease is defined by SC 1.1.1(h) as including a sub-lease, a tenancy and an agreement for a lease or sub-lease, and should thereby cover all forms of lettings but not licences.) The seller is obliged by SC 3.3.2(a) to provide full particulars of the letting, with copies of any documents relating thereto, so as to ensure that the buyer enters into the contract 'knowing and fully accepting those terms'. To comply with this provision, the seller should supply, with the draft contract, a copy of any relevant lease or tenancy agreement along with any deeds or documents that are supplementary to them, such as a deed of variation. SC 3.3.2(b) requires the seller to inform the buyer of any lease or tenancy termination after exchange but before completion, as well as to act as the buyer reasonably directs with the buyer indemnifying the seller against any consequent loss or damage. Similarly, SC 3.3.2(c) prohibits the seller from agreeing any changes to the lease or tenancy terms, and requires the seller to advise the buyer of any proposed or agreed changes. Further, the buyer is, by SC 3.3.2(d), to indemnify the seller against claims arising from the lease or tenancy for the period following completion. Indeed, SC 3.3.2(f) puts the burden of enquiry upon the buyer as to what rent is lawfully recoverable and what legislation affects the lease or tenancy. It is for this reason, where the SCs are adopted, that the buyer must make particular enquiries about the rent and legislation as they affect the lessee in occupation (these particular matters are considered in detail below).

If the sale is of a reversion subject to residential long leases, the sale cannot proceed without **9.36** careful consideration of the effects of the Landlord and Tenant Act 1987, which gives the lessees in occupation a right of pre-emption. The contract will therefore need to show that the necessary steps have been taken to comply with the Act and that the lessees are not going to exercise their rights. In these circumstances a buyer is receiving contractual reassurance on this statutory requirement and that as a consequence the sale to the non-occupant buyer may proceed.

9.37 Where the letting is of a commercial nature, the same approach set out above can be adopted but further elements are of concern in particular:

(a) Where there is a substantial commercial rental income from the property, the contract will need to cover the question of rent arrears and the apportionment of rent at completion. Arrears can be dealt with by a special condition requiring the buyer to pay to the seller a sum equivalent to any subsisting rent arrears at the date of completion so that the buyer can then sue the lessee for those arrears. *Re King, Robinson v Gray* [1963] 1 All ER 781, throws doubt on whether a lessor who has sold the reversion can after the sale still sue the lessee for rent arrears that arose prior to the sale. This case therefore makes such a clause judicious; at the very least, there should be a contractual clause making the buyer assign to the seller the right to sue the lessee for those arrears.

(b) Special contractual provisions should be included if a rent review is due at the time of the contract, or if the lease is about to terminate and Part II proceedings under the Landlord and Tenant Act 1954 are anticipated. In both cases the seller should agree not to do anything without consulting the buyer and should agree to act as the buyer reasonably directs.

(c) There may be a rental deposit paid by the lessee to the seller. If there is, the buyer will want to take control of those monies. However, whether this will be possible will depend upon the terms of the actual deposit deed. This will need to be considered prior to exchange, with the necessary steps required to effect a transfer covered in the special conditions.

Other contractual concerns for the seller

9.38 There are other concerns that a seller should have in mind when preparing a contract for sale.

Post-1995 leases

9.39 The Landlord and Tenant (Covenants) Act 1995 allows for a release of a landlord from all lease covenants on a sale of the reversion but, unlike the release for a tenant, this release is not automatic. Section 8 of the 1995 Act covers the requisite procedure. It may be that a landlord does not request or obtain a release, and if this is the case then the landlord can apply for a release on the occasion of a future assignment of the lease (see ss 7 and 11(3)(b) of the 1995 Act). The contract for the original sale should therefore be drafted in such a way as to ensure that the lessor/seller is informed of any subsequent assignment of the lease, thereby enabling the former lessor to seek a release under the terms of the 1995 Act.

Pre-1996 leases

9.40 When a reversion is sold where a lease of the subject property is governed by the pre-Landlord and Tenant (Covenants) Act 1995 law, an original lessor will remain liable for the landlord's covenants for the full term of the lease. As a result, a prudent lessor/seller will seek an indemnity from the buyer for future breaches of covenant. The indemnity provision can either be expressed as a special condition, or a seller might rely upon SC 4.6.4 or SCPC 6.6.4. It is a common convention in practice to state an express provision for indemnity so that the fullest cover can be obtained.

Service charge funds

It is possible that service charge provisions call for the lessor to maintain a reserve fund or **9.41** sinking fund, paid by the tenants in occupation but held by the landlord. If the reversion is sold, the lessor should include in the contract a provision for the transfer of funds to the buyer to be held on the same terms as required by the leases.

1954 Act renewal cases

It is possible that after exchange but before completion lease renewal proceedings could **9.42** commence pursuant to the terms of Pt II of the Landlord and Tenant Act 1954. This is particularly so where there is an extended period between exchange and completion. In these circumstances the seller may wish to reassure the buyer by inserting in the contract provisions concerning the new lease negotiations that go beyond anything in SC 3.3. In particular, the contract should permit the buyer to lead the renewal negotiations, and with the seller agreeing to co-operate to ensure that the buyer's reasonable requirements in this connection are met. This is different in SCPC 5 that deals with rent reviews, see para 9.13 above for details.

The choice of contract conditions

Should a prudent practitioner adopt these new commercial conditions for all their seller **9.43** clients? In theory there is no reason why this should not be done, although in practice there could be substantial resistance to this practice from buyers when they come to approve the draft agreement. In reality the same effect can be achieved by adopting the SCs and by making specific amendments to the draft contract to take into account those changes made by the SCPCs that are relevant to the specific transaction in hand. Indeed, some of the new conditions may not be very sensible in the context of a residential sale. We take the view that the right approach is to adopt whichever set of conditions is best for the subject property and specifically to amend them further to make the selected conditions thoroughly appropriate to that particular property. Best practice dictates that in general a prudent practitioner should always alter a standard contract form to suit a specific property. In particular, practitioners acting for a buyer should always amend the SCPCs to ensure that interest will be a part of the selection of contractual remedies available to the buyer should the seller default. (See paras 9.16 to 9.17 above on condition 7, where it should be noted that SCPC 9.3.1 provides that liability for interest arises only on the default of the buyer.)

Selling by auction

Procedure

Contracts made at auction are not governed by s 2 of the Law of Property (Miscellaneous **9.44** Provisions) Act 1989, and thus a binding and enforceable auction contract arises immediately the auctioneer's hammer has fallen. Confirmatory written contracts are then signed at the end of the auction. As a consequence, a prudent buyer will ensure that a survey is carried out and that financial arrangements, including the deposit to be paid if the buyer's bid is successful, are in place before the auction. If the contract provides for the risk in the property to pass to the buyer once the contract is in force (eg, if SC 5.1 is deleted), the buyer must also make arrangements for the property to be insured immediately the buyer's bid is knocked down, ie, accepted.

9.45 Before the auction, the buyer's conveyancer should inspect and approve the title, the draft contract, answers to standard enquiries and all requisite searches. The seller's practitioner will usually produce these items for prior inspection, often at the auction itself (beware of out-of-date local searches!). The buyer's conveyancer should raise any additional enquiries which are considered to be relevant. The seller's practitioner should also be present at the auction to deal with questions of a legal nature which may arise.

9.46 The contract will comprise the particulars, the conditions of sale and a memorandum of sale. The particulars—which describe the property—are usually prepared by the auctioneer and approved by the seller's conveyancer. The conditions of sale are usually prepared by the seller's conveyancer (although auctioneers often have their own printed conditions which they ask the conveyancer to approve). A memorandum of sale is then attached to the particulars and conditions of sale, which the parties sign after the auction.

Conditions of sale in an auction contract

9.47 The principal concern for the seller's practitioner is, of course, to ensure that the conditions of sale in the contract adequately protect the seller. SC 2.3/SCPC 2.3 incorporates provisions which assist in the contract complying with the Sale of Land by Auction Act 1867:

- SC/SCPC 2.3.2—the sale is subject to a reserve price, ie, an undisclosed price below which the property will not be sold. Without a reserve price the auctioneer is bound to sell to the highest bidder
- SC/SCPC 2.3.3—the seller (or a person on the seller's behalf, known as a 'puffer') may bid up to the reserve price. Given this option, the seller is more likely to achieve the reserve price
- SC/SCPC 2.3.4—the auctioneer may refuse any bid
- SC/SCPC 2.3.5—if there is any dispute about a bid, the auctioneer may resolve the dispute or restart the auction at the last undisputed bid.

9.48 In addition to SC/SCPC 2.3, the seller's practitioner will need to consider whether any additional special conditions are appropriate. The following is a summary of the special conditions which are recommended for use when acting for a seller at auction:

(a) payment of deposit only by cash, or banker's draft or solicitors' clients' account cheque (although SC 2.2.1 deals with methods of payment of deposit, sales by auction are excluded);

(b) the deposit to be held by the auctioneer as agent for the seller (otherwise the auctioneer must hold as stakeholder: *Harrington v Hoggart* (1830) 1 B & Ad 577);

(c) the buyer is not entitled to withdraw a bid once made;

(d) full disclosure of any tenancies subject to which the property is sold;

(e) the seller reserves the right to withdraw the property from sale at any time during the auction;

(f)   the buyer will not raise any enquiries, objection or make any requisition after the auction;

(g)   no sub-sales permitted by the buyer;

(h)   the buyer to reimburse the seller for any search fees and any purchase deed engrossment charges.

If the SCPCs are being used in an auction contract, SCPC 2.3.6 provides for the auctioneer to **9.49** hold the deposit as agent for the seller. It then goes on to deal with the situation where a cheque tendered in payment of all or part of the deposit is dishonoured when first presented. The position is that the seller may, within seven working days of being notified that the cheque has been dishonoured, give notice to the buyer that the contract is discharged by the buyer's breach.

Occasionally, last-minute alterations may be necessary to the auction particulars or **9.50** conditions. If so, an oral statement can be made just before the auction begins, advising prospective bidders of the changes.

C   TENANTED PROPERTIES: THE BUYER'S PERSPECTIVE; PRE-CONTRACT ENQUIRIES

Preliminary enquiries: an introduction

A buyer will need to find out as much as possible about the subject property before contracts **9.51** are exchanged. The simple yet compelling reason for this is that the buyer must take the property whatever condition it is in, at the point when there is a binding contract for the purchase. The law imposes a clear obligation upon the buyer to find out as much about the property as possible, because the common law recognizes that the seller has only a limited duty of disclosure. The buyer must carry out all appropriate enquiries before entering into a binding contract to purchase the subject property. If a buyer does make all necessary enquiries of the seller, and gets sensible answers, an informed decision can then be taken as to the nature and suitability of the property based on all the information obtained prior to exchange.

The use and format of preliminary enquiries has been greatly affected by procedural changes **9.52** ushered in by the Law Society's National Conveyancing Protocol. Practitioners should acquaint themselves with the contents of the conventional pre-printed traditional forms of enquiries before contract, as well as with the new Property Information Forms. By doing this they will come to appreciate that perhaps the Property Information Forms are best used only in the simplest of transactions where tenanted property is being bought or sold. Many conveyancing practitioners have adopted the Protocol 'enquiry' forms even when they are not actually using the full Protocol process. However, many remain traditionally minded and use pre-printed, or their own in-house, preliminary enquiry forms. Where the buying and selling of tenanted property is concerned, the use of tailored-made enquiries is of value as the nature of each letting is likely to be highly distinctive. Whatever form is used, the intention remains the same—to seek out answers from the seller, about any matters that affect or could affect the subject property.

9.53 It is clear that when a conveyancer is involved in the buying or selling of tenanted properties, the heavier burden rests with the buyer's practitioner. This is because the buyer will
want to have full details of the title approved, as well as details of the tenancy or tenancies
affecting the subject property. A buyer will expect a good and marketable title to the subject
property, as well as a letting that is upon terms that the buyer deems acceptable. This will of
course centre on the rental due, but will also cover other terms of the tenancy or letting.
Therefore, this particular form of conveyancing transaction in particular requires extra care
when raising preliminary enquiries. This is also the case when looking at the title and when
raising requisitions. These matters are considered further in the following paragraphs. One
sensible way of selecting appropriate enquiries is to adopt a set that will be issued for
all properties, ie, core enquiries, with a second, more selective set tailored to the subject
property. A detailed examination of the nature and extent of such core or standard enquiries
can be found in Abbey, R. and Richards, M., *A Practical Approach to Conveyancing* (7th edn,
OUP, 2005). The idea of using a set of core enquiries has been adopted for the Commercial
Property Standard Enquiries drafted by members of the London Property Support Lawyers
Group under the sponsorship of the British Property Federation. They are considered at
paras 9.80 et seq below and are set out in appendix 18. In summary, the following matters
should always form the subject of preliminary enquiries:

(a) *Disputes*. Clearly, a buyer will want to know all about past and present disputes of all
kinds affecting the property. Buying into a current dispute may not be what the buyer
wants!

(b) *Notices*. Similarly, a buyer will want to know about and see copies of all notices affecting
the subject property; and clearly, if the seller has received any, it must be under a duty to
disclose. The buyer may seek to ensure that the seller complies with the requirements of
all known notices prior to completion. This could form a term of the contract.

(c) *Boundaries and fences*. The buyer will want to know about the ownership of all the
boundary walls and fences, as well as repairing responsibility if this differs from
ownership.

(d) *Services*. The buyer will want to know about the gas, electricity and water supply and
whether or not mains drainage is available. A recent development is the growing installation of water meters. Again, in these circumstances, a buyer will want to know about
this possibility, especially if the lessee is likely to be a high-volume consumer of water
(eg, a manufacturer that uses water in its manufacturing process).

(e) *Exclusive facilities*. The subject property may enjoy an exclusive facility, such as a right of
way to and from it, and the buyer will most certainly want full details. These details will
need to cover the cost of maintenance and any conditions attached to the exercise of
these facilities.

(f) *Shared facilities*. Following on from the previous enquiry, a buyer will need to know
about facilities used in common with owners or occupiers of adjoining or adjacent land.
The same kind of detail will be required as for exclusive facilities.

(g) *Occupiers*. This is a critical enquiry. A question should be raised that refers to any possible rights accruing to a non-lessee occupant. The immediate example is, of course, a
squatter, who could very well have rights of occupation which might not be highlighted
in the copy deeds supplied. The replies given by sellers in answer to enquiries concerning this topic are likely to be somewhat non-committal, and as such the onus is on the

buyer to make its own enquiries and to rely upon its own inspection (and indeed survey). This is also true for the next enquiry regarding user.

(h) *User*. A buyer will want to be reassured that the permitted use for planning purposes is the use for which the lessee in occupation actually uses the property; in other words, that the actual use is the permitted use for the purposes of the Town and Country Planning Acts.

(i) *Relevant names/identities, etc*. It is a great help for the buyer and the buyer's conveyancer if the seller can accurately confirm the names and addresses of the lessor, any superior lessor, the superior lessor's managing agent, if any, and the superior lessor's solicitors. If there is a management company mentioned in any of the leases of the subject property, full details of the management company, its officers, agents and solicitors should be requested.

(j) *Service charges*. This is a critical area for buyers, who will want to be sure that they are not taking over any service charge arrears (or indeed, disputes about service charges yet unpaid). This could apply to both commercial and residential cases.

(k) *Insurance arrangements*. This is another important concern, as lending institutions will always want to be sure that the property is insured for the full reinstatement value and for a comprehensive set of perils. This being so, a full copy of the current policy should be requested. Again, this could apply to both commercial and residential cases.

(l) *Covenants*. The buyer will want the seller's written confirmation of the absence of breaches of covenant known to the lessor, and indeed any that exist but have not come to the attention of the lessor. This should apply to almost all transactions, be they residential or commercial.

(m) *Flooding*. The buyer should always enquire about whether the subject property has ever been subject to flooding.

Additional enquiries: a general introduction

In addition to the standard enquiries that need to be made in all conveyancing transactions, **9.54** it is critical that enquiries be made with regard to the lessees in occupation and their rents paid or in arrears for both residential and commercial leases. It is therefore appropriate to request details of previous rent reviews, if any, along with copies of rent review memoranda recording the previous changes in rent. If the rent for a residential tenant is regulated by statute, it may be that there is some form of registration covering the rental payment and details should be obtained. For example, the Rent Act 1977 created a register of 'fair rents' which are statutory maxima for tenancies covered by the Act. Copy registration details can be obtained and should be requested from the seller. Service charge accounts should be requested for the last three years with details of sinking funds, along with details of arrears that may exist in respect of these payments. Details should also be requested of any authorized changes of use, as these too could materially affect the future (or indeed current) rental potential. If the property is subject to VAT (ie, the owner has elected to charge VAT on the rents), details of the VAT position will need to be investigated along with accounts of VAT payments made by lessees or details of arrears. Insurance details need to be investigated, particularly if the lessor insures the block and the lessee repays the premium, or indeed if the management company insures.

9.55 It was reported in (2001) 98(10) LS Gaz 8 that a group of 15 city law firms have pooled their existing precedents in an effort to produce the first set of standard pre-contract enquiries for the commercial property sector. These are now the Commercial Property Standard Enquiries (see appendix 18) and are considered at paras 9.80 et seq below.

Additional enquiries: commercial

9.56 In addition to the standard enquiries or the questions contained with the Law Society Protocol Property Information Forms that should always be raised in any conveyancing transaction, it is appropriate to issue further enquiries in relation to specific commercial lettings. The topics that can be covered are legion, but should cover at least the following:

Is the potential renewal of the tenancy in the subject property regulated by legislation?

9.57 In essence, a buyer will want to know how far, if at all, the lease is influenced by Pt II of the Landlord and Tenant Act 1954. Business lessees can claim security of tenure and the scrutiny of their rental on renewal by the courts. Buyers will want to know if there has been a court application; and if so, they will want to see the court order for the lease renewal terms, if any, to confirm the same. (The parties to a business lease can agree to exclude these rights. A court order confirming the agreement is required. The lease terms then need to be checked, because if there is no clause in the lease confirming the court order then the contracting out will be to no effect.)

9.58 If the lease has been recently renewed under the terms of the 1954 Act, a prudent buyer will want details to ascertain how the length of the term eventually granted was settled along with the other terms of the lease. Perhaps of more consequence would be to see the basis upon which the rental was finally settled. Valuers' reports would be of use, and copies should be requested. A buyer will also want to know if the lessor originally sought to oppose the grant of the lease and why. The ground (or grounds) for possession would be of material interest to the buyer, especially if it related to an alleged breach of covenant and/or for arrears of rent. In the circumstances, detailed enquiries should be directed to the seller's practitioner seeking as much information as possible about the circumstances of any recent statutory renewal.

Enquiries relating to tenancies granted after 1 January 1996

9.59 After this date, tenancies will be subject to the release provisions of the Landlord and Tenant (Covenants) Act 1995. Enquiries will need to elicit information about any authorized guarantee agreements obtained as a consequence of the operation of the statute, as well as about any enforcement action taken by the lessor/seller to obtain monies pursuant to such an agreement.

Enquiries relating to possible sub-lettings

9.60 The seller should be asked if it is aware of any sub-lettings of part or all of the subject property. This is important in the context of the renewal provisions mentioned in paras 9.57 to 9.58 above. Any notice to terminate issued under the terms of s 25 of the Landlord and Tenant Act 1954 should be served upon the lessee in occupation. It should be carefully noted that this could mean a sub-lessee where the whole property has been sub-let, thereby cutting out the intermediate non-occupying head tenant. Where the subject premises have been sub-let as to part, the lessor can either serve notice on the lessor's tenant and require that lessee to take a lease of the whole of the premises (s 32(2)), or the lessor can give notice to the immediate and sub-tenants. In this second case, each lessee will be entitled to renew; while in the first case, the new lease will be granted to the lessor's direct lessee, subject to the sub-letting of part (see chapter 7 generally regarding s 25 notices).

Accordingly, it is prudent to seek from answers to preliminary enquiries the full names and addresses of all sub-tenants, along with full details of the terms of the sub-lettings.   **9.61**

The terms of the tenant's business

Enquiries should be made of the seller to try to ascertain how long the tenant has carried on   **9.62** a business at the subject premises. The reason for this relates to possible compensation payments that the law requires the lessor to pay to the lessee where the lessee has sought to renew under the terms of the 1954 Act but the lessor has successfully opposed that renewal application. In essence, the longer the period, the more compensation may be payable. Compensation may be payable if the lessor is successful in opposing the grant of a new tenancy on grounds (e) (where there is a sub-letting of part, that possession is required for the letting or disposing of the property as a whole), (f) (where there is an intention on the lessor's part to demolish or reconstruct the subject premises) or (g) (where the lessor intends to occupy the premises) (see paras 7.110 et seq above). Moreover, if the lessor relies upon one of these three grounds and the lessee does not apply to court, compensation will still be payable (s 37(1)). The appropriate level of compensation is related to the rateable value for the property and is dictated by the Landlord and Tenant Act 1954 (Appropriate Multiplier) Order 1990, SI 1990/363.

In most cases the appropriate multiplier is $1 \times$ the rateable value. The multiplier can be $2 \times$ **9.63** the rateable value when the lessee, or the lessee and the lessee's predecessors in title for the same business have been in occupation of the subject premises for at least 14 years prior to the date of termination. It is therefore critical to ascertain how long the lessee has carried on business at the subject property where the buyer considers that there is a possibility that on a future renewal application the buyer intends to oppose it. Clearly, a short-term occupation will be less costly in compensation terms than is the case for a long-term occupant. Furthermore, while the parties to a lease can agree to exclude a right to compensation, if the lessee, or the lessee and predecessors in title have been in occupation for more than five years, any agreement to exclude a right to compensation is void (s 38(2)).

Purchase during renewal

Additional enquiries will be necessary if a purchase takes place during renewal negotiations.   **9.64** In particular, enquiries should be made about the issue and service of 1954 Act notices, about the commencement of court proceedings and about the negotiation of renewal terms. If terms have been agreed, any document recording the agreement (such as a Heads of Agreement document) should be requested.

Environmental concerns

Enquiries should be considered to seek out information about the nature of the construction   **9.65** of the subject property as well as its environment. Questions therefore need to be posed about what was used in the erection of the property that might now be considered hazardous (such as asbestos or high alumina cement). Similarly, questions need to be put to the seller about the environment to see if there is or has been anything hazardous now or recently upon the property. This could cover highly inflammable items such as petrol or old chemicals, or waste by-products that are dangerous such as can be found on land previously occupied by old coal-gas plants, ie, old town gas buildings and the land around them. The essence of this kind of environmental question seeks to ascertain whether or not the land may be considered contaminated such that it could have adverse repercussions upon the rental value or subsequent redevelopment (say) for residential purposes. (See generally paras 8.51 et seq regarding contaminated land and appendix 16 for examples of environmental enquiries.)

9.66   In regard to environmental concerns but relating to searches covering commercial properties, two additional factors should be considered. First, when making a water and drainage search the water companies try to limit their liability arising from the search result. There purports to be a £5,000 limit on liability for non-domestic properties. Several such water companies, as a response to concerns expressed about this limit, have indicated that their indemnity cover is now £2 million. However, as a commercial conveyancing practitioner you need to mark your search request 'Commercial property' to enjoy the benefit of this higher cover. (Inevitably higher cover will mean higher search fees, see <http://www.drainageandwater.co.uk>.)

9.67   Secondly, conveyancing support companies are now offering extra search facilities for commercial conveyancers. Sitescope offer the option of an environmental risk assessment along with a sitescope environmental search: see <http://www.sitescope.co.uk>. Jordans offer 'plansearch commercial'. This will give details of planning applications within 500 metres of the subject property as well as land use policies and flood plain details within the same area. It will also provide details of current and emerging development plans relevant to the search area: see <http://www.jordansproperty.co.uk>. In both cases they are specifically designed to provide information for commercial conveyancers in relation to commercial property.

Fire certificate

9.68   Some buildings require a fire certificate to confirm that all fire safety requirements are in place and approved by the appropriate authority. It is always prudent to ask if there is a certificate and to request a copy of it.

Capital allowances

9.69   Capital allowances are a tax relief that can be available on commercial property. The amount of a capital allowance that a lawyer may claim can be limited by similar allowances claimed by a previous owner. Enquiries need to be made about claims for allowances back to July 1996, being the start date for such allowances in their current form.

Additional enquiries: residential lettings

9.70   In addition to the standard enquiries that are always raised, and the additional enquiries mentioned above, it is appropriate to make further enquiries in relation to residential lettings in so far as they may be affected or regulated by legislation. Furthermore, additional specific enquiries will have to be raised if the residential tenancy is of a particular nature, such as a Crown Estate tenancy or a tenancy granted by a housing association. This is because the special nature of the letting may have repercussions on the security of tenure (or lack of it) for the tenant in occupation. For example, a Crown tenancy cannot be an assured tenancy by reason of Sch 1, para 11 to the Housing Act 1988, and therefore cannot benefit from the statutory security provisions the Act provides.

As a result, a buyer will want to enquire as to the status of the tenant in occupation, and in **9.71** particular whether the tenant can claim any form of statutory protection affording the tenant any element of security of tenure. After 28 February 1997, s 96 of the Housing Act 1996 makes most subsequent residential tenancies assured shorthold tenancies without the need to comply with any particular formalities such as formal notices, etc. This is not retrospective, though, and only applies to new tenancies granted after this date. Accordingly, the date of creation of the tenancy is a crucial item of information that needs to be disclosed to the buyer and should be elicited through a specific preliminary enquiry. All the more so since different forms of security of tenure will apply to tenancies depending upon when they were created. If the tenancy arose prior to 28 November 1980, the tenancy will be covered by the Rent Acts and will be a protected tenancy with full security of tenure. If the tenancy commenced after this date but before 15 January 1989, it could be either a protected tenancy under the Rent Acts, or it might also be a protected shorthold where there is limited security with the lessor being entitled to a mandatory ground for possession. Accordingly, further enquiries will be necessary to ascertain which form of tenancy will be involved. If the tenancy arose after 15 January 1989, the Housing Act 1988 applies and the tenancy will usually be an assured tenancy with full security, or an assured tenancy again with limited security. This is not a complete listing as this is an area of great complexity, and practitioners should consult specialist texts for further information on which element of housing law may apply. However, as highlighted above, you should note that there are some tenancies that will not be covered at all, such as those at a low rent (eg, outside London, not exceeding £250), or a business tenancy, agricultural holding, student or holiday letting, or a letting by the Crown or a local authority.

Further enquiries should be made as to the statutory control of the rents payable by a **9.72** residential tenant. Tenancies granted after 28 February 1997 will have minimal control as a consequence of the effect of the Housing Act 1996. Tenants in these circumstances can merely, and only during the first six months of their tenancy, refer the rent to a Rent Assessment Committee for scrutiny. Tenancies created previously will have differing elements of statutory control of rents depending on when the tenancy was first created.

Lastly, perhaps almost as a matter of history, it may be that an older tenancy falls within the **9.73** Rent Act 1977 (s 12 of the Housing Act 1988), which relates to tenancies granted by resident landlords. If the tenancy is one covered by this form of security, it will be lost to a purchaser that does not take up residency. Questions should be asked to see if this area of regulation applies and whether or not there is a resident landlord.

Enquiry disclaimers

Some printed forms of preliminary enquiries try to limit liability by including a disclaimer **9.74** of responsibility for inaccuracies. Practitioners will immediately appreciate that if such a disclaimer were allowed, it would greatly enhance the chances of limiting liability when dealing with replies to enquiries. It would seem that s 11(3) of the Unfair Contract Terms Act 1977 puts the burden of proof on practitioners in these circumstances, which militates against the effectiveness of such a clause. In *First National Commercial Bank plc v Loxleys (a firm)* (1996) 93 (43) LSGaz 20, it was held that the solicitors were required by the Act to show that it was fair and reasonable for the firm to rely upon the standard disclaimer to release them from all liability having regard to all the circumstances of the case. The decision in the case was to show that there was a reasonable cause of action and that the disclaimer did not prevent the case from going to trial. In effect, it is clear that the courts will not view disclaimers with any great sympathy and will use the 1977 Act to strike them down wherever possible. The moral for the busy practitioner is to ensure the accuracy of all answers given, rather than to rely upon a disclaimer.

New buildings

9.75　Developers of new buildings often do not retain them once they have been built and fully let. By selling the reversion at this stage, the developer can realize the capital element in the building and utilize that capital for further acquisitions and developments, as well as realizing a profit from the original venture. (It is also possible that a lender will, as a condition of the funding scheme made available to the developer, require the reversion to be transferred to the lender once the property is fully let.) In the circumstances, a buyer will have additional requirements when the property is newly built.

9.76　Apart from a survey, the buyer will want to submit enquiries that cover the method of construction as well as the materials used to build the structure. The buyer's concern is to obtain information that might assist should a latent defect materialize in future. This is because a buyer may wish to pursue an action against the developer's builders, or indeed against any architect or other element of the developer's design team that might be responsible for the defect. It is true that if the tenant in occupation has a full repairing obligation, it may be that the lessor will be able to require the lessee to repair any such defect, but this may not always be possible. To ensure that there is some form of redress available to the buyer, steps need to be taken to protect him or her.

9.77　The buyer will require collateral warranties from the builders and the designers, as well as an assignment of all rights that the developer may have against these parties. The buyer can also obtain a latent defects insurance policy for a newly erected commercial property. These policies give cover against latent defects for a period of ten years from the completion of the building. The premiums are normally quite steep and the policies will be subject to pecuniary excesses, but they do offer a measure of cover that might not otherwise be available without the need to prove liability or to resort to litigation. However, such policies are not widely used. (Practitioners should bear in mind that no cover is afforded to new commercial properties by the NHBC scheme and so warranties can offer replacement protection.)

9.78　It will be clear, therefore, that the best method of protection for the buyer is the collateral warranties approach. This is an agreement whereby either a builder (including subcontractors) or a designer (including all consultants) involved in the creation of the new property accepts a contractual duty of care to the buyer with regard to the integrity of the new structure. There is a statutory limitation, though. The provisions of the Latent Damage Act 1986 are such that if latent defects do not appear until six years after the making of a collateral warranty in a contract, or until 12 years after one given by deed, any action would be statute barred. All such collateral warranty arrangements should require that the warrantor has a current professional indemnity insurance policy. Subsequent buyers may be able to resort to these warranties under the terms of the Contracts (Rights of Third Parties) Act 1999. A third party may sue under the terms of the Act where, on a proper consideration of the contract, the parties intended that he or she should be able to do so (see s 1). If the intentions are unclear, the court can construe and rule as it deems appropriate.

If warranties are taken, the buyer should also obtain a copy of the developer's contracts with **9.79** the builders and the designers as (of course) the rights accruing to the buyer stem from the terms of those agreements. The buyer should also seek written confirmation of the level of cover for the professional indemnity insurance policies covered by the collateral agreement. A form of warranty approved by the British Property Federation and other professional bodies is available. See also chapter 8 regarding collateral warranties and other property development issues.

Commercial Property Standard Enquiries

The Commercial Property Standard Enquiries (CPSEs) are a set of documents that have been **9.80** drafted by members of the London Property Support Lawyers Group under the sponsorship of the British Property Federation (BPF). Contributions were also made by a number of other firms and individuals. The CPSEs are endorsed by the BPF and it is anticipated that they might become industry standard pre-contract enquiries for commercial property conveyancing. The following explanation and details are taken from the guidance notes to the Commercial Property Standard Enquiries issued with the enquiries themselves.

The CPSEs comprise the following documents: **9.81**

- GN/CPSE—Guidance notes on the Commercial Property Standard Enquiries.
- CPSE.1—General pre-contract enquiries for all commercial property transactions.
- CPSE.2—Supplemental pre-contract enquiries for commercial property subject to tenancies.
- CPSE.3—Supplemental pre-contract enquiries for commercial property on the grant of a new lease.
- CPSE.4—Supplemental pre-contract enquiries for commercial leasehold property on the assignment of the lease.
- STER—Solicitor's title and exchange requirements.
- SCR—Solicitor's completion requirements.

These documents can be used freely and without charge subject to the user identifying them **9.82** as being part of the suite of documents comprising the CPSE. Details of the CPSEs can be seen at <http://www.practicallaw.com> and in appendix 18. Any reproduction of it must bear the BPF logo. Any user of the forms must not change the text of the documents. If a user wishes to raise any additional enquiries in the documents comprising the CPSEs, the user must do so in a separate document that identifies clearly those additional enquiries as being separate from and additional to the CPSEs. The enquiries in the CPSEs are intended as a standard minimum for use in any commercial property transaction. It is expected that some add-itional enquiries will be necessary for any that relate specifically to the subject property and also in relation to transactions involving newly constructed or altered buildings.

9.83   CPSE.1 is designed to cover all commercial property transactions and will, together with any additional enquiries relevant to the particular transaction, be sufficient if the transaction deals only with a freehold sold with vacant possession. The following supplemental enquir-ies are intended to be used in conjunction with CPSE.1. Which particular additional form or forms will be required will depend upon the individual circumstances of each transaction. The following supplemental forms are available:

- CPSE.2—where the property is sold subject to existing tenancies.
- CPSE.3—where a lease of a property is being granted.
- CPSE.4—where the property being sold is leasehold.

9.84   The enquiries in CPSE.1 cover the following topics and are reproduced in full in appendix 18. (The details and explanations for these enquiries are taken from the guidance notes on CPSE.1 (version 2.2). General pre-contract enquiries for all commercial property transactions can be found at <http://www.practicallaw.com/Article_ID=32021>.)

1   *Boundaries and extent*: this enquiry is concerned with verifying the extent of the pro-perty. The buyer also needs to know who is responsible for maintaining boundary features and so questions are posed to cover this aspect.

2   *Party walls*: the joint owners of a party structure are given some statutory protection to prevent one owner carrying out work to the structure unilaterally without regard to the needs and wishes of the other. This enquiry therefore seeks detail about party walls.

3   *Rights benefiting the property*: because generally rights benefiting the property will pass to the buyer, an enquiry is raised to ascertain details of all such matters.

4   *Adverse rights affecting the property*: because generally the burden of adverse rights to which the property is subject will pass to the buyer, an enquiry is raised to ascertain details of all such matters.

5   *Title policies*: insurance may be available to cover restrictive covenants where the nature of the covenant or the identity of the person having the benefit of the covenant is unknown, lost title deeds, or defects in title where the title to the land is unregistered. In these cases the buyer is entitled to see the policy terms to check whether cover passes on sale.

6   *Access to neighbouring land*: the buyer will want details of all requests for access made and permissions given, whether made informally or by the court under the Access to Neighbouring Land Act 1992.

7   *Access to and from the property*: enquiries are made to ensure that the buyer can be satisfied that there are adequate rights of access to and from the property.

8   *Physical condition*: the seller is asked about the condition of the subject property and, in answering, may be willing to give full details even where it considers that a defect or problem would be apparent on an inspection or would be revealed by a survey or has been treated or resolved. The seller may of course (as with any enquiry) decline to give an answer. The buyer can deduce what it wishes from any such refusal. If, however, the seller does provide an answer, it may be liable for misrepresentation if the answer is not complete or is misleading in some way.

9   *Contents*: the buyer and the seller need to agree what items will be left at the subject property on completion of the transaction and what items will be removed, and any effect this may have on the price. This enquiry seeks to make these items plain to both sides of the transaction.

10 *Utilities and services*: this enquiry asks for details of the utilities and other services connected to or serving the property, including water, drainage, oil and communications systems.

11 *Fire certificates and means of escape*: the following require a fire certificate:
    — hotels and boarding houses with sleeping accommodation for more than six people (whether guest or staff), or where there is sleeping accommodation above first floor or below ground floor levels;
    — premises at which highly flammable substances covered by the Fire Certificates (Special Premises) Regulations 1976, SI 1976/2003 are manufactured or stored;
    — factories, offices, shops, and railway premises where more than 20 people work of whom ten work somewhere other than on the ground floor;
    — buildings in multiple occupation containing two or more individual factory, office, shop, or railway units and where more than 20 people work of whom ten work somewhere other than on the ground floor.
    Clearly all these premises may be of a commercial nature and as such an enquiry is necessary to obtain details of any fire certificate and means of escape in case of fire.

12 *Planning and building regulations*: full details of all consents and approvals are requested through these questions along with confirmation of user. Questions are also asked about any planning enforcement issues.

13 *Statutory agreements and infrastructure*: this enquiry covers various matters including agreements under s 38 of the Highways Act 1980, agreements under s 104 of the Water Industry Act 1991 and planning obligations under s 106 of the Town and Country Planning Act 1990. Moreover, the local authority search may not disclose all relevant agreement and notices. As a result, these questions seek further details of these matters.

14 *Statutory and other requirements*: enquiry 14 addresses potential liabilities in connection with the property and concentrates mainly on statutory liabilities—statute will provide who is responsible for compliance.

15 *Environmental*: enquiry 15 is a general enquiry about environmental issues, aimed at sites with no known environmental problems. More relevant questions specific to the subject property can be raised where there are known problems.

16 *Occupiers and employees*: enquiry 16 is concerned with the rights, statutory or otherwise, of anyone who will remain in occupation of the property following completion of the transaction.

17 *Insurance*: enquiry 17 concerns buildings insurance as opposed to contents insurance or title insurance. The information which will be given in reply to this enquiry is likely to be of interest where the buyer is to rely on the seller's insurance between exchange of contracts and completion or where the existing insurance arrangements will remain in place following completion of the transaction.

18 *Rates and other outgoings*: the buyer will need to know its liability for periodic payments following completion of the transaction. The main liabilities are likely to be business rates and water and sewerage charges, but there may be others.

19 *Capital allowances*: the buyer may be entitled to claim capital allowances on any fixed

plant and machinery within the subject property. The amount on which such a claim may be based may be an apportionment of the total consideration, but in many cases there are limiting factors. In particular, the amount of the claim may be limited where the seller has itself claimed allowances. Enquiry needs to be made as to what claims have been made.

20 *VAT registration information*: it is essential to establish if the seller is registered for VAT to ensure that any charge to VAT is valid. The information is also important in deciding whether an election should be made to waive exemption.

21 *Transfer of a business as a going concern*: the sale of an investment property subject to one or more leases can constitute the transfer of a business as a going concern (TOGC) for the purposes of VAT. In such a case no VAT is payable.

22 *Other VAT treatment.* This enquiry is designed to assist in verifying the correct VAT treatment.

23 *Standard-rated supplies.* This is used in the same way as 22 above.

24 *Exempt supplies.* This is used as above.

25 *Zero-rated supplies*: these four enquiries (22–25) are intended to help the buyer to verify the seller's view of the correct VAT treatment of the transaction.

26 *Transactions outside the scope of VAT (other than TOGCs)*: certain property transactions (other than TOGCs) may be outside the scope of VAT. This would apply if, for example, the transaction is not made in the furtherance of a business. It is important to establish the reasoning to avoid any disputes if it is subsequently discovered that a VAT charge was appropriate. By way of example, the sale of a church by a religious movement which has no business activities is likely to be a transaction which is non-business and outside the scope of VAT.

27 *Notices*: the buyer needs details of every notice affecting the subject property to ensure the buyer understands the nature and effect of all such notices.

28 *Disputes*: the buyer needs details of every dispute relating to the subject property to ensure the buyer understands the nature and effect of all such disputes.

29 *Stamp Duty Land Tax (SDLT) on assignment of a lease.* The grant of a lease on or after 1 December 2003 is a land transaction for SDLT purposes unless the lease was granted pursuant to an agreement for lease exchanged on or before 10 July 2003 which has not been subsequently assigned or varied. The grant of a lease is notifiable to the Inland Revenue if the term is for seven years or more and was granted for chargeable consideration. If the grant of a lease was not notifiable to the Inland Revenue, a self-certification certificate may have been produced in order to enable the registration at the Land Registry of any easements granted to the tenant under the lease. The buyer will need to know the date of the grant of the lease for SDLT purposes. The buyer will need to ensure that all SDLT payable on the lease has been paid and retain evidence that shows the total amount that has been paid

30 *Deferred payments of SDLT.* Where the whole or part of the consideration for a land transaction is contingent, uncertain or unascertained, the taxpayer is under an obligation to pay SDLT on completion of the transaction on its reasonable estimate of the amount of contingent, uncertain or unascertained consideration that will be payable.

D TENANTED PROPERTIES: THE BUYER'S PERSPECTIVE; THE TITLE AND RAISING REQUISITIONS

The accepted practice today is to deduce and investigate title before exchange of contracts. **9.85**
This is all the more so for the buying and selling of tenanted properties when there is a core
element of acquisition for investment that drives the transaction forward. The SCPC
6.1.1 merely says that the seller is to provide the buyer with proof of the title and his
ability to transfer it. Indeed, the contract will often contain a special condition preventing
the buyer from raising requisitions on the title and thereby compelling the buyer to investigate title before exchange. Condition 4.1.1 (SCPC 6.3) also lays down time limits for
deducing title and raising requisitions. These are only of academic interest where deduction
and investigation of title occur before exchange. However, the time limits could in theory
result in the buyer being out of time for raising objections when an unregistered title is
verified, normally on completion.

In general, the basics of title investigation will be much the same as for domestic transac- **9.86**
tions; for further detail, see Abbey and Richards, op cit at para 9.53 above, ch 5. However, the
distinctive title component that will apply to the purchase of tenanted property relates to
the lease, or other deed or document that gives the occupant the title or right to remain
within the subject premises. The following paragraphs therefore consider the fundamentals
that need to be covered for both commercial and residential transactions.

Commercial leases

Many of the basic requirements of a commercial lease have been covered in earlier chapters. **9.87**
However, here we set out what we believe should never be overlooked when acting for
a client that is purchasing a commercial property for a profit rental.

In all cases the buyer will want to be sure that the terms of the lease, leases or other deeds and **9.88**
documents under which the tenant occupies the property are acceptable to it as well as
to any mortgagee. In commercial terms, the basic lease requirements are a term of at least
15 years with three-yearly upward-only rent reviews. When the market is strong, this could
extend to 25-year terms, possibly with five-yearly upward-only rent reviews.

In all cases, where a single tenant occupies a commercial property, the buyer will want to be **9.89**
satisfied that the tenant is responsible for all repairs to and maintenance of the subject
property. If there are several separate lettings of part in the one building, the leases should
incorporate comprehensive service charge covenants under which the lessees reimburse any
expenditure by the buyer/lessor for the maintenance and repair of the subject property. In
all commercial lease cases, if the lessor insures there must be a covenant on the part of the
lessees to reimburse the premium in whole or in part, as the case may be. The ultimate aim is,
of course, to maximize the buyer's income generated from the rents paid by the lessee(s)
without deduction for repairs and or insurance. A modern commercial lease should also
include a penalty clause charging interest on all sums paid late under the terms of the lease,
including rent, insurance rents and service charges.

Perhaps of greatest concern to the lessor/buyer is the nature and extent of the rent review **9.90** provision. (For a detailed consideration of rent review points, see chapter 2.) The lease rent review clauses should contain a definition of a formula by which the new, reviewed rent should be ascertained. That formula is normally prepared incorporating detailed assumptions upon which the review is to be based. If the lease stipulates assumptions to be made on a rent review, they will be central to the valuation process for the subject property. Typical assumptions are that the rent is to be reviewed at the renewal date assuming the property is vacant for a term equal either to that originally granted, or to the residue of the term and for the permitted user stated in the lease. (As to the term, it can be argued that a higher rental will arise if the term is longer than the unexpired residue at the time of review, although this may depend upon market conditions at any one time.) Modern rent review clauses will also allow the valuer to ignore any diminution in the value of the rental as a result of the lessee having failed to repair the subject property properly. Some review clauses also import assumptions with regard to improvements made by the lessee. If the lease is silent on the point then the rent review will be based on the nature of the premises at the time of review, including any improvements made by the lessee even though they were made at the lessee's cost (see *Ponsford v HMS Aerosols Ltd* [1979] AC 63). Assumptions can also cover sub-lettings to take into account any profit rental the lessee may be receiving from sub-lessees. All of these elements need to be carefully considered when approving the title (see chapter 2). Many buyers/lessors will only buy or accept leases where the rent, on review, can only increase or remain the same. They will reject a lease that allows a reduction in rent at the time of review.

9.91 The procedure for the rent review, prescribed by the lease, must also be checked to make sure that it does not disadvantage the lessor/buyer. An example arises in relation to the timing of the procedure. Lessors can also be late calling for review by not complying with a timescale stated in the lease rent review provisions. The decision in *United Scientific Holdings Ltd v Burnley BC* [1978] AC 904 held that unless the clause makes it so, time is *not* of the essence for a rent review clause. If the clause makes all of it subject to time being of the essence (or part of the procedure) then the time limits are absolute and incapable of extension. In the absence of express provision, though, delay will not defeat a lessor's claim for a rent review. Time can be of the essence even if the rent review provision does not include that actual wording. If the words of the rent review clause are such that it is possible to show that there was an intention to make time limits absolute then the courts will infer time to be of the essence (see *Henry Smith's Charity Trustees v AWADA Trading & Promotion Services Ltd* [1984] 1 EGLR 116). Time being of the essence can also arise if other wording in the lease supports this possibility. For example, if the lessee can, by notice, terminate the tenancy at the review date, it has been held that this means that time is of the essence for the review (see *Al Saloom v Shirley James Travel Services Ltd* (1981) 42 P & CR 181).

9.92 Connected to the payment of rent is one of the lease provisions to cover non-payment by the tenant, ie, surety covenants. In the absence of express agreement to the contrary, the benefit of surety covenants will pass to a buyer (see *P&A Swift Investments v Combined English Stores Group plc* [1988] 2 All ER 885). Agreement to the contrary will, of course, include covenants that are expressed to be personal to the original parties. Personal covenants covered by a surety provision will not automatically pass to the buyer. These are covenants that do not touch and concern the reversion. In these circumstances, and perhaps to be quite sure in all cases, it would be best to obtain an explicit assignment of the surety covenants in favour of the buyer. As mentioned at para 2.09 above, should there be non-payment then a modern lease should include interest on late rent.

A conveyancer should also look at other important lease clauses for any impact they might **9.93** have on the rent review. For example, a highly restrictive use clause can have a limiting effect on the level of rent payable. This will in turn reduce the capital value of the subject property. This is also true for a very restrictive alienation clause. It therefore follows that a careful check should be made of the user and alienation clauses to make sure that they are neither too harsh nor too weak.

While considering the lease for title features, a practitioner for a buyer should also consider **9.94** the alienation terms, the covenants affecting the use of the property, and any covenants on structural alterations that may be permitted. Leases may contain extensive provisions regulating these areas and they should be considered carefully before exchanging contracts.

The nature of the tenant and its status can have an effect upon the rental value (and hence **9.95** the capital value of a property). It is clear that a blue-chip public company tenant is going to be more highly regarded than a mere individual. As a result, a lessor will want to control the alienation provisions to try to regulate who might become a tenant of the subject property. This being so, at the very least, a lessor will want to ensure that an alienation clause is as comprehensive as possible and, where appropriate, completely excludes dealings with part so as to avoid sub-division of the subject premises. Alienation clauses are considered at length in paras 3.54 et seq above.

Similarly, the use of the subject property could affect the rental and capital value of the **9.96** premises. Furthermore, there may be some uses that the lessor would not want to allow in the property. To that end a buyer will want to review the user provisions carefully to ensure that once again there is maximum influence over the use of the property in the control of the landlord. This is also true for alterations to the property. These provisions are considered in detail in paras 3.36 et seq above.

Lastly, and because it is such an obvious requirement in a commercial lease it should **9.97** therefore never be overlooked, always check for a complete forfeiture clause that includes forfeiture on the bankruptcy or liquidation of the lessee.

Residential lettings

These break into two types: (i) the purchase of a whole property subject to a residential **9.98** tenancy; or (ii) the purchase of the freehold or superior title subject to several lettings on either short- or long-term leases. The purpose of any such acquisition is to receive the rents from the occupants. Consequently, the buyer will want to be sure that the terms of the lease, leases, tenancy agreement or other deeds and/or documents under which the tenant occupies the property are acceptable to it as well as to any mortgagee. Where the subject property is occupied by residential short-term tenants, the terms of the tenancy agreements will have to be considered. A buyer will also need to be sure about the effect of statute upon any such tenancies, and this depends upon the date of the creation of each and every tenancy (see para 9.71 above). The only other major consideration is to check that the residential letting is not a breach of any of the covenants affecting the title being purchased, and that the planning user of the subject property allows multiple occupation by residential tenants where there is more than one such tenant in occupation.

9.99   Rent deposits are common for residential short-term lettings. Prior to 1 January 1996, in the absence of agreement to the contrary, such an agreement was personal to the parties to it. After that date, and in the absence of agreement to the contrary, the benefit and burden of a rent deposit agreement will pass to successors in title (see s 3 of the Landlord and Tenant (Covenants) Act 1995). Consequently, a solicitor acting for a buyer/lessor will need to see all rent deposit agreements to check the date of creation and the provisions covering successors in title. Also in relation to the payment by a tenant of a deposit, consideration should be given to the effects of the Unfair Terms in Consumer Contracts Regulations 1999, SI 1999/2083. These govern, inter alia, residential tenancies other than those to a company. The effect of the Regulations is to make void any term that is 'unfair'. A term is unfair if it is significantly to the detriment of the consumer/tenant. There should not be any significant imbalance in the division of obligations between the parties to the tenancy; but if this is the case, as a consequence of the terms upon which the rental deposit is required, the Regulations could strike down the whole provision. (However, practitioners should note that these Regulations do not apply to contractual terms that reflect mandatory statutory or regulatory provisions.)

9.100 There are various other, more specific items that should always be considered in relation to a purchase of this nature, and of these the following should be particularly noted.

The effect of the Landlord and Tenant Act 1987

9.101 Where a buyer intends purchasing a property subject to long leases, title checks need to include matters relating to one specific statute, the effect of which could negative the contract itself. This may not be a strict matter of title, but it could have such a catastrophic effect upon a buyer that it should form an early part of a 'title' check.

9.102 The Landlord and Tenant Act 1987 gives tenants in a block, ie, a property in multiple occupation, a right of pre-emption where the lessor intends to dispose of the freehold. This means that if the lessor intends to sell, the lessees must first be offered the chance of buying the reversionary title before there is a sale on the open market. A block will cover a house split into two flats where the freeholder intends to sell the reversionary title. In effect, the statute applies to property containing two or more flats. Where the premises are mixed in use, ie, residential and commercial, the Act may still apply, depending upon the percentages of occupation. If the non-residential use does not exceed 50 per cent of the whole, the statute will apply. The lessor must give notice of the proposed disposal to the lessees (s 5 of the 1987 Act) and the notice will give them the right to buy the lessor's interest. At least 50 per cent of the flats must be held by qualifying tenants (ie, long leaseholders) and the block must contain two or more flats. An auction is clearly a disposal contemplated by the Act (see s 4 of the Act), and if the freeholder wishes to sell by auction, he or she will be obliged to offer the reversion to the lessees before the auction. If at least half of the qualifying lessees take up the offer, the lessor will be obliged to sell on the same terms as those that gave rise to the notice. It is presumed that the price will therefore be not less than the auction reserve price.

9.103 The 1987 Act contains clear provisions should the lessor sell without serving the necessary notices. Under the Housing Act 1996 it became a criminal offence not to give notice to the tenants of a proposed disposal; (new s 10A of the 1987 Act). Section 11 provides for a notice to be served by the lessees on the purchaser requiring information about the sale; and s 12 then contains a provision to force the buyer to transfer the freehold to the lessees on the same terms as were made for the disposal to that purchaser. However, any dispute about the terms, including the price, can be referred to and decided by a tribunal. A further practical problem is that the time constraints contemplated by the Act are lengthy. For example, the period during which the lessees must respond to the notice is in effect two months, with further time delays possible. Accordingly the timing of any proposed disposal by the freeholder may be greatly delayed by the effect of this Act. Lastly, it should be noted that the 1987 Act has other weaknesses. For example, if the freehold is owned by a company as its only asset, the owner of that company can avoid the effect of the Act should there be a desire to dispose of the property. This is achieved by selling the shares in the company rather than the freehold title.

Repairs

Where the residential letting is for a term of less than seven years, s 11 of the Landlord and   **9.104**
Tenant Act 1985 imposes upon the lessor an obligation to repair the structure and exterior of the subject property. However, the letting agreement should still make the tenant responsible for all internal repairs of a non-structural nature. The terms of the letting agreement should be reviewed to check whether or not this provision has been included.

Alienation

If there is a written short-term letting agreement, there should be a complete prohibition   **9.105**
upon assignment. This will ensure that the lessor has complete control over who occupies the subject premises and avoids the effect of common law that, in the absence of any written provision to the contrary, allows the tenant to assign without the lessor's consent being required.

Forfeiture

Because it is such an obvious requirement in any lease or fixed-term tenancy agreement, and   **9.106**
should therefore never be overlooked, always check for a forfeiture clause. Of course, statute will intervene in many cases and override the provision (eg, because of the effect of statute, it is not possible to forfeit an assured tenancy), but this may not always be the case. It is therefore prudent to include such a provision, even where statute may currently prevail.

Certificates of title

There is an alternative to the traditional title approval arrangements set out above, and this   **9.107**
is the provision by the seller's solicitor of a certificate of title. The purpose of such a certificate is to move to completion as quickly as possible, and in particular without having to expend the amount of time normally taken up by traditional procedures. Furthermore, the certificate operates so as to put the person receiving the benefit of the certification in a similar position to that he or she would have been in had the traditional conveyancing approach been adopted. It is in effect a guarantee as to all the contents of the certificate by the solicitor issuing it. This being so, the solicitor will of course seek to qualify all assertions,

while the recipient's solicitor will seek to ensure that all assertions are unqualified. It therefore follows that the negotiations may focus more on the nature and content of the certificate than on the subject property.

9.108 The extent of the topics covered by the certificate is a crucial area, in that it will have to extend beyond the simple title details to cover matters that would normally be dealt with through searches and preliminary enquiries. A solicitor acting for the seller will seek to restrict the firm's liability. One way of achieving this is to exempt the firm from any liability in respect of any errors within detail supplied by the client company. In this way the lawyers seek to restrict liability for information gleaned from the title, from the client, or from information that would be available had the normal searches actually been made.

9.109 A certificate of title can prove to be of great use in two particular circumstances: (i) where there are a large number of tenanted properties being sold within one portfolio; and (ii) where there is a portfolio being offered to a lender as security for a loan. There is also a third, somewhat indirect situation where such a certificate is usually adopted, ie, where a property-owning limited company is itself being sold. Rather than go through each title for each property owned by the company in the traditional conveyancing format, the buyer's solicitors will seek a certificate of title for the properties to accompany any other requirements they may have in relation to the company itself.

E   COMPLETION MATTERS

9.110 We set out below two aspects of the transaction in relation to completion matters. The first is a reminder of one pre-completion element that must not be overlooked, and the other is a consideration of what must be done on the day of completion for the sale and purchase of tenanted property.

Buying from a company

9.111 As is likely to be the case in many transactions where tenanted property is being bought or sold, if the seller is a limited company then there will be an important pre-completion search that will apply to both registered and unregistered land that must not be overlooked. Where a company is selling, a search of the companies register at Companies House should be carried out. This can be done either in person, or through search agents. There is no formal or prescribed method or form for this search, which is carried out at the Companies Registration Office. It should be noted that there is no priority period of protection available for a company search. Because of this lack of protection for a buyer, this search should therefore be made just before completion to ensure as far as possible that the information to be relied upon is up-to-date at completion. Certainly, in large-scale commercial conveyancing transactions two company searches should be made—one just before exchange and the second on the morning of completion. If you, as the buyer's representative, have any cause to doubt the standing of the selling company, we recommend, wherever possible, that you carry out a company search on the day of completion.

9.112 In the case of registered land, if a particular charge in question is not registered at the Land

Registry the buyer can take free of it. It is therefore plain that no company charge of whatever kind, be it fixed or floating, will affect a buyer unless it is protected by some form of registration at the Land Registry (such as registration in the charges register, or even possibly a notice or restriction).

However, a company search will still be necessary, because a buyer may wish to be sure that **9.113** the company still subsists and has not been struck off the register, perhaps for failing to file returns. If it has been struck off the companies register, the company ceases to exist in law and cannot therefore enter into a deed, transfer or conveyance. Of course, if the company is subject to winding-up proceedings these too will be shown by a company search; and this is information of which a buyer needs to be aware in the context of the imminence of completion. (Pursuant to s 522 of the Companies Act 1985, any disposition of property owned by a company will be void if made after the commencement of winding-up proceedings.)

In the case of unregistered land the company search is very important. The search will reveal **9.114** subsisting floating charges, specific (or fixed) charges created before 1 January 1970, and also the commencement of any winding-up proceedings. All three are of material importance to a buyer, and if disclosed in the search result would clearly be adverse. No purchaser should proceed until the seller has in the appropriate way shown how and when the adverse entry is to be dealt with. Bearing in mind that any disposition by a company subject to winding-up proceedings is void (s 127, Insolvency Act 1986), it will be appreciated just how important a company search can be.

The mechanics of completion

On completion the seller must hand over not merely the reversionary title deeds and **9.115** documents, but also the counterpart lease(s) or tenancy agreement(s) as well as rental authorities. These authorities should be completed in letter format and signed by the seller, and addressed to the lessees authorizing them to pay all future rents to the buyer or as the buyer directs. (Standard pre-printed requisitions normally include a request that such authorities be made available on completion.) Practitioners should bear in mind that where the subject property constitutes a dwelling, s 3 of the Landlord and Tenant Act 1985 compels the buyer to give written notice of the change of ownership to the lessee or tenant in occupation within two months of completion. Furthermore, where a dwelling has been sold, s 48 of the Landlord and Tenant Act 1987 compels the lessor buyer to provide the lessee in occupation with an address within England and Wales that can be used for the service of notices.

As well as all leases or tenancy agreements, the buyer will expect to receive all allied deeds **9.116** and documents relating to them, such as licences to assign or for alterations, rent deposit deeds, and authorized guarantee agreements. All licences to sub-let should be handed over with copies of the sub-lease or agreement, as should all rent review memoranda along with any side letters or deeds of variation that affect any of the tenants in occupation of the subject property. If the buyer has obtained a formal assignment of the seller's right to sue for rent arrears then the deed of assignment should, of course, be obtained upon completion. If the subject property is newly built, the buyer should also seek to receive at completion the plans and/or the architect's drawings of the property.

9.117   If the buyer is taking over the seller's insurance policy, the buyer's conveyancer should ensure that the policy document and all correspondence relating to it are handed over at completion. The insurance may form part of the service charge payable by a tenant or tenants in occupation of the subject property. Detailed copies or the originals of all service charge receipts and invoices for the current year should be made available to the buyer at completion so that the buyer can refer to them later should a dispute arise.

9.118   Because the pace of and demands on the conveyancing system have increased, the last time for completion on the contractual completion date must now be negotiated and will appear in all conveyancing agreements. SC 6.1.2 (and SCPC 8.1.3) now, in effect, set a final time of 2 pm on the day of completion. It does so by providing that if completion does not take place by that time, interest will be payable. Of course, this does not mean that completion cannot take place that day. However, if completion cannot take place before 2 pm, interest will be payable (if demanded) for late completion.

9.119   We recommend personal completion in all cases where the transaction is complicated, or where the price is substantial. We do so because a personal completion will enable the buyer's practitioner to inspect and approve all the deeds and documents before paying over or releasing the completion monies. If for nothing else, this ensures certainty. There can be no doubt as to whether or not all the buyer's requirements have been fulfilled as they will have been checked through at the completion meeting. Reliance need not be placed upon an agent, or indeed on the seller's practitioner. Of course personal completions take more time and cost more, but, by the same token, the risk of errors or omissions is minimized. Indeed, the buyer's practitioner should also take the complete file, just in case a query should arise during completion that, without the file, might hold up the conclusion of the meeting. If you intend to complete in person and the contract incorporates the SCs or the SCPCs, send the completion monies by electronic transfer. You should then arrange to complete in person prior to the time in the contract for completion, and release the monies once satisfied with the documentation. The draft contract can be amended to allow for this style of completion.

9.120   Normally completion will take place at the offices of the practitioner acting for the seller. SC 6.2/SCPC 8.2 both provide that completion is to be effected somewhere in England and Wales, being either the offices of the seller's solicitor or some other place which the seller reasonably specifies. Sometimes the deeds will remain with solicitors acting solely for a lender. This will happen if the lender is separately represented, or possibly if the lender has commenced repossession proceedings. In these circumstances, completion may have to take place at the lender's solicitor's offices, although efforts should be made to persuade such solicitors to allow the seller's solicitors to deal with completion and redemption together. They cannot be compelled to agree to this arrangement, however.

9.121   Lastly, it is worth repeating that a final check of all searches should be made just before completion, and the buyer should make one last inspection of the property.

KEY POINTS SUMMARY: SELLING AND BUYING TENANTED PROPERTIES

- What extra questions need to be asked that are specific to the subject property, and what **9.122** specific enquiries should you raise consequent upon any particular instructions you may have received from the client? Always advise your client of any onerous or unusual replies or results to any of the preliminary enquiries, and request written instructions in response.
- Should you adopt the Commercial Property Standard Enquiries? If so, do you need to include any of the additional standard forms and/or any extra enquiries?
- If the sale is of a reversion subject to residential long leases, the sale cannot proceed without careful consideration of the effects of the Landlord and Tenant Act 1987, which may give the lessees in occupation a right of pre-emption. If the right exists, the contract will need to show that steps have been taken to comply with the Act.
- Where there is a substantial commercial rental income from the property, the contract will need to cover the question of rent arrears and the apportionment of rent at completion.
- Remember that SC 3.3.2(b) requires the seller to inform the buyer of any lease or tenancy termination after exchange but before completion, as well as to act as the buyer reasonably directs with the buyer indemnifying the seller against any consequent loss or damage; and that these provisions are altered substantially in SCPC 4.
- If you are acting for the buyer and the SCPCs are used in the contract, remember to ensure that the property is fully insured at the moment of exchange. It is good practice to check the insurance position at exchange, irrespective of which set of conditions is adopted.
- Bear in mind that where the property constitutes a dwelling, s 3 of the Landlord and Tenant Act 1985 compels the buyer to give written notice of the change of ownership to the lessee or tenant in occupation within two months of completion. Section 48 of the Landlord and Tenant Act 1987 compels the lessor buyer to provide the lessee in occupation with an address within England and Wales that can be used for the service of notices.

F COMPANY ACQUISITIONS

As has been noted at para 9.103 above, there will be occasions when a tenanted property **9.123** may be bought by way of a company acquisition. The Landlord and Tenant Act 1987 has an obvious weakness in this respect, in that the effect of the Act can be circumvented by a company acquisition. For example, if there is a freehold which is owned by a company as its only asset, and which is subject to a tenancy covered by the Act (see paras 9.98 et seq above), the owner of that company can avoid the effect of the Act by selling the shares in the company rather than the freehold title. If the shares are sold then the property remains in the ownership of the company; it is simply the share ownership that has changed. However, there can be problems associated with such a transaction.

First, it will still be necessary to carry out an investigation of title and to raise all appropriate **9.124** enquiries and to make all relevant searches. Notwithstanding that the transaction is going to be by way of share acquisition, a prudent buyer will still want to be sure that the asset of the company is actually in the ownership of the company and that there are no defects in title. All enquiries and searches will be required to support the position in relation to the title for all the reasons set out previously in this chapter.

9.125 Secondly, when buying via a share acquisition the buyer will take on not only the liabilities arising from the subject property, but also those arising from the company. This means that as well as irremovable encumbrances that affect the property, such as restrictive covenants, the sale transfer of shares would also pass to the buyer any outstanding tax liabilities of the company and unpaid company debts that could have nothing to do with the subject property. Past liabilities could come back to haunt an otherwise unblemished company. For example, the company might have been a lessee under pre-1996 leases, and as original lessee might still be held liable under the lease covenants should the present lessee default.

9.126 Nonetheless, there may be certain tax benefits from purchasing via a share acquisition. A share acquisition is not normally liable to VAT as share transfers are exempt supplies. A company acquisition may therefore escape VAT. Stamp duty will be payable at the normal, tiered rates on a property transfer up to the top rate of 4 per cent. The stamp duty on share transfers is at the much lower rate of 0.5 per cent. This option could therefore give rise to a substantial saving of duty. Furthermore, while not a tax or a duty, Land Registry fees could be saved on a share acquisition as there is no need for a transfer or registration at the Land Registry. Nevertheless, a Land Registry search against the title to the company property would still be possible utilizing form OS3 (although this does not confer priority).

PRACTICAL CHECKLIST: TENANTED PROPERTIES

9.127
- Have all appropriate standard enquiries been sent to the seller and to the local planning authority?
- What specific enquiries should you raise consequent upon any particular instructions you may have received from the client and as a result of the nature of the letting or lettings within the subject property?
- Always raise extra enquiries before contract when acting for a buyer of tenanted property; and ensure that those enquiries are employed to ascertain as much detail about the tenant and tenancy as possible.
- Should you use the Commercial Property Standard Enquiries?
- Always raise questions about any statutory controls affecting the tenant or the terms of the tenancy.
- Ask specifically about security of tenure provisions that may affect the lessee, as well as any specific statutory controls on the passing rental.
- Do you need to raise supplementary enquiries in the light of the answers given to the first tranche of enquiries?
- Make sure that the contract terms specifically cover the nature of the letting, be it commercial or residential; and if the tenant in occupation uses it for commercial purposes, consider utilizing the SCPCs.
- If either the SCs or SCPCs are used, remember that a deposit and the completion monies

must be paid by bank telegraphic transfer. If you intend to complete in person, send the electronic transfer and then arrange to complete in person prior to the time in the contract for completion, and release the monies once satisfied with the documentation.

- Always advise clients of any onerous or unusual replies or results to any of the enquiries in so far as they relate to the subject property or the tenancy, and request the clients' written instructions in response. Do not exchange contracts until all enquiries have been answered satisfactorily and the client has been supplied with full details and approves the position as reported.

KEY DOCUMENTS

- Land Registration Act 2002   **9.128**
- Commonhold and Leasehold Reform Act 2002
- Landlord and Tenant Act 1987
- Landlord and Tenant Act 1954
- Law of Property Act 1925
- Code of Practice for Commercial Leases in England and Wales (2nd edn)
- Commercial Property Standard Enquiries
- Standard Commercial Property Conditions (2nd edn)
- Standard Property Conditions (4th edn)

Printed copies of legislation can be ordered from The Stationary Office (<http://www.tso.co.uk>). Legislation from 1988 onwards can be downloaded free of charge from <http://www.opsi.gov.uk/acts.htm>.

The Code of Practice for Commercial Leases in England and Wales is set out in appendix 17.

The Commercial Property Standard Enquiries are set out in appendix 18 with guidance notes on the Enquiries set out in appendix 19.

The Standard Commercial Property Conditions are set out in appendix 4.

10

REVENUE LAW AND COMMERCIAL CONVEYANCING

A INTRODUCTION

10.01 Commercial conveyancing requires a practitioner to focus upon commercial property and business leases. Therefore, because the conveyancing practices involved in this speciality concentrate upon commercial investments or acquisitions and disposals, the tax regime is very different to that which prevails in residential conveyancing. Consequently, it is critical that practitioners are aware of the implications of the basics of revenue law when dealing with commercial transactions. Because of the *Hurlingham Estates* case (see paras 10.42 and 10.75 below for further details), it is now vital that practitioners know and understand their limitations in this area. Should they fail to do so, they may be held liable in negligence even though they did not offer any advice touching upon the taxation of the particular transaction in question.

B VAT ON COMMERCIAL PROPERTY

10.02 Value added tax (VAT) is a tax that manifests itself across Europe and is in effect a tax on turnover. VAT payments could arise both in a commercial lease and in a commercial property purchase. In these circumstances, a practitioner should in both transactions take all necessary steps to ensure that the VAT position is known, quantified and understood by the client before the transaction is finalized. HM Revenue and Customs deal with VAT, which is currently payable at 17.5 per cent on chargeable items. A chargeable item is called a 'supply'. In the context of commercial property, if a lease is granted, there can be the supply of a lease by the lessor to the lessee. If a commercial property is to be sold then there can be a supply of the subject property by the seller to the buyer. If a lease is assigned or transferred, there can be a supply of the residue of the term granted by the lease by the assignor/transferor to the assignee/transferee. However, there is no such supply where a lessee pays compensation to a lessor on a dilapidations claim, or on the sale of a business as a going concern where the sale includes freehold or leasehold property.

10.03 The general rule is that property transactions such as transfers, conveyances, assignments or the granting of leases can all be exempt supplies, ie, they do not attract a VAT charge. However, this can be reversed by written election (see para 10.08 below). Accordingly, practitioners should appreciate that conveyancing and VAT are a complex mix. On the face of it, conveyancing transactions are exempt. Nevertheless, as will be seen, some transactions can be compulsorily standard-rated (ie, paying the full rate of tax), some are zero-rated (ie, subject to VAT but at 0 per cent), and the taxpayer always has the option to elect to tax.

Parties can register as taxable persons who can pay and receive VAT. The Revenue sets a **10.04** threshold at which they are obliged so to register (of the value of taxable supplies, usually the business turnover figures). In the context of commercial transactions the tax can be payable either on the price paid for a commercial property, or on the rent payable by the terms of a commercial lease. Thus if the rent is £100 the VAT is added to it in the sum of £17.50, making £117.50 payable by the lessee. Where a person or company is required to pay VAT on a purchase price or rent, they should receive an invoice (a VAT invoice) showing how much VAT has been charged. This amount of VAT is called 'input tax'. That person or company may also charge VAT to someone else; this is called 'output tax'. VAT is payable quarterly (being a 'prescribed accounting period' by s 25(1) of the Value Added Tax Act 1994). The taxpayer can, when accounting to HM Revenue and Customs for the output tax received, deduct input tax paid. The net balance is then actually paid, and if input tax exceeds output tax the full amount is recoverable (see s 25(3) of the 1994 Act).

The rate of VAT presently at 17.5 per cent is called the standard rate. There is another rate, **10.05** called the zero rate, where there is a taxable supply but the rate of tax is zero. Otherwise a supply can be exempt, ie, not subject to VAT at all. So, the sale of a greenfield site for development is exempt (but there is an option to tax, see below). The surrender of a lease is exempt, as is the assignment of a lease (but again, in both cases there is an option to tax). However, the charges levied by a solicitor or other professional instructed in a commercial transaction will involve fees together with standard-rate VAT. Similarly, construction services for the building of a commercial development are standard-rated. (There is also a lower rate of 5 per cent. This has a limited application to conversion and renovation works in dwellings and also in relation to the insertion of insulation and energy-saving materials.)

Practitioners will immediately appreciate that they should ensure that their clients can **10.06** recover in full all their input tax. Nevertheless, there are parties who have to pay input tax and yet cannot recover it. Parties who are general consumers (as opposed to business persons or companies) cannot register as taxable persons entitled to recover input tax. Some parties make exempt supplies, ie, they are exempt from VAT. Examples are banks, building societies and insurance companies. Additionally, some parties can be 'partially exempt', ie, they have supplies that are both exempt and not exempt, and must therefore charge VAT on part of their business activities and can recover only a proportion of their input tax. If some or all of the paid VAT cannot be recovered, clients will seek to arrange matters so as to pay as little tax as possible (see paras 10.15 et seq below).

Although of no direct relevance to commercial conveyancing, it is worth noting that the **10.07** Law Society Conveyancing Protocol stipulates that the price paid for a property shall always be deemed to be exclusive of VAT. However, for the sake of certainty, if it is intended that VAT shall be paid in addition to any consideration then there should be a clear and unambiguous condition in the documentation to that effect. (See paras 10.08 et seq and 10.15 et seq below for a more detailed look at how this operates in practice, first where a lease might be involved and thereafter when a commercial sale is the transaction in question.)

VAT and leases generally

10.08 If a commercial lease is granted, the rule is that it is generally exempt from VAT (ie, there is an exempt supply), but it is nevertheless subject to the option to tax, ie, to make the letting taxable. The option to tax arises when the lessor decides voluntarily to give up the exemption and to opt for VAT liability at the standard rate (see s 89 of the Value Added Tax Act 1994). Notice of the election must be given to HM Revenue and Customs within 30 days of its being exercised and best practice dictates the use of customs form VAT 1614. The building or premises concerned will thereafter be a taxable supply instead of an exempt supply. If it is a taxable supply, on a lease of the subject premises VAT will be chargeable to the lessee. An election must be for the whole of the subject premises; an election in respect of part is not possible. This is also true for assignments and surrenders. It is in effect an option to waive the standard exemption. The lessor must be registered for VAT; and if there is such a registration, written notice must be given to HM Revenue and Customs within 30 days of the election having been made. As it will be for the lessees to pay the VAT on their rent, it is vital that at the same time they are advised of the VAT election. This election is personal to the elector. This means that if there are sub-lessees, the sub-lessor must also elect for VAT to be payable on the sub-lessees' rents.

10.09 Electing to charge VAT will only suit a lessor who wishes to recover VAT. Careful consideration should be given to the effect of charging VAT on the rent, as many prospective lessees will be put off taking the premises where they are not registered for VAT and cannot therefore recover the VAT themselves. Consequently, the election can be seen very much as a double-edged sword, and one that needs to be handled with care.

10.10 As will be seen below, there should always be a covenant in all leases to require payment of VAT in addition to the rent. On the assumption that there is an existing lease and it is silent as to the payment of VAT, the lessee will nevertheless have to pay VAT on the rent should the lessor decide to opt to tax. However, there is one vital point to note where you are acting for a lessor who intends to grant a new lease and also intends to opt to tax. You must advise the lessor not to make the election before the grant of the new lease. If the election precedes the grant, HM Revenue and Customs will deem the new rent to be *inclusive* of VAT. This pitfall can be avoided by electing immediately *after* the grant of the lease, but including in the lease a covenant requiring the lessee to pay any VAT on all the rents. Lastly, bear in mind that HM Revenue and Customs view any rent-free period, or periods that are granted as an inducement to a new lessee, as subject to VAT. VAT will be payable on the unpaid rent (see below).

10.11 If VAT is payable on a rent, it will also be payable upon any service charge under the terms of the same lease by which the rent is paid. In both cases the lessor can issue mere demands (and not VAT invoices), and when the rents and service charges are actually paid receipted VAT invoices should then be issued. In this way the lessor can delay accounting for VAT to HM Revenue and Customs until the lessor receives the actual payments. This has the benefit of delaying payment of tax, as well as ensuring that no VAT payments are made on supplies where monies have yet to reach the lessor, ie, rent arrears.

10.12 It is commonplace for lessees to be responsible for the payment of the fees of the lessor's solicitor or surveyor in respect of work effected by them and arising out the terms of the lease. For example, if the lessor is obliged to instruct its surveyor to prepare a schedule of dilapidations and its solicitor to arrange for service of that schedule upon the lessee, the fees of the surveyor and solicitor will almost certainly be payable by the lessee. This will usually be as a direct consequence of a covenant to that effect in the lease. If the lessor has not elected, the professionals' fee accounts are likely to include VAT and the lessee will have to bear the full cost including the VAT without the possibility of recovering that component. (The invoices will be addressed to the lessor but expressed to be payable by the lessee.) In the alternative, if the lessor has elected and the building is therefore taxable, the lessor's professionals will still render a VAT invoice to the lessor. The lessor will then issue a VAT invoice direct to the lessee to enable recovery to be possible. In practice the lessee will usually pay the professionals direct, with VAT invoices following the event.

The lessor may allow the lessee a rent-free period at the beginning of the term to enable the lessee to prepare the subject premises for business, or perhaps as an inducement for the lessee to take the lease if the lessor is having difficulty finding a tenant. There are no VAT implications if the purpose of the rent-free period is genuinely to permit the tenant to fit out in readiness for trading or to arrange a sub-letting; in this case the tenant is giving the landlord nothing in return for the rent-free period. However, the position is different either if the lessee is obliged by the lessor to do the fitting-out works (ie, they are for the lessor's benefit), or if the rent-free period is an inducement for the lessee to take the lease. In these situations HM Revenue and Customs will treat the tenant as making a supply to the lessor of an amount equivalent to the rent foregone; thus the lessee must pay VAT on the rent not paid during the rent-free period (see *Ridgeons Bulk v Commissioners of Customs and Excise* [1992] 37 EG 97). **10.13**

Other than a rent free period it is possible for a lessor to induce a lessee into taking on a lease by offering a reverse premium, ie, a payment by the lessor to the lessee on the grant of the new lease. If such a payment is made then it will be subject to VAT. Furthermore, if a deed of surrender is completed and consideration is paid for the surrender, that too could attract VAT. However it will be an exempt supply by reason of the Value Added Tax (Land) Order 1995, SI 1995/282. **10.14**

VAT and buying/selling a commercial property

If the commercial property to be sold or purchased is not new (ie, not less than three years old), there is an exempt supply of the property on sale. A building is said to be VATable when the lessor has made an election and collects rent and VAT on the rent payable by the lessee(s) of the subject premises. The option to tax arises when the lessor decides voluntarily to give up the standard exemption and to opt for a VAT liability at the standard rate (see s 89 of the 1994 Act). Notice of the election must be given to HM Revenue and Customs within 30 days of its being exercised and best practice dictates the use of customs form VAT 1614. The building concerned will thereafter be a taxable supply instead of an exempt supply. If it is a taxable supply, on sale of the subject premises VAT will be chargeable to the buyer. An election must be for the whole of the subject premises as an election in respect of part is not possible. **10.15**

When buying a commercial investment property, the buyer will want to know whether VAT will be payable on top of the proposed purchase price. Both the Standard Conditions of Sale **10.16**

(SC 1.4) and the Standard Commercial Property Conditions of Sale (SCPC 1.4) provide for all sums payable under the contract to be exclusive of VAT, ie, any VAT is *added* to the purchase price. If the buyer wishes to avoid paying VAT, it will require a special condition to this effect. The condition will say either that the purchase price is to be inclusive of any VAT, or that the seller warrants that it has not elected to waive any exemption to VAT and will not do so on or before completion. This is especially important for buyers who make exempt supplies in the course of their businesses, eg, banks, building societies and insurance companies, because they are unable to recover their VAT payments. Typical clauses protecting the buyer might read:

> All sums payable under this agreement are inclusive of VAT

or,

> The Seller warrants that it has not prior to the date of this agreement and will not before completion elect to waive any exemption for VAT in respect of the Property

10.17   If a new freehold building (ie, less than three years old) is sold it is subject to the standard rate of VAT. Accordingly, if a client instructs you to sell a new commercial property, the seller will be making a supply that will be standard-rated. This being so, the consideration will attract VAT at the standard rate. However, the client will want to know whether the stated price includes or excludes the standard rate of VAT. Clearly the seller will want the VAT to be on top of the consideration. Unless there is evidence or documentation to the contrary, there will be a presumption that the stated consideration is to *include* VAT. Practitioners acting for a seller in these circumstances should therefore ensure that there is a clear contractual term making the consideration exclusive of VAT so that the full price is paid to the seller with VAT on top of it. To omit such a clause in these circumstances would amount to a clear act of negligence. Therefore, as a matter of course, a VAT exclusive clause should be included in all such contracts.

10.18   The second edition of the Standard Commercial Property Conditions (SCPC) is divided into two parts. Part 1 contains general conditions building upon those in the first edition, while Part 2 contains new clauses and in particular detailed provisions covering VAT, capital allowances and reversionary interests in flats. In general Part 1 applies unless expressly excluded while Part 2 will only apply if expressly incorporated. Completing tick boxes on the back page of the agreement effects express incorporation, see SCPC 1.1.4 (a) and (b).

10.19   The standard position in Part 1 is that the seller warrants that the sale of the property does not constitute a supply that is taxable for VAT purposes. Part 2 changes this in two possible ways. First, A1 states that the sale does constitute a supply that is taxable for VAT purposes. A1.3 requires the buyer to pay VAT on top of the purchase price in exchange for a proper VAT invoice. Secondly, Condition A2 covers a transfer of a going concern. In this case the seller warrants that it is using the property for the business of letting to produce a rental income.

VAT and improvements

10.20   Where a property is let on a commercial basis, and in relation to improvements to the subject property, there is a concern for the lessee in relation to the payment and recovery of

VAT. Under the terms of the Landlord and Tenant Act 1927, the lessee can apply to the lessor to carry out improvements. In response, the lessor can opt to carry out the proposed works of improvement itself and rentalize the expense of those works (see s 27 of the Act). If this occurs, the lessee will not be in a position to recover any element of the VAT on the cost of the improvements made by and paid for by the lessor. The consequence is that payments equivalent to the VAT will have to be made but without the possibility of recovering all or any part of the VAT element.

Making the election

As has been noted above, a client can opt to pay and receive VAT. The option to tax arises **10.21** when the client decides voluntarily to give up the standard exemption and to opt for a VAT liability at the standard rate (see s 89 of the Value Added Tax Act 1994). Notice of the election must be given in writing to HM Revenue and Customs within 30 days of its being exercised and best practice dictates the use of customs form VAT 1614. Strictly speaking, the option is to waive exemption from VAT, but of course it has become known as the option to tax. To make the election the client should first ensure that it is registered for VAT. Thereafter the client should simply write to HM Revenue and Customs using VAT 1614 informing them of the election to waive exemption. The election is personal to the elector and is in respect of individual properties. The consent of HM Revenue and Customs is not required, save where an exempt supply has been made by the party seeking the election. In these circumstances consent will be required, and will only be forthcoming if HM Revenue and Customs are satisfied that any potential recovery of input tax is going to be fair and reasonable.

The client can have second thoughts and revoke the option, but only within three months **10.22** of the original election. Revocation within the three-month period can arise only if there is no tax due and HM Revenue and Customs give their consent to it. Alternatively, the option can be revoked at the end of a 20-year period (see, in both cases, the Value Added Tax (Buildings and Land) Order 1995, SI 1995/ 279).

KEY POINTS SUMMARY: VAT AND COMMERCIAL CONVEYANCING

- If a commercial lease is granted, the rule is that it is generally exempt from VAT but is **10.23** nevertheless subject to the option to tax, ie, to make the letting VATable.
- In a commercial lease, where VAT is to be charged on the rent the lessor must be registered for VAT; and if there is such a registration, written notice must be given to the Revenue within 30 days of the election having been made.
- If the election precedes the grant of a new commercial lease, the Revenue will deem the new rent to be *inclusive* of VAT.
- The election to tax is personal to the elector and is in respect of individual properties.
- On the assumption that there is an existing lease and it is silent as to the payment of VAT, the lessee will nevertheless have to pay VAT on the rent should the lessor decide to opt to tax. For certainty, always ensure that there is a covenant requiring the lessee to pay VAT on rent if required.
- If a commercial property is to be sold or purchased that is not new (not less than three

years old), there is an exempt supply of the property on sale and VAT will not be payable unless the seller opts to tax.

- If a new freehold building is to be sold it will be subject to the standard rate of VAT. Accordingly, if a client instructs you to sell a new commercial property the seller will be making a supply that will be standard-rated.

- Practitioners acting for sellers should always draft contracts so as to make all sums exclusive of VAT. Both the Standard Conditions of Sale (SC 1.4) and the Standard Commercial Property Conditions of Sale (SCPC 1.4) provide for all sums payable under the contract to be exclusive of VAT, ie, any VAT is *added* to the purchase price.

- The Customs national advice service can be contacted on 0845 010 9000 where they will deal with general VAT enquiries. The HMRC website contains guidance on VAT at <http://www.hmrc.gov.uk>.

C   STAMP DUTY LAND TAX

Introduction

10.24   Stamp duty land tax is a new tax based on the taxation of transactions in place of deeds or documents which was the case for the old stamp duty regime. It is assessed directly against the buyer rather than the property being purchased. The 2003 Budget set out details of this reform to the taxation of residential and commercial property transactions. Those details created a new tax, called stamp duty land tax ('Land Tax' or SDLT)). It would seem that the new tax was introduced for three reasons. First, to further the present government's desire to modernize; secondly, to anticipate the needs of e-conveyancing; and thirdly to try to limit tax avoidance.

Stamp duty land tax practice and procedure

10.25   The new regime came into force on 1 December 2003. Section 43 of the Finance Act 2003 defines land transactions as being the focus for Land Tax and is an extremely wide definition covering dealings in estates and interests including those that are equitable. The following tables set out SDLT rates from 17 March 2005.

(a)   SDLT on the consideration paid for transfers of land and buildings

Rate	Land in disadvantaged areas		Land not in disadvantaged areas	
	Residential	Commercial	Residential	Commercial
0%	£0–£150,000	£0–£150,000	£0–£120,000	£0–£150,000
1%	Over £150,000–£250,000	Over £150,000–£250,000	Over £120,000–£250,000	Over £150,000–£250,000
3%	Over £250,000–£500,000	Over £250,000–£500,000	Over £250,000–£500,000	Over £250,000–£500,000
4%	Over £500,000	Over £500,000	Over £500,000	Over £500,000

Disadvantaged Area Relief for non-residential land transactions is not available for non-residential land transactions on or after 17 March 2005, ie, the commercial property exemption is now lost.

(b) New leases—lease duty, duty on rent

Rate	Net present value of rent	
	Residential	Commercial
Zero	£0–£120,000	£0–£150,000
1%	Over £120,000	Over £150,000

Conveyancers should note that when calculating duty payable on the 'NPV' (Net Present **10.26** Value) of leases, you must reduce the 'NPV' calculation by the following before applying the 1 per cent rate: residential—£120,000, non-residential—£150,000. NPV is discussed below.

If a property is used as a residence then the Revenue will of course consider the subject **10.27** property on sale to be residential. Alternatively, if an office or shop is sold then it will be considered non-residential. Practitioners also need to be aware that transactions under the threshold (£120,000 or £150,000), will be taxed at 0 per cent but will still require a land transaction return to be completed for these transactions. Details of the land transaction returns are set out below. Land Tax will be at 1 per cent on a consideration up to the value of £250,000, 3 per cent for £250,001 to £500,000 and 4 per cent from £500,001. The Revenue will be implementing a regime of random checks to verify that the correct Land Tax has been paid.

In many disadvantaged areas across England and Wales Land Tax will not be payable on **10.28** residential transactions where the consideration does not exceed £150,000. This does not apply at all on non-residential land or commercial transactions. This disadvantaged area relief is also available on new residential leases but not commercial ones. You can phone the Revenue's enquiry line 0845 6030135 for assistance.

For transactions in land and buildings in the UK, completed on or after 1 December 2003, **10.29** practitioners do not need to arrange for documents to be physically stamped. Instead the Revenue will require the completion and submission of a land transaction return to their data capture centre in Merseyside within 30 days of the completion of the transaction. (Payment is required either on completion or when there is substantial performance of the contract. This will be if the buyer goes into possession or pays a substantial amount, probably 90 per cent of the price.) The centre address is Inland Revenue (Stamp/Taxes MSD), Comben House, Farriers Way, Netherton, Merseyside L30 4RN. If a return is filed late the buyer will be liable to a fixed penalty of £100, or if more than three months late, £200. The buyer may also be liable to a tax-related penalty, not to exceed the tax payable.

When should a land transaction return be completed?

The land transaction return should be submitted to notify: **10.30**

(a) Any transfer of a freehold or assignment of a lease for consideration, whether or not giving rise to a charge.
(b) Any transaction for which relief is being claimed.
(c) The grant of a lease for a contractual term of seven years or more or which gives rise to a charge.
(d) Any other transaction giving rise to a charge.

10.31   The following transactions are not notifiable and as such no Land Tax return is required. However, a self-certificate will be required to enable the transaction to be registered at Land Registry.

- The acquisition of a freehold or leasehold interest in land for no chargeable consideration. (Note that there will normally be chargeable consideration where there is a gift of property subject to an existing debt such as a mortgage.)
- Transactions made in connection with the ending of a marriage.
- Transactions varying the dispositions made, whether effected by will or laws of intestacy, within two years after the person's death not involving any consideration in money or money's worth.
- A transaction which affects something other than a major interest in land chargeable with tax at 0 per cent. An example of such a transaction would be an interest, which is not a major interest in land, such as the grant of an easement where the consideration does not exceed £120,000. This would attract Land Tax at 0 per cent, provided it is not linked to any other transaction that would bring the total consideration to more than £120,000. Notification would not be required.

10.32   The land transaction return, Form SDLT1 (supplemented by SDLT2 and 3 and 4) replaces the previous 'Stamps L(A)451' (the 'Particulars Delivered' or PD form). The effect of this is to abolish the need for and the use of the PD form. Furthermore the Land Tax system means that certificates of value are now redundant and can be excluded from all purchase deeds.

10.33   For most transactions, the submission of the land transaction return and the correct payment will be all that is required. Payment may be made by cheque, enclosed with the return or electronic payment (BACS, CHAPS, etc) or at a bank, Post Office or by Alliance and Leicester/Giro account using the payslip included in the return.

10.34   The supplementary forms deal with the following circumstances:

(a)   SDLT2—where there are more than two sellers and/or two buyers.
(b)   SDLT3—where land is involved and further space is required in addition to the space provided on SDLT1.
(c)   SDLT4—for complex commercial transactions and leases.

Completion of the stamp duty land tax forms

10.35   The land transaction return must be completed in black ink and must be signed by the buyer(s). The buyer's solicitor or conveyancer must not sign the return. This is because it is the buyer's responsibility to ensure that the information contained in the land transaction return is correct and complete. However, the buyer may request that their solicitor or conveyancer be authorized to handle correspondence on their behalf, by completing box 59 of the land transaction return. It is also vital for practitioners to remember to complete box 58. This will enable them to receive the certificate of payment from the Revenue (rather than the buyer), which will be required to enable the application for registration to the Land Registry to be completed. Of particular importance to practitioners is the provision that each land transaction return has a unique reference number, so photocopies cannot be used. Furthermore the form requires each national insurance number for every buyer if buying in person. This being so it would seem prudent for practitioners to ask for this information when taking instructions from the client at the start of the transaction.

HM Revenue and Customs have distributed a CD-Rom to conveyancers to enable the elec-   **10.36**
tronic completion on screen of SDLT forms. Drop down menus are used and if a box is missed in error the form cannot be printed until properly completed.

Stamp duty land tax and leases

The changes to stamp duty also usher in a new regime for the rental element of commercial   **10.37**
leases. The new charge will be at a rate of 1 per cent on the net present value (NPV) of the total rent payable over the term of the lease. Future rents will be discounted at 3.5 per cent per annum in order to arrive at the NPV. Leases where the NPV of the rent over the term of the lease does not exceed £150,000 will be exempt. The Revenue have suggested that change in the regime could mean that some 60 per cent of all commercial leases could avoid any stamp duty land tax on the rental element.

The SDLT5 or certificate of payment

Once the Revenue has received and processed a proper Land Tax return and payment it will   **10.38**
issue a certificate of payment. This is called a Land Transaction Return Certificate or SDLT5. The certificate is issued under s 79 of the Finance Act 2003 and evidences that Land Tax has been accounted on the particular transaction notified to the Revenue. This must be sent to the Land Registry to enable an application to register to proceed (alternatively where appropriate a self-certificate will be all that is required, see above for self-certificates). Finally the rule that deeds were inadmissible in court if they were not stamped will no longer apply. Unstamped deeds and documents (dated on or after 1 December 2003) can therefore be relied upon in court should reference to them be required.

An attempt to evade stamp duty land tax can amount to a criminal offence. An obvious   **10.39**
example is to try to apportion inappropriately the consideration in the contract between the property being purchased and fixtures and fittings within it. If the value ascribed to the fixtures and fittings is not accurate, eg, it is inflated well beyond the true value, this could be seen to be a fraud on the Revenue (and see *Saunders v Edwards* [1987] 1 WLR 1116). If there is such an apportionment, the values must be accurate as between the property and the fixtures and fittings. Where there is such an apportionment, it is recommended that the contract contains a list of the fixtures and fittings, showing the true value for each item in the list as well as the total.

KEY POINTS SUMMARY: STAMP DUTY LAND TAX

- It is assessed directly against the buyer rather than the property being purchased.   **10.40**
- The Revenue will require the completion and submission of a land transaction return to their data capture centre in Merseyside within 30 days of the completion of a transaction.
- If a return is filed late the buyer will be liable as a minimum to a fixed penalty of £100, or if more than three months late, £200.
- Section 43 of the Finance Act 2003 defines land transactions as being the focus of Land

Tax and is an extremely wide definition covering dealings in estates and interests (including easements and equitable interests).

• The starting threshold for the payment of Land Tax is £150,001 for non-residential or commercial properties.

• Transactions under the threshold (£150,001), will be taxed at 0 per cent but will still require a land transaction return to be completed.

• The land transaction return, Form SDLT1 (supplemented by SDLT2 and 3 and 4) replaces the previous 'Stamps L(A)451' (the 'Particulars Delivered' form) which is now redundant.

• The Land Tax system means that certificates of value are also now redundant and can be excluded from all purchase deeds.

• The land transaction return must be completed in black ink or by using the HMRC CD-Rom and must be signed by the buyer(s). The buyer's solicitor or conveyancer is not permitted to sign the return.

• The buyer may request that his or her conveyancer be authorized to handle correspondence on their behalf, by completing box 59 of the land transaction return. It is also vital for practitioners to remember to complete box 58. This will enable them to receive the certificate of payment from the Revenue (rather than the buyer), which will be required to enable the application for registration to the Land Registry to be completed.

• Each land transaction return has a unique reference number, so photocopies of the tax forms cannot be used.

• The rule that deeds were inadmissible in court if they were not stamped will no longer apply for deeds dated on or after 1 December 2003.

D   OTHER TAXES

10.41 Although from a perspective of commercial conveyancing practitioners will most commonly encounter stamp duty land tax and VAT, it is important that they are also aware of other taxes that might have an effect on their clients and their property transactions. Although a detailed examination of other taxes is beyond the scope of this book, we set out below some of the basics that a commercial conveyancer should consider, as well as some more detailed concerns.

Introduction

10.42 All conveyancing practitioners should be aware of the implications of the decision in *Hurlingham Estates Ltd v Wilde & Partners* (1997) 147 NLJ 453. Lightman J made it clear that a solicitor will be liable in negligence for adverse revenue implications for a client that arise from a transaction effected by the solicitor, even though the solicitor was not expressly instructed to consider the revenue implications. This is also true even if the solicitor assumed that the client had previously sought the advice of an accountant. The consequence of this decision is to make it quite clear that if a solicitor feels unable to cover the revenue implications of a commercial transaction, he or she should explain to the client, at the commencement of instructions, that this is so and that the client should separately seek professional advice on the tax implications of the proposed transaction. To do otherwise might court just the kind of negligence liability found in the *Hurlingham* case. Accordingly, the safest course of action would be to include such a caveat in the initial letter to the client.

Having set out the above warning, it is clear that many practitioners will nevertheless wish **10.43** to assist clients in commercial matters notwithstanding this potential liability. A brief overview of other taxes that might need to be considered in the context of commercial conveyancing and property is therefore given below.

Capital gains tax matters

Capital gains tax is payable upon 'profits' or gains made on the disposal of an asset that is not **10.44** otherwise taxable as income. If a client sells and receives a capital payment that exceeds the price at which the client purchased, there may be a possible liability for capital gains tax. This is also the case should a client receive a payment for the assignment of a lease. There can also be capital gains tax implications on the receipt of a premium for the grant of a commercial lease. If a gain is made on a conveyance or assignment then tax could arise either as:

(a) capital gains tax under the Taxation of Chargeable Gains Act 1992; or
(b) income tax under Case 1 of Sch D, ie, in respect of a trade (s 18 of the Income and Corporation Taxes Act 1988).

Practitioners should remember that if the seller is a company, its profits will be subject to **10.45** corporation tax and not income and capital gains taxes, but the rules of income and capital gains tax have been taken up for corporation tax calculations. (Indeed, since 5 April 1998 the tax has been chargeable at income tax rates for individuals, although at corporation tax rates for companies.)

Whether the client is an individual or a corporation, a practitioner will need, for capital **10.46** gains tax purposes, to pinpoint:

(a) the acquisition cost;
(b) incidental costs of the acquisition (such as cost of transfer, including stamp duty);
(c) any 'enhancement' expenditure that can be seen in the nature or state of the property at the time of sale; and
(d) sale expenses, as well as the amount to come in to the seller on completion.

By identifying these elements, the conveyancer can advise the client or its professional **10.47** advisers of the gross profit (or loss) made by the seller client having taken into account the other elements of the acquisition and disposal listed above. There is the possibility of reducing the liability to tax by offsetting any previous losses, both capital and trading. An individual can set a trading loss against capital gains in the same year of assessment so long as it cannot be set against income for that year. Capital gains losses from previous years have to be set against capital gains before any trading losses. When calculating the gain it should be remembered that there is also an indexation allowance to offset the effects of inflation. The indexation benefit can only be used to reduce or clear a gain, it cannot be used to form or exaggerate a loss. After 5 April 1998, the indexation amount is fixed at its value at that time. There is also Taper relief. Furthermore, s 152 of the Taxation of Chargeable Gains Act 1992 allows rollover relief for land. To qualify, the taxpayer must enter into an unconditional contract to buy the replacement property no later than three years after the disposal of the old property (or indeed, not earlier than one year before the disposal of the old property).

10.48 Capital gains tax is calculated in relation to disposals made in any one year up to 5 April. This has relevance for a conveyancer, in that tax planning may be required with reference to timing, and hence the timing of the exchange of contracts giving rise to a potential gain. Thus although the gain is realized at the time of completion, ie, when all the consideration is in the hands of the seller, for capital gains tax purposes the date of the contract is the date the Revenue will consider as the date of the disposal. The contract date is therefore the date of the gain. An exception to this is where there are certain types of conditional contracts. The conditionality required is of a fundamental nature, ie, the condition would have to be of such consequence that it has to take place failing which the contract will be completely thwarted. Where there is a contract for the sale of development land that is expressed to be conditional upon the obtaining from the local planning authority of a suitable planning consent, the Revenue will normally accept this as such a fundamental conditionality. This being so, where there is such a conditional contract, the date of disposal will not be until completion actually occurs.

10.49 If a seller enters into a contract to sell land or property and the buyer pays a deposit but then fails to complete, a question arises as to the tax treatment of the deposit monies. The Revenue require the deposit to be treated in the same way as option monies (see paras 10.52 to 10.53 below for the taxation of options). In effect, the Revenue consider that the deposit monies are treated as a separate asset in the hands of the recipient, ie, the seller, with the full sum being liable to capital gains tax. (This is because there is in effect no acquisition cost for the deposit and so all the monies will be subject to tax; see s 144 of the Taxation of Chargeable Gains Act 1992.)

Capital gains tax and leaseholds

10.50 If a lessor charges and receives a premium for the granting of a commercial lease, that premium will be potentially liable to tax as a capital gain. As premiums are uncommon in the context of commercial leases, this tax liability is unlikely to be a frequent occurrence. (The granting of a lease at a premium will be considered by the Revenue as a 'part disposal', to the extent that the lessor retains an element of value, namely the freehold reversion.) However, the lessor's profit rental income will be liable to tax either as income (ie, income tax), or (if a company) as corporation tax. The Revenue also deem a premium paid on a lease for a term of less than 50 years to be partly taxable as income. There is no double charge to tax as that element deemed to be income will be excluded from the capital gains element. Lastly, a premium paid on assignment will, potentially, attract capital gains tax as it is (of course) a 'disposal' which attracts this tax liability. Where the lease being assigned has less than 50 years left to run then the Revenue will regard this to be a 'wasting asset', and as such will apply special rules in calculating any gain liable to tax. In essence, the acquisition cost is subject to a formula that writes off the cost progressively. This is meant to take into account the fact that lease values decline with their shortening term (ie, a lease with a term of 125 years but with 99 years to run will be worth much more than one with just nine years to run).

If a receiver or liquidator is required to pay to a lessor rent arrears accumulated by the   **10.51**
defaulting party, to enable the lessor to grant licence to assign, those rent arrears will not be a
permitted deduction from any gain made on the sale of the relevant lease (see *Emmerson v
Computer Time International Limited* [1997] 1 WLR 734). If a commercial lease is renewed
pursuant to the terms of Pt II of the Landlord and Tenant Act 1954, the courts have held that
the new lease is not derived from the old one and as such stands alone as a separate entity.
This will have relevance to calculations of lease lengths. (A lessee may be more successful in
reducing the notional value of a lease that is shorter than if the previous term had also to be
taken into account.)

Options and capital gains tax

Options are looked at in detail at paras 8.20 et seq above. The capital gains tax implications   **10.52**
of granting an option can be complicated. The Revenue regard the grant of an option as the
disposal of an entirely separate asset from the land or property over which it is granted.
However, should the option be exercised then the original option and the exercise are
regarded as a unified transaction. Thus, the money that was paid by the buyer to acquire the
option will be treated by the Revenue as part of the buyer's costs of acquiring the land or
property in total. As far as the seller is concerned, the receipt of the monies paid for the
option will be considered by the Revenue as a constituent element of the proceeds of sale (in
both cases, see s 144 of the Taxation of Chargeable Gains Act 1992). Put options are treated
in a similar way.

The abandonment of an option, ie, by the non-exercise of the option within the prescribed   **10.53**
period, will not be treated as a disposal of an asset (see s 144 of the Taxation of Chargeable
Gains Act 1992). Section 144 also stipulates that an option that requires a lessor to grant a
lease at a premium is to be treated in the same way as an option to sell. This is so even
though the option is in effect over an estate or interest that is not formed or in existence at
the time the option is granted, ie, the term of years appears only once the option is actually
exercised.

Taxes on income

A lessor will, it is hoped, make an annual profit on the rents received from lessees. For   **10.54**
income tax or corporation tax purposes, that rental profit will be assessed for tax on a current
year basis under Sch A to the Income and Corporation Taxes Act ('ICTA') 1988. Furthermore,
payments made in respect of the use or enjoyment of land that include a licence to occupy or
use land, or in the exercise of rights over land, are all receipts taxable under Sch A. This will
also include rent charges, ground rents and other annual payments made for the use or
occupation or benefit in or over land. This has been extended to payments made for the
occupation of a caravan on land or a houseboat. If an occupant of either moveable form of
habitation pays money to a landowner then the money in the hands of the recipient, ie, the
lessor, will be taxed as income under Sch A to ICTA 1988.

The situation outlined above should be distinguished from that of a person making profits   **10.55**
that arise from the occupation of land. The difference is that in this case there is a trade from
which the profits are made, and they are then taxable under Case 1 of Sch D to ICTA 1988.

This exception will exclude hotel owners and property dealings. There are other exceptions that are not taxed within Sch A, and these include farming and mining. Rents paid to a landlord for serviced accommodation will also be outside the scope of Sch A and are deemed to be profits within the ambit of Sch D to the 1988 Act. In the event of a Sch A loss, it can be carried forward against any future profits from a Sch A business.

Income tax and service charge reserve and sinking funds

10.56   There can be complex taxation difficulties for both parties in connection with service charge reserve and sinking funds, the details of which are beyond the scope of this book. However, very broadly, the potential difficulties are as follows. For the lessor, if the fund is payable to the lessor 'as rent' (ie, not into a trust), the lessor will be liable to income tax under Sch A to ICTA 1988. The lessor can of course offset its annual expenditure against income, but in the case of these funds it probably cannot do so until the year in which the expenditure is actually incurred. Likewise for a lessee, service charge payments are normally deductible for income tax purposes. However, if the monies are paid into a trust, it is likely that they will not be deductible from income until the year in which the trust actually lays out the monies (see generally, ss 25–31 of ICTA 1988). There may also be inheritance tax implications for the lessee, as the trust could amount to a settlement for inheritance tax purposes. The parties should each take specialist tax advice before setting up and agreeing the terms of any sinking or reserve fund.

Income tax and lease premiums

10.57   The Revenue have put in place statutory provisions to stop lessors taking premiums or other capital sums in place of rent, ie, to stop the taking of a capital profit instead of income profit. Where a lease term does not exceed 50 years, the lessor will have to pay income tax on part of any premium paid for the lease as if that element of the premium were rent. The lessor can deduct from the value of the premium (and in doing so it will take it out of a liability to income tax) 2 per cent for each full year of the term, other than the first year. So the maximum exemption could be as much as 98 per cent.

10.58   These obligations extend not just to cash premiums. The income tax element will also apply to lump sums paid on the sale of land with a right to reconveyance, sums paid for an assignment of a lease made at an undervalue, sums paid for a variation of lease terms and sums paid for the surrender of a lease required by the lease terms in lieu of rents otherwise due. This taxation provision can also apply where a lease is granted which imposes upon the lessee an obligation to carry out works to the subject premises. The premium element is deemed to be equivalent to the value of the improvements to the lessor at the end of the lease. See s 34 of ICTA 1988.

Property investment companies

10.59   A property investment company buys properties to receive rents from lessees in occupation, ie, the property will be viewed as an asset to be held for the purposes of making the owner a profit rental income. Should the asset, ie, a property, be sold, the disposal will amount to a capital gain. (The opposite type of company will be a property dealing company that buys and then sells properties with a view to making a turn, ie, a profit on sale from the increased value at the time of disposal. The company is trading in property and is taxed as a trading company in much the same way as if the company were trading in the purchase and sale of any other commodity (such as clothes or foodstuffs).)

Because an investment company is not carrying on a trade, it therefore calculates total rental income in accordance with usual Sch A rules for each accounting period and with regard to the rents income. If other income is involved, this too must be brought into account along with capital gains made during the relevant accounting year, and this will then amount to the company's total gross profits for tax purposes. Management expenses can be deducted. However, a clear distinction must be made between expenses incurred in managing the company's portfolio of properties and those incurred in the management of the company itself.   **10.60**

Local taxes

All the taxes mentioned above relate to levies imposed by central government. Local authorities have the power to impose two taxes on property: **10.61**

(a) From 1 April 1993, local authorities can impose on residential properties a council tax that replaces the community charge or poll tax. It is authorized by the Local Government Finance Act 1992.

(b) Non-domestic rates—the uniform business rate. If a property is not one on which council tax is payable then it will attract non-domestic rates. This is the tax that will normally be paid for business premises.

Commercial properties subject to rates are allotted a rateable value. This value is said to be based upon the rental value of the subject premises for a notional annual letting and with the notional lessee responsible for repairs and insurance. The valuation is made on a five-year cycle. There is an exemption for land that is used for agricultural purposes, as well as for agricultural buildings. Various other exemptions are also available for other, less common land uses such as religious worship. Furthermore, local authorities can exempt charities and non-profit making bodies from paying business rates. They can also agree reduced amounts of rates for such parties rather than a full exemption.   **10.62**

The rate payable is calculated by multiplying the rateable value by a figure that is decreed annually by central government. (Domestic council tax figures are different, in that the local authorities and not central government fix the annual figure for the levy.) Because government sets the figure for the business rate, it has been termed a uniform business rate. Occupants of commercial properties will be required to pay the amount of the annual rate to the local authority, although there is usually a facility available to pay it either by lump sum, or by instalments throughout the year.   **10.63**

Capital allowances

Capital allowances are a tax relief that can be available on commercial property. They are meant to be an incentive to the investment in capital equipment that includes commercial property. Capital allowances will be seen by the Revenue as an expense and, as such, will be accepted as a legitimate deduction and therefore reduce taxation.   **10.64**

The capital allowance most commonly encountered is in respect of 'plant and machinery'.   **10.65**

This will cover heating equipment, fire safety installations and air conditioning machinery. Allowances are valued under s 562 of the Capital Allowances Act 2001. This permits the apportionment of a purchase price between the land and non-qualifying items (including the building), and qualifying items of plant and machinery. Under s 196(1) of this Act the same apportionment process can be made on a sale.

10.66   The amount of a capital allowance that a lawyer may claim can be limited by similar allowances claimed by a previous owner. Enquiries need to be made about claims for allowances going back to 24 July 1996. Accordingly, when acting on a sale or purchase of commercial property, consideration should be given to the possible inclusion in the contract of an apportionment as outlined above. In any event practitioners should at an early stage in the transaction advise their client to consider this topic and to take additional professional advice as required.

10.67   The second edition of the Standard Commercial Property Conditions (SCPC) is divided into two parts. Part 1 contains general conditions while Part 2 contains new clauses and in particular detailed provisions covering capital allowances. In general Part 1 applies unless expressly excluded while Part 2 will only apply if expressly incorporated. Completing tick boxes on the back page of the agreement effects express incorporation, see SCPC 1.1.4 (a) and (b). Condition B of the second part of the contract deals with capital allowances. Condition B supports a buyer in any claims it may make pursuant to the terms of the Capital Allowances Act 2001. In doing so it requires the seller to provide copies of relevant information as well as co-operation and assistance as the buyer may reasonably require.

KEY POINTS SUMMARY: REVENUE LAW AND COMMERCIAL CONVEYANCING

10.68   • A solicitor may be liable in negligence for adverse revenue implications for a client that arise from a transaction effected by the solicitor, even though the solicitor was not expressly instructed to consider the revenue implications. Therefore, always consider what your attitude is, and state it in your first letter to the client.
   • Although a capital gain is realized at the time of completion, ie, when all the consideration is in the hands of the seller, for tax purposes the Revenue will consider the date of the contract as the date of the disposal and thus the taxable gain.
   • If there is a development contract conditional upon obtaining planning permission, the Revenue will normally accept the completion date as the date of the gain and not the date of the agreement.
   • The Revenue regard the grant of an option as the disposal of an entirely separate asset from the land or property over which it is granted.
   • For income tax or corporation tax purposes, a rental profit will be assessed for tax on a current year basis under Sch A to the Income and Corporation Taxes Act 1988.
   • Lease service charge reserves and sinking funds—if the fund is payable to the lessor 'as rent' (ie, not into a trust), the lessor will be liable to income tax under Sch A to the 1988 Act.
   • Consider the need to involve capital allowance in a commercial transaction.

E TAXATION ISSUES FOR YOUR CLIENT

Introduction

There can be varied and sometimes quite complex issues for clients in the context of **10.69** taxation, and we set out below some examples as well as some thoughts and guidance on how to advise clients when confronted with differing sets of circumstances affecting them or their property.

Clients and tax effectiveness

There is a common perception, when dealing with a commercial transaction, that the best **10.70** entity for your client to adopt would be to select a corporate vehicle for the deal as opposed to your individual client. This may not always be the best choice, notwithstanding the commercial nature of the transaction. For example, a company has been seen as a poor vehicle for holding property that represents an appreciating asset in the context of capital gains tax (see below for further details). On the other hand, the limited liability of a company may have its benefits for your client. Even here, though, conveyancing practice has whittled down the effectiveness of limited liability. For example, should a company take a lease, we have seen in chapter 3 that lessors will require the directors of that company to guarantee the rent personally on behalf of their company. Similarly, if a company buys a commercial property to make a profit, but with a loan, lending institutions regularly ask the directors of the company to guarantee the loan or offer other, personal collateral. Perhaps the only time a limited company may offer some degree of protection is where there is a development and where the directors have not been called upon to offer guarantees to the builders or other contractors.

A commercial property that is an asset of a limited company may well prove to be an **10.71** appreciating asset. If it does, there can be a problem in capital gains tax terms. If the value increases then there can be a capital gains tax liability on sale. However, the increased value also has a knock-on effect on the value of the shares in the company, as it too will increase. If you take into account the potential taxation upon both these elements then there is a significant increase on what might otherwise be paid by an individual on his or her own capital gain.

You need to consider your client's ultimate intentions for the assets to be held by him or her. **10.72** For example, if the company is being proposed as a vehicle in which to lodge assets that it is hoped will appreciate and eventually form a source of a pension for the client, there may be better ways to give effect to the client's wishes. If the 'pension fund' were owned by a self-administered pension fund, this would be more efficient from a tax perspective and would certainly reduce the tax liability that might otherwise arise should the fund remain within a company. On the other hand, if the client intends to build up an asset that will eventually be floated on the stock market or sold to other investors, plainly a limited company is going to be the only choice available to the client.

F   TAXATION ISSUES FOR THE SUBJECT PROPERTY

10.73   Some types of land are treated differently for special economic reasons. Agricultural land is a good example of this. Farming is an activity arising from the use of agricultural land that the Revenue considers to be a trade. The occupant, the farmer, is therefore carrying on a trade that will be taxable on Case 1 of Sch D to ICTA 1988. (Farming excludes market gardening; see s 823 of ICTA 1988.) The Revenue will also permit writing down allowances at the rate of 4 per cent per annum deductible over 25 years against capital payments for the building of farm buildings. (However, in relation to any payments made for the farmhouse, the Revenue limit the allowance to one third for the construction works to this building only. The relief otherwise applies to capital payments for the construction of all other farm buildings, or farm cottages and boundary fences.) Within the context of inheritance tax, there is a substantial benefit from agricultural property relief. On death or early transfer there can be up to 100 per cent relief in respect of such property passing, or in the worst case scenario a 50 per cent relief. Either way, there is a powerful benefit available to an owner/occupier of agricultural land. In the context of the uniform business rate authorized by the Local Government Finance Act 1992, there is an exemption available for land that is used for agricultural purposes as well as agricultural buildings.

10.74   For the purposes of VAT, practitioners should bear in mind that the construction of new dwellings is zero-rated, as is the conversion of commercial premises to residential use. In detail, this applies to the first grant or assignment in relation to a building designed for dwellings, or for residential or charitable purposes. Again in detail, this applies to the grant or assignment of a building being converted from commercial to residential purposes. To qualify for zero-rating the sale or the grant of a new lease must be by the constructor. The 'constructor' covers not just an owner/builder, but also an owner who contracts with a builder provided the owner is able to exert some control over the construction works. Proof of control would include the owner being able to dictate the required design and planning applications. To ensure that your client can obtain the benefit of zero-rating, you should make it clear to the client that the measure of control should be obvious and realistic. So if the client has in effect devolved all the construction and development work and decisions to another party, the right to claim zero-rating might be lost. If, however, the client merely selects an architect and then a builder, and has control incorporated into their contracts, that client will be able to claim zero-rating. It is interesting to note that HM Revenue and Customs have said that the grant of an interest in a development that is incomplete, ie, only partially built, will qualify to be zero-rated. However, this will be the case only if building and construction works have passed the stage of putting in and completing the foundations.

G   TAXATION ISSUES FOR PRACTITIONERS

10.75   Following *Hurlingham Estates Ltd v Wilde & Partners* (1997) 147 NLJ 453 (see para 10.42 above), practitioners on receiving instructions have to make an important decision in the light of the nature of the proposed transaction. Do you consider that you have enough knowledge of the taxation implications of the proposed transaction? If you think not, or are in any doubt, we suggest that you make it quite clear to the client in writing how far your advice and assistance will go, and where the boundaries lie as to how you can assist. You should at the same time urge the client to seek specialist help and advice elsewhere. From your own commercial perspective this is a sensitive step, as you will not want to do anything that might estrange your client from you or your practice. However, to avoid a potential negligence claim and to act in a responsible and professional manner, this letter must be written. It may be that the client will confirm that it is relying upon the advice of retained accountants. If this is so then you should make it clear to the client that the accountants should be informed that they will be responsible for all taxation issues arising from the proposed transaction. If necessary, you should write to the accountants to confirm this understanding so that there can be no blurring of responsibilities. Furthermore, before contracts are exchanged or a lease completed, full details of the proposed transaction should be disclosed to the accountants so that they can then confirm in writing that they have considered the tax implications for the client and that the transaction can proceed without detriment to the client.

Practitioners should be aware that there is a procedure to advise the Revenue of the details of a proposed transaction and to require the Inspector of Taxes to state whether a particular tax provision relating to the taxation of a capital gain will or will not apply to that specific deal. If the Inspector states that the tax provisions do not catch the transaction then the Revenue are not permitted to raise an assessment on the transaction in respect of that particular tax point. However, if there has been inadequate disclosure then of course the Revenue will not be prohibited from making such an assessment (see s 776(11) of ICTA 1988). The procedure is that the taxpayer should write to the Inspector with details of how the gain is to arise. The Inspector then has to advise the taxpayer, within 30 days from the receipt of the taxpayer's details, of his or her decision. The response must indicate whether the section does not apply. The major fault of this system is that the Inspector is under no obligation to say why a clearance is being refused. There is also the problem of not really being sure of the extent and nature of the detail that the Inspector might require in order to decide whether or not to grant a clearance. In these circumstances, we would recommend informal discussions before actually submitting your client's papers. The Revenue have said that in seeking a response from the Revenue, the taxpayer should 'put all his cards face up on the table' when indicating the guidance required, as well as stipulating how the taxpayer intends to use the guidance issued by the Revenue. **10.76**

Before an application for such a clearance is considered, a property practitioner should first decide whether to seek the advice and opinion of tax counsel. It may well be that counsel should vet complex or novel schemes before any contact is made with the Revenue. This is particularly so if there is an element of tax avoidance within the scheme. (This is particularly important in the light of considerable efforts by the Revenue to design and promulgate statutory anti-avoidance measures.) **10.77**

Once completion of a transaction has taken place, a practitioner should of course remember to pay stamp duty land tax within 30 days and to obtain all appropriate VAT invoices for the use of a VAT registered client. Copy completion statements should be retained, as clients **10.78** inevitably ask for details for their tax returns many months after the completion of the particular transaction.

H   REVENUE LAW AND COMMERCIAL CONVEYANCING—A CONCLUDING ISSUE

10.79   To conclude, we feel that we should underline the need for practitioners to consider what is best for the client when reflecting upon how taxation implications should be dealt with in commercial transactions. If you consider that your knowledge is insufficient you should either seek expertise within your firm or from tax counsel, or you should advise the client to seek specialist tax advice elsewhere. Alternatively, you may consider that you can assist within limited boundaries, eg, you might consider that you are able to assist with stamp duty and VAT but not with income and capital tax implications. If this is so, you should write to the client at the start, setting out your position so that the client may appreciate what you can and cannot do. That way your indemnity policy is likely to see fewer claims as the years progress. It is a beneficial example of defensive lawyering; it should mean that negligence claims are held in check but that you are still managing to act in the best interests of your client. Lastly, practitioners should remember that commercial clients should now appreciate that pockets of expertise exist in different locations. Clients should be prepared to accept that a practitioner cannot be a 'jack of all trades' and that they will be better served by consulting several professionals to achieve their commercial goals.

PRACTICAL CHECKLISTS

Revenue law and commercial conveyancing

10.80   • In the light of *Hurlingham Estates Ltd v Wilde & Partners* (1997) 147 NLJ 453, if you feel unable to cover the revenue implications of a commercial transaction, make this quite clear to the client at the outset. Advise the client to seek professional advice on the tax implications of the proposed transaction.
   • For capital gains tax purposes, pinpoint the consideration paid to buy the subject property, the acquisition cost, incidental costs of the acquisition, any 'enhancement' expenditure that can be seen in the nature or state of the property at the time of sale, and sale expenses.
   • If your client is entitled to seek roll-over relief, remember that to qualify the taxpayer must enter into an unconditional contract to buy the replacement property no later than three years after the disposal of the old property, or not earlier than one year before.
   • Stamp duty land tax is payable at a flat rate of 1 per cent on the net present value (NPV) of the total rent payable over the term of the lease. No duty is payable where the NPV of the total rent does not exceed £150,000.
   • Consider whether a company is really the most tax-efficient vehicle for the client in the context of the particular commercial venture to be dealt with by you. If limited liability is

unavailable, would a different holding entity be more appropriate in the prevailing circumstances?

- Decide upon the nature of a client company. Is it a vehicle for property investment or for dealing? A property investment company buys properties to receive rents from lessees in occupation. Should the property be sold the disposal will amount to a capital gain. The opposite will be a property dealing company that buys and then sells properties with a view to making a turn. The company is trading in property and is taxed as a trading company.
- If your client's proposals include an element of tax avoidance, is it appropriate to apply to the Revenue for a clearance certificate pursuant to the terms of s 776(11) of ICTA 1988, or should you first seek the advice of tax counsel?
- Once completion of a transaction has taken place a practitioner should, of course, remember to stamp all documents within 30 days and to obtain all appropriate VAT invoices for the use of a VAT registered client.
- Copy completion statements should be retained, as clients often ask for details for their tax returns many months after the completion of the particular transaction.

VAT rates

Exempt from VAT (but subject to the option to tax)

- Disposal of a greenfield site for development **10.81**
- Grant of a lease
- Assignment or surrender of a lease
- Disposal of a freehold (that is not new, ie, building not completed within three years preceding the disposal)

Zero-rated (VAT payable but at 0 per cent)

- New house sale **10.82**
- Building and construction services (but not for commercial properties, where they are standard-rated)

Standard-rated (VAT payable at the standard rate, currently 17.5 per cent variable)

- Works of repair or alterations **10.83**
- Services rendered by professional advisers
- Building and construction services (but not for residential properties, where they are zero-rated)
- Disposal of a freehold (that is new, ie, building completed within three years preceding the disposal)

KEY DOCUMENTS

- Finance Act 2003 **10.84**
- Value Added Tax Act 1994
- Taxation of Chargeable Gains Act 1992

- Income and Corporation Taxes Act 1988
- Customs Form VAT 1614 (Notice of election in respect of VAT)
- Standard Commercial Property Conditions (2nd edn)

Printed copies of legislation can be ordered from The Stationary Office (<http://www.tsoshop.co.uk>). Legislation from 1988 onwards can be downloaded free of charge from <http://www.opsi.gov.uk/acts.htm>.

Information about Customs forms can be found at <http://www.hmrc.org.uk>.

The Standard Commercial Property Conditions are set out in appendix 4.

11

YOUR PRACTICE

A INTRODUCTION

At the start of this book we said that all areas of legal work carried out by solicitors have, in **11.01** recent years, become so complex that specialization is the key to the future success of the profession. Residential conveyancing, until recently the backbone of many firms' fee income, can no longer be seen as a protected area of practice where fees will continue to roll in. To compensate there has developed over the years a particular area of expertise that services and supports the market in and for commercial property. It is the growth of specific expertise in this complex area that we have examined in this book and which we now consider from the perspective of your practice. Accordingly we will consider what is important for a basic practice library, what you might wish to collate as practice materials, such as a database of forms and precedents, and then what other research materials might be of assistance to your practice. Finally we make some suggestions about how you might continue your professional development within the area of commercial conveyancing and practice and about how you can keep up to date.

This book has necessarily concentrated on several different topics that all relate to com- **11.02** mercial property. We think this demonstrates that any practitioner who wishes to concentrate on this area of legal work will need to command a broad base of specialist knowledge or in the larger practices may specialize in specific areas within those covered in our book. Commercial leases will remain the main topic for consideration and as such anyone in your practice who works in this area must be able to keep up to date with the complex procedures for the payment and review of rent as well as the covenants frequently entered into by both lessor and lessee. However one area of potential confusion can arise in the difficult but crucial area relating to the renewal of business leases and the effects of the Landlord and Tenant Act 1954, Pt II. Business leases are clearly within the sphere of a commercial conveyancer but the renewal procedure requires a thorough knowledge of court procedure and practice tactics. Should this renewal element remain in the control of the conveyancer or should he or she pass this element to a specialist within the litigation department? A policy decision is required by the partners and must be adhered to for all cases involving renewal. The authors favour the work remaining with the commercial conveyancers as there is no risk of files or cases being lost or confused between departments. If the renewal cases remain with the conveyancers then they will need regular training and professional development in this extension to their practice knowledge. One refinement of responsibility within this area could be regarding how far each renewal case progresses. Since the recent reforms to the renewal process it is anticipated that few cases will actually make it to a full hearing. This being so, conveyancers could cover the simple application-only renewal cases while the firm's litigation department could take over the few cases that fail to settle terms by negotiation and which end up being heard before a court. Certainly cases where the lessor seeks repossession should be passed to a specialist litigator within your firm.

11.03   As for site acquisitions and funding, and the selling and buying of tenanted property with both commercial and residential lessees, this too should be covered by the commercial conveyancing department. As such, practitioners must be able to make a careful examination of the new contractual Standard Commercial Property Conditions and contrast them with the long established Standard Conditions with the intention of seeking to ascertain which set better suits the type of conveyancing transaction. These are all policy decisions that are required to ensure your practice is efficient and cost effective and are twin demands of a successful practice.

B   LIBRARY, PRACTICE, AND RESEARCH MATERIALS

11.04   We set out below details of the spread of versatile resources that are available to commercial property practitioners, both free as well as subscription based. We also make some suggestions about your continuing professional development and how you might keep up to date with your chosen area of practice.

Practitioner texts and Internet resources

11.05   There really is no single practitioner text that covers in depth all the elements that make up the area of practice that is Commercial Property. There are various single topic practitioner texts and their selection is really a matter of choice for the partnership when building up the practice library. Of course some texts will spill over from mainstream conveyancing such as *Emmet on Title* or *Ruoff and Roper on the Law and Practice of Registered Conveyancing*. Similarly, if you wanted a text that covers all aspects of Landlord and Tenant work then there is either *Hill and Redman's Law of Landlord and Tenant* published by Butterworths or *Woodfall's Law of Landlord and Tenant* published by Sweet and Maxwell. Online access is available at <http://www.sweetandmaxwell.co.uk>. They will of course continue to be of relevance for commercial transactions. However we can recommend Ross, *Drafting and Negotiating Commercial Leases*, specifically for commercial leases and Reynolds and Clark, *Renewal of Business Tenancies*, for lease renewals.

Developments in information technology affect all aspects of commercial conveyancing. **11.06** The Internet is a significant and versatile source of research data that can assist commercial conveyancers in their daily tasks. There are free sites and subscription sites that are of help to commercial conveyancers. To assist we set out in appendix 1 a list of useful free access web sites. The subscription sites are made available usually by commercial publishing houses that have made their reference works available on the Internet. If you wish to access Internet sites please note, to save time, when using most of the leading web browsers, you can leave out the prefix http:// when inputting one of these site addresses. Web site addresses change frequently. If you have difficulty in locating any of these sites try searching for them using a web search site such as <http://www.google.co.uk> or <http://www.yahoo.co.uk> and by searching against the main title of the site itself, as listed in the appendix. This should produce a search result that will take you to the correct location.

Statutory detail

Printed copies of all legislation can be ordered from The Stationery Office (<http:// **11.07** www.tsoshop.co.uk>) Alternatively, online access is available for all statutes that are of interest to a commercial conveyancer from 1988 onward at <http://www.opsi.gov.uk>. Otherwise publishers such as the Oxford University Press regularly produce bound volumes of statutes relevant to a particular area of practice. While such a volume may not be specifically available for commercial conveyancing, they will certainly exist for Land or Property Law and if compiled with care should extend to the kinds of statutes covered in this book. Law publishers will also produce commentaries upon major reforming statutes such as the Land Registration Act 2002 with detailed commentary on each section of the particular Act in question. It is sometimes of benefit to see proposed new statutes and to do so Bills passing through Parliament can also be accessed online at <http://www.parliament. the-stationery-office.co.uk/pa/pabills.htm>.

Law reports

Bearing in mind the spread of topics that make up the specialism of commercial property, **11.08** most important decisions in this area will be covered by the Weekly Law Reports or the All England law reports or those published in the press such as The Times and The Independent. As you might anticipate, most of these reports are available on a subscription basis over the Internet. The publishers Butterworths provide such a service for The Times and All England while the Weekly Law Reports can be accessed through <http://www.justis.com>. Perhaps of more specialized interest to the commercial conveyancer will be the law reports in The Estates Gazette or the Property and Conveyancing Reports. Practitioners should bear in mind that cases reported may be those in the county court and as such are reports of decisions at first instance. It is entirely possible that decisions may be reversed or altered at the Court of Appeal or indeed in the House of Lords. Consequently, it is suggested that not too much reliance should be placed upon first instance decisions.

Forms and precedents

11.09 An up to date library of precedents will be a core resource for any successful practitioner. Inevitably the larger practices will have their own online database of commercial precedents covering most if not all of the typical transactions covered by the topics in this book. However, smaller practices may rely on other resources. For example, a subscription to the online Encyclopaedia of Forms and Precedents (available at <http://www.butterworths.com>) would be a cost effective solution and would make available many other precedents that will be of use to a busy practitioner. Furthermore each time you formulate a bespoke precedent, save it in a precedent area on your computer network so that you can build up your own library of useful precedents that will be available to you and your firm for future use.

11.10 Court forms relevant to lease renewal proceedings should be available from <http://www.hmcourts-service.gov.uk>.

Journals

11.11 Commercial conveyancers should subscribe to The Estates Gazette not just for the law reports it contains but also for the detailed articles it features regularly on the major topics of concern in the field of commercial property. The Landlord and Tenant Review can be of use as can the Law Society's Gazette. Indeed several of the generic legal publications such as the New Law Journal, the Solicitors Journal and The Lawyer can sometimes contain useful and provocative articles on relevant topics for commercial conveyancers.

C   CONTINUING YOUR PROFESSIONAL DEVELOPMENT

11.12 Every solicitor is required by the Law Society to participate in annual continuing professional development. It is an attempt by a regulator of the profession to ensure that practitioners do not allow their knowledge to become stale. However, any effective or successful commercial conveyancer will want to ensure his or her knowledge is as up to date as possible even without this element of compulsion. We set out below some ways in which this may be achieved.

Keeping yourself up to date

11.13 To do this a commercial conveyancer will need to keep up to date with statute, cases, and changes in practice. All these can be covered by making reference to practitioner updating journals such as The Practical Lawyer edited by John Pritchard and published monthly by Legalease Ltd and by attending accredited continuing professional development courses. The Practical Lawyer contains sections each month on developments in areas such as 'Landlord and Tenant—Commercial', 'Planning and Environment' and 'Conveyancing' generally. As such it seeks to cover many of the areas of concern for a commercial conveyancer. Otherwise reference to journals and publications listed above will assist in keeping knowledge current.

Further professional development

Another popular and effective way of participating in further professional development is to **11.14** attend a conference or course that offers updating information. This can be by internal or external courses. The larger practices will arrange their own internal courses while other firms can support their staff by encouraging them to attend external courses. They can be of value particularly if they are accredited, ie, when they provide points that contribute to a practitioner completing his or her annual requirements. Topics provided by external providers will cover virtually all the subject areas in this book and will naturally focus upon recent developments. There are several commercial providers of continuing professional development courses and these include:

Central Law Training—<http://www.clt.co.uk>
BPP—<http://www.bpp.co.uk>
Hawksmere Limited—<http://www.hawksmereltd.co.uk>
Henry Stewart Conference Studies—<http://www.henrystewart.com>
Quorum Training Limited—<http://www.quorumtraining.co.uk>

Law Society authorized CPD providers

There is a list of accredited course providers maintained by the Law Society at <http:// **11.15** www.lawsociety.org.uk/professional/continuing/accredited.law>.

The Law Society has authorized approximately 1,200 providers to offer training—on an **11.16** external basis—for Continuing Professional Development purposes, including providers of accredited distance-learning courses and accredited long-term courses. Details can be found via the Law Society website referred to above.

APPENDIX 1

Commercial Property Related Web Sites

The Internet web sites are listed alphabetically in this appendix. If you wish to access Internet sites, please note, to save time, when using most of the leading web browsers, that you can leave out the prefix 'http://' when inputting one of these site addresses. Web site addresses change frequently. If you have difficulty in locating any of these sites, try searching for them using a web search site such as <http://uk.yahoo.com> and by searching against the main title of the site itself. This should produce a search result that will take you to the correct location. Other search sites available include <http://www.alltheweb.com>, <http://www.lycos.co.uk>, <http://www.google.co.uk>, <http://uk.altavista.com> and <http://www.excite.co.uk>.

Acts of Parliament, <http://www.opsi.gov.uk/acts.htm>
Association of British Insurers, <http://www.abi.org.uk>
Association for Consultancy and Engineering, <http://www.acenet.co.uk>
Association for Geographic Information, <http://www.agi.org.uk>
Bank of England, <http://www.bankofengland.co.uk>
British Bankers Association, <http://www.bba.org.uk>
British Property Federation, <http://www.bpf.org.uk>
Centre for Ecology and Hydrology, <http://www.ceh.ac.uk>
Chartered Institute of Arbitrators, <http://www.arbitrators.org>
Chartered Institute of Bankers, <http://www.eubfn.com/cib-con.htm>
Chartered Institute of Taxation, <http://www.tax.org.uk>
Code of Practice for Commercial Leases in England and Wales, <http://www.commercial-leasecodeew.co.uk>
Companies House, <http://www.companieshouse.gov.uk>
Confederation of British Industry, <http://www.cbi.org.uk>
Council for Licensed Conveyancers, <http://www.conveyancer.org.uk>
Council of Mortgage Lenders, <http://www.cml.org.uk>
Department for Constitutional Affairs, <http://www.dca.gov.uk>
Department for Environment, Food and Rural Affairs, <http://www.defra.gov.uk>
Estates Gazette, <http://www.egi.co.uk>
Financial Services Authority, <http://www.fsa.gov.uk>
HM Revenue and Customs, <http://www.hmrc.gov.uk>
HM Treasury, <http://www.hm-treasury.gov.uk>
Health and Safety Executive, <http://www.hse.gov.uk>
Highways Agency, <http://www.highways.gov.uk>
Homecheck, <http://www.homecheck.co.uk>
House of Lords judgments, <http://www.parliament.the-stationery-office.co.uk/pa/ld199697/ldjudgmt/ldjudgmt.htm>
Housing Corporation, <http://www.housingcorp.gov.uk>
Housing Forum, <http://www.constructingexcellence.org.uk/sectors/housingforum>
International Union for Housing Finance, <http://www.housingfinance.org>
Land Registry, <http://www.landreg.gov.uk>
Land Registry internet register access, <http://www.landregistrydirect.gov.uk>
Landmark Information Group, <http://www.landmark-information.co.uk>

Lands Tribunal, <http://www.landstribunal.gov.uk>
Law Commission, <http://www.lawcom.gov.uk>
Law Gazette, <http://www.lawgazette.co.uk>
Law Society, <http://www.lawsociety.org.uk>
Location statistics, <http://www.upmystreet.com>
National Archives, <http://www.nationalarchives.gov.uk>
National Association of Estate Agents, <http://www.naea.co.uk>
National House Building Council, <http://www.nhbc.co.uk>
National Housing Federation, <http://www.housing.org.uk>
National Land Information Service, <http://www.nlis.org.uk>
National Statistics Online, <http://www.statistics.gov.uk>
Office of Public Sector Information, <http://www.opsi.gov.uk> (locate official documents)
Ordnance Survey, <http://www.ordnancesurvey.co.uk>
Practical Law Company, <http://www.practicallaw.com>
Registers of Scotland, <http://www.ros.gov.uk>
Royal Institute of British Architects, <http://www.riba.org>
Royal Institution of Chartered Surveyors, <http://www.rics.org.uk>
Royal Town Planning Institute, <http://www.rtpi.org.uk>
Service charges: Good Practice Guide, <http://www.servicechargeguide.propertymall.com>
Society of Construction Law, <http://www.scl.org.uk>
Street maps of the UK, <http://www.streetmap.co.uk>
UK Parliament, <http://www.parliament.uk>
Valuation Office Agency, <http://www.voa.gov.uk>
VAT Practitioners Group, <http://www.vpgweb.com>

Authorized Guarantee Agreement Precedent

Here we set out the basic terms that might be encountered in an Authorized Guarantee Agreement. It is in the condition that might be encountered in the office after it has been issued by the solicitor acting for the lessor, and after it has been reviewed and amended by the practitioners acting for the lessee and the proposed assignee. You will see improvements made to the original style as well as substantive changes, eg, the removal of the assignee as a party. This has been done because the assignee is not entering into any obligation by way of a covenant or otherwise and so the inclusion of the assignee is in effect superfluous. As is the convention in this book, deletions are shown with strike throughs and insertions with underlining.

This **AUTHORIZED GUARANTEE AGREEMENT** is made the   day

of   2006

Between:

(1)

of

(~~hereinafter called~~ 'the Lessor' which expression where the context admits includes its ~~(successors or assigns)~~ and

(2)

of

(~~hereinafter called~~ 'the Lessee')

~~(3)~~

~~of~~

~~(hereinafter called 'the Assignee')~~

WHEREAS:

(1) The reversion immediately expectant upon the determination of the term created by the lease of [*repeat the lease demise*] (~~hereinafter called~~ 'the Property') dated [*date of lease*] and made between [*original lease parties*] for a term of [*original term length*] (~~hereinafter called~~ 'the Term') commencing on [*start date*] (~~hereinafter called~~ 'the Lease') is vested in the Lessor.

(2) The Term created by the Lease is vested in the Lessee.

(3) The Lessee has applied to the Lessor for consent to an assignment of the residue of the Term to [*name and address of assignee*] ('the Assignee').

(4) The Lease terms require the consent of the Lessor prior to an assignment of the residue of the Term and the Lessor has agreed to give consent on condition that the Lessee enters into a form of Guarantee pursuant to the terms of s. 16 of the Landlord and Tenant (Covenants) Act 1995.

NOW IT IS AGREED AS FOLLOWS:

1. This agreement will take effect from the date of the giving of the Lessor's written consent to the assignment of the residue of the Term to the Assignee and shall remain in force while the Assignee is bound to comply with the covenants and conditions in the Lease.

2. The Lessee hereby guarantees that the Assignee will observe and perform all the covenants and conditions contained or referred to in the Lease for the tenant to perform from the date of the giving of the Lessor's written consent to the assignment of the residue of the Term to the Assignee until such time as the Assignee is released from those covenants and conditions pursuant to the terms of the Landlord and Tenant (Covenants) Act 1995.

3.   The Lessee covenants with the Lessor that:—

(1)   should the Lease assigned by ~~it~~ the Lessee be disclaimed by either a trustee in bankruptcy or a liquidator ~~it~~ the Lessee will enter into a new lease ('the New Lease') of the Property for a term commencing on the date of disclaimer and ending on the expiry date of the Lease at the rent payable at the time of disclaimer and upon the same terms and conditions of the Lease, and

(2)   the Lessee shall pay the Lessor's solicitor's reasonable costs for the preparation and completion of the New Lease.

4.   The liability of the Lessee under the terms of this agreement is not released or waived:—

(1)   because of any delay or failure by the Lessor at any time to enforce the terms of this agreement or

(2)   because the Lessor has refused rent from the Assignee as a consequence of ~~the lessor~~ there being subsisting breaches of any of the terms of the Lease.

AS WITNESS the hands of the parties ~~hereto set~~ the day and year first above written

Signed ~~for and on behalf of~~ by the Lessor
in the presence of:—

Signed ~~for and on behalf of~~ by the Lessee
in the presence of:—

APPENDIX 3

Law Society Standard Form Leases

Appendix 3

The Law Society

THE LAW SOCIETY BUSINESS LEASE (PART OF BUILDING)

DATE

LANDLORD

OF _____

LETS TO

TENANT

OF _____

THE PROPERTY KNOWN AS

PROPERTY

WHICH IS PART OF

BUILDING

(WHICH, WHEN REFERRED TO IN THIS LEASE, INCLUDES ITS GROUNDS) FOR THE PERIOD STARTING ON

LEASE PERIOD
_____ AND ENDING ON

USE ALLOWED
FOR USE AS

OR ANY OTHER USE TO WHICH THE LANDLORD CONSENTS (AND THE LANDLORD IS

NOT ENTITLED TO WITHHOLD THAT CONSENT UNREASONABLY)

THE TENANT PAYING THE LANDLORD RENT AT THE RATE OF

RENT
_____ POUNDS

(£ _____)

A YEAR BY THESE INSTALMENTS:

(A) ON THE DATE OF THIS LEASE, A PROPORTIONATE SUM FOR THE PERIOD

STARTING ON

_____ TO

_____ AND THEN

(B) EQUAL MONTHLY INSTALMENTS IN ADVANCE ON THE

RENT DAYS
_____ DAY OF EACH MONTH

THE RENT MAY BE INCREASED (UNDER CLAUSE 9) WITH EFFECT FROM EVERY

RENT REVIEW DATES
_____ ANNIVERSARY OF THE START OF THE LEASE PERIOD

This lease is granted on the terms printed on pages 2 to 5, as added to or varied by any terms appearing on page 6 or any attached continuation page.

Oyez   7 Spa Road, London SE16 3QQ
Oyez is an approved Law Society Supplier

2.2004 F42089
5037404

L.S.1 (Part)

TENANT'S OBLIGATIONS

1 PAYMENTS

1. The Tenant is to pay the Landlord:

1.1 the rent

1.2 the service charge in accordance with clause 3 (and this is to be paid as rent)

and the following sums on demand:

1.3 a fair proportion (decided by a surveyor the Landlord nominates) of the cost of repairing maintaining and cleaning:

party walls, party structures, yards, gardens, roads, paths, gutters, drains, sewers, pipes, conduits, wires, cables and things used or shared with other property

1.4 the cost (including professional fees) of any works to the property which the Landlord does after the Tenant defaults

1.5 the costs and expenses (including professional fees) which the Landlord incurs in:

(a) dealing with any application by the Tenant for consent or approval, whether or not it is given

(b) preparing and serving a notice of a breach of the Tenant's obligations, under section 146 of the Law of Property Act 1925, even if forfeiture of this lease is avoided without a court order.

(c) preparing and serving schedules of dilapidations either during the lease period or recording failure to give up the property in the appropriate state of repair when this lease ends

1.6 interest at the Law Society's interest rate on any of the above payments when more than fourteen days overdue, to be calculated from its due date

and in making payments under this clause:

(a) nothing is to be deducted or set off

(b) any value added tax payable is to be added.

2. The Tenant is also to make the following payments, with value added tax where payable:

2.1 all periodic rates, taxes and outgoings relating to the property, including any imposed after the date of this lease (even if of a novel nature), to be paid promptly to the authorities to whom they are due

2.2 the cost of the grant, renewal or continuation of any licence or registration for using the property for the use allowed, to be paid promptly to the appropriate authority when due

2.3 a registration fee of £20 for each document which this lease requires the Tenant to register to be paid to the Landlord's solicitors when presenting the document for registration

3 SERVICE CHARGE

3. The Landlord and the Tenant agree that:

3.1 the service charge is the Tenant's fair proportion of each item of the service costs

3.2 the service costs:

(a) are the costs which the Landlord fairly and reasonably incurs in complying with his obligations under clauses 12 and 13

(b) include the reasonable charges of any agent contractor consultant or employee whom the Landlord engages to provide the services under clauses 12 and 13

(c) include interest at no more than the Law Society's interest rate on sums the Landlord borrows to discharge his obligations under clauses 12 and 13

3.3 the Tenant is to pay the Landlord interim payments on account of the service charge within 21 days of receiving a written demand setting out how it is calculated

3.4 an interim payment is to be the Tenant's fair proportion of what the service costs are reasonably likely to be in the three months following the demand

3.5 the Landlord is not entitled to demand interim payments more than once in every three months

3.6 the Landlord is to keep full records of the service costs and at least once a year is to send the Tenant an account setting out, for the period since the beginning of the lease period or the last account as the case may be:

(a) the amount of the service costs

(b) the service charge the Tenant is to pay

(c) the total of any interim payments the Tenant has paid

(d) the difference between the total interim payments and the service charge

3.7 within 21 days after the Tenant receives the account, the amount mentioned in clause 3.6(d) is to be settled by payment between the parties except that the Landlord is entitled to retain any overpayment towards any interim payments he has demanded for a later accounting period

3.8 the Landlord is either:

(a) to have the account certified by an independent chartered accountant, or

(b) to allow the Tenant to inspect the books records invoices and receipts relating to the service costs

3.9 disagreements about the amounts of the service charge or the service costs are to be decided by arbitration under clause 17.5

4 USE

4. The Tenant is to comply with the following requirements as to the use of the building and any part of it, and is not to authorise or allow anyone else to contravene them:

4.1 to use the property only for the use allowed

4.2 not to obstruct any part of the building used for access to the property or any other part of the building

4.3 not to do anything which might invalidate any insurance policy covering any part of the building or which might increase the premium

4.4 not to hold an auction sale in the property

4.5 not to use any part of the building for any activities which are dangerous, offensive, noxious, illegal or immoral, or which are or may become a nuisance or annoyance to the Landlord or to the owner or occupier of any other part of the building or of any neighbouring property

4.6 not to display any advertisements on the outside of the property or which are visible from outside unless the Landlord consents (and the Landlord is not entitled to withhold that consent unreasonably)

4.7 not to overload the floors or walls of the property

4.8 to comply with the terms of every Act of Parliament, order, regulation, bye-law, rule, licence and registration authorising or regulating how the property is used, and to obtain, renew and continue any licence or registration which is required

5 ACCESS

5. The Tenant is to give the Landlord, or anyone authorised by him in writing, access to the property:

5.1 for these purposes:

(a) inspecting the condition of the property, or how it is being used

(b) doing works which the Landlord is permitted to do under clauses 6.11(c) or 13

(c) complying with any statutory obligation

(d) viewing the property as a prospective buyer, tenant or mortgagee

(e) valuing the property

(f) inspecting, cleaning or repairing neighbouring property, or any sewers, drains, pipes, wires, cables serving the building or any neighbouring property

5.2 and only on seven days' written notice except in an emergency

5.3 and during normal business hours except in an emergency

5.4 and the Landlord is promptly to make good all damage caused to the property and any goods there in exercising these rights

6 CONDITION AND WORK

6. The Tenant is to comply with the following duties in relation to the property:

6.1 to maintain the state and condition of the inside of the property but the Tenant need not alter or improve it except if required in clause 6.10

6.2 to decorate the inside of the property:

(a) in every fifth year of the lease period

(b) in the last three months of the lease period (however it ends) except to the extent that it has been decorated in the previous year

6.3 where the property has a shop front to maintain and decorate it

6.4 when decorating, the Tenant is to use the colours and the types of finish used previously

6.5 but the Tenant need only make good damage caused by an insured risk to the extent that the insurance money has not been paid because of any act or default of the Tenant

6.6 the inside of the property is to include all ceilings, floors, doors, door frames, windows, window frames and plate glass and the internal surfaces of all walls but is to exclude joists immediately above the ceilings and supporting floors

6.7 not to make any structural alterations, external alterations or additions to the property

6.8 not to make any other alterations unless with the Landlord's consent in writing (and the Landlord is not entitled to withhold that consent unreasonably)

6.9 to keep any plate glass in the property insured for its full replacement cost with reputable insurers, to give the Landlord details of that insurance on request, and to replace any plate glass which becomes damaged

6.10 to do the work to the property which any authority acting under an Act of Parliament requires even if it alters or improves the property. Before the Tenant does so, the Landlord is to:

(a) give his consent in writing to the work

(b) contribute a fair proportion of the cost of the work taking into account any value to him of that work

6.11 if the Tenant fails to do any work which this lease requires him to do and the Landlord gives him written notice to do it, the Tenant is to:

(a) start the work within two months, or immediately in case of emergency, and

(b) proceed diligently with the work

(c) in default, permit the Landlord to do the work

6.12 any dispute arising under clause 6.10(b) is to be decided by arbitration under clause 17.5

7 TRANSFER ETC.

7. The Tenant is to comply with the following:

7.1 the Tenant is not to share occupation of the property and no part of it is to be transferred, sublet or occupied separately from the remainder

7.2 the Tenant is not to transfer or sublet the whole of the property unless the Landlord gives his written consent in advance, and the Landlord is not entitled to withhold that consent unreasonably

7.3 any sublease is to be on terms which are consistent with this lease, but is not to permit the sub-tenant to underlet

7.4 within four weeks after the property is transferred mortgaged or sublet, the Landlord's solicitors are to be notified and a copy of the transfer mortgage or sublease sent to them for registration with the fee payable under clause 2.3

7.5 If the Landlord requires, a Tenant who transfers the whole of the property is to give the Landlord a written guarantee, in the terms set out in the Guarantee Box, that the Transferee will perform his obligations as Tenant

8 OTHER MATTERS

8. The Tenant:

8.1 is to give the Landlord a copy of any notice concerning the property or any neighbouring property as soon as he receives it

8.2 is to allow the Landlord, during the last six months of the lease period, to fix a notice in a reasonable position on the outside of the property announcing that it is for sale or to let

8.3 is not to apply for planning permission relating to the use or alteration of the property unless the Landlord gives written consent in advance

9 RENT REVIEW

9.1 On each rent review date, the rent is to increase to the market rent if that is higher than the rent applying before that date

9.2 The market rent is the rent which a willing tenant would pay for the property on the open market, if let to him on the rent review date by a willing Landlord on a lease on the same terms as this lease without any premium and for a period equal to the remainder of the lease period, assuming that at that date:

(a) the willing Tenant takes account of any likelihood that he would be entitled to a new lease of the property when the lease ends, but does not take account of any goodwill belonging to anyone who had occupied the property;

(b) the property is vacant and had not been occupied by the Tenant or any sub-tenant;

(c) the property can immediately be used;

(d) the property is in the condition required by this lease and any damage caused by any of the risks insured under clause 12 has been made good;

(e) during the lease period no Tenant or sub-tenant has done anything to the property to increase or decrease its rental value and "anything" includes work done by the Tenant to comply with clause 6.10, but nothing else which the Tenant was obliged to do under this lease

9.3 If the Landlord and the Tenant agree the amount of the new rent, a statement of that new rent, signed by them, is to be attached to this lease

9.4 If the Landlord and the Tenant have not agreed the amount of the new rent two months before the rent review date, either of them may require the new rent to be decided by arbitration under clause 17.5

9.5

(a) The Tenant is to continue to pay rent at the rate applying before the rent review date until the next rent day after the new rent is agreed or decided

(b) Starting on that rent day, the Tenant is to pay the new rent

(c) On that rent day, the Tenant is also to pay any amount by which the new rent since the rent review date exceeds the rent paid, with interest on that amount at 2% below the Law Society's interest rate

10 DAMAGE

10. If the property is or the common parts are damaged by any of the risks to be insured under clause 12 and as a result of that damage the property, or any part of it, cannot be used for the use allowed:

10.1 the rent, or fair proportion of it, is to be suspended for three years or until the property or the common parts are fully restored, if sooner

10.2 if at any time it is unlikely that the property or the common parts will be fully restored within three years from the date of the damage, the Landlord (so long as he has not wilfully delayed the restoration) or the Tenant may end this lease by giving one month's notice to the other during the three year period, in which case:

(a) the insurance money belongs to the Landlord and

(b) the Landlord's obligation to make good damage under clause 12 ceases

10.3 a notice given outside the time limits in clause 10.2 is not effective

10.4 The Tenant cannot claim the benefit of this clause to the extent that the insurers refuse to pay the insurance money because of his act or default

10.5 any dispute arising under any part of this clause is to be decided by arbitration under clause 17.5

LANDLORD'S OBLIGATIONS AND FORFEITURE RIGHTS

11 QUIET ENJOYMENT

11. While the Tenant complies with the terms of this lease, the Landlord is to allow the Tenant to possess and use the property without lawful interference from the Landlord, anyone who derives title from the Landlord or any trustee for the Landlord

12 INSURANCE

12. The Landlord agrees with the Tenant:

12.1 the Landlord is to keep the building (except the plate glass) insured with reputable insurers to cover:

(a) full rebuilding, site clearance, professional fees, value added tax and three years' loss of rent

(b) against fire, lightning, explosion, earthquake, landslip, subsidence, heave, riot, civil commotion, aircraft, aerial devices, storm, flood, water, theft, impact by vehicles, damage by malicious persons and vandals and third party liability and any other risks reasonably required by the Landlord

so far as cover is available at the normal insurance rates for the locality and subject to reasonable excesses and exclusions

12.2 and to take all necessary steps to make good as soon as possible damage to the building caused by insured risks except to the extent that the insurance money is not paid because of the act or default of the Tenant

12.3 and to give the Tenant at his request once a year particulars of the policy and evidence from the insurer that it is in force

12.4 and that the Tenant is not responsible for any damage for which the Landlord is compensated under the insurance policy

13 SERVICES

13. The Landlord is to comply with the following duties in relation to the building:

13.1 to maintain the state and condition (including the decorations) of:

(a) the structure, outside, roof, foundations, joists, floor slabs, load bearing walls, beams and columns of the building

(b) those parts of the building which Tenants of more than one part can use ("the common parts")

13.2 to decorate the common parts and the outside of the building every five years, using colours and types of finish reasonably decided by the Landlord

13.3 to pay promptly all periodic rates, taxes and outgoings relating to the common parts, including any imposed after the date of this lease (even if of a novel nature)

13.4 to pay or contribute to the cost of repairing, maintaining, and cleaning party walls, party structures, yards, gardens, roads, paths, gutters, drains, sewers, pipes, conduits, wires, cables and other things used or shared with other property

13.5 to provide the services listed on page 5, but the Landlord is not to be liable for failure or delay caused by industrial disputes, shortage of supplies, adverse weather conditions or other causes beyond the control of the Landlord

14 FORFEITURE

14. This lease comes to an end if the Landlord forfeits it by entering any part of the property, which the Landlord is entitled to do whenever:

(a) payment of any rent is fourteen days overdue, even if it was not formally demanded

(b) the Tenant has not complied with any of the terms in this lease

(c) the Tenant if an individual (and if more than one, any of them) is adjudicated bankrupt or an interim receiver of his property is appointed

(d) the Tenant if a company (and if more than one, any of them) goes into liquidation (unless solely for the purpose of amalgamation or reconstruction when solvent), or has an administrative receiver appointed or has an administration order made in respect of it

The forfeiture of this lease does not cancel any outstanding obligation of the Tenant or a Guarantor

15 END OF LEASE

15. When this lease ends the Tenant is to:

15.1 return the property to the Landlord leaving it in the state and condition in which this lease requires the Tenant to keep it

15.2 (if the Landlord so requires) remove anything the Tenant fixed to the property and make good any damage which that causes

PROPERTY RIGHTS

16 BOUNDARIES

16.1 This lease does not let to the Tenant the external surfaces of the outside walls of the property and anything above the ceilings and below the floors

FACILITIES

16.2 The Tenant is to have the use, whether or not exclusive, of any of the following facilities:

the right for the Tenant and visitors to come and go to and from the property over the parts of the building designed or designated to afford access to the property, the rights previously enjoyed by the property for shelter and support and for service wires, pipes and drains to pass through them, and the right to park vehicles in any designated parking area subject to any reasonable rules made by the Landlord

16.3 The Landlord is to have the right previously enjoyed over the property by other parts of the building for shelter and support and for service wires, pipes and drains to pass through it, and the right for the Landlord and his Tenants and their visitors to come and go to and from the other parts of the property over the parts of the property designated for that purpose

GENERAL

17 PARTIES' RESPONSIBILITY

17.1 Whenever more than one person or company is the Landlord, the Tenant or the Guarantor, their obligations can be enforced against all or both of them jointly and against each individually

LANDLORD

17.2

(a) The obligations in this lease continue to apply to the Landlord until he is released by the Tenant or by a declaration of the court

(b) The current owner of the Landlord's interest in the property must comply with the Landlord's obligations in this lease

TENANT

17.3

(a) A transfer of this lease releases the Tenant from any future obligations under it. This does not apply in the case of a transfer made without the Landlord's consent or as a result of the Tenant's death or bankruptcy

(b) After a transfer, the Tenant's successor must comply with the Tenant's obligations in this lease

SERVICE OF NOTICE

17.4 The rules about serving notices in Section 196 of the Law of Property Act 1925 (as since amended) apply to any notice given under this lease

ARBITRATION

17.5 Any matter which this lease requires to be decided by arbitration is to be referred to a single arbitrator under the Arbitration Act 1996. The Landlord and the Tenant may agree the appointment of the arbitrator, or either of them may apply to the President of the Royal Institution of Chartered Surveyors to make the appointment

HEADINGS

17.6 The headings do not form part of this lease

18 STAMP DUTY

This lease has not been granted to implement an agreement for a lease

These are the services mentioned in clause 13.5
(delete or add as required)

Cleaning of the common parts

Lighting of the common parts

Heating of the common parts

Lift maintenance

Hot and cold water to wash hand basins in the common parts

Porterage

Fire extinguishers in the common parts

Heating in the property

Window cleaning for the building

Furnishing the common parts

GUARANTEE BOX

The terms in this box only take effect if a guarantor is named and then only until the Tenant transfers this lease with the Landlord's written consent. The Guarantor must sign this lease.

'Guarantor':

of

agrees to compensate the Landlord for any loss incurred as a result of the Tenant failing to comply with an obligation in this lease during the lease period or any statutory extension of it. If the Tenant is insolvent and this lease ends because it is disclaimed, the Guarantor agrees to accept a new lease, if the Landlord so requires, in the same form but at the rent then payable. Even if the Landlord gives the Tenant extra time to comply with an obligation, or does not insist on strict compliance with terms of this lease, the Guarantor's obligation remains fully effective.

THIS DOCUMENT CREATES LEGAL RIGHTS AND LEGAL OBLIGATIONS. DO NOT SIGN IT UNTIL YOU HAVE CONSULTED A SOLICITOR. THERE IS A CODE OF PRACTICE CONCERNING COMMERCIAL LEASES IN ENGLAND AND WALES PUBLISHED UNDER THE AUSPICES OF THE DEPARTMENT OF THE ENVIRONMENT.

Signed as a deed by/on behalf of the
Landlord and delivered in the presence of:

....

Landlord

Witness

....

Witness's occupation and address

....

Signed as a deed by/on behalf of the
Tenant and delivered in the presence of:

....

Tenant

Witness

....

Witness's occupation and address

....

Signed as a deed by/on behalf of the
Guarantor and delivered in the presence of:

....

Guarantor

Witness

....

Witness's occupation and address

....

The Law Society

DATE

LANDLORD

OF

LETS TO

TENANT

OF

THE PROPERTY KNOWN AS

PROPERTY

RESIDENTIAL
ACCOMMODATION

[WHICH INCLUDES

]

FOR THE PERIOD STARTING ON

LEASE PERIOD

AND ENDING ON

FOR USE (EXCEPT ANY RESIDENTIAL ACCOMMODATION) AS

USE ALLOWED

OR ANY OTHER USE TO WHICH THE LANDLORD CONSENTS (AND THE LANDLORD IS

NOT ENTITLED TO WITHHOLD THAT CONSENT UNREASONABLY)

THE TENANT PAYING THE LANDLORD RENT AT THE RATE OF

RENT

POUNDS

(£   )

A YEAR BY THESE INSTALMENTS:

(A) ON THE DATE OF THIS LEASE, A PROPORTIONATE SUM FOR THE PERIOD

STARTING ON

TO

AND THEN

(B) EQUAL MONTHLY INSTALMENTS IN ADVANCE ON THE

RENT DAYS

DAY OF EACH MONTH

THE RENT MAY BE INCREASED (UNDER CLAUSE 8) WITH EFFECT FROM EVERY

RENT REVIEW DATES

ANNIVERSARY OF THE START OF THE LEASE PERIOD

This lease is granted on the terms printed on pages 2 to 4, as added to or varied by any terms appearing on any attached continuation page.

Oyez 7 Spa Road, London SE16 3QQ
Oyez is an approved Law Society Supplier

4.2004 F42306
5037446

L.S.2 (Whole)

TENANT'S OBLIGATIONS

1 PAYMENTS

1. The Tenant is to pay the Landlord:

1.1 the rent

1.2 the amount of every premium which the Landlord pays to insure the property under this lease, to be paid within 14 days after the Landlord gives written notice of payment (and this amount is to be paid as rent)

and the following sums on demand:

1.3 a fair proportion (decided by a surveyor the Landlord nominates) of the cost of repairing maintaining and cleaning:

party walls, party structures, yards, gardens, roads, paths, gutters, drains, sewers, pipes, conduits, wires, cables and things used or shared with other property

1.4 the cost (including professional fees) of any works to the property which the Landlord does after the Tenant defaults

1.5 the costs and expenses (including professional fees) which the Landlord incurs in:

(a) dealing with any application by the Tenant for consent or approval, whether or not it is given

(b) preparing and serving a notice of a breach of the Tenant's obligations, under section 146 of the Law of Property Act 1925, even if forfeiture of this lease is avoided without a court order

(c) preparing and serving schedules of dilapidations either during the lease period or recording failure to give up the property in the appropriate state of repair when this lease ends

1.6 interest at the Law Society's interest rate on any of the above payments when more than fourteen days overdue, to be calculated from its due date

and in making payment under this clause:

(a) nothing is to be deducted or set off

(b) any value added tax payable is to be added.

2

2. The Tenant is also to make the following payments, with value added tax where payable:

2.1 all periodic rates, taxes and outgoings relating to the property, including any imposed after the date of this lease (even if of a novel nature), to be paid promptly to the authorities to whom they are due

2.2 the cost of the grant, renewal or continuation of any licence or registration for using the property for the use allowed, to be paid promptly to the appropriate authority when due

2.3 a registration fee of £20 for each document which this lease requires the Tenant to register, to be paid to the Landlord's solicitors when presenting the document for registration

3 USE

3. The Tenant is to comply with the following requirements as to the use of the property and any part of it and is not to authorise or allow anyone else to contravene them:

3.1 to use the property, except any residential accommodation, only for the use allowed

3.2 to use any residential accommodation only as a home for one family

3.3 not to do anything which might invalidate any insurance policy covering the property or which might increase the premium

3.4 not to hold an auction sale in the property

3.5 not to use the property for any activities which are dangerous, offensive, noxious, illegal or immoral, or which are or may become a nuisance or annoyance to the Landlord or to the owner or occupier of any neighbouring property

3.6 not to display any advertisements on the outside of the property or which are visible from the outside unless the Landlord consents (and the Landlord is not entitled to withhold that consent unreasonably)

3.7 not to overload the floors or walls of the property

3.8 to comply with the terms of every Act of Parliament, order, regulation, bye-law, rule, licence and registration authorising or regulating how the property is used, and to obtain, renew and continue any licence or registration which is required

4 ACCESS

4. The Tenant is to give the Landlord, or anyone authorised by him in writing, access to the property:

4.1 for these purposes:

(a) inspecting the condition of the property, or how it is being used

(b) doing works which the Landlord is permitted to do under clause 5.8(c)

(c) complying with any statutory obligation

(d) viewing the property as a prospective buyer or mortgagee or, during the last six months of the lease period, as a prospective Tenant

(e) valuing the property

(f) inspecting, cleaning or repairing neighbouring property, or any sewers, drains, pipes, wires, cables serving neighbouring property

4.2 and only on seven days' written notice except in an emergency

4.3 and during normal business hours except in an emergency

4.4 and the Landlord is promptly to make good all damage caused to the property and any goods there in exercising these rights

5 CONDITION AND WORK

5. The Tenant is to comply with the following duties in relation to the property:

5.1 to maintain the state and condition of the property but the Tenant need not alter or improve it except if required under clause 5.7

5.2 to decorate the inside and outside of the property:

(a) in every fifth year of the lease period

(b) in the last three months of the lease period (however it ends) except to the extent that it has been decorated in the previous year

and on each occasion the Tenant is to use the colours and the types of finish used previously

5.3 but the Tenant need only make good damage caused by an insured risk to the extent that the insurance money has not been paid because of any act or default of the Tenant

5.4 not to make any structural alterations, external alterations or additions to the property

5.5 not to make any other alterations unless with the Landlord's consent in writing (and the Landlord is not entitled to withhold that consent unreasonably)

5.6 to keep any plate glass in the property insured for its full replacement cost with reputable insurers, to give the Landlord details of that insurance on request, and to replace any plate glass which becomes damaged

5.7 to do the work to the property which any authority acting under an Act of Parliament requires, even if it alters or improves the property. Before the Tenant does so, the Landlord is to:

(a) give his consent in writing to the work

(b) contribute a fair proportion of the cost of the work taking into account any value to him of that work

5.8 if the Tenant fails to do any work which this lease requires him to do and the Landlord gives him written notice to do it, the Tenant is to:

(a) start the work within two months, or immediately in case of emergency, and

(b) proceed diligently with the work

(c) in default, permit the Landlord to do the work

5.9 any dispute arising under clause 5.7(b) is to be decided by arbitration under clause 14.5

6 TRANSFER ETC.

6. The Tenant is to comply with the following:

6.1 the Tenant is not to share occupation of the property and no part of it is to be transferred, sublet or occupied separately from the remainder.

6.2 the Tenant is not to transfer or sublet the whole of the property unless the Landlord gives his written consent in advance, and the Landlord is not entitled to withhold that consent unreasonably

6.3 any sublease is to be in terms which are consistent with this lease, but is not to permit the sub-tenant to underlet

6.4 within four weeks after the property is transferred mortgaged or sublet, the Landlord's solicitors are to be notified and a copy of the transfer mortgage or sublease sent to them for registration with the fee payable under clause 2.3

6.5 if the Landlord requires, a Tenant who transfers the whole of the property is to give the Landlord a written guarantee, in the terms set out in the Guarantee Box, that the Transferee will perform his obligations as Tenant

7 OTHER MATTERS

7. The Tenant:

7.1 is to give the Landlord a copy of any notice concerning the property or any neighbouring property as soon as he receives it

7.2 is to allow the Landlord, during the last six months of the lease period, to fix a notice in a reasonable position on the outside of the property announcing that it is for sale or to let

7.3 is not to apply for planning permission relating to the use or alteration of the property unless the Landlord gives written consent in advance

8 RENT REVIEW

8.1 On each rent review date, the rent is to increase to the market rent if that is higher than the rent applying before that date

8.2 the market rent is the rent which a willing Tenant would pay for the property on the open market, if let to him on the rent review date by a willing Landlord on a lease on the same terms as this lease without any premium and for a period equal to the remainder of the lease period, assuming that at that date:

(a) the willing Tenant takes account of any likelihood that he would be entitled to a new lease of the property when the lease ends, but does not take account of any goodwill belonging to anyone who had occupied the property

(b) the property is vacant and had not been occupied by the Tenant or any sub-tenant

(c) the property can immediately be used

(d) the property is in the condition required by this lease and any damage caused by any of the risks insured under clause 11 has been made good

(e) during the lease period no Tenant or sub-tenant has done anything to the property to increase or decrease its rental value and "anything" includes work done by the Tenant to comply with clause 5.7, but nothing else which the Tenant was obliged to do under this lease.

8.3 If the Landlord and the Tenant agree the amount of the new rent, a statement of that new rent signed by them, is to be attached to this lease

8.4 If the Landlord and the Tenant have not agreed the amount of the new rent two months before the rent review date, either of them may require the new rent to be decided by arbitration under clause 14.5

8.5

(a) the Tenant is to continue to pay rent at the rate applying before the rent review date until the next rent day after the new rent is agreed or decided

(b) starting on that rent day, the Tenant is to pay the new rent

(c) on that rent day, the Tenant is also to pay any amount by which the new rent since the rent review date exceeds the rent paid, with interest on that amount at 2% below the Law Society's interest rate

9 DAMAGE

9. If the property is damaged by any of the risks to be insured under clause 11 and as a result of that damage the property, or any part of it, cannot be used for the use allowed:

9.1 the rent, or a fair proportion of it, is to be suspended for three years or until the property is fully restored, if sooner

9.2 if at any time it is unlikely that the property will be fully restored within three years from the date of the damage, the Landlord (so long as he has not delayed the restoration) or the Tenant can end this lease by giving one month's notice to the other during the three year period, in which case

(a) the insurance money belongs to the Landlord and

(b) the Landlord's obligation to make good damage under clause 11 ceases

9.3 a notice given outside the time limits in clause 9.2 is not effective

9.4 the Tenant cannot claim the benefit of this clause to the extent that the insurers refuse to pay the insurance money because of his act or default

9.5 any dispute arising under any part of this clause is to be decided by arbitration under clause 14.5

10 LANDLORD'S OBLIGATIONS AND FORFEITURE RIGHTS

QUIET ENJOYMENT

10. While the Tenant complies with the terms of this lease, the Landlord is to allow the Tenant to possess and use the property without lawful interference from the Landlord, anyone who derives title from the Landlord or any trustee for the Landlord

11 INSURANCE

11. The Landlord agrees with the Tenant:

11.1 the Landlord is to keep the property (except the plate glass) insured with reputable insurers to cover:

(a) full rebuilding, site clearance, professional fees, value added tax and three years' loss of rent

(b) against fire, lightning, explosion, earthquake, landslip, subsidence, heave, riot, civil commotion, aircraft, aerial devices, storm, flood, water, theft, impact by vehicles, damage by malicious persons and vandals and third party liability and any other risks reasonably required by the Landlord

so far as cover is available at the normal insurance rates for the locality and subject to reasonable excesses and exclusions

11.2 and to take all necessary steps to make good as soon as possible damage to the property caused by insured risks except to the extent the insurance money is not paid because of the act or default of the Tenant

11.3 and to give the Tenant at his request once a year particulars of the policy and evidence from the insurer that it is in force

11.4 and that the Tenant is not responsible for any damage for which the Landlord is compensated under the insurance policy

12 FORFEITURE

12. This lease comes to an end if the Landlord forfeits it by entering any part of the property, which the Landlord is entitled to do whenever:

(a) payment of any rent is fourteen days overdue, even if it was not formally demanded

(b) the Tenant has not complied with any of the terms in this lease

(c) the Tenant if an individual (and if more than one, any of them) is adjudicated bankrupt or an interim receiver of his property is appointed

(d) the Tenant if a company (and if more than one, any of them) goes into liquidation (unless solely for the purpose of amalgamation or reconstruction when solvent), or has an administrative receiver appointed or has an administration order made in respect of it

The forfeiture of this lease does not cancel any outstanding obligation of the Tenant or a Guarantor

13 END OF LEASE

13. When this lease ends the Tenant is to:

13.1 return the property to the Landlord leaving it in the state and condition in which this lease requires the Tenant to keep it

13.2 (if the Landlord so requires) remove anything the Tenant fixed to the property and make good any damage which that causes

GENERAL

14 PARTIES' RESPONSIBILITY

14.1 Whenever more than one person or company is the Landlord, the Tenant or the Guarantor, their obligations can be enforced against all or both of them jointly and against each individually

LANDLORD

14.2 (a) The obligations in this lease continue to apply to the Landlord until he is released by the Tenant or by a declaration of the court

(b) The current owner of the Landlord's interest in the property must comply with the Landlord's obligations in this lease

TENANT

14.3 (a) A transfer of this lease releases the Tenant from any future obligations under it. This does not apply in the case of a transfer made without the Landlord's consent or as a result of the Tenant's death or bankruptcy

(b) After a transfer, the Tenant's successor must comply with the Tenant's obligations in this lease

SERVICE OF NOTICES

14.4 The rules about serving notices in Section 196 of the Law of Property Act 1925 (as since amended) apply to any notice given under this lease

ARBITRATION

14.5 Any matter which this lease requires to be decided by arbitration is to be referred to a single arbitrator under the Arbitration Acts. The Landlord and the Tenant may agree the appointment of the arbitrator, or either of them may apply to the President of the Royal Institution of Chartered Surveyors to make the appointment

HEADINGS

14.6 The headings do not form part of this lease.

15 STAMP DUTY

This lease has not been granted to implement an agreement for a lease

---

GUARANTEE BOX

The terms in this box only take effect if a guarantor is named and then only until the Tenant transfers this lease with the Landlord's written consent. The Guarantor must sign this lease.

'Guarantor':

of

agrees to compensate the Landlord for any loss incurred as a result of the Tenant failing to comply with an obligation in this lease during the lease period or any statutory extension of it. If the Tenant is insolvent and this lease ends because it is disclaimed, the Guarantor agrees to accept a new lease, if the Landlord so requires, in the same form but at the rent then payable. Even if the Landlord gives the Tenant extra time to comply with an obligation, or does not insist on strict compliance with terms of this lease, the Guarantor's obligation remains fully effective.

THIS DOCUMENT CREATES LEGAL RIGHTS AND LEGAL OBLIGATIONS. DO NOT SIGN IT UNTIL YOU HAVE CONSULTED A SOLICITOR. THERE IS A CODE OF PRACTICE CONCERNING COMMERCIAL LEASES IN ENGLAND AND WALES PUBLISHED UNDER THE AUSPICES OF THE DEPARTMENT OF THE ENVIRONMENT.

Signed as a deed by/on behalf of the
Landlord and delivered in the presence of:

Landlord

Witness

Witness's occupation and address

Signed as a deed by/on behalf of the
Tenant and delivered in the presence of:

Tenant

Witness

Witness's occupation and address

Signed as a deed by/on behalf of the
Guarantor and delivered in the presence of:

Guarantor

Witness

Witness's occupation and address

The Law Society

APPENDIX 4

Standard Commercial Property Conditions (2nd edn)

CONTRACT
Incorporating the Standard Commercial Property Conditions (Second Edition)

Date   :

Seller

Buyer   :

Property   :
(freehold/leasehold)

Title Number/Root of title   :

Specified incumbrances   :

Completion date   :

Contract rate   :

Purchase price   :

Deposit   :

The seller will sell and the buyer will buy:

(a) the property, and

(b) any chattels which, under the special conditions, are included in the sale

for the purchase price.

WARNING	Signed
This is a formal document, designed to create legal rights and legal obligations. Take advice before using it.	Authorised to sign on behalf of Seller/Buyer

Standard Commercial Property Conditions (2nd edn)

PART 1

1. GENERAL

1.1 Definitions

1.1.1   In these conditions:

   (a)   "accrued interest" means:

      (i)   if money has been placed on deposit or in a building society share account, the interest actually earned

      (ii)   otherwise, the interest which might reasonably have been earned by depositing the money at interest on seven days' notice of withdrawal with a clearing bank less, in either case, any proper charges for handling the money

   (b)   "apportionment day" has the meaning given in condition 8.3.2

   (c)   "clearing bank" means a bank which is a shareholder in CHAPS Clearing Co. Limited

   (d)   "completion date" has the meaning given in condition 8.1.1

   (e)   "contract rate" is the Law Society's interest rate from time to time in force

   (f)   "conveyancer" means a solicitor, barrister, duly certified notary public, licensed conveyancer or recognised body under sections 9 or 23 of the Administration of Justice Act 1985

   (g)   "direct credit" means a direct transfer of cleared funds to an account nominated by the seller's conveyancer and maintained at a clearing bank

   (h)   "election to waive exemption" means an election made under paragraph 2 of Schedule 10 to the Value Added Tax Act 1994

   (i)   "lease" includes sub-lease, tenancy and agreement for a lease or sub-lease

   (j)   "notice to complete" means a notice requiring completion of the contract in accordance with condition 8

   (k)   "post" includes a service provided by a person licensed under the Postal Services Act 2000

   (l)   "public requirement" means any notice, order or proposal given or made (whether before or after the date of the contract) by a body acting on statutory authority

   (m)   "requisition" includes objection

   (n)   "transfer" includes conveyance and assignment

   (o)   "working day" means any day from Monday to Friday (inclusive) which is not Christmas Day, Good Friday or a statutory Bank Holiday.

1.1.2   In these conditions the terms "absolute title" and "official copies" have the special meanings given to them by the Land Registration Act 2002.

1.1.3   A party is ready, able and willing to complete:

   (a)   if it could be, but for the default of the other party, and

   (b)   in the case of the seller, even though a mortgage remains secured on the property, if the amount to be paid on completion enables the property to be transferred freed of all mortgages (except those to which the sale is expressly subject).

1.1.4   (a)   The conditions in Part 1 apply except as varied or excluded by the contract.

   (b)   A condition in Part 2 only applies if expressly incorporated into the contract.

1.2 Joint parties

If there is more than one seller or more than one buyer, the obligations which they undertake can be enforced against them all jointly or against each individually.

1.3   Notices and documents

1.3.1   A notice required or authorised by the contract must be in writing.

1.3.2   Giving a notice or delivering a document to a party's conveyancer has the same effect as giving or delivering it to that party.

1.3.3   Where delivery of the original document is not essential, a notice or document is validly given or sent if it is sent:

   (a)   by fax, or

   (b)   by e-mail to an e-mail address for the intended recipient given in the contract.

1.3.4   Subject to conditions 1.3.5 to 1.3.7, a notice is given and a document delivered when it is received.

1.3.5   (a)   A notice or document sent through the document exchange is received when it is available for collection

   (b)   A notice or document which is received after 4.00 p.m. on a working day, or on a day which is not a working day, is to be treated as having been received on the next working day

   (c)   An automated response to a notice or document sent by e-mail that the intended recipient is out of the office is to be treated as proof that the notice or document was not received.

1.3.6   Condition 1.3.7 applies unless there is proof:

   (a)   that a notice or document has not been received, or

   (b)   of when it was received.

1.3.7   Unless the actual time of receipt is proved, a notice or document sent by the following means is treated as having been received as follows:

   (a)   by first class post: before 4.00 pm on the second working day after posting
   (b)   by second-class post: before 4.00 pm on the third working day after posting
   (c)   through a document   before 4.00 pm on the first working day after the day on which
         exchange: it would normally be available for collection by the addressee
   (d)   by fax: one hour after despatch
   (e)   by e-mail: before 4.00 p.m. on the first working day after despatch.

1.3.8   In condition 1.3.7, "first class post" means a postal service which seeks to deliver posted items no later than the next working day in all or the majority of cases.

1.4   VAT

1.4.1   The seller:

   (a)   warrants that the sale of the property does not constitute a supply that is taxable for VAT purposes

   (b)   agrees that there will be no exercise of the election to waive exemption in respect of the property, and

   (c)   cannot require the buyer to pay any amount in respect of any liability to VAT arising in respect of the sale of the property, unless condition 1.4.2 applies.

1.4.2   If, solely as a result of a change in law made and coming into effect between the date of the contract and completion, the sale of the property will constitute a supply chargeable to VAT, the buyer is to pay to the seller on completion an additional amount equal to that VAT in exchange for a proper VAT invoice from the seller.

1.4.3   The amount payable for the chattels is exclusive of VAT and the buyer is to pay to the seller on completion an additional amount equal to any VAT charged on that supply in exchange for a proper VAT invoice from the seller.

1.5 Assignment and sub-sales

1.5.1 The buyer is not entitled to transfer the benefit of the contract.

1.5.2 The seller may not be required to transfer the property in parts or to any person other than the buyer.

2. FORMATION

2.1 Date

2.1.1 If the parties intend to make a contract by exchanging duplicate copies by post or through a document exchange, the contract is made when the last copy is posted or deposited at the document exchange.

2.1.2 If the parties' conveyancers agree to treat exchange as taking place before duplicate copies are actually exchanged, the contract is made as so agreed.

2.2 Deposit

2.2.1 The buyer is to pay a deposit of 10 per cent of the purchase price no later than the date of the contract.

2.2.2 Except on a sale by auction the deposit is to be paid by direct credit and is to be held by the seller's conveyancer as stakeholder on terms that on completion it is to be paid to the seller with accrued interest.

2.3 Auctions

2.3.1 On a sale by auction the following conditions apply to the property and, if it is sold in lots, to each lot.

2.3.2 The sale is subject to a reserve price.

2.3.3 The seller, or a person on its behalf, may bid up to the reserve price.

2.3.4 The auctioneer may refuse any bid.

2.3.5 If there is a dispute about a bid, the auctioneer may resolve the dispute or restart the auction at the last undisputed bid.

2.3.6 The auctioneer is to hold the deposit as agent for the seller.

2.3.7 If any cheque tendered in payment of all or part of the deposit is dishonoured when first presented, the seller may, within seven working days of being notified that the cheque has been dishonoured, give notice to the buyer that the contract is discharged by the buyer's breach.

3. MATTERS AFFECTING THE PROPERTY

3.1 Freedom from incumbrances

3.1.1. The seller is selling the property free from incumbrances, other than those mentioned in condition 3.1.2.

3.1.2 The incumbrances subject to which the property is sold are:

(a) those specified in the contract

(b) those discoverable by inspection of the property before the contract

(c) those the seller does not and could not reasonably know about

(d) matters, other than monetary charges or incumbrances, disclosed or which would have been disclosed by the searches and enquiries which a prudent buyer would have made before entering into the contract

(e) public requirements.

3.1.3 After the contract is made, the seller is to give the buyer written details without delay of any new public requirement and of anything in writing which he learns about concerning a matter covered by condition 3.1.2.

3.1.4 The buyer is to bear the cost of complying with any outstanding public requirement and is to indemnify the seller against any liability resulting from a public requirement.

3.2 Physical state

3.2.1 The buyer accepts the property in the physical state it is in at the date of the contract unless the seller is building or converting it.

3.2.2 A leasehold property is sold subject to any subsisting breach of a condition or tenant's obligation relating to the physical state of the property which renders the lease liable to forfeiture.

3.2.3 A sub-lease is granted subject to any subsisting breach of a condition or tenant's obligation relating to the physical state of the property which renders the seller's own lease liable to forfeiture.

3.3 Retained land

Where after the transfer the seller will be retaining land near the property:

(a) the buyer will have no right of light or air over the retained land, but

(b) in other respects the seller and the buyer will each have the rights over the land of the other which they would have had if they were two separate buyers to whom the seller had made simultaneous transfers of the property and the retained land.

The transfer is to contain appropriate express terms.

4. LEASES AFFECTING THE PROPERTY

4.1 General

4.1.1 This condition applies if any part of the property is sold subject to a lease.

4.1.2 The seller having provided the buyer with full details of each lease or copies of documents embodying the lease terms, the buyer is treated as entering into the contract knowing and fully accepting those terms.

4.1.3 The seller is not to serve a notice to end the lease nor to accept a surrender.

4.1.4 The seller is to inform the buyer without delay if the lease ends.

4.1.5 The buyer is to indemnify the seller against all claims arising from the lease after actual completion; this includes claims which are unenforceable against a buyer for want of registration.

4.1.6 If the property does not include all the land let, the seller may apportion the rent and, if the lease is a new tenancy, the buyer may require the seller to apply under section 10 of the Landlord and Tenant (Covenants) Act 1995 for the apportionment to bind the tenant.

4.2 Property management

4.2.1 The seller is promptly to give the buyer full particulars of:

(a) any court or arbitration proceedings in connection with the lease, and

(b) any application for a licence, consent or approval under the lease.

4.2.2 Conditions 4.2.3 to 4.2.8 do not apply to a rent review process to which condition 5 applies.

4.2.3 Subject to condition 4.2.4, the seller is to conduct any court or arbitration proceedings in accordance with written directions given by the buyer from time to time (for which the seller is to apply), unless to do so might place the seller in breach of an obligation to the tenant or a statutory duty.

4.2.4 If the seller applies for directions from the buyer in relation to a proposed step in the proceedings and the buyer does not give such directions within 10 working days, the seller may take or refrain from taking that step as it thinks fit.

4.2.5   The buyer is to indemnify the seller against all loss and expense resulting from the seller's following the buyer's directions.

4.2.6   Unless the buyer gives written consent, the seller is not to:

(a)   grant or formally withhold any licence, consent or approval under the lease, or

(b)   serve any notice or take any action (other than action in court or arbitration proceedings) as landlord under the lease.

4.2.7   When the seller applies for the buyer's consent under condition 4.2.6:

(a)   the buyer is not to withhold its consent or attach conditions to the consent where to do so might place the seller in breach of an obligation to the tenant or a statutory duty

(b)   the seller may proceed as if the buyer has consented when:

(i)   in accordance with paragraph (a), the buyer is not entitled to withhold its consent, or

(ii) the buyer does not refuse its consent within 10 working days.

4.2.8   If the buyer withholds or attaches conditions to its consent, the buyer is to indemnify the seller against all loss and expense.

4.2.9   In all other respects, the seller is to manage the property in accordance with the principles of good estate management until completion.

4.3   Continuing liability

At the request and cost of the seller, the buyer is to support any application by the seller to be released from the landlord covenants in a lease to which the property is sold subject.

5.   RENT REVIEWS

5.1   Subject to condition 5.2, this condition applies if:

(a)   the rent reserved by a lease of all or part of the property is to be reviewed,

(b)   the seller is either the landlord or the tenant,

(c)   the rent review process starts before actual completion, and

(d)   no reviewed rent has been agreed or determined at the date of the contract.

5.2   The seller is to conduct the rent review process until actual completion, after which the buyer is to conduct it.

5.3   Conditions 5.4 and 5.5 cease to apply on actual completion if the reviewed rent will only be payable in respect of a period after that date.

5.4   In the course of the rent review process, the seller and the buyer are each to:

(a)   act promptly with a view to achieving the best result obtainable,

(b)   consult with and have regard to the views of the other,

(c)   provide the other with copies of all material correspondence and papers relating to the process,

(d)   ensure that its representations take account of matters put forward by the other, and

(e)   keep the other informed of the progress of the process.

5.5   Neither the seller nor the buyer is to agree a rent figure unless it has been approved in writing by the other (such approval not to be unreasonably withheld).

5.4   The seller and the buyer are each to bear their own costs of the rent review process.

5.7   Unless the rent review date precedes the apportionment day, the buyer is to pay the costs of a third party appointed to determine the rent.

5.8   Where the rent review date precedes the apportionment day, those costs are to be divided as follows:

(a) the seller is to pay the proportion that the number of days from the rent review date to the apportionment day bears to the number of days from that rent review date until either the following rent review date or, if none, the expiry of the term, and

(b) the buyer is to pay the balance.

6.   TITLE AND TRANSFER

6.1   Proof of title

6.1.1   Without cost to the buyer, the seller is to provide the buyer with proof of the title to the property and of his ability to transfer it, or to procure its transfer.

6.1.2   Where the property has a registered title the proof is to include official copies of the items referred to in rules 134(1)(a) and (b) and 135(1)(a) of the Land Registration Rules 2003, so far as they are not to be discharged or overridden at or before completion.

6.1.3   Where the property has an unregistered title, the proof is to include:

(a) an abstract of title or an epitome of title with photocopies of the documents, and

(b) production of every document or an abstract, epitome or copy of it with an original marking by a conveyancer either against the original or an examined abstract or an examined copy.

6.2   Requisitions

6.2.1   The buyer may not raise requisitions:

(a) on the title shown by the seller taking the steps described in condition 6.1.1 before the contract was made

(b) in relation to the matters covered by condition 3.1.2

6.2.2   Notwithstanding condition 6.2.1, the buyer may, within six working days of a matter coming to his attention after the contract was made, raise written requisitions on that matter. In that event steps 3 and 4 in condition 6.3.1 apply.

6.2.3   On the expiry of the relevant time limit under condition 6.2.2 or condition 6.3.1, the buyer loses his right to raise requisitions or to make observations.

6.3   Timetable

6.3.1   Subject to condition 6.2 and to the extent that the seller did not take the steps described in condition 6.1.1 before the contract was made, the following are the steps for deducing and investigating the title to the property to be taken within the following time limits:

Step	*Time limit*
1. The seller is to comply with condition 6.1.1	Immediately after making the contract
2. The buyer may raise written requisitions	Six working days after either the date of the contract or the date of delivery of the seller's evidence of title on which the requisitions are raised whichever is the later
3. The seller is to reply in writing to any requisitions raised	Four working days after receiving the requisitions
4. The buyer may make written observations on the seller's replies	Three working days after receiving the replies

The time limit on the buyer's right to raise requisitions applies even where the seller supplies incomplete evidence of its title, but the buyer may, within six working days from delivery of any further evidence, raise further requisitions resulting from that evidence.

6.3.2   The parties are to take the following steps to prepare and agree the transfer of the property within the following time limits:

Step	Time limit
A. The buyer is to send the seller a draft transfer	At least twelve working days before completion date
B. The seller is to approve or revise that draft and either return it or retain it for use as the actual transfer	Four working days after delivery of the draft transfer
C. If the draft is returned the buyer is to send an engrossment to the seller	At least five working days before completion date

6.3.3   Periods of time under conditions 6.3.1 and 6.3.2 may run concurrently.

6.3.4   If the period between the date of the contract and completion date is less than 15 working days, the time limits in conditions 6.2.2, 6.3.1 and 6.3.2 are to be reduced by the same proportion as that period bears to the period of 15 working days. Fractions of a working day are to be rounded down except that the time limit to perform any step is not to be less than one working day.

6.4   Defining the property

6.4.1   The seller need not, further than it may be able to do from information in its possession:

(a)   prove the exact boundaries of the property

(b)   prove who owns fences, ditches, hedges or walls

(c)   separately identify parts of the property with different titles.

6.4.2   The buyer may, if to do so is reasonable, require the seller to make or obtain, pay for and hand over a statutory declaration about facts relevant to the matters mentioned in condition 6.4.1. The form of the declaration is to be agreed by the buyer, who must not unreasonably withhold its agreement.

6.5   Rents and rentcharges

The fact that a rent or rentcharge, whether payable or receivable by the owner of the property, has been or will on completion be, informally apportioned is not to be regarded as a defect in title.

6.6   Transfer

6.1.1   The buyer does not prejudice its right to raise requisitions, or to require replies to any raised, by taking steps in relation to the preparation or agreement of the transfer.

6.6.2   Subject to condition 6.6.3, the seller is to transfer the property with full title guarantee.

6.6.3   The transfer is to have effect as if the disposition is expressly made subject to all matters covered by condition 3.1.2.

6.6.4   If after completion the seller will remain bound by any obligation affecting the property and disclosed to the buyer before the contract was made, but the law does not imply any covenant by the buyer to indemnify the seller against liability for future breaches of it:

(a)   the buyer is to covenant in the transfer to indemnify the seller against liability for any future breach of the obligation and to perform it from then on, and

(b)   if required by the seller, the buyer is to execute and deliver to the seller on completion a duplicate transfer prepared by the buyer.

6.6.5   The seller is to arrange at its expense that, in relation to every document of title which the buyer does not receive on completion, the buyer is to have the benefit of:

(a)   a written acknowledgement of the buyer's right to its production, and

(b)   a written undertaking for its safe custody (except while it is held by a mortgagee or by someone in a fiduciary capacity).

7.   INSURANCE

7.1   Responsibility for insuring

7.1.1   Conditions 7.1.2 and 7.1.3 apply if:

(a) the contract provides that the policy effected by or for the seller and insuring the property or any part of it against loss or damage should continue in force after the exchange of contracts, or

(b) the property or any part of it is let on terms under which the seller (whether as landlord or as tenant) is obliged to insure against loss or damage.

7.1.2   The seller is to:

(a) do everything required to continue to maintain the policy, including the prompt payment of any premium which falls due

(b) increase the amount or extent of the cover as requested by the buyer, if the insurers agree and the buyer pays the additional premium

(c) permit the buyer to inspect the policy, or evidence of its terms, at any time

(d) obtain or consent to an endorsement on the policy of the buyer's interest, at the buyer's expense

(e) pay to the buyer immediately on receipt, any part of an additional premium which the buyer paid and which is returned by the insurers

(f) if before completion the property suffers loss or damage:

(i) pay to the buyer on completion the amount of policy moneys which the seller has received, so far as not applied in repairing or reinstating the property, and

(ii) if no final payment has then been received, assign to the buyer, at the buyer's expense, all rights to claim under the policy in such form as the buyer reasonably requires and pending execution of the assignment, hold any policy moneys received in trust for the buyer

(g) on completion:

(i) cancel the insurance policy

(ii) apply for a refund of the premium and pay the buyer, immediately on receipt, any amount received which relates to a part of the premium which was paid or reimbursed by a tenant or third party. The buyer is to hold the money paid subject to the rights of that tenant or third party.

7.1.3   The buyer is to pay the seller a proportionate part of the premium which the seller paid in respect of the period from the date when the contract is made to the date of actual completion, except so far as the seller is entitled to recover it from a tenant.

7.1.4   Unless condition 7.1.2 applies:

(a) the seller is under no obligation to the buyer to insure the property

(b) if payment under a policy effected by or for the buyer is reduced, because the property is covered against loss or damage by an insurance policy effected by or for the seller, the purchase price is to be abated by the amount of that reduction.

7.1.5   Section 47 of the Law of Property Act 1925 does not apply.

8.   COMPLETION

8.1   Date

8.1.1   Completion date is twenty working days after the date of the contract but time is not of the essence of the contract unless a notice to complete has been served.

8.1.2   If the money due on completion is received after 2.00 p.m., completion is to be treated, for the purposes only of conditions 8.3 and 9.3, as taking place on the next working day as a result of the buyer's default.

8.1.3 Condition 8.1.2 does not apply if:

(a) the sale is with vacant possession of the property or a part of it, and

(b) the buyer is ready, willing and able to complete but does not pay the money due on completion until after 2.00 p.m. because the seller has not vacated the property or that part by that time.

8.2 Place

Completion is to take place in England and Wales, either at the seller's conveyancer's office or at some other place which the seller reasonably specifies.

8.3 Apportionments

8.3.1 Subject to condition 8.3.6 income and outgoings of the property are to be apportioned between the parties so far as the change of ownership on completion will affect entitlement to receive or liability to pay them.

8.3.2 The day from which the apportionment is to be made ('apportionment day') is:

(a) if the whole property is sold with vacant possession or the seller exercises its option in condition 9.3.4, the date of actual completion, or

(b) otherwise, completion date.

8.3.3 In apportioning any sum, it is to be assumed that the buyer owns the property from the beginning of the day on which the apportionment is to be made.

8.3.4 A sum to be apportioned is to be treated as:

(a) payable for the period which it covers, except that if it is an instalment of an annual sum the buyer is to be attributed with an amount equal to 1/365th of the annual sum for each day from and including the apportionment day to the end of the instalment period

(b) accruing—

(i) from day to day, and

(ii) at the rate applicable from time to time.

8.3.5 When a sum to be apportioned, or the rate at which it is to be treated as accruing, is not known or easily ascertainable at completion, a provisional apportionment is to be made according to the best estimate available. As soon as the amount is known, a final apportionment is to be made and notified to the other party. Subject to condition 8.3.8, any resulting balance is to be paid no more than ten working days later, and if not then paid the balance is to bear interest at the contract rate from then until payment.

8.3.6 Where a lease of the property requires the tenant to reimburse the landlord for expenditure on goods or services, on completion:

(a) the buyer is to pay the seller the amount of any expenditure already incurred by the seller but not yet due from the tenant and in respect of which the seller provides the buyer with the information and vouchers required for its recovery from the tenant, and

(b) the seller is to credit the buyer with payments already recovered from the tenant but not yet incurred by the seller.

8.3.7 Condition 8.3.8 applies if any part of the property is sold subject to a lease and either:

(a) (i) on completion any rent or other sum payable under the lease is due but not paid.

(ii) the contract does not provide that the buyer is to assign to the seller the right to collect any arrears due to the seller under the terms of the contract, and

(iii) the seller is not entitled to recover any arrears from the tenant, or

(b) (i) as a result of a rent review to which condition 5 applies a reviewed rent is agreed or determined after actual completion, and

    (ii) an additional sum then becomes payable in respect of a period before the apportionment day.

8.3.8 (a) The buyer is to seek to collect all sums due in the circumstances referred to in condition 8.3.7 in the ordinary course of management, but need not take legal proceedings or distrain.

    (b) A payment made on account of those sums is to be apportioned between the parties in the ratio of the amounts owed to each, notwithstanding that the tenant exercises its right to appropriate the payment in some other manner.

    (c) Any part of a payment on account received by one party but due to the other is to be paid no more than ten working days after the receipt of cash or cleared funds and, if not then paid, the sum is to bear interest at the contract rate until payment.

8.4 Amount payable

The amount payable by the buyer on completion is the purchase price (less any deposit already paid to the seller or its agent) adjusted to take account of:

(a) apportionments made under condition 8.3

(b) any compensation to be paid under condition 9.3

(c) any sum payable under condition 7.1.2 or 7.1.3.

8.5 Title deeds

8.5.1 As soon as the buyer has complied with all its obligations on completion the seller must hand over the documents of title.

8.5.2 Condition 8.5.1 does not apply to any documents of title relating to land being retained by the seller after completion.

8.6 Rent receipts

The buyer is to assume that whoever gave any receipt for a payment of rent which the seller produces was the person or the agent of the person then entitled to that rent.

8.7 Means of payment

The buyer is to pay the money due on completion by direct credit and, if appropriate, by an unconditional release of a deposit held by a stakeholder.

8.8 Notice to complete

8.8.1 At any time on or after completion date, a party who is ready, able and willing to complete may give the other a notice to complete.

8.8.2 The parties are to complete the contract within ten working days of giving a notice to complete, excluding the day on which the notice is given. For this purpose, time is of the essence of the contract.

9. REMEDIES

9.1 Errors and omissions

9.1.1 If any plan or statement in the contract, or in the negotiations leading to it, is or was misleading or inaccurate due to an error or omission, the remedies available are as follows.

9.1.2 When there is a material difference between the description or value of the property as represented and as it is, the buyer is entitled to damages.

9.1.3 An error or omission only entitles the buyer to rescind the contract:

(a) where the error or omission results from fraud or recklessness, or

(b) where the buyer would be obliged, to its prejudice, to accept property differing substantially (in quantity, quality or tenure) from that which the error or omission had led it to expect.

9.2 Rescission

If either party rescinds the contract:

(a) unless the rescission is a result of the buyer's breach of contract the deposit is to be repaid to the buyer with accrued interest

(b) the buyer is to return any documents received from the seller and is to cancel any registration of the contract.

(c) the seller's duty to pay any returned premium under condition 7.1.2(e) (whenever received) is not affected.

9.3 Late completion

9.3.1 If the buyer defaults in performing its obligations under the contract and completion is delayed, the buyer is to pay compensation to the seller.

9.3.2 Compensation is calculated at the contract rate on the purchase price (less any deposit paid) for the period between completion date and actual completion, but ignoring any period during which the seller was in default.

9.3.3 Any claim by the seller for loss resulting from delayed completion is to be reduced by any compensation paid under this contract.

9.3.4 Where the sale is not with vacant possession of the whole property and completion is delayed, the seller may give notice to the buyer, before the date of actual completion, that it will take the net income from the property until completion as well as compensation under condition 9.3.1

9.4 After completion

Completion does not cancel liability to perform any outstanding obligation under the contract.

9.5 Buyer's failure to comply with notice to complete

9.5.1 If the buyer fails to complete in accordance with a notice to complete, the following terms apply.

9.5.2 The seller may rescind the contract, and if it does so:

(a) it may

(i) forfeit and keep any deposit and accrued interest

(ii) resell the property

(iii) claim damages

(b) the buyer is to return any documents received from the seller and is to cancel any registration of the contract.

9.5.3 The seller retains its other rights and remedies.

9.6 Seller's failure to comply with notice to complete

9.6.1 If the seller fails to complete in accordance with a notice to complete, the following terms apply:

9.6.2 The buyer may rescind the contract, and if it does so:

(a) the deposit is to be repaid to the buyer with accrued interest

(b) the buyer is to return any documents it received from the seller and is, at the seller's expense, to cancel any registration of the contract.

9.6.3 The buyer retains its other rights and remedies.

10.   LEASEHOLD PROPERTY

10.1   Existing leases

10.1.1 The following provisions apply to a sale of leasehold land.

10.1.2 The seller having provided the buyer with copies of the documents embodying the lease terms, the buyer is treated as entering into the contract knowing and fully accepting those terms.

10.1.3 The seller is to comply with any lease obligations requiring the tenant to insure the property.

10.2   New leases

10.2.1 The following provisions apply to a contract to grant a new lease.

10.2.2 The conditions apply so that:

"seller" means the proposed landlord
"buyer" means the proposed tenant
"purchase price" means the premium to be paid on the grant of a lease.

10.2.3 The lease is to be in the form of the draft attached to the contract.

10.2.4 If the term of the new lease will exceed seven years, the seller is to deduce a title which will enable the buyer to register the lease at the Land Registry with an absolute title.

10.2.5 The seller is to engross the lease and a counterpart of it and is to send the counterpart to the buyer at least five working days before completion date.

10.2.6 The buyer is to execute the counterpart and deliver it to the seller on completion.

10.3   Consents

10.3.1 (a) The following provisions apply if a consent to let, assign or sub-let is required to complete the contract

(b) In this condition "consent" means consent in a form which satisfies the requirement to obtain it.

10.3.2 (a) The seller is to:

(i) apply for the consent at its expense, and to use all reasonable efforts to obtain it

(ii) give the buyer notice forthwith on obtaining the consent.

(b) The buyer is to comply with all reasonable requirements, including requirements for the provision of information and references.

10.3.3 Where the consent of a reversioner (whether or not immediate) is required to an assignment or sub-letting, then so far as the reversioner lawfully imposes such a condition:

(a) the buyer is to:

(i) covenant directly with the reversioner to observe the tenant's covenants and the conditions in the seller's lease

(ii) use reasonable endeavours to provide guarantees of the performance and observance of the tenant's covenants and the conditions in the seller's lease

(iii) execute or procure the execution of the licence

(b) the seller, in the case of an assignment, is to enter into an authorised guarantee agreement.

10.3.4   Neither party may object to a reversioner's consent given subject to a condition:

(a)   which under section 19A of the Landlord and Tenant Act 1927 is not regarded as unreasonable, and

(b)   which is lawfully imposed under an express term of the lease.

10.3.5   If any required consent has not been obtained by the original completion date:

(a)   the time for completion is to be postponed until five working days after the seller gives written notice to the buyer that the consent has been obtained or four months from the original completion date whichever is the earlier

(b)   the postponed date is to be treated as the completion date.

10.3.6   At any time after four months from the original completion date, either party may rescind the contract by notice to the other, if:

(a)   consent has still not been given, and

(b)   no declaration has been obtained from the court that consent has been unreasonably withheld.

10.3.7   If the contract is rescinded under condition 10.3.6 the seller is to remain liable for any breach of condition 10.3.2(a) or 10.3.3(b) and the buyer is to remain liable for any breach of condition 10.3.2(b) or 10.3.3(a). In all other respects neither party is to be treated as in breach of contract and condition 9.2 applies.

10.3.8   A party in breach of its obligations under condition 10.3.2 or 10.3.3 cannot rescind under condition 10.3.6 for so long as its breach is a cause of the consent's being withheld.

11.   COMMONHOLD

11.1   Terms used in this condition have the special meanings given to them in Part 1 of the Commonhold and Leasehold Reform Act 2002.

11.2   This condition applies to a disposition of commonhold land.

11.3   The seller having provided the buyer with copies of the current versions of the memorandum and articles of the commonhold association and of the commonhold community statement, the buyer is treated as entering into the contract knowing and fully accepting their terms.

11.4   If the contract is for the sale of property which is or includes part only of a commonhold unit:

(a)   the seller is, at its expense, to apply for the written consent of the commonhold association and is to use all reasonable efforts to obtain it

(b)   either the seller, unless it is in breach of its obligation under paragraph (a), or the buyer may rescind the contract by notice to the other party if three working days before completion date (or before a later date on which the parties have agreed to complete the contract) the consent has not been given. In that case, neither party is to be treated as in breach of contract and condition 9.2 applies.

12.   CHATTELS

12.1   The following provisions apply to any chattels which are included in the contract.

12.2   The contract takes effect as a contract for the sale of goods.

12.3   The buyer takes the chattels in the physical state they are in at the date of the contract.

12.4   Ownership of the chattels passes to the buyer on actual completion but they are at the buyer's risk from the contract date.

PART 2[1]

A.   VAT

A1   Standard rated supply

A1.1   Conditions 1.4.1 and 1.4.2. do not apply.

A1.2   The seller warrants that the sale of the property will constitute a supply chargeable to VAT at the standard rate.

A1.3   The buyer is to pay to the seller on completion an additional amount equal to the VAT in exchange for a proper VAT invoice from the seller.

A2   Transfer of a going concern

A2.1   Condition 1.4 does not apply.

A2.2   In this condition "TOGC" means a transfer of a business as a going concern treated as neither a supply of goods nor a supply of services by virtue of article 5 of the Value Added Tax (Special Provisions) Order 1995.

A2.3   The seller warrants that it is using the property for the business of letting to produce rental income.

A2.4   The buyer is to make every effort to comply with the conditions to be met by a transferee under article 5(1) and 5(2) for the sale to constitute a TOGC.

A2.5   The buyer will, on or before the earlier of:

(a)   completion date, and

(b)   the earliest date on which a supply of the property could be treated as made by the seller under this contract if the sale does not constitute a TOGC,

notify the seller that paragraph (2B) of article 5 of the VAT (Special Provisions) Order 1995 does not apply to the buyer.

A2.6   The parties are to treat the sale as a TOGC at completion if the buyer provides written evidence to the seller before completion that it is a taxable person and that it has made an election to waive exemption in respect of the property and has given a written notification of the making of such election in conformity with article 5(2) and has given the notification referred to in condition A2.5.

A2.7   The buyer is not to revoke its election to waive exemption in respect of the property at any time.

A2.8   If the parties treat the sale at completion as a TOGC but it is later determined that the sale was not a TOGC, then within five working days of that determination the buyer shall pay to the seller:

(a)   an amount equal to the VAT chargeable in respect of the supply of the property, in exchange for a proper VAT invoice from the seller; and

(b)   except where the sale is not a TOGC because of an act or omission of the seller, an amount equal to any interest or penalty for which the seller is liable to account to HM Customs and Excise in respect of or by reference to that VAT.

A2.9   If the seller obtains the consent of HM Customs and Excise to retain its VAT records relating to the property, it shall make them available to the buyer for inspection and copying at reasonable times on reasonable request during the six years following completion.

---

[1] The conditions in Part 2 do not apply unless expressly incorporated. See condition 1.1.4(b).

B.   CAPITAL ALLOWANCES

B1   To enable the buyer to make and substantiate claims under the Capital Allowances Act 2001 in respect of the property, the seller is to use its reasonable endeavours to provide, or to procure that its agents provide:

    (a)   copies of all relevant information in its possession or that of its agents, and

    (b)   such co-operation and assistance as the buyer may reasonably require.

B2.1   The buyer is only to use information provided under condition B1 for the stated purpose.

B2.2   The buyer is not to disclose, without the consent of the seller, any such information which the seller expressly provides on a confidential basis.

B3.1   On completion, the seller and the buyer are jointly to make an election under section 198 of the Capital Allowances Act 2001 which is consistent with the apportionment in the Special Conditions.

B3.2   The seller and the buyer are each to submit the amount fixed by that election to the Inland Revenue for the purposes of their respective capital allowance computations.

C.   REVERSIONARY INTERESTS IN FLATS

C1   No tenants' rights

C1.1   In this condition, sections refer to sections of the Landlord and Tenant Act 1987 and expressions have the special meanings given to them in that Act.

C1.2   The seller warrants that:

    (a)   it gave the notice required by section 5,

    (b)   no acceptance notice was served on the landlord or no person was nominated for the purposes of section 6 during the protected period, and

    (c)   that period ended less than 12 months before the date of the contract.

C2   Tenants' right of first refusal

C2.1   In this condition, sections refer to sections of the Landlord and Tenant Act 1987 and expressions have the special meanings given to them in that Act.

C2.2   The seller warrants that:

    (a)   it gave the notice required by section 5, and

    (b)   it has given the buyer a copy of:

        (i)   any acceptance notice served on the landlord and

        (ii) any nomination of a person duly nominated for the purposes of section 6.

C2.3   If the sale is by auction:

    (a)   the seller warrants that it has given the buyer a copy of any notice served on the landlord electing that section 8B shall apply,

    (b)   condition 8.1.1. applies as if "thirty working days" were substituted for "twenty working days",

    (c)   the seller is to send a copy of the contract to the nominated person as required by section 8B(3), and

    (d)   if the nominated person serves notice under section 8B(4):

        (i)   the seller is to give the buyer a copy of the notice, and

        (ii) condition 9.2 is to apply as if the contract had been rescinded.

SPECIAL CONDITIONS

1. This contract incorporates the Standard Commercial Property Conditions (Second Edition).

2. The property is sold with vacant possession.

(or) 2. The property is sold subject to the leases or tenancies set out on the attached list but otherwise with vacant possession on completion.

3. The chattels at the Property and set out on the attached list are included in the sale. [The amount of the purchase price apportioned to those chattels is £   ]

4. The conditions in Part 2 shown against the boxes ticked below are included in the contract:

☐   Condition A1 (VAT: standard rate)

[or]   ☐   Condition A2 (VAT: transfer of a going concern)

☐   Condition B (capital allowances). The amount of the purchase price apportioned to plant and machinery at the property for the purposes of the Capital Allowances Act 2001 is £

☐   Condition C1 (flats: no tenants' rights of first refusal)

[or]   ☐   Condition C2 (flats: with tenants' rights of first refusal)

Seller's Conveyancers*:

Buyer's Conveyancers*:

* Adding an e-mail address authorises service by e-mail: see condition 1.3.3(b)

Copyright in this form and its contents rests jointly in SLSS Limited (Oyez) and The Law Society

The Law Society
© 2004 OYEZ and The Law Society

'Green Card' Warning on Property Fraud—Practice Information

Could you be involved or implicated?

Could you be unwittingly assisting in a fraud? The general assumption is that if there has been a property fraud a solicitor *must* have been involved. Solicitors should therefore be vigilant to protect both their clients and themselves. Steps can be taken to minimise the risk of being involved or implicated in a fraud (see below).

Could you spot a property fraud?

The signs to watch for include the following (but this list is not exhaustive):

- **Fraudulent buyer or fictious solicitors**—especially if the buyer is introduced to your practice by a third party (for example a broker or estate agent) who is not well known to you. Beware of clients whom you never meet and solicitors not known to you.
- **Unusual instructions**—for example a solicitor being instructed by the seller to remit the net proceeds of sale to anyone other than the seller.
- **Misrepresentation of the purchase price**—ensure that the true cash price actually to be paid is stated as the consideration in the contract and transfer and is identical to the price shown in the mortgage instructions and in the report on title to the lender.
- **A deposit or any part of purchase price paid direct**—a deposit or the difference between the mortgage advance and the price, paid direct, or said to be paid direct, to the seller.
- **Incomplete contract documentation**—contract documents not fully completed by the seller's representative, ie, dates missing or the identity of the parties not fully described or financial details not fully stated.
- **Changes in the purchase price**—adjustments to the purchase price, particularly in high percentage mortgage cases, or allowances off the purchase price, for example, for works to be carried out.
- **Unusual transactions**—transactions which do not follow their normal course or the usual pattern of events:
  - (a) client with current mortgage on two or more properties
  - (b) client using alias
  - (c) client buying several properties from same person or two or more persons using same solicitor
  - (d) client reselling property at a substantial profit, for which no explanation has been provided.

What steps can I take to minimise the risk of fraud?

Be vigilant: if you have any doubts about a transaction, consider whether any of the following steps could be taken to minimise the risk of fraud:

- **Verify the identity and *bona fides* of your client and solicitors' firms you do not know**— meet the clients where possible and get to know them a little. Check that the solicitor's firm and office address appear in the *Directory of Solicitors and Barristers* or contact the Law Society's Regulation and Information Services (tel: 0870 606 2555).

- **Question unusual instructions**—if you receive unusual instructions from your client discuss them with your client fully.
- **Discuss with your client any aspects of the transaction which worry you**—if, for example, you have any suspicion that your client may have submitted a false mortgage application or references, or if the lender's valuation exceeds the actual price paid, discuss this with your client. If you believe that the client intends to proceed with a fraudulent application, you must refuse to continue to act for the buyer and the lender.
- **Check that the true price is shown in all documentation**—check that the actual price paid is stated in the contract, transfer and mortgage instructions. Where you are also acting for a lender, tell your client that you will have to cease acting unless the client permits you to report to the lender all allowances and incentives. See also the guidance printed in [1990] *Gazette*, 12 December 16 [see Annex 25F, p. 500 in the Guide].
- **Do not witness pre-signed documentation**—no document should be witnessed by a solicitor or his or her staff unless the person signing does so in the presence of the witness. If the document is pre-signed, ensure that it is re-signed in the presence of a witness.
- **Verify signatures**—consider whether signatures on all documents connected with a transaction should be examined and compared with signatures on any other available documentation.
- **Make a company search**—where a private company is the seller, or the seller has purchased from a private company in the recent past, and you suspect that the sale may not be on proper arm's length terms, you should make a search in the Companies Register to ascertain the names and addresses of the officers and shareholders, which can then be compared with the names of those connected with the transaction and the seller and buyer.

Remember that, even where investigations result in a solicitor ceasing to act for a client the solicitor will still owe a duty of confidentiality which would prevent the solicitor passing on information to the lender. It is only where the solicitor is satisfied that there is a strong *prima facie* case that the client was using the solicitor to further a fraud or other criminal purpose that the duty of confidentiality would not apply.

Any failure to observe these signs and to take the appropriate steps may be used in court as evidence against you if you and your client are prosecuted, or if you are sued for negligence.

Further guidance can be obtained from the Law Society's Practice Advice Service (tel: 0870 606 2522).

March 1991, revised January 1996, updated February 1999.

APPENDIX 6

Forms of Notice under the Landlord and Tenant (Covenants) Act 1995, s 17

SCHEDULE
FORM 1
NOTICE TO FORMER TENANT OR GUARANTOR OF INTENTION TO RECOVER FIXED CHARGE[1]
(Landlord and Tenant (Covenants) Act 1995, section 17)

To [name and address]: ....
....

> IMPORTANT—THE PERSON GIVING THIS NOTICE IS PROTECTING THE RIGHT TO RECOVER THE AMOUNT(S) SPECIFIED FROM YOU NOW OR AT SOME TIME IN THE FUTURE. THERE MAY BE ACTION WHICH YOU CAN TAKE TO PROTECT YOUR POSITION. READ THE NOTICE AND ALL THE NOTES OVERLEAF CAREFULLY. IF YOU ARE IN ANY DOUBT ABOUT THE ACTION YOU SHOULD TAKE, SEEK ADVICE IMMEDIATELY, FOR INSTANCE FROM A SOLICITOR OR CITIZENS ADVICE BUREAU.

1.   This notice is given under section 17 of the Landlord and Tenant (Covenants) Act 1995. *[see Note 1]*

2.   It relates to (address and description of property) ....
....
let under a lease dated .... and made between ....
....
....
[of which you were formerly tenant] [in relation to which you are liable as guarantor of a person who was formerly tenant].[2]

3.   I/we as landlord[3] hereby give you notice that the fixed charge(s) of which details are set out in the attached Schedule[4] is/are now due and unpaid, and that I/we intend to recover from you the

---

[1] The Act defines a fixed charge as (a) rent, (b) any service charge (as defined by section 18 of the Landlord and Tenant Act 1985, disregarding the words 'of a dwelling') and (c) any amount payable under a tenant covenant of the tenancy providing for payment of a liquidated sum in the event of failure to comply with the covenant.

[2] Delete alternative as appropriate.

[3] 'Landlord' for these purposes includes any person who has the right to enforce the charge.

[4] The Schedule must be in writing, and must indicate in relation to each item the date on which it became payable, the amount payable and whether it is rent, service charge or a fixed charge of some other kind (in which case particulars of the nature of the charge should be given). Charges due before 1 January 1996 are deemed to have become due on that date, but the actual date on which they became due should also be stated.

amount(s) specified in the Schedule [and interest from the date and calculated on the basis specified in the Schedule][5]. *[see Notes 2 and 3]*

4.[6]   There is a possibility that your liability in respect of the fixed charge(s) detailed in the Schedule will subsequently be determined to be for a greater amount. *[see Note 4]*

5.   All correspondence about this notice should be sent to the landlord/landlord's agent at the address given below.

Date . . . . Signature of landlord/landlord's agent . . . .
Name and address of landlord . . . .
. . . .
. . . .
[Name and address of agent . . . .
. . . .
. . . .]

NOTES

1.   The person giving you this notice alleges that you are still liable for the performance of the tenant's obligations under the tenancy to which this notice relates, either as a previous tenant bound by privity of contract or an authorised guarantee agreement, or because you are the guarantor of a previous tenant. By giving you this notice, the landlord (or other person entitled to enforce payment, such as a management company) is protecting his right to require you to pay the amount specified in the notice. There may be other sums not covered by the notice which the landlord can also recover because they are not fixed charges (for example in respect of repairs or costs if legal proceedings have to be brought). If you pay the amount specified in this notice in full, you will have the right to call on the landlord to grant you an 'overriding lease', which puts you in the position of landlord to the present tenant. There are both advantages and drawbacks to doing this, and you should take advice before coming to a decision.

Validity of notice
2.   The landlord is required to give this notice within six months of the date on which the charge or charges in question became due (or, if it became due before 1 January 1996, within six months of that date). If the notice has been given late, it is not valid and the amount in the notice cannot be recovered from you. The date of the giving of the notice may not be the date written on the notice or the date on which you actually saw it. It may, for instance, be the date on which the notice was delivered through the post to your last address known to the landlord. If you are in any doubt, you should seek advice immediately.

Interest
3.   If interest is payable on the amount due, the landlord does not have to state the precise amount of interest, but he must state the basis on which the interest is calculated to enable you to work out the likely amount, or he will not be able to claim interest at all. This does not include interest which may be payable under rules of court if legal proceedings are brought.

---

[5] Delete words in brackets if not applicable. If applicable, the Schedule must state the basis on which interest is calculated (for example, rate of interest, date from which it is payable and provision of Lease or other document under which it is payable).

[6] Delete this paragraph if not applicable. If applicable (for example, where there is an outstanding rent review or service charge collected on account) a further notice must be served on the former tenant or guarantor within three (3) months beginning with the date on which the greater amount is determined. If only applicable to one or more charge of several, the Schedule should specify which.

Change in amount due

4.   Apart from interest, the landlord is not entitled to recover an amount which is more than he has specified in the notice, with one exception. This is where the amount cannot be finally determined within six months after it is due (for example, if there is dispute concerning an outstanding rent review or if the charge is a service charge collected on account and adjusted following final determination). In such a case, if the amount due is eventually determined to be more than originally notified, the landlord may claim the larger amount *if and only if* he completes the paragraph giving notice of the possibility that the amount may change, and gives a further notice specifying the larger amount within three months of the final determination.

FORM 2

FURTHER NOTICE TO FORMER TENANT OR GUARANTOR OF REVISED AMOUNT DUE IN RESPECT OF A FIXED CHARGE[1]

(Landlord and Tenant (Covenants) Act 1995, section 17)

To [name and address]: ....
....

IMPORTANT—THE PERSON GIVING THIS NOTICE IS PROTECTING THE RIGHT TO RECOVER THE AMOUNT(S) SPECIFIED FROM YOU NOW OR AT SOME TIME IN THE FUTURE. THERE MAY BE ACTION WHICH YOU CAN TAKE TO PROTECT YOUR POSITION. READ THE NOTICE AND ALL THE NOTES OVERLEAF CAREFULLY. IF YOU ARE IN ANY DOUBT ABOUT THE ACTION YOU SHOULD TAKE, SEEK ADVICE IMMEDIATELY, FOR INSTANCE FROM A SOLICITOR OR CITIZENS ADVICE BUREAU.

---

1.   This notice is given under section 17 of the Landlord and Tenant (Covenants) Act 1995. *[see Note 1]*

2.   It relates to (address and description of property) ....
....
let under a lease dated .... and made between ....
....
....
[of which you were formerly tenant] [in relation to which you are liable as guarantor of a person who was formerly tenant].[2]

3.   You were informed on .... (date of original notice) of the amount due in respect of a fixed charge or charges, and of the possibility that your liability in respect of the charge(s) might subsequently be determined to be for a greater amount.

4.   I/we as landlord[3] hereby give you notice that the fixed charge(s) of which details are set out in the attached Schedule[4] has/have now been determined to be for a greater amount than specified in the original notice, and that I/we intend to recover from you the amount(s) specified in the Schedule [and interest from the date and calculated on the basis specified in the Schedule].[5] *[see Notes 2 and 3]*

5.   All correspondence about this notice should be sent to the landlord/landlord's agent at the address given below.

---

[1] The Act defines a fixed charge as (a) rent, (b) any service charge (as defined by section 18 of the Landlord and Tenant Act 1985, disregarding the words 'of a dwelling') and (c) any amount payable under a tenant covenant of the tenancy providing for payment of a liquidated sum in the event of failure to comply with the covenant.

[2] Delete alternative as appropriate.

[3] 'Landlord' for these purposes includes any person who has the right to enforce the charge.

[4] The Schedule can be in any form, but must indicate in relation to each item the date on which it was revised, the revised amount payable and whether it is rent, service charge or a fixed charge of some other kind (in which case particulars of the nature of the charge should be given).

[5] Delete words in brackets if not applicable. If applicable, the Schedule must state the basis on which interest is calculated (for example, rate of interest, date from which it is payable and provision of Lease or other document under which it is payable).

Date . . . . Signature of landlord/landlord's agent . . . .

Name and address of landlord . . . .

. . . .

. . . .

[Name and address of agent . . . .

. . . .

. . . .]

NOTES

1.   The person giving you this notice alleges that you are still liable for the performance of the tenant's obligations under the tenancy to which this notice relates, either as a previous tenant bound by privity of contract or an authorised guarantee agreement, or because you are the guarantor of a previous tenant. You should already have been given a notice by which the landlord (or other person entitled to enforce payment, such as a management company) protected his right to require you to pay the amount specified in that notice. The purpose of this notice is to protect the landlord's right to require you to pay a larger amount, because the amount specified in the original notice could not be finally determined at the time of the original notice (for example, because there was a dispute concerning an outstanding rent review or if the charge was a service charge collected on account and adjusted following final determination).

Validity of notice

2.   The notice is not valid unless the original notice contained a warning that the amount in question might subsequently be determined to be greater. In addition, the landlord is required to give this notice within three months of the date on which the amount was finally determined. If the original notice did not include that warning, or if this notice has been given late, then this notice is not valid and the landlord cannot recover the greater amount, but only the smaller amount specified in the original notice. The date of the giving of this notice may not be the date written on the notice or the date on which you actually saw it. It may, for instance, be the date on which the notice was delivered through the post to your last address known to the person giving notice. If you are in any doubt, you should seek advice immediately.

Interest

3.   If interest is chargeable on the amount due, the landlord does not have to state the precise amount of interest, but he must have stated the basis on which the interest is calculated, or he will not be able to claim interest at all.

APPENDIX 7

Landlord's Requests for Release from Covenants

FORM 3

PART I

LANDLORD'S NOTICE APPLYING FOR RELEASE FROM LANDLORD COVENANTS OF A TENANCY ON ASSIGNMENT OF WHOLE OF REVERSION

(Landlord and Tenant (Covenants) Act 1995, sections 6 and 8)

To [name and address]: . . . .
. . . .

> IMPORTANT—THIS NOTICE IS INTENDED TO RELEASE YOUR LANDLORD FROM HIS OBLI-
> GATIONS WHEN HE TRANSFERS HIS INTEREST TO A NEW LANDLORD. IF YOU CONSIDER
> THAT THERE IS GOOD REASON FOR YOUR LANDLORD **NOT** TO BE RELEASED, YOU MUST
> ACT QUICKLY. READ THE NOTICE AND ALL THE NOTES OVERLEAF CAREFULLY. IF YOU ARE
> IN ANY DOUBT ABOUT THE ACTION YOU SHOULD TAKE, SEEK ADVICE IMMEDIATELY,
> FOR INSTANCE FROM A SOLICITOR OR CITIZENS ADVICE BUREAU.

1. This notice is given under section 8 of the Landlord and Tenant (Covenants) Act 1995. *[see Note 1]*

2. It relates to (address and description of property) . . . .
. . . .
let under a lease dated . . . . and made between . . . .
. . . .
. . . .
of which you are the tenant.

3. I/we [propose to transfer] [transferred on . . . .]¹
the whole of the landlord's interest and wish to be released from the landlord's obligations under the
tenancy with effect from the date of the transfer. *[see Note 2]*

4. If you consider that it is reasonable for me/us to be released, you do not need to do anything, but
it would help me/us if you notify me/us using Part II of this Form. *[see Note 3]*

5. If you do **not** consider it reasonable for me/us to be released, you **must** notify me/us of your
objection, using Part II of this Form, within the period of **FOUR WEEKS** beginning with the giving of
this notice, or I/we will be released in any event. You may withdraw your objection at any time by
notifying me/us in writing. *[see Notes 4–6]*

6. All correspondence about this notice should be sent to the landlord/landlord's agent at the
address given below.

---

¹ Delete alternative as appropriate.

Date . . . . Signature of landlord/landlord's agent . . . .

Name and address of landlord . . . .

. . . .

. . . .

[Name and address of agent . . . .

. . . .

. . . .]

NOTES TO PART I

Release of landlord

1.   The landlord is about to transfer his interest to a new landlord, or has just done so, and is applying to be released from the obligations of the landlord under your tenancy. You have a number of options: you may expressly agree to the landlord's being released; you may object to his being released (with the option of withdrawing your objection later); or you may do nothing, in which case the landlord will automatically be released, with effect from the date of the transfer, once four weeks have elapsed from the date of the giving of the notice. If you choose to oppose release, you must act within four weeks of the giving of the notice.

Validity of notice

2.   The landlord must give this notice either before the transfer or within the period of four weeks beginning with the date of the transfer. If the notice has been given late, it is not valid. You should read Note 4 below concerning the date of the giving of the notice.

Agreeing to release

3.   If you are content for the landlord to be released, you may notify him of this using Part II of this Form, and the landlord will then be released as from the date of the transfer. If you do this, you may not later change your mind and object.

Objecting to release

4.   If you think that it is not reasonable for the landlord to be released, you may object to release by notifying the landlord, using Part II of this Form. You must, however, do this within four weeks of the date of the giving of the notice. The date of the giving of the notice may not be the date written on the notice or the date on which you actually saw it. It may, for instance, be the date on which the notice was delivered through the post to your last address known by the landlord. If there has been any delay in your seeing this notice you may need to act very quickly. If you are in any doubt, you should seek advice immediately. If you change your mind after objecting, you may consent instead, at any time, by notifying the landlord *in writing* that you now consent to his being released and that your objection is withdrawn.

5.   If you object within the time limit, the landlord will only be released if *either* he applies to a court and the court decides that it is reasonable for him to be released, *or* you withdraw your objection by a notice in writing as explained in Note 4 above.

6.   In deciding whether to object, you should bear in mind that if the court finds that it is reasonable for the landlord to be released, or if you withdraw your objection late, you may have to pay costs.

FORM 4

PART I

LANDLORD'S NOTICE APPLYING FOR RELEASE FROM LANDLORD COVENANTS OF A TENANCY ON ASSIGNMENT OF PART OF REVERSION

(Landlord and Tenant (Covenants) Act 1995, sections 6 and 8)

To [name and address]: ....
....

> IMPORTANT—THIS NOTICE IS INTENDED TO RELEASE YOUR LANDLORD PARTLY FROM HIS OBLIGATIONS WHEN HE TRANSFERS PART OF HIS INTEREST TO A NEW LANDLORD. IF YOU CONSIDER THAT THERE IS GOOD REASON FOR YOUR LANDLORD **NOT** TO BE RELEASED, YOU MUST ACT QUICKLY. READ THE NOTICE AND ALL THE NOTES OVER LEAF CAREFULLY. IF YOU ARE IN ANY DOUBT ABOUT THE ACTION YOU SHOULD TAKE, SEEK ADVICE IMMEDIATELY, FOR INSTANCE FROM A SOLICITOR OR CITIZENS ADVICE BUREAU.

1. This notice is given under section 8 of the Landlord and Tenant (Covenants) Act 1995. *[see Note 1]*

2. It relates to (address and description of property) ....
....
let under a lease dated .... and made between ....
....
of which you are the tenant.

3. I/we [propose to transfer] [transferred on ....]¹
part of the landlord's interest, namely ....
and wish to be released from the landlord's obligations under the tenancy, to the extent that they fall to be complied with in relation to that part, with effect from the date of the transfer. *[see Note 2]*

4. If you consider that it is reasonable for me/us to be released, you do not need to do anything, but it would help me/us if you notify me/us using Part II of this Form. *[see Note 3]*

5. If you do **not** consider it reasonable for me/us to be released, you **must** notify me/us of your objection, using Part II of this Form, within the period of **FOUR WEEKS** beginning with the giving of this notice, or I/we will be released in any event. You may withdraw your objection at any time by notifying me/us in writing. *[see Notes 4–6]*

6. All correspondence about this notice should be sent to the landlord/landlord's agent at the address given below.

Date .... Signature of landlord/landlord's agent ....
Name and address of landlord ....
....
....
[Name and address of agent ....
....]

---

¹ Delete alternative as appropriate.

NOTES TO PART I

Release of landlord

1.   The landlord is about to transfer part of his interest to a new landlord, or has just done so, and is applying to be released from the obligations of the landlord under your tenancy, to the extent that they fall to be complied with in relation to that part. You have a number of options: you may expressly agree to the landlord's being released; you may object to his being released (with the option of withdrawing your objection later); or you may do nothing, in which case the landlord will automatically be released, with effect from the date of the assignment, once four weeks have elapsed from the date of the giving of the notice. If you choose to oppose release, you must act within four weeks of the giving of the notice.

Validity of notice

2.   The landlord must give this notice either before the transfer or within the period of four weeks beginning with the date of the transfer. If the notice has been given late, it is not valid. You should read Note 4 below concerning the date of the giving of the notice.

Agreeing to release

3.   If you are content for the landlord to be released, you may notify him of this using Part II of this Form, and the landlord will then be released as from the date of the transfer. If you do this, you may not later change your mind and object.

Objecting to release

4.   If you think that it is not reasonable for the landlord to be released, you may object to release by notifying the landlord, using Part II of this Form. You must, however, do this within four weeks of the date of the giving of the notice. The date of the giving of the notice may not be the date written on the notice or the date on which you actually saw it. It may, for instance, be the date on which the notice was delivered through the post to your last address known to the person giving the notice. If there has been any delay in your seeing this notice you may need to act very quickly. If you are in any doubt, you should seek advice immediately. If you change your mind after objecting, you may consent instead, at any time, by notifying the landlord *in writing* that you now consent to his being released and that your objection is withdrawn.

5.   If you object within the time limit, the landlord will only be released if *either* he applies to a court and the court decides that it is reasonable for him to be released, *or* you withdraw your objection by a notice in writing as explained in Note 4 above.

6.   In deciding whether to object, you should bear in mind that if the court finds that it is reasonable for the landlord to be released, or if you withdraw your objection late, you may have to pay costs.

FORM 5

PART I

FORMER LANDLORD'S NOTICE APPLYING FOR RELEASE FROM LANDLORD COVENANTS OF A TENANCY

(Landlord and Tenant (Covenants) Act 1995, sections 7 and 8)

To [name and address]: ....
....

IMPORTANT—THIS NOTICE IS INTENDED TO RELEASE THE FORMER LANDLORD OF THE PROPERTY FROM HIS OBLIGATIONS UNDER YOUR TENANCY. IF YOU CONSIDER THAT THERE IS GOOD REASON FOR THE FORMER LANDLORD **NOT** TO BE RELEASED, YOU MUST ACT QUICKLY. READ THE NOTICE AND ALL THE NOTES OVERLEAF CAREFULLY. IF YOU ARE IN ANY DOUBT ABOUT THE ACTION YOU SHOULD TAKE, SEEK ADVICE IMMEDIATELY, FOR INSTANCE FROM A SOLICITOR OR CITIZENS ADVICE BUREAU.

---

1. This notice is given under section 8 of the Landlord and Tenant (Covenants) Act 1995. *[see Note 1]*

2. It relates to (address and description of property) ....
....

let under a lease dated .... and made between ....
....
....

of which you are the tenant.

3. I/we was/were formerly landlord of the property of which you are tenant and remained bound by the landlord's obligations under the tenancy after transferring the landlord's interest. The landlord's interest, or part of it [is about to be transferred] [was transferred on][1]. I/we wish to be released from my/our obligations with effect from the date of that transfer. *[see Note 2]*

4. If you consider that it is reasonable for me/us to be released, you do not need to do anything, but it would help me/us if you notify me/us using Part II of this Form. *[see Note 3]*

5. If you do **not** consider it reasonable for me/us to be released, you **must** notify me/us of your objection, using Part II of this Form, within the period of **FOUR WEEKS** beginning with the giving of this notice, or I/we will be released in any event. You may withdraw your objection at any time by notifying me/us in writing. *[see Notes 4–6]*

6. All correspondence about this notice should be sent to the former landlord/former landlord's agent at the address given below.

Date .... Signature of former landlord/agent ....
Name and address of former landlord ....
....
....

---

[1] Delete alternative as appropriate.

[Name and address of agent ....
....
....]

NOTES TO PART I

Release of former landlord

1.   Your landlord is about to transfer his interest, or part of it, to a new landlord, or has just done so, and a former landlord of the property is applying to be released from his obligations, from which he was not released when he transferred the landlord's interest himself. You have a number of options: you may expressly agree to the former landlord's being released; you may object to his being released (with the option of withdrawing your objection later); or you may do nothing, in which case the former landlord will automatically be released, with effect from the date of the present transfer, once four weeks have elapsed from the date of the giving of the notice. If you choose to oppose release, you must act within four weeks of the giving of the notice.

Validity of notice

2.   The former landlord is required to give this notice either before the transfer by the present landlord takes place or within the period of four weeks beginning with the date of the transfer. If the notice has been given late, it is not valid. You should read Note 4 below concerning the date of the giving of the notice.

Agreeing to release

3.   If you are content for the former landlord to be released, you may notify him of this using Part II of this Form, and the former landlord will then automatically be released as from the date of the present transfer. If you do this, you may not later change your mind and object.

Objecting to release

4.   If you think that it is not reasonable for the former landlord to be released, you may object to release by notifying the former landlord, using Part II of this Form. You must, however, do this within four weeks of the date of the giving of the notice. The date of the giving of the notice may not be the date written on the notice or the date on which you actually saw it. It may, for instance, be the date on which the notice was delivered through the post to your last address known to the person giving the notice. If there has been any delay in your seeing this notice you may need to act very quickly. If you are in any doubt, you should seek advice immediately. If you change your mind after objecting, you may consent instead, at any time, by notifying the former landlord *in writing* that you now consent to his being released and that your objection is withdrawn.

5.   If you object within the time limit, the former landlord will only be released if *either* he applies to a court and the court decides that it is reasonable for him to be released, *or* you withdraw your objection by a notice in writing as explained in Note 4 above.

6.   In deciding whether to object, you should bear in mind that if the court finds that it is reasonable for the former landlord to be released, or if you withdraw your objection late, you may have to pay costs.

FORM 6

PART I

FORMER LANDLORD'S NOTICE APPLYING FOR RELEASE FROM LANDLORD COVENANTS OF A TENANCY (FORMER LANDLORD HAVING ASSIGNED PART OF REVERSION)

(Landlord and Tenant (Covenants) Act 1995, sections 7 and 8)

To [name and address]: ....
....

IMPORTANT—THIS NOTICE IS INTENDED TO RELEASE THE FORMER LANDLORD OF THE PROPERTY PARTIALLY FROM HIS OBLIGATIONS UNDER YOUR TENANCY. IF YOU CONSIDER THAT THERE IS GOOD REASON FOR THE FORMER LANDLORD **NOT** TO BE RELEASED, YOU MUST ACT QUICKLY. READ THE NOTICE AND ALL THE NOTES OVERLEAF CAREFULLY. IF YOU ARE IN ANY DOUBT ABOUT THE ACTION YOU SHOULD TAKE, SEEK ADVICE IMMEDIATELY, FOR INSTANCE FROM A SOLICITOR OR CITIZENS ADVICE BUREAU.

---

1. This notice is given under section 8 of the Landlord and Tenant (Covenants) Act 1995. *[see Note 1]*

2. It relates to (address and description of property) ....
....

let under a lease dated .... and made between ....
....
....

of which you are the tenant.

3. I/we was/were formerly landlord of the property of which you are tenant and remained bound by all the landlord's obligations under the tenancy after transferring part of the landlord's interest, namely ....
....
The landlord's interest, or part of it [is about to be transferred] [was transferred on][1]
I/we wish to be released from my/our obligations with effect from the date of that transfer. *[see Note 2]*

4. If you consider that it is reasonable for me/us to be released, you do not need to do anything, but it would help me/us if you notify me/us using Part II of this Form. *[see Note 3]*

5. If you do **not** consider it reasonable for me/us to be released, you **must** notify me/us of your objection, using Part II of this Form, within the period of **FOUR WEEKS** beginning with the giving of this notice, or I/we will be released in any event. You may withdraw your objection at any time by notifying me/us in writing. *[see Notes 4–6]*

6. All correspondence about this notice should be sent to the former landlord/former landlord's agent at the address given below.

---

[1] Delete alternative as appropriate.

Date . . . . Signature of former landlord/agent . . . .

Name and address of former landlord . . . .

. . . .

. . . .

[Name and address of agent . . . .

. . . .

. . . .]

NOTES TO PART I

Release of former landlord

1.   Your landlord is about to transfer his interest, or part of it, to a new landlord, or has just done so, and a former landlord of the property is applying to be released from his obligations in relation to part of the landlord's interest, from which he was not released when he transferred that part himself. You have a number of options: you may expressly agree to the former landlord's being released; you may object to his being released (with the option of withdrawing your objection later); or you may do nothing, in which case the former landlord will automatically be released, with effect from the date of the present transfer, once four weeks have elapsed from the date of the giving of the notice. If you choose to oppose release, you must act within four weeks of the giving of the notice.

Validity of notice

2.   The former landlord is required to give this notice either before the transfer by the present landlord takes place or within the period of four weeks beginning with the date of the transfer. If the notice has been given late, it is not valid. You should read Note 4 below concerning the date of the giving of the notice.

Agreeing to release

3.   If you are content for the former landlord to be released, you may notify him of this using Part II of this Form, and the former landlord will then automatically be released as from the date of the present transfer. If you do this, you may not later change your mind and object.

Objecting to release

4.   If you think that it is not reasonable for the former landlord to be released, you may object to release by notifying the former landlord, using Part II of this Form. You must, however, do this within four weeks of the date of the giving of the notice. The date of the giving of the notice may not be the date written on the notice or the date on which you actually saw it. It may, for instance, be the date on which the notice was delivered through the post to your last address known to the person giving the notice. If there has been any delay in your seeing this notice you may need to act very quickly. If you are in any doubt, you should seek advice immediately. If you change your mind after objecting, you may consent instead, at any time, by notifying the former landlord *in writing* that you now consent to his being released and that your objection is withdrawn.

5.   If you object within the time limit, the former landlord will only be released if *either* he applies to a court and the court decides that it is reasonable for him to be released, *or* you withdraw your objection by a notice in writing as explained in Note 4 above.

6.   In deciding whether to object, you should bear in mind that if the court finds that it is reasonable for the former landlord to be released, or if you withdraw your objection late, you may have to pay costs.

APPENDIX 8

Tenant's Responses to Landlord's Requests for Release from Covenants

PART II

TENANT'S RESPONSE TO LANDLORD'S NOTICE APPLYING FOR RELEASE FROM LANDLORD COVENANTS OF A TENANCY ON ASSIGNMENT OF WHOLE OF REVERSION

(Landlord and Tenant (Covenants) Act 1995, section 8)

To [name and address]: ....
....

1. This notice is given under section 8 of the Landlord and Tenant (Covenants) Act 1995.

2. It relates to (address and description of property)
....
let under a lease dated . . . . and made between . . . .
....
....
Of which you are the landlord or have just transferred the landlord's interest.

3. You [propose to transfer] [transferred on . . . .][1]
the landlord's interest and have applied to be released from the landlord's obligations under the tenancy with effect from the date of the transfer.

4.[2] I/we agree to your being released from the landlord's obligations with effect from the date of the transfer. *[see Note 1]*

OR

4. I/we do **not** consider it reasonable that you should be released from the landlord's obligations, and object to the release. *[see Notes 2 and 3]*

5. All correspondence about this notice should be sent to the tenant/tenant's agent at the address given below.
Date . . . . Signature of tenant/tenant's agent . . . .
Name and address of tenant . . . .
....
....
[Name and address of agent . . . .
....
. . . .]

---

[1] Delete alternative as appropriate.
[2] The tenant should select one version of paragraph 4 and cross out the other.

NOTES TO PART II

Agreement to release

1.   If the tenant has indicated agreement in paragraph 4 of the notice, you will automatically be released from the landlord's obligations under the tenancy with effect from the date of your transfer of the landlord's interest.

Objection to release

2.   If the tenant has indicated an objection in paragraph 4 of the notice, you will not be released unless either the tenant later withdraws his objection *or* you apply to the Country Court to declare that it is reasonable for you to be released, and the court so declares. If you are not released, you may still apply for release when the landlord's interest, or part of it, is next transferred, and it may therefore be sensible to make arrangements for the person to whom you are making the transfer to inform you when he intends to transfer the landlord's interest in his turn.

Validity of notice of objection

3.   A notice of objection by the tenant is only valid if he has given it to you within the period of four weeks beginning with the date on which you gave him your notice applying for release. If you are in any doubt, you should seek advice before applying to the court.

PART II

TENANT'S RESPONSE TO LANDLORD'S NOTICE APPLYING FOR RELEASE FROM LANDLORD COVENANTS OF A TENANCY ON ASSIGNMENT OF PART OF REVERSION

(Landlord and Tenant (Covenants) Act 1995, section 8)

To [name and address]: ....
....

1.   This notice is given under section 8 of the Landlord and Tenant (Covenants) Act 1995.

2.   It relates to (address and description of property) ....
....
let under a lease dated .... and made between ....
....
....
of which you are the landlord or have just transferred part of the landlord's interest.

3.   You [propose to transfer] [transferred on..]¹
part of the landlord's interest, namely ....
and have applied to be released from the landlord's obligations under the tenancy, to the extent that
they fall to be complied with in relation to that part, with effect from the date of the transfer.

4.²   I/we agree to your being released from the landlord's obligations to that extent with effect from
the date of the transfer. *[see Note 1]*

OR

4.   I/we do **not** consider it reasonable that you should be released from the landlord's obligations,
and object to the release. *[see Notes 2 and 3]*

5.   All correspondence about this notice should be sent to the tenant/tenant's agent at the address
given below.

Date .... Signature of tenant/tenant's agent ....
Name and address of tenant ....
....
....
[Name and address of agent ....
....
....]

NOTES TO PART II

Agreement to release

1.   If the tenant has indicated agreement in paragraph 4 of the notice, you will automatically
be released from the landlord's obligations under the tenancy, to the extent that they fall to be

---

¹   Delete alternative as appropriate.

²   The tenant should select one version of paragraph 4 and cross out the other.

complied with in relation to the part of your interest being transferred, with effect from the date of the transfer.

Objection to release

2.   If the tenant has indicated an objection in paragraph 4 of the notice, you will not be released unless *either* the tenant later withdraws his objection *or* you apply to the County Court to declare that it is reasonable for you to be released, and the court so declares. If you are not released, you may still apply for release when the landlord's interest, or part of it, is next transferred, and it may therefore be sensible to make arrangements for the person to whom you are making the transfer to inform you when he intends to transfer the landlord's interest in his turn.

Validity of notice of objection

3.   A notice of objection by the tenant is only valid if he has given it to you within the period of four weeks beginning with the date on which you gave him your notice applying for release. If you are in any doubt, you should seek advice before applying to the court.

PART II

TENANT'S RESPONSE TO FORMER LANDLORD'S NOTICE APPLYING FOR RELEASE FROM LANDLORD COVENANTS OF A TENANCY

(Landlord and Tenant (Covenants) Act 1995, section 8)

To [name and address]: ....

....

1.   This notice is given under section 8 of the Landlord and Tenant (Covenants) Act 1995.

2.   It relates to (address and description of property) ....

....

let under a lease dated . . . . and made between ....

....

....

of which you were formerly landlord.

3.   You have applied to be released from the landlord's obligations under the tenancy with effect from the date of a [proposed transfer] [transfer on . . . .][1] of the landlord's interest.

4.[2]   I/we agree to your being released from the landlord's obligations with effect from the date of that transfer. *[see Note 1]*

OR

4.   I/we do **not** consider it reasonable that you should be released from the landlord's obligations, and object to your being so released. *[see Notes 2 and 3]*

5.   All correspondence about this notice should be sent to the tenant/tenant's agent at the address given below.

Date . . . . Signature of tenant/tenant's agent ....

Name and address of tenant ....

....

....

[Name and address of agent ....

....

....]

NOTES TO PART II

Agreement to release

1.   If the tenant has indicated agreement in paragraph 4 of the notice, you will automatically be released from the landlord's obligations under the tenancy with effect from the date of the transfer by the present landlord.

---

[1] Delete alternative as appropriate.

[2] The tenant should select one version of paragraph 4 and cross out the other.

Objection to release

2.   If the tenant has indicated an objection in paragraph 4 of the notice, you will not be released unless *either* the tenant later withdraws his objection *or* you apply to the County Court to declare that it is reasonable for you to be released, and the court so declares. If you are not released, you may still apply for release when the reversion, or part of it, is next assigned, and it may therefore be sensible to make arrangements for you to be informed when the present landlord's transferee intends to transfer the landlord's interest in his turn.

Validity of notice of objection

3.   A notice of objection by the tenant is only valid if he has given it to you within the period of four weeks beginning with the date on which you gave him your notice applying for release. If you are in any doubt, you should seek advice before applying to the court.

PART II

TENANT'S RESPONSE TO FORMER LANDLORD'S NOTICE APPLYING FOR RELEASE FROM LANDLORD COVENANTS OF A TENANCY (FORMER LANDLORD HAVING ASSIGNED PART OF REVERSION)

(Landlord and Tenant (Covenants) Act 1995, section 8)

To [name and address]: ....

....

1.   This notice is given under section 8 of the Landlord and Tenant (Covenants) Act 1995.

2.   It relates to (address and description of property) ....

....

let under a lease dated .... and made between ....

....

....

of which you were formerly landlord.

3.   You remain bound by the landlord's obligations under the tenancy in relation to a part of the landlord's interest which you previously assigned, namely ....

....

You have applied to be released from those obligations, to the extent that they relate to that part, with effect from the date of a [proposed transfer] [transfer on ....]¹ of the landlord's interest.

4.² I/we agree to your being released from the landlord's obligations to that effect from the date of that transfer. *[see Note 1]*

OR

4.   I/we do **not** consider it reasonable that you should be released from the landlord's obligations, and object to your being so released. *[see Notes 2 and 3]*

5.   All correspondence about this notice should be sent to the tenant/tenant's agent at the address given below.

Date .... Signature of tenant/tenant's agent ....

Name and address of tenant ....

....

....

[Name and address of agent ....

....

....]

---

¹ Delete alternative as appropriate.
² The tenant should select one version of paragraph 4 and cross out the other.

NOTES TO PART II

Agreement to release
1.   If the tenant has indicated agreement in paragraph 4 of the notice, you will automatically be released from the landlord's obligations under the tenancy to the appropriate extent with effect from the date of the transfer by the present landlord.

Objection to release
2.   If the tenant has indicated an objection in paragraph 4 of the notice, you will not be released unless *either* the tenant later withdraws his objection *or* you apply to the County Court to declare that it is reasonable for you to be released, and the court so declares. If you are not released, you may still apply for release when the reversion, or part of it, is next transferred, and it may therefore be sensible to make arrangements for you to be informed when the present landlord's transferee intends to transfer the landlord's interest in his turn.

Validity of notice of objection
3.   A notice of objection by the tenant is only valid if he has given it to you within the period of four weeks beginning with the date on which you gave him your notice applying for release. If you are in any doubt, you should seek advice before applying to the court.

Notice for Binding Apportionment on Assignment of Part

FORM 7

PART I

JOINT NOTICE BY TENANT AND ASSIGNEE FOR BINDING APPORTIONMENT OF LIABILITY UNDER NON-ATTRIBUTABLE TENANT COVENANTS OF A TENANCY ON ASSIGNMENT OF PART OF PROPERTY

(Landlord and Tenant (Covenants) Act 1995, sections 9 and 10)

To [name and address]: ....
....

IMPORTANT—THIS NOTICE IS INTENDED TO AFFECT THE WAY IN WHICH YOU CAN ENFORCE THE TENANT'S OBLIGATIONS UNDER THE TENANCY AS BETWEEN THE TENANT AND THE NEW TENANT. IF YOU CONSIDER THAT THERE IS GOOD REASON WHY YOU SHOULD **NOT** BE BOUND BY THEIR AGREEMENT, YOU MUST ACT QUICKLY. READ THE NOTICE AND ALL THE NOTES OVERLEAF CAREFULLY. IF YOU ARE IN ANY DOUBT ABOUT THE ACTION YOU SHOULD TAKE, SEEK ADVICE IMMEDIATELY, FOR INSTANCE FROM A SOLICITOR OR CITIZENS ADVICE BUREAU.

---

1. This notice is given under section 10 of the Landlord and Tenant (Covenants) Act 1995. *[see Note 1]*

2. It relates to (address and description of property) ....
....
let under a lease dated .... and made between ....
....
....
of which you are the landlord.[1]

3. We are the parties to a [proposed transfer] [transfer on ....]²
of part of the property comprised in the tenancy, namely ....
....
We are jointly and severally liable to perform the obligation(s) specified in the attached Schedule and have agreed to divide that liability between us in the manner specified in the Schedule.³ We wish

---

¹ 'Landlord', for these purposes, includes any person for the time being entitled to enforce the obligations in question (for example, a management company).
² Delete alternative as appropriate.
³ The Schedule must be in writing, and must specify the nature of the obligation, the term or condition of the Lease or other instrument under which it arises and the manner in which liability to perform it is divided under the agreement (for example, an obligation to pay service charge under a specific provision of the lease might be divided equally). It may be helpful to attach a copy of the agreement to the notice.

this agreement to be binding on you as well as between us, with effect from the date of the transfer. *[see Note 2]*

4. If you consider that it is reasonable for you to be bound by this agreement, you do not need to do anything, but it would help us if you notify us using Part II of this Form. *[see Note 3]*

5. If you do **not** consider it reasonable for you to be bound by this agreement, you **must** notify both of us of your objection, using Part II of this Form, within the period of **FOUR WEEKS** beginning with the giving of this notice. You may withdraw your objection at any time by notifying us in writing. *[see Notes 4–6]*

6. All correspondence about this notice should be copied, one copy sent to each of the parties to the agreement, at the addresses given below.

Signature of tenant/tenant's agents . . . .

Name and address of tenant . . . .

. . . .

. . . .

[Name and address of agent . . . .

. . . .

. . . .]

Signature of new tenant/agent . . . .

Name and address of new tenant . . . .

. . . .

. . . .

[Name and address of agent . . . .

. . . .

. . . .]

Date . . . .

NOTES TO PART I

Apportionment of liability

1. The tenant is about to transfer, or has just transferred, part of his interest to a new tenant, but they are jointly and severally liable for a particular obligation or obligations covering the whole of the property. They have agreed to divide that liability between them, and are applying for you as the landlord to be bound as well, so that you can only enforce the liability against each of them as set out in their agreement. If you are bound, any subsequent landlord to whom you may transfer your interest will also be bound. You have a number of options: you may expressly agree to be bound; you may object to being bound (with the option of withdrawing your objection later); or you may do nothing, in which case you will automatically be bound, with effect from the date of the transfer, once four weeks have elapsed from the date of the giving of the notice. If you choose to object, you must act within four weeks of the giving of the notice.

Validity of notice

2. This notice must be given either before the transfer or within the period of four weeks beginning with the date of the transfer. If the notice has been given late, it is not valid. You should read Note 4 below concerning the date of the giving of the notice.

Agreeing to be bound

3. If you are content to be bound, you may notify the tenant and new tenant using Part II of this Form (sending a copy to each of them), and all of you will be bound with effect from the date of the transfer. If you do this, you may not later change your mind and object.

Objecting to being bound

4.   If you think that it is not reasonable for you to be bound, you may object by notifying the tenant and new tenant, using Part II of this Form (sending a copy to each of them). You must, however, do this within four weeks of the date of the giving of this notice. The date of the giving of the notice may not be the date written on the notice or the date on which you actually saw it. It may, for instance, be the date on which the notice was delivered through the post to your last address known to the person giving the notice. If there has been any delay in your seeing this notice you may need to act very quickly. If you are in any doubt, you should seek advice immediately. If you change your mind after objecting, you may consent instead, at any time, by notifying *both* the tenant and new tenant *in writing* that you now consent to be bound and that your objection is withdrawn.

5.   If you object within the time limit, the apportionment will only bind you if *either* the tenant and new tenant apply to a court and the court decides that it is reasonable for you to be bound, *or* you withdraw your objection by notice in writing as explained in Note 4 above.

6.   In deciding whether to object, you should bear in mind that if the court finds that it is reasonable for you to be bound, *or* if you withdraw your objection late, you may have to pay costs.

APPENDIX 10

Request for an Overriding Lease by Former Tenant Pursuant to s 19 of the Landlord and Tenant (Covenants) Act 1995

To: [name and address of landlord]

From: [name and address of former tenant]

The Property: [address of property]

The Lease: A lease dated [insert date] made between [insert name of original landlord] and [insert name of original tenant]

TAKE NOTICE that on [insert date] I/we received from you a notice under section 17 of the Landlord and Tenant (Covenants) Act 1995 ('the Act') requiring me/us to pay a fixed charge of [insert amount] (the 'Qualifying Payment').

I/we duly paid the qualifying Payment to you on [insert date] and am/are entitled to request an overriding lease of the Property from you in accordance with section 19 of the Act.

I/we request that within a reasonable time of your receipt of this notice you grant to me/us an overriding lease of the Property.

Signed [Former Tenant]

Dated [insert date]

APPENDIX 11

Precedent for an Overriding Lease Granted Pursuant to s 19 of the Landlord and Tenant (Covenants) Act 1995

[Insert Land Registry heading for registered lease]

This lease is dated the   day of   200_

1. In this lease:
    1.1 'the Act' means the Landlord and Tenant (Covenants) Act 1995
    1.2 'the Landlord' means [insert name and address]
    1.3 'the Tenant' means [insert name and address]
    1.4 'the Demised Property' means [insert address] being the premises demised by the Original Lease
    1.5 'the Original Lease' means the lease of the Demised Property dated [   ] made between the Original Landlord and the Original Tenant
    1.6 'the Original Landlord' means [insert name and address]
    1.7 'the Original Tenant' means [insert name and address]
    1.8 'the Term' means the unexpired residue at the date of this lease of the term granted by the Original Lease plus three days
2. This lease is an overriding lease granted pursuant to section 19 of the Act and is [not] a new tenancy for the purposes of section 1 of the Act[1]
3. In consideration of [insert amount] being the sum payable by the Tenant to the Landlord pursuant to section 17 of the Act[2] (receipt of which the Landlord hereby acknowledges) and of the covenants set out below the Landlord hereby demises unto the Tenant the Demised Property for the Term [together with the rights granted to the Original Tenant by the Original Lease]
4. This lease is granted subject to and with the benefit of the Original Lease
5. The Tenant covenants with the Landlord:
    5.1 to pay the rent payable under the Original Lease in accordance with the terms for payment in the Original Lease
    5.2 to perform and observe all the covenants and conditions on the part of the Original Tenant in the Original Lease except those which are expressed to be personal or which have been spent[3]
    5.3 In conformity with s. 19(6) of the Act to pay the Landlord's surveyors' and solicitors' costs in connection with the negotiation and grant of this lease[4]

---

[1] This statement is obligatory in an overriding lease under the 1995 Act (s. 20(2) of the Act and the Land Registration (Overriding Leases) Rules 1995). The overriding lease will be a new tenancy under the Act only if the original lease was granted on or after 1 January 1996.

[2] Under s. 17 of the Act, where a landlord wishes to recover a fixed charge (which includes rent or service charge) from a former tenant, the landlord must serve notice on the tenant within six months of the charge becoming due.

[3] Covenants in the original lease which are expressed to be personal or which have been spent should not be included in the overriding lease (s. 19(3) and s. 19(4)(b) of the Act).

[4] Payment of the landlord's reasonable costs is obligatory (s. 19(6) of the Act).

6.   The Landlord covenants with the Tenant to perform and observe all the covenants and conditions on the part of the Original Landlord in the Original Lease except for those which are expressed to be personal or which have been spent

7.   If the rent or any part of it shall be unpaid for twenty one days after becoming due (whether formally demanded or not) or if any of the Tenant's covenants shall not be performed or observed or if the Tenant shall become bankrupt or go into liquidation (otherwise than for the purpose of amalgamation or reconstruction) or enter into an arrangement or composition for the benefit of its creditors then and in any such case the Landlord or any person authorised by the Landlord may re-enter the Demised Property or any part of it in the name of the whole and thereupon this lease shall absolutely determine

8.   The parties hereby agree and declare that the Contracts (Rights of Third Parties) Act 1999 shall not apply to this lease

9.   It is hereby certified that there is no Agreement for Lease to which this lease gives effect within the meaning of section 240 of the Finance Act 1994

IN WITNESS whereof this lease has been executed by the parties as a deed the day and year first before written

[SIGNED as a deed by the said
in the presence of
Witness
Address

Occupation   ]

[THE COMMON SEAL of
was hereunto affixed in the presence of

Director

Secretary   ]

Specimen Notices under the Law of Property Act 1925, s 146

SECTION 146 NOTICE FOR REMEDIABLE BREACH
(eg, UNAUTHORISED CHANGE OF USE)

To [tenant's name] of [tenant's address] the tenant of the property known as [address of subject property] ('the Property').

We [landlord's solicitors' name] of [landlord's solicitors' address] as solicitors and agents for your landlord [name of landlord] ('the Landlord') hereby give you notice as follows:

1.   The lease dated [date of lease] ('the Lease') and made between (1) [name of original landlord] and (2) [name of original tenant] contains covenants binding on you as follows:
    (i)   Not to use the Property otherwise than for [permitted user]
    (ii)   Not to commit a breach of planning control.
2.   The above covenants have been broken and the particular breaches complained of are the use of the Property for [insert unauthorised use] and without having obtained planning permission for the change of use.
3.   We require you to remedy all those breaches and to pay compensation to the Landlord for them.
4.   If you fail to comply with this notice within [28 days] [a reasonable time] it is the intention of the Landlord to forfeit the Lease and to claim damages for breach of covenant.

Dated

Signed

SECTION 146 NOTICE FOR IRREMEDIABLE BREACH
(eg, UNAUTHORISED SUB-LETTING)

To [tenant's name] of [tenant's address] the tenant of the property known as [address of subject property] ('the Property').

We [landlord's solicitors' name] of [landlord's solicitors' address] as solicitors and agents for your landlord [name of landlord] ('the Landlord') hereby give you notice as follows:

1.   The lease dated [date of lease] ('the Lease') and made between (1) [name of original landlord] and (2) [name of original tenant] contains a covenant binding on you not to sub-let the Property without the written consent of the Landlord.

2.   The above covenant has been broken and the particular breach complained of is the sub-letting of the Property to [name of sub-tenant] without the consent of the Landlord.

3.   The breach is one which is not capable of remedy. [We require you to remedy the breach if it is capable of remedy.]

4.   We require you to pay compensation to the Landlord for the breaches.

5.   If you fail to comply with this notice within [28 days] [a reasonable time] it is the intention of the Landlord to forfeit the Lease and to claim damages for breach of covenant.

Dated

Signed

SECTION 146 NOTICE FOR DILAPIDATIONS WHERE LEASEHOLD PROPERTY (REPAIRS) ACT 1938 DOES NOT APPLY

To [tenant's name] of [tenant's address] the tenant of the property known as [address of subject property] ('the Property').

We [landlord's solicitors' name] of [landlord's solicitors' address] as solicitors and agents for your landlord [name of landlord] ('the Landlord') hereby give you notice as follows:

1.   The lease dated [date of lease] ('the Lease') and made between (1) [name of original landlord] and (2) [name of original tenant] contains covenants binding on you as follows:
[set out relevant repairing covenants]

2.   The above covenants have been broken and the particular breaches complained of are committing or permitting the dilapidations specified in the Schedule of Dilapidations annexed hereto.

3.   We require you to remedy all those breaches and to pay compensation to the Landlord for them.

4.   If you fail to comply with this notice within [three months] [a reasonable time] it is the intention of the Landlord to forfeit the Lease and to claim damages for breach of covenant.

Dated

Signed

SECTION 146 NOTICE FOR DILAPIDATIONS WHERE LEASEHOLD PROPERTY (REPAIRS) ACT 1938 APPLIES

To [tenant's name] of [tenant's address] the tenant of the property known as [address of subject property] ('the Property').

We [landlord's solicitors' name] of [landlord's solicitors' address] as solicitors and agents for your landlord [name of landlord] ('the Landlord') hereby give you notice as follows:

1.   The lease dated [date of lease] ('the Lease') and made between (1) [name of original landlord] and (2) [name of original tenant] contains covenants binding on you as follows:
[set out relevant repairing covenants]

2.   The above covenants have been broken and the particular breaches complained of are committing or permitting the dilapidations specified in the Schedule of Dilapidations annexed hereto.

3.   We require you to remedy all those breaches and to pay compensation to the Landlord for them.

4.   If you fail to comply with this notice within [three months] [a reasonable time] it is the intention of the Landlord to forfeit the Lease and to claim damages for breach of covenant.

5.   Under the Leasehold Property (Repairs) Act 1938 ('the Act') you are entitled to serve on the Landlord a counter-notice claiming the benefit of the Act.

6.   The counter-notice may be served within 28 days from the date of service of this notice.

7.   The counter-notice may be served in any of the following ways:
   • By handing it to the Landlord personally;
   • By leaving it at the Landlord's last known place of abode or business in the United Kingdom;
   • By sending it by post in a registered letter or by the recorded delivery service addressed to the Landlord by name at that place of abode or business if the letter is not returned through the post undelivered; and service in this manner is deemed to be made at the time when in the ordinary course of post the letter would be delivered.

8.   The Landlord's name and address for service is [insert details]

Dated

Signed

Notices under the Landlord and Tenant Act 1954, s 40

Landlord and Tenant Act 1954, Part 2 (Notices) (Regulations) 2004 - Schedule 2 - Form 4

LT4

Landlord's Request for Information About Occupation and Sub-tenancies

Section 40(1) of the Landlord and Tenant Act 1954

(insert name and address of tenant)   To:

(insert name and address of landlord)   From:

(insert address or description of premises)   1. This notice relates to the following premises:

2. I give you notice under section 40(1) of the Landlord and Tenant Act 1954 that I require you to provide information -

    (a) by answering questions (1) to (3) in the Table below;

    (b) if you answer "yes" to question (2), by giving me the name and address of the person or persons concerned;

    (c) if you answer "yes" to question (3), by also answering questions (4) to (10) in the Table below;

    (d) if you answer "no" to question (8), by giving me the name and address of the sub-tenant; and

    (e) if you answer "yes" to question (10), by giving me details of the notice or request.

TABLE

(1)	Do you occupy the premises or any part of them wholly or partly for the purposes of a business that is carried on by you?
(2)	To the best of your knowledge and belief, does any other person own an interest in reversion in any part of the premises?
(3)	Does your tenancy have effect subject to any sub-tenancy on which your tenancy is immediately expectant?
(4)	What premises are comprised in the sub-tenancy?
(5)	For what term does it have effect or, if it is terminable by notice, by what notice can it be terminated?
(6)	What is the rent payable under it?
(7)	Who is the sub-tenant?

(8) To the best of your knowledge and belief, is the sub-tenant in occupation of the premises or of part of the premises comprised in the sub-tenancy?

(9) Is an agreement in force excluding, in relation to the sub-tenancy, the provisions of sections 24 to 28 of the Landlord and Tenant Act 1954?

(10) Has a notice been given under section 25 or 26(6) of that Act, or has a request been made under section 26 of that Act, in relation to the sub-tenancy?

3. You must give the information concerned in writing and within the period of one month beginning with the date of service of this notice.

4. Please send all correspondence about this notice to:

Name:

Address:

Signed: .... Date: ....

*(*delete whichever*
is inapplicable)

*[Landlord] *[On behalf of the landlord]

IMPORTANT NOTE FOR THE TENANT

This notice contains some words and phrases that you may not understand. The Notes below should help you, but it would be wise to seek professional advice, for example, from a solicitor or surveyor, before responding to this notice.

Once you have provided the information required by this notice, you must correct it if you realise that it is not, or is no longer, correct. This obligation lasts for six months from the date of service of this notice, but an exception is explained in the next paragraph. If you need to correct information already given, you must do so within one month of becoming aware that the information is incorrect.

The obligation will cease if, after transferring your tenancy, you notify the landlord of the transfer and of the name and address of the person to whom your tenancy has been transferred.

If you fail to comply with the requirements of this notice, or the obligation mentioned above, you may face civil proceedings for breach of the statutory duty that arises under section 40 of the Landlord and Tenant Act 1954. In any such proceedings a court may order you to comply with that duty and may make an award of damages.

NOTES

The sections mentioned below are sections of the Landlord and Tenant Act 1954, as amended, (most recently by the Regulatory Reform (Business Tenancies) (England and Wales) Order 2003)

Purpose of this notice

Your landlord (or, if he or she is a tenant, possibly your landlord's landlord) has sent you this notice in order to obtain information about your occupation and that of any sub-tenants. This information may be relevant to the taking of steps to end or renew your business tenancy.

Time limit for replying

You must provide the relevant information within one month of the date of service of this notice (section 40(1), (2) and (5)).

Information required

You do not have to give your answers on this form; you may use a separate sheet for this purpose. The notice requires you to provide, in writing, information in the form of answers to questions (1) to (3) in the Table above and, if you answer "yes" to question (3), also to provide information in the form of answers to questions (4) to (10) in that Table. Depending on your answer to question (2) and, if applicable in your case, questions (8) and (10), you must also provide the information referred to in paragraph 2(b), (d) and (e) of this notice. Question (2) refers to a person who owns an interest in reversion. You should answer "yes" to this question if you know or believe that there is a person who receives, or is entitled to receive, rent in respect of any part of the premises (other than the landlord who served this notice).

When you answer questions about sub-tenants, please bear in mind that, for these purposes, a sub-tenant includes a person retaining possession of premises by virtue of the Rent (Agriculture) Act 1976 or the Rent Act 1977 after the coming to an end of a sub-tenancy, and "sub-tenancy" includes a right so to retain possession (section 40(8)).

You should keep a copy of your answers and of any other information provided in response to questions (2), (8) or (10) above.

If, once you have given this information, you realise that it is not, or is no longer, correct, you must give the correct information within one month of becoming aware that the previous information is incorrect. Subject to the next paragraph, your duty to correct any information that you have already given continues for six months after you receive this notice (section 40(5)). You should give the correct information to the landlord who gave you this notice unless you receive notice of the transfer of his or her interest, and of the name and address of the person to whom that interest has been transferred. In that case, the correct information must be given to that person.

If you transfer your tenancy within the period of six months referred to above, your duty to correct information already given will cease if you notify the landlord of the transfer and of the name and address of the person to whom your tenancy has been transferred.

If you do not provide the information requested, or fail to correct information that you have provided earlier, after realising that it is not, or is no longer, correct, proceedings may be taken against you and you may have to pay damages (section 40B).

If you are in any doubt about the information that you should give, get immediate advice from a solicitor or a surveyor.

Validity of this notice

The landlord who has given you this notice may not be the landlord to whom you pay your rent (sections 44 and 67). This does not necessarily mean that the notice is invalid.

If you have any doubts about whether this notice is valid, get advice immediately from a solicitor or a surveyor.

Further information

An explanation of the main points to consider when renewing or ending a business tenancy, "Renewing and Ending Business Leases: a Guide for Tenants and Landlords", can be found at www.odpm.gov.uk. Printed copies of the explanation, but not of this form, are available from 1st June 2004 from Free Literature, PO Box 236, Wetherby, West Yorkshire, LS23 7NB (0870 1226 236).

Landlord and Tenant Act 1954, Part 2 (Notices) Regulations 2004 - Schedule 2 - Form 5

LT5

Tenant's Request for Information from Landlord or Landlord's Mortgagee about Landlord's Interest

Section 40(3) of the Landlord and Tenant Act 1954

(insert name and address of reversioner or reversioner's mortgagee in possession [see the first note below])

To:

(insert name and address of tenant)

From:

(insert address or description of premises)

1. This notice relates to the following premises:

2. In accordance with section 40(3) of the Landlord and Tenant Act 1954 I require you-

   (a) to state in writing whether you are the owner of the fee simple in respect of the premises or any part of them or the mortgagee in possession of such an owner,

   (b) if you answer "no" to (a), to state in writing, to the best of your knowledge and belief-

      (i) the name and address of the person who is your or, as the case may be, your mortgagor's immediate landlord in respect of the premises or of the part in respect of which you are not, or your mortgagor is not, the owner in fee simple;

      (ii) for what term your or your mortgagor's tenancy has effect and what is the earliest date (if any) at which that tenancy is terminable by notice to quit given by the landlord; and

      (iii) whether a notice has been given under section 25 or 26(6) of the Landlord and Tenant Act 1954, or a request has been made under section 26 of that Act, in relation to the tenancy and, if so, details of the notice or request;

   (c) to state in writing, to the best of your knowledge and belief, the name and address of any other person who owns an interest in reversion in any part of the premises;

   (d) if you are a reversioner, to state in writing whether there is a mortgagee in possession of your interest in the premises; and

   (e) if you answer "yes" to (d), to state in writing, to the best of your knowledge and belief, the name and address of the mortgagee in possession.

3. You must give the information concerned within the period of one month beginning with the date of service of this notice.

4. Please send all correspondence about this notice to:

Name:

Address:

Signed: .... Date:..

*(*delete whichever is inapplicable)*

*[Tenant] *[On behalf of the tenant]

IMPORTANT NOTE FOR LANDLORD OR LANDLORD'S MORTGAGEE

This notice contains some words and phrases that you may not understand. The Notes below should help you, but it would be wise to seek professional advice, for example, from a solicitor or surveyor, before responding to this notice.

Once you have provided the information required by this notice, you must correct it if you realise that it is not, or is no longer, correct. This obligation lasts for six months from the date of service of this notice, but an exception is explained in the next paragraph. If you need to correct information already given, you must do so within one month of becoming aware that the information is incorrect.

The obligation will cease if, after transferring your interest, you notify the tenant of the transfer and of the name and address of the person to whom your interest has been transferred.

If you fail to comply with the requirements of this notice, or the obligation mentioned above, you may face civil proceedings for breach of the statutory duty that arises under section 40 of the Landlord and Tenant Act 1954. In any such proceedings a court may order you to comply with that duty and may make an award of damages.

NOTES

The sections mentioned below are sections of the Landlord and Tenant Act 1954, as amended, (most recently by the Regulatory Reform (Business Tenancies) (England and Wales) Order 2003)

Terms used in this notice

The following terms, which are used in paragraph 2 of this notice, are defined in section 40(8):

"mortgagee in possession" includes a receiver appointed by the mortgagee or by the court who is in receipt of the rents and profits;

"reversioner" means any person having an interest in the premises, being an interest in reversion expectant (whether immediately or not) on the tenancy; and

"reversioner's mortgagee in possession" means any person being a mortgagee in possession in respect of such an interest.

Section 40(8) requires the reference in paragraph 2(b) of this notice to your mortgagor to be read in the light of the definition of "mortgagee in possession".

A mortgagee (mortgage lender) will be "in possession" if the mortgagor (the person who owes money to the mortgage lender) has failed to comply with the terms of the mortgage. The mortgagee may then be entitled to receive rent that would normally have been paid to the mortgagor.

The term "the owner of the fee simple" means the freehold owner.

The term "reversioner" includes the freehold owner and any intermediate landlord as well as the immediate landlord of the tenant who served this notice.

Purpose of this notice and information required

This notice requires you to provide, in writing, the information requested in paragraph 2(a) and (c) of the notice and, if applicable in your case, in paragraph 2(b), (d) and (e). You do not need to use a special form for this purpose.

If, once you have given this information, you realise that it is not, or is no longer, correct, you must give the correct information within one month of becoming aware that the previous information is incorrect. Subject to the last paragraph in this section of these Notes, your duty to correct any information that you have already given continues for six months after you receive this notice (section 40(5)).

You should give the correct information to the tenant who gave you this notice unless you receive notice of the transfer of his or her interest, and of the name and address of the person to whom that interest has been transferred. In that case, the correct information must be given to that person.

If you do not provide the information requested, or fail to correct information that you have provided earlier, after realising that it is not, or is no longer, correct, proceedings may be taken against you and you may have to pay damages (section 40B).

If you are in any doubt as to the information that you should give, get advice immediately from a solicitor or a surveyor.

If you transfer your interest within the period of six months referred to above, your duty to correct information already given will cease if you notify the tenant of that transfer and of the name and address of the person to whom your interest has been transferred.

Time limit for replying

You must provide the relevant information within one month of the date of service of this notice (section 40(3), (4) and (5)).

Validity of this notice

The tenant who has given you this notice may not be the person from whom you receive rent (sections 44 and 67). This does not necessarily mean that the notice is invalid.

If you have any doubts about the validity of the notice, get advice immediately from a solicitor or a surveyor.

Further information

An explanation of the main points to consider when renewing or ending a business tenancy, "Renewing and Ending Business Leases: a Guide for Tenants and Landlords", can be found at www.odpm.gov.uk. Printed copies of the explanation, but not of this form, are available from 1st June 2004 from Free Literature, PO Box 236, Wetherby, West Yorkshire, LS23 7NB (0870 1226 236).

APPENDIX 14

Landlord's Notices under the Landlord and Tenant Act 1954, s 25

Appendix 14

Landlord and Tenant Act 1954, Part 2 (Notices) Regulations 2004 - Schedule 2 - Form 2

LT2

Landlord's Notice Ending a Business Tenancy and Reasons for Refusing a New One

Section 25 of the Landlord and Tenant Act 1954

IMPORTANT NOTE FOR THE LANDLORD: If you wish to oppose the grant of a new tenancy on any of the grounds in section 30(1) of the Landlord and Tenant Act 1954, complete this form and send it to the tenant. If the tenant may be entitled to acquire the freehold or an extended lease, use form 7 (Laserform LT7) in Schedule 2 to the Landlord and Tenant Act 1954, Part 2 (Notices) Regulations 2004 instead of this form.

(insert name and address of tenant)

To:

(insert name and address of landlord)

From:

(insert address or description of property)

1. This notice relates to the following property:

(insert date)

2. I am giving you notice under section 25 of the Landlord and Tenant Act 1954 to end your tenancy on

3. I am opposed to the grant of a new tenancy.

*(insert letter(s) of the paragraph(s) relied on)

4. You may ask the court to order the grant of a new tenancy. If you do, I will oppose your application on the ground(s) mentioned in paragraph(s)*   of section 30(1) of that Act. I draw your attention to the Table in the Notes below, which sets out all the grounds of opposition.

5. If you wish to ask the court for a new tenancy you must do so before the date in paragraph 2 unless, before that date, we agree in writing to a later date.

6. I can ask the court to order the ending of your tenancy without granting you a new tenancy. I may have to pay you compensation if I have relied only on one or more of the grounds mentioned in paragraphs (e), (f) and (g) of section 30(1). If I ask the court to end your tenancy, you can challenge my application.

7. Please send all correspondence about this notice to:

Name:

Address:

Signed: .... Date: ....

(*delete if inapplicable)

*[Landlord] *[On behalf of the landlord] *[Mortgagee] *[On behalf of the mortgagee]

IMPORTANT NOTE FOR THE TENANT

This notice is intended to bring your tenancy to an end on the date specified in paragraph 2.

Your landlord is not prepared to offer you a new tenancy. **You will not get a new tenancy unless you successfully challenge in court the grounds on which your landlord opposes the grant of a new tenancy.**

If you want to continue to occupy your property you must act quickly. The notes below should help you to decide what action you now need to take. If you want to challenge your landlord's refusal to renew your tenancy, get advice immediately from a solicitor or a surveyor.

NOTES

The sections mentioned below are sections of the Landlord and Tenant Act 1954, as amended, (most recently by the Regulatory Reform (Business Tenancies) (England and Wales) Order 2003)

Ending of your tenancy

This notice is intended to bring your tenancy to an end on the date given in paragraph 2. Section 25 contains rules about the date that the landlord can put in that paragraph.

Your landlord is not prepared to offer you a new tenancy. If you want a new tenancy you will need to apply to the court for a new tenancy and successfully challenge the landlord's grounds for opposition (see the section below headed *"Landlord's opposition to new tenancy"*). If you wish to apply to the court you must do so before the date given in paragraph 2 of this notice, unless you and your landlord have agreed in writing, before that date, to extend the deadline (sections 29A and 29B).

If you apply to the court your tenancy will continue after the date given in paragraph 2 of this notice while your application is being considered (section 24). You may not apply to the court if your landlord has already done so (section 24(2A) and (2B)).

You may only stay in the property after the date given in paragraph 2 (or such later date as you and the landlord may have agreed in writing) if before that date you have asked the court to order the grant of a new tenancy or the landlord has asked the court to order the ending of your tenancy without granting you a new one.

If you are in any doubt about what action you should take, get advice immediately from a solicitor or a surveyor.

Landlord's opposition to new tenancy

If you apply to the court for a new tenancy, the landlord can only oppose your application on one or more of the grounds set out in section 30(1). If you match the letter(s) specified in paragraph 4 of this notice with those in the first column in the Table below, you can see from the second column the ground(s) on which the landlord relies.

Paragraph of section 30(1)	Grounds
(a)	Where under the current tenancy the tenant has any obligations as respects the repair and maintenance of the holding, that the tenant ought not to be granted a new tenancy in view of the state of repair of the holding, being a state resulting from the tenant's failure to comply with the said obligations.
(b)	That the tenant ought not to be granted a new tenancy in view of his persistent delay in paying rent which has become due.
(c)	That the tenant ought not to be granted a new tenancy in view of other substantial breaches by him of his obligations under the current tenancy, or for any other reason connected with the tenant's use or management of the holding.
(d)	That the landlord has offered and is willing to provide or secure the provision of alternative accommodation for the tenant, that the terms on which the alternative accommodation is available are reasonable having regard to the terms of the current tenancy and to all other relevant circumstances, and that the accommodation and the time at which it will be available are suitable for the tenant's requirements (including the requirement to preserve goodwill) having regard to the nature and class of his business and to the situation and extent of, and facilities afforded by, the holding.
(e)	Where the current tenancy was created by the sub-letting of part only of the property comprised in a superior tenancy and the landlord is the owner of an interest in reversion expectant on the termination of that superior tenancy, that the aggregate of the rents reasonably obtainable on separate lettings of the holding and the remainder of that property would be substantially less than the rent reasonably obtainable on a letting of that property as a whole, that on the termination of the current tenancy the landlord requires possession of the holding for the purposes of letting or otherwise disposing of the said property as a whole, and that in view thereof the tenant ought not to be granted a new tenancy.
(f)	That on the termination of the current tenancy the landlord intends to demolish or reconstruct the premises comprised in the holding or a substantial part of those premises or to carry out substantial work of construction on the holding or part thereof and that he could not reasonably do so without obtaining possession of the holding.
(g)	On the termination of the current tenancy the landlord intends to occupy the holding for the purposes, or partly for the purposes, of a business to be carried on by him therein, or as his residence.

In this Table "the holding" means the property that is the subject of the tenancy.

In ground (e), "the landlord is the owner an interest in reversion expectant on the termination of that superior tenancy" means that the landlord has an interest in the property that will entitle him or her, when your immediate landlord's tenancy comes to an end, to exercise certain rights and obligations in relation to the property that are currently exercisable by your immediate landlord.

If the landlord relies on ground (f), the court can sometimes still grant a new tenancy if certain conditions set out in section 31A are met.

If the landlord relies on ground (g), please note that "the landlord" may have an extended meaning. Where a landlord has a controlling interest in a company then either the landlord or the company can rely on ground (g). Where the landlord is a company and a person has a controlling interest in that company then either of them can rely on ground (g) (section 30(1A) and (1B)). A person has a "controlling interest" in a company if, had he been a company, the other company would have been its subsidiary (section 46(2)).

The landlord must normally have been the landlord for at least five years before he or she can rely on ground (g).

Compensation

If you cannot get a new tenancy solely because one or more of grounds (e), (f) and (g) applies, you may be entitled to compensation under section 37. If your landlord has opposed your application on any of the other grounds as well as (e), (f) or (g) you can only get compensation if the court's refusal to grant a new tenancy is based solely on one or more of grounds (e), (f) and (g). In other words, you cannot get compensation under section 37 if the court has refused your tenancy on *other* grounds, even if one or more of grounds (e), (f) and (g) also applies.

If your landlord is an authority possessing compulsory purchase powers (such as a local authority) you may be entitled to a disturbance payment under Part 3 of the Land Compensation Act 1973.

Validity of this notice

The landlord who has given you this notice may not be the landlord to whom you pay your rent (sections 44 and 67). This does not necessarily mean that the notice is invalid.

If you have any doubts about whether this notice is valid, get advice immediately from a solicitor or a surveyor.

Further information

An explanation of the main points to consider when renewing or ending a business tenancy, "Renewing and Ending Business Leases: a Guide for Tenants and Landlords", can be found at www.odpm.gov.uk. Printed copies of the explanation, but not of this form, are available from 1st June 2004 from Free Literature, PO Box 236, Wetherby, West Yorkshire, LS23 7NB (0870 1226 236).

Landlord and Tenant Act 1954, Part 2 (Notices) Regulations 2004 - Schedule 2 - Form 1

LT1

Landlord's Notice Ending a Business Tenancy with Proposals For a New One

Section 25 of the Landlord and Tenant Act 1954

> **IMPORTANT NOTE FOR THE LANDLORD**: If you are willing to grant a new tenancy, complete this form and send it to the tenant. If you wish to oppose the grant of a new tenancy, <u>use form 2 (Laserform LT2) in Schedule 2 to the Landlord and Tenant Act 1954, Part 2 (Notices) Regulations 2004 or, where the tenant may be entitled to acquire the freehold or an extended lease, form 7 (Laserform LT7) in that Schedule, instead of this form.</u>

(insert name and address of tenant)

To:

(insert name and address of landlord)

From:

(insert address or description of property)

1. This notice applies to the following property:

(insert date)

2. I am giving you notice under section 25 of the Landlord and Tenant Act 1954 to end your tenancy on

3. I am not opposed to granting you a new tenancy. You will find my proposals for the new tenancy, which we can discuss, in the Schedule to this notice.

4. If we cannot agree on all the terms of a new tenancy, either you or I may ask the court to order the grant of a new tenancy and settle the terms on which we cannot agree.

5. If you wish to ask the court for a new tenancy you must do so by the date in paragraph 2, unless we agree <u>in writing</u> to a later date and do so before the date in paragraph 2.

6. Please send all correspondence about this notice to:

Name:

Address:

Signed: .... Date: ....

*(*delete if inapplicable)*

*[Landlord] *[On behalf of the landlord] *[Mortgagee] *[On behalf of the mortgagee]

SCHEDULE

Landlord's Proposals for a New Tenancy

(attach or insert proposed terms of the new tenancy)

IMPORTANT NOTE FOR THE TENANT

This Notice is intended to bring your tenancy to an end. If you want to continue to occupy your property after the date specified in paragraph 2 you must act quickly. If you are in any doubt about the action that you should take, get advice immediately from a solicitor or a surveyor.

The landlord is prepared to offer you a new tenancy and has set out proposed terms in the Schedule to this notice. <u>You are not bound to accept these terms.</u> They are merely suggestions as a basis for negotiation. In the event of disagreement, ultimately the court would settle the terms of the new tenancy.

It would be wise to seek professional advice before agreeing to accept the landlord's terms or putting forward your own proposals.

NOTES

The sections mentioned below are sections of the Landlord and Tenant Act 1954, as amended, (most recently by the Regulatory Reform (Business Tenancies) (England and Wales) Order 2003).

Ending of tenancy and grant of new tenancy

This notice is intended to bring your tenancy to an end on the date given in paragraph 2. Section 25 contains rules about the date that the landlord can put in that paragraph.

However, your landlord is prepared to offer you a new tenancy and has set out proposals for it in the Schedule to this notice (section 25(8)). You are not obliged to accept these proposals and may put forward your own.

If you and your landlord are unable to agree terms either one of you may apply to the court. You may not apply to the court if your landlord has already done so (section 24(2A)). If you wish to apply to the court you must do so by the date given in paragraph 2 of this notice, unless you and your landlord have agreed in writing to extend the deadline (sections 29A and 29B).

The court will settle the rent and other terms of the new tenancy or those on which you and your landlord cannot agree (sections 34 and 35). If you apply to the court your tenancy will continue after the date shown in paragraph 2 of this notice while your application is being considered (section 24).

If you are in any doubt as to what action you should take, get advice immediately from a solicitor or a surveyor.

Negotiating a new tenancy

Most tenancies are renewed by negotiation. You and your landlord may agree in writing to extend the deadline for making an application to the court while negotiations continue. Either you or your landlord can ask the court to fix the rent that you will have to pay while the tenancy continues (sections 24A to 24D).

You may only stay in the property after the date in paragraph 2 (or if we have agreed in writing to a later date, that date), if by then you or the landlord has asked the court to order the grant of a new tenancy.

If you do try to agree a new tenancy with your landlord remember:

- that your present tenancy will not continue after the date in paragraph 2 of this notice without the agreement in writing mentioned above, unless you have applied to the court or your landlord has done so, and

- that you will lose your right to apply to the court once the deadline in paragraph 2 of this notice has passed, unless there is a written agreement extending the deadline.

Validity of this notice

The landlord who has given you this notice may not be the landlord to whom you pay your rent (sections 44 and 67). This does not necessarily mean that the notice is invalid.

If you have any doubts about whether this notice is valid, get advice immediately from a solicitor or a surveyor.

Further information

An explanation of the main points to consider when renewing or ending a business tenancy, "Renewing and Ending Business Leases: a Guide for Tenants and Landlords", can be found at www.odpm.gov.uk. Printed copies of the explanation, but not of this form, are available from 1st June 2004 from Free Literature, PO Box 236, Wetherby, West Yorkshire, LS23 7NB (0870 1226 236).

APPENDIX 15

Tenant's Request under the Landlord and Tenant Act 1954, s 26

Landlord and Tenant Act 1954, Part 2 (Notices) Regulations 2004 - Schedule 2 - Form 3

LT3

Tenant's Request for a New Business Tenancy

Section 26 of the Landlord and Tenant Act 1954

(insert name and address of landlord)   To:

(insert name and address of tenant)   From:

(insert address or description of property)

1. This notice relates to the following property:

(insert date)

2. I am giving you notice under section 26 of the Landlord and Tenant Act 1954 that I request a new tenancy beginning on

3. You will find my proposals for the new tenancy, which we can discuss, in the Schedule to this notice.

4. If we cannot agree on all the terms of a new tenancy, either you or I may ask the court to order the grant of a new tenancy and settle the terms on which we cannot agree.

5. If you wish to ask the court to order the grant of a new tenancy you must do so by the date in paragraph 2, unless we agree in writing to a later date and do so before the date in paragraph 2.

6. You may oppose my request for a new tenancy only on one or more of the grounds set out in section 30(1) of the Landlord and Tenant Act 1954. You must tell me what your grounds are within two months of receiving this notice. If you miss this deadline you will not be able to oppose renewal of my tenancy and you will have to grant me a new tenancy.

7. Please send all correspondence about this notice to:

Name:

Address:

Signed:.. Date:..

(*delete whichever is inapplicable)   *[Tenant] *[On behalf of the tenant]

SCHEDULE

Tenant's Proposals for a New Tenancy

(attach or insert proposed terms of the new tenancy)

IMPORTANT NOTE FOR THE LANDLORD

This notice requests a new tenancy of your property or part of it. If you want to oppose this request you must act quickly.

Read the notice and all the Notes carefully. It would be wise to seek professional advice.

NOTES

The sections mentioned below are sections of the Landlord and Tenant Act 1954, as amended, (most recently by the Regulatory Reform (Business Tenancies) (England and Wales) Order 2003)

Tenant's request for a new tenancy

This request by your tenant for a new tenancy brings his or her current tenancy to an end on the day before the date mentioned in paragraph 2 of this notice. Section 26 contains rules about the date that the tenant can put in paragraph 2 of this notice.

Your tenant can apply to the court under section 24 for a new tenancy. You may apply for a new tenancy yourself, under the same section, but not if your tenant has already served an application. Once an application has been made to the court, your tenant's current tenancy will continue after the date mentioned in paragraph 2 while the application is being considered by the court. Either you or your tenant can ask the court to fix the rent which your tenant will have to pay whilst the tenancy continues (sections 24A to 24D). The court will settle any terms of a new tenancy on which you and your tenant disagree (sections 34 and 35).

Time limit for opposing your tenant's request

If you do not want to grant a new tenancy, you have <u>two months from the making of your tenant's request</u> in which to notify him or her that you will oppose any application made to the court for a new tenancy. You do not need a special form to do this, but <u>the notice must be in writing and it must state on which of the grounds set out in section 30(1) you will oppose the application.</u> If you do not use the same wording of the ground (or grounds), as set out below, your notice may be ineffective.

If there has been any delay in your seeing this notice, you may need to act very quickly. If you are in any doubt about what action you should take, get advice immediately from a solicitor or a surveyor.

Grounds for opposing tenant's application

If you wish to oppose the renewal of the tenancy, you can do so by opposing your tenant's application to the court, or by making your own application to the court for termination without renewal. However, you can only oppose your tenant's application, or apply for termination without renewal, on one or more of the grounds set out in section 30(1). These grounds are set out below. <u>You will only be able to rely on the ground(s) of opposition that you have mentioned in your written notice to your tenant.</u>

In this Table "the holding" means the property that is the subject of the tenancy.

Paragraph of section 30(1)	Grounds
(a)	Where under the current tenancy the tenant has any obligations as respects the repair and maintenance of the holding, that the tenant ought not to be granted a new tenancy in view of the state of repair of the holding, being a state resulting from the tenant's failure to comply with the said obligations.
(b)	That the tenant ought not to be granted a new tenancy in view of his persistent delay in paying rent which has become due.
(c)	That the tenant ought not to be granted a new tenancy in view of other substantial breaches by him of his obligations under the current tenancy, or for any other reason connected with the tenant's use or management of the holding.
(d)	That the landlord has offered and is willing to provide or secure the provision of alternative accommodation for the tenant, that the terms on which the alternative accommodation is available are reasonable having regard to the terms of the current tenancy and to all other relevant circumstances, and that the accommodation and the time at which it will be available are suitable for the tenant's requirements (including the requirement to preserve goodwill) having regard to the nature and class of his business and to the situation and extent of, and facilities afforded by, the holding.
(e)	Where the current tenancy was created by the sub-letting of part only of the property comprised in a superior tenancy and the landlord is the owner of an interest in reversion expectant on the termination of that superior tenancy, that the aggregate of the rents reasonably obtainable on separate lettings of the holding and the remainder of that property would be substantially less than the rent reasonably obtainable on a letting of that property as a whole, that on the termination of the current tenancy the landlord requires possession of the holding for the purposes of letting or otherwise disposing of the said property as a whole, and that in view thereof the tenant ought not to be granted a new tenancy.
(f)	That on the termination of the current tenancy the landlord intends to demolish or reconstruct the premises comprised in the holding or a substantial part of those premises or to carry out substantial work of construction on the holding or part thereof and that he could not reasonably do so without obtaining possession of the holding.
(g)	On the termination of the current tenancy the landlord intends to occupy the holding for the purposes, or partly for the purposes, of a business to be carried on by him therein, or as his residence.

Compensation

If your tenant cannot get a new tenancy solely because one or more of grounds (e), (f) and (g) applies, he or she is entitled to compensation under section 37. If you have opposed your tenant's application on any of the other grounds mentioned in section 30(1), as well as on one or more of grounds (e), (f) and (g), your tenant can only get compensation if the court's refusal to grant a new tenancy is based solely on ground (e), (f) or (g). In other words, your tenant cannot get compensation under section 37 if the court has refused the tenancy on *other* grounds, even if one or more of grounds (e), (f) and (g) also applies.

If you are an authority possessing compulsory purchase powers (such as a local authority), your tenant may be entitled to a disturbance payment under Part 3 of the Land Compensation Act 1973.

Negotiating a new tenancy

Most tenancies are renewed by negotiation and your tenant has set out proposals for the new tenancy in paragraph 3 of this notice. You are not obliged to accept these proposals and may put forward your own. You and your tenant may agree in writing to extend the deadline for making an application to the court while negotiations continue. Your tenant may not apply to the court for a new tenancy until two months have passed from the date of the making of the request contained in this notice, unless you have already given notice opposing your tenant's request as mentioned in paragraph 6 of this notice (section 29A(3)).

If you try to agree a new tenancy with your tenant, remember:

- that one of you will need to apply to the court before the date in paragraph 2 of this notice, unless you both agree to extend the period for making an application.
- that any such agreement must be in writing and must be made before the date in paragraph 2 (sections 29A and 29B).

Validity of this notice

The tenant who has given you this notice may not be the person from whom you receive rent (sections 44 and 67). This does not necessarily mean that the notice is invalid.

If you have any doubts about whether this notice is valid, get advice immediately from a solicitor or a surveyor.

Further information

An explanation of the main points to consider when renewing or ending a business tenancy, "Renewing and Ending Business Leases: a Guide for Tenants and Landlords", can be found at www.odpm.gov.uk. Printed copies of the explanation, but not of this form, are available from 1st June 2004 from Free Literature, PO Box 236, Wetherby, West Yorkshire, LS23 7NB (0870 1226 236).

APPENDIX 16

Environmental Enquiries of Seller's Solicitors

The enquiries below are listed to show examples of the kind of questions that should be considered. The actual list used should be tailored to suit each individual property under negotiation.

1.   Is the seller aware of any part of the land within the property which may be contaminated by any substance, or which may be passing under, on or through the property? If so, please provide details.

2.   Is the seller aware of any land within the surrounding area of the property (ie, within 200 metres) which may be contaminated by any substance, or which may be passing under, on or through the property? If so, please provide details.

3.   Is the seller aware of any land within the surrounding area of the property (ie, within 200 metres) which may be contaminated or may have been put to such a use that it is included or proposed for inclusion on the register of contaminated land pursuant to s 143 of the Environmental Protection Act 1990? If so, please provide full details.

4.   Please provide a copy of all statutory consents in relation to the property or buildings on it that relate to pollution or environmental controls.

5.   Has any radioactive waste or other hazardous substance been stored or disposed of on the property and has any radioactive material or other hazardous substance or waste been kept, used, stored or disposed of on any land within 200 metres of the property?

6.   Have any other hazardous, toxic, flammable, explosive, corrosive or harmful substances been stored or disposed of at or under the property? If so, please provide details.

7.   In relation to the property or any building on it please confirm that the seller has complied with all requirements relating to the following:

    7.1   sewage disposal,
    7.2   water pollution,
    7.3   trade or industrial waste,
    7.4   gas emissions or releases of any kind whatsoever,
    7.5   discharges of radioactive waste,
    7.6   chemical or other pollutants or contaminants,
    7.7   toxic or hazardous substances or waste,
    7.8   the regulation of noise and noise pollution,
    7.9   health and safety at work.

8.   If there has been failure to comply with any of the above requirements, please provide full details.

9.   Is there now or has there at any time been present on the property any hazardous substance (as defined in regulations made under s 5 of the Planning (Hazardous Substances) Act 1990 or the Notification of Installations Handling Hazardous Substances Regulations 1982?

10.   Have any works been undertaken to alter, divert or put underground any watercourse within the property or has any such watercourse been blocked? If so, please provide full details.

11.   Has a person or organization with responsibility for flood prevention undertaken any flood alleviation measures on the property?

12.   Please confirm that discharges from the property into the public sewer do not contravene the provisions of any statutes governing such discharges.

13.   Is there, or has there at any time been, on the property any underground reservoirs or tanks used for the storage of any substance? Please provide full details.

14. Has any building on the property ever been affected by radon gas, and is the seller aware of any migration of gases normally associated with landfill operations under, in or through the property? If so, please provide details.

15. In respect of any buildings on the property please confirm that none of the following materials were used in their construction:

    15.1   high alumina cement,

    15.2   asbestos or asbestos based products,

    15.3   materials containing chloro-fluorocarbons ('CFCs'), extruded polystyrenepolyurethane, polyisocyanurate phenolic foam and CFCs in refrigerants,

    15.4   any other substances not in accordance with British Standards and codes of practice and good building practice current at the relevant time.

    15.5   If any such materials have been used, please provide details.

16. Has the property previously been used for the treatment, storage, disposal, burial or burning of any form of waste as defined by s 75 of the Environmental Protection Act 1990? If so please give full details.

17. Has any testing or sampling of the soil, or groundwater, been carried out in the property? If so, please provide full details.

18. Is the seller aware of any insurance claim made or being made in respect of any damage, the basis for which arises from any contamination of the land or the use of the land?

19. If any building on the subject property has air conditioning, when was the system last inspected for bacterial contamination and with what result?

A Code of Practice for Commercial Leases in England and Wales (2nd edn)

This updated Code and Explanatory Guide has been produced, at the request of the Department for Transport, Local Government and the Regions, by the Commercial Leases Working Group comprising the Association of British Insurers, Association of Property Bankers, British Retail Consortium, British Property Federation, Confederation of British Industry, Forum of Private Business, Law Society, National Association of Corporate Real Estate Executives (UK chapter), Property Market Reform Group, Royal Institution of Chartered Surveyors and Small Business Bureau. In addition, this code has received support from the British Council for Offices, the British Chambers of Commerce, Council for Licensed Conveyancers and the Federation of Small Businesses.

This Code replaces the First Edition produced by the Commercial Leases Group in December 1995.

INTRODUCTION

This updated Code contains recommendations for landlords and tenants when they negotiate new leases of business premises and where they deal with each other during the term of a lease.

The Code consists of twenty-three recommendations which an industry-wide working party, including landlord and tenant representatives, consider reflect current 'best practice' for landlords and tenants negotiating a business tenancy.

Explanatory guidance notes, set out on pages 4 to 12, provide the background to each of the recommendations.

Landlords and tenants should have regard to the recommendations of this Code when they negotiate lease renewals. Under current legislation if a court has to fix terms for a new lease it may decide not to change the terms from those in the existing lease.

NEGOTIATING A BUSINESS TENANCY (LEASE)

Recommendation 1; Renting premises

Both landlords and tenants should negotiate the terms of a lease openly, constructively and considering each other's views.

Recommendation 2; Obtaining professional advice

Parties intending to enter into leases should seek early advice from property professionals or lawyers.

Recommendation 3; Financial matters

Landlords should provide estimates of any service charges and other outgoings in addition to the rent. Parties should be open about their financial standing to each other, on the understanding that information provided will be kept confidential unless already publicly available or there is proper need for disclosure. The terms on which any cash deposit is to be held should be agreed and documented.

Recommendation 4; Duration of lease

Landlords should consider offering tenants a choice of length of term, including break clauses where appropriate and with or without the protection of the Landlord and Tenant Act 1954. Those funding property should make every effort to avoid imposing restrictions on the length of lease that landlords, developers and/or investors may offer.

Recommendation 5; Rent and value added tax

Where alternative lease terms are offered, different rents should be appropriately priced for each set of terms. The landlord should disclose the VAT status of the property and the tenant should take professional advice as to whether any VAT charged on rent and other charges is recoverable.

Recommendation 6; Rent Review

The basis of rent review should generally be to open market rent. Wherever possible, landlords should offer alternatives which are priced on a risk-adjusted basis, including alternatives to upwards only rent reviews; these might include up/down reviews to open market rent with a minimum of the initial rent, or another basis such as annual indexation. Those funding property should make every effort to avoid imposing restrictions on the type of rent review that landlords, developers and/or investors may offer.

Recommendation 7; Repairs and services

The tenant's repairing obligations, and any repair costs included in service charges, should be appropriate to the length of the term and the condition and age of the property at the start of the lease. Where appropriate the landlord should consider appropriately priced alternatives to full repairing terms.

Recommendation 8; Insurance

Where the landlord is responsible for insuring the property, the policy terms should be competitive. The tenant of an entire building should, in appropriate cases, be given the opportunity to influence the choice of insurer. If the premises are so damaged by an uninsured risk as to prevent occupation, the tenant should be allowed to terminate the lease unless the landlord agrees to rebuild at his own cost.

Recommendation 9; Assigning and subletting

Unless the particular circumstances of the letting justify greater control, the only restriction on assignment of the whole premises should be obtaining the landlord's consent which is not to be unreasonably withheld. Landlords are urged to consider requiring Authorised Guarantee Agreements only where the assignee is of lower financial standing than the assignor at the date of the assignment.

Recommendation 10; Alterations and changes of use

Landlord's control over alterations and changes of use should not be more restrictive than is necessary to protect the value of the premises and any adjoining or neighbouring premises of the landlord. At the end of the lease the tenant should not be required to remove and make good permitted alterations unless this is reasonably required.

CONDUCT DURING A LEASE

Recommendation 11; Ongoing relationship

Landlords and tenants should deal with each other constructively, courteously, openly and honestly throughout the term of the lease and carry out their respective obligations fully and on time. If either party faces a difficulty in carrying out any obligations under the lease, the other should be told without undue delay so that the possibility of agreement on how to deal with the problem may be explored. When either party proposes to take any action which is likely to have significant consequences for the other, the party proposing the action, when it becomes appropriate to do so, should notify the other without undue delay.

Recommendation 12; Request for consents

When seeking a consent from the landlord, the tenant should supply full information about his/her proposal. The landlord should respond without undue delay and should where practicable give the tenant an estimate of the costs that the tenant will have to pay. The landlord should ensure that the request is passed promptly to any superior landlord or mortgagee whose agreement is needed and should give details to the tenant so that any problems can be speedily resolved.

Recommendation 13; Rent review negotiation

Landlords and tenants should ensure that they understand the basis upon which rent may be reviewed and the procedure to be followed, including the existence of any strict time limits which could create pitfalls. They should obtain professional advice on these matters well before the review date and also immediately upon receiving (and before responding to) any notice or correspondence on the matter from the other party or his/her agent.

Recommendation 14; Insurance

Where the landlord has arranged insurance, the terms should be made known to the tenant and any interest of the tenant covered by the policy. Any material change in the insurance should be notified to the tenant. Tenants should consider taking out their own insurance against loss or damage to contents and their business (loss of profits etc.) and any other risks not covered by the landlord's policy.

Recommendation 15; Varying the lease—effect on guarantors

Landlords and tenants should seek the agreement of any guarantors to proposed material changes to the terms of the lease, or even minor changes which could increase the guarantor's liability.

Recommendation 16; Holding former tenants and their guarantors liable

When previous tenants or their guarantors are liable to a landlord for defaults by the current tenant, landlords should notify them before the current tenant accumulates excessive liabilities. All defaults should be handled with speed and landlords should seek to assist the tenant and guarantor in minimising losses. An assignor who wishes to remain informed of the outcome of rent reviews should keep in touch with the landlord and the landlord should provide the information. Assignors should take professional advice on what methods are open to them to minimise their losses caused by defaults by the current occupier.

Recommendation 17; Release of landlord on sale of property

Landlords who sell their interest in premises should take legal advice about ending their ongoing liability under the relevant leases.

Recommendation 18; Repairs

Tenants should take the advice of a property professional about their repairing obligations near the end of the term of the lease and also immediately upon receiving a notice to repair or a schedule of dilapidations.

Recommendation 19; Business Rates

Tenants or other ratepayers should consider if their business rates assessment is correct or whether they need to make an appeal. They should refer to the DTLR Business Rates—a Guide or obtain advice from a rating specialist. The RICS provides a free rating help line service (see below) and advice is available also from the Institute of Revenues Rating and Valuation (IRRV).

Recommendation 20; Service charges

Landlords should observe the Guide to Good Practice on Service Charges in Commercial Properties. Tenants should familiarise themselves with that Guide and should take professional advice if they think they are being asked to pay excessive service charges.

Recommendation 21; Dispute resolution

When disputes arise, the parties should make prompt and reasonable efforts to settle them by agreement. Where disputes cannot be settled by agreement, both sides should always consider speed and economy when selecting a method of dispute resolution. Mediation may be appropriate before embarking on more formal procedures.

Recommendation 22; Repossession by the landlord

Tenants threatened with repossession or whose property has been repossessed will need professional advice if they wish to try to keep or regain possession. Similarly, landlords should be clear about their rights before attempting to operate a forfeiture clause and may need professional advice.

Recommendation 23; Renewals under the Landlord and Tenant Act 1954

The parties should take professional advice on the Landlord and Tenant Act 1954 and the PACT (Professional Arbitration on Court Terms) scheme at least six months before the end of the term of the lease and also immediately upon receiving any notice under the Act from the other party or their agent. Guidance on the Act can be found in the Department for Transport, Local Government and the Region's "Guide to the Landlord and Tenant Act 1954".

A CODE OF PRACTICE FOR COMMERCIAL LEASES IN ENGLAND AND WALES—EXPLANATORY GUIDE

The Code of Practice for Commercial Leases consists of the Recommendations set out in this Guide. This Guide gives a brief explanation of the background to the recommendations. Further sources of advice and explanation are listed at the end.

NEGOTIATING A BUSINESS TENANCY (LEASE)

Renting premises

Roughly a third of business premises in the UK are occupied by rent-paying tenants holding a lease (also called a "tenancy") of the premises. Tenants should choose premises suitable for their short to medium term business plans, in respect of size, location, property and the terms of the lease. Premises might be rented, depending on the individual circumstances, either by the owner granting a new lease, by an existing tenant assigning the lease or by an existing tenant granting a sublease. The terms of a lease should reflect the type, location and condition of the property, the needs and status of the parties, and the state of the property market. All the terms in a commercial lease are normally negotiable.

For business reasons, the landlord or the tenant may wish to keep the details of their transaction confidential, but parties should avoid unnecessary secrecy. This will help the availability of market data.

Recommendation 1

Both landlords and tenants should negotiate the terms of a lease openly, constructively and considering each other's views.

Obtaining professional advice

Unless landlords and tenants are fully experienced in these matters they will benefit from the advice of professional property advisers. Each party should be separately advised by independent advisers as the same person should not advise both parties. Tenants should not place reliance on advice offered by a letting agent acting for the landlord.

The main recognised property professionals are chartered surveyors regulated by the Royal Institution of Chartered Surveyors (RICS) and solicitors regulated by the Law Society and Licensed Conveyancers regulated by the Council for Licensed Conveyancers.

A surveyor can conduct, or assist in, the negotiations and can advise on the terms, including the appropriate level of rent taking into account the other terms of the letting, the location, size and quality of the property, the state of the property market, the level of business rates and other outgoings, and other relevant matters. A building surveyor can advise about the present condition of the property and about any necessary repairs. For lettings of part of a building, this can include advice about the need for major repairs and renewals of the structure or common parts which might increase service charges. A solicitor can negotiate the detailed text of the lease once the main terms have been agreed. Lease documents often run to many pages and there are no standard forms of lease. A solicitor can also check important matters such as town planning and the landlord's ownership of the property.

Recommendation 2

Parties intending to enter into leases should seek early advice from property professionals or lawyers.

Financial matters

The tenant should find out about the total cost of occupying the premises—rent, service charges, insurance, business rates, utility costs etc.—and ensure that they can be afforded within the budget of the business.

As the landlord will wish to assess the tenant's ability to pay those costs, particularly the rent and any service charge, the tenant should provide written references from accountants, trade suppliers and any previous landlord. If the tenant is a limited company, the landlord may also wish to see audited accounts for the last few years' trading. If this information does not exist or fails to show that the tenant has an adequate financial standing, the landlord may refuse to accept that tenant or may require guarantees from financially viable guarantors, covering not only the rent but also all other liabilities under the lease.

The landlord may also require a cash deposit, frequently of three or six months' rent. This "rent deposit" will generally be required as security for service charges and the cost of remedying disrepair or other defaults as well as rent. There should be a proper written agreement covering the amount deposited, whether it can vary, who can hold it, how and when it can be paid over to the landlord or returned to the tenant and which party will receive any interest accruing.

The drawing up of commercial leases involves legal costs. The question of payment is a matter for negotiation between the parties. The Costs of Leases Act 1958 provides that, in the absence of agreement, each side pays its own costs.

Recommendation 3

Landlords should provide estimates of any service charges and other outgoings in addition to the rent. Parties should be open about their financial standing to each other, on the understanding that information provided will be kept confidential unless already publicly available or there is proper need for disclosure. The terms on which any cash deposit is to be held should be agreed and documented.

Duration of lease

The length of the letting is called the "term". Leases are commonly granted for three, five, ten or fifteen year terms, but can be for terms of twenty or twenty-five years or more. A lease carries the protection of the Landlord and Tenant Act 1954, unless the parties agree to its exclusion. If the tenant occupies all or part of the premises when the lease ends, the Act enables a tenant to ask the county court to order the landlord to grant a new lease at a market rent.

The landlord can refuse to grant a new lease in certain circumstances set out in the Act, for example if the tenant has seriously defaulted under the lease, or if the property is to be redeveloped or used for the landlord's own business. The tenant can ask the county court to examine the landlord's refusal to grant a new lease. In some cases, the tenant may be entitled to be paid compensation if a new lease is refused. If the lease excludes the Act, the tenant will not have the right to seek a new lease through the courts when the term expires.

Leases can contain a provision (break clause) allowing either the landlord or the tenant (or both) to terminate the lease at a specified date without waiting for the term to expire. This may be advantageous to the party who wishes to end the lease early—such as a tenant who wants to vacate without finding an assignee or subtenant, or a landlord who wants to redevelop—but early termination may cause problems and/or loss to the other party.

Recommendation 4

Landlords should consider offering tenants a choice of length of term, including break clauses where appropriate and with or without the protection of the Landlord and Tenant Act 1954. Those funding property should make every effort to avoid imposing restrictions on the length of lease that landlords, developers and/or investors may offer.

Rent and value added tax

The appropriate level of rent will depend upon the state of the property market, the location, type, age, size, character and condition of the premises and the terms on which the lease is to be granted, especially the duration of the lease and the burden of repairing obligations. Rent is usually payable by quarterly installments in advance; the usual quarter days being 25 March, 24 June, 29 September and 25 December.

One quarter of the yearly rent will usually be payable on these dates. This is not invariable. In some cases, particularly for short term lettings, monthly payments might be appropriate. Value Added Tax

(VAT) will be payable on the rent (and on service charges) if the landlord has elected to waive the building's exemption from VAT. If the landlord has not already done this, it could be done at any time during the lease unless the lease forbids it. If this waiver is made, VAT will be payable by the tenant in addition to the rent and service charge. Many tenants will be entitled to recover the VAT through their business VAT returns.

Recommendation 5

Where alternative lease terms are offered, different rents should be appropriately priced for each set of terms. The landlord should disclose the VAT status of the property and the tenant should take professional advice as to whether any VAT charged on rent and other charges is recoverable.

Rent Review

For leases over five years, it is usual for the rent to be reviewed at stated intervals. Usually rent is reviewed to open market rent level – the rent that a new tenant would pay if the property was being let in the open market at the time of the review (the most appropriate basis for review). Alternatives include fixed increases or linking the rent to a published index (such as the Index of Retail Prices) or to the annual turnover of the tenant's business at the premises. Reviews to open market rent normally occur every five years whilst rents linked to indices or turnover are commonly recalculated annually.

Not all these methods of review are suitable for every tenant or appropriate to every type of property or business. If the review is on "upwards only" terms, the rent will not reduce at review but will remain at its existing level even if the market rent or index has fallen. Tenants may find that they would have to pay a higher initial rent where the rent review is to be up or down compared with upwards only, as this transfers the risk of downward movements to the landlord. Financers of property require landlords to ensure that rental income will not fall below a particular level and this may restrict a landlord's ability to agree an upwards/downwards basis.

Recommendation 6

The basis of rent review should generally be to open market rent. Wherever possible, landlords should offer alternatives which are priced on a risk-adjusted basis, including alternatives to upwards only rent reviews; these might include up/down reviews to open market rent with a minimum of the initial rent, or another basis such as annual indexation. Those funding property should make every effort to avoid imposing restrictions on the type of rent review that landlords, developers and/or investors may offer.

Repairs and services

Leases generally state which party will be responsible for carrying out, or for meeting the cost of, repairing and maintaining the fabric and services of the property. The degree to which these burdens are placed on the tenant should take into account the initial condition of the premises and the duration of the lease.

A "full repairing" lease makes the tenant of an entire building responsible for all internal and external repairs and redecoration that become necessary during the term. This includes the roof, foundations, main walls and other structural parts, irrespective of whether or not they are in good condition at the start of the lease. A "full repairing" lease for part of a building requires the tenant to maintain and decorate the inside of the premises and to pay, through a service charge, towards the landlord's costs of maintaining and repairing the common parts and structure and providing services such as porterage, lifts, central heating, etc. Such obligations might require the tenant to carry out, or pay towards the cost of, work to remedy an inherent construction defect which becomes apparent during the term.

Alternatives to "full repairing" terms might include limiting the tenant's repairs to the maintenance of the property in its existing condition, excluding certain categories of repair, and the remediation of inherent defects. The scope or amount of any service charge can be limited or there can be a fixed rent which is inclusive of service costs.

If the lease refers to the existing condition of the property, it will be in both parties' interests for a schedule of condition (which can be photographic) to be professionally prepared and kept with the lease documents. Professional advice should be sought when the tenant is required to carry out initial improvements and repairs, as there may be implications for tax and rent review.

Recommendation 7

The tenant's repairing obligations, and any repairs costs included in service charges, should be appropriate to the length of the term and the condition and age of the property at the start of the lease. Where appropriate the landlord should consider appropriately priced alternatives to full repairing terms.

Insurance

It is usual for the landlord to insure the building and require the tenants to pay the premiums. In the case of multi-occupied buildings, each tenant would be expected to contribute towards the total insurance premium; this may be included in the service charge or may be charged separately. Leases may give the landlord discretion to choose the insurer. Alternatives include allowing the tenant to influence the selection of the insurer (if their lease covers the entire building), or providing that the landlord must arrange the insurance on competitive rates.

The lease should contain provisions covering the situation where there is damage by an uninsured risk or where there is a large excess. These risks vary from time to time and might include terrorist damage. If suitable provisions are not included in the lease the tenant might have to meet the cost of rebuilding in that situation.

Alternatives include allowing the tenant to terminate the lease following uninsured damage, although it may be appropriate to allow the landlord to choose to rebuild at his own cost in order to keep the lease in force.

Recommendation 8

Where the landlord is responsible for insuring the property, the policy terms should be competitive. The tenant of an entire building should, in appropriate cases, be given the opportunity to influence the choice of insurer. If the premises are so damaged by an uninsured risk as to prevent occupation, the tenant should be allowed to terminate the lease unless the landlord agrees to rebuild at his own cost.

Assigning and subletting

There are two ways in which the tenant may pass on the lease obligations to a third party; one is by assignment (selling, giving away or paying someone to take over, the lease) and the other is by subletting (remaining as tenant of the lease with the lease obligations but granting a sublease to another tenant who undertakes the same or similar obligations). Leases generally control assignment and subletting. Most require the tenant to obtain the landlord's consent (which cannot be unreasonably withheld) but some leases completely prohibit certain acts such as subletting part of the premises.

A new lease, and an existing lease granted since 1995, may expand the landlord's right to control assignments by imposing credit ratings or other financial criteria for assignees. It may also require the assigning tenant to stand as guarantor for any assignee by giving the landlord an "Authorised Guarantee Agreement"; alternatives include giving this guarantee only if it is reasonably required by the landlord, such as where the assignee is of lower financial standing than the assigning tenant.

Recommendation 9

Unless the particular circumstances of the letting justify greater control, the only restriction on assignment of the whole premises should be obtaining the landlord's consent which is not to be unreasonably withheld. Landlords are urged to consider requiring Authorised Guarantee Agreements only where the assignee is of lower financial standing than the assignor at the date of the assignment.

Alterations and changes of use

Leases generally restrict the tenant's freedom to make alterations and often impose tighter control over external and structural alterations than over internal non-structural alterations or partitioning. The lease may absolutely prohibit the work.

Alternatives may require the landlord's consent which must not be unreasonably withheld, or may permit the particular type of alteration without consent. The lease may entitle the landlord to require the tenant to reinstate the premises (remove alterations) at the end of the lease; or alternatively reinstatement need only take place if it is reasonable for the landlord to require it.

The permitted use of the premises may be very narrowly defined or there may be a wide class of use. Consent for changes of use can be at the landlord's discretion or, alternatively, the lease may provide that consent is not to be unreasonably withheld.

If the provisions of the lease are very restrictive this can hinder the assignment of the lease or the subletting of the property to a different business.

Recommendation 10

Landlord's control over alterations and changes of use should not be more restrictive than is necessary to protect the value of the premises and any adjoining or neighbouring premises of the landlord. At the end of the lease the tenant should not be required to remove and make good permitted alterations unless this is reasonably required.

CONDUCT DURING A LEASE

Ongoing relationship

The relationship between landlord and tenant will continue after the lease has been signed; for example, there may be rent review negotiations or discussions about varying the terms. The landlord may be contemplating planning applications, redevelopment, improvements or making changes in the provision of services.

Recommendation 11

Landlords and tenants should deal with each other constructively, courteously, openly and honestly throughout the term of the lease and carry out their respective obligations fully and on time. If either party faces a difficulty in carrying out any obligations under the lease, the other should be told without undue delay so that the possibility of agreement on how to deal with the problem may be explored. When either party proposes to take any action which is likely to have significant consequences for the other, the party proposing the action, when it becomes appropriate to do so, should notify the other without undue delay.

Request for consents

There may be occasions when the tenant seeks a consent (licence) from the landlord, when for example, the tenant proposes to assign the lease, grant a sublease, change the use of the property, make alterations or display signs. The effect on the landlord will vary with the exact details. In some cases, the landlord will have to pass the request to a superior landlord or to a mortgagee. Most leases require the tenant to pay any costs incurred by the landlord in dealing with such an application.

Recommendation 12

When seeking a consent from the landlord, the tenant should supply full information about his/her proposal. The landlord should respond without undue delay and should where practicable give the tenant an estimate of the costs that the tenant will have to pay. The landlord should ensure that the request is passed promptly to any superior landlord or mortgagee whose agreement is needed and should give details to the tenant so that any problems can be speedily resolved.

Rent review negotiation
Many leases contain provisions for the periodic review of rent; these may be highly technical and may lay down procedures and time limits.

Recommendation 13

Landlords and tenants should ensure that they understand the basis upon which rent may be reviewed and the procedure to be followed, including the existence of any strict time limits which could create pitfalls. They should obtain professional advice on these matters well before the review date and also immediately upon receiving (and before responding to) any notice or correspondence on the matter from the other party or his/her agent.

Insurance
Directly or indirectly, the tenant will usually pay the cost of insuring the premises and the lease will state whether the tenant or the landlord has to arrange this. Where the landlord has arranged insurance, the terms should be made known to the tenant and any interest of the tenant covered by the policy.

Sometimes the lease allows the landlord or the tenant to end the lease if the premises are very badly damaged. If damage occurs but is covered by the insurance, there may be important questions about how, why and by whom the insurance money is spent and the parties should take professional advice as soon as the damage occurs.

Recommendation 14

Where the landlord has arranged insurance, the terms should be made known to the tenant and any interest of the tenant covered by the policy. Any material change in the insurance should be notified to the tenant. Tenants should consider taking out their own insurance against loss or damage to contents and their business (loss of profits etc.) and any other risks not covered by the landlord's policy.

Varying the lease—effect on guarantors
A guarantor may not be liable if the terms of the lease are changed without the guarantor's consent. In some cases the variation may release a guarantor from all liability.

Recommendation 15

Landlords and tenants should seek the agreement of any guarantors to any proposed material changes to the terms of the lease, or even minor changes which could increase the guarantor's liability.

Holding former tenants and their guarantors liable
A tenant who assigns a lease may remain liable for a period for any subsequent breach of the lease terms including failure to pay rent. This liability may also apply to a guarantor for the former tenant. Where payment is made to the landlord under this liability, the former tenant may be entitled to take an overriding lease of the property in order to have some control over the current tenants; legal advice can be obtained about these matters. In certain circumstances, insurance against losses

following an assignment may be possible. Landlords must notify previous tenants about arrears of rent and service charges within six months of the amount becoming due, in order to make them liable.

Recommendation 16

When previous tenants or their guarantors are liable to a landlord for defaults by the current tenant, landlords should notify them before the current tenant accumulates excessive liabilities. All defaults should be handled with speed and landlords should seek to assist the tenant and guarantor in minimising losses. An assignor who wishes to remain informed of the outcome of rent reviews should keep in touch with the landlord and the landlord should provide the information. Assignors should take professional advice on what methods are open to them to minimise their losses caused by defaults by the current occupier.

Release of landlord on sale of property
A landlord who sells his interest in the building may remain liable to the tenants to perform any obligations in the lease (for example, in repairing or insuring the building) in the event of failure on the part of the new landlord.

It is possible, in certain circumstances, for landlords to terminate their obligations on selling the property through provisions in the lease or, in some cases by seeking the agreement of their tenants and, in the event of objection, decision by a county court.

Recommendation 17

Landlords who sell their interest in premises should take legal advice about ending their ongoing liability under the lease.

Repairs
The landlord may be entitled to serve a notice requiring the tenant to undertake repairing obligations which the tenant has failed to carry out. This notice may be served near or at the end of the term or earlier. The list of repairs is called a "schedule of dilapidations". Disagreements about these are not uncommon and the law on repairing obligations is complex.

Recommendation 18

Tenants should take the advice of a property professional about their repairing obligations near the end of the term of the lease and also immediately upon receiving a notice to repair or a schedule of dilapidations.

Business Rates
Uniform Business Rates (UBR) are payable to local authorities and are the responsibility of the occupier (the ratepayer) of the property. In certain circumstances the amount payable can be reduced by appealing against the business rates assessment.

Ratepayers should be aware time limits apply to certain appeal procedures and advice on these may be obtained from a rating specialist, who is usually a chartered surveyor.

Recommendation 19

Tenants or other ratepayers should consider if their business rates assessment is correct or whether they need to make an appeal. They should refer to the DTLR Business Rates—a Guide or obtain advice from a rating specialist. RICS provides a free rating help line service (see inside back-cover) and advice is available also from the Institute of Revenues Rating and Valuation (IRRV)

Service charges

Where the lease entitles the landlord to levy a service charge, details of the services covered are usually set out in the lease and it may contain provisions requiring the landlord to act reasonably or economically. Some leases lay down strict time limits for the tenant to query service charges. Several leading property industry and professional bodies have agreed a Guide to Good Practice in relation to service charges which is available free.

Recommendation 20

Landlords should observe the Guide to Good Practice on Service Charges in Commercial Properties. Tenants should familiarise themselves with that Guide and should take professional advice if they think they are being asked to pay excessive service charges.

Dispute resolution

Disputes between landlords and tenants can be expensive, time-consuming and divisive. If the lease does not state how a particular dispute is to be settled, the parties may have to go to court. Leases often provide for certain types of dispute to be resolved by particular procedures; for example, it is common to provide that a dispute about rent review is to be referred to an independent surveyor acting either as an arbitrator or as an expert. Professional advice should be obtained about any procedures laid down in the lease.

The parties can agree to appoint a mediator to try to resolve a particular dispute even though the lease does not provide for it. The mediator will consult both parties separately and advise them on the strengths or weaknesses of their case and work towards a settlement. Mediators should be able to keep costs down and achieve an outcome within a short timescale; but if mediation fails, delay and cost will have been incurred and the parties still have to resort to the formal procedures of arbitration, expert determination or court proceedings.

Recommendation 21

When disputes arise, the parties should make prompt and reasonable efforts to settle them by agreement. Where disputes cannot be settled by agreement, both sides should always consider speed and economy when selecting a method of dispute resolution. Mediation may be appropriate before embarking on more formal procedures.

Repossession by the landlord

The lease will contain a clause giving the landlord the right ("forfeiture" or "re-entry") to repossess the property if the tenant breaks any obligations under the lease or becomes insolvent. When a landlord seeks repossession under a forfeiture clause, the tenant (or sub-tenant) may be entitled to claim "relief from forfeiture" from a court, i.e. the right to retain the property despite the breach.

Recommendation 22

Tenants threatened with repossession or whose property has been repossessed will need professional advice if they wish to try to keep or regain possession. Similarly, landlords should be clear about their rights before attempting to operate a forfeiture clause and may need professional advice.

Renewals under the Landlord and Tenant Act 1954

Unless it is excluded, this Act may give the tenant a right to renew the lease when it ends (see under Duration of lease). It contains procedures and time limits that must be strictly followed by both landlords and tenants. Disputes under the Act about whether the tenant should be granted a new lease and about its terms are adjudicated by the county court, but the parties may agree to ask the court to refer all or some aspects to be decided by an independent surveyor or solicitor under the Professional Arbitration on Court Terms scheme operated by the RICS and the Law Society.

Recommendation 23

The parties should take professional advice on the Landlord and Tenant Act 1954 and the PACT scheme at least six months before the end of the term of the lease and also immediately upon receiving any notice under the Act from the other party or their agent. Guidance on the Act can be found in the Department for Transport, Local Government and the Regions, "Guide to the Landlord and Tenant Act 1954" (see inside back-cover).

PROPERTY ADVICE

For a selection of local professional property advisers who could represent you call: The Royal Institution of Chartered Surveyors (RICS) Contact Centre on 020 7222 7000.

For a free rent review and lease renewal helpline service for businesses not already professionally represented call the RICS on 020 7334 3806. For the rating helpline call 020 7222 7000. Rating advice also available from the Institute of Revenues Rating and Valuation on 020 7831 3505.

Also free from the RICS: "Rent review—a guide for small businesses". Send a large stamped, self addressed envelope to Corporate Communications, The Royal Institution of Chartered Surveyors, 12 Great George Street, London SWIP 3AD, or contact the RICS Rent Review and Lease Renewal helpline on 020 7334 3806.

For a "Guide to Good Practice on Service Charges in Commercial Properties", contact the RICS Commercial Property Faculty at the address above (with a large stamped SAE) or the website found at <www.servicechargeguide.co.uk>.

LEGAL ADVICE

For a free Guide to the Landlord and Tenant Act 1954 write to the
Department for Transport,
Local Government and the Regions,
Eland House,
Bressenden Place,
London SW1E 5DU.

For information on local solicitors who could represent you, call The Law Society on 020 7242 1222.

For information on local licensed conveyancers who could represent you, call The Council for Licensed Conveyancers on 01245 349599.

PROPERTY OWNERS

The trade association which looks after the interests of property owners is:
The British Property Federation,
1 Warwick Row,
7th Floor,
London SW1E 5ER,
Tel: 020 7828 0111
Fax: 020 7834 3442.

OCCUPIERS

Several trade associations look after the interests of occupiers, including the British Retail Consortium and the Property Market Reform Group.

The BRC can be contacted on 020 7854 8900.

Contact details for the PMRG and other organisations supporting the code may be obtained from the Commercial Leases Working Group Secretariat.

The Secretariat for the Commercial Leases Working Group can be contacted at:
Policy Unit
The Royal Institution of Chartered Surveyors
12 Great George Street
Parliament Square
London
SW1P 3AD
United Kingdom
T. +44 (0)20 7695 1535
F.+44 (0)20 7334 3795

APPENDIX 18

British Property Federation Commercial Property Standard Enquiries

COMMERCIAL PROPERTY STANDARD ENQUIRIES
CPSE.1 (VERSION 2.2)
GENERAL PRE-CONTRACT ENQUIRIES FOR ALL COMMERCIAL PROPERTY TRANSACTIONS

These enquiries are designed to cover all commercial property transactions. Guidance notes have been prepared to assist the Buyer and the Seller and are available in GN/CPSE.1. These enquiries stand on their own and do not depend on the guidance notes for interpretation.

Supplemental enquiries should be raised if leases are involved: CPSE.2 where an investment property is sold subject to existing tenancies, CPSE.3 where a lease is being granted, and CPSE.4 where a lease is being assigned.

CPSE.1 consists of:

- Particulars.
- Conditions of use.
- Introduction.
- Enquiries 1–30.

PARTICULARS

Seller:
Buyer:
Property:
Development (if appropriate):
Transaction:
Seller's solicitors:
Buyer's solicitors:
Date:

CONTENTS
1. Boundaries and extent
2. Party walls
3. Rights benefiting the Property
4. Adverse rights affecting the Property
5. Title policies

  6.   Access to neighbouring land
  7.   Access to and from the Property
  8.   Physical condition
  9.   Contents
  10.   Utilities and services
  11.   Fire certificates and means of escape
  12.   Planning and building regulations
  13.   Statutory agreements and infrastructure
  14.   Statutory and other requirements
  15.   Environmental
  16.   Occupiers and employees
  17.   Insurance
  18.   Rates and other outgoings
  19.   Capital allowances
  20.   Value Added Tax (VAT) registration information
  21.   Transfer of a business as a going concern (TOGC)
  22.   Other VAT treatment
  23.   Standard-rated supplies
  24.   Exempt supplies
  25.   Zero-rated supplies
  26.   Transactions outside the scope of VAT (other than TOGCs)
  27.   Notices
  28.   Disputes
  29.   Stamp duty land tax on assignment of a lease
  30.   Deferred payments of stamp duty land tax

CONDITIONS OF USE

This document may be used freely and without charge subject to the following:

- The user identifies this document, and any part or parts of it, as CPSE.1 (version 2.2) and as being part of the suite of documents comprising the Commercial Property Standard Enquiries (CPSEs). Details of these documents can be seen at <www.practicallaw.com/Article_ID=32021>.
- Use of the CPSEs, including the guidance notes, is at the user's own risk. Neither the participating law firms who prepared the CPSEs, their partners and employees, the British Property Federation nor Practical Law Company Limited represent that the CPSEs, including the guidance notes, reflect or will be kept up-to-date to reflect modern law or practice relating to commercial property transactions, that the guidance notes comprise complete or accurate statements of the law to which they relate or that comments and suggestions within the guidance notes are appropriate or sufficient for any particular transaction. Such law firms, their partners and employees, the British Property Federation and Practical Law Company Limited exclude all liability to the user and the user's clients for any losses, liabilities, damage or other consequences arising from the CPSEs, including the guidance notes, failing to reflect modern law or practice relating to commercial property transactions, the guidance notes not comprising complete or accurate statements of the law to which they relate or for comments and suggestions within the guidance notes not being appropriate or sufficient for any particular transaction. A list of the participating law firms can be seen at <www.practicallaw.com/Article_ID=16220>.
- The user acknowledges that use of this document is with the consent of the Practical Law Company Limited, the British Property Federation and the participating law firms. Any reproduction of it must be marked © MEMBER FIRMS OF LPSLG AND PRACTICAL LAW COMPANY LIMITED 2002–4 and must bear the logo of the British Property Federation.

- The user will not change the text of this document (including these Conditions of use) or represent that it or any part or parts of it is anything other than CPSE.1 (version 2.2). If the user wishes to raise any enquiries additional to those contained in this document or in the other documents comprising the CPSEs, the user will do so in a separate document that identifies clearly those additional enquiries as being separate from and additional to the CPSEs.
- The user can use this document in connection with the provision of legal advice or legal training, including advice or training given for reward or commercial gain, but otherwise the user will not sell or publish for reward or commercial gain either this document, whether in whole or part, or any document which incorporates it, whether in whole or part.

INTRODUCTION

(A)   In interpreting these enquiries the terms set out in the Particulars have the meanings given to them in the Particulars and the following interpretation also applies:

Buyer: includes tenant and prospective tenant.
Conduits: means the pipes, wires and cables through which utilities and other services are carried.
Property: includes any part of it and all buildings and other structures on it.
Seller: includes landlord and prospective landlord.

(B)   The replies to the enquiries will be given by the Seller and addressed to the Buyer. Unless otherwise agreed in writing, only the Buyer and those acting for it may rely on them. References in these enquiries to '**you**' mean the Seller and to '**we**' and '**us**' mean the Buyer. In replies to the enquiries, references to '**you**' will be taken to mean the Buyer and to '**we**' and '**us**' will be taken to mean the Seller.

(C)   The replies are given without liability on the part of the Seller's solicitors.

(D)   The Buyer acknowledges that even though the Seller will be giving replies to the enquiries, the Buyer should still inspect the Property, have the Property surveyed, investigate title and make all appropriate searches and enquiries of third parties.

(E)   In replying to each of these enquiries and any supplemental enquiries, the Seller acknowledges that it is required to provide the Buyer with copies of all documents and correspondence and to supply all details relevant to the replies, whether or not specifically requested to do so.

(F)   The Seller confirms that pending exchange of contracts or, where there is no prior contract, pending completion of the Transaction, it will notify the Buyer on becoming aware of anything which may cause any reply that it has given to these or any supplemental enquiries to be incorrect.

ENQUIRIES

1. Boundaries and extent

1.1   In respect of all walls, fences, ditches, hedges or other features (**Boundary Features**) that form the physical boundaries of the Property:

    (a)   are you aware of any discrepancies between the boundaries shown on or referred to in the title deeds and the Boundary Features; and

    (b)   have any alterations been made to the position of any Boundary Features during your ownership or, to your knowledge, earlier?

1.2   To whom do the Boundary Features belong if they do not lie wholly within the Property?

1.3   In relation to each of the Boundary Features:

    (a)   have you maintained it or regarded it as your responsibility;

    (b)   has someone else maintained it or regarded it as their responsibility; or

    (c)   have you treated it as a party structure or jointly repaired or maintained it with someone else?

1.4   Please supply a copy of any agreement for the maintenance of any of the Boundary Features.

1.5   Please supply a plan showing any parts of the Property that are situated beneath or above adjoining premises, roads or footpaths and supply copies of any relevant licences for projections.

1.6   Are there any adjoining or nearby premises or land which you use or occupy in connection with the Property?

1.7   If the answer to enquiry 1.6 is 'yes', please:

    (a)   provide a plan showing the area occupied;

    (b)   provide evidence of the basis of such occupation; and

    (c)   state when such occupation commenced.

2. Party walls

In respect of any party structures which form part of the Property and also in respect of any works of the kind which require notices to be served under the Party Wall etc. Act 1996 (**1996 Act**) please:

    (a)   confirm that there have been no breaches of the 1996 Act or any earlier legislation governing party structures;

    (b)   supply copies of any notices, counternotices, awards and agreements relating to party structures, whether made under the 1996 Act or otherwise; and

    (c)   confirm that there have been no breaches of any of the terms, notices, counternotices, awards or agreements.

3. Rights benefiting the property

3.1   Unless apparent from the copy documents supplied, are there any covenants, agreements, rights or informal arrangements of any kind (including any which you may be in the course of acquiring) which benefit the Property (Rights)?

3.2   In respect of any Rights benefiting the Property, and unless apparent from the copy documents supplied, please:

    (a)   if the Right is formally documented, show title and supply copies of all relevant documents, plans and consents;

    (b)   if the Right is not formally documented, supply evidence as to entitlement together with a plan showing the area over which the Right is exercised;

    (c)   state to what extent any Rights are exercised, whether they are shared and if so by whom;

    (d)   state whether they can be terminated and, if so, by whom;

    (e)   state who owns and/or occupies the land over which any Rights are exercisable;

    (f)   give details of the maintenance (including costs) of any land, Conduits or equipment used in connection with any Rights;

    (g)   give details of any interference with any Rights, whether past, current or threatened; and

    (h)   confirm that all terms and conditions relating to the exercise of any Rights have been complied with or, if they have not, give details.

3.3   Have you (or, to your knowledge, has any predecessor in title):

    (a)   registered against any other titles at the Land Registry any unilateral notices to protect the priority of any of the Rights revealed in response to enquiry 3.1; or

    (b)   registered any cautions against first registration in respect of any of the Rights revealed in response to enquiry 3.1?

4. Adverse rights affecting the property

4.1   Unless apparent from the copy documents supplied, are there any covenants, restrictions, agreements, rights or informal arrangements of any kind to which the Property is subject (whether public or private and whether existing or in the course of acquisition) (**Adverse Rights**)?

4.2   In respect of any Adverse Rights to which the Property is subject, and unless apparent from the copy documents supplied, please:

- (a)   give full details and supply copies of all relevant documents, plans and consents;
- (b)   state to what extent any Adverse Rights have been exercised;
- (c)   state who has the benefit of any Adverse Rights;
- (d)   state whether any Adverse Rights can be terminated and, if so, by whom;
- (e)   give details of the maintenance (including costs) of any land, Conduits or equipment used in connection with any Adverse Rights; and
- (f)   confirm that all terms and conditions relating to the exercise of any Adverse Rights have been complied with or, if they have not, give details.

4.3   Unless apparent from the copy documents supplied, does any person use any part of the Property with or without your permission?

4.4   Have you, or to your knowledge has anyone else, applied to have any restrictive covenant affecting the Property modified or discharged?

4.5   Unless full details appear from the copy documents already supplied, please supply details of any interests to which the Property is subject under Schedules 1, 3 or 12 to the Land Registration Act 2002.

4.6   For the purposes of Part I of the Countryside and Rights of Way Act 2000:

- (a)   is the Property 'access land' within the meaning of section 1(1) of that Act;
- (b)   if the answer to 4.5(a) is 'no', are you aware of anything that might result in the Property becoming 'access land'; and
- (c)   if the answer to enquiry 4.5(a) is 'yes', are there any exclusions or restrictions in force under Chapter II of Part I of the Countryside and Rights of Way Act 2000?

5. Title policies

5.1   Has anyone obtained or been refused insurance cover in respect of any defect in title to the Property, including any restrictive covenant or any lost title deed?

5.2   If insurance cover has been obtained, please:

- (a)   supply copies of all policy documents including the proposal form;
- (b)   confirm that the conditions of all such policies have been complied with; and
- (c)   give details of any claims made and supply copies of all relevant correspondence and documents.

5.3   If insurance cover has been refused, please give details and supply copies of all relevant correspondence and documents.

6. Access to neighbouring land

6.1   Has the owner or occupier of any neighbouring premises ever requested or been allowed or been refused access to the Property to carry out repairs, alterations or other works to any neighbouring premises or the Conduits serving them? If so, please give details, including copies of any access orders granted under the Access to Neighbouring Land Act 1992 (**1992 Act**).

6.2   Have you or, to your knowledge, has any previous owner or occupier of the Property ever requested or been allowed or been refused access to neighbouring premises to carry out repairs, alterations or other works to the Property or the Conduits serving it? If so, please give details, including copies of any access orders granted under the 1992 Act.

7. Access to and from the property

7.1 Does the boundary of the Property (or, if applicable, the Development) immediately adjoin a highway maintainable at public expense at, and for the full width of, each point of access?

7.2 Are there any barriers to access to the Property that are controlled by a third party? If so, please give details.

8. Physical condition

8.1 If the Property has been affected by any of the following, please supply details:

    (a) structural or inherent defects;

    (b) subsidence, settlement, landslip or heave;

    (c) defective Conduits, fixtures, plant or equipment;

    (d) rising damp, rot, any fungal or other infection or any infestation; or

    (e) flooding.

8.2 Has asbestos been used in the present structures forming part of the Property or of any premises of which the Property forms part, including Conduits, fixtures, plant and equipment?

8.3 Please supply a copy of the most recent survey or assessment carried out in relation to the Property (whether by the Seller or by any other person) for the purposes of complying with regulation 4 of the Control of Asbestos at Work Regulations 2002, or advise us when and where it can be inspected.

8.4 Please supply a copy of the written plan and any other records prepared for managing asbestos in the Property or in any premises of which the Property forms part, or advise us when and where they can be inspected.

8.5 Has any substance (other than asbestos) known or suspected to be unsuitable for its purpose, unstable or hazardous, been used in the present structures forming part of the Property, including Conduits, fixtures, plant and equipment.

8.6 Has any asbestos or other substance known or suspected to be unsuitable for its purpose, unstable or hazardous, been removed from the Property in the past?

8.7 Please identify:

    (a) any buildings

    (b) any extensions or major alterations to existing buildings, and

    (c) any other major engineering works

which have been erected, made or carried out at the Property within the last 12 years.

8.8 In respect of anything identified in reply to enquiry 8.7, please supply copies of any subsisting guarantees, warranties and insurance policies.

8.9 In respect of all Conduits, fixtures, plant or equipment which will remain part of the Property or which will serve the Property after completion of the Transaction:

    (a) please confirm that they have been regularly tested and maintained;

    (b) please confirm that, so far as you are aware, there are no items requiring significant expenditure within the next three years;

    (c) please supply a copy of the most recent maintenance report relating to each of them;

    (d) please supply copies of any subsisting guarantees, warranties and insurance policies.

8.10 In relation to the guarantees, warranties and insurance policies identified in reply to enquiries 8.8 and 8.9, please confirm that:

(a) all the terms have been complied with;

(b) there have been no claims made under any of them, whether or not those claims are current or have been settled; and

(c) there are no apparent defects in respect of which a claim might arise under them.

9. Contents

9.1 Please list any items which are currently attached to the structure of the Property in some way (e.g. wired, plumbed, bolted) and which you propose removing from the Property prior to completion of the Transaction.

9.2 Please list any items (other than those belonging to an occupational tenant) that are not attached to the structure of the Property, and which you propose leaving at the Property after completion of the Transaction.

9.3 In respect of each item listed in reply to enquiry 9.2, please:

(a) confirm that the item is included in the purchase price agreed for the Transaction;

(b) confirm that the item belongs to you free from any claim by any other party; and

(c) supply copies of any subsisting certificates, guarantees and warranties relating to it.

9.4 Please list any item that will remain at the Property after completion but which belongs to any third party other than an occupational tenant (e.g. meters).

10. Utilities and services

10.1 Please provide details of the utilities and other services connected to or serving the Property.

10.2 In respect of each utility or service listed in reply to enquiry 10.1, please state:

(a) whether the connection is direct to a mains supply;

(b) whether the connection is metered and if so whether the meter is on the Property and relates only to your use in relation to the Property;

(c) who makes the supply; and

(d) whether the Conduits run directly from a highway maintainable at public expense to the Property without passing through, under or over any other land.

10.3 Please provide details of any supply contracts and any other relevant documents.

10.4 Please provide details of any contracts for the supply of services carried out at the Property (e.g. security or cleaning).

11. Fire certificates and means of escape

11.1 Is there any breach of the current fire regulations in relation to the Property?

11.2 If a fire certificate is required for the existing use of the Property, please:

(a) provide a copy of the certificate and any ancillary documents, or tell us where they can be inspected;

(b) confirm that it remains in force and that you are not aware of anything which may lead to it being revoked, terminated or not renewed; and

(c) supply a letter addressed to the fire officer authorising the fire officer to correspond directly with us concerning the Property.

11.3 If a fire certificate is required for the existing use of the Property but none has been granted, please explain why.

11.4 Please provide copies of any risk assessments relating to the Property carried out by you or any occupier of the Property under the Fire Precautions (Workplace) Regulations 1997 or tell us where they can be inspected.

11.5 If there are any insurance requirements in relation to fire safety, please give us details and confirm that the requirements have been complied with.

11.6 In relation to means of escape from the Property in case of emergency:

(a) what are the current means of escape from the Property in case of emergency?

(b) if any means of escape passes over any land other than the Property or a public highway, please provide copies of any agreements that authorise such use; and

(c) please confirm that all conditions in any such agreements have been complied with.

11.7 Please tell us when and where any reports by the fire officer, the Health and Safety Executive or any other regulatory authority can be inspected and give us authority, if required, to inspect. Have all requirements and recommendations in these reports been complied with?

11.8 Have there been any physical alterations that might affect the validity of the current fire certificate or any other licences relating to the Property or has anything else occurred that may lead to any fire certificate, licence or any agreement for means of escape being revoked, terminated or not renewed?

12. Planning and building regulations

12.1 Please supply a copy of any planning permission, approval of reserved matters, building regulations approval, building regulations completion certificate, listed building consent and conservation area consent which relates to the Property, and of any consent for the display of advertisements at or from the Property (each a **Consent**).

12.2 In respect of any Consents disclosed, please identify:

(a) those which have been implemented and if so, indicate whether fully or partially;

(b) those which authorise existing uses and buildings; and

(c) those which have not yet been implemented but are still capable of implementation.

12.3 Please supply a copy of any of the following certificates (each a **Certificate**) which relate to the Property:

(a) established use certificate;

(b) certificate of lawfulness of existing use or development; and

(c) certificate of lawfulness of proposed use or development.

12.4 How are the existing buildings on the Property authorised if not by a Consent or a Certificate?

12.5 How is the existing use of the Property authorised if not by a Consent or a Certificate?

12.6 What is the existing use of the Property, when did it start and has it been continuous since? If there is more than one existing use please specify each use and indicate which are main and which are ancillary, and when each use started.

12.7 Where the Property is not listed under the Planning (Listed Buildings and Conservation Areas) Act 1990, please provide details of any building works, demolition, mining or other engineering works that have taken place at the Property within the past ten years, and confirm that all necessary Consents were obtained for them.

12.8 Where the Property is listed under the Planning (Listed Buildings and Conservation Areas) Act 1990, please provide:

(a) a copy of the listing particulars where available; and

(b)   details of any building works, demolition, mining or other engineering works that have taken place at the Property since the date when the Property was listed, and confirm that all necessary Consents were obtained for them.

12.9   Have there been any actual or alleged breaches of the conditions and limitations and other terms in any Consents or Certificates?

12.10   Is any Consent or Certificate the subject of a challenge in the courts either by way of judicial review or statutory proceedings? If not, is a challenge expected?

12.11   Please provide details of any application for a Consent or a Certificate which:

(a)   has been made but not yet decided;

(b)   has been refused or withdrawn; or

(c)   is the subject of an outstanding appeal.

12.12   If there is any existing outline planning permission relating to the Property or other planning permission with conditions which need to be satisfied in order for development to proceed, what has been done to obtain approval of reserved matters and/or satisfaction of those conditions?

12.13   Please supply a copy of any letters or notices under planning legislation which have been given or received in relation to the Property.

13. Statutory agreements and infrastructure

13.1   In relation to any agreements affecting the Property that have been entered into with any planning, highway or other public authority or utilities provider:

(a)   please supply details;

(b)   confirm that there are no breaches of any of their terms; and

(c)   confirm that there are no outstanding obligations under them.

13.2   Are you required to enter into any agreement or obligation with any planning, highway or other public authority or utilities provider?

13.3   Are there any proposals relating to planning, compulsory purchase powers, infrastructure (including parking, public transport schemes, road schemes and traffic regulation) or environmental health which, if implemented, would affect the continued use of the Property for its present purposes?

13.4   Is there anything affecting the Property that is capable of being registered on the local land charges register but that is not registered?

13.5   Please confirm that the Property is not subject to any charge or notice remaining to be complied with.

13.6   Please supply details of any grant made or claimed in respect of the Property, including any circumstances in which any grant may have to be repaid.

13.7   Please supply details of any compensation paid or claimed in respect of the Property under any planning legislation or following the exercise of compulsory purchase powers.

14. Statutory and other requirements

14.1   Are you aware of any breach of, alleged breach of or any claim under any statutory requirements or byelaws affecting the Property, its current use, the storage of any substance in it or the use of any fixtures, machinery or chattels in it?

14.2   Please give details of any notices that require works to be carried out to the Property under any statute, covenant, agreement or otherwise and state to what extent these notices have been complied with.

14.3   Other than any already supplied, please provide details of any licences or consents required to authorise any activities currently carried out at the Property, including any required under local legislation (e.g. London Building Act).

14.4   Was the construction of the Property, or of any subsequent alteration or addition to the Property, subject to the Construction (Design and Management) Regulations 1994? If so, with respect to the Health and Safety file, please:

    (a)   confirm that it has been compiled in accordance with the Regulations;

    (b)   advise when and where it can be inspected; and

    (c)   confirm that the original will be handed over on completion.

15. Environmental

15.1   Please supply a copy of all environmental reports that have been prepared in relation to the Property or indicate where such reports may be inspected.

15.2   Please supply:

    (a)   a copy of all licences and authorisations given in relation to the Property under environmental law and confirm that the terms of all such licences and authorisations have been complied with; and

    (b)   details of any licences and authorisations for which application has been made but that have not yet been given.

15.3   What (if any) authorisations are required under environmental law for activities currently carried out or processes occurring at the Property, including storage of materials, water abstraction, discharges to sewers or controlled waters, emissions to air and the management of waste?

15.4   Please give details (so far as the Seller is aware) of:

    (a)   past and present uses of the Property and of activities carried out there; and

    (b)   the existence of any hazardous substances or contaminative or potentially contaminative material in, on or under the Property, including asbestos or asbestos-containing materials, any known deposits of waste, existing or past storage areas for hazardous or radioactive substances, existing or former storage tanks (whether below or above ground) and any parts of the Property that are or were landfill.

15.5   Please provide full details of any notices, correspondence, legal proceedings, disputes or complaints under environmental law or otherwise relating to real or perceived environmental problems that affect the Property, or which have affected the Property within the last ten years, including any communications relating to the actual or possible presence of contamination at or near the Property.

15.6   Please provide full details of how any forms of waste or effluent from the Property (including surface water) are disposed of, including copies of any relevant consents, agreements and correspondence.

15.7   Please give details of any actual, alleged or potential breaches of environmental law or licences or authorisations and any other environmental problems (including actual or suspected contamination) relating to:

    (a)   the Property; or

    (b)   land in the vicinity of the Property that may adversely affect the Property, its use or enjoyment or give rise to any material liability or expenditure on the part of the owner or occupier of the Property.

15.8   Please provide copies of any insurance policies that specifically provide cover in relation to contamination or other environmental problems affecting the Property. If such insurance cover has at any time been applied for and refused, please provide full details.

16. Occupiers and employees

16.1   Please give the names of anyone in actual occupation of the Property or receiving income from it. Except where apparent from the title deeds, please explain what rights or interests they have in the Property.

16.2   Except where apparent from the title deeds or revealed in reply to enquiry 16.1, please state whether any person, apart from you, has or claims to have any right (actual or contingent) to use or occupy the Property or any right to possession of the Property or to any interest in it.

16.3   If the Property is vacant, when did it become vacant?

16.4   Is there anyone to whom the Transfer of Undertakings (Protection of Employment) Regulations 1981 will or might apply, who is:

    (a)   employed at the Property by you; or

    (b)   employed at the Property by someone other than you; or

    (c)   is otherwise working at or is providing services at or to the Property?

16.5   In respect of each person identified in reply to enquiry 16.4, please provide copies of the current contract of employment, service agreement and (if applicable) service occupancy agreement for resident employees.

17. Insurance

17.1   Have you experienced any difficulty in obtaining insurance cover (including cover for public liability and, where relevant, for loss of rent) for the Property at normal rates and subject only to normal exclusions and excesses?

17.2   Please give details of the claims history and any outstanding claims.

17.3   Is there any insurance benefiting the Property, other than buildings insurance and any policy disclosed in reply to enquiry 5.1 (defect in title) or 15.8 (environmental insurance)?

17.4   If an existing buildings insurance policy will remain in place after completion of the Transaction, or is to be relied on by the Buyer until completion, please supply a copy of the policy including the proposal form (if available) and schedule of insurance cover and (where not shown on the schedule) provide the following information:

    (a)   the insurer's name and address;

    (b)   the policy number;

    (c)   the risks covered and the exclusions and the excesses payable;

    (d)   the sums insured (showing separately, where applicable, the sums for buildings, plant and machinery, professionals' fees, loss of rent and public liability);

    (e)   the name(s) of the insured(s) and of all other persons whose interests are (or will be) noted on the policy;

    (f)   the current premium;

    (g)   the next renewal date;

    (h)   the name and address of the brokers; and

    (i)   details of any separate terrorism insurance arrangements.

17.5   Please confirm that all premiums have been paid that are required to maintain the cover referred to in enquiry 17.4 up to the next renewal date following the date of the Seller's replies to these enquiries.

17.6   Please provide details of any circumstances that may make the policy referred to in the reply to enquiry 17.4 void or voidable.

18. Rates and other outgoings

18.1   What is the rateable value of the Property?

18.2   Please confirm that the Property is not assessed together with other premises or, if it is, please give details.

18.3   Please provide copies of any communications received in connection with:

   (a)   the latest rating revaluation and any returns made; and

   (b)   any proposal or pending appeal.

18.4   Please give details of:

   (a)   any works carried out to, or any change of use of, the Property that may cause the rateable value to be revised; and

   (b)   any application made for the rateable value to be revised.

18.5   In the current year what is payable in respect of the Property for:

   (a)   uniform business rates; and

   (b)   water rates, sewerage and drainage rates?

18.6   Have you made any claim for void period allowance or for exemption from liability for business rates? If so, please give details.

18.7   Is the Property the subject of transitional charging arrangements? If so, please give details.

18.8   Except where apparent from the title deeds, please give details of all outgoings (other than business, water, sewerage and drainage rates) payable by the owner or occupier of the Property, and confirm that all payments due to date have been made.

19. Capital allowances

19.1   Do you hold the Property as an investor (i.e. on capital account) or as a trader as part of your trading stock?

19.2   Does the Property form part of an area either currently or formerly designated as an enterprise zone? If so, when was the area designated? Please supply details of any claims made for capital allowances on an enterprise zone building forming part of the Property.

19.3   Have you or any other person claimed (or is any person entitled to claim) industrial building allowances on the Property? If so, please provide the following details in relation to all expenditure on the original construction of the Property and on any alteration to it (and where items of expenditure have been incurred at different times, please provide the details in respect of each separate amount of expenditure incurred):

   (a)   the relevant interest (within the meaning of section 286 of the Capital Allowances Act 2001 (**CAA 2001**));

   (b)   the amount of expenditure;

   (c)   the date when the expenditure was incurred;

   (d)   the date of first use;

   (e)   the name of any current tenant;

   (f)   the use made of the building by current and previous occupiers (with dates);

   (g)   any periods of non-qualifying use;

   (h)   the value of the claim;

   (i)   the residue of qualifying expenditure;

   (j)   the value of any balancing allowance;

   (k)   the value of any balancing charge; and

   (l)   whether any expenditure was incurred by a trader holding the Property as part of its trading stock.

19.4   Have you or any other person claimed (or, in relation to any period prior to completion, will any person claim) research and development or scientific research allowances in respect of the Property or any other asset to be included in the Transaction?

19.5   Has the Inland Revenue accepted, or has the Seller or any person connected to the Seller (within the meaning of section 839 of the Income and Corporation Taxes Act 1988) submitted to the Inland Revenue, any claim for capital allowances in respect of any item of plant or machinery installed in or fixed to the Property so as to become, in law, a fixture (a **Fixture**) to be included in the Transaction? If so, for each such claim please state:

> (a)   the date the Fixture was acquired;
> (b)   whether the claim was in respect of Fixtures installed by the Seller or already installed by a previous owner;
> (c)   the value of the claim; and
> (d)   the proposed disposal value.

19.6   If the Seller or any person connected to the Seller (within the meaning of section 839 of the Income and Corporation Taxes Act 1988), has not submitted a claim to the Inland Revenue for capital allowances in respect of any Fixtures to be included in the Transaction, will the Seller be willing to agree in the contract not to make such a claim?

19.7   If the Seller acquired the Property on or after 24 July, 1996, is the Seller aware of any claims for capital allowances in respect of any Fixtures to be included in the Transaction accepted or submitted to the Inland Revenue by a previous owner? If so, for each such prior claim please state:

> (a)   the date the Fixture was acquired by the previous owner;
> (b)   the name of the previous owner;
> (c)   whether the claim was in respect of Fixtures installed by the previous owner or already installed by a prior owner;
> (d)   the value of the claim; and
> (e)   the disposal value.

19.8   Have any of the Fixtures included in the Transaction been included in an election either under section 198 or section 199 of the CAA 2001 or section 59B of the Capital Allowances Act 1990? If so, please provide a copy of such election notice(s).

19.9   If requested by us, will you enter into an agreement with us to make an election under section 198 or section 199 of the CAA 2001?

19.10   Have you or any predecessor in title made a contribution to another person's expenditure which is either expenditure on or relating to the Property on which industrial building allowances are available or expenditure on any fixed plant or machinery installed in the Property? If so, please provide details.

19.11   Please provide details of any plant or machinery that is not a Fixture but is included in the Transaction.

19.12   Please confirm that none of the plant and machinery (whether or not a Fixture) included in the Transaction has been or is likely to be treated as a long-life asset in accordance with Part 2, Chapter 10 CAA 2001.

19.13   Please provide details of any Fixtures upon which expenditure has been incurred by a tenant or that are subject to an equipment lease.

19.14   Where the Transaction is the grant of a lease:

> (a)   if requested, will you make a joint election with us under section 290 of the CAA 2001 in respect of the Transaction; and
> (b)   if requested, will you make a joint election with us under section 183 of the CAA 2001 enabling us to claim capital allowances on fixed plant or machinery installed in the Property and included in the Transaction?

20. Value added tax (VAT) registration information

20.1   Are you registered for VAT?

20.2   If so, please provide details of your VAT registration number.

20.3   If you are registered as part of a VAT group, please provide the name of the representative member.

21. Transfer of a business as a going concern (TOGC)

21.1   Do you expect the Transaction to be treated as a TOGC and so to be outside the scope of VAT?

If you answered no, please go to enquiry 22 below; otherwise please answer enquiries 21.2–21.6 below.

21.2   Why do you think TOGC treatment will apply?

21.3   Are there any factors (other than those solely within our control) that may affect the availability of this treatment?

21.4   Is the Transaction partly within and partly outside the scope of VAT (being a TOGC)? If so, how do you propose to apportion the price between the two elements?

21.5   Is the Property a Capital Goods Scheme item? If so, and if the period of adjustment has not yet expired, please supply the following:

> (a)   the start date of the adjustment period and of any intervals that have started or will start before completion of the Transaction;
>
> (b)   the original deductible percentage;
>
> (c)   the total input tax attributable to the Property (whether or not recoverable) that is subject to adjustment in accordance with the Capital Goods Scheme and the amount of that input tax that has been recovered by you, or by anyone previously responsible for making adjustments during the current period of adjustment; and
>
> (d)   details of any adjustment of the input tax recovered in relation to the Property by you or anyone previously responsible for making adjustments.

21.6   Do you intend to apply to HM Customs & Excise for permission to retain the VAT records relating to the Property following completion of the Transaction?

22. Other VAT treatment

If and to the extent that the Transaction may not be a TOGC (however unlikely this may be) or TOGC status is not available, will the Transaction (or any part of it) be treated for VAT purposes as:

> (a)   standard-rated (*if yes, please go to enquiry 23 below*);
>
> (b)   exempt (*if yes, please go to enquiry 24 below*);
>
> (c)   zero-rated (*if yes, please go to enquiry 25 below*); or
>
> (d)   outside the scope of VAT (*other than by reason of being a TOGC*)? (*if yes, please go to enquiry 26 below*).

23. Standard-rated supplies

23.1   Why do you think that the Transaction (or any part of it) is standard-rated?

23.2   If the Transaction (or any part of it) is compulsorily standard-rated (as the freehold sale of a new or uncompleted building or civil engineering work), please state:

> (a)   the date of the certificate of practical completion of the Property (or each relevant part);
>
> (b)   if different, the date on which it was first fully occupied; and
>
> (c)   whether the Property (or any part of it) is not yet completed.

23.3   Has an election to waive the exemption from VAT been made in respect of, or which affects, the Property by you or any relevant associate within the meaning of paragraph 3(7) Schedule 10 to the Value Added Tax Act 1994? If so, please:

(a)   supply a copy of the election and the notice of election given to HM Customs & Excise and any notices and correspondence received from HM Customs & Excise in relation to the election;

(b)   supply a copy of any permission required from HM Customs & Excise for the election or, where relevant, details of any automatic permission relied upon, and provide confirmation that any conditions for such permission have been satisfied; and

(c)   confirm that the election applies to the whole of the Property and has not been and cannot be disapplied or rendered ineffective for any reason and cannot or will not be revoked.

23.4   Where the Transaction is the assignment of a lease, has the landlord or any relevant associate (as above) made an election to waive the exemption from VAT in respect of the Lease?

Unless you also answered yes to enquiry 22 (b), (c) or (d), please now go to enquiry 27.

24. Exempt supplies

24.1   Why do you think the Transaction (or any part of it) will be exempt?

24.2   Does the Transaction involve both standard-rated and exempt supplies? If so, how do you propose to apportion the price between the two elements?

Unless you also answered yes to enquiry 22(c) or (d), please now go to enquiry 27.

25. Zero-rated supplies

25.1   Why do you think that the Transaction (or any part of it) is zero-rated?

25.2   Does the Transaction involve both standard-rated and zero-rated supplies? If so, how do you propose to apportion the price between the two elements?

Unless you also answered yes to enquiry 22(d), please now go to enquiry 27.

26. Transactions outside the scope of VAT (other than TOGCs)

26.1   Why do you think that the Transaction (or any part of it) is outside the scope of VAT?

26.2   Is the Transaction partly within and partly outside the scope of VAT (other than by reason of being a TOGC)? If so, how do you propose to apportion the price between the two elements?

27. Notices

27.1   Except where details have already been given elsewhere in replies to these enquiries, please supply copies of all notices and any subsequent correspondence that affect the Property or any neighbouring property and have been given or received by you or (to your knowledge) by any previous owner, tenant or occupier of the Property.

27.2   Are you expecting to give or to receive any notice affecting the Property or any neighbouring property?

28. Disputes

Except where details have already been given elsewhere in replies to these enquiries, please give details of any disputes, claims, actions, demands or complaints that are currently outstanding, likely or have arisen in the past and that:

(a)   relate to the Property or to any rights enjoyed with the Property or to which the Property is subject; or

(b)   affect the Property but relate to property near the Property or any rights enjoyed by such neighbouring property or to which such neighbouring property is subject.

29. Stamp duty land tax on assignment of a lease

In this enquiry, **Lease** *has the same meaning as in CPSE.4 ("the lease under which the Property is held and which is to be assigned by the Seller to the Buyer")*

29.1   If the grant of the Lease or any event since the grant of the Lease was a land transaction for Stamp Duty Land Tax purposes,

(a)   what was the date of the grant of the lease for Stamp Duty Land Tax purposes?

(b)   was the transaction notifiable?

(c)   if the transaction was notifiable, please provide a copy of each land transaction return made to the Inland Revenue and copy of each certificate issued by the Inland Revenue certifying that the transaction was notified to them;

(d)   if the transaction was not notifiable, please provide a copy of any self-certification certificate made on the grant of the lease or otherwise certify the effective date of the grant of the lease.

29.2   Is there a potential or outstanding obligation to make an additional land transaction return to the Inland Revenue as a result of any of the following occurring during the first five years from the date given in the answer to Enquiry 29.1(a):

(a)   the settlement or determination of any rent reviews or any other provision for varying the rent; or

(b)   the settlement or determination of any contingent, uncertain or unascertained rents?

If there is, please provide a full schedule of the rents payable and paid in each quarter since the date given in the answer to Enquiry 29.1(a).

29.3   If a premium was paid for the grant of the lease or any assignment of the lease to you

(a)   was the whole or any part of that premium contingent, uncertain or unascertained;

(b)   if it was, does the whole or any part of that premium remain contingent, uncertain or unascertained; and

(c)   have you made any application to the Inland Revenue to defer payment of Stamp Duty Land Tax on that contingent, uncertain or unascertained consideration?

29.4   Were any Stamp Duty Land Tax reliefs claimed on the grant of the Lease and, if applicable, on the assignment of the Lease to you, that would result in the assignment of the Lease by you being deemed to be the grant of a new Lease?

30. Deferred payments of stamp duty land tax

30.1   If you have made any application to defer the payment of Stamp Duty Land Tax on any contingent, uncertain or unascertained consideration and you are seeking an indemnity from the buyer in respect of the deferred payment:

(a)   please provide a copy of the original land transaction return made to the Inland Revenue and a copy of the certificate issued by the Inland Revenue certifying that the transaction was notified to them;

(b)   please provide a copy of all correspondence with the Inland Revenue regarding the application to defer the payment of Stamp Duty Land Tax;

(c) what is the amount of Stamp Duty Land Tax on which payment has been deferred;

(d) when does the period of deferral end; and

(e) has any event occurred that quantifies the amount of the contingent, uncertain or unascertained consideration that would impose an obligation on you to make a further land transaction return to the Inland Revenue?

APPENDIX 19

British Property Federation Commercial Property Standard Enquiries Guidance Notes

COMMERCIAL PROPERTY STANDARD ENQUIRIES
GN/CPSE.1 (VERSION 2.2)
GUIDANCE NOTES ON CPSE.1 GENERAL PRE-CONTRACT ENQUIRIES FOR ALL COMMERCIAL PROPERTY TRANSACTIONS

CPSE.1 enquiries should be raised in every transaction where commercial property is being acquired, whether freehold or leasehold.

These guidance notes:

- Enable the enquiries to be presented in a concise form without the need for illustrative examples.
- Are intended to help the legal advisers, the Buyer and the Seller to understand why individual enquiries are raised, how the enquiry should be answered and what may need to be done depending on the nature of the reply.

The Buyer may wish to keep a set of the guidance notes with the Seller's replies to the enquiries to assist the Buyer in understanding and using the information in the replies both during the period of the Buyer's ownership and later on a subsequent sale of the Property.

The enquiries stand on their own and do not depend on the guidance notes for interpretation.

CONTENTS
Conditions of use
Guidance Notes
Boundaries and extent
Party walls
Rights benefiting the Property
Adverse rights affecting the Property
Title policies
Access to neighbouring land
Access to and from the Property

Physical condition

Contents

Utilities and services

Fire certificates and means of escape

Planning and building regulations

Statutory agreements and infrastructure

Statutory and other liabilities

Environmental

Occupiers and employees

Insurance

Rates and other outgoings

Capital allowances

Value Added Tax (VAT) registration information

Transfer of a business as a going concern (TOGC)

Other VAT treatment

Standard-rated supplies

Exempt supplies

Zero-rated supplies

Transactions outside the scope of VAT (other than TOGCs)

Notices

Disputes

Stamp Duty Land Tax on assignment of a lease

Deferred payments of Stamp Duty Land Tax

CONDITIONS OF USE

This document may be used freely and without charge subject to the following:

- The user identifies this document, and any part or parts of it, as GN/CPSE.1 (version 2.2) and as being part of the suite of documents comprising the Commercial Property Standard Enquiries (CPSEs). Details of these documents can be seen at <www.practicallaw.com/Article_ID=32021>.
- Use of the CPSEs, including the guidance notes, is at the user's own risk. Neither the participating law firms who prepared the CPSEs, their partners and employees, the British Property Federation nor Practical Law Company Limited represent that the CPSEs, including the guidance notes, reflect or will be kept up-to-date to reflect modern law or practice relating to commercial property transactions, that the guidance notes comprise complete or accurate statements of the law to which they relate or that comments and suggestions within the guidance notes are appropriate or sufficient for any particular transaction. Such law firms, their partners and employees, the British Property Federation and Practical Law Company Limited exclude all liability to the user and the user's clients for any losses, liabilities, damage or other consequences arising from the CPSEs, including the guidance notes, failing to reflect modern law or practice relating to commercial property transactions, the guidance notes not comprising complete or accurate statements of the law to which they relate or for comments and suggestions within the guidance notes not being appropriate or sufficient for any particular transaction. A list of the participating law firms can be seen at <www.practicallaw.com/Article_ID=16220>.
- The user acknowledges that use of this document is with the consent of the Practical Law Company Limited, the British Property Federation and the participating law firms. Any reproduction of it must be marked © MEMBER FIRMS OF LPSLG AND PRACTICAL LAW COMPANY LIMITED 2002–4 and must bear the logo of the British Property Federation.
- The user will not change the text of this document (including these Conditions of use) or represent that it or any part or parts of it is anything other than GN/CPSE.1 (version 2.2).

If the user wishes to raise any enquiries additional to those contained in this document or in the other documents comprising the CPSEs, the user will do so in a separate document that identifies clearly those additional enquiries as being separate from and additional to the CPSEs.

- The user can use this document in connection with the provision of legal advice or legal training, including advice or training given for reward or commercial gain, but otherwise the user will not sell or publish for reward or commercial gain either this document, whether in whole or part, or any document which incorporates it, whether in whole or part.

GUIDANCE NOTES

Boundaries and extent

Verifying extent
This enquiry is concerned with verifying the extent of the Property. The questions are aimed at matching the title description of the Property with what appears on the ground as the physical extent of the Property, often marked by features such as walls, trees, ditches and hedges.

The Property will be defined in the title deeds and, if title is registered, the extent of the Property will be shown on the title plan. However, the Land Register is not conclusive as to boundaries and the boundary features may not correspond exactly with the title description. They may:

- Lie wholly within the legal boundaries of the Property in which case the Buyer will need to establish that nobody else has been using the land which lies between the legal boundaries and the boundary features; or
- Lie outside the legal boundaries in which case the Buyer will wish to establish whether the Seller has acquired additional land by "adverse possession" or long usage. To do this, the Buyer needs to know:
  - For how long any land beyond the legal boundaries has been used as part of the Property.
  - Whether there has been any objection to this use.
  - Who has maintained the boundary features.

Responsibility for boundary features
The Buyer also needs to know who is responsible for maintaining boundary features. The title deeds may not contain information about the ownership of the boundary features or their maintenance, and in the absence of any clear indication the Buyer must find out what the Seller and others have regarded as their responsibilities.

If available, the Seller should include details of:

- What works to boundary features have been carried out.
- What costs have been incurred.
- Who contributed and in what proportions.

Plans
Although it is up to the Buyer to obtain suitable plans, the Seller should supply copies of whatever plans it has in the interests of speeding up the Transaction. It would be helpful if the Seller were to mark all the boundaries on a plan and indicate which belong to the Property using "T" marks along the inside of the boundary line.

Enquiry 1 If there is any boundary dispute, the Seller should give details here or in response to enquiry 28.

Enquiry 1.5 Examples of what may be included in the reply to this enquiry include: vaults beneath a pavement; overhanging eaves; projecting signs; canopies; and flying freeholds.

Enquiry 1.6 Examples of what might be included in the reply to this enquiry include: storehouses, car parking areas, plant and equipment rooms, and strips of land alongside boundaries which are used although they fall outside the legal title.

Enquiry 1.7 The Buyer needs to establish whether there is any issue of adverse possession by the Seller. Enquiry 1.7 is, therefore, concerned with land or premises which do not actually form part of the Property to which the Seller has paper title, but which the Seller is nevertheless still using or enjoying. The reply to enquiry 1.7 will help identify whether the Buyer will acquire title to additional land by reason of the Seller's adverse possession, as well as whether use or occupation of other property will be needed by the Buyer to enjoy the Property once acquired.

Party walls

Where a boundary structure is jointly owned by the owners of the properties on either side of it, the structure may be a party structure. The joint owners of a party structure are given some statutory protection to prevent one owner carrying out work to the structure unilaterally without regard to the needs and wishes of the other. The statutory protection is in the Party Wall etc. Act 1996. Prior to the 1996 Act, party walls were governed by the London Building Acts if they were in London; outside London they were usually subject to the common law.

Under the 1996 Act, certain notice procedures must be followed for:

- The construction of a new wall (including the wall of a building) over or up to the boundary.
- Works affecting existing party structures, and
- Excavations within certain distances of neighbouring buildings.

Non-compliance with the legislation may mean that the construction has to be dismantled and the land reinstated. The London Building Acts contained similar notice requirements.

The Seller should give the Buyer copies of all notices, awards and agreements, whether made under the 1996 Act, the London Building Acts or by private agreement, and including any which are the subject of negotiation and settlement.

The Buyer should check all the terms, particularly those relating to payment of compensation, costs, or security. To speed the Transaction, the Seller could anticipate further questions about outstanding payments and arrangements for securing payments.

Rights benefiting the property

Generally rights benefiting the Property will pass to the Buyer.

Examples of rights benefiting the Property are rights of way (including those over emergency escape routes), rights of support, rights to light and rights to use conduits serving the Property (e.g. water, drainage and gas pipes, electricity and telephone cables).

Rights may have been granted:

- Formally by deed.
- Informally by agreement but not documented, or
- Informally through long use, with or without the knowledge or consent of the person over whose property the right is exercised.

If the title deeds do not show that the Seller has good title to exercise a right, the Buyer may be able to establish that the right has been granted informally or is in the course of being acquired. To do this the Buyer needs to establish:

- For how long and to what extent the right or purported right has been exercised (and this includes the frequency of exercise and whether the exercise has been over the whole or part of the relevant land or conduits).
- Whether this has been with the knowledge or consent of the person over whose land the right has been exercised.
- Whether there has been any objection to the exercise.
- Whether there are any maintenance obligations associated with the rights or whether anyone has assumed any responsibility for maintenance (for example, in relation to drains or footpaths).
- What costs have been incurred in exercising the rights, how costs are dealt with and the amount of any recent expenditure.

The Seller should supply details of all rights and arrangements benefiting the Property, even where these would be evident to the Seller from an inspection. What is legally required may be different from what happens in practice, which may not be apparent. The Seller should supply copies of all relevant documents and correspondence.

Enquiry 3.2(b) Express reference is made to plans because if the Right is an easement that is not formally documented, the Buyer will need to know the exact position, line or route of the easement. This is necessary to enable the Buyer to check the title to the servient tenement to ascertain whether the burden of the easement has been properly noted on it (without which the easement may not be binding on the owner of the servient tenement).

Enquiry 3.3 If for some reason an easement has been protected by a Unilateral Notice, the Buyer will need to change the identity of the beneficiary of the Unilateral Notice. Where the servient tenement is unregistered and a caution against first registration has been registered to protect the easement, the Buyer may need to change the name and address on the cautions register or, if this is not possible, lodge a new caution in the Buyer's own name. Failure to change the beneficiary's name and address will result in any warning-off notice not being received.

Adverse rights affecting the property

Generally the burden of adverse rights to which the Property is subject will pass to the Buyer.

Examples of adverse rights affecting the Property are rights of way (including emergency escape routes), rights of support, rights to light and rights to use conduits serving the neighbouring premises (e.g. water, drainage and gas pipes, electricity and telephone cables).

Adverse rights may have been granted:

- Formally by deed.
- Informally by agreement but not documented, or
- Informally through long use, with or without the knowledge or consent of the person over whose property the right is exercised.

Please see the notes to enquiry 3 as similar considerations apply.

Public rights may be acquired over property where, for example, an open forecourt forming part of the property is regularly crossed by members of the public. Car parks and private passageways between buildings are similarly vulnerable. It is possible to negative dedication as part of the highway by the display of a notice to that effect. If there are or have been any such signs erected, further enquiry should be made as to the extent of public use, its duration and as to how long the sign has been displayed.

Even if the title deeds are silent on third party rights affecting the Property, the Buyer will still need to establish that no such rights have been created informally or are in the course of being created. This is not confined to the acquisition of rights by private landowners. Public rights may also be in the course of acquisition, as explained in the preceding paragraph.

Enquiry 4.5 This enquiry concerns registered title and overriding interests. The Property may be subject to third party rights and interests, which will not necessarily be apparent from the title deeds or from any inspection of the Property, but which will still bind the Buyer whether or not the Buyer knows of them.

Land Registry Practice Guide 15 describes the law relating to overriding interests and how it has changed under the Land Registration Act 2002.

Enquiry 4.6 Part I of the Countryside and Rights of Way Act 2000 gives a public right of access to land that comes within the definition of "access land" in section 1(1) of that Act. Land that is wholly or predominantly mountain, moor, heath or down is defined as "open country" (so long as it is not improved or semi-improved grassland) but this definition may be extended to include "coastal land" (within the meaning of section 3 of the Act) in the future.

Open country will qualify as access land if it has been shown on a map of open country issued by the countryside bodies. The countryside bodies will be responsible for deciding the extent of any mountain, moor, heath and down. Land over 600 metres above sea level and registered common land immediately qualifies as access land without any requirement for mapping by the countryside bodies, but the bodies will in due course also include these categories of land on their maps. Access land will also include land which under section 16 is irrevocably dedicated by the owner to public access.

The definition of "access land" excludes the 13 categories of land listed in Schedule 1 to the Act, defined as "excepted". This includes cultivated land, land covered by buildings and land within 20 metres of a dwelling. In particular cases, landowners are entitled to exclude or restrict the public's right to enter access land. The principal exclusion is a right to exclude the public for up to 28 days in any calendar month, on terms that have yet to be prescribed by regulations (as at September, 2002).

The Seller may not know whether the Property has been designated as access land because the designation procedure does not include any requirement for service of a notice on the landowner. The Buyer will, therefore, also need to make its own inspection of the public maps that indicate the extent of access land. These can be inspected at <www.countryside.gov.uk/access/mapping> for England and <www.ccw.gov.uk/mapping/ index.cfm> for Wales. At the time of publication of the Commercial Property Standard Enquiries (September, 2002), no maps have yet been finalised in either England or Wales.

Title policies

Insurance may be available to cover:

- Restrictive covenants where, for example, the nature of the covenant or the identity of the person having the benefit of the covenant is unknown, or
- Lost title deeds (for example, in relation to rights benefiting the Property) or defects in title where the title to the land is unregistered.

Title insurance policies may benefit subsequent owners and mortgagees of the Property as well as the person who originally took out the insurance. The Buyer needs to be satisfied that the level of cover is still adequate. Any increase in the market value of the Property may make the level of cover inadequate, irrespective of any index-linking of the sum insured.

Enquiry 5.2(a) "Policy documents" generally comprise the policy and schedule showing the level of cover. Copies of any other documents referred to in the policy documents should also be produced (e.g. any opinion of counsel).

Enquiry 5.3 The Seller should include details of any application for insurance that has been refused as this is relevant information that must be disclosed on a future insurance application and may also be useful in making any subsequent re-application.

Access to neighbouring land

It is often difficult or impossible for an owner or occupier to carry out repairs, alterations or other works to its own premises without going onto neighbouring land. If access is necessary but neighbours cannot agree arrangements, an application may be made to the court for an order giving access under the Access to Neighbouring Land Act 1992.

The Buyer will want details of all requests for access made and permissions given, whether made informally or by the court, including any applications and permissions relating to conduits (e.g. for unblocking drains or laying cables) so that it is aware of any potential difficulties that are likely to arise.

Access to and from the property

Enquiry 7.1 The Buyer needs to be satisfied that there are adequate rights of access to the Property. If access is direct to a public highway, no additional rights of way will be necessary and the Buyer will need to check only that there are no outstanding maintenance charges in respect of the highway (see enquiry 13).

Local authority enquiries should reveal whether roadways and footpaths are public highways, and therefore maintainable at public expense. They are unlikely, however, to reveal whether the public highway directly abuts the boundary of the Property and it may not be possible for the Buyer to establish this from an inspection.

Following *Gooden v Northamptonshire County Council* [2001] 49 EG 116 (CS) if adoption of a road or footpath is crucial to a buyer's proposed use or development of the property, it is prudent not to rely solely on information obtained from local authority searches and enquiries, which may be unreliable. Further independent checks should be made, for example, of adjoining landowners.

Enquiry 7.2 Access may be controlled by a third party (e.g. by means of a locked gate). Enquiries should be made as to availability of keys, times when the barrier is attended by an operator and access arrangements when the barrier is not attended.

Physical condition

Enquiry 8 relates to the physical condition of the Property.

A survey or inspection may not reveal past or intermittent defects and not everything can be inspected, for example, hidden structure and conduits. For this reason, the Seller is asked about the condition of the Property and, in answering, may be willing to give full details even where it considers that a defect or problem would be apparent on an inspection or would be revealed by a survey or has been treated or resolved. The Seller may of course (as with any enquiry) decline to give an answer. The Buyer can deduce what it wishes from any such refusal. If, however, the Seller does provide an answer, it may be liable for misrepresentation if the answer is not complete or is misleading in some way.

A significant part of Enquiry 8 is devoted to enquiries about asbestos. Asbestos was extensively used in building materials providing protection from heat, fire and sound, until the dangers from exposure to asbestos became known. It was used extensively, for example, in floor tiles, as insulation around pipes, for wall and ceiling panels, roofing, and decorative plasters. It is now illegal to use any form of asbestos in the construction or refurbishment of any buildings, but much of what was used in the past is still in place, constituting a significant health risk to those involved in building, renovation or maintenance work.

The Control of Asbestos at Work Regulations 2002 (CAWR 2002) consolidate previous regulations and replace the Control of Asbestos at Work Act Regulations 1987. Whilst most of CAWR 2002 came into force on 21 November 2002, Regulation 4 did not come into force until 21 May 2004. Regulation 4 imposes a new duty on all "dutyholders" to:

- Determine whether asbestos is present in a building or is likely to be present; and
- Manage any asbestos that is or is likely to be present

"Dutyholders" are all those who have some contractual responsibility for the maintenance or repair of the property, or can exercise some control over access to and from the property. A number of people may have regulation 4 duties in respect of the same property, as for example where a property is let: the freeholder, the tenant, the sub-tenant and any licensee could each be responsible. Where there is joint liability, each party's relative liability is determined by the "nature and extent of the maintenance and repair obligations" that it owes.

There is also a duty on "every person" to co-operate with the dutyholder "so far as necessary to enable the dutyholder to comply" with its duties. This would extend, for example, to landlords, tenants and licensees co-operating with each other, and also to surveyors, architects and building contractors.

There is no definition of "non-domestic premises" in the CAWR 2002, but the Health and Safety Executive (HSE) is advising that a broad approach should be taken, which may include certain parts of blocks of flats, houses that have been converted into flats, and flats over shops.

The duty is first to carry out an assessment of the property to identify the presence or possible presence of asbestos. The assessment must be recorded and kept under review. If the result of the assessment is that asbestos is or is liable to be in the property, the dutyholder must determine the risk posed by the asbestos, prepare a written plan to identify those parts of the property affected and to specify what measures should be taken for managing the risk. It may be appropriate in the circumstances for the asbestos to be removed, but it may be sufficient for the asbestos to be encapsulated and effectively made safe.

The written plan must be kept under review and the dutyholder must ensure that information about the location and condition of any asbestos, or any substance containing or suspected of containing asbestos, is provided to everyone liable to disturb it and to the emergency services.

Detailed guidance on the application and extent of the duty to manage under regulation 4 is contained in the Approved Code of Practice, "*The management of asbestos in non-domestic premises*" prepared by the Health and Safety Executive (HSE). For details on how to obtain this, see the HSE website, <http://www.hse.gov.uk/asbestos/>.

Enquiry 8.1(a) An inherent defect (sometimes referred to as a latent defect) is one that exists because of some fault or limitation in the construction or design of the building or the materials used to construct it. It may not be apparent on completion of the construction of the building, but may become apparent with time or because an intervening event triggers symptoms of the defect.

Enquiry 8.1(c) The Seller should include in any reply information about all defective conduits affecting the Property, whether or not they form part of the Property.

Enquiry 8.2 This enquiry focuses on asbestos and the present construction of the Property, which includes the original construction, any subsequent alteration or addition to it, and fixtures, plant, equipment or conduits, which serve the Property, whether or not they form part of it.

Enquiry 8.3 The Buyer will want as much information as possible about the presence and condition of asbestos. Enquiry 8.3 therefore asks the Seller to supply a copy of the most recent survey or assessment carried out in relation to the Property for the purposes of complying with regulation 4 of the CAWR 2002. The Seller may decline to provide this. A record of assessment may not be a particularly useful document if the Seller has simply made a presumptive inspection (i.e. presumed the presence of asbestos, which effectively the Seller must do unless it can establish that there is no asbestos present). The infotmation can effectively be obtained by the Buyer's own survey and once the Buyer completes on the acquisition, the Buyer will become a dutyholder and liable to make its own assessment. The Buyer is unlikely to be in compliance with regulation 4 merely by relying on the Seller's assessment.

Enquiry 8.4 Enquiry 8.4 is concerned with the written plan and other records prepared in relation to the duty to manage asbestos. This will provide the Buyer with useful background information, but the Buyer will be under a duty to prepare its own written plan once it has completed the transaction; the Buyer will not be able to rely on the Seller's written plan. The Seller's written plan may be of limited use on the purchase of the freehold because the scope of it will be determined in part by the Seller's use of the property, proposals for alterations, finances and current condition. However, on the acquisition of leasehold property, the Seller's written plan will provide valuable information about what works the Seller may need to do, and so may be able to charge the tenant for under the service charge provisions. It may also give an indication of the landlord's likely attitude to proposed alterations to the Property, and the need for the landlord to gain access to the Property to carry out works to remove or make safe asbestos in the Property.

The Seller's written plan will also be highly relevant to the Buyer in the context of a business acquisition.

Enquiry 8.5: Enquiry 8.5 is concerned with the presence of substances other than asbestos. It was common practice in pre-contract enquiries to ask the Seller to list what were referred to as "deleterious materials" used in the construction of the Property. This practice was been criticised for concentrating attention on the materials themselves rather than on the way in which they have been used. A substance on its own or used in a particular manner may present no risk but used in a different way, or in conjunction with another material, may be unstable or hazardous.

In May 1997, Ove Arup & Partners, in conjunction with the British Council of Offices and the British Property Federation, launched a guide entitled *"Good Practice in the Selection of Construction Materials"*, providing guidance on good practice for the selection of materials in construction. The preamble explains the need to adopt a new approach to dealing with such materials so that, rather than prohibiting the use of certain materials automatically, good practice is followed in their selection to ensure that they are used appropriately. Adopting this approach, the enquiries do not list particular materials. The function of this enquiry is to ascertain whether a potential problem exists. Whether there is an actual problem will be a matter for appropriately qualified consultants, having regard to British, European and International Standards and Codes of Practice.

Enquiry 8.6: This enquiry is concerned with materials (asbestos or other materials) that have already been removed from the Property. The Buyer should be concerned that any removal of asbestos, for example, has been done in accordance with relevant codes of practice.

Enquiry 8.7: If the reply to this enquiry indicates that buildings have been erected on the Property or that any extensions or major alterations have been carried out within the previous 12 years, the Buyer may wish to raise further specific enquiries. To avoid delay the Seller may consider volunteering details and any relevant information without specifically being asked to do so.

Enquiry 8.9: "Plant and equipment" may include security, access and alarm systems, lifts, escalators, CCTV, building management systems, air conditioning and heating systems. "Reports" may include reports that take the form of answers to formal questionnaires and may relate to construction, alteration, maintenance, repair, replacement, treatment or improvements. The Buyer is primarily concerned with current state and condition but maintenance reports may be the only practical source of information. The Buyer will be interested in all guarantees, warranties and insurance policies under which it may be able to claim in the event of a defect.

Contents

The Buyer and the Seller need to agree what items will be left at the Property on completion of the Transaction and what items will be removed, and any effect this may have on the price.

This enquiry is to clarify what the Buyer expects to receive and what the Seller must do to give vacant possession of the Property. The general rule, unless the parties agree otherwise, is that:

- Fixtures remain in the Property and pass to the Buyer.
- Chattels do not pass and the Seller is legally obliged to remove them prior to completion.

The distinction between fixtures and chattels can be difficult to determine, which is why the enquiries avoid these terms in favour of "item". The courts have evolved tests by reference to the degree and purpose of annexation to the property. Generally if something has been fixed to a property so that it is difficult to remove without causing damage and was fixed to improve that property permanently, it will be a fixture. Rather than rely on this imprecise test, however, it is prudent for the parties to come to a clear agreement.

In the case of telecommunications links and equipment, replies should clearly set out what will be removed, what will remain, and what is the undertaker's property.

Enquiries 9.1 and 9.2 It is particularly important that the parties agree whether fixed plant is to be removed on completion or is to remain in the Property. Fixed plant tends to be heavy, difficult to move and expensive and generally will play a significant part in the business or use of the Property. It may not be clear whether it should be treated as a fixture or a chattel, and any misunderstanding between the parties as to whether it stays in the Property on completion or is removed may have serious consequences.

Enquiry 9.3(b) Examples of third party claims which may affect items that the Seller is proposing to leave at the Property following completion include credit or conditional sale agreements, hire and hire purchase agreements, finance and leasing agreements. Some of these may contain title retention clauses, which would mean that the Seller does not own the item in question. In relation to such items there may be some overlap with enquiry 9.4.

Enquiry 9.4 Items which will remain in the Property but which will belong to a third party include telecommunication masts, advertising hoardings, metering equipment and street signs fixed to exterior walls.

Utilities and services

Enquiry 10.1 Utilities and services may include:

- Water.
- Drainage of foul and surface water.
- Gas.
- Oil.
- Electricity.

- District heating schemes.
- Telecommunications.
- Cable and satellite communications systems.

Enquiry 10.2 Although usual for a property to be connected to mains utilities (such as water, drainage, gas and electricity), this is not always so. Also, there may be more than one source of the utility supply. Water may come from a mains supply and a well or be drawn directly from a river or lake. Electricity may come from a private generator instead of or in addition to the mains supply.

If conduits do not run directly from a highway maintainable at public expense, details of the rights to use the conduits should be given in reply to enquiry 3.

Enquiry 10.3 and 10.4 Although the Buyer will not generally be concerned to see supply contracts for mains utilities, it will need to see copies of all supply contracts and consents which either will continue to affect the Property after completion or which it may wish to take over. An example would be a water abstraction licence. Details of all contracts and licences are requested so that the Buyer can decide what may be of interest.

Fire certificates and means of escape

Fire safety is dealt with under several statutory regimes. The age and use of the Property and the number of occupiers determine which requirements apply. The following require a fire certificate:

- Hotels and boarding houses with sleeping accommodation for more than six people (whether guests or staff), or where there is sleeping accommodation above first floor or below ground floor levels.
- Premises at which highly flammable substances covered by the Fire Certificates (Special Premises) Regulations 1976 are manufactured or stored.
- Factories, offices, shops and railway premises where more than 20 people work of whom ten work somewhere other than on the ground floor.
- Buildings in multiple occupation containing two or more individual factory, office, shop or railway units and where more than 20 people work of whom ten work somewhere other than on the ground floor.

Regardless of any requirement for a fire certificate, the Fire Precautions (Workplace) Regulations 1997 may apply to protect employees in non-domestic premises used for the purposes of an employer's business.

The burden of compliance with fire requirements generally rests with the occupier but, if the building is in multiple occupation, the owner of the building may also be liable. An owner for these purposes is the person who receives rent for the building and may include a trustee and/or a managing agent.

Enquiry 11.1 A breach of fire regulations may be punishable as a criminal offence with a fine and/or a term of imprisonment.

Enquiry 11.2 A breach of fire certificate requirements may result in the cancellation of the certificate, which in turn may lead to a breach of fire regulations.

Without a letter to the fire officer authorising the fire officer to correspond directly with the Buyer, the fire officer may refuse to correspond with anyone other than the Seller in relation to the Property.

Enquiry 11.6 A fire certificate, if there is one, will specify the means of escape and may impose obligations to maintain an escape route and keep it free from obstruction. It is deemed to be a requirement of a fire certificate that the means of escape will be kept in accordance with the specification in the fire certificate. The means of escape may be direct from the Property or may be over adjoining premises, in which case the Seller should give full details of any rights or agreements with the owners of the adjoining premises.

Enquiry 11.7 Fire certificates are issued by the Fire and Civil Defence Authority for the area in which the Property is situated. Consideration must be given when answering this enquiry to other regulatory bodies such as licensing bodies for cinemas, pubs, theatres and sports grounds and to Building Regulation requirements.

Enquiry 11.8 It is an offence to carry out any material alterations to premises for which there is a current fire certificate without the prior approval of the Fire Authority. "Material" means any alteration that, in case of fire, could render the means of escape from the premises inadequate given the use of the premises for which the fire certificate was issued. A letter of consent should be obtained prior to making any alterations.

Planning and building regulations

Planning law is contained in a number of statutes and subordinate legislation, principally the Town and Country Planning Act 1990, the Planning (Listed Buildings and Conservation Areas) Act 1990, the Planning (Hazardous Substances) Act 1990 and the Planning (Consequential Provisions) Act 1990.

Planning permission is required for "development", which encompasses either of two elements:

- Building works on the land or to buildings (which includes building, engineering, mining, demolition and other operations on, in, over or under a property), or
- A material change of use of the land or buildings.

A planning permission authorising the construction of a building will at the same time authorise its use.

Enquiry 12.1 The importance of establishing that building regulation consent was obtained, where required, and that works were carried out in accordance with the approved plans, was illustrated in *Cottingham v Attey Bower & Jones* [2000] EGCS 48 (ChD).

Building Regulations completion certificates were introduced into the Buildings Regulations in 1991. The production by the Seller of a completion certificate will be evidence (but not conclusive evidence) that works were carried out in accordance with Building Regulations.

Enquiry 12.2 A planning permission must generally be implemented within five years from the date of its grant.

Enquiries 12.3, 12.4, 12.5 Established use certificates are no longer granted. Since 27 July, 1992, the equivalent is a certificate of lawfulness of existing use or development (CLEUD) or a certificate of lawfulness of proposed use or development (CLOPUD) (sections 191 and 192, Town and Country Planning Act 1990). Existing established use certificates are still valid and can be relied upon, however, and so their existence is still relevant for the Buyer. There is a procedure for converting an established use certificate into a CLEUD.

A CLEUD or a CLOPUD will establish that:
- An existing use is or a proposed use would be lawful.
- Any operations that have been carried out or which are proposed, in, on, over or under the land are, or will be, lawful.
- Any other matter that constitutes a breach of condition or limitation subject to which planning permission has been granted, is lawful.

A use, an operation or a breach of condition or limitation will be lawful if:

- No enforcement action can be taken in respect of it, and
- The use or development or the breach does not contravene any of the requirements of any enforcement notice in force.

The power to issue enforcement notices is subject to time limits (section 171B, Town and Country Planning Act 1990).

- Four years: No enforcement action can be taken after four years where the breach of planning control relates to building, engineering, mining or other operations in, on or over land.
- Four years: No enforcement action can be taken after four years where the breach of planning control relates to the change of use of any building to use as a single dwelling-house.
- Ten years: No enforcement action can be taken after ten years where the breach of planning control relates to anything else.

Enquiry 12.4 The existing buildings on the Property may be authorised by means of an express planning permission, or by a CLEUD or by virtue of the Town and Country Planning (Use Classes) Order 1987 (as amended) or the Town and Country Planning (General Permitted Development) Order 1995 (as amended).

Enquiry 12.5 and 12.6 The existing use of the Property may be authorised by means of an express planning permission, under a CLEUD or under the Town and Country Planning (Use Classes) Order 1987 (as amended) or the Town and Country Planning (General Permitted Development) Order 1995 (as amended). The Property may have a single use or a single use with an ancillary use. Where one use is ancillary to another (for example, storage associated with a shop) a separate permission for the ancillary use will not generally be required. It is possible for the Property to have more than one use where the further uses are not ancillary but are main uses in their own right as, for example, a shop at ground level with a flat above. Separate permissions are required for each main use but each main use may still have its own ancillary uses.

Enquiries 12.7, 12.8 and 12.9 Where planning consent is required for a development (whether building works or a change of use), the local planning authority can take enforcement action if the development is carried out without planning consent. There are time limits for enforcement action. No enforcement action can be brought in relation to building works after four years have passed following substantial completion of the building works. Where the development is a change of use (other than a change of use to a single dwelling house), no enforcement action can be brought after ten years from the date of the breach. Works that need to be considered include both external works to any buildings, and also works with the curtilage of the building.

Where, however, a building is listed under the Planning (Listed Buildings and Conservation Areas) Act 1990, there is no time limit for enforcement action in respect of a breach. A breach of listed building control can be enforced against an owner no matter when or by whom the breach was committed. A practical problem may arise because when a property is listed, the listing may fail to record the state and extent of the listing, making it difficult for buyers, sellers and local authorities to establish whether any breach has occurred.

Enquiry 12.10 Third parties may challenge the grant of a consent or a certificate either by judicial review or by appeal in the courts under procedures provided in the Planning Acts.

Enquiry 12.12 Outline planning permissions are permissions for the construction of a building that are granted in principle, subject to certain "reserved matters". The outline planning permission cannot be implemented until the reserved matters have been approved.

Statutory agreements and infrastructure

The Buyer will make a local authority and local land charges search. The results should disclose agreements and notices relating to roads, drains, public health matters and repair obligations. The following are examples of the types of agreement and notice about which the Buyer will need information:

- Agreements under section 38 of the Highways Act 1980

  These impose obligations on a developer to make up roads and footpaths to a standard required by the local highway authority and to maintain them for a specified period. The road or footpath is then adopted by the highway authority and maintained at public expense. Normally the agreement is supported by a bond to pay for completion of the works if the developer fails to carry them out. Section 38 agreements do not run with the land so, if the Seller is party to one, the Buyer may need to take an assignment of it otherwise the highway authority may close the road which may affect access to the Property.

  A local highway authority may agree or resolve to make up roadways or footpaths at the cost of owners of premises fronting the roadway. Full details will be required so that the Buyer is aware of potential liabilities.

- Agreements under section 104 of the Water Industry Act 1991

  These impose obligations in relation to sewers similar to those relating to roads under section 38 above.

- Planning obligations under section 106 of the Town and Country Planning Act 1990

  These may require a landowner to carry out specified works or impose restrictions on the development or use of land or require money to be paid to a local planning authority. Such obligations are normally entered into as part of negotiations for planning permission and may provide for the making up and adoption of roads and footpaths.

The local authority search may not disclose all relevant agreements and notices.

Enquiry 13.1 Examples of the types of agreement to which this enquiry relates include:

- Agreements relating to the construction and adoption of roads, footpaths, drains and sewers.
- Agreements relating to the laying of gas pipes, electricity and telecommunications cables, wires and other equipment including transformer substations.
- Water abstraction licences.

Enquiry 13.2 This enquiry covers, for example, obligations on the Seller to enter into any highway, water or sewerage agreements or a section 106 planning agreement.

Enquiry 13.3 Examples of what might be included in the reply to this enquiry include a road closure order, a diversion order, a traffic flow order which, if implemented, might affect access to the Property or the ability to park near or deliver to the Property or a food hygiene order, of particular relevance if the Property is a restaurant or hotel.

Enquiry 13.4 Some agreements, such as section 106 and section 38 agreements, cannot be registered by the local authority until they have been completed. Until registered they will not be disclosed by a local authority search but will still constitute overriding interests (see enquiry 4). If the Seller is aware of anything which is not yet, but will be, registered it should be disclosed here, unless it has already been disclosed in reply to enquiry 13.1. There are some matters which are not required to be registered as a local land charge, for example, planning contravention notices and notices of intention to adopt a highway.

Enquiry 13.6 The local authority or other public or private bodies, such as English Partnerships, can make financial grants. These are generally made to promote development and improvement and may be subject to repayment obligations in certain circumstances. The Buyer needs to know what grants have been made, by whom, for how much and the terms of the grant and in particular will need to know about repayment obligations so that appropriate provisions can be made in the contract.

Statutory and other liabilities

Enquiry 14 addresses potential liabilities in connection with the Property and concentrates mainly on statutory liabilities.

Liability under statute may be strict, which means that the person responsible for the breach will be liable regardless of the state of their knowledge about the breach. This is often the case with health and safety legislation, which is designed to protect the welfare of employees and occupiers of premises.

Liability may, in other cases, depend on the state of knowledge of the person responsible for the breach.

Statute will provide who is responsible for compliance. Liability may rest with the occupier and/or the owner. The owner may be defined to include the landlord, any superior landlord and/or the freeholder. Some legislation, such as fire regulations, extends the meaning of owner to include anyone in receipt of rents and so may include a trustee of the landlord or a managing agent.

Enquiry 14.1 The enquiry is wide and addresses all legislation that may affect the Property. Depending on the nature of the Property and its use, particular consideration should be given to the Occupiers' Liability Acts 1957 and 1984, the Defective Premises Act 1972, health and safety legislation (including the Shops Act 1950, the Factories Acts, the Offices, Shops and Railway Premises Act 1963 and the Health and Safety at Work etc. Act 1974), and liquor and gambling licensing. To the extent not covered elsewhere, the reply should cover breaches of building regulations, breaches of fire regulations, gas safety legislation, highway and drainage obligations, section 106 agreements, planning control, waste storage and management, hazardous substances, advertising control, bye-laws relating to trading and advertisement control.

Enquiry 14.2 This enquiry is not limited to statutory matters. It does not cover works to be carried out to anything other than the Property and so will not include section 38 highway agreements or section 106 agreements unless the land over which the works are to be carried out is included within the definition of the Property.

Enquiry 14.3 This enquiry is designed to catch such things as liquor licences, betting and gaming licences, water abstraction licences and any other activity controlled by law.

Enquiry 14.4 Subject to specific exceptions, the Construction (Design and Management) Regulations 1994 (which came into force on 31 March, 1995), apply to all construction work, which includes demolition, construction, alteration, fitting-out, commissioning, repair, maintenance and decoration. Their objective is to improve management, information and co-ordination of work on site. The Regulations do not apply to small construction projects where the number of people working on the project at any one time is/was not expected to exceed four and the project is/was not expected to last longer than 30 days. The Health and Safety file for the project should contain all health and safety related information necessary for the proper maintenance, repair, alteration, decoration and demolition of the building. The Buyer needs the information requested as it could have an impact on the Buyer's ability or method of doing works or on the value of the Property and its marketability.

Environmental

The primary objectives of the environmental legislation are:

- Protection of the environment from pollution.

- Remediation of existing contamination.
- Prevention of future contamination.
- Better management of natural resources and promotion of sustainable development.

Enquiry 15 is a general enquiry about environmental issues, aimed at sites with no known environmental problems. More specific questions can be raised if the Buyer's requirements, or the state of the Property, demand.

The fundamental principle of the environmental legislation is that "the polluter pays". The definition of polluter is wide so that it can include parties who have not been directly responsible for the contamination, including a subsequent owner of the land. This is particularly important since Part IIA of the Environmental Protection Act 1990, dealing with contaminated land, came into force on 1 April, 2000.

These enquiries are intended to alert the Buyer to any matter which may need further investigation so the Buyer can be fully aware of what environmental liabilities it may inherit as a result of the Transaction. The cost of remedying damage caused by contamination may be significantly more than the value of the Property and this can make it difficult to identify any arbitrary value below which it can be said that any form of environmental investigation is unnecessary.

The following are examples of the types of hazard with which these enquiries are concerned:

- Pollution and protection of the environment.
- Health and safety.
- Emissions and releases.
- Disposal of industrial, commercial or household waste.
- Discharges of radioactive waste or chemical or other pollutants or contaminants or toxic or hazardous substances.
- Manufacture, processing, distribution, use, treatment, storage, disposal, transport or handling of any discharges or waste materials.
- Control of noise and noise emissions.
- Water pollution, including pollution by trade and sewage effluent.

Enquiry 15.2 If any authorisations are disclosed then the Buyer should consider asking for confirmation that:

- The authorisations have not been breached.
- No upgrade of plant or equipment and no capital expenditure is needed before authorisations can be complied with.
- No notice or other communication has been received from an enforcement authority which may materially affect the terms of such authorisations or their continued validity.

Enquiry 15.4 This enquiry focuses on whether the Property has been subject to potentially contaminative uses or whether there is any hazardous material in the Property. It has been deliberately framed widely to avoid the Seller having to form a view on whether or not information given is indicative of a contaminative use.

Enquiry 15.5 The reply should cover both statutory notices and complaints from neighbours.

Enquiry 15.6 The enquiry does not expressly ask for sight of transfer notes relating to waste (which might be numerous) but if there were a concern as to whether waste was being disposed of properly, these could be requested.

Enquiry 15.7 The reply to this should reveal matters such as migrating contamination, dust, noise and other forms of nuisance.

Occupiers and employees

Enquiry 16 is concerned with the rights, statutory or otherwise, of anyone who will remain in occupation of the Property following completion of the Transaction.

Occupiers may have specific rights of occupation which need to be addressed as part of the Transaction and where there are leases and licences conferring these occupational rights, the Buyer may need to raise additional enquiries (e.g. CPSE.2, CPSE.3 and CPSE.4).

Occupiers may have rights which go beyond those set out in a formal lease or licence and these rights may be protected as overriding interests, information about which should have been included in reply to enquiry 4.

There may be people in occupation who are employed to work at the Property and they may have rights as employees under the Transfer of Undertakings (Protection of Employment) Regulations 1981 ("TUPE") (see enquiry 16.5).

Enquiry 16.1 Where the Seller is a company, firm or partnership or some other corporate body, the Seller is not required to give the names of all shareholders, partners or employees but should give details of any other body in occupation including a company in the same group. The Seller should explain whether occupation is by virtue of lease or licence or whether there is no formal right to occupy, in which case the Seller should give details of the length of occupation, any payments received in respect of it and any objections made to it.

Enquiry 16.3 Whether the Property is vacant, and the period during which it has been vacant, may be relevant for a number of reasons. For example, it may have an impact on the validity of insurance cover, affect liability to pay business rates and may put the Buyer on notice that squatters may be in occupation.

Enquiry 16.4 The purpose of TUPE is to protect the jobs and terms and conditions of employment of employees where the undertaking by, or in respect of which, they are employed is transferred. TUPE applies to any transaction considered to be the transfer of an economic entity and can include the transfer of premises as part of a business sale and transfers of investment properties such as shopping centres or office buildings.

TUPE applies to staff employed in respect of the business or property which is being sold and extends to managers, managing agents, caretakers, cleaners, maintenance staff and security guards employed in respect of buildings which may otherwise be empty.

All employees employed in the undertaking automatically transfer to the Buyer on their existing terms and conditions (save for pension schemes) and their employment is treated as being continuous for purposes of claims for redundancy or unfair dismissal. Any dismissals connected with the transfer are automatically considered to be unfair.

Under TUPE, the Buyer takes on all rights, liabilities and responsibilities for anything done by the Seller in respect of the employee and may therefore inherit liability for unfair dismissals, claims in relation to sex discrimination and any failure to pay wages or bonuses which arise before the time of the transfer.

TUPE may also apply to contracted-out services provided under contracts for services (such as security or cleaning contractors). Employees of contractors may be protected if, after completion of the Transaction, the services are to be provided by another contractor or where the contract is to be terminated and the services provided in-house.

Insurance

Enquiry 17 concerns buildings insurance as opposed to contents insurance or title insurance. The convention is that once contracts are exchanged, the Buyer takes over the risk in the Property and must therefore insure from that date. In transactions where there is no contract, the Buyer will usually assume the risk on completion.

The information which will be given in reply to this enquiry is likely, therefore, to be of interest where the Buyer is to rely on the Seller's insurance between exchange of contracts and completion or where the existing insurance arrangements will remain in place following completion of the Transaction. This might be so where, for example, the sale is between related companies and the insurance is dealt with under a group company policy, or where the Property is leasehold and the landlord insures.

Where the Buyer is to rely on the Seller's insurance between exchange of contracts and completion, the contract may need to cover noting the Buyer's interest on the policy and the Buyer will need to be clear as to exactly what the cover includes (e.g. loss of rent).

Where the insurance arrangements will remain in place following completion of the Transaction, the Buyer will need full details of the insurance cover effected to check that cover is satisfactory, particularly in relation to the adequacy of the sum insured and whether this is index-linked, the adequacy of insured risks and acceptability of any exclusions. It will also be concerned to check that the policy complies with the requirements of any relevant lease or mortgage, whether the policy is and will continue in force and that the proposed use of the Property will not render the policy void or voidable.

The Buyer will need to check who has the benefit of the insurance policy and ensure that its own interest is adequately protected.

Enquiry 17.3 The types of insurance referred to here may include public liability and employers' liability insurance and insurance for specific items of machinery or equipment.

Enquiry 17.6 Circumstances which may make the policy void or voidable include non-payment of premiums and failure to give all relevant information to the insurance company.

Rates and other outgoings

The Buyer will need to know its liability for periodic payments following completion of the Transaction. The main liabilities are likely to be business rates and water and sewerage charges, but there may be others.

Enquiry 18.1 The rateable value of the Property is the value attributed to it for the purpose of calculating the local authority business rates payable on it. This information will be on the rating assessment of the Property and on the rate demands received from the local authority but can also be obtained from the local authority.

Enquiry 18.2 Whether or not the Property is separately assessed is important because if it is assessed as part of other premises that are not included in the Transaction, it may have to be reassessed following completion of the Transaction.

Enquiry 18.3 Local rating lists, which were compiled initially on 1 April, 1990, are revised on every fifth anniversary of that date, most recently on 1 April, 2000. A revaluation will be made on each date the list is revised. To enable the valuation officers to prepare the list, notice may be served on an occupier or owner of a property requiring information about that property. Any correspondence passing between the owner or occupiers of the property and the valuation officer regarding a revaluation should be disclosed in response to this enquiry, including copies of all relevant proposals, notices, returns and appeals.

Enquiry 18.4 The rateable value of a property may be revised at any time due to a material change in circumstances. An owner or occupier of a property can at any time apply to the valuation officer requesting an alteration to the rateable value shown in the rating list or an alteration to any other statement made in the rating list about the property. The valuation officer may also propose an alteration if there have been any alterations or improvement works, works to extend or enlarge the property or a change of use of the property. Copies of all relevant correspondence and documentation should be produced including all proposals, notices, returns and appeals.

Enquiry 18.5 The amount payable for uniform business rates, water rates, sewerage and drainage charges can be obtained from the local authority and the water supply company. If the Property forms part of other premises for which there is only one assessment for business rates and for water, sewerage and drainage rates, that fact should be disclosed in this reply. Local authorities and water companies have a financial year that runs from 1 April of each calendar year. Accordingly, reference to the current year in this enquiry will mean the financial year that started on the most recent 1 April.

Enquiry 18.6 If a property is vacant, the owner or occupier may be entitled to empty rate relief for a period of three months following the date on which the property becomes vacant. After that three-month period, empty rates are charged. If the property has been left vacant for any period of time and relief has been claimed for that period, full details should be provided. If the property is currently vacant, the date on which the property was vacated should also be provided. Exemption from local authority rates may be given to certain qualifying premises in designated enterprise zones.

Enquiry 18.7 Transitional charging arrangements are concerned with phasing in new rates bills when they are significantly above or below the previous year's bills.

Enquiry 18.8 Examples of the types of periodic charges envisaged by this enquiry include payments in respect of private water supplies, private sewers and private access routes to the Property, rent tithe agreements and chancel repairs. The reply is not expected to include details of rent and service charges payable under a lease of the Property.

Capital allowances

A deduction from profits can be claimed for certain types of capital expenditure under the Capital Allowances Act 2001. The deduction is called a capital allowance. Some expenditure, such as that on assets used for scientific research or situated in an enterprise zone, may be written off in full in the year in which it is incurred. Most capital expenditure, however, is written off over a number of years. The most common capital allowances are those in respect of plant and machinery, and on certain "industrial" buildings, which expression generally relates to buildings or structures used for manufacturing and processing together with some types of storage and also includes hotels built after April 1978 with ten or more bedrooms and certain statutory and other undertakings.

Note that where the Transaction involves the seller paying for or carrying out works to the Property for a buyer as an inducement, the buyer's capital allowances entitlement may be affected.

Enquiry 19.1 If the Seller is holding the Property as a trader as part of trading stock, because, for example, the Seller is a developer or dealer, it will not have been able to claim capital allowances as any expenditure incurred will not have been on capital account. However the remaining enquiries in enquiry 19 should still be answered as there may be relevant information relating to an earlier owner of the Property.

Enquiry 19.2 Expenditure on the construction of a building in an enterprise zone qualifies for an allowance equal to 100% of the cost. Subsequent buyers may also be entitled to this allowance, if the enterprise zone is not more than twenty-two years old, and the building is either unused, or has been used for less than two years.

Enquiry 19.3 An allowance is available in respect of "industrial" buildings, as defined in the legislation.

When a building that is classified for these purposes as being "industrial" is acquired second-hand but within twenty-five years after its first use, the allowance is generally calculated by writing-off the original cost (or the current consideration, if lower) over the remainder of this twenty-five year life. The allowance is given not only in respect of the original construction of the building, but also in respect of subsequent alterations and enhancements. Each addition is regarded for the purposes of allowances as a new building, with its own twenty-five year life. This enquiry therefore asks for information not only about the original construction of the Property but also in relation to alterations made to it.

The Buyer must acquire the "relevant interest" in the Property to be entitled to make a claim for industrial buildings allowances attached to that relevant interest. If the interest acquired is not a relevant interest as defined in section 286 of the CAA 2001, the Buyer has no entitlement to industrial buildings allowances. The "relevant interest" is generally the interest held by the person who incurred the expenditure at the time of construction of the building. However, it can be an interest that is subordinate to that interest, if the Property has been subject to an election pursuant to section 290 of the CAA 2001.

Enquiry 19.4 An allowance of 100% of cost is given in respect of expenditure on assets (including buildings), which are for scientific research under the Capital Allowances Act 1990, or research and development under CAA 2001. The allowance is not available to a subsequent buyer of the Property but a previous claim for scientific research allowances may affect the Buyer's entitlement to claim the allowance on fixtures.

If the answer to this enquiry is "yes", the Buyer will need to make further specialist enquiries about this expenditure.

Enquiry 19.5 The Buyer may be entitled to claim capital allowances on any fixed plant and machinery within the Property. The amount on which such a claim may be based may be an apportionment of the total consideration, but in many cases there are limiting factors. In particular, the amount of the claim may be limited where the Seller has itself claimed allowances.

If the answer to enquiry 19.5 is "no", the Buyer should request details of the previous owner and ask whether the contract between the former owner and the Seller allocated any sum to machinery and plant.

The original qualifying expenditure in most cases will be the maximum allowable amount upon which the Buyer can claim allowances on those assets for which a capital allowances claim has been made. It may be possible, however, to increase the Seller's claim and there may also be assets within the Property upon which a claim has not previously been made.

Where assets are subject to a sale and leaseback or similar arrangements, the amount of the Buyer's claim may be similarly restricted.

Enquiry 19.6 The Seller is still entitled to make a claim for capital allowances on the Property after completion of the Transaction for a previous accounting period when the Property was still owned by the Seller.

Enquiry 19.7 Even if the Seller has not claimed allowances, the Buyer's claim may still be restricted if allowances have been claimed by any former owner of the Property, provided that the former owner disposed of the Property on or after 24 July, 1996. It is therefore necessary for the Buyer to be aware of the recent history of ownership and details of any transaction affecting the plant and machinery now included in the sale.

Enquiry 19.8 For transactions made on or after 19 March 1997, it has been possible for the parties to make a joint election, fixing the amount to be allocated to the Fixtures within a building. This is subject to certain limits, and must not be motivated by tax avoidance. If the Fixtures have been subject to a previous election notice, then the value of that election will limit the level of allowances available to subsequent buyers.

Enquiry 19.9 The Buyer and the Seller can agree to elect between themselves an amount at which the Fixtures will transfer from the Seller to the Buyer. The procedure is set out in section 201 of the CAA 2001.

Enquiry 19.10 Capital allowances are available for both fixtures and industrial buildings in respect of contributions towards another person's expenditure, and the written-down value of any such allowances will pass to the buyer of the contributor's interest.

Enquiry 19.11 Any loose (i.e. not fixed) plant or machinery included in the sale may be the subject of a claim by the Buyer, based on open market value. This may be restricted if sale and leasebacks or other similar arrangements are envisaged.

Enquiry 19.12 Allowances on plant and machinery are generally given at a rate of 25% per annum. This is reduced to 6% per annum, however, for plant and machinery that has a useful economic life, when new, in excess of 25 years. Various exemptions for plant within a hotel, office, shop or showroom apply.

Enquiry 19.13 Allowances will not be available to the Buyer in respect of any plant or machinery within the building upon which a tenant has incurred expenditure, or subject to an equipment lease.

Enquiry 19.14 Where a landlord grants a long leasehold (over 50 years) interest in a property for a premium, the tenant acquiring that long leasehold interest will not be acquiring the Relevant Interest that entitles it to make a claim for any Industrial Building Allowances available on the property. In order for the tenant as opposed to the landlord to be treated as the owner of the Relevant Interest, both parties must within two years from the grant of the long leasehold interest enter into an election under section 290 of the CAA 2001.

Similarly, where a landlord grants a long leasehold interest in a property for a premium, the tenant acquiring that long leasehold interest will not be acquiring the interest that entitles it to make a claim for any plant and machinery allowances on any fixtures within the property. In order for the tenant as opposed to the landlord to be treated as the owner of the fixtures, both parties must within two years from the grant of the long leasehold interest enter into an election under section 183 of the CAA 2001.

Value added tax (VAT) Registration information

Most property transactions in the course of a business are within the VAT regime, but this does not necessarily mean that VAT must be added to the price. The most common VAT classifications are standard-rated supplies, exempt supplies and transfers as a going concern. Transactions involving certain types of property may occasionally be zero-rated supplies.

This and the following VAT enquiries will not elicit all necessary information about the VAT position but the replies should trigger a series of additional enquiries as appropriate, which can then be referred to VAT experts. To avoid delay, these notes suggest relevant additional enquiries and the Seller is encouraged to volunteer the replies before waiting to be asked.

It is essential to establish if the Seller is registered for VAT to ensure that any charge to VAT is valid. The information is also important in deciding whether an election should be made to waive exemption. If the Seller is registered as part of a VAT group, the name of the group representative member is needed, as the Transaction will be deemed for the purposes of VAT to be made by that company.

Transfer of a business as a going concern (TOGC)

The sale of an investment property subject to one or more leases can constitute the transfer of a business as a going concern (TOGC) for the purposes of VAT. In such a case no VAT is payable.

Qualification for treatment as a TOGC requires that:

- The asset or assets are to be used by the Buyer in carrying on the same kind of business as that carried on by the Seller;
- Where the Seller is a taxable person (that is registered or liable to be registered for VAT), the Buyer must already be a taxable person or immediately become, as a result of the transfer, a taxable person;
- In relation to a part transfer, that part is capable of separate operation;
- The effect of the transfer must be to put the Buyer in possession of a business which can be operated as a business;
- The business, or part, transferred must be a "going concern" at the time of transfer, which in essence means that it is a business, whether profit-making or not;
- There should not be a series of immediately consecutive transfers of the business; there should be no significant break in the normal trading pattern before or immediately after the transfer; and
- Where the Seller has made an election to waive exemption, or the supply is the freehold sale of new buildings or civil engineering works which are less than three years old, the Buyer must make an election to waive exemption in relation to the land and buildings concerned and notify HM Customs & Excise of that election before the first occasion on which a supply of the property is made. This may mean that the Buyer must make an election in respect of the Property before exchange, if, for example, it is to pay a deposit on exchange of contracts to the Seller's representative as agent for the Seller (as often happens in auction sales) rather than to a stakeholder (see *Higher Education Statistics Agency v Customs and Excise Commissioners* [2000] STC 332).

Enquiry 21.2 Sufficient detail should be provided to enable the Buyer to satisfy itself on the treatment of the Transaction as a TOGC. This will include, for example, providing details of:

- Any elections to waive exemption;
- The precise use of the Property by the Seller; and
- On a freehold sale, the period that has elapsed since practical completion or occupation.

Enquiry 21.3 The availability of treatment as a TOGC can be affected by the Seller's circumstances or actions. For example TOGC treatment may not be available if:

- The Property is entirely let to a company within the same VAT group as the Seller;
- The Seller transfers the Property to another of its corporate group companies which is not within the same VAT group registration and this transfer takes place immediately before the Transaction itself; or
- The Seller makes an election to waive exemption before the Transaction takes place and the Buyer does not make an election.

Enquiry 21.5 If the Transaction is a TOGC, it is important to determine if the Property is a capital item for VAT purposes and is within its adjustment period. The Capital Goods Scheme adjustments are designed to ensure that the VAT reclaimed on the original cost of development or acquisition is adjusted over a five or ten year period (dependent upon the length of the interest held or acquired). This is done through clawbacks and it will be important for the Buyer to be aware of any clawback liability.

Enquiry 21.6 It is normally the responsibility of the Buyer to take over and maintain the VAT records relating to a property acquired as a TOGC. If the Seller is unwilling to transfer the records it should apply to Customs & Excise for permission to retain them. In practice it is often difficult to transfer the records relating to one property which is part of a portfolio and consequently applications to retain the records are commonplace.

Other VAT treatment

If the Transaction is not a TOGC, it is important to identify its correct VAT treatment, as certain actions may be required to validate that treatment.

This enquiry is intended to help the Buyer to verify the Seller's view of the correct VAT treatment of the Transaction. The legislation is extremely complex and specific expert advice should always be sought.

Standard-rated supplies

This enquiry is intended to help the Buyer to verify the Seller's view of the correct VAT treatment of the Transaction. The legislation is extremely complex and specific expert advice should always be sought.

Exempt supplies

This enquiry is intended to help the Buyer to verify the Seller's view of the correct VAT treatment of the Transaction. The legislation is extremely complex and specific expert advice should always be sought.

Zero-rated supplies

This enquiry is intended to help the Buyer to verify the Seller's view of the correct VAT treatment of the Transaction. The legislation is extremely complex and specific expert advice should always be sought.

Transactions outside the scope of VAT (other than TOGCs)

Certain property transactions (other than TOGCs) may be outside the scope of VAT. This would apply if, for example, the Transaction is not made in the furtherance of a business. It is important to establish the reasoning to avoid any disputes if it is subsequently discovered that a VAT charge was appropriate. By way of example, the sale of a church by a religious movement which has no business activities is likely to be a transaction which is non-business and outside the scope of VAT.

Notices

The Buyer needs details of every notice affecting the Property so that it:

- Knows what may affect the Property;
- Can take steps in the contract to ensure that the Seller deals with all notices as appropriate;

- Is prepared to take appropriate action following completion of the Transaction; and
- May negotiate an indemnity.

Examples of notices which may affect the Property include planning notices, compulsory purchase notices, public utilities' notices, repair notices, landlords' notices of intention to sell the freehold, tenants' notices of intention to buy the freehold or to enfranchise, notices about a change of landlord or tenant, mortgages and rent review.

Notices about disputes should be included in the reply to enquiry 28.

If the Buyer raises supplemental enquiries in forms CPSE.2, CPSE.3 or CPSE.4, it may be more appropriate to give details of landlords' and tenants' notices in response to those supplemental enquiries. Alternatively the information can be given here and a cross-reference made in the replies to the supplemental enquiries.

Disputes

The Buyer needs details of every dispute relating to the Property so that it may:

- Appreciate what liabilities it may be taking on.
- Be aware of potential obstacles to the use and enjoyment of the Property.
- Take steps in the contract to ensure that the Seller deals with all disputes as may be appropriate.
- Be prepared to take appropriate action following completion of the Transaction.
- Negotiate an indemnity.

Disputes include those that have arisen in the past, whether or not they have been resolved. The existence of a dispute in the past may indicate a potential problem for the future and also may explain facts and circumstances about the Property. Information should be included on anticipated disputes, even where there is nothing formally on record.

Stamp duty land tax on assignment of a lease

Enquiry 29.1 The grant of a lease on or after 1 December 2003 is a land transaction for Stamp Duty Land Tax purposes unless the lease was granted pursuant to an agreement for lease exchanged on or before 10 July 2003 which has not been subsequently assigned or varied.

The grant of a lease is notifiable to the Inland Revenue if:

- the term is for seven years or more and was granted for chargeable consideration, regardless of whether any Stamp Duty Land Tax is payable; or
- Stamp Duty Land Tax is payable on the grant of the lease or would be payable but for any Stamp Duty Land Tax relief claimed by the tenant.

If the grant of a lease was not notifiable to the Inland Revenue, a self-certification certificate may have been produced in order to enable the registration at the Land Registry of any easements granted to the tenant under the lease.

Subsequent events under the lease may give rise to a further obligation to notify the Inland Revenue of a land transaction. Examples include:

- the variation of the lease that creates a surrender and regrant or which increases the rent payable under the lease;
- the settlement or determination of a rent review during the first five years of the term (disregarding rent reviews by reference to the Retail Prices Index);
- any contingent, uncertain or unascertained rents payable during the first five years of the term becoming payable, certain or ascertained; and

- the first assignment of a lease that is not itself exempt from Stamp Duty Land Tax where certain Stamp Duty Land Tax reliefs were claimed on the grant of the lease (see the notes for Enquiry 1.4 below).

The buyer will need to know the date of the grant of the lease for Stamp Duty Land Tax purposes. This is:

- the actual date of grant unless certain Stamp Duty Land Tax reliefs were claimed on the grant of the lease (see the notes for Enquiry 29.4 below);
- if the original grant was exempt under one of those reliefs, the date of the deemed grant of a lease where a non-exempt assignment has followed the original exempt grant.

The buyer will need to ensure that all Stamp Duty Land Tax payable on the lease has been paid and retain evidence that shows the total amount that has been paid. This is because the buyer will be responsible for the payment of any future Stamp Duty Land Tax due and, where that future transaction is linked to the grant of the original lease, the extent of the buyer's liability to Stamp Duty Land Tax (if any) may depend on the amount of Stamp Duty Land Tax already paid.

If Stamp Duty Land Tax was not payable on the grant of the lease or the grant of the lease was not notifiable, the buyer will need to know this as subsequent events under the terms of the lease may bring the original grant of the lease within the requirements for notification and the payment of Stamp Duty Land Tax; for example where the lease comes to an end and the buyer remains in occupation of the property.

For the purposes of any additional land transaction returns that need to be made, the buyer will need to know the "effective date" of the lease. This will be the earlier of the date of actual completion of the lease and, if there was a preceding agreement for lease, the date of substantial performance of that agreement, for example the date the buyer was given occupation of the premises.

Enquiry 29.2. This enquiry is relevant where a lease is assigned during the first five years of the term and the grant of the lease was a land transaction for the purposes of Stamp Duty Land Tax. It applies also on the assignment of a lease where a previous assignment of the lease has resulted in the deemed grant of a new lease (see the notes for Enquiry 29.3 below).

For the purposes of Stamp Duty Land Tax, the tenant of a lease may be under an obligation to make two land transaction returns where any of the following conditions apply:

- there is a rent review during the first five years of the term, excluding for these purposes any RPI rent reviews;
- there is any other mechanism in the lease to vary the rent payable under that lease; or
- there are contingent, uncertain or unascertained rents payable, for example where there is a turnover rent.

Where any of these conditions apply, the tenant makes an initial land transaction return on the grant of the lease based on a reasonable estimate of the sums that will become payable and, if additional Stamp Duty Land Tax is payable or the transaction becomes notifiable, a further land transaction return at the end of the fifth year of the term or, where a rent review is agreed or determined before the end of the fifth year of the term or the mechanism for varying the rent is operated, on completion of the rent review or variation.

If the lease is assigned during the first five years of the term, the potential obligation to make the additional land transaction return passes to the buyer. In order to make any additional land transaction return, the buyer will need to know the highest amount of rent paid by the seller in any consecutive twelve-month period.

These provisions apply equally where the lease was granted for a term of less than five years; for example they would apply to a turnover rent lease for a term of four years.

Enquiry 29.3 This enquiry is relevant where there has been the grant or assignment of a lease at a premium and the whole or any part of that that premium is contingent, uncertain or unascertained.

An adjustment to the seller's land transaction return may be required when the contingency occurs (or it is clear that it will not occur) or the amount of the premium becomes certain or ascertained.

On the assignment of a lease, the buyer inherits the seller's obligation to make any additional land transaction return required once contingency occurs or the amount of the premium becomes certain or ascertained.

The position is different if the seller has made an application to defer payment as the obligation then remains with the seller.

Enquiry 29.4 This enquiry is relevant where one of the following Stamp Duty Land Tax reliefs was claimed on the grant of the lease:

- sale and leaseback relief;
- group company, reconstruction or acquisition relief;
- transfers involving public bodies;
- charities relief; or
- any of the reliefs set out in The Stamp Duty Land Tax (Consequential Amendment of Enact-ments) Regulations 2003.

On the first assignment of the lease where one of these reliefs has been claimed on the grant of the lease, the assignment of the lease is treated as the deemed grant of a new lease from the seller to the buyer for the unexpired residue of the term of the original lease unless similar reliefs are claimed on the assignment. If similar reliefs are claimed on the first assignment of the lease, the next assignment of the lease on which none of the relevant reliefs is claimed will be treated as the deemed grant of the new lease from the seller to the buyer.

Where the assignment of the lease is treated as the grant of a new lease, the buyer will be under an obligation to pay Stamp Duty Land Tax based on the net present value of the deemed new lease.

The Inland Revenue has stated that these provisions do not apply if stamp duty, and not Stamp Duty Land Tax, applied on the grant of the lease and it was the corresponding stamp duty reliefs that were claimed on the grant of the lease.

Deferred payments of stamp duty land tax

Enquiry 30 Where the whole or part of the consideration for a land transaction is contingent, uncertain or unascertained, the taxpayer is under an obligation to pay Stamp Duty Land Tax on completion of the transaction on its reasonable estimate of the amount of contingent, uncertain or unascertained consideration that will be payable. Where the payment of additional consideration is contingent, the taxpayer must assume that the additional consideration will become payable (regard-less of the likely outcome of the contingent event).

If the contingent, uncertain or unascertained consideration will not be payable within the first six months of completion of the transaction, the taxpayer can make an application to the Inland Revenue to defer the payment of Stamp Duty Land Tax on the contingent or uncertain amount. The application for deferral must be made before the taxpayer makes its land transaction return in accordance with The Stamp Duty Land Tax (Administration) Regulations 2003.

If an application for deferral is successful, the taxpayer remains liable for any additional Stamp Duty Land Tax payable but the taxpayer may want an indemnity from any buyer from him where that buyer, and not the taxpayer, becomes liable for the payment of the additional consideration to the original seller. The buyer will therefore need to know the additional amount of Stamp Duty Land Tax that may be payable.

INDEX